PALESTINE,

ISRAEL,

AND THE

POLITICS OF

POPULAR

CULTURE

Rebecca L. Stein and

Ted Swedenburg, editors

PALESTINE,

ISRAEL,

AND THE

POLITICS OF

POPULAR

CULTURE

Duke University Press

Durham & London

2005

© 2005 Duke University Press

All rights reserved

Printed in the United States of America on acid-free paper ⊚

Designed by Rebecca Giménez

Typeset in Scala by Tseng Information Systems

Library of Congress Cataloging-in-Publication Data appear

on the last printed page of this book.

CONTENTS

ACKNOWLEDGMENTS

This volume has been long in the making and depended on the assistance of many friends and colleagues. We found critical inspiration for this project in the work of Ammiel Alcalay, Edward Said, and Ella Shohat; while none of these scholars was able to contribute to the volume, their early interest and support for the initiative was critical in its realization. Portions of this volume were originally presented as papers in a panel that we organized for the American Anthropological Association Meetings in November 2001. Thanks to Nadia Abu El-Haj and Susan Slyomovics, who offered insightful critiques in their capacity as discussants and helped shape the volume to come. Joel Beinin, Yael Ben-Zvi, Robert Blecher, Elliott Colla, Andrew Janiak, Zachary Lockman, and Shira Robinson provided generous consultation and constructive commentary during the course of the volume's production. Particular thanks are due to the contributors, whose pioneering work on issues of popular culture in Palestine and Israel made this volume possible; we thank them for their incredibly hard work in bringing this text to publication. Elizabeth Angel did extensive editorial work on the manuscripts and helped all of us to clarify and strengthen our arguments. At Duke Press, Ken Wissoker's enthusiasm for the project, intellectual support, and critical advice was this volume's backbone. Courtney Berger's enormous editorial care and heavy lifting was invaluable as the volume went into production. Kate Lothman skillfully moved the manuscript into its final stages. Thanks also to our partners and families for their patience, encouragement, and support. And to our colleagues and friends at *Middle East Report*; this volume grows out of our collective struggle for justice in Palestine and Israel.

Introduction

REBECCA L. STEIN &
TED SWEDENBURG

Popular Culture,

Transnationality, and

Radical History

T raditionally, most radical scholarship on Palestine and Israel has ignored questions of popular culture, or, at best, consigned popular culture forms and processes to the margins of scholarly debate and investigation.[1] For many scholars, the act of marginalization has seemed a
necessary response to the severity of the national conflict, the harsh violence of the Israeli occupation, and the enduring struggle for Palestinian
national liberation. Popular culture's frequent appearance in commodity
form has made the labor of marginalization seem all the more necessary,
particularly for scholars wedded to classic Marxist analytics, in which mass
production and commodification are thought to render the cultural form
"inauthentic." For scholars concerned primarily with questions of nationalism and national conflict in Palestine and Israel, the global circuits of
the popular cultural commodity have further removed it from the scholarly
agenda. Popular culture, in all these approaches, is deemed epiphenomenal to questions of politics and power.

In the past decade, scholars in the field of Middle East studies have
begun to rethink these presumptions, taking popular culture seriously as
a space, practice, or discourse.[2] Our volume grows out of this larger effort.
In the most basic terms, we are arguing that the question of popular culture in Palestine and Israel is fundamentally one of politics and power. In
turn, we suggest that the marginalization of popular culture in progressive scholarship on the region is symptomatic of the conceptual and meth-
odological limits that still define much of this scholarship: the pervading
logic of the nation or nation-state, on the one hand, and the analytic tools

of traditional Marxist historiography and political economy, on the other. In what follows, we turn to a notion of cultural politics as a way to think beyond these limits. At stake is an attempt to broaden our understanding of the terrain of power in Palestine and Israel and thereby the possible arenas and modalities of struggle.

Radical Genealogies

Together, the essays in this volume grow out of, and pay homage to, at least three decades of radical scholarship on Palestine, Israel, and the history of Zionism, by which we mean scholarship that has been framed through questions of colonization, occupation, and the Palestinian self-determination struggle.[3] At the turn of the twenty-first century, as new scholarship on the region proliferates, it is perhaps easy to forget the relatively recent appearance of this radical agenda in the U.S. academy. As recently as the 1980s and into the early 1990s, efforts to publish on or speak critically about Zionism and its histories were frequently met with fierce opposition in institutions of higher education, academic advisors cautioned graduate students with Palestine-based projects of certain difficulties on the job market, and research funding for such projects was difficult to secure.[4] The parameters of permissible discourse on Palestine and Israel have shifted significantly since this period, evidenced by the widespread use of the colonial paradigm by scholars in both the United States and Israel.[5] Thus, despite the current "war on terror" and its effects in the academy, radical scholarship on the region is no longer the "lonely" enterprise described by Said in *The Question of Palestine* in 1979.[6]

By our accounting, there are six key moments in the history of this radical scholarly agenda as it pertains to the U.S. academy. The first was what we might call the documentary moment, which took place in the wake of the June 1967 war and emerged out of the Palestinian resistance movement and its nascent affiliated institutions. These emergent institutions, largely based in Beirut, began the unprecedented labor of publishing a body of literature on the Palestinian question from the Palestinian perspective, produced in Western languages and aimed at export. These various centers of research and publication (such as the Institute for Palestine Studies and the PLO-affiliated Palestine Research Center) provided key sources for emerging U.S. radical journalism and scholarship.[7]

The second moment, crucially enabled by the first, was the gradual radicalization of U.S. Middle East studies, beginning in the mid-1970s and continuing through the 1980s. Deeply influenced by the political ferment of the 1960s and deploying what Said has called "antithetical knowledge," a younger generation of U.S. scholars began to draw parallels between U.S. imperialist intervention in Vietnam and U.S. support for Israel in the Middle East—an analogy that emerged forcefully only after the 1967 war. This radicalized generation began to enter the professoriate and, in turn, the Middle East Studies Association and to shift the overall terms of the debate on the Middle East and its histories.[8]

The third moment, and in a sense the culmination of the first two, was the appearance of Said's *The Question of Palestine* in 1979, a book that, published by a trade press and thus widely available, sought to redress the invisibility of Palestinians in state and academic accounts of the Middle East and to unsettle the presumed isomorphism of "Palestinian" and "terrorist" in the popular U.S. lexicon of the period. Said's text played a major role in bringing the Palestinian viewpoint into public visibility.

The Israeli invasion of Lebanon (1982) and the first Palestinian uprising or Intifada (1987–1993) mark the fourth and fifth discursive shifts. Although the 1982 Lebanon war provided an incentive for increased organizing on the Palestine question in both academic and activist arenas in the United States, the left liberal public was primarily consumed with cold war concerns (nuclear disarmament, U.S. covert intervention in Central America, etc.). The U.S. response to the uprising of 1987 was quite different. The heightened media visibility of a Palestinian struggle waged by stone-hurling youth against a heavily armed Israeli army helped to educate the public about Palestinian demands for self-determination and to displace the iconic image of the Palestinian terrorist. The Intifada also gave rise to a substantial body of solidarity literature produced in the West. Blurring the lines between activist/journalistic and academic writing on Palestine and Israel, this literature sought to promote the legitimacy of the Palestinian struggle against occupation and to document and expose Israeli human rights violations.[9]

In Israel, by contrast, the Lebanon War of 1982 had substantial political effects—effects that eventually rebounded back into the United States. The violence of the Israeli invasion and occupation, culminating with the massacres at Sabra and Shatila, generated massive antiwar mobilization in the country.[10] Coupled with the state's declassification of information in 1948, this unprecedented culture of protest created the conditions necessary for a radical revisionist trend in the Israeli academy. Israeli Scholars working in the fields of history and sociology undertook projects that seriously rethought the foundational myths of Zionism and state building, myths long hegemonic in Israeli historiography and popular discourse, particularly those pertaining to the 1948 war and the mass dispossession of the Palestinians.[11] This revisionist literature grew in magnitude and force after the outbreak of the first Intifada and began to produce effects in the U.S. academy, a trend that was also enabled by the popular politics and knowledges that the uprising had generated in U.S. activist and academic spaces.[12] By the end of the 1980s and early 1990s, Israeli revisionism had helped to make it legitimate for U.S.-based scholars to talk about Zionism as a colonial movement and to argue that Palestinians were indeed *expelled* from their lands in 1947–48. Graduate students and faculty were able to safely pursue Palestine-centered research and secure funds from major granting institutions; scholars could *begin* to critique Zionist history and ideology in classrooms and conferences without institutional retribution; and academics enjoyed wider audiences for works on Palestine that spoke in a critical, decolonizing idiom.[13] By this time, the focus of revisionist and revisionist-inspired scholarship began to broaden beyond questions of nationalist conflict and occupation to those of gender, citizenship, and minoritarian struggles in the Israeli state, particularly those of Israel's Mizrahi and Palestinian communities.[14]

The sixth moment in our account is the Oslo Accords of 1993. Despite its failure to bring an end to the Israeli occupation, the Oslo process further advanced the academic epistemic shift already underway. In Israel, revisionist scholarship grew in scope and acceptability after 1993; under the Rabin-Peres administration (1992–1996), the work of radical scholars was aired in the pages of Israeli newspapers and on state-run television and catalyzed a brief rethinking of state-sponsored historical textbooks and curriculum (a Ministry of Education initiative that ended when the Likud came to power in 1996). In the United States, the influence of revisionist scholarship grew as government support for the Oslo "peace process" authorized an increased openness toward critiques of Zionism and Israeli history. In tandem, an increasing number of U.S.-based Palestinian scholars were researching and publishing on Palestine and Israel, and their works were circulating in unprecedented ways.[15] It should be noted that the broadening of public debate on Palestine and Israel in both the North American and Israeli academies during this period was partially made possible by a misreading of Oslo as ruptural, that is, as able to inaugurate a just and lasting peace. That the Arab academies were not marked by analogous shifts was partially due to the legacy of a very different political relationship to Oslo, one marked by a fierce critique of normalized relations with Israel and Israeli actions in the Occupied Territories.

Hegemonic Scholarly Paradigms

As this history suggests, scholarship on Palestine and Israel has changed dramatically over the course of the past few decades. The changes are not in political idiom alone. Rather, a new generation of scholars has begun to take up historical questions that "move beyond the narrowly political to explore the social, economic, and cultural histories of each community."[16] These scholars, situated mainly in anthropology and literary studies, have begun to focus on new objects of analysis and to rethink questions of power and knowledge through critical and poststructural theory.[17] Yet, despite such innovations and despite the growing strength of a radical, decolonizing voice in the field, left scholarship is still dominated by relatively traditional methodologies and lines of questioning that have tended to remove or severely marginalize issues of cultural politics.

We argue that such marginalization stems from the analytic paradigms that have long dominated left scholarship on Palestine and Israel in the U.S. academy—paradigms that are imbricated and often articulate through each other. The first may be termed the national paradigm, and the second the Marxist historiographical or political economic paradigm. The former is characterized by a scholarly narrative that installs the nation or nation-state as the inherent logic guiding the critical analysis (that is, Palestine or Israel). In this paradigm, the nation-state figures as both politically determinative and largely enclosed and discrete. Perhaps remarkably, this paradigm remains active in both scholarship that canvasses the international dimension and scholarship that addresses internal heterogeneity within the nation-state—along the lines, for example, of ethnonational difference (notably, as per Palestinian citizens of Israel)[18] and gender. In turn, while the notion of diaspora (both Jewish and Palestinian) has been prominent in this literature, it largely functions as a sign of separation from the national rather than as an analytic tool for deterritorializing the nation-state. While the Marxist model may complicate the narrative of national conflict through attention to political economy, it tends to retain the dyadic model of Israel versus Palestine, albeit configured as a struggle over control of the state and the means of production. The presence of an international dimension in such narratives proceeds according to the logic of class or economic determinism (and, as we noted above, often works to reinscribe the nation-state logic).[19]

Infrequently discussed by scholars in Middle East studies, although heavily debated in other fields, is the rather limited theory of politics and power that these analytic paradigms presume.[20] In both, power is understood in relatively monolithic terms, and its location is presumed to be relatively singular, taking shape in the state (Israeli) or the ruling classes. In the Marxist paradigm, power is rooted primarily in control of the economy, with class struggle understood as the primary locus of political action. In the nation-state model, control of the economy is coupled with control of territory and the coercive and administrative bases of state power (military, police, judiciary, bureaucracy, etc.). What these analytic frameworks share is a notion of power as something that can be held, or at least potentially grasped. The nature of progressive political action is likewise seen as locatable and relatively singular, cohering in the practices of disenfranchised communities and actors, be they Palestinian or Israeli, and aimed explicitly at the creation or defense of the state and nation. Both frameworks presume a binary notion of struggle revolving around the poles of domination and resistance, variously configured.

Cultural practices, objects, and circuits sometimes have a place in these left scholarly frameworks, but in highly circumscribed ways.[21] More often than not, the relative importance of culture is directly proportional to its perceived ability to reflect, serve, and exemplify the political, either in the instrumental service of hegemony or when deployed as a weapon in political struggles. This has been particularly true in the case of literature on Palestine, in which much of the attention accorded to resistance culture (notably, poetry, folk dance, and graffiti) has turned on its ability either to mobilize the masses or to reflect broader oppositional efforts.[22] A similar logic accounts for the proliferation of scholarly work on early Zionist culture—scholarship that has explored the crucial role of culture (e.g., *Shirei Eretz Yisrael*, Songs of the Land of Israel) in building Hebrew character and collective identity in the early state era.[23] Yet, in much of this scholarship, culture is positioned as an effect of broader processes and forms, in peripheral relation to, or as a symptom of, the wider context. And if expressive culture has figured only marginally in this literature, popular culture has been perceived as even more insignificant. This is due, we hypothesize, to assumptions made about the nature of *the commodity*, the form taken by much popular culture. Lurking here is the influence of deterministic Marxist arguments about the ways commodification and mass production effectively denude culture of its political role or potential, even as commodities are deployed as tools with which to control the "stupefied" and consuming masses. When coupled with the scholarly agenda of the national narrative, the problem of the commodity form becomes more intransigent still. The fact that culture as commodity is frequently produced and circulated via global circuits and interests is often thought to endow it with a troubled, even treasonous relation to national interests and struggle agendas.

For many Middle East studies scholars, particularly those who focus on issues of Palestinian society and politics, the instrumentalization or peripheralization of culture is motivated by the exigencies of the occupation and the history of Palestinian dispossession. The argument runs like this: when Palestinians lack a state, when 5 million refugees are without a home, when West Bank residents are cut off from each other and ghettoized in some 220 cantons—what is the possible relevance of an academic study of Palestinian fitness clubs? In an atmosphere of torture, land expropriations, suicide bombings, and massive poverty, isn't it simply frivolous and perhaps even politically irresponsible to devote one's scholarly energies to Israeli punk bands or Palestinian villagers' consumption of U.S. television soap operas? The violence and catastrophe that so frequently prevail in the landscape of Palestine and Israel give added weight to analytical tendencies to read culture as outside of or strictly determined by the realm of the political, and thus of subsidiary importance to the radical scholarly agenda.

The Turn to Cultural Politics

Where, then, might we look for alternatives? In rethinking the theoretical limits of Palestine and Israel scholarship, we begin by turning to the work of the Birmingham School (otherwise known as British cultural studies), particularly that of Stuart Hall and his critical engagement with the writings of Antonio Gramsci. What one encounters in Hall's work is an insistence on the cultural as a crucial terrain of power and struggle that articulates with broader social forces and political economic processes. Counter to the rigid structural determinism of orthodox Marxism, culture has no singular location or function in Hall's account, nor are subcultural or popular cultural forces or actors necessarily inscribed with counterhegemonic meanings or effects. Rather, the terrain of the cultural is contradictory and changeable, "always capable of being dearticulated and rearticulated."[24] It should be noted that even as British cultural studies rejected both the class determinism and base-superstructure dyad of orthodox Marxism, it nonetheless remained within the problematic of Marxism, with an attention to the ways that culture articulates with the "materialities of power and inequality" in differently situated communities.

For scholars of the Birmingham School, the interest in explicitly popular cultural forms has not been incidental. Rather, it has been a crucial component of their attempt to rethink classic Marxist paradigms and analytics with a view toward expanding theoretical conceptions of power. In turn, it has represented an effort to think beyond the high-culture/low-culture dyad that characterized much previous cultural scholarship,[25] according to which high culture carried notions of bourgeois self-cultivation, and low or folk culture carried notions of populist authenticity and was thought to be located "outside of corrupting influences."[26] Instead, Birmingham scholars proposed a popular culture stripped of rigid class location, determining function, or fixed political valence; a form that articulated through multiple and sometimes contradictory modalities of difference (e.g., class, gender, ethnonationality, religion, and place) in ways that were perpetually subject to reinscription. As Tony Bennett has argued, the unfixed nature of popular culture has frustrated attempts at a rigid definition of this term.[27] Nonetheless, Birmingham scholars have insisted on the crucial importance of popular culture in modern mass-mediated societies as a site in and through which people's commonsense interpretations of the world, as well as their own identities, are constructed.[28]

As we have noted, such theorizations of popular culture—to which the framework of this volume is indebted—have relied heavily on Gramsci's work on hegemony. Gramsci argued that the struggle for hegemony, as opposed to that over domination, ranged over a wide array of fronts.[29] Hegemonic power was not something that rulers "held" over the ruled, but the result of complex and shifting interactions between dominant and subordinate. Power, in this model, was not the provenance of a static ruling class, but theorized as transactional, a joint construction, without a fixed or permanent location, inherently unstable and constantly shifting.[30] Central to Gramsci's model was a practice of politics in which would-be hegemonic forces actively work in the domains of the economy, society, and culture in order to produce and secure power.[31] The political struggle between hegemonic powers and subaltern resistant forces, proceeding across the vast array of modern institutions, spaces, and practices, Gramsci termed the "war of position."[32] Culture was deemed integral to such political processes, an essential element in the struggle for gaining consent of the ruled, always working together with and indissoluble from coercion.[33]

To take seriously the theory of cultural politics advanced by the Birmingham School, with particular attention to its reliance on Gramsci, is to substantially rethink the story of culture advanced by radical literature on Palestine and Israel, a rethinking that, again, proceeds within the problematic of Marxism even as it pushes beyond the limits of classic Marxist formulations. The work of Stuart Hall and others enables us to theorize culture as frequently constitutive rather than merely epiphenomenal, as a crucial locus of political engagement, although not in static or necessarily resistive ways, and always working in articulation with broader social forces, political process, and modalities of difference in fluid and variable ways across a range of institutional locations. Such a rethinking entails a substantial retheorization of the nature of the political field. What emerges in such a reconsideration is not merely a proliferation of sites of power but also an expanded conception of the possible avenues and modalities of resistance.

Nations and Relationalities

Yet, what of the "national" paradigm that remains dominant in the field of radical scholarship on Palestine and Israel, with its story of a "conflict" between two discrete national entities? This narrative also requires revision, and though the work of British cultural studies does offer us countermodels,[34] we prefer the historically specific alternatives available in the field of Middle East studies. In particular, we propose a turn to what Zachary Lockman has described, after Perry Anderson, as "relational history."[35] In Lockman's work, relationality was a response to the ways much Palestinian and Zionist historiography, in keeping with the logic of the national paradigm, virtually occluded histories of contact between Palestinian Arabs and Jews. Relational history opened up the space to narrate interdependence and to dismantle the Palestinian Arab/Jew binary (often figured as an Arab/Jew binary)[36] that national logics have tended to presume.

Building on the work of Lockman, this volume is committed to a notion of relationality that works more expansively in both scale and kind. First, although we certainly aim to consider what Lockman calls the "mutually formative interactions" *between* Palestinian Arabs and Jews in the pre- and poststate period (see Tamari and LeVine, both this volume), we also aim to account for divides and histories of contact *within* each nation and national formation.[37] An attention to what one might call *intranational relationality* helps to pluralize the story of interaction by considering the ways that gender, religion, ethnoracial identity and country of origin cut across nations and nationalisms in ways that further destabilize the fiction of the Palestinian Arab/Jew divide.[38] Second, even as we concern ourselves with interactions and forms of relationality at the intranational and national levels, we are also interested in the place of Palestine and Israel in larger geopolitical networks and geographies: cultural, economic, and political (see Layoun, this volume). At issue here is an attention to what could be called *transnational relationality*, that is, to forms of contact, community, and mutual contingency that span checkpoints, walls, and histories of interstate enmity and that circulate with the commodity form and the Internet through increasingly global channels of commerce and culture.

Although we deploy the keyword *transnational*, this volume positions itself in contrast to much of the recent scholarship on transnationalism, with its frequently celebratory narrative of politics and social forms situated "beyond the nation-state." Instead, we insist on the continuing importance and reemergence of the nation-state as an ideological-political form in the midst of globalizing processes, a tension that is particularly acute in the case of Palestinians and their struggle for liberation, the still unrealized aim of which remains the nation-state. We argue that rather than illustrating a logic of deterritorialization, the present-day (and past) conflict between Palestine and Israel illustrates the ongoing violence associated with the enduring, exclusivist ideologies of the national. Thus it is that attention to transnational and intranational forms of border crossing and mutual contingency within and across Palestine and Israel must also be accompanied by attention to histories and emerging forms of division, both territorial and ideological in nature. The challenge is to consider the two in tandem: both (for example) the rising popularity among Israeli audiences of Jewish and Palestinian rap artists, with their syncretic mix of local idioms and global musical aesthetics, and the rising support, among Israeli Jews, for total separation from the Palestinians, premised on a desire for ethnonational purity; both the alternative structures of transnational Palestinian and pan-Arab community made possible by new media and technologies (e.g., satellite television and the Internet; see Khalili, this volume) and the new forms of spatial incarceration and division that the separation barrier is forcing on the Palestinian population in the West Bank and Gaza Strip.

This attention to relationality in its multiple forms is also an attempt to rethink the place of Israel in the field of Middle East studies. Historically,

Rebecca L. Stein and Ted Swedenburg

much scholarship in the field has avoided sustained engagement with the state of Israel, apart from its legacy as a Western colonial outpost.[39] Avoidance was thought to do the work of radical anti-Zionist critique, effectively removing the Jewish state from the map of the region. Perhaps ironically, this mapping echoed the imagined geography of much Zionist ideology, with its fantasy of Israel as a European nation-state apart from the Arab Middle East. This volume proposes a different cartography, one that reinscribes Israel within the region and the purview of Middle East studies scholarship. While we are in agreement with critiques of area studies that have attended to the fiction of the hermetic geographic area and its arbitrary borders as imagined territorial unit, we are also interested in questions of interiority and inclusion within a given area. At issue in the case of Middle East studies is not simply the area per se, but the question of what has been excluded from within its parameters and the conditions of possibility for this exclusion.

Popular Culture and the Challenge to History

Central to this volume is the claim that attention to popular culture configures both politics and history differently, providing a significant alternative to some of the political narratives and paradigms that have dominated academic, activist, and popular discourse on Palestine and Israel. The history of the past decade is a case in point, for although major political shifts and struggles have been carefully documented and critiqued by scholars and activists alike, concurrent changes in cultural production and consumption have been granted far less attention. Attention to such cultural trends, we argue, yields a fuller chronicle of politics and power than political economy or diplomatic history models alone can provide.

The Oslo or Middle East "peace process" of the 1990s profoundly affected popular cultural trends in the region even as it was, in part, propelled by these trends. In Israel, the cultural changes were marked. One witnessed, for example, a radicalization in the film industry. After a history of largely phobic cinematic engagements with Palestinian Arab culture, feature films and documentaries began to critically reassess the founding myths of Zionism (see Pappé and Bardenstein, both this volume).[40] Such new forms of representation were effects of the Oslo process and also spawned both political support for and resistance to the ambiguous trajectory of the Oslo process itself. One also saw the emergence of a new Euro-Israeli curiosity in the commodity value of Arab things (food, music, dress) and places as tourist sites—a curiosity made possible by Israeli diplomacy with its Arab neighbors (see Stein, this volume).[41] At the same time, as Mizrahi political power grew, Mizrahi cultural figures acquired greater visibility in Israel and the broader Middle East (see Horowitz, this volume).[42] Shifting demography also altered the popular cultural landscape. By the turn of the twenty-first century, the massive influx of Russian immigrants, combined with a growing population of legal and illegal workers from the third world, was introducing new musical forms, sports practices, and culinary traditions into Israeli cities (e.g., South Asian cricket teams and Thai and Chinese groceries in Israel's new urban peripheries).

The Palestinian popular cultural landscape was also changing, although in very different ways. With the onset of "peace" talks, the "Intifada culture" of struggle, sacrifice, austerity, and seriousness gradually lifted, and repressed forms of everyday culture (re)emerged.[43] Weddings were extravagantly celebrated; pop bands that had disbanded during the Intifada reappeared. New sites of cultural consumption sprang up, although selectively and often meeting with resistance catering to the growing Palestinian middle class (bars in Ramallah, cinemas and cinema clubs in Ramallah, Bethlehem, and Gaza City). As part of its state-building efforts, the Palestinian Authority fostered new national media institutions that enabled the creation and dissemination of novel or submerged cultural forms (songs, radio talk shows, television serials, and movies; on the last, see Alexander, this volume).[44] Although few cultural commodities crossed the Green Line during this period, audiences in both Israel and Palestine were conjoined through the consumption of shared global commodities, media, and popular icons. At the same time, the proliferation of satellite television allowed Palestinians in the Territories to turn away from Israeli Arabic-language TV and toward satellite networks based in the Arab world (such as al-Jazeera), which effectively incorporated Palestinians into pan-Arab cultural and political trends.

Since the onset of the al-Aqsa Intifada in October 2000, both Israeli and Palestinian societies have returned to conflict mode. In the West Bank and Gaza, frequent curfews and closures, extreme restrictions on mobility, army violence, the decline in disposable income, and the return of the "struggle atmosphere" have virtually closed down the spaces of popular sociality and consumption that had expanded during the 1990s, except in cosmopolitan Ramallah and, to a lesser degree, Bethlehem. In Ramallah, cultural institutions (e.g., the National Conservatory of Music) continued to flourish, testimony to the continued growth of the emerging middle class; likewise, audiences remained strong at film showings, art exhibits, and concerts, albeit with the occasional interruptions caused by curfew and invasion.[45] In less central or wealthy Palestinian localities, the second uprising produced an interiorization of the social, as families and individuals incarcerated in the domestic sphere turned to television, video games, and the Internet as modes of entertainment and communication between communities separated by the (re)occupation, trends that intensified after the Israeli military incursion in March 2002 (see Khalili, this volume). At the same time, Palestinian society has witnessed the emergence of a popular culture of "martyrdom operations" ("suicide bombings," in Western parlance), celebrated with posters, graffiti, popular music, and song, all of which raises significant challenges to the secular nationalist culture that developed during the 1990s.[46]

In Sharon's Israel, the pervasive fear (both real and imagined) of random Palestinian violence has increasingly curtailed prior rituals and geographies of consumption, even as it has generated new ones. Flight from the urban periphery to escape possible attacks has catalyzed the growth and popularity of U.S.-style malls as loci of middle-class consumption and leisure.[47] These carefully guarded and fully contained consumptive spaces, emerging for the first time in the 1990s as the fruits of "peace through globalization," have been re-marked and revalued as safe havens from terror.[48] The 1990s' popularity of "Arab" culture, restaurants, and places among Ashkenazi Israelis has now been eclipsed by the rise of anti-Arab phobia and racism and by the nostalgic return to canonical Zionist cultural practices (as in the renewed popularity of the sing-along). In turn, an angry culture of hip-hop has emerged among Palestinian Israeli youth, raising such issues as Jewish Israeli racism, unemployment, and endemic poverty (see Massad, this volume). And as levels of army violence have swelled, along with growing numbers of conscientious objectors and army evaders, Jewish youth cultures of escapism have also grown, cultures centered on trance music, drug use, and the aesthetics of the so-called Far East.[49] This period has also seen the disintegration of many cooperative cultural projects between Israelis and Palestinians from the Occupied Territories.[50] Yet, on both sides of the Green Line or wall, the nationalist tendencies of popular culture coexist with the increasing globalization of media and culture (e.g., the growing prevalence of international cable and satellite television)[51] and, in Israel, of labor (e.g., the growing populations of non-Palestinian foreign workers).

Finally, in this period since the outset of the second Palestinian uprising, we have also witnessed a change in the ways Palestine and Israel are understood and deployed as signifiers in regional and international arenas of popular culture. The Arab Middle East has seen the growth of an anti-normalization discourse (decrying "normalized" relations with Israel) that often takes popular cultural forms and institutions as its target of scrutiny (film, television, and music).[52] In turn, in the Middle East, "Palestine" once more circulates as tragic-heroic fetish object (see Colla and Swedenburg, both this volume). In the era of the "war on terror," anti-Arab discourses have acquired renewed popularity in the United States, as manifest in the renaissance of the antiterrorism movies on cable television that have returned the iconic figure of the "Arab terrorist" to popular culture's center stage. Simultaneously, the popular culture of the Christian right, with its apocalyptic Zionist message, has grown in scale and consumer popularity in the form of comic books, graphic novels, and film (see McAlister, this volume). The complexities of these cultural landscapes defy a singular reading.

Alternative Futures

To read this history through the lens of Birmingham School analytics is to be attentive both to the ways culture of the past two decades has necessarily articulated through contemporaneous social and political processes, and to insist on the highly variable effects of such articulations. Popular culture has constituted a site of struggle against hegemonic discourses (as in post-Zionist cinema and Palestinian Israeli rap music); has been crucial to processes of class formation and class consolidation (as in the growth and expression of middle-class Palestinian taste); has been used as a tool to fortify nationalist ideologies and hatreds; and has functioned to undercut the hegemony of secular-nationalist ideologies (as per "martyrdom" culture). All instances, however variable in their forms and effects, problematize the fiction of popular culture as the constitutive other of politics.

The project of this volume is multiple: to read Palestinian and Israeli popular cultures closely in articulation with the histories and processes in which they are embedded; to chronicle the social life of popular cultural forms in the region and its diasporas, both as they traverse borders, checkpoints, walls, and ethnonational difference, and are confined by them; and, finally, to consider the ways such cultural forms and practices circulate within and articulate with broader regional and global spheres and contexts. Together, the essays speak diachronically (beginning as early as the late nineteenth century and concluding in the present) and trans-spatially (from the Middle East to the United States and beyond). We seek to unmoor popular culture from a particular historical period, and Palestine and Israel from a rigid geographic grid, in an effort to think more expansively about culture-power relations.

A project of this kind and scope, we believe, requires an interdisciplinary approach. Thus, the essays in this volume draw on a wide range of scholarly methodologies and traditions, bringing together scholars from the fields of history, sociology, ethnomusicology, literary studies, anthropology, and political science. By bridging intellectual traditions that are not usually conjoined in the field of Middle East studies, by spanning a diverse set of historical periods, and by situating our study in national, regional, and global contexts, we aim to imagine and stimulate new kinds of approaches in the field and new sets of conceptual paradigms in which Palestine and Israel might be thought.

Notes

Thanks to Joel Beinin, Yael Ben-Zvi, Robert Blecher, Elliott Colla, Andrew Janiak, Penny Johnson, Zachary Lockman, Negar Mottahedeh, and several anonymous readers for their careful readings and helpful suggestions on earlier versions. A shortened version of this introduction appeared as "Popular Culture, Relational History, and the Question of Power in Palestine and Israel," *Journal of Palestine Studies* 33, no. 4 (summer 2004): 5–20. Thanks to Linda Butler for helping us work out our arguments prior to the appearance of this volume.

1. In this introduction, when we speak of Israel, we are referring to the country within its pre-1967 borders. When we speak of Israeli culture, we are also including settler culture in the West Bank and Gaza Strip.

2. The most important exception is the foundational work of Ella Shohat, particularly *Israeli Cinema: East/West and the Politics of Representation* (Austin: University of Texas Press, 1989). Additional work in this area, much of it recent, includes the following: Husayn al-'Awdat, *Al-sinima wa-al-qadiya al-Filastiniya* [Cinema and the Palestinian question] (Damascus: al-Ahali, 1987); Oz Almog, *The Sabra: The Creation of the New Jew* (Berkeley: University of California Press, 2000); Nurith Gertz, *Myths in Israeli Culture: Captives of a Dream* (London: Valentine Mitchell, 2000); Yosefa Loshitzky, *Identity Politics on the Israeli Screen* (Austin: University of Texas Press, 2002); Motti Regev and Edwin Seroussi, *Popular Music and National Culture in Israel* (Berkeley: University of California Press, 2004); Raz Yosef, *Beyond Flesh: Queer Masculinities and Nationalisms in Israeli Cinema* (New Brunswick, N.J.: Rutgers University Press, 2004); Walid Shamit and Guy Hennebelle, eds., *Filastin fi al-sinima* [Palestine in cinema] (Beirut: Fajr, 1980). As this list suggests, one sees growing attention to Israeli popular culture, particularly to film and television, in the U.S. and Israeli academies.

There has been considerably less new work on Palestinian popular culture. Recent monographs on Middle Eastern popular culture in broader terms include the following: Walter Armbrust, *Mass Culture and Modernism in Egypt* (Cambridge, England: Cambridge University Press, 1996) and *Mass Mediations: New Approaches to Popular Culture in the Middle East and Beyond* (Berkeley: University of California Press, 2000); Mai Ghoussoub and Emma Sinclair-West, *Imagined Masculinities: Male Identity and Culture in the Modern Middle East* (London: Saqi Books, 2000); Joel Gordon, *Revolutionary Melodrama: Popular Film and Civic Identity in Nasser's Egypt* (Chicago: University of Chicago Press, 2002); Melani McAlister, *Epic Encounters: Culture, Media, and U.S. Interests in the Middle East, 1945–2000* (Berkeley: University of California Press, 2001); Hamid Naficy, *An Accented Cinema: Exilic and Diasporic Filmmaking* (Princeton: Princeton University Press, 2001) and *The Making of Exile Cultures: Iranian Television in Los Angeles* (Minneapolis: University of Minnesota Press, 1993); Viola Shafik, *Arab Cinema: History and Cultural Identity* (Cairo: American University Press, 1998); Martin Stokes, *The Arabesk Debate: Music and Musicians in Modern Turkey* (New York: Oxford University Press, 1992). These lists are by no means exhaustive.

3. The section that follows outlines the genealogy of this scholarship.

4. At the first annual Middle East Studies Association (MESA) meetings in 1967 and for several years thereafter, as MESA's 2002 president recently noted, the Israel-Palestine conflict was considered too "controversial" a subject for discussion. Joel Beinin, "2002 Presidential Address: Middle East Studies after September 11, 2001," *Middle East Studies Association Bulletin* 37, no. 1 (2003): 15. As late as the early 1990s, as an article in the *Chronicle of Higher Education* put it, it "was not always a wise career move" for aspiring U.S. scholars to work on the (so-called) question of Palestine. See Ellen K. Coughlin, "As Perceptions of the Palestinian People Change, Study of Their History and Society Grows," *Chronicle of Higher Education*, 19 February 1992, A8.

5. Recent examples include Nadia Abu El-Haj, *Facts on the Ground: Archeological Practice and Territorial Self-Fashioning in Israeli Society* (Chicago: University of Chicago Press, 2001) and Gershon Shafir and Yoav Peled, *Being Israeli: The Dynamics of Multiple Citizenship* (Cambridge, England: Cambridge University Press, 2002).

6. In his introduction, Said writes: "To the West, which is where I live, to be a Palestinian is in political terms to be an outlaw of sorts, or at any rate very much an outsider. But that is a reality, and I mention it today only as a way of indicating the peculiar loneliness of my undertaking in this book." Edward Said, *The Question of Palestine* (New York: Vintage Books, 1979), xviii. Examples of recent radical scholarship on Palestine and Palestinian society include the following: Abu El-Haj, *Facts on the Ground*; George Bisharat, *Palestinian Lawyers and Israeli Rule: Law and Disorder in the West Bank* (Austin: University of Texas Press, 1989); Beshara Doumani, *Rediscovering Palestine: Merchants and Peasants in Jabal Nablus, 1700–1900* (Berkeley: University of California Press, 1995); Joost Hiltermann, *Behind the Intifada: Labor and Women's Movements in the Occupied Territories* (Princeton: Princeton University Press, 1991); Rhoda Ann Kanaaneh, *Birthing the Nation: Strategies of Palestinian Women in Israel* (Berkeley: University of California Press, 2002); Rashid Khalidi, *Palestinian Identity: The Construction of Modern National Consciousness* (New York: Columbia University Press, 1997); Julie M. Peteet, *Gender in Crisis: Women and the Palestinian Resistance*

Movement (New York: Columbia University Press, 1991); Susan Slyomovics, *The Object of Memory: Arab and Jew Narrate the Palestinian Village* (Philadelphia: University of Pennsylvania Press, 1998); Ted Swedenburg, *Memories of Revolt: The 1936–1939 Rebellion and the Palestinian National Past* (Minneapolis: University of Minnesota Press, 1995; reprinted Fayetteville: University of Arkansas Press, 2003); Judith Tucker, *In the House of the Law: Gender and Islamic Law in Ottoman Syria and Palestine* (Berkeley: University of California Press, 1998).

7. Such institutions also included the Fifth of June Society and the American Friends of the Middle East. The *Journal of Palestine Studies*, which began publication in Beirut in 1971 under the auspices of the Institute for Palestine Studies, is also critical in this regard. Additional important publications from the Institute for Palestine Studies include Nevill Barbour, *Nisi Dominus: A Survey of the Palestine Controversy*, 1969; Henry Cattan, *The Dimensions of the Palestine Problem, 1967*, 1968; Peter Dodd and Halim Barakat, *River without Bridges: A Study of the Exodus of the 1967 Palestinian Arab Refugees*, 1969; Michael E. Jansen, *United States and the Palestinian People*, 1970; Sabri Jiryis, *The Arabs in Israel, 1948–1966*, 1969; Walid Khalidi, ed., *From Haven to Conquest: Readings in Zionism and the Palestine Problem until 1948*, 1971; Hisham Sharabi, *Palestine Guerrillas: Their Credibility and Effectiveness*, 1970; Richard P. Stevens, *Zionism and Palestine before the Mandate: A Phase of Western Imperialism*, 1972; Alan Taylor, *Prelude to Israel: An Analysis of Zionist Diplomacy, 1897–1947*, 1970. Many of these books remain in print.

8. Key actors in this development include the Association of Arab-American University Graduates (which publishes the *Arab Studies Quarterly*), the Alternative Middle East Studies Seminar, and the Middle East Research and Information Project (publisher of MERIP *Reports*, later renamed *Middle East Report*).

9. See Ebba Augustin, ed., *Palestinian Women: Identity and Experience* (London: Zed Books, 1993); Phyllis Bennis, *From Stones to Statehood: The Palestinian Uprising* (New York: Olive Branch Press, 1990); Sherna Berger Gluck, *An American Feminist in Palestine: The Intifada Years* (Philadelphia: Temple University Press, 1994); Zachary Lockman and Joel Beinin, eds., *Intifada: The Palestinian Uprising against Israeli Occupation* (Boston: South End Press, 1989); Jamal R. Nassar and Roger Heacock, eds., *Intifada: Palestine at the Crossroads* (New York: Praeger, 1990); Don Peretz, *Intifada: The Palestinian Uprising* (Boulder, Colo.: Westview Press, 1990); Elise G. Young, *Keepers of the History* (New York: Teachers College Press, 1992); Kitty Warnock, *Land before Honour: Palestinian Women in the Occupied Territories* (New York: Monthly Review Press, 1990).

10. On this period of protest, see Adam Keller, *Terrible Days: Social Divisions and Political Paradoxes in Israel* (Amstelveen, Netherlands: Cypres, 1987).

11. For a brief history of the emergence of Israeli revisionist scholarship and the political conditions that made this emergence possible, see Zachary Lockman, "Original Sin," in *Intifada*, ed. Lockman and Beinin (Boston: South End Press, 1989), 185–204. Useful surveys of Israeli revisionist scholarship include Laurence Silberstein, *The Postzionism Debates: Knowledge and Power in Israeli Culture* (New York: Routledge, 1998) and the special issue of *History and Memory* 7, no. 1 (1995).

12. As Joel Beinin argues, the initial breach in the Israeli national consensus, and

therein the possibility for the demthyologizing of history, occurred as a result of the "shock over the 'lapse' which allowed Egypt and Syria to seize the intiative in the first stages of 1973." In turn, Beinin suggests that the shift in Israeli history, memory, and scholarship in the 1980s and 1990s is propelled by "quality of life issues" and the "senseless deaths of Israeli soldiers" in Lebanon, rather than by a concern about the continuing Israeli occupation or the invasion of Lebanon per se. Joel Beinin, "Intellectual and Political Limits of New Israeli History," unpublished manuscript, 14.

13. See n. 5 for examples of this work.

14. The scholarship on Israel, occupation, and the politics of gender that emerged during this period includes the following: Ayala H. Emmett, *Our Sisters' Promised Land: Women, Politics, and Israeli-Palestinian Coexistence* (Ann Arbor: University of Michigan Press, 1996); Tamar Mayer, ed. *Women and the Israeli Occupation: The Politics of Change* (New York: Routledge, 1994); Simona Sharoni, *Gender and the Israeli Palestinian Conflict: The Politics of Women's Resistance* (Syracuse: Syracuse University Press, 1995); Barbara Swirski and Marilyn P. Safir, eds., *Calling the Equality Bluff: Women in Israel* (New York: Teachers College Press, 1991). Much of the extensive literature on gender in Palestinian society belongs to another intellectual and political genealogy, one not marked, in the same ways, by the Israeli revisionist tradition.

New and foundational scholarship on the Mizrahi and Sephardi communities includes Shohat, *Israeli Cinema*; Sammy Smooha, *Israel: Pluralism and Conflict* (London: Routledge and Kegan Paul, 1978); Shafir and Peled, *Being Israeli*; Shlomo Swirski, *Israel: The Mizrahi Majority* (London: Zed Books, 1989); Alex Weingrod, ed., *Studies in Israeli Ethnicity: After the Ingathering* (New York: Routledge, 1985); Oren Yiftachel and Avinoam Meir, eds., *Ethnic Frontiers and Peripheries: Landscapes of Development and Inequality in Israel* (Boulder, Colo.: Westview, 1998).

Recent scholarship on Palestinians within the Israeli state includes As'ad Ghanem, *The Palestinian-Arab Minority in Israel, 1948–2000: A Political Study* (Albany: State University of New York Press, 2001); Kanaaneh, *Birthing the Nation*; Nadim N. Rouhana, *Palestinian Citizens in an Ethnic Jewish State* (New Haven: Yale University Press, 1997); Dan Rabinowitz, *Overlooking Nazareth: The Ethnography of Exclusion in Galilee* (Cambridge, England: Cambridge University Press, 1997); Oren Yiftachel, "State Policies, Land Control and an Ethnic Minority: The Arabs in the Galilee, Israel," *Society and Space* 9 (1991): 329–362. The earlier, foundational literature includes Sabri Jiryis, *The Arabs in Israel* (New York: Monthly Review Press, 1976); Ian Lustick, *Arabs in the Jewish State: Israel's Control of a National Minority* (Austin: University of Texas Press, 1980); and Sammy Smooha, *The Orientation and Politicization of the Arab Minority in Israel* (Haifa: Haifa University Press, 1980).

15. In addition to the work of Edward Said, see, for instance, El-Haj, *Facts on the Ground*; Doumani, *Rediscovering Palestine*; Ghanem, *The Palestinian-Arab Minority in Israel, 1948–2000*; Kanaaneh, *Birthing the Nation*; R. Khalidi, *Palestinian Identity*; and Rouhana, *Palestinian Citizens in an Ethnic Jewish State*.

16. Zachary Lockman, *Comrades and Enemies: Arab and Jewish Workers in Palestine, 1906–1948* (Berkeley: University of California Press, 1996), 8.

17. An instance of the former includes Susan Martha Kahn, *Reproducing Jews: A Cultural Account of Assisted Conception in Israel* (Durham, N.C.: Duke University Press,

2000). Instances of the latter include Daniel Bertrand Monk, *An Aesthetic Occupation: The Immediacy of Architecture and the Palestine Conflict* (Durham, N.C.: Duke University Press, 2002) and El-Haj, *Facts on the Ground*.

18. As Robert Blecher has argued, recent scholarship on the state's Palestinian citizens still privileges political formations, struggles, and alliances *within* Israel's borders, emphasizing their status as Israeli citizens rather than Palestinian nationals. See Blecher, "Citizens without Sovereignty: Ethnic Cleansing and Transfer in Israel," forthcoming, *Comparative Studies in Society and History*.

19. Examples of Marxist-inflected scholarship include Joel Beinin, *Was the Red Flag Flying There? Marxist Politics and the Arab-Israeli Conflict in Egypt and Israel, 1948–1965* (Berkeley: University of California Press, 1990); Adel Samara, *Industrialisation in the West Bank: A Marxist Socio-economic Analysis, 1967–1991* (Jerusalem: Al-Mashriq Publications for Economic and Development Studies, 1992); Michael Shalev, *Labour and the Political Economy in Israel* (Oxford: Oxford University Press, 1992); Gershon Shafir, *Land, Labor and the Origin of the Israeli-Palestinian Conflict: 1882–1914* (Cambridge, England: Cambridge University Press, 1989); and Elia Zureik, *Israel: A Study in Internal Colonialism* (London: Routledge and Kegan Paul, 1979). Examples of the national paradigm include Helena Cobban, *The Palestinian Liberation Organisation: People, Power and Politics* (Cambridge, England: Cambridge University Press, 1984); Norman Finkelstein, *Image and Reality of the Israel-Palestine Conflict* (New York: Verso, 1995); Simha Flapan, *The Birth of Israel: Myths and Realities* (New York: Pantheon, 1987); 'Abd al-Wahhab Kayyali, *Palestine: A Modern History* (London: Croom Helm, 1978); R. Khalidi, *Palestinian Identity*; Walid Khalidi, *All That Remains: The Palestinian Villages Occupied and Depopulated by Israel in 1948* (Washington, D.C.: Institute for Palestine Studies, 1992); Baruch Kimmerling and Joel S. Migdal, *The Palestinian People: A History* (Cambridge, Mass.: Harvard University Press, 2003); Muhammad Y. Muslih, *The Origins of Palestinian Nationalism* (New York: Columbia University Press, 1988); William Quandt, Fuad Jabber, and Ann Mosely Lesch, eds., *The Politics of Palestinian Nationalism* (Berkeley: University of California Press, 1973); Yezid Sayigh, *Armed Struggle and the Search for State: The Palestinian National Movement 1949–1993* (Oxford: Oxford University Press, 1997). This list is by no means exhaustive.

20. Arguably, this concern with rethinking the parameters of the political was at the center of Edward Said's work in *Orientalism* (New York: Vintage, 1979); yet, despite Said's enormous influence on Palestine scholarship, this concern remains marginal to most scholars in the field. On the other hand, critical literature in other areas has extensively addressed the limits of both nationalist and Marxist paradigms with regard to the question of the political. In our discussion, we particularly draw on the work of postcolonial theorists aimed at conceptualizing power beyond progressivist and determinist Marxist narratives. For a particularly clear articulation of how postcolonial theory has tried to move beyond these frameworks in its account of coloniality, see David Scott, *Refashioning Futures* (Princeton: Princeton University Press, 1999). It should also be noted that, in the past decade, scholars in the field have begun seriously to rethink the conceptual limitations of the nation-state paradigm, just as they have the area studies rubric more generally, with a concern for the ways the fiction

of a hermetic nation-state forecloses attention to forms and processes not contained by its real and imagined boundaries. The work of Zachary Lockman is of particular importance in this regard. We take up his argument in the next section of this essay.

21. It should be noted that many anthropologists working in the Palestine and Israel have been attentive to daily cultural practices and the ways they intersect with political processes. Such scholarship includes Eyal Ben Air and Yoram Bilu, *Grasping Land: Space and Place in Contemporary Israeli Discourse and Experience* (Albany: State University of New York Press, 1997); Jonathan Boyarin, *Palestine and Jewish History: Criticism at the Borders of Ethnography* (Minneapolis: University of Minnesota Press, 1996); Virginia R. Domínguez, *People as Subject, People as Object: Selfhood and Peoplehood in Contemporary Israel* (Madison: University of Wisconsin Press, 1989); Kanaaneh, *Birthing the Nation*; Rabinowitz, *Overlooking Nazareth*; Slyomovics, *The Object of Memory*; Swedenburg, *Memories of Revolt*.

22. An example of such a reading is Hanan Ashrawi's article, "The Contemporary Palestinian Poetry of Occupation," *Journal of Palestine Studies* 7, no. 3 (1978): 77–101. Ashrawi divides Palestinian poets into the "nationalist, committed, and politically aware poets, who view poetry primarily as a means of moving the masses" and the "individualistic" poets, whom she essentially dismisses. The latter, among whom she includes Anton Shammas (subsequently much celebrated for his novel *Arabesques*), are accused of being "totally detached from their setting." See also Barbara Harlow, *Resistance Literature* (London: Routledge, 1987).

23. For an excellent review of the history of the Shirei Eretz Yisrael, see Regev and Serousi, *Popular Music and Culture in Israel*, 49–70. This fine work is an exception to the trend in reading music, or popular culture more broadly, instrumentally.

24. Lawrence Grossberg, "History, Politics, and Postmodernism: Stuart Hall and Cultural Studies," in *Stuart Hall: Critical Dialogues in Cultural Studies*, ed. David Morley and Kuan-Hsing Chen (London: Routledge 1996), 158.

25. Tony Bennett, "Introduction," in *Popular Culture and Social Relations*, ed. Tony Bennett, Colin Mercer, and Janet Woollacott (Milton Keyes, England: Open University Press, 1986), xi–xii.

26. See Raymond Williams, *Keywords: A Vocabulary of Society and Culture*, revised ed. (Oxford: Oxford University Press, 1985). Hall goes further in refusing the myth of folk culture: "Since the inception of commercial capitalism and the drawing of all relations into the net of market transactions, there has been little or no 'pure' culture of the people—no separate folk-realm of the authentic popular, where 'the people' existed in their pure state, outside of the corrupting influences" (Grossberg, "History, Politics, and Postmodernism," 163).

27. Tony Bennett, "The Politics of the 'Popular' and Popular Culture," *Popular Culture and Social Relations*, Bennett, Mercer, and Woollacott, eds., 8.

28. Lawrence Grossberg, "Pedagogy in the Present," in *Popular Culture, Schooling, and Everyday Life*, ed. Henry Giroux and Roger Simon (New York: Bergin and Garvey, 1989), 94.

29. All systems of rule, in Gramsci's schema, were based on a combination of coercion and persuasion. "Domination" (*dominio*) was the term Gramsci used to identify

a mixture of persuasion and coercion decisively weighted in favor of force and repression (i.e., dictatorships, monarchies, and colonial regimes). "Hegemony" (*egemonia*), in turn, identified systems of political authority (i.e., modern "bourgeois democracies") where persuasion, or gaining the active consent of the ruled, was the predominant feature. See Antonio Gramsci, *Selections from the Prison Notebooks*, ed. Quintin Hoare and Geoffrey Nowell-Smith (London: Lawrence and Wishart, 1970) and Antonio Gramsci, *Selections from Cultural Writings*, ed. David Forgacs and Geoffrey Nowell-Smith (Cambridge, Mass.: Harvard University Press, 1991).

30. Given the expansion of civil society characteristic of the modern nation-state, these locations and modalities, sites and institutions included educational establishments, the mass media, workplaces, legal apparatuses, government bureaucracies, spaces of consumption and entertainment, and so on.

31. The hegemony of a class or class fraction depends on its capacity to actively win consent and thereby to gain the ability to claim that it represents the "universal" interests of the entire society. See Anne Showstack Sassoon, "Hegemony, War of Position and Political Intervention," in *Approaches to Gramsci*, ed. Anne Showstack Sassoon (London: Writers and Readers, 1982), 111.

32. According to Gramsci, in political systems characterized by *dominio* (see n. 29), open political struggle involved two relatively fixed sides in opposing and discrete trenches. Such a struggle he termed "war of maneuver."

33. It should be apparent that the work of Michel Foucault and his conceptualization of power is critical to our rethinking of popular culture and informs our reading of Gramsci. It is important to stress, however, that Foucault's notion(s) of power cannot simply be assimilated to those of Gramsci's hegemony; see Timothy Mitchell, "The Limits of the State: Beyond Statist Approaches and Their Critics," *American Political Science Review* 85, no. 1 (1991): 77–96. To turn primarily to Gramscian scholarship, as opposed to Foucaultian scholarship, to do the work of rethinking culture is also to suggest ways radical scholarship on Palestine and Israel can work "within shouting distance of Marxism" (as Stuart Hall argues), even as it rethinks the more orthodox tenets associated with the Marxist tradition.

34. The critique of such national paradigms is also at issue for scholars of the Birmingham School, particularly Paul Gilroy. See his *The Black Atlantic: Modernity and Double Consciousness* (Cambridge, Mass.: Harvard University Press, 1993).

35. Lockman, *Comrades and Enemies*, 8.

36. On the history of this binary in Zionist thought and ideology, and the ways it has rendered the Mizrahim invisible, see Ella Shohat, "Reflections of an Arab Jew," *Emergences* 3, no. 4 (1992): 39–45, and "Sephardim in Israel: Zionism from the Standpoint of Its Jewish Victims," in *Dangerous Liaisons: Gender, Nation, and Postcolonial Perspectives*, ed. Anne McClintock, Aamir Mufti, and Ella Shohat (Minneapolis: University of Minnesota Press, 1997).

37. Ibid., 9.

38. Thanks to an anonymous reader for pushing us on this point.

39. The emergence of Israel studies as a field outside of Middle East studies is was an effect of this trend in the scholarship.

40. See Ilan Pappé, "Post-Zionist Critique on Israel and the Palestinians: Popular Culture," *Journal of Palestine Studies* 26, no. 4 (1997): 60–69; Livia Alexander, "Conflicting Images: Palestinian and Israeli Cinemas, 1988–1998," PhD diss., New York University, 2001.

41. It should be noted that only certain forms of "Arab" culture became popular among Euro-Jewish consumers: those whose story or semiotics of Palestinianness did not pose a fundamental threat to the Jewish state. See Rebecca Stein, "National Itineraries, Itinerant Nations: Israeli Tourism and Palestinian Cultural Production," *Social Text* 56 (1998): 91–124.

42. On the growing popularity of Mizrahi popular rock during this era, see Motti Regev, "*Musica Mizrakhit*, Israeli Rock and National Culture in Israel," *Popular Music* 15, no. 3 (1996): 275–284.

43. On the everyday culture of the first Intifada, see Rema Hammami, "Women's Political Participation in the Intifada: A Critical Overview," in *The Intifada and Some Women's Social Issues* (Ramallah: Bisan Center for Research and Development, 1991), 77.

44. See Lena Jayyusi, "The Voice of Palestine and the Peace Process: Paradoxes in Media Discourse after Oslo," in *After Oslo: New Realities, Old Problems*, ed. George Giacaman and Dag Jrund Lonning (London: Pluto Press, 1998), 189–211.

45. Expressive culture at these venues tends to draw from the paradoxes, tragedies, and even comedies of Intifada quotidian life. One example is Vera Tamari's art installation *"Going for a Ride?"* at the Friends' Boys School Playground in El Bireh, 23 June–23 July 2002. The installation was created out of cars destroyed in the April 2002 invasion of Ramallah. See Penny Johnson, "Ramallah Dada: The Reality of the Absurd," *Jerusalem Quarterly File* 16, 2002. Available at: http://www.jqf-jerusalem.org/2002/jqf16/dada.html.

46. Lori Allen, "There Are Many Reasons Why: Suicide Bombers and Martyrs in Palestine," *Middle East Report* 32 no. 2 (summer 2002): 34–37.

47. On the growth of McDonald's culture in Israel as part of the Americanizing trend, see Uri Ram, "Glocommodification: How the Global Consumes the Local. McDonald's in Israel," *Current Sociology* 52, no. 1 (2004): 11–31.

48. At the same time, Israeli consumptive practices, deemed an affront to Palestinian terror and its labors of disturbing the Israeli everyday, have been invested with a discourse of Israeli patriotic defiance. See Rebecca L. Stein, "Israeli Leisure, 'Palestinian Terror,' and the Question of Palestine (Again)," *Theory and Event* 6, no. 3 (2002).

49. This aesthetic is a byproduct of the popular postarmy trip to India, and the ways it has altered popular culture domestically, in Israel. For an intimate portrait of this Israeli tourist phenomenon, see the documentary *Thank God for India*, directed by Nisan Katz (2000).

50. On everyday life in Ramallah during the al-Aqsa Intifada, see Raja Shehadeh, *When the Birds Stopped Singing: Life in Ramallah under Siege* (South Royalton, Vt.: Steerforth Press, 2003). For Intifada life in a refugee camp, see Muna Hamza-Muhaisen's Dheisheh diary, available at: http://xii.net/intifada2000/deardiary/.

51. On general trends in satellite television consumption and popularity in the

region, see Naomi Sakr, "Satellite Television and Development in the Middle East," *Middle East Report* 29, no. 1 (1999): 6–10.

52. Boycott campaigns, often co-articulating with classic anti-Semitic rhetorics, have increasingly been launched against cultural producers accused of collaborating with Zionist forces; indeed, such campaigns have preoccupied the cultural arena in Egypt, and to a lesser degree in Jordan, Lebanon, and Algeria.

HISTORICAL
ARTICULATIONS

SALIM TAMARI

Wasif Jawhariyyeh,

Popular Music,

and Early Modernity

in Jerusalem

The great singer Shaykh Salama Hijazi was already half paralyzed when he was invited by Mayor Hashim al-Husayni to come from Cairo to Jerusalem to celebrate the Constitutional Revolution of 1908. His orchestra was led by George Abyad, and a huge tent (*surdaq*) was set up for him in the terrace facing Jaffa Gate on the road to the train station. Shaykh Salama performed sketches from several of his musicals, including *Salah al-Din al-Ayyubi* and *Romeo and Juliet*. At the time I was eleven and was lucky enough to attend (with my father) several of his performances. Salama was dragging himself on stage, yet despite his handicap the audience was ecstatic with delight. People were moved to tears as he sang "Hata li khamarata al-shifa" [Pour me the wine of deliverance]. Even the Greeks in the audience, who did not understand a word, were crying. At night after some begging I was admitted to meet the Shaykh where I kissed his hands. Admission to Shaykh Salama's concerts was half a French Pound, a fortune in those days. —WASIF JAWHARIYYEH, *Ahwal al-Quds al-'Uthmaniya fil-Mudhakkarat al-Jawhariya* [Ottoman Jerusalem in the Jawhariyah memoirs]

Conventional approaches to the study of modernity in Jerusalem regard the city in the late nineteenth century as a provincial capital city in the Ottoman hinterland whose social fabric was basically communitarian and confessional. Ethnicity and sectarian identities were identical in that confessional consciousness was defined by ethnic-religious terms and the boundaries of these identities were physically delineated by habitat in the confines of the Old City quarters.[1] The quartered city corresponded, in this approach, to the ethnoconfessional divisions of the four communities: Muslim, Christian, Armenian, and Jewish. In these quarters, conventional accounts argue, social nodes were more or less exclusive, physically defined, and reinforced by mechanisms of mutual aid, craft specialization, ritual celebrations, internal schooling systems, and, above all, the rules of confessional endogamy. Although a substantial degree of interaction existed in the city, it was confined mainly to the marketplace and ritual social visitations. The modernity of the city is seen as the product of the breakup of the Ottoman system under the triadic impact of European penetration, Zionist emigration, and the modernizing schemes of the British Mandate.

In this essay, I use my reading of the diaries of a Jerusalem musician, Wasif Jawhariyyeh, to suggest substantial weaknesses in this paradigm (see figure 1). I suggest that Jerusalem's modernity was a feature of internal dynamics in the Ottoman city and propose that the social structure of the walled city was much more fluid than is generally believed; further, I suggest that the quarter system signaling the division of the Old City into confessional bounded domains was introduced and imposed retroactively on the city by British colonial regulations. On the eve of the First World War, although Jerusalem had a strong communitarian makeup in which religious identity was highly pronounced, communal boundaries were not defined primarily by confession or ethnicity (except for the Armenians, who congregated around the Armenian patriarchate) but by the *Mahalla*, the neighborhood unit. This unit was reconstituted under the British Mandate in favor of the quarter system (*hayy* or *hara*), which was based on distinctly religious sectarian identity, and within it of denominational subidentity. The communal bonds of confessional affiliation were superseded and supplemented by bonds of patronage and clientalism.

Jawhariyyeh, who was a musician and an interpreter of popular Arabic music, left memoirs (together with his unpublished "Musical Notebooks") that can be gainfully read as a record illustrating the formation of a regional tradition in *Mashriqi* music. This transformation transcended the regional boundaries of greater Syria and Egypt through the interaction between a new technology (the gramophone and the vinyl record) and the creation of a novel arena for the diffusion of a new musical market and new musical tastes enhanced by the increased mobility of performers between Egypt and Bilad al-Sham. However, I focus on Jawhariyyeh's exposition of quotidian life in Late Ottoman Jerusalem. His vignettes of daily life allow us to

FIGURE I. Wasif Jawhariyyeh. Cover of the Arabic edition of *Ahwal al-Quds al-'Uthmaniya fil-Mudhakkarat al-Jawhariya* [Ottoman Jerusalem in the Jawhariya memoirs].

(re)discover a community that is no longer with us, and his account sheds significant light on the modernity of Palestinian urban life, both in the confines of the seemingly ghettoized old city and in the emancipated environment of greater Jerusalem. The memoirs tell a tale of a Late Ottoman and early Mandate Jerusalem with a thriving nightlife and a considerable degree of intercommunal interaction and cultural hybridity.

I am aware of conceptual problems in using the term "hybridity" to describe the city's cultural scene in the period around the time of the First World War. The current usage of this term generally refers to the proliferation of multiethnic identities sharing the same space and creating creolized cultural forms as a result of their interaction, the reference here being to lifestyle, dress codes, cuisine, and even language.[2] The main arena of this hybridity is the postindustrial metropolitan city that has witnessed large-scale third world migrations in recent decades, creating multiple ethnicities of habitations and dual categories of identity-citizenships.[3] In the case of prewar Ottoman Jerusalem, by contrast, the city fostered a communitarian identity, a prenationalist confessional consciousness competing with emergent but vigorous Arab nationalist and localized (Syrian Palestinian) sentiments, as well as an embryonic Jewish-Zionist movement vying for the allegiance of native Jewish communities. A local narrative like that of Wasif Jawhariyyeh compels us to rethink these categories of analysis and ultimately to reimagine the city's social history.

The *Memoirs* are mostly written in the anecdotal style of the street *haka-wati* (storyteller) that mesmerized Wasif's childhood. The stories told by the traveling performers of the *Sanduq al-Ajab* (Magic box) and *Qara Qoz* (Shadow theater), in Turkish and Arabic, are described in vivid details as he recalls them from the alleys of Mahallat al-Sa'diya and the Damascus Gate of Jerusalem before the Great War. This style tends to camouflage a profundity in the narrative precisely because of its simplicity and seeming frivolity. One can capture its panoramic depth only after delving into the networks of social and personal webs that are woven by the author. The reader is reminded of F. W. Dupee's remarks about Flaubert's *Sentimental Education*: "It was [his] feat, and one that followed from his comic aims, to have made an epic novel out of the accumulation of anecdotes. The novel is epic because the fates of numerous characters and a major revolution are embraced in the action; it is anecdotal because each episode recounts, as I think anecdotes do by nature, the momentary defeat or the equivocal victory of someone in a particular situation."[4] In Jawhariyyeh's case, the revolution was the Great War, and the fictional characters are the infinite but real Jerusalem people he encountered in his neighborhood, in the new city outside the walls, and during his convoluted career as a musician.

The 'Ud Player and His Family

> I was born on Wednesday morning the 14th of January 1897, according to the Western calendar, which happened to be the eve of the Ortho-dox New Year.[5] At the moment my father was preparing a tray of *kunafa* [a dessert made with vermicelli and cheese], as was customary then in Eastern Orthodox households. I was named Wasif after the Damascene Wasif bey al-'Azm who was then my father's close friend and the sitting judge in Jerusalem's Criminal Court.[6]

Thus opens the memoirs of Wasif Jawhariyyeh, one of Jerusalem's most illustrious citizens: composer, 'ud player, poet, and chronicler. They span a period of forty-four years (1904–1948) of Jerusalem's turbulent modern history, covering four regimes and five wars. More significant, they mark the transition of Palestinian society into modernity and the breaking out of its Arab population beyond the ghettoized confines of the walled city.

Where do we place the Jawhariyyehs in the social hierarchies of Jeru-salem at the turn of the nineteenth century? Wasif's father and grand-father both occupied important public positions, but the men of the family also passed through a number of more modest occupations. Wasif's father, Jiryis (Girgis), was the mukhtar of the Eastern Orthodox Christian community in the Old City (1884) and a member of Jerusalem's municipal council under the mayoralty of Salim al-Husayni and Faidy al-'Alami. Trained as a lawyer, he was well versed in Muslim Shari'a law and spoke several languages, including Greek, Turkish, and Arabic. He worked briefly as a government tax assessor but later turned to private business as a silk farmer and café proprietor. He was also a skilled icon maker and amateur musician, which accounts for his encouragement of Wasif's musical talents. Wasif's mother, Hilana Barakat, descended from a leading Orthodox family from what later became known as the Christian Quarter. The Jawhariyyehs' social position in pre-Mandate Palestine must be understood in relation to their critical bonds as protégés of the Husayni family, feudal landlords and patricians in Jerusalem's inner circle of *a'yan* (notables). We can say with some certainty that the family members skirted that precarious space between artisanal work and the middle ranks of the civil service.

Wasif traces the beginning of his musical career to the "year of the seven snowstorms," a typical mode of chronicling in semiliterate cultures, which he later figures was either 1906 or 1907. He was nine years old, and on the festival of St. Dimitri the Jawhariyyeh household was celebrating the birthday of his namesake, their neighbor and friend Mitri 'Abdallah. Khalil (Wasif's older brother), then an apprentice carpenter, constructed for Wasif his first tambourine.

> Qustandi al-Sus was one of the most famous singers in the Mahalla—he sang for Shaykh Salama al-Hijazi on his renowned 'ud most of the evening, then they allowed me to perform; I danced the dabke, then I sang a piece of "Romeo and Juliet" to the melodies composed by Sheik Salama and the accompaniment of Qustandi's 'ud. When the latter heard me he was so pleased that he handed me his precious 'ud—which drove me into a frenzy—and I began to play it and sing to the tune of "Zeina . . . Zeina." The next day my father took a barber's blade and forged me a beautiful handle for my tambourine . . . thus began my musical career at the age of nine. (41)

The Jawhariyyeh house was the perfect setting for his budding musical talents. All the family members, with the exception of Wasif's younger brother Tawfiq, who was tone deaf, either played instruments, or sang, or enjoyed good music. Jiryis was one of the few Jerusalemites who owned a His Master's Voice phonograph, and he had a number of early recordings by leading Egyptian singers, such as Shaykh Minyalawi and Salama Hijazi. He encouraged his children to lip-synch in accompaniment to these records, and was particularly severe with Wasif when he made mistakes. Jiryis was also keen to host prominent singers and musicians visiting Jerusalem. One of those, the Egyptian 'udist Qaftanji, spent a week with the Jawhariyyehs, and from him Wasif learned a number of melodies that he used to sing during summer nights on the roof or in the outhouse (19). Jiryis was sufficiently moved by his son's desire to allow him to accompany a number of well-known performers in Mahallat al-Sa'diya to learn their art. They included Hanna Fasha, who crafted his own instruments, and Sabri 'Abd Rabbu, who sold Wasif his first 'ud when he was eleven.[7] Jiryis was so impressed with Wasif's persistence that he hired one of Jerusalem's best-known 'ud tutors, Abdul Hamid Quttayna, to give him lessons twice a week.

As was customary in the Old City, Wasif was apprenticed to a number of jobs during his boyhood. These assignments supplemented his formal schooling and often furthered his evolving musical career. In the summer of 1907, at the age of nine, Wasif became an apprentice in the barbershop of Mattia al-Hallaq (Abu 'Abdallah). A barber in Ottoman Jerusalem was much more than a hairstylist: he was an herbalist, was trained to apply leeches for bloodletting and vacuum cups for congestion relief, and in general performed the function of a local doctor. It is possible that Jiryis wanted one of his sons to acquire such a vocation, but Wasif had other ambitions.

> I would hold the customer by the neck while Abu 'Abdallah was washing his hair so that the water would not drip down his shirt. Water was poured from a brass pot and would flow directly from his head to another brass container that was clasped around the customer's neck. [Initially] I was delighted with this first job. In the evening my brother Khalil would pass by in the company of Muhammad al-Maddah—a *qabaday* [tough guy] and grocer from Mahallat Bab al-'Amud. Muhammad was initiating Khalil into the arts of manhood and both of them would take me to their uda [a bachelor's apartment equivalent to the French garçonierre] where we would play the tambourine and sing.[8] (46)

Wasif learned creative truancy during this period. He would escape his master's shop to listen to the 'ud played by Hussayn Nashashibi at another barber salon, that of Abu Manwil, whose shop was owned by the Nashashibi family. It was in this period that Wasif's obsession with 'ud performance began, and he started to seek out musical instruction.

Contrary to the impression conveyed by Wasif's comments about his truancy and rebelliousness, he had a substantial degree of formal schooling in addition to his musical training. This education is reflected in his polished language, rich poetic imagination, and elegant handwriting. References abound in his diaries to classical poetry and contemporary literature by figures such as Khalil Sakakini, Ahmad Shawqi, Khalil Jibran, and others. Wasif and Tawfiq first attended the Dabbagha School, which was governed by the Lutheran Church next to the Holy Sepulcher. At the Dabbagha, Wasif was taught basic Arabic grammar, dictation, reading, and arithmetic. He also studied German and Bible recitation. His school uniform was the *qumbaz* (traditional robe) and the Damascene red leather shoes known as *balaghat* (17). In 1909, when Wasif was twelve, the brothers were taken out of the Dabbagha after being savagely beaten by the mathematics teacher for mocking him. For several years thereafter, Wasif accompanied his father in his work as overseer of the Husayni estates, occasionally performing as a singer (and later as 'ud player) in the neighborhood.

When Khalil Sakakini established his progressive Dusturiya National School in Musrara, Jiryis intervened with the mayor to have Wasif admitted as an external student. Sakakini had acquired a reputation for using radical methods of pedagogy in his school and for strictly banning physical punishment and written exams. In addition to advanced grammar, literature, and mathematics, the curriculum included English, French, and Turkish. Sakakini was a pioneer in introducing two disciplines unique to his school at the time: physical education and Qur'anic studies for Christians. Wasif was strongly influenced by his study of the Qu'ran.

> I received my copy of the Qur'an from al-Hajja Umm Musa Qadim Pasha al-Husayni . . . who taught me how to treat it with respect and maintain its cleanliness. My Qur'anic teacher was Shaykh Amin Al-Ansar, a well-known *faqih* in Jerusalem. Sakakini's idea was that the essence of learning Arabic lies in mastering the Qur'an, both reading and incantation. My Muslim classmates and I would start with Surat al-Baqara and continue . . . I can say in all frankness today that my mastery of Arabic music and singing is attributed to these lessons—especially my ability to render classical poetry and *muwashshahat* in musical form. (125–126)

Sakakini was a music lover, and had a special fondness for the 'ud and the violin. Some of the Dusturiya students had seen Wasif performing in local weddings and taunted him for being "a paid street singer" (*ajir*), but Sakakini defended him and taught the students to enjoy Wasif's music.

Eventually, despite his love for the Dusturiya's liberal environment, Wasif was compelled at the insistence of his patron, Husayn al-Husayni, to enroll in al-Mutran School (St. George's) in Shaykh Jarrah "in order to gain knowledge of the English language and build a solid base for my future" (145–146). At St. George's Wasif excelled in acting in school plays, where he was able to develop his musical talents. He remained there for two years (1912–1914), until the school was closed at the beginning of the First World War. Wasif finished the fourth secondary class (his tenth year of studies) and ended his formal schooling without a secondary school certificate.

During the war, Wasif continued his musical education in the company of Jerusalem's foremost 'ud players and composers, including his first tutor, Abdul Hamid Quttayna, Muhammad al-Sibasi, and Hamada al-Afifi, who taught him the art of muwashshahat in the Turkish tradition. But Wasif's most important mentor was the great master 'ud player 'Umar al-Batsh. In the spring of 1915, after his father's death, Wasif was attending a party in the company of Husayn Effendi al-Husayni and several Turkish officers. A section of the army military band known as the Izmir Group was performing Andalusian muwashshahat. Wasif was mesmerized by the playing of a young 'ud player wearing a military uniform, who was introduced to him as 'Umar al-Batsh. For the duration of the war 'Umar became Wasif's constant companion. Wasif prevailed on Husayn Effendi, now his official patron, to hire 'Umar to give him four 'ud lessons a week at the headquarters of the army orchestra in Maskubiya. From 'Umar, Wasif learned how to read musical notation and considerably expanded his repertoire of classical Arabic music. Wasif eventually wrote a chapter on the adaptation of Western notational system for the 'ud.[9] 'Umar began to bring Wasif to sing and accompany him on the 'ud in his performances, but above all, he taught him to be a critical and discriminating listener and instructed him in the performance of the classical muwashshah.[10] In his diaries Wasif refers to 'Umar as "my teacher" and "my master."

Throughout his adult career, Wasif saw himself as a musician and 'ud player above all else. His musical career occupies a substantial part of the diaries. We are fortunate to have his "Musical Notebook," which he began just prior to the war.[11] It reflects the progression of Wasif's interests in Arabic music, from classical *Andalusiyat* and Aleppo muwashshahat, to choral music (which he performed at weddings and family celebrations), love songs, melodies based on classical poetry, and finally *taqatiq* and erotic songs.[12] Although he sought employment in various government and municipal authorities, it was only to survive and free him for his obsession: the 'ud and the company of men and women who shared his vision.

Wasif's first paid job, as a clerk in the Jerusalem municipality in charge of recording contributions for the Ottoman war effort, was arranged by his patron, Husayn Effendi al-Husayni. Wasif briefly served in the Ottoman navy, but after the war's end and the start of the British Mandate, he resumed his career in the municipality. He was promoted to the position of court clerk in the Ministry of Justice, serving under the judgeship of 'Ali bey Jarallah in Maskubiya. After the death of Husayn Effendi (whom he called "my second father"), he resigned from his job at the central court to help Husayn's widow, Umm Salim, with the administration of the Hussayni estates in Deir Amr.

Thus continued a series of jobs based on his patronage. Wasif's relationships with the Husayni family, and later with the Nashashibis (who became ascendant under British rule), helped him continue his career as a musician while maintaining a steady income from public coffers.

Musa Qadhim Pasha [al-Hysayni], then Mayor of Jerusalem, sent after me through sergeant 'Arif al-Nammari. I went to meet him in city hall, then located at Jaffa Gate. He rebuked me for not staying in touch since the death of the late Husayn Effendi, and asked about my family's condition, especially about the health of my mother. Then he appointed me as Assistant Inspector [mufattish baj] with a temporary income of 24 Egyptian pounds per month, until the position was institutionalized. I kissed his hands and signed for the new position working under the late 'Abd al-Qadi al-Afifi Effendi. My job consisted of the following: I had to inspect all animals sold in Jerusalem at the animal market [suq al-juma'] every Friday near the Sultan's Pool area. I was to work under the supervision of the late Mustafa al-Kurd, known as Abu Darwish, a top expert in this fine art. Abu Darwish would say to me: "Do not burden yourself! Sit there, drink your coffee and smoke the arghila [water pipe]. I will do all the inspection and will hand you the receipts on a daily basis." This suited me very well. I would start my day at the Ma'arif Café with friends drinking the arghila until 10 or 11 in the morning when Abu Darwish would arrive and order his first smoke, then his second, then his third. Then he would pull five pounds from his 'ajami belt: "Here, Wasif Effendi, this is your spending money for the day," then he would pay me another sum against a signed receipt which I would hand over to the municipality. (335–336)

Musa Qadhim al-Husayni's mayoralty was followed by that of Raghib Bey Nashashibi, who held the position throughout the 1920s and into the next decade. Raghib was an amateur 'ud player and socialite, and he hired Wasif to give 'ud and singing lessons to him and his mistress, Umm Mansur. As a reward, Wasif was added to the payroll of the Tax Bureau with a monthly salary of 20 Egyptian pounds. At the end of each month he would go to the Regie (tobacco state monopoly) Department and collect his salary, performing no further duties.

Wasif called the early Mandate years "the period of total anarchy in my life." He lived like a vagabond, sleeping all day and partying all night. "I only went home to change my clothes, sleeping in a different house every day. My body totally exhausted from drinking and merrymaking. One moment I am in Mahallat Bab Hatta . . . in the morning I am picnicking with members of Jerusalem's 'ayan [notable] families, the next day I am holding an orgy with thugs and gangsters in the alleys of the Old City. My only source of livelihood was my salary from the Regie Department arranged by Raghib Bey." When his mother complained that he came home late at night, if at all, he retorted with the famous line: "Man talaba al-'ula sahar al-layali" (He who seeks glory, must toil the nights; 335).

His brother Khalil opened a café in 1918 that became one of the centers of Jerusalem nightlife. In the Late Ottoman years, especially during the war, and in the Mandate period that followed, Wasif thus was deeply involved in a libertine popular culture and café scene, an aspect of Jerusalem life elided in previous accounts of the city's modernity. His account of his childhood and adult life in the city tell us about the advent of modernity in this urban context and hint at the complex nature of the interactions among Jerusalem's communities.

Urban Life and Communal Boundaries in Jerusalem

Wasif's vivid rendition of daily life in Mahallat al-Sa'diya (situated between Bab al-Sahira and Via Dolorossa) during the first decades of the twentieth century marks one of the most valuable records of Palestinian urban life that exists anywhere. The bourgeoisification of domestic living arrangements, for instance, is periodized and described in detail:

> During the summer months [of 1904] we would sit around the lowered table for the main meal. Food was served in enameled zinc plates. That year we stopped eating in wooden spoons imported from Anatolia and

Greece and replaced them with brass ones that were oxidized periodically. We replaced the common drinking *tasa* [water container] tied to the pottery jar with individualized crystal glasses. In 1906 my father acquired single iron beds for each of my siblings, thus ending the habit of sleeping on the floor. What a delight it was to get rid of the burden of having to place our mattresses into the wall enclaves every night. (14)

For the social historian, the Jawhariyyeh diaries also provide a contemporary record for the growth of the city outside the city walls. Although Shaykh Jarrah, Yemin Moshe, and Wa'riya were established before his time, Wasif narrates the growth of Musrara and the Maskubiya neighborhoods along Jaffa Road during his boyhood, followed by Talbiya and Katamon in the 1930s. These expansions, and the similar one that preceded them in Baq'a, saw hundreds of families move to modern tiled buildings, built of mortar fortified by iron railings. It was in these neighborhoods that the implements of modernity were introduced: electricity, first in the Notre Dame compound just opposite the new Gate, the automobile on Jaffa Road, the cinematograph, and, above all, the phonograph, which introduced Jawhariyyeh to the world of Salama Hijazi and Sayyid Darwish.

Jawhariyyeh's cognitive map of Jerusalem's neighborhoods and his identification of communal boundaries prevalent in his youth clearly suggest that the division of the city into four confessional quarters was a late development. The new boundaries were demarcated by the British to create a modern sectarian balance among the four ancient communities. The basis of this balance was the preservation of the status quo in the administration of Jerusalem's holy sites that was carefully negotiated during the Late Ottoman period and elaborated and codified during early Mandate rule.

The diaries implicitly challenge this notion of quarters based on the regulation of relations among Jerusalemites in terms of their religious and ethnic habitat. Wasif's recollection of daily life in the alleys of the Old City shows the weakness of this concept in two respects. First, it suggests that there was no clear delineation between neighborhood and religion; instead, a substantial intermixing of religious groups existed in each quarter. Second, the primary unit of habitation was the Mahalla, the neighborhood network of social demarcations, within which a substantial amount of communal solidarity was exhibited. Such cohesiveness was clearly articulated in periodic visitations and by the sharing of ceremonies, including weddings and funerals but also active participation in religious festivities. These solidarities undermined the fixity of the confessional system with a premodern (perhaps even primordial) network of affinities.

But confessional boundaries were also being undermined by the rise of the nationalist movement in Palestine, initially in the context of the constitutional Ottoman movement at the turn of the century, then after the 1908 coup, which received a lot of support among intellectual circles in Jerusalem, and later by the anti-Turkish trends in greater Syrian nationalism. Wasif's memoirs depict such shifts in a haphazard and selective manner. Although he was not involved in any political party, he was an Ottoman patriot, and later a Palestinian nationalist, and he clearly believed that the move toward modernity (and presumably post-Ottoman nationalism) was linked to the migration to the outskirts of the city by the rising middle class.[13] By the mid-nineteenth century members of the notable clans had established bases in Shaykh Jarrah to the north and in Wa'riya to the south.[14] There was a similar move in the Jewish population, originating with the construction of the new neighborhoods of Mea She'arim and Yemin Moshe, signaling a separation of ways between modern Palestinian Arab nationalism and Jewish communal consciousness even before the entrenchment of Zionism.[15]

Jawhariyyeh's relationship with the Jewish community of Jerusalem is complex. His narrative is no doubt colored by retroactive memories of clashes during the 1920s and in 1936–1939 between Palestinian Arabs and the Zionist movement, and his perspective is mediated by the events of the 1948 war. But he also recalls a different era, when as a teenager he participated in the events of Purim (which he describes in great detail, including the costumes he used to wear with his brother Khalil), and in family picnics in the spring to the shrine of Shimon al-Siddiq in Wadi al-Juz. He also mentions a number of Sephardic families with whom his family was on intimate terms, including the Eliashars, Hazzans, Anteibis, Manis (from Hebron), and Navons.

Deeply involved in the affairs of the Arab Orthodox community, Jawhariyyeh nevertheless exhibits a unique affinity for the Muslim culture of his city. His narrative compels us to rethink the received wisdom about Jerusalem's communal and confessional structure in Ottoman times. For example, endless stories, many scandalous and satirical, draw a picture of profound triadic coexistence of Christian and Jewish families in the heart of what came to be known as the Muslim Quarter. This was not merely a tolerant cohabitation of protected *dhimmi* minorities (Jews and Christians), but a positive engagement in the affairs of neighbors whose religion was coincidental to their wider urban heritage. There is no doubt that the Jawhariyyeh family, though deeply conscious of its Orthodox heritage, was immersed in Muslim culture. Jiryis made his sons read and memorize the Qur'an at an early age. When he died in September 1914 he was eulogized by Khalil Sakakini ("With the death of Jawhariyyeh the era of wit has come to an end") and by Shaykh 'Ali Rimawi, who lamented: "I cannot believe that Jawhariyyeh's soul will remain in Zion [cemetery] . . . for tonight surely it will move to Mamillah [referring to the Muslim cemetery]" (172–173). This attitude clearly transcended the current normative rules of coexistence at the time.

Many of Jawhariyyeh's anecdotes challenge social and religious taboos that would appear unthinkable in today's puritanical atmosphere.[16] An example is the anecdote titled "A Dog's Religion":

> My father was strolling with his intimate companion Salih al-Jamal, who died a bachelor. They passed several elderly gentlemen who were sitting by the wooden enclave built by the Municipality opposite the special opening constructed at Jaffa Gate to receive the German Emperor. After saluting them a dog happened to pass by. One of the notables asked my father: "Ya Abu Khalil, would you say this dog is Muslim or Christian?" This question was an obvious provocation since the enquirer was a well-known Muslim, and my father was clearly a Christian. But his quick wit saved him from aggravating the situation further: "It should be easy to find out my dear sir. Today, Friday, is our [i.e., the Orthodox] fasting day. You can throw him a bone, if he picks it up then he is definitely not a Christian." (197)[17]

Jawhariyyeh's teasing attitude toward religious sensibilities recalls a period in which religious and ethnic boundaries were blurred in the neighborhoods of Ottoman Jerusalem.

Cultural Hybridity: A Christian Ramadan and a Muslim Purim

The Jawhariyyeh diaries invite the reader to share a world of religious syncretism and cultural hybridity that is difficult to imagine in today's prevailing atmosphere of ethnic exclusivity and religious fundamentalism. It was a prenationalist era in which religious identity incorporated the Other in its festivals and rituals. Jawhariyyeh describes the feast of Easter/Pesach as an occasion for Muslim-Christian-Jewish celebrations. He details the Muslim processions of Palm Sunday (which proceeded from the Abrahamic Mosque in Hebron toward Jerusalem). The festival of Nabi Musa is recalled as a Muslim popular celebration that merged with the Christian Orthodox Easter. The fantasia of Sabt al-Nur (Fire Saturday, commemorating the resurrection of Christ) was the greatest popular Christian celebration in Palestine, and was closely coordinated with Muslim folk festivals. Purim was celebrated by Christian and Muslim youth in Jewish neighborhoods, and Wasif describes in detail the costumes they wore on this occasion. Twice a year Muslim and Christian families, including the Jawhariyyeh family, joined the Jewish celebrations at the shrine of Simon the Just in Shaykh Jarrah (an event known as *shat'hat al-Yahudiya*, "the Jewish outing"), where "Haim the 'ud player and Zaki the tambourine player would sing to the accompaniment of Andalusian melodies."

But the greatest celebrations of all happened during Ramadan. Wasif devotes a substantial section of his diaries to the street festivals, the foods, and the dramatic displays of *Qara Qoz* (shadow plays) and magic lantern shows. Many of the shadow plays were performed in a mixture of Ottoman Turkish and Aleppo dialects, and some of the plays performed included daring social satire and veiled political criticism of the regime, although Wasif does not explicitly mention these displays of dissent. To enhance their sales, manufacturers of goods and confectionary establishments (such as Zalatimo) used the performances to introduce commercial presentations sung by the shadow players.

The city also celebrated seasonal occasions that were not tied to religious feasts. Wasif identifies two such secular occasions: the summer outings (*shat'hat*) of Sa'd wa Sa'id, and the spring visits to Bi'r Ayyub. In the pre–World War I era Sa'd wa Sa'id became the choice location for the Old City's Christian and Muslim families to picnic on hot summer afternoons. These excursions were especially encouraged by the growth of the new mansions around Musrara and the American Colony area. The picnickers consumed large quantities of 'araq and food during these outings, which usually lasted until the late evening hours, when revelers had to go back before the city gates were closed. In the spring, similar parties were held at Bi'r Ayyub, in the springs of Lower Silwan, where Jerusalem families found an outlet from the severe winters.

With the implementation of the Balfour Declaration in the British Mandate, this era of religious syncretism came to a close. Palestinian nationalism, previously a secular movement, started to become infused with religious fervor. The new colonial authority interpreted the protocols regarding religious control and access in terms of confessional exclusivity. Christians were banned by military edict from entering Islamic holy places, and Muslims from Christian churches and monasteries. It had been customary for young Jerusalemites—of all religions—to picnic in the green meadows in the Haram area, but now the area was off-limits. Wasif describes an adventure on a spring day in April 1919, during the early days of the British military government, when he passed as a "Musilman" to the Indian Guards of the Haram area, while his blue-eyed companion, Muhammad Marzuqa, was barred because Wasif explained to them that he was Jewish.

The complexity of Jerusalem's Ottoman identity is also shown in Wasif's account of his involvement with the Red Crescent Society, which was founded in 1915 ostensibly to garner local support in Palestine for the Ottoman armed forces against the Allies.[18] Through public musical events and direct solicitations, the Red Crescent was able to raise substantial funds for the war effort. Jawhariyyeh also believed that the Society could create a bridge between the interests of the Jewish community in Palestine and the Ottoman government before the appearance of Zionism as an active force. Both Ibrahim Entaibi, the director of the Alliance Israelite school system in Jerusalem, and a Miss Landau, described as "the liaison between the Jewish community in Jerusalem and the Ottoman military leadership," were pivotal in cementing those ties. With this objective they mobilized a large number of young Jerusalem women, who wore ceremonial Ottoman military uniforms with Red Crescent insignia, to solicit contributions for the army. Wasif describes several of them as "attractive ladies" who developed intimate relations with the high-ranking Ottoman officials: Miss Tenanbaum ("one of the most beautiful Jewish women in Palestine"; 226) became the mistress of Jamal Pasha, commander of the Fourth Army (after the war, she married Michael Abcarius, the famous Jerusalem attorney); Miss Sima al-Maghribiya became the mistress of Sa'd Allah Bey, the commander of the Jerusalem garrison; and Miss Cobb became the mistress of Majid Bey, the Mutasarrif (governor) of the city.

During the war years, personal as well as political links thus played a part in the complex interaction of Jerusalem's communities. Through his literary and enormously entertaining narrative of the events, Wasif reveals the radical transformations that were encompassing Palestinian and Syrian society in that period: the emergence of secular Arab nationalism, the separation of Palestinian national identity from its Syrian context, and the enhancement of Jerusalem as a capital city.

The memoirs devote an extended section to musical and artistic life in Jerusalem during the Ottoman period. Wasif provides a long list of 'ud makers, 'ud players, dancers, and singers. Many of these musicians performed as family teams in local weddings, and later, during the Mandate, in cafés and cabarets outside the walled city. In combination with his special compendium on the typology of musical traditions that prevailed in Palestine at the turn of the century, Jawhariyyeh's observations provide us with an original and unique source on the modernization of Arabic music in Bilad al-Sham and the influence of such great innovators as Shaykh Yusif al-Minyalawi and Sayyid Darwish on provincial capitals like Jerusalem.[19]

The members of Wasif's household were amateur musicians, 'ud players, and sophisticated listeners who did not restrict their musical interests to any particular religious community. Jiryis treated Qur'anic incantations as a form of music and taught his children to distinguish a good *Adhan* (call to prayer) from a bad one. Once Jiryis led a delegation from Harat al-Sa'diya to the Awqaf Department to request the replacement of a local imam whose voice he could not stand. When the official in charge questioned Abu Khalil's credentials as a Christian to request the removal of the *mu'adhdhin* he responded in verse that was replete with double entendre:

> I hear the call to prayer in a voice, which keeps buzzing in my ears . . .
> I wondered as my ears were humming,
> Is this a sacred prayer, or did he mean to damage my ears [*Adhana*]?[20]

When it was pointed out to him that the mu'adhdhin was a poor orphan who had a large family to support, the elder Jawhariyyeh suggested that they relocate him to the mosque by the American Colony (Sa'd wa Sa'id), where there were fewer people living to suffer from his voice (162). The Awqaf people were so amused by this outrageous attitude that they obliged Jawhariyyeh and replaced the Shaykh.

Wasif also performed or associated with a number of Jewish musicians (64), including Shihada, Badi'a Masabni's 'ud player. He also mentions the prominent role played by groups of Aleppo Jews, known as Dallatiya, who resided in Jerusalem and were choral musicians who performed Andalusian music in weddings of Jerusalem Arabs (155). Before the onset of the Mandate, Wasif played in a number of Jewish communities surrounding Jerusalem (e.g., 327). In one such episode, he accompanied an Ashkenazi choral group at the house of Khawaja Salmon the tailor in Montefiore (i.e., Yemin Moshe), performing what appears to be Oriental music. The group's Arabic rendition of a well-known skit at the time ("Na'im Na'im hal-Rihan") was so convoluted that Wasif assumed it was "a new Ashkenazi ballad." His mock-Ashkenazi version of this song became a popular item in his own comical repertoire, which he often performed. "This," he adds sadly, "was before the onset of the cursed Balfour Declaration" (328).

A self-taught chronicler, Wasif had a photographic memory that enabled him to recall not only the dramatic (the entries of Jamal Pasha and Lord Allenby to Jerusalem) but also the thrill of the seemingly mundane. As Wasif forged for himself a local reputation as one of the city's foremost 'ud players and composer-musicians, he immersed himself in its musical and artistic scene. Playing in the mansions of Jerusalem's urban notables, he recorded with great wit and satire the musings and tribulations of the city's patricians and paupers.

What emerges is an intimate portrait of Jerusalem's Ottoman modernity at the very moment when Zionism was about to clash with an emerging Palestinian nationalism. Wasif's memoirs often view this modernity through the lens of his musical interests. He recounts the introduction of the phonograph and cinematograph to the city's cafés in 1910, and the wonderment he experienced as he saw moving images for the first time in the Russian compound. In 1912 he saw for the first time a horseless car (a Ford) driven by Mr. Vester of the American Colony at the Municipal Park by Jaffa Street. In the summer of 1914 he rode a donkey with his father to Baq'a in Jerusalem's southern suburbs to watch the landing of an Ottoman military airplane. Unfortunately, the plane crashed in Samakh (Tiberias) and its two Turkish pilots were killed. Wasif composed a special eulogy in their honor, which, he claims, was sung throughout the country.

Jawhariyyeh's writings introduce us to the rich social milieu of Jerusalem in the postwar period and the early 1920s, which can only be described as hedonistic. Nightly episodes of drinking, dancing, and sometimes hashish smoking recur throughout the period. Wasif's family made a significant contribution to this milieu with the opening of Café Jawhariyyeh in 1918 near the Russian compound at the southern entrance of Jaffa Road. Wasif's brother Khalil brought to the management of this café the skills he had acquired in Beirut while serving in the Turkish army. He created a special mezzeh menu including 'araq and iced-water, the latter a new innovation for Jerusalem, made possible by the introduction of electric power. Within months after its opening the café became a major attraction for pleasure seekers all over the city and was renowned for hiring the best singers in the country, including Shaykh Ahmad Tarifi, Muhammad al-'Ashiq, Zaki Effendi Murad, and Badi'a Masabni. Wasif's association with the Syrian Lebanese cabaret dancer Badi'a Masabni and her husband, Nagib al-Rihani, dates to this period.[21] Masabni used to visit Jaffa periodically in the summer en route from Cairo to Beirut, and she occasionally came to Jerusalem. Wasif met her in the summer of 1920 (361), when she performed at the al-Ma'arif theater-café just outside Jaffa Gate. He describes several of her risqué song-and-dance sketches, performed in what he terms "transparent costume." She also sang several Sayyid Darwish songs, which were very popular, especially her social satire of the rich, "Al-Haqq 'al-Aghniya." One stanza often moved her popular audience to ask for encores:

Aymta baqa nshuf qirsh al-sharqi
Yifdal bi baladu u-mayitla'shi.

[When will we ever see the piaster of the Eastern man
remain in his homeland and not depart (to Europe).]

Wasif, Badi'a, and others often met at intimate parties, either in the mansions of Jerusalem notables such as Fakhri Nashishibi and Mustafa al-Jabsha, or in the Hotel St. John.[22] Heavy drinking and cannabis enhanced the atmosphere of these evenings, and both Masabni and Rihani habitually used cocaine. On one occasion Wasif himself accompanied Badi'a on his 'ud in an all-night party that started in the Jawhariyyeh café, and continued in his father's house—a night of which he fondly kept a photographic record. Badi'a was one of several Egyptian and Lebanese performers whom Wasif associated with, including Salama Hijazi, Da'ud Husni, and Shaykh Yusif al-Minyalawi.[23] Many of these singers became popular in Palestine with the importation of the new music machines: first the cylindrical wax record machine, and then the hand-propelled gramophone using the 78 rpm vinyl records that Wasif calls Edison Phonographs. At the beginning of the First World War there were only ten such gadgets in Jerusalem, costing about 25 French pounds apiece, a small fortune that made them accessible only to an exclusive number of owners.[24] During the war, several Jerusalem cafés began to attract customers by purchasing phonographs and playing selected pieces on demand.

> I would take a *matleek* [the smallest Ottoman coin] from my father and go to 'Ali Izhiman's café near Damascus gate. A blind man by the name

of Ibrahim al-Bayruti operated a phonograph in Izhiman's café. The machine was raised on a wooden cabinet full of 78 rpm records and covered by red velvet to protect it from the evil eye. I used to throw my matleek in a brass plate and cry to the blind man: "Uncle let us hear 'Ballahi Marhamatan wa-Sabran lil-Ghad' " by Salama Hijazi. The blind man would immediately pull the requested record from the cabinet—only God knows how—and would play it on the phonograph. Later my music teacher Kamil al-Qal'i used to say: Listening to this music is like eating with false teeth! (51)

This postwar libertinism of the early Mandate era was not a novelty; Wasif's memoirs recount his involvement in similar cultural spheres at the behest of his patrons during and before the war. Wasif was blessed with an exquisite voice that even as a teenager placed him in high demand for performances at weddings. He played and sang mainly for male members of the city's elites, usually in special homes kept by and for their mistresses. Several members of Jerusalem's patrician families, including the Husaynis and the Nashashibis, kept special apartments for their mistresses (many of them Greeks, Armenians, and Jews) in suburban areas of the new city. The most famous of these concubines was Persephone, a Greek Albanian seamstress who in 1895 became the mistress of Husayn Effendi al-Husayni. She lived in a special apartment on Jaffa Road and used her clout with Husayn Effendi to trade in cattle in Bayt Susen and Dayr Amr, both Husayni estates. Wasif became her musical companion and helped her market za'tar (thyme) oil. When Husayn Effendi became mayor of Jerusalem in 1909, he distanced himself from Persephone and gave her permission to marry Khawaja Yenni, a Greek confectioner. During the war, Persephone became sick and was brought to the Jawhariyyeh household after her husband's desertion, where Wasif took care of her until her death. The Jawhariyyeh diaries relate numerous episodes of festive events spent in the company of members of the social elites and their concubines. Muslim, Christian, and Jewish entertainers all catered to these events.

Another feature of cultural life in Ottoman Jerusalem recounted in the diaries is the uda. It was customary for middle-class single men from the Old City to rent a furnished one-room apartment where they would spend their evening playing cards, smoking, drinking and, in the long winter nights, host 'ud sessions. The apartments were also used to conduct love affairs or to bring in the occasional prostitute. The uda did not necessarily have a negative reputation, although it is clear from Wasif's narrative that older family members, especially the females, were not privy to what took place in them. Jawhariyyeh lists a number of well-known udas in the Old City and in Shaykh Jarrah, where he used to perform his music. For several years he had a key to Husayn Hashim's uda behind Ma'milla Cemetery, where he used to entertain "Russian and Greek ladies" in the company of Raghib Bey Nashashibi (later the mayor of Jerusalem) and Isma'il al-Husayni.

These episodes compel us to rethink the image of Jerusalem at the turn of the century. It is often (falsely) characterized as a grim, conservative, and joyless city by visitors and natives alike. ("The only thing he ever said about it [Jerusalem] was that it reminded him of death," says Edward Said about his father's recollections of the city.)[25] How do we account for this incongruity? We have to remember that Jerusalem was a city of religion, but not an excessively religious city, meaning that its religious status generated a large number of industries and services that catered to a visiting population of pilgrims, but its native population was not necessarily more religious than those of other urban centers in the hill country. Nablus, Hebron, and Nazareth, for example, all had decidedly more religious reputations than Jerusalem.

Jawhariyyeh's narrative comes from an era of the city's history when class boundaries and seigniorial privilege created an atmosphere in which the upper crust felt relatively insulated in their behavioral patterns from the public's moral judgment. In many cases, they even flaunted this behavior, as with public drinking and the keeping of concubines, without fear of retribution. Another source of protection for this latitude was that Jerusalem was still a reasonably closed city, exhibiting limited influx from the surrounding villages or from Mount Hebron. Peasant migrants who arrived later established the conservative influence on the city's norms for which it became renowned. During the Late Ottoman and early Mandate period, however, the thriving cultural scene of udas, cafés, and cabarets described by Jawhariyyeh was an integral part of Jerusalem's popular culture.

Conclusion: Syncretic Religion and Secular Culture

Jawhariyyeh's memoirs contest the conventional picture of Jerusalem as a grim and conservative city dominated by religious endowments and institutions of pilgrimage. They illustrate the syncretic character of popular religion in the city, in which popular celebrations and processionals were shared by members of the three religious communities. This sharing occurred both at the level of popular involvement in the activities of the other and in the presence of deities and saints, *maqamat awlia'* (saints' shrines), whose veneration was common to all three communities; these included St. George (al-Khidr) and St. Elijah (Nabi Ilyas). For example, Jawhariyyeh describes how biblical prophets (such as Moses and Reuben) became both popularized and Islamicized in these ceremonials.

The life of Wasif Jawhariyyeh underscores the significance of aristocratic patronage in the Late Ottoman period for the survival and success of musicians and other performers. In this case, patronage involved the securing of employment possibilities (municipal jobs, often on paper), the provision of entertainments venues (in the mansions of the upper classes, and wedding ceremonies), and intercession with the central authorities (periodic leaves from army service and rank promotion). The memoirs demonstrate the extent to which the patricians of Jerusalem and other regional capitals were integrated into the Ottoman system and their influence as patrons.

The diaries also bear witness to the emergence of a new and *secular* middle-class celebratory culture. This popular culture was enhanced by the spread of secular education (both missionary and state-supported) and the movement of the new professional and salaried classes to the new city outside the city walls just before the First World War. A new cultural space was opened through the proliferation of cafés and institutions of public performance involving musicians and singers visiting Palestine from Egypt and Syria. Local vocal and instrumental performers entertained in many new venues and via new technology, including the phonograph and vinyl records.

The public café-cabaret was the most significant of these new cultural spaces. Also important were the military bands of the Ottoman army, which recruited local talent to perform at wedding and betrothal ceremonies and private functions in the udahs. Traditional celebrations of popular holidays such as Nabi Musa festivals and Sabt al-Nur rituals in Jerusalem were now enhanced by the spread of modern transport routes and vehicles. Religious syncretism and hybridity gave way to new forms of ethnic nationalism in which the clash between the emergent territorial Zionism and Palestinian nationalism became more pronounced during the early Mandate period. On the other hand, secular popular culture persisted well into the 1940s as Jerusalem became the capital of the country and attracted thousands of newcomers: job seekers, entertainers, entrepreneurs, civil servants, and villagers coming to the city in search of a new life.

Notes

This essay is based on Wasif Jawhariyyeh's handwritten memoirs (three volumes). Volume I has been published as *Ahwal al-Quds al-Uthmaniya fil-Mudhakkarat al-Jawhariya* [Ottoman Jerusalem in the Jawharia memoirs], edited by Issam Nassar and Salim Tamari (Jerusalem: Institute of Jerusalem Studies, 2003) (Jawhariya). This essay deals only with the first volume of the diaries.

I would like to thank Mr. George Jawhariyyeh (in Athens) and Mrs. Aya Jawhariyyeh Musa (in Jerusalem) for making Jawhariyyeh's manuscripts and photographic collection available to the Institute and for their invaluable help during the editing of the manuscript.

1. See Ben-Arieh, Yehoshua, *Jerusalem in the 19th Century*, vol. I, *The Old City in Context* (New York: St. Martin's Press, 1986), 390–401.

2. Ayse Oncu and Petra Weyland, *Space, Culture and Power: New Identities in Globalizing Cities* (London: Zed Press, 1997), 8–9; see also Michael Smith, *Transnational Urbanism* (London: Blackwell, 2001), 136–140.

3. Benedict Anderson, "Exodus," *Critical Inquiry* 20, no. 2 (1994): 314–327.

4. F. W. Dupee, afterword to *Sentimental Education* by Gustave Flaubert (New York: New American Edition, 1972), 427.

5. Jawhariyyeh refers to the Gregorian and Julian calendars, respectively. It was common in this period to use both in Palestine. Both Muslim and Christian farmers used the Julian calendar in marking the agricultural cycle.

6. Wasif Jawhariyyeh began writing his memoirs systematically in 1947 at the Agricultural Development Society in Jericho on the basis of earlier notes he had in his possession. He continued writing in Beirut during the 1960s. That he began writing in the 1940s can be gleaned from his comment on the Maskubiya during the Ottoman period, where he mentions in passing, "Today these quarters serve as the center of British intelligence" (220). Subsequent references to the diaries are cited parenthetically in the text. Unless otherwise noted, all translations are mine.

In addition to the three-volume manuscript, he has left a collection of musical notes and notations, a compendium of poetry, and a large collection of popular proverbs and their interpretation. His late daughter Yusra Arnita (d. March 2000) used the collection of proverbs in her book on Palestinian folklore.

7. Wasif had saved 20 piasters from his work and borrowed the rest from his father's friend Hussein al-Husseini (87). His first 'ud cost 4 majidis (80 Ottoman qirsh). To appreciate the value of Wasif's beginner's 'ud, a *ratl* (3 kilograms) of lamb's meat was valued at the time at 7.5 piasters. The amount of money paid for the 'ud was equivalent to 32 kilograms of meat. That would be equivalent to $320 at 2000 prices in Jerusalem, certainly a huge sum for a family of modest means at the time. See Jawhariyyeh, "A price list of basic commodities in Ottoman Jerusalem: 1900–1914" (101).

8. Muhammad was a *futuwwa*, a street gang member entrusted with the protection of his neighborhood. The Arabic term used by Jawhariyyeh is *min ashawis mahallat bab al-'Amud*, plural of *ashwas*, which literally means "tough guy" or "brave man." It is not clear what "initiation into manhood" means here, but the context indicates that he was being introduced to the ways of the street. As for uda, see the discussion below.

9. See "Tarkib al-Nota al-Ifranjiya 'ala Awtar al 'ud," in "Musical Notebook," 9–10.

10. "My master 'Umar was widely recognized as a grand master in the performance of the *muwashshah*, a genre which is almost extinct today in the Arab world, except perhaps in Aleppo. 'Umar used to tell me about his teacher, 'Ali Darwish, who was a world authority in this genre" (diary, 221–223). Wasif's characterization of muwash-shahat as extinct was premature, for it witnessed a major rebirth in the 1960s.

11. It was salvaged from its hiding place in the family's Botta Street house in West Jerusalem after the 1967 war.

12. *Andalusiyat* and *muwashshahat* are classical musical forms (melodies and songs) that originated in Islamic Andalusia and were imported to North Africa and Syria after the sixteenth century. *Taqatiq* are ditties that often (but not always) accompany dance routines.

13. Although he was clearly a protégé of the Husayni family, he does not indicate that he was a sympathizer of the Palestine Arab Party, which they founded in the 1930s. When his patron, Husayn al-Husayni, died he allied himself with Raghib al-Nashashibi, the antagonist of Haj Amin al-Husayni, without identifying himself with the Nashashibi-led Defense Party (founded in 1934). These shifts should not be read as a mark of Jawhariyyeh's opportunism, especially because both families conceived of Wasif as an artist and musician and had no political expectations of him.

14. See Rochelle Davis, "Ottoman Jerusalem," in *Jerusalem 1948: The Arab Neighbourhoods and Their Fate in the War* (Jerusalem: Institute of Jerusalem Studies, 1999), 10–29.

15. Ben-Arieh, *Jerusalem in the 19th Century*, 152–172.

16. In this they resemble the freethinking reflections of Khalil al-Sakakini from the Mandate period, particularly in *Kadha Ana Ya Dunia* [Such Is My Life] (Beirut: al-Ittihad al-'Amm lil-Kuttab wa-al-Suhufiyin al-Filastiniyin, al-Amana al-'Amma, 1982).

17. It is unclear whether Wasif heard such recollections from his father, read them in a diary kept by his father, or by recording them from memory.

18. For a discussion of these contested loyalties, see Rashid Khalidi, "Competing and Overlapping Loyalties in Ottoman Jerusalem," in his *Palestinian Identity: The Construction of Modern National Consciousness* (New York: Columbia University Press, 1997), 63–88; see also James Glevin, *Divided Loyalties: Nationalism and Mass Politics in Syria at the Close of Empire* (Berkeley: University of California Press, 1998), 141–195; and for a "revisionist" perspective, see Hasan Kayali, *Arabs and Young Turks: Ottomanism, Arabism, and Islamism in the Ottoman Empire, 1908–1918* (Berkeley: University of California Press, 1997), 81–115.

19. Wasif Jawhariyyeh, "Musical Notebook" (untitled, undated, and unpublished, 576 pages). This handwritten manuscript, dedicated to the Ottoman Sultan and signed "Wasif Jawhariyyeh—Quds Sharif," was clearly written in the Ottoman period. It is divided into five sections: 1. Muwashshahat and Anashid, 2. Madhahib and Adwar, 3. "Love Songs," 4. Ballads and Quartets, 5. Taqatiq [ditties] and Erotic Songs. Darwish and Minyalawi were leading modernist Egyptian composers who revolutionized Arabic music at the turn of the century.

20. There is a play on words here: *adhana* means both "our ears" and "to injure."

21. Both were well-known Syrian actors and comedy performers. Eventually,

Rihani married Bad'ia Masabni and together they formed a comedy team in Cairo. Rihani appeared in several Egyptian films during the 1930s.

22. Fakhri Nashashibi was a leading figure in the Defense Party (pro-British) and led the opposition to Haj Amin al-Husayni. He was assassinated in Baghdad in the early 1940s.

23. Leading Egyptian composers and singers during the WWI period. Da'ud Husni was Jewish.

24. The author calculates that this was the annual equivalent of a judge's salary for the same period.

25. Edward Said, *Out of Place: A Memoir* (New York: Vintage, 1999), 6.

MARK LeVINE

The Palestinian

Press in Mandatory

Jaffa: Advertising,

Nationalism, and

the Public Sphere

In this essay, I examine the intersection of popular cultures and public spheres among the Palestinian residents of the city of Jaffa during the Mandate period. Jaffa and its neighbor, Tel Aviv, were the economic, cultural, and political capitals of two rival communities. I argue that the production, circulation, and consumption of popular culture in Jaffa, as expressed in the city's vibrant press, was a crucial vehicle for transmitting normative identities and political discourses of the Palestinian Arab national movement to its constituents. Yet, at the same time, significant disjunctures emerged between the more exclusivist discourses of the nationalist movement and the transnational imagery and ideologies deployed by the advertisements. Together they reflected the complex, sometimes conflictual, and often productive interaction between the various levels of the public sphere and popular cultures of Mandatory Palestine.

My research uses this interaction to elucidate the ambivalent dynamics of pre-1948 Palestinian nationalism, specifically as it emerged in the juxtaposition of nationalist and advertising discourses. I argue that the Palestinian Arab press of Jaffa constitutes an important site for examining the conflicts between Jaffa and Tel Aviv. The textual and visual discourses of the press helped shape Palestinian popular culture through its function as a primary location of the public sphere. I first discuss how conflicts between Jaffa and Tel Aviv were portrayed in the press. Next, I examine the kinds of advertising that were featured in two of Palestine's leading newspapers, *Filastin* and *al-Difa'*, exploring how the images, messages, and activities they represented both supported and challenged the dominant nationalist imaginary of the papers' editors and readers. I also contextualize these images via the actual economic dynamics of the Jaffa–Tel Aviv region (particularly via an analysis of the level and types of imports arriving at Jaffa port) and former residents' recollections of how the advertised products actually circulated in and were consumed by the local community. I suggest that the indigenous press in Palestine (and, by extension, in the colonial-Mandatory Middle East at large) played a dual role as simultaneously a popular and a public text. As such, it was a crucial site for the formation and contestation of popular culture in Palestine, on its own terms and through its relationship with other popular media.

The Public Sphere in Mandatory Jaffa

In their imagination and representation of Jaffa and Tel Aviv, the newspapers and periodicals of the two cities were important loci of communication and conflict between the public sphere and popular culture. In contrast to the paradigmatic case of Great Britain, where there was an early and obvious difference between the "quality" and "popular" presses, the Palestinian Arab press was small enough to contain elements of both genres. As Anderson has famously argued, the press was a primary vehicle for the articulation and dissemination of modern nationalist discourses.[1] The Palestinian Arab press gave significant voice to all the main classes in society *together*, a particularly important dynamic in Palestinian society at a time when, in other spheres—especially the economically determined civil society— the interests of the bourgeoisie did not coincide with those of nonelites.[2] Many members of the local Palestinian Arab bourgeoisie literally sold the ground out from under the feet of their poorer concitoyens,[3] evidence of a double identity that had a profound impact on the nature and success of Palestinian resistance against Zionist colonization in the Jaffa–Tel Aviv region. This dynamic made the interjectory role of popular culture within the larger public sphere a particularly important component in the larger national(ist) discourses. The one bourgeois institution where the interests of the larger society were consistently represented and served was the press, precisely because it reflected the public opinion of the city's popular culture.[4]

The public sphere could, and in Palestine often did, perform both the buffering function against the power of the British colonial (and Zionist para-) state that Palestinian civil society was too weak to perform, and the mediating function within Palestinian Arab society that was necessary for the construction of Palestinian national consciousness and institutions. Its capacity to perform this function derived from the intersection of the press and popular culture;[5] in Palestine, however, the relative weakness of the Palestinian public sphere played an important role in the outcome of the contest between the two nationalisms. It was the Jewish Zionist intellectual and political classes whose relationship to the British Mandate state was most similar to the relationship between reformers and state elites in other Middle Eastern societies of the colonial period.[6] The imbalance in favor of the Zionists was strengthened by the absence of an indigenous hereditary Palestinian Arab ruling class with religious and traditional, cultural, and political prestige, with whom the Palestinian Arab intellectual and cultural elite could forge a symbiotic relationship to make undeniable demands on the colonial state. In this situation, Palestinian popular culture necessarily had to play a more determinedly political role, yet it also remained an arena where various competing aesthetic and economic forces vied for a share of individual and communal Palestinian attention and loyalty. The politically active journalist was a central player in this drama, helping to "create an imagined community among a specific assemblage of fellow-readers" among citizens of London and Cairo, Tel Aviv and Jaffa.[7] Newspapers produced meanings linguistically and visually at the same time, thereby reinforcing their power to demarcate the interiority and exteriority of the nation and making this imagination a more powerful force.[8] In Palestine, the normal channels of political power acquisition for intellectuals were blocked, leading to a situation in which the Jaffan press became a site for "resistance vernaculars" that challenged the privileged and hegemonic political and economic discursive vernaculars shared by Zionist and British ideologies (and sometimes by Palestinian Arab leaders).[9] Such a language was constructed out of the meeting of popular cultures and public spheres in the Arab press of the Jaffa–Tel Aviv region and, through them, in Zionist and Palestinian Arab nations at large.

Popular culture is often conceived as including the press, which has traditionally been considered central to the public sphere.[10] Moreover, despite oppositions of popular and learned or elite culture, the reality is that most popular culture is consciously and continuously learned, is complex and difficult to comprehend fully and immediately, and is dependent on conventions and traditions for meaning. Finally, popular culture is assumed to comprise commercial, mass-mediated forms of art and entertainment. This was certainly true of much popular culture in Jaffa and Tel Aviv, though it is less accurate in the case of the press. Arabic newspapers in particular were hardly money-making ventures; they were often distributed for free by their publishers to fulfill a national(ist) obligation. On the other hand, we can learn a great detail about the culture of the time and place of Mandate Jaffa by critically examining the blending of aesthetic and commodity discourses in the press via the paid advertisements that increasingly graced its pages. As critical scholarship attempts to analyze popular culture in the Middle East, the case of the Jaffan press shows the relevance of such approaches for historical analyses as well.

"We are in a state of war":
The Jaffan Press under the British Mandate

The Palestinian Arab press was an important institution in the Late Ottoman period, but it grew even more rapidly with the onset of the Mandatory period, in large part because of the improved road and mass communication systems instituted by the British.[11] The press saw its most important mission as covering and promoting Palestinian resistance to Zionism by "creat[ing an] environment and affect[ing the] viewpoint" in its community.[12] The two aspects of this mission were explicitly political and cultural-aesthetic, and the economic considerations reflected in the advertisements often came into implicit conflict with both goals. I have elsewhere explored the crucial role played by the Zionist press, particularly through the deployment of Tel Aviv as the epitome of Zionist modernity and of Jaffa as its backward, stagnant other, in the shaping of both the Zionist public sphere and popular culture. The Palestinian Arab press was aware of the manner in which Zionist discourses were deployed in the Hebrew-language press. In response, Tel Aviv was continually criticized as corrupt and dangerous, while Jaffa was described as the "jewel" of Arab Palestine. The Palestinian press depicted Jaffa as the country's most beautiful and important Arab city; as *Filastin* described it, "No one doubts that Jaffa is the greatest Arab city in Palestine, and it is inevitable that visitors to Palestine will stop by to see the model of Palestine's cities" (May 9, 1946, 2).

Jaffa was also described as the economic and cultural center for Palestine's Arab community, its "gate of entrance and liberation."[13] In fact, the city's position as the cultural center of Palestine was intimately tied to its role as a center for the country's press, which "was formed in Jaffa."[14] Yet, whatever the hostility toward Tel Aviv on the part of those attempting to mold Palestinian Arab public opinion, Tel Aviv was nonetheless a major site for cultural consumption of fashion, food, and film by Palestinian Arabs from Jaffa and beyond. Numerous interviews, recollections, and memoirs of Palestinian men who lived in Jaffa during the pre-1948 period recount their trips to the beach, cinemas, shops, and even brothels in Tel Aviv. It is in this as yet too little explored context that we must understand the role of the Palestinian Arab press as a crucial component of both the popular culture and the public sphere of the community. That is, the more people from the two communities mixed together, the more important it was for the public spheres and popular cultures to reinforce the boundaries between them.[15]

The British government recognized the "inflammatory" power of the press and its influence on public opinion, because "in almost every village there is someone who reads from the papers to the gatherings of those villagers who are illiterate. The Arab *fallaheen* and villagers are therefore probably more politically-minded than many of the people in Europe."[16] This observation was even truer in the Jaffa–Tel Aviv region, where free copies of *Filastin* were sent to the mukhtar of every village in the Jaffa district with more than a hundred inhabitants. This practice helped inform the residents of the six Arab villages surrounding Tel Aviv of the continuous battles with the city over the land and resources of the region. Despite its best efforts, the British government could not control the international flow of information made possible by new media technologies such as the telegraph and telephone. When the government banned *Filastin*, the "youth of Jaffa" submitted a memorandum to the high commissioner opposing the move, and in 1924 they established a new paper, *al-Jazira* (The island), to give voice to the "youth movement in Jaffa, attempting to revive and lead the nationalist movement."[17] Soon after its reappearance, *Filastin* defiantly called on its people to preserve their land and not sell it to Jews. The press, *Filastin* in particular, both reflected and helped to shape the popular mood and the "norms of right thinking" for Palestinians of all classes vis-à-vis the struggle against Zionism.[18] As epitomized by *Filastin*, the Palestinian press performed an "agenda-setting function" for the larger nationalist movement, with journalists acting as "leaders of public opinion" and defenders of the "people's cause" by sounding "revolutionary tones" against British and Zionist imperialism.[19] The press's unique location at the intersection of the popular cultures and public spheres of the emerging Palestinian nation made this complex role possible.

Responses to Zionism in the Jaffan Arab Press

The Palestinian Arab press in Jaffa employed nationalist cartoons and inflammatory rhetoric in its struggle against Tel Aviv. Newspapers campaigned against the "judaization of the Port" and other British policies supporting Zionism. In response to the organization of Jewish labor, the press argued, Palestinian Arabs had to maintain Jaffa as a "pure Arab port," as it supposedly had been since "time immemorial" (*al-Difa'*, February 2, 1936; October 23, 1936, 2). Such language brings together the "reasoned discourse" of the bourgeois public sphere with the more emotive and "inflammatory" language of the plebian sphere and its popular cultures. Vivid cartoons were especially important because of the large number of illiterate or semiliterate "readers."[20] They shaped and reinforced visual markers of separation in the larger popular culture by depicting such images as Tel Aviv's Mayor Dizengoff presenting a Jewish Star to High Commissioner Lord Wauchope (*Filastin*, July 24, 1936) or disingenuously saying "Shalom" to the mayor of Nablus.[21] Other cartoons portrayed Jewish women as dangerous seductresses, in one cartoon causing Britain (in the guise of John Bull) to divorce its first wife, Palestine, for a Zionist mistress. One particularly evocative cartoon depicted, among a group of animals, a Jewish Tel Avivan mouse and an Arab Jaffan cat, the power imbalance between the two clearly implying Jaffa's hoped-for victory over Tel Aviv in the ongoing 1936–39 Revolt. The mouse is wearing a Hassidic-looking hat and the cat, naturally, wears a kufiya. All the animals are listening to radios that are broadcasting a speech by the colonial secretary, who stands astride the whole country while informing the world that "the whole object of His Britannic Majesty's Government is that Arabs and Jews should be able to live together in peace and amity."[22]

The press did not imagine such an amicable resolution. For Jaffa's Arab press, Tel Aviv's and Zionism's corruption was contagious.[23] The entrance of Arabs or Arab symbols into this Jewish space was viewed negatively, unless such penetration was an act of defiance against the city and what it symbolized. The press engaged in a clear attempt to police the Jaffan Palestinian population, for whom Tel Aviv was a site of popular cultural consumption. Thus, in an article titled "The Fez in Tel Aviv," *al-Jam'ia al-*

Islamiya explained, "We are in a state of war . . . and [cannot] deny ourselves any weapon or means to defend ourselves. And there is no [better] weapon than . . . holding on to our eastness [*sharqiatna*]. And I will confirm for you that the presence of the fez in Tel Aviv will be a great influence . . . I am the first to hold on to the fez" (September 6, 1932, 2).

Most Palestinian Arabs who wore their fezzes in Tel Aviv, however, did not intend to make a nationalist statement; they simply wanted to shop, eat, or go to a movie. The most important act of resistance occurred through the ritual and performance involved in reading and buying the daily paper. The young boys who sold the papers would shout aloud the headlines in the streets and even embellish the stories of the exploits of Palestinian Arab heroes in order both to sell more papers and to motivate people to engage in violent resistance.[24] In this way, the press served as the voice of the masses and of the popular culture they represented (*Filastin*, January 5, 1930, 3) and shored up the popular will in difficult times, such as during the 1936–39 Revolt. The Jaffan Arabic newspapers energetically resisted Zionist encroachment on Jaffa, mobilizing their readers through the use of highly emotive images and language to resist the obvious allure of Tel Aviv. In this regard, urban development was a primary concern, given Jaffa's sense of the need to keep up with its wealthier neighbor. Thus, the press covered the numerous privately and publicly sponsored development projects in Jaffa during the Mandate period, particularly in the 1930s and 1940s, discussing the "need to quickly implement plans to beautify the city and widen its streets" so that the "black stain" might be removed from Jaffa (*Filastin*, January 4, 1936, 3). (One of the city's main streets was called Shari'at al-hilwa, or Beautiful Street, and the name Yafa itself means beautiful in Aramaic and Hebrew, a sentiment reflected in the popular nickname of the city as the "Bride of the Sea.") Even when skeptical of their feasibility, the press reported various development plans with great fanfare.[25] Such positive descriptions of the city were important to sustain a sense of modernity for Jaffa that would be congruent with the claims of the advertisements in the newspapers' pages.

Advertising and the Cosmopolitan Jaffan

The two most important Palestinian papers based in Jaffa, *Filastin* and *al-Difa'*, carried a wide variety of advertisements; in this section, I compare advertising of commodities with actual circulation and consumption of these goods in Jaffa.[26] Advertisements were crucial sources of cultural information in the Palestinian Arab newspapers, because unlike their Jewish Zionist counterparts, which featured columns dealing with food, films, and other types of cultural activities, the columns in Arabic papers focused almost exclusively on political and economic issues. Advertisements are thus one of the only sources that reveal the kinds of foods, goods, and entertainment sold to and consumed by Palestinian Arabs in Jaffa. Although the press coverage of the Palestinian-Zionist conflict was important in supporting a specifically nationalist Palestinian agenda and consciousness, the advertisements located between the articles were much less nationalistic. Indeed, most ads did not even promote Palestinian products. Ultimately, business concerns seem to have trumped nationalist concerns. As Salim Tamari, Issa Khalaf, and Sarah Graham-Brown have demonstrated, the factionalized structure of Palestinian society prevented subaltern social actors from challenging the power and class-based policies of the elite at the same time that they left the society as a whole too weak to meet the combined external (Zionist and British) and internal (a weak and atomized bourgeoisie) challenges confronting them.[27] Thus, in August 1936, two months after the Arab Relief Committee in Jaffa placed an ad to inform readers about a "Jaffa Day" to raise funds for victims of the British reprisals against the 1936–39 Revolt, an advertisement started running in al-Difa' asking Jaffa's merchants, "What will come after the strike? The competition of life!" (al-Difa', August 10, 1936, 6; October 18, 1936, 7; November 17, 1936, 11).

Both newspapers, especially Filastin, regularly ran front-page photo montages highlighting major world and regional events of the previous day(s). The primary subjects of these montages were invariably important political or military figures in the process of some kind of public spectacle or examples of the latest technological advances, such as the newest plane or radio. These images helped connect Palestinians to events around the world, as the headlines exclaimed that these "world pictures . . . came to us in the rapid air mail" (al-Difa', January 1, 1935, 1). For Jaffa's businessmen, particularly orange exporters, the latest news could not arrive quickly enough as they attempted to stay one step ahead of the volatile citrus market. In fact, these collages ultimately served an economic purpose: the selling of advertising space, as captions imbedded between the photos urged readers to "announce your products in Filastin."[28] Similarly, ads for the most important accoutrements of modern life, from raincoats to shotguns (presumably for hunting), lamps, radios, carriages, shoes, and bicycles appeared next to each other, often within larger, full-page ads for department stores, sometimes on page 1 of the paper (see Filastin, January 23, 1930, 6).

Part of what made life complete, according to the advertisers in *Filastin* and, to a lesser extent, *al-Difaʻ*, was travel. Jaffa contained Palestine's chief port for several millennia (until it was displaced by Haifa with the opening of the Hijaz pipeline in 1934) and Jaffans had long had access to overseas travel. In the Mandate period, Jaffans were exposed to innumerable travel advertisements, including full-page ads for the first flights to Egypt on Egypt Air and KLM airlines (*Filastin*, February 4, 1930, 4), for Palestine Railways's less exciting service to Egypt, for trips to Lebanon (where many Jaffans, especially Christians, had family and vacation homes), and for cruises to Europe, especially Italy. The Lloyd Triestino Steamship Company and the Steamship Company Genoa regularly advertised cruises to Italy (which was depicted with the most modern skyscrapers imaginable and a skyline that resembled New York City more than any Italian city circa 1937). Asia, Africa, and Australia were also listed as destinations (*Filastin*, October 3, 1937, 2). But Italy's predominance is particularly interesting because most of the architects who designed the homes of the Jaffan Palestinian bourgeoisie, including the most modern house in all of Jaffa–Tel Aviv, belonging to one of the most conservative Muslim men in Jaffa, were Italian. Palestine, or more specifically, elite bourgeois Palestinians, were incorporated into larger Middle Eastern *and* European (and even global) circuits of aesthetic production and consumption.[29] But while the bourgeoisie were the main active consumers of travel and architectural design, such cultural consumption clearly had an impact on the social and spatial imaginaries of all classes of the population, including the popular classes, who referred to Jaffa as the "mother of strangers" because of its long participation in international flows of people and commodities.

Another sign of Jaffa's incorporation into these larger circuits of cultural production and consumption is the large number of advertisements for radios and phonographs in the two papers, the second largest class of advertisements throughout the period under review. The cartoon in *Filastin* featuring cats and mice (i.e., Palestinians and Jews) listening to the radio highlights its importance. Radio and phonograph ads featured some of the most modern(ist) imagery of any ads in the press. Ownership of the latest radio and phonograph technology symbolized the modern brain of the consumer. One drawing places the newest vacuum tubes and dials right inside a modernist drawing of a human head (*Filastin*, April 10, 1936, 8; see figure 2); the "new magic brain" of the "radio with the magic eye and metal tubes" is described in Arabic and English. Yet another ad features a photograph of an old man in traditional village dress standing next to the newest

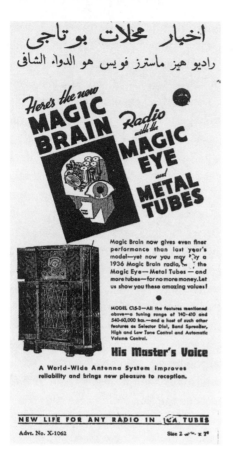

FIGURE 2. "News from Boutaji
Stores: Radio Is Healing Medicine."
Advertisement in *Filastin*, 1936.

radio on the market.[30] Car radios were advertised as a crucial component
in the most modern car.[31]

The most common advertisements in the two papers were for automobiles and related products. The most frequently advertised brands were
Ford, Buick, Studebaker, REO Speedwagon, Auckland, and other U.S. and
British brands; as a rule, the cars were drawn in stylized modern graphics
(e.g., *Filastin*, November 4, 1937, 3). Ads for cars were sometimes juxtaposed with pictures of war and military pageantry on the same page, linking automobile owners to world circuits of political, financial, and military power. The car and related ads often took up half a page or more and
featured Arabic translations of English-language ad copy; even the ads for
motor oil featured the most modern styles and graphics. Car dealers such
as the International Car Agents in Jaffa started their ad copy with the salu-
tation "Dear Brothers," attempting to link potential customers to the larger

Palestinian nation through the consumption of their relatively expensive product.

If travel and automobile ads showed the means to see the world, films brought the world to a much larger number of Palestinians. By the 1920s Jaffa was a center of the film industry in Palestine and screened all the first-run Arab-language films. The photos in film ads invariably depicted actors and actresses such as Umm Kulthum and 'Abd al-Wahhab in modern and upscale Western attire and settings. A film ad might address readers as "Dear Palestinians" and stress a film's qualities as "the most powerful and greatest Arabic film produced for the people till today," or as featuring themes of national importance. Moreover, when advertising screenings in Jaffa, the ad copy would describe the city as "civilized" or "prosperous" (*Filastin*, May 11, 1935, 11; June 5, 1935, 7). Advertisements for films from Egypt (the center of the burgeoning Arab film industry) depicted strong connections between Egypt and Palestine (*al-Difa'*, January 11, 1935, 3). Arabic-language films would occasionally run in Tel Aviv, one example being the screening of *Sultan 'Abdulhamid* at the Majd al-Nar cinema, only two days before the outbreak of the 1936 Revolt (*Filastin*, April 16, 1936, 2). Although the press carried few ads for cinemas in Tel Aviv, interviews with numerous residents of Jaffa of the pre-1948 period revealed that going to Tel Aviv to see the latest U.S. or European film was a favorite pastime of all classes of the Palestinian Arab population of Jaffa.

Business-related products and services were another prominent group of advertisements in the two papers. Citrus importers in Germany (or Tel Aviv) announced their desire to pay the best possible prices, and merchants advertised agricultural tools, motors for factories, sewing machines and "Celanese fashion fabrics" for the local textile industry, office products (the latest Vacumatic fountain pens and typewriters being perennial favorites), and furniture sales. Other ads featured real estate sold by Arab owners (even in Tel Aviv; *Filastin*, August 3, 1929, 8), life insurance, and vocational schools such as the Tanning Arts Institute, which described its role as fostering "economic independence as the basis for political independence" (*Filastin*, January 1, 1929, 2). All of these products gave the impression that the Palestinian businessman could emulate (or anticipate) his European colleagues to whatever degree he desired. Jaffan consumers could purchase Lipton tea, Wrigley's Gum, Nestlé's children's food, chocolate, Farina, Ovaltine, Black and White Scotch Whisky, HMV refrigerators, Amstel Beer, and Pellegrino water, all regularly featured in advertisements. The food ads were accompanied by ads for medicines and personal hygiene products (indeed, in one poorly placed juxtaposition, an ad for the Maghrebi coffeehouse and restaurant in Jaffa ran directly above an ad for Recto-Serol hemorrhoid cream). These ads promoted almost entirely European or U.S. remedies.

The ads depicted gender roles in a similarly modernized and Westernized fashion. Thus, an ad for Colgate's Ribbon Dental Cream featured a man and a woman smoking and smiling, with the woman holding her arm up suggestively and the caption explaining that with this toothpaste people could smoke without fear of discoloring their teeth (*Filastin*, May 15, 1935, 8). She might easily have been friends with the Jewish woman so negatively—but not dissimilarly—drawn in the nationalist cartoon described earlier. Similarly, Umm Kulthum appeared in several film ads in various types of European or Gypsy dress, looking more like Ingrid Bergman than a symbol of the Egyptian Arab woman, or even nation. Indeed, all the ads for women's products featured women in the latest European fashions. Thus, an ad for Tangee lipstick, "imported from New York," was intended to create an image of the modern woman. Most telling was a 1929 ad for Whippet Holeproof Extoe Hosiery, which shows a woman's shapely legs suggestively walking down the stairs of what appears to be either a restaurant or an alley in an old *medina*, with a background of Moorish architecture (*Filastin*, March 5, 1929, 7; see figure 3). The ad implies that, with her uncovered legs, she is walking away from her Oriental past to a modern Western and European future.

Cleaning products, both for personal hygiene and household use, also featured stylized images of modern femininity. There is a significant body of scholarship on the production of the "modern, scientific" housewife as a centerpiece of the "new women" refashioned by proto-feminist discourses in the Middle East.[32] In colonial discourses, images and emerging technologies of hygiene focused significant attention on women as the locus of transmission of modern health concepts and practices to colonized peoples. The ads in *Filastin* and, to a lesser extent, *al-Difa'* reveal how these discourses were reflected in the types of products advertised to women of the period. Perhaps the most frequently advertised product was Palmolive soap, appearing among many ads for complexion, acne, and anti-aging cream, all featuring European (and usually blonde) faces. Interestingly, until the British Mandate, olive oil soap was one of the principal industries of Palestine, especially Jaffa.

Ultimately, it was a "matter of class and cosmopolitanism" that divided the population in terms of how various social groups perceived these dis-

FIGURE 3. "Holeproof Stockings." Advertisement in *Filastin*, 1929.

جرابات هولبروف

courses and made use of new technologies.³³ Jaffa had been a cosmopolitan city for decades before the onset of British rule. The city generated a transcultural network of relationships that linked producers, distributors, and consumers of commodities in ways that transcended nationalistically sanctioned and imagined identities. The use of modern technologies and hygiene products did not necessarily determine one's sense of modernity, but was judged and consumed based on a combination of economic, aesthetic, and cultural-political factors. The Jaffan elites' consumption of Western products was interpreted as a sign of modernity, and in the contest between Palestinian Arabs and Zionists, such modernity may have had nationalist meaning.

Yet, the papers also featured a number of ads for Jewish products, department stores, and services, although they would disappear in times of violence.³⁴ It is striking that a paper like *al-Difaʿ*, which clearly took an anti-Zionist position and warned its audience that "Jaffa [is] on the way to Judaization," would run ads by Jewish businesses, such as orange exporters "offering great prices for oranges to orange growers of Jaffa" and the Levy and Emanuel Department Store, all of whose ads were in Arabic (*Filastin*, November 8, 1930, 6; January 6, 1935, 13; January 25, 1935, 4). Even Hebrew lessons were advertised, one ad urging readers to "Study Hebrew in the Easiest Way, by comparing with Arabic. Ben Horim, Tel Aviv, Mea Shearim Street, 26" (*Filastin*, April 2, 1936, 7). There are few places more public, yet at the same time more intimate, than a public bath, and the fact that a Jewish-owned bath (*Hamei Hadarom*, with its name in Hebrew, English, and Arabic in its ads) would advertise in a Palestinian paper named *al-Difa'* (Defense) suggests that intercommunal relations were much more complex than the editorial content suggested. Nationalist rhetoric aside, the populations of Jaffa and Tel Aviv were not homogeneous. Jaffa in particular had an increasingly large Jewish population, at least half of whom lived in several "Jewish" neighborhoods.[35] Much less is known about Tel Aviv's non-Jewish Arab population, although one source from 1933 explains, "The Arabs living in Tel Aviv are those who didn't sell their land and still live and work on it."[36] I was told by older former residents that intercommunal use of the baths was an everyday occurrence apart from times of explicit tension or violence, especially for poorer (and often Arab) Jews and Palestinian Arabs. These ads, which sold many of the same products advertised in the Hebrew press, raise the interesting question of how separate the two communities actually were on a day-to-day level. As one former resident explained, there were always some "individualist Jews," men and women, who shopped in the Arab wholesale markets and fruit stands, a "certain type" who would also have frequented the baths regardless of the social strictures against mixing with Palestinian Arabs.[37]

Advertising suggests that the readers of these papers were imbued with modern European notions of taste, fashion, health, nutrition, travel, and business. In fact, the only local products regularly advertised were cigarettes, orange juice, flour, and, in *al-Difa'*, soap from Nablus and textiles. Almost all these ads were in Arabic, as opposed to the varying levels of English in the ads for foreign products. The predominance of foreign products, compared to the greater representation of local Jewish products in the Jewish press, raises the question of how local Palestinian small industries survived into the Mandate period. Their absence in the press may have been a calculated decision that such advertising was either not necessary or not productive, a possibility that seems more likely given the importance of "direct marketing" for most Palestinian producers. On the other hand, by the early Mandate period, Jaffa (even more than Haifa), was the "trade center [of Palestine], the main town supplying Palestine's consumers with imported goods . . . almost all the leading firms of Palestine have their branches or agencies there," and thus most major local stores, especially department stores, Arab, foreign, and Jewish, did regularly advertise in *Filastin* and *al-Difa'*.[38] I would argue that such depictions of Jaffa's cosmopolitanism and modernity drove the decision to commission the chief city planner of Cairo to create a new and modern town plan for Jaffa as a tourism-centered "city on the sea" in the 1940s. If implemented, the plan would have led to the uprooting of numerous poor and middle-class neighborhoods in the city and to conflicts with the working-class residents, who could consume the images of Jaffa's bourgeois modernity but not afford the products themselves.

Beyond sociopolitical issues, the ads in the two papers reveal what could be described as an executive or businessmen's popular culture, which offered the public all the requirements to lead a solidly respectable bourgeois life—from the best new car to buy to the best hard liquor to drink (and Bayer Aspirin for the hangover), to furnishings for one's office on Jaffa–Tel Aviv Street (home to most of the city's major businesses, pointing to the deep commercial relations between Jaffa and Tel Aviv even in the midst of growing conflict) to the oatmeal to eat to stay regular, the toothpaste to get rid of those ugly cigarette teeth, and facial creams to keep skin clear and young looking. Moreover, although the self-described goal of papers such as *Filastin* was to reach and preach to the widest Palestinian audience possible, the ads suggest that the primary readership, or at least the group the ads were primarily interested in reaching, was the bourgeoisie, particularly businessmen.

Representations of Consumption

The number and frequency of ads for consumer products in Jaffa's Arabic newspapers might seem to suggest that products such as imported soap, radios, and cars were actually consumed in large quantities by the population, but actual patterns of consumption do not support this. Limited documentation (port and customs records) reveals the extent of importation and circulation of such goods; more broadly, it places Palestinian, especially Jaffan, consumption in the larger context of high colonial political economies in other regions, such as Africa. Sa'id Himadeh's statistics from 1938 indicate a general (but not uniform) increase in imports of already manufactured articles from 51.5 percent of total imports in 1923 to 65.4 percent in 1938.[39] A breakdown of the value of manufactured articles reveals that "cotton piece goods" was the predominant import in this category throughout most of the period, with industrial machinery and clothing surpassing it around 1933. Significantly, the importation of electrical goods rapidly increased, from 23,000 to 208,000 pounds in the 1927–1936 period, while drugs and medicine rose from 46,000 to 160,000 pounds by 1935. Although much of this increase was attributed to greater Jewish immigration, it is clear that Palestinian Arabs also partook of these products, especially in the Jaffa region. Jaffa's elites benefited economically from the citrus trade (which accounted for over 70 percent of the total exports of Palestine) and Jewish immigration, which brought demand for European capital and commodities into the country. The main sources of imports were Britain, Germany, and the United States. Palestinian trade with the surrounding Arab countries, significant in the Late Ottoman period, decreased to not more than 10 percent of imports (mostly food products) by the mid-1930s, suggesting that Palestine was fully incorporated into European circuits of trade by this time.[40] Yet, if Western, primarily European, drugs and medicines were increasingly integrated into the arsenal of Palestinian Arab health aids, the same could not be said about one of the most advertised commodities in the Arabic press: soaps and cleansers. In his examination of the circulation of personal hygiene products in colonial Rhodesia, Timothy Burke demonstrates the importance of studying advertisements to gain new perspectives on the nature and role of commodities, consumption, and needs in the history of colonized societies. In Africa, the appearance of "new needs" played an important role in the transformation to European colonial rule as the "taste transfer" from Europe to Africa helped turn once "discretionary" into "necessary" requirements. No such dynamic manifested in Jaffa, as the "prior meanings" of these commodities had decades earlier ceased to be mere "cultural and social raw material from which the colonized social life of things" could be shaped. Jaffa's substantial incorporation into European and Ottoman and regional trade networks meant a significant portion of the population was already infused with some degree of European taste.[41] Indeed, a film shot at the port around the turn of the century shows the mélange of fashions (and peoples) that already reflected Jaffa's emergence as a cosmopolitan setting.

The British and Zionists did not display the ambivalent response to rapid changes in Palestinian Arab consumption that in other colonial settings triggered fears of an uncontrollable hybridity, challenging colonial privilege and rule.[42] Nor were the Mandate authorities trying to change "the nature of [Palestinian] selfhood" by pushing British commodities onto the market as "commonsense" replacements for only partially commodified indigenous products. In the case of hygiene and cleaning products, this contrast is especially apparent. Unlike colonial Zimbabwe, there was no sudden increase in the power of Western ideals of cleanliness, appearance, and bodily behavior in the Jaffan Palestinian Arab community with the onset of British rule or Zionist colonization (although in the villages such a change might have been stronger).[43] Moreover, the relatively strong nationalist consciousness and relatively independent press provided little opportunity to inculcate colonial notions of domesticity and womanhood. The appeal of local cleaning products (as opposed to cars and radios, which did not face local competition) did not weaken in the face of British and European imports, as occurred in Africa. In fact, there is a clear indication that price, availability of local alternatives, and importance as a status symbol combined to determine whether a product was actually consumed in proportion to its prominent depiction in the newspapers. The three main products discussed earlier—cars, radios, and cleaning products—demonstrate the complexity of the situation.

Former residents of Jaffa during the 1930s and 1940s help construct a biography of consumption, although the lack of documentary evidence makes it difficult to piece together the specific dynamics of their acquisition and cultural sedimentation. It appears that in Jaffa, the middle and upper classes did purchase a fairly large number of new automobiles in the 1930s and 1940s, although during the Second World War many people sold their cars or had them requisitioned by the army. Most of the people associated with the citrus industry—growers, exporters, packers—could afford and owned cars. Private cars were unnecessary in Jaffa, suggesting that they functioned mainly as a status symbol and only secondarily as a business tool. Still, cars were numerous in the city. According to one informant, there were different types of car buyers. At the top end was the upper class, usually associated with the citrus industry or real estate, who bought Studebakers or Buicks and were especially fond of convertibles. The middle class, such as bank managers, lawyers, store owners, and other white-collar professionals, usually bought Chryslers, DeSotos, Austins, or Morrises, less expensive but still relatively nice. The main reason there were so many cars in Jaffa, I was told, was because the city was "mostly populated by entrepreneurs; wholesalers, retailers, dry goods purveyors, and pharmacists."[44] We can be skeptical of overly nostalgic recollections of Jaffa as a primarily bourgeois city, as it was clearly a major working-class town, yet it is clear that there was a fairly good business for dealerships in Jaffa.

Radios and similar goods were also foreign-made, so there was little competition by local producers. The most famous brand was His Master's Voice, whose products were found in practically all homes, including those of poor families. Several former residents recall listening to the Near East Broadcasting Service, which was run by the British. Until late 1947 its headquarters and antenna for the entire Near East were located in central Jaffa.[45] The station played mostly Arabic music, with a bit of Western classical music as well as news and even theatrical productions part of the regular programming. Jaffans also listened to Egyptian and Lebanese radio, but whichever station they tuned to, they were usually looking for the latest compositions of Farid al-Atrash, 'Abd al-Wahhab, or Umm Kulthum, with the more generic Arab Andalusian music to fill in the gaps. Explicitly religious programming was fairly rare. Phonographs were also quite popular; people played them at parties, weddings, and similar events. As with the radio, most of the records people bought featured Arab artists.

For cleaning and soap products, the complicated dynamic between local and foreign producers is clearer. In Palestine, as in Africa, the British implemented significant hygiene programs aimed ostensibly at modernizing the bodies, identities, and consumption habits of the colonized population. The government went so far as to hold annual fairs in major cities and send inspectors to neighborhoods to teach residents modern techniques for bathing and cleaning.[46] The British ardor for hygiene promotion was not dampened by Jaffa's status as a major indigenous center of soap production. According to my informants, everyone used local soaps for the bathroom and laundry, and thus there was no need for the local producers to advertise. As for the offerings of major foreign companies like Lever Bros. and Palmolive, they both "cost more and didn't go as far as the local soaps . . . the local soap was better quality. It's just like the local ice cream shops. They never advertised but were always bustling."[47] It was typically the nouveau riche and others concerned with status who bought imported soaps. Not surprisingly, these were the same people who most often put status and money ahead of local or national communal interests in other matters.

Conclusion: Jaffa's Popular Culture across Time and Place

In her seminal study of popular culture in British-ruled India, Sandria Freitag demonstrates that the public arena that arose out of the "politicization of the everyday" gave institutions such as the press a particular importance in indigenous popular culture, even when the forces of political constraint were strongest. The press played a similar role in the solidification of imagined and invented traditions of Palestinian nationalism, via both the communal reading of newspapers in villages and the more solitary bourgeois reading of the morning *Filastin* in Jaffa proper, "rel[ying] particularly on the interplay of public sphere and ritual." From this evidence, we can argue that what makes colonized spaces such as Palestine and India distinct vis-à-vis the history of the bourgeois public sphere in Europe was that the colonial state was specifically not "the framework of citizens' collective actions"; there was never the kind of shift (in Habermasian terminology, "disintegration") from "confrontational" to "consolational" popular cultural expressions.[48] It took the brute force of war to pacify the Palestinian Arab population.

Yet, the dynamics of the press in Mandatory Palestine were somewhat different from those in other colonial settings. The specificities of the public sphere and popular culture gave the press, especially the Palestinian Arab press, a vital role in shaping the national consciousness among its readers, specifically a consciousness of the need for resistance to Zionism. Moreover, through the press the colonized Palestinian Arab public could attempt to "mount a critical surveillance of Government and society."[49] In the process, they often saw through the positivistic, "civilizing" façades of colonial modernity more clearly than did their British and Zionist antagonists. The differences between Palestine and India or Africa in this particular instance demonstrate the importance of comparative research not just between European and colonized societies, but also *among* colonized societies in order to understand the variable manner in which class, ethnicity, religion, gender, and nation interacted at different points along the axis of colonial modernity. Such a project would necessarily involve an exploration of how popular culture functioned in and influenced these various nodes of identity and meaning formation.

From our initial and limited comparison of the advertisement and consumption of commodities in Jaffa, we can posit two reasons for its residents' significant degree of experience and autonomy when choosing between local and imported goods: (1) the city's long-standing interaction with local, regional, Mediterranean, and European markets and circuits of production and consumption, and (2) the fact that neither the British colonial state nor the Zionist movement exerted much energy to "conquer" Palestine's markets (despite the Zionist labor movement's attempt to conquer other aspects of the economy and space of Palestine). Indeed, an examination of advertisements in the Palestinian press immediately before, during, and after moments of heightened conflict (1921, 1929, 1936) suggests that even in the nationalist spaces of newspapers such as *Filastin* and *al-Difa'*, commodities flowed across the boundaries of the nation in all but the most intense periods of conflict. On the one hand, such movement can be understood as reflecting a failure of the Palestinian elite either to police the boundaries of the nation or to successfully incorporate the voices of local, popular cultures into its public narrative. A kind of political and sociological entropy was perhaps the natural state of interaction among the various communities living in the Jaffa–Tel Aviv region, one where various class and communal interests intersected through multiple spheres of the public and its cultures in a manner that required considerable effort to manage, let alone direct toward a goal of independence against the combined power of the British empire and the Zionist movement.

The Palestinian bourgeoisie that constituted the nationalist elite clearly did not have the power or commitment to direct such a struggle, particularly when it challenged the elites' own political and economic position. In this context, studying the intersections of the public sphere, civil society, and popular culture in the press of Mandatory Palestine can help us understand the poetics of conquest and memory and the dynamics behind the evisceration of popular culture in contemporary Jaffa. Such investigations are a fundamental component of the "rewriting of history" in Palestine-Israel.[50]

This revision is particularly important given that after decades of neglect, the city-turned-neighborhood has recently become Tel Aviv's "chic," "ancient," or "quaint" tourist destination in a process that, as half a century earlier, has entailed further "erasure and reinscription" of a Palestinian Arab into a Zionist Israeli Jewish presence. Despite incessant attempts to raise consciousness among the remaining Palestinian Jaffan community through poignant and powerful discourses of memory and resistance, community leaders have been unable to motivate the local Palestinian community with the same degree of success as in the Mandate period.[51] I would argue that an important reason for this failure is the lack of a local Arabic-language press, as none of the papers that made Jaffa famous have existed for decades; the former headquarters of *Filastin* is now a coffee and *nargila* (water pipe or hookah) house frequented by illegal Egyptian workers.[52] We can imagine what the wealthy residents of the al-'Ajami Quarter of Jaffa thought while reading the latest news about the "Great Revolt" (which began in Jaffa) in their morning paper, or what the (supposedly) semiliterate residents of the village of Summel, which was surrounded by and gradually annexed to Tel Aviv during the 1930s and 1940s, thought as they heard the news about the latest struggle to control the land, water, or resources of the Jaffa–Tel Aviv region. Until 1948, Jaffa and its people still had a vibrant popular culture and a functioning, if handicapped, public sphere with which to disseminate and respond to such information. They also had their own, locally produced products to imagine and consume alongside those arriving from distant shores. Today, this rich local culture is a fading memory.

Notes

1. Benedict Anderson, *Imagined Communities: Reflections on the Origin and Spread of Nationalism* (London: Verso, 1991), 35.

2. Stuart Hall, "Popular Culture and the State," in *Popular Culture and Social Relations*, edited by Tony Bennett, Colin Mercer, and Janet Woollacott (Milton Keynes, England: Open University Press, 1986), 22–49.

3. For a discussion of how the political and economic elite of Jaffa sold the land of the Jaffa–Tel Aviv region to Jews against the interests of the less wealthy inhabitants, see Mark LeVine, *Overthrowing Geography: Jaffa, Tel Aviv and the Struggle for Palestine* (Berkeley: University of California Press, 2005), especially chs. 4 and 7.

4. See Jürgen Habermas, *The Structural Transformation of the Public Sphere: An Inquiry into a Category of Bourgeois Society*, translated by Thomas Burger (Cambridge, Mass.: MIT Press, 1991), ch. 5, section 19.

5. However fragile and insufficient the public spheres that emerged during the colonial period in most Middle Eastern societies may have been, they nevertheless were crucial in forging hegemonizing (and thus cohesive) national identities capable of achieving independence. The press helped shape popular culture as a primary site for the expression and redefinition of community through collective activities in public spaces. See Sandria B. Freitag, *Collective Action and Community: Public Arenas and the Emergence of Communalism in North India* (Berkeley: University of California Press, 1989), 6.

6. Existing theoretical frameworks for criticism of popular culture have missed these qualities precisely to the degree that they have not considered its relationship to the public sphere, which helps clarify them. Such clarification is crucial in the case of Palestine because the people in the plebian or working/peasant category that were the primary consumers—if not producers—of popular culture were in fact *two* peoples-in-the-making (i.e., Zionist Jew and Palestinian Arab). Their respective popular cultures both informed and contested one another as they developed in and through their respective public spheres, which themselves were deeply implicated by British colonial Mandatory rule. See Tony Bennett, "The Politics of the 'Popular' and Popular Culture," *Popular Culture and Social Relations*, edited by Tony Bennett, Colin Mercer, and Janet Woollacott (Milton Keynes, England: Open University Press, 1986), 6–21.

7. Anderson, *Imagined Communities*, 61, 62.

8. Peter Sinnema, *Dynamics of the Picture Page: Representing the Nation in the "Illustrated London News"* (Aldershot, England: Ashgate, 1998), 2, 85.

9. For a discussion of "resistance vernaculars," see Russell A. Potter, *Spectacular Vernaculars: Hip-Hop and the Politics of Postmodernism* (Syracuse: State University of New York Press, 1995), 57; B. Anderson, *Imagined Communities*, especially ch. 5.

10. Walter Armbrust, *Mass Culture and Modernism in Egypt* (Cambridge, England:

Cambridge University Press, 1996), 221. If we consider popular culture as comprising a set of mass-mediated expressive discourses that define the scale and character of social interaction, then mass media, including the print media, cinema, and recorded music (and today television) are clearly its primary texts. Walter Armbrust, ed., *Mass Mediations: New Approaches to Popular Culture in the Middle East and Beyond* (Berkeley: University of California Press, 2000).

11. Armbrust, *Mass Culture and Modernism in Egypt*, 58.

12. Miton Israel, *Communications and Power: Propaganda and the Press in the Indian Nationalist Struggle, 1920–1947* (Cambridge, England: Cambridge University Press, 1994). For example, the editor of *Filastin*, referring to his readers as "my people," encouraged them to have the last word against Zionist or British plans for their dispossession. See *Filastin*, May 4, 1921 and May 21, 1921; see also Aida Ali Najjar, "The Arabic Press and Nationalism in Palestine, 1920–1948," PhD diss., Syracuse University, 1975, 62.

Subsequent references to newspapers are cited in the text in parentheses. All translations of newspaper articles and advertisements are mine.

13. A. S. Marmarji Dumaniki, "Nazra fi ta'rikh Yafa" [A view of the history of Jaffa], *al-Mashriq*, no. 10 (1928): 729–735; no. 11 (1928): 826–833. He further describes Jaffa as "beautiful" in myriad ways, "important" strategically, and very "fertile" (833).

14. Recollection of Dr. Akram al-Dajani, in Imtiyaz Diyab, *Yafa: 'Utr Madina* [Jaffa: Perfume of a city] (Beirut: Dar al-Fata al-'Arabi, 1991), 152. There was an important link between cultural, sport, and military/nationalist activities, both actually and discursively (recollection of 'Abd al-Rahman al-Habbab, in ibid., 200; *Filastin*, 29 August 1940, 1). Beginning in 1911, three of Palestine's most important Arab newspapers were centered there: *Filastin*, *al-Jam'ia al-Islamiya*, and *al-Difa'*. For an in-depth review of the politics of these newspapers, although, curiously, *al-Difa'* is missing from his analysis, see Rashid Khalidi, *Palestinian Identity: The Construction of Modern National Consciousness* (New York: Columbia University Press, 1997), ch. 6. All told, there were eight newspapers founded in Jaffa in the Late Ottoman period and thirty-three during the middle of the Mandate. See series on Jaffa's history in *al-Quds*, August 12, 16, and 25, 1997.

15. By the Late Ottoman period the press, more than other institutions, "had perhaps the most widespread impact on society" of all its public and popular institutions. Arab Palestinian journalists saw Palestine as "a special case"; in so doing they helped to create the consciousness of Palestine as a separate geographic and national entity (see R. Khalidi, *Palestinian Identity*, 31, 53). The founders and editors of the major Palestinian, particularly Jaffan newspapers, such as *Filastin* (clearly the most important paper in the country), *al-Difa'*, and *al-Jam'ia al-Islamiya*, were all politically active and used their papers as organs for various nationalist parties (like Ben Franklin more than a century earlier, journalists and members of the intelligentsia played multiple roles); see R. Khalidi, *Palestinian Identity*, 19.

16. Royal Institute of International Affairs, *Great Britain and Palestine, 1915–1945* (London: Oxford University Press, 1946), 28; see also Najjar, "The Arabic Press and Nationalism in Palestine," 80.

17. *Filastin*, September 29, 1913, 1; R. Khalidi, *Palestinian Identity*, 57. Specifically,

the object of the memorandum was "to acquaint the fallah with what is happening in the country, and to teach him his rights, in order to prevent those who do not fear God and his prophets from dominating him and stealing his goods." Najjar, "The Arabic Press and Nationalism in Palestine," 66, 71.

18. Najjar thus argues that "the press in Palestine proved to play an important role not only by reflecting public opinion, but by shaping it" ("The Arabic Press and Nationalism in Palestine," 79).

19. Ibid., 103, 108. *Filastin, al-Difaʻ,* and *al-Jamʻia al-Islamiya* during the 1933 and 1936–1939 revolts often spoke on behalf of "the people" and engaged in well-thought-out "agitation campaigns" against the government.

20. As Sandra Sufian demonstrates, political cartoonists were central players in the shaping of popular opinion, especially during the times of heightened tension such as the 1936–1939 Revolt. Sandy Sufian, "Anatomy of the 1936–1939 Revolt: Images of the Body in Political Cartoons of Mandatory Palestine," *Journal of Palestine Studies,* forthcoming.

One reason for the cartoons' power was their deployment of physiognomic ideas about the bodies and faces of Palestinian Arabs and Jews, which used the constructed hierarchy of race to visually represent and criticize the Other, to present recognizable yet stereotypical images of well-known personalities or groups. Thus, fattened stomachs, long and beaked noses, large hands, and exaggerated facial expressions were all used to convey "an overarching theme of deviancy" of both Zionist leaders and opposing Palestinians. (Ibid.)

21. Who would have none of it, replying, "No Shalom, No Salam, and no negotiation till Jewish immigration ends" (*Filastin,* July 14, 1936). It is important to note the physiognomic characteristics of Dizengoff and Wauchope (especially Dizengoff), which clearly play on existing European stereotypes that have found their way into the Palestinian Arab press: Tel Aviv's mayor is slightly hunched over, with big hands signifying lack of intelligence and integrity.

22. Reproduced in Sufian, "Anatomy of the 1936–1939 Revolt," 2.

23. Thus, when an Arab National Conference was held in Tel Aviv in 1933 (for reasons not explained in the article), *al-Jamʻia al-Islamiya* labeled it "reckless," "scornful," and "contemptible," and, in conjunction with the incidences of Arabs going to cafés or engaging in other activities in Tel Aviv, saw it as "signing a contract of slavery and servitude to the Jews."

24. Najjar, "The Arabic Press and Nationalism in Palestine," 141.

25. *Filastin,* July 22, 1931, 1; July 23, 1931, 1. For the text of each plan, see *Palestine Gazette,* June 16, 1931 (no. 285), and January 5, 1933 (no. 337), which also dutifully reported the smallest details of budget allocations, port, hospitals, infrastructure, and related issues, including a major project to "mold the face of Jaffa as a 'Garden City' on the sea" (*Palestine Post,* August 9, 1934, 2). See also *Filastin,* June 18, 1932, 3; July 22, 1932, 1; July 23, 1932, 1; January 4, 1936, 2; January 9, 1940, 3; January 27, 1940, 3; August 1, 1941, 3; January 12, 1945, 3; Dov Gavish, "The Old City of Jaffa 1936: A Colonial Urban Renewal Project" [Mivtz'a Yafo: Shipur Coloniali shel Pnei 'Ir], *Eretz Israel* 17 (1984): 66–73.

26. My samples are drawn from the two-year periods immediately prior to and

after the major intercommunal violence of 1921, 1929, and 1936, the reason for which was my desire to determine if the violence changed the kinds of ads in the papers or the images and messages they contained, particularly when riots and allied popular culture activities often reveal the sinews of urban life that provide the basic elements of community and popular culture. It turned out that there was no discernable difference in the types of ads or their messages or images, with the exception of a reduction in the number of ads by Jewish businesses, and thus I do not follow up on this question in the text. Moreover, there were no analytically important changes over time. The only development worth noting was that in the early 1920s, there were no real cultural ads, such as for movies and concerts (not surprising, given the nascent development of these industries), although record companies such as Odeon Records were already regularly advertising for surveyors and equipment. Also in the early 1920s there were a few ads for engineers and land surveyors, whose primary work would have been derived from documenting land sales, many of whom *Filastin* would no doubt have disapproved of (see *Filastin*, August 1, 1922, 4). A final development of note is that while in the early 1920s most newspaper photos were of Arab nationalist meetings, the more "worldly" photos and montages began to be used toward the end of the 1920s. Sandria B. Freitag, "Popular Culture in the Rewriting of History: An Essay in Comparative History and Historiography," *Peasant Studies* 16, no. 3 (1989): 186.

27. Sarah Graham-Brown, "The Political Economy of the Jabal Nablus, 1920–48," in *Studies in the Economic and Social History of Palestine in the Nineteenth and Twentieth Centuries*, edited by Roger Owen (Carbondale: Southern Illinois University Press, 1982), 88–176; Salim Tamari, "Factionalism and Class Formation in Recent Palestinian History," in *Studies in the Economic and Social History of Palestine*, 177–202; Issa Khalaf, *Politics in Palestine: Arab Factionalism and Social Disintegration 1939–1948* (Albany: State University of New York Press, 1991).

28. See *Filastin*, May 12, 1935, 1, for a seminal montage and text.

29. On the other hand, it appears that the cruise business was mostly a sideline for the Jaffan shipping companies, and some of the larger concerns that moved to Beirut in 1948 became more successful there than in Jaffa.

30. *Filastin*, April 11, 1936, 4; April 10, 1936, 8; October 1, 1936, 6; *al-Difaʿ*, February 8, 1935, 8; March 11, 1935, 1.

31. Philco Car Radio, advertised in *al-Difaʿ*, September 3, 1935, 6. The car is very modern in its depiction. It should also be noted that ads for cameras, mostly Polaroid brand, were also featured in the two papers, especially in *al-Difaʿ*.

32. See, among others, Margot Badran, *Feminists, Islam, and Nation: Gender and the Making of Modern Egypt* (Princeton: Princeton University Press, 1995); Lila Abu-Lughod, ed., *Remaking Women: Feminism and Modernity in the Middle East* (Princeton: Princeton University Press, 1998).

33. See Sufian, "Anatomy of the 1936–39 Revolt."

34. For example, the Yitzhak Cohen department store published an Arabic ad only days before the outbreak of the 1929 violence (*Filastin*, February 8, 1928, 4).

35. Their population was a combination of spillover from the official borders of Tel

Aviv as the city expanded, and of Jaffan Jews who no longer wanted to live in "Arab" neighborhoods as intercommunal hostility increased.

36. *Yedi'ot Tel Aviv*, no. 10 (1933): 341.

37. Interview with former resident of Jaffa, February 2002.

38. B. Veicmanas, "Internal Trade," in *Economic Organization of Palestine*, edited by Sa'id Himadeh (Beirut: AUB Press, 1938), 345–383.

39. Food, drink, and tobacco held fairly steady between 25 percent and 28 percent during this period, and raw materials and unclassified items each took up around 10 percent of the total imports. Husni Sawwaf, "Foreign Trade," in *Economic Organization of Palestine*, edited by Sa'id Himadeh (Beirut: AUB Press, 1938), 398 table.

40. Ibid., 402 table, 425–431.

41. Timothy Burke, *Lifebuoy Men, Lux Women: Commodification, Consumption and Cleanliness in Modern Zimbabwe* (Durham, N.C.: Duke University Press, 1996), 140, 2, 3.

42. Lee V. Cassanelli, "Qat: Changes in the Production and Consumption of a Quasilegal Commodity in Northeast Africa," in *The Social Life of Things: Commodities in Cultural Perspective*, edited by Arjun Appadurai (Cambridge, England: Cambridge University Press, 1986), 236–260. That is, there was never the backlash from white residents who felt the consumption of European(-style) goods by the "native" Jaffan or larger Palestinian Arab population was a threat to the boundaries of racial and class privilege as elite or aspiring Palestinians consumed goods that had previously been used only by whites. See ibid., 99, 104.

43. See ibid., 11, 43; Sufian, "Anatomy of the 1936–1939 Revolt."

44. Interviews with former residents of Jaffa, March 2003.

45. The NEBS remained largely apolitical until 1947, when the soon-to-depart British loosened their control of the station and it quickly became oriented more toward Palestinian nationalism and the looming war with the Zionist Jewish community.

46. See Sufian, "Anatomy of the 1936–39 Revolt."

47. Interview with former resident of Jaffa, February 2003.

48. Freitag, "Popular Culture in the Rewriting of History," 179, 181, 183.

49. C. A. Bayly, *Empire and Information: Intelligence Gathering and Social Communication in India, 1780–1870* (Cambridge, England: Cambridge University Press, 1996), 182. Indeed, the press in Mandatory Palestine bears many similarities to that of India, which did not go unnoticed by Palestinian Arab journalists, as there were numerous articles on India in *Filastin*. Both colonized societies were "literacy-aware . . . if not yet a society of mass literacy," and each used written media in complex and creative ways to reinforce oral culture and debate, which was both "popular and political" (180).

50. Freitag, "Popular Culture in the Rewriting of History," 169–199.

51. One group, al-Rabita (the Society for Jaffa's Arabs), published a children's book entitled *Yafa: 'Arus al-Bahr*, which is filled with poems, stories, and recollections by older people about Jaffa's beauty and past glory. The book's young narrators inform children that Jaffa was a "thriving, flourishing, and blossoming city that always loved the stranger"; see Muhammad Badarna, *Yafa: 'Arus al-Bahr* [Jaffa: Bride of the sea]

(Jaffa: Rabita Publications, 1997), 56. Most recently, in 1997 the Jerusalem-based Arabic newspaper *al-Quds* ran a nineteen-part series on Jaffa and its history by 'Abbas Nimr, the director of Pious Endowments (*Awqaf*) and Religious Affairs for the Palestinian National Authority; see Abbas Nimr, "Jaffa . . . The Eternal Longing," *al-Quds*, May 17, 1997, no page on offprint.

52. The one locally produced Arabic newspaper, *al-Sabbar* (which is in fact a biweekly publication), is published by a dedicated staff of muckraking journalists whose investigations are of inestimable value for activists and scholars. Yet the paper has very few readers among the local Palestinian Arab population.

ILAN PAPPÉ

Post-Zionism and Its

Popular Cultures

In the 1990s, Israeli universities became the venue for a lively debate on Israeli history and sociology. By the end of the decade, the debate had spread to the public arena and become the subject of heated discussions in the popular press and electronic mass media. At the debate's core was the willingness of many academics in Israel to re-evaluate hegemonic Zionist ideology—a project of reassessment that many labeled as "post-Zionist." This reassessment began in earnest in the 1980s, with the appearance of a number of scholarly works that presented images of Israeli society and history that were strongly at odds with the Israeli public's self-image and collective memory. These works challenged the most sacred histori-cal "truths" of Zionism in a body of scholarship that traced its roots to the histories and struggles of the Israeli communities that had histori-cally been systematically marginalized within the state, namely, the Pal-estinian citizens of Israel and the Mizrahim. Such scholarship also criti-cized the role played by the country's academic institutions in shaping the Zionist self-image and interpretation of Palestinian history and iden-tity. Although the critique varied in form and strength, and was voiced by self-identified Zionists as well as anti-Zionists, it was termed post-Zionist because of the ways it challenged the dominant Zionist narrative.[1] The post-Zionist rubric therefore included those who criticized Zionism's short-comings, even if they did not possess a clearly non-Zionist vision of Israel's future.

The search for alternative interpretations of Zionism and Israeli history signaled a crisis in the Jewish state. In the 1990s, Jewish society in Israel found itself at a critical ideological juncture: it could either move toward a more extreme form of Zionism or remake itself as a civic, non-Jewish state. Whereas the majority of Israeli Jews opted for the former ideological path, the majority of cultural producers in Israel advocated the latter. By the turn of the twenty-first century, with the rise of Ariel Sharon to power, the onset of the second Palestinian uprising, and the beginning of a general shift in Israeli public opinion to the right, the post-Zionist age had come to something of an end.[2] Yet during its heyday in the early to mid-1990s, post-Zionism boldly confronted the hegemonic culture of a very indoctrinated and ideological society.

Post-Zionism is typically described as an intellectual movement and discourse. In this essay, I argue that it was in fact a much wider phenomenon. Although the debate centered in the universities, it also occurred in the arena of popular culture, particularly in the film industry, where it both preceded and catalyzed the academic debate, and in the arenas of television, visual arts, poetry, literature, and the theater. This essay argues that popular cultural production in Israel has functioned as a radical and important political intervention, one whose role in the post-Zionist discussion has been largely overlooked.

Historical and Social Precursors

Both the cultural and intellectual challenges to Zionism of the last few decades owe a great deal to an earlier history of protest, both political and cultural, that emerged in the 1950s during the early years of Israeli statehood. This decade was an era of a mostly unchallenged Zionist consensus, when what was recognized as Israeli "culture" consisted of a well-defined canon of books, popular songs, poetry, plays, and ceremonies commemorating heroic chapters in Zionist history. But the 1950s were also uneasy days of economic scarcity that produced the first social rebellion in the nation-state—the 1959 riots of Mizrahis in Wadi Salib as well as other similar outbreaks. During this period, Mizrahi Jews were largely ghettoized in the *maabarot* (makeshift camps for newly arrived immigrants), in the slums of the big towns, and in the isolated settlements established near the borders. Concurrently, Palestinian citizens were living under a military administration (1948–1966); they were cordoned off in military-ruled areas, denied freedom of mobility, and faced even more difficult social, political, and economic conditions than did their Mizrahi co-nationals. Taken together, these Arabs—Jews, Muslims, and Christians—made up almost half of the total population, but they lacked representation in either the dominant political or the cultural branches of Israeli society.

The undercurrents of Mizrahi dissatisfaction and antagonism erupted in the early 1970s in open social protests. The 1973 war played a key role in creating cracks in Israel's wall of moral smugness and self-satisfaction. In the relative calm that followed, tensions between Israel's multicultural and multiethnic fabric and the melting pot ideal of the state came to the fore. Young Mizrahi activists, emulating the dissent voiced by African Americans, established their own Black Panther movement (thus named) to demand a fairer distribution of economic resources and a share in the definition of Israeli cultural identity. Although this movement failed to attract the political attentions of the Israeli left, it did draw the interest of the right, which was able to skillfully channel Mizrahi discontent into a mass movement that brought the Likud, led by Menachem Begin, to power in 1977. Mizrahi social protest also coincided with a growing sense of activism and Palestinian nationalism among the Palestinian population in Israel. Key manifestations of this struggle were protests against ongoing confiscation of the Palestinian lands, launched in the 1976 Land Day protests, and the growth in significance of progressive nationalist organizations like the Communist Party and Ibna' al-Balad.

The Mizrahi political rebellion of 1977 spelled an end to the predominately Ashkenazi Labor Party's reign of power. However, the political revolution did not bring about any significant change in the socioeconomic conditions of North African and Middle Eastern Jews, who instead found an ideology of redemption in a mixture of Orthodox Jewish fundamentalism, anti-Arab racism, and ethnic politics of identity.[3] Meanwhile, Palestinian citizens of Israel continued with their own national struggles, which were for the most part disconnected from and sometimes antagonistic to the political directions taken by most Mizrahi politics and social movements. These disparate struggles constituted an important but usually ignored element of the backdrop out of which academic post-Zionism emerged.

The Post-Zionist Academic Debate

In the Israeli academy of 1948 to 1967, most Jewish-Israeli scholars ignored the Palestinians as an academic subject, except to occasionally mention their status as refugees. After 1967, with the rise of the Palestinian resistance movement, and through the 1980s, Palestinians appeared in Israeli academic writings largely as "terrorists" or as pawns in a pan-Arab conspiracy to annihilate the Jewish state. Concurrently, most Israeli scholars

approached the events of 1948 as the culmination of a teleological process of Jewish redemption and renaissance—as a war in which Zionists
prevailed against overwhelming odds, and in which Palestinians fled without a fight. Scholarship about the 1947–48 war conferred on Zionism a
status equivalent to that of a third world liberation movement. Accordingly,
scholars described the war as a process of gaining "independence" from
the British and as "liberation" from the yoke of the diaspora—terms that
effectively ignored any direct conflict with the Arabs. Scholarly accounts
described the war as the result of an unequal military confrontation between a small Jewish community, with a stress on the Holocaust survivors
among them, and a hostile British colonial government and united Arab
world bent on its annihilation. In this narrative, the Zionist victory was configured as a miracle due to the ingenuity of David Ben-Gurion and the heroism of his soldiers.[4] As for the task of describing and analyzing Arab culture
and history during this era, this was entrusted to the Israeli "Orientalist"
establishment—most of whose members were uninterested in either the
Palestinians or the 1948 war.[5] The few scholars who did write about the war
avoided dealing with the Nakba ("the Catastrophe," the Palestinian name
for the events of 1948) as a human or national tragedy, and instead focused
on political and military maneuvering in the Arab world before and after
the war.[6]

The post-Zionist wave radically shifted the tenor of prevailing Israeli
academic discourse.[7] The phenomenon can be traced back to the work of
a handful of sociologists at Haifa University in the 1970s that echoed the
protests of the Mizrahim and the Palestinians in Israel of that period—
work that gathered strength among historians in the wake of the Lebanon
war of 1982 and during the first Palestinian uprising or Intifada (1987–
1993). These historians made their mark when they challenged the Zionist
historiographical picture of the 1948 war, adopting major chapters of the
Palestinian historiographical narrative as well as adding new elements—a
project made possible both by political shifts in Israel and the region and
by the opening of state archives dealing with the 1948 war.

The works of the new historians radically undermined the notion that
the Jewish community in Palestine had been in danger of annihilation
on the eve of the 1948 war. Indeed, their works described a fragmented
Arab world, unable to lend effective support to the poorly armed and badly
trained paramilitary Palestinian groups in their battle for post-Mandatory
Palestine.[8] In turn, they argued that an important factor in Jewish success

on the battlefield was the Jewish Agency's tacit understanding with Trans-jordan which allowed the Hashemites to take over the West Bank. Some of these scholars attributed Jewish success on the diplomatic front to a rare moment of cooperation between the two superpowers (the United States and the Soviet Union), each of which supported the Zionist cause. These works directly contradicted both the Zionist narrative of a heroic libera-tion movement that succeeded despite the overwhelming strength of the enemy, and the Israeli myth of a voluntary Palestinian exodus in 1948 — the latter famously explored in the groundbreaking work of Benny Morris.[9] It should be noted that despite the radical intervention of Jewish-Israeli scholarship of this period, a gap remained between the claims of such scholarship and those made within the Palestinian national narrative.[10]

The work of many such scholars provoked angry reactions from Jewish-Israeli public figures and press commentators. Israeli policy before 1967 had never before been described as aggressive, to say nothing of brutal, inhuman, and morally unjustifiable. Although none of the new historians had dealt explicitly with the Israeli academic establishment in their schol-arly works, they openly blamed mainstream academia for concealing these unpleasant chapters in their accounts of 1948 in the ensuing public media debate.[11] The research carried out on 1948 during the 1980s eventually paved the way for a more fundamental criticism of Zionism and its role in Israeli academia, and this critique slowly made its way into public con-sciousness.

The first Palestinian Intifada also opened a new chapter in Israeli-Palestinian dialogue, one that was conducted mainly by scholars. Most Jew-ish Israeli scholars of the late 1980s were not connected to radical po-litical groups, and few had encountered the historical narratives of their Palestinian academic counterparts. These scholars' exchanges with Pales-tinians resulted in the exposure of unpleasant and often shocking chapters in Israeli history—making visible the basic contradiction between Zionist national ambitions, historically, and the lives and aspirations of the indige-nous Arab population in Palestine.

In the 1990s, post-Zionist scholars turned their attention to more meta-historical and theoretical questions.[12] During this period, there was a grow-ing tendency to embrace postmodernist (i.e., relativist) historiography and multiculturalist interpretations of Israeli society. Some of the scholars working in this vein aimed to expose the role played by the academic estab-lishment in the nation-building process and the consequent demise of freedom of thought and self-criticism. Employing Said's critique of Orientalism, some exposed the underlying biases in Israeli sociological, anthropological, and historiographical discourses on Arabs, whether Israeli Palestinians, Egyptians, or Sephardic Jews.[13] The very grouping of Palestinians and Oriental Jews in a common category, as was done in the work of Shlomo Swirski and Sammy Smooha, posed a fundamental challenge to conventional Zionist academic norms.[14] Other scholars, focusing on dominant texts, explored the ways that museums, ceremonies, school curricula, and national emblems had been deployed by dominant Ashkenazi society to excise others from the national memory.[15]

A number of additional questions and issues occupied post-Zionist scholars of the 1990s. Some began to explore the Holocaust and its impact on Israeli society, as in the work of Tom Segev and Idit Zertal.[16] Others approached the highly sensitive subject of militarism in Israeli society, in a scholarly assault on Israel's most sacred cow: "security." In tandem, Israeli political scientists began to reject government explanations that security and national defense considerations had been responsible for consigning North African Jews to the geographic and social margins of society, or for the imposition of an apartheid regime on Palestinians in Israel.[17] Yet perhaps the most significant contribution of post-Zionist scholars was their application of a colonialist perspective to the historical study of Zionism, as in the work of Gershon Shafir.[18] Other scholars followed suit. Much post-Zionist scholarship, with its attempts to critically discuss the essence of Zionism in historical and contemporary terms, was denounced in Israel as the work of self-hating Jews writing in the service of the enemy; yet, both despite and because of such denunciations, the impact of the critique was significant, and it quickly spread to more popular and more cultural realms.[19]

Post-Zionist Fiction and Poetry

Not all critiques of Zionism emanated from the Israeli academy, nor were all of these scholarly critiques entirely novel. Some cultural fields had long histories of dissent—histories that ultimately served to make post-Zionist scholarship possible. Such was the case with poetry, particularly that produced by Palestinians with Israeli citizenship. Beginning in the 1950s, and increasingly during the 1970s, this community turned to cultural protest as a means of challenging the glass ceiling that had denied them any chance of social equality or economic improvement. While Palestinian-Israeli politicians debated the issue of "collaboration" with, or resistance to, the Jewish state, poets like Samih al-Qasim, Salim Jubran, and Tawfiq Zayyad turned to nationalist verse, written in a high cultural idiom but recited in the streets as a popular form. Poetry was one of the few fields of narrative or knowledge production open to the expression of Palestinian national identity after the Nakba. It was the medium through which daily Palestinian interests of love and hate, birth and death, marriage and family could be intertwined with those of land confiscation and state oppression, and such poems circulated broadly within the Palestinian arena via special poetry festivals.[20]

It was Palestinian prose, however, that had the greatest impact on the Jewish public. In the 1980s, the Palestinian counternarrative on Zionism in Israel began to make its way to readers of Hebrew-language fiction through the novels of Palestinian-Israeli writers like Emile Habiby and Anton Shammas. Indeed, many critics regarded Shammas's 1986 novel *Arabesques*, describing the life of a family excluded and discriminated against by the Hebrew-speaking majority, as the best work ever written in Hebrew.[21] Hebrew translations of the novels of the late Emile Habiby (most notably by Shammas), which describe the military regime imposed on Palestinians of Israel between 1948 and 1966, exposed readers to an Israeli-Palestinian view of the past and future.[22] Translations produced by a fringe-publishing house, Mifras, created an even more direct link to works of Palestinian and Arab writers in the Middle East at large. By the end of the 1990s, a limited number of canonical Arabic works (including the writing of Naguib Mahfouz) became available in Hebrew and sold well. In 2002, Mifras's successor, Andalus, published Elias Khoury's epic novel about the Nakba, *Bab ul-Shums*.

Jewish-Israeli poets found it easier than did novelists to experiment with alternative viewpoints. During the Lebanon war, some wrote antiwar poems, while a number explicitly criticized the occupation during the first Intifada.[23] Yet these were infrequently collected or anthologized and thus did not circulate widely in Israel. Post-Zionist fiction was a more marginal cultural form. Several writers, including Yitzhak Laor, Leah Iny, and Savion Librecht, produced non-Zionist fictional narratives that dealt with Israeli history and identity at odds with Zionist truisms. The more substantial post-Zionist perspectives came mainly from outside the Ashkenazi-Israeli mainstream. Immigrant writers like Shimon Ballas and Sami Michael from

Iraq and Albert Swissa from Morocco offered counternarratives that they traced to their self-declared identities as "Arab Jews," which most Israeli Zionists perceived as something of a betrayal to the Zionist dream.[24]

Post-Zionist Theater

Before the 1970s, most Israeli plays portrayed Arabs as shallow, one-dimensional figures, drawing their characters using classically racist tropes, such as sloppy dress and lisped speech. After the 1973 war, a younger generation of playwrights and directors began to incorporate paci-fist viewpoints into their works.[25] Among the first to criticize Israel's mili-taristic society was Hanoch Levin. The main theme of his most celebrated play, the 1970 satirical cabaret *The Queen of the Bath* (*Hamalkat ambatia*), was corruption in the army; the play was quickly censored. Yet the focus of the theater's critique during this period was largely limited to post-1967 Israel and the immoral implications of the continued occupation of Palestine. Many cultural workers in the theater identified primarily with Peace Now and shared the movement's dichotomous conception of Pales-tine's history—that is, of a pre-1967 period when Zionism and Israel were morally right and just, and a post-1967 period when Palestinians were treated with brutality and insensitivity. Plays produced in this vein envi-sioned a majority of young Jews agonizing about their society, vacillating between callous inhumanity and passionate manifestations of their care and concern when they came into contact with Palestinians under occupa-tion. The Palestinians who appeared in the plays of writers like Yehoushu'a Sobol or Benny Barabash remained enigmatic and shallow figures playing secondary roles; Jews were entrusted with the roles of heroes who shot, killed, and tortured—and always regretted their actions.[26]

Post-Zionist criticism also inflected the Israeli theater of the 1990s, but only marginally so. Its influences could be seen in translated plays by Palestinian writers, in original post-Zionist plays, and in onstage adapta-tions of earlier novels—among them, the work of Sami Michael.[27] As in his novels, Michael's plays humanized the Palestinians and endowed them with names, histories, and ambitions. The fringe theater scene also pro-duced plays written by Palestinian Israelis that depicted the occupation and the lives of Palestinians in Israel, always testing the boundaries of free speech. In 1994, a theater in Jerusalem launched an Israeli-Palestinian co-production of *Romeo and Juliet*, but such cooperative projects were few and far between.[28]

If one includes the long history of Mizrahi cultural production and cultural dissent within the post-Zionist cultural rubric, then the phenomenon of critique through popular music can be construed quite broadly. During the 1970s, in response to their social, political, and economic depravation, Mizrahim developed an underground musical movement revolving chiefly around a black or informal market in cassettes of Arabic and so-called Mediterranean music.[29] This movement emerged as a powerful tool of social protest as well as a career vehicle for Mizrahi pop stars; it was an attempt to articulate a particularistic ethnic identity, in addition to satisfying the cravings of a new generation of Jewish-Israeli youth for a more global popular culture.

During the 1990s, Mizrahi popular music gained new kinds of Israeli and international audiences. Indeed, during this decade Euro-Israeli audiences began to turn toward Arabic music in unprecedented ways. Music from all over the Arab World, ranging from Umm Kulthum to North African rai, began to enjoy broad audiences in Israel. Arguably the new popularity of Middle Eastern music did not signify a significant change in Euro-Israeli attitudes toward Arab culture. Rather, the Zionist political elite appropriated Mizrahi music as a means of gaining an important constituency. Even the most extreme right-wing radio stations (among them Gush Emunim's *Arutz Sheva*) aired such music, and extreme-right parties played Middle Eastern music at their political rallies, even as both preached the expulsion and destruction of Arabs and Palestinians.

Even in the more open society of the 1990s, few Ashkenazi Israeli pop singers risked their relationship with the wider public by being openly political. One important exception was pop star Aviv Gefen, one of the country's most popular singers, whose lyrics contained sharp but simplistic criticisms of Israeli militarism—criticism echoed in his own refusal to serve in the army. His appeal, in fact, was based largely on the spectacle of his performances, rather than the substance of his message, but his popularity created the impression of growing public tolerance for nonconformist pop music lyrics. In truth, Gefen's popularity did not herald a wider acceptance of post-Zionist ideas, and he returned to the political consensus after Rabin's assassination in November 1995. During the same period, Chava Alberstein and Nurit Galron produced songs that criticized the inhuman behavior of soldiers in the Occupied Territories during the first Intifada. Galron was particularly bold, singing, "Do not tell me you don't care about a little girl who lost her eye," referring to the large number of Palestinian children blinded by Israeli rubber bullets. This song was banned for almost a year from Israeli radio stations.[30] Although Alberstein and Galron were extremely popular, they represented a decisive minority in the Israeli pop music world.

Post-Zionist Cinema

The film and television industries in Israel went through a similar process, and in many respects went further than any other cultural media in adopting the post-Zionist counternarrative. In order to do so, both industries had to battle an intense history of racism and Zionist stereotyping. Until the early 1970s, commercial film had closely followed the nationalist agenda— more closely than any other cultural agency or institution within the country, save that of children's literature. Historically, Mizrahi Jews and Palestinians had been ridiculed and degraded whenever they were represented in Israeli cinema—as in one of Israel's most popular films, Efraim Kishon's *Salah Shabati* (1964). The film depicts Mizrahi Jews with the ambivalence acutely described by Homi Bhabha: as the "other oriental: the noble native and the childish brutal primitive."[31] The same ambivalence later appeared in the *bourekas* genre, popular feature films of the seventies that dealt with the lives of Mizrahi Jews.[32] Most of the films dealing with history or the conflict depicted the Palestinians or the Arabs as pathetic stereotypical figures who always yielded to the superior Euro-Jewish Israeli hero. The story of Jewish schoolchildren single-handedly capturing armed Arab terrorists or invaders was a common plot within this storyline. As Ella Shohat has noted, the ideology of Zionism and its politics of representation in Israeli cinema either excluded Mizrahis and Palestinians or misrepresented them in one-dimensional and derogatory ways.[33] Yet during the 1960s and 1970s, the hegemony of Zionist ideology began to erode in the feature film industry. Directors began to depict private lives in ways that challenged the cinema's prior commitment to nation, homeland, and army. Existentialism became a principle way for films to enunciate a critique of Zionism, as in Dan Wolman's adaptation of Amos Oz's *My Michael*. But it was still some time before Mizrahi, Palestinian, and women's narratives would make their way to the celluloid screen.[34]

As in other cultural and intellectual fields, the Lebanon war and the first Palestinian uprising had a catalytic effect on the cinema. Both in quantity and quality, commercial feature films began to adopt a critical view of Israel's past and present attitude toward the Arabs in general and the Palestinians in particular. Some of the first attempts to revise the place of the Palestinian narrative in the Israeli film industry were broadcast on Israeli television. The most courageous of these films were produced during the 1970s. At a time when Israel still had only one national television channel, and budgets for production were not at issue, officials managing television production could experiment relatively freely. A prime example was Ram Loevy's (also spelled Levi) 1976 screen adaptation of S. Yizhar's "Siper Hirbet Hizah" (The story of Hirbet Hizah), a famous short story that depicted the maltreatment of an Arab prisoner of war. Yizhar had situated his story in an undefined and possibly fictional locale, thus making it easier for readers to contemplate the possibility of Israeli soldiers committing atrocities. Levi's film adaptation made the story more concrete by linking the tale to Israeli behavior toward Palestinians in the Occupied Territories. Despite the canonical status of Yizhar's story, television executives prevented the film's screening. In the wake of the 1982 Lebanon War, film producers began to rethink Israel's relationship to the Arabs—particularly to the Palestinians. The first film to explore these issues was *Hiuh Hagedi* (The smile of the lamb), a 1983 adaptation of a novel by David Grossman, directed by Shimon Dotan. It was one of the first commercial features to feature an Arab hero with whom viewers could easily identify.[35] The effort to give a voice to the Palestinian point of view became common in Israeli cinema in the following years—as in Ram Loevy's 1986 TV drama *Ani Ahmad* (I am Ahmad), which criticized the treatment of Israel's Palestinian population. Yet, the critique at work was of the Peace Now variety; that is, one that concentrated on post-1967 Israel and thus failed to deviate substantially from the Zionist metanarrative. Nevertheless, these films represented a radical departure from Israeli cinema of the 1960s, given their desire both to humanize and, at times, heroize Palestinians.

Beginning in the late 1980s, film directors used romance and sex to prepare the Jewish-Israeli palate for new kinds of critiques and viewpoints. Typical of this period were films modeled on a *Romeo and Juliet*–type plot, in which a Jewish woman falls in love with a Palestinian man against the wishes of their respective families and societies. Despite their problematic sexual narratives, these films challenged the dominant image of the Arab in the Zionist metanarrative by switching the conventional roles of heroes and villains. One of the earliest films of this genre, 1989's *Esh Tzolevet* (Crossfire), offered an unprecedented Palestinian perspective on the 1948 war, dramatizing the despair and bewilderment of the Palestinian population through a story of cross-cultural romance. The late 1980s also witnessed new kinds of films, much more angry than their predecessors, produced by a second generation of Mizrahi directors that portrayed the Arab Jews' growing frustration with the prospering Ashkenazi upper classes, their continued geographic and social marginality in the development towns and peripheral slums and limited access to financial resources, and their distorted image in the national narrative.[36] A prominent example is Ram Loevy's 1985 film *Lehem* (Bread), an exposition of the dismal reality of Mizrahi life in a development town. Such films gained relevance against the backdrop of other seemingly "radical" films of the decade—ones that concentrated largely on relations between Jewish-Israelis and Palestinian-Arabs. For all their radicalism, most of the latter reflected the lives and views of the Ashkenazi hegemony, portraying the conflict from the perspective of yuppies in Tel Aviv. Thus, while these films explored Others' perspectives in important ways, their treatment of the Palestinians was still radically circumscribed.[37] Some of the films depicting the Israelis as occupiers and colonizers and the Palestinians as victims, and those exposing the discrimination against the Mizrahim, attracted considerable public attention, an indication that they may have created public empathy.[38]

The ideological manipulation of the Holocaust in the service of Zionist and Israeli politics also came under scrutiny in the film industry—albeit in relatively few instances. Ilan Moshensons's 1979 movie *Roveh Huliot* (A wooden gun) exposed Israeli uneasiness over the possible connection between the Nazi wish to annihilate the Jews in Europe and the Zionist desire to expel the Palestinians for the sake of the Jewish community in Palestine. Some of these same themes were treated in television programming. A documentary film by Benny Bruner based on Tom Segev's *The Seventh Million* aired on television in 1995; it focused on the cynical aspects of Zionist policy toward the Holocaust. Asher Tlalim's *Al Tigu Li Bashoah* (Don't touch my Holocaust) was even more progressive in its challenge to the ethos of the Holocaust in Israel, discussing the role of Holocaust representations in consolidating Ashkenazi domination.[39]

The 1990s and 2000s continued to produce challenging and overtly post-Zionist films. Films like 2002's *Ruah Qadim* (Kaddim wind) by David Benchetrit and *The Black Panthers (in Israel) Speak* by Sami Shalom Chetrit (both 2002) were unusual in their political directness in treating the Mizrahi experience. In turn, a new wave of films was produced for television whose representations of the Palestinian experience directly contradicted the dominant Zionist narrative. Most prominent of these was Amos Gitai's

1998 film *Bait* (House); the film told the story of a house that had belonged to a Palestinian doctor in 1948, confiscated by the Israelis, and sold to Jewish immigrants from Algiers. Although Gitai's film did not question the immigrants' rights to the house, it recognized the legitimacy of the Palestinian claim—a relatively new posture for films of this period. In 2002, a small cable channel screened Ram Loevy's documentary *Close, Closed, Closure* (Seger), which depicted the misery of life under occupation at a time when Israeli news bulletins were blocking their viewers' access to the sights and sounds of a quarantined Palestinian population under siege.

Among Palestinian-Israeli filmmakers, Nizar Hassan pried open issues relating to Palestinians in Israel that had never been examined on the screen. His *Istiqlal* (Independence), in Arabic with Hebrew subtitles, told the story of a village in Israel that remained Palestinian despite coercion, denial, cooptation, and confiscation. Yet for the Israeli Jewish public, films about the "discovery" of past Israeli "sins" had the greatest impact. One such film was David Benchetrit's 1992 powerful documentary *Miba'ad Lire'alat Hagalut* (Behind the veil of exile). In addition to Benchetrit's rethinking of the notion of exile (*galut*), a term usually reserved for the Jewish diaspora, his film followed the lives of three Palestinian women from a Palestinian historical perspective. The film marked the first time that the expulsion of Palestinians was represented on Israeli television. Finally, in 1998, Muhammad Bakri screened his documentary *1948*, a chilling tale of Israel's ethnic cleansing operation as reported by Palestinian survivors and Jewish perpetrators. Yet by the time the film had reached the stage of marketing and distribution, the public mood had already shifted and few Israeli Jews were willing to confront the Nakba or examine its relevance in the present.

Post-Zionist TV: The Case of Tekuma

Perhaps the most significant artifact of post-Zionism in the realm of either television or feature film was the 1998 documentary television series *Tekuma* (Revival). The show's screening provided one of the first opportunities to gauge the impact of post-Zionism on the wider public. The series—a survey of founding trends, moments, and movements in Israeli history and society such as the question of Zionism, the 1948 war, and the treatment of Israeli Palestinians and Mizrahi Jews in the early 1950s—was proudly presented as the centerpiece of Israeli television's contribution to the fiftieth anniversary celebrations of the founding of the state. The very name of the documentary—*Tekuma*, meaning the resurrection of the Jewish people in the redeemed land of Palestine—was very much in line with Zionist mythology. But this explicitly Zionist title was affixed to a television program that delivered a post-Zionist message, or, at least, one that experimented seriously with post-Zionist interpretations.

The series was characterized by a tension between the wish to tell a Zionist story, on the one hand, and the desire to present the Palestinian and Mizrahi view on the other. Although each segment was narrated from a Zionist perspective, it was at times interrupted and challenged by Palestinian, Egyptian, and Jordanian as well as Mizrahi eyewitnesses. Although many episodes, particularly those relating to the 1948 war, did rely on the findings of the new histories, the series' account of pre-1967 events was very much in keeping with the Peace Now version of the Zionist narrative. Segments dealing with the 1950s, particularly the state's attitude toward Jews from Arab countries and toward its Palestinian citizens, presented Ashkenazi condescension as an instance of pure racism with regard to anything Arab—an attitude that translated into colonialist policies in education and welfare. The segment on the Palestinian citizens in Israel, entitled "The Pessoptimist" after the novel by Emile Habiby's book,[40] was the clearest in its critique, presenting no excuses or alibis for the abuse and maltreatment the Palestinians suffered during eighteen years of emergency rule.

Interestingly, although *Tekuma* held the Zionist left responsible for the expulsions, massacres, and discrimination, it was the rightist Likud that spearheaded the protests against what it termed a post-Zionist program. According to the minister of communication, Limor Livnat (Likud), the deeds of the Israeli nation had to be presented as just and moral. Propelling the wrath of the Likud government were the program's very high ratings and good tape sales, this despite the Ministry of Education's explicit instructions not to include the series within the national curriculum. Interestingly, many of the series' shocking stories and images failed to move much of its Jewish-Israeli audience, as similar images were beginning to appear on television with the outbreak of the second Intifada in September 2000 and audiences were growing immune to their effects.

Post-Zionist Discourse: Its Impact and Demise

By the end of the twentieth century—with the rise of Ariel Sharon to power, the onset of the second Palestinian uprising, and the beginning of a general shift in Israeli public opinion to the right—the mainstream Zionist per-spective had returned with force. After this point, most of the novels, plays, and films produced in Israel refused to seriously transcend the Zionist nar-rative with its negative portrayal of Arabs, and those cultural producers who did articulate post-Zionist messages in their work were no longer among the leaders of the Israeli cultural scene. The scholarly debate in Israel still continued, it should be noted, even after the post-Zionist trends in culture had begun to weaken, although its impact had lessened and its claims were increasingly under fire.

Despite its dissolution, the post-Zionist cultural debate, particularly that of the 1990s, had provided a glimpse of what might occur within Israeli society if and when a genuine chance for peace emerges. In the 1990s, in the wake of the Oslo Accords of 1993, the debate had signaled both a rift in academy, and an identity crisis in the wider society—a crisis produced by the possibility of seriously confronting peace. Peace had opened up the possibility for academics, cultural producers, and others to undermine the national consensus and its narrative about the need to act in unison (that is, as Jews) against common enemies. Relative economic success and security during this decade had also led deprived groups inside Israel (e.g., Miz-rahim gays and lesbians) to demand their fair share, just as it had encour-aged the Palestinians in Israel to lay bare the tension between the state's pretension to democracy and its insistence on remaining a Jewish state. In the era of post-Zionism, challenges to Zionist identity had come from many quarters within the state: from the Palestinians, from Mizrahim, from feminists, from Ultra-Orthodox Jews, and from a small number of scholars, including this writer, who were born in post-1948 Israel and were now ready to voice their dissent. In 2002, at the time of this writing, few of these critiques are audible. But should the bloody clashes subside, they may be heard again, and perhaps with even greater force.

Notes

1. Ilan Pappé, "Post-Zionist Critique: Part 1. The Academic Debate," *Journal of Palestine Studies* 26, no. 2 (winter 1997): 29–41.

2. The end of post-Zionism and the shift of the Jewish public to the right is dis-cussed in Ilan Pappé, "The Post-Zionist Discourse in Israel, 1991–2000," *Holy Land Studies* 1, no. 1 (September 2002): 9–35.

3. A thorough study of this development can be found in a collection of essays: Yoav Peled, ed., *Shas: The Challenge of Israelism* (Tel Aviv: Yediot Aharanot, 2001) (in Hebrew).

4. A detailed description is provided in Ilan Pappé, "The New History of the 1948 War," *Teoria vebikoret* 3 (1993): 95–114 [in Hebrew].

5. Even Yehoshua Porath, who provided the first balanced Israeli view of the Palestinians, never wrote about 1948 and instead dealt only with the period up to 1939. See his *The Emergence of the Palestinian-Arab National Movement, 1918–1929* (London: Frank Cass, 1974) and *The Palestinian Arab National Movement, 1929–1939* (London: Frank Cass, 1977).

6. See, for instance, Yoseph Nevo, "The Palestinians and the Jewish State, 1947–48," in *We Were Like Dreamers*, edited by Y. Wallach (Tel Aviv: Massada, 1985) [in Hebrew], and recently, Itamar Rabinovich, *The Road Not Taken: Early Arab Negotiations* (New York: Oxford University Press, 1991), which ignores the Palestinian side of the story altogether. Similarly, when more recent generations of Orientalists dealt with the PLO, they did not take 1948 as a starting point. The notable exception is Moshe Shemesh, *The Palestinian Entity, 1959–1974: Arab Politics and the PLO* (London: Frank Cass, 1988). Otherwise, the Palestinians of 1948 were erased from the academic scene in Israel.

7. See n. 1. On the history and dominant trends of post-Zionism, see Lawrence J. Silberstein, *The Postzionism Debates: Knowledge and Power in Israeli Culture* (New York: Routledge, 1999).

8. Ilan Pappé, *The Making of the Arab-Israeli Conflict, 1947–1951* (New York: I.B. Tauris, 1992), 102–135.

9. Benny Morris was the first to argue, on the basis of newly declassified documents, that many of the Palestinians had been expelled in the course of the 1948 war, although he did not accept the Palestinian historiographical claim that expulsion was part of a master plan. Benny Morris, *The Birth of the Palestinian Refugee Problem, 1947–1949* (Cambridge, England: Cambridge University Press, 1989).

10. The work of the "new historians" on 1948 in a sense built upon important earlier rewritings of the official Zionist narratives about the Yishuv (Jewish community in Palestine) during the Mandatory period. In the early 1980s, scholars such as Baruch Kimmerling and Yonathan Shapiro had used domination and co-optation theories to expose the dictatorial and arbitrary nature of the Jewish political system that developed during the Mandatory period. Their work challenged the myth embraced by Israeli Zionist historians that the actions of Zionist leaders during the Mandate had been motivated by altruistic socialist and liberal ideologies. See Sami Smooha, *Israel: Pluralism and Conflict* (London: Routledge and Kegan Paul, 1978), and Yonathan Shapiro, "The Historical Origins of Israeli Democracy," in *Israeli Democracy under Stress*, ed. Ehud Sprinzak and Larry Diamond (Boulder, Colo.: Lynne Rienner, 1993). This claim about Zionist leaders' altruism during the mandate continues to be made by leading Israeli historians today; see in particular Anita Shapira, *Visions in Conflict* (Tel Aviv: 'Am 'Oved, 1987) [in Hebrew].

11. See Uri Ram, "The Colonization Perspective in Israeli Sociology," *Journal of Historical Sociology* 6, no. 3 (September 1993): 327, n. 50; and Gershon Shafir, *Land, Labor and the Origins of the Israeli-Palestinian Conflict, 1882–1914* (Cambridge, England: Cambridge University Press, 1989).

12. Moshe Lissak in an interview with *Davar*, March 18, 1994; Yaakov Katz in an interview with *Ha'aretz*, November 18, 1994.

13. On Israeli Orientalism, see Azmi Beshara, "On the Question of the Palestinian Minority in Israel," *Teoria vebikoret* 3 (1993): 7–21; Gil Eyal, "Between East and West: The Discourse on the Arab Village in Israel," *Teoria vebikoret* 3 (1993): 39–56; Dan Rabinowitz, "Oriental Nostalgia: The Transformation of the Palestinians into 'Israeli Arabs,'" *Teoria vebikoret* 4 (1993): 141–152. Other academics, such as Uri Ram, exposed the role played by the academy in providing scholarly justifications for repression by unconditionally accepting the governmental axis of inclusion and exclusion.

14. Smooha and Swirski had already aired these positions in the late 1970s; see Smooha, *Israel* and Sara Kazir and Shlomo Swirski, "Ashkenazim and Sephardim: The Making of Dependence," *Mahbarot lemehkar vebikoret* 1 (1978): 21–59 [in Hebrew].

15. Common to all these challenges was the underlying assumption that collective memory was officially constructed by the educational system and the media. This assumption was first voiced in the early 1970s at Haifa University, when post-Zionist scholars accused mainstream sociologists of employing methodologies that suited the Zionist ideological claims on the land and the Jewish people. Pappé, *The Making of the Arab-Israeli Conflict*, 18–25. On museums, see Tamar Katriel, "Remaking Place: Cultural Production in an Israeli Pioneer Settlement Museum," *History and Memory* 5, no. 2 (fall–winter 1993): 104–135; Ariela Azoulay, "With Open Doors: Museums and History and the Israeli Public Space," *Teoria vebikoret* 4 (1993): 79–96 [in Hebrew].

16. Tom Segev, *The Seventh Million: The Israelis and the Holocaust* (New York: Henry Holt, 2000); Idit Zertal, *Zhavam shel hayehudim: hahagirah hayehudit hamahtartit le-Erets Yisrael, 1945–1948* (From catastrophe to power: Jewish illegal immigration to Palestine, 1945–1948) (Tel Aviv: Am Oved, 1996).

17. Yail Levy, "A Militaristic Policy, Interethnic Relationship and Domestic Expansion of the State: Israel 1948–1956," *Teoria vebikoret* 8 (1996): 203–224 [in Hebrew].

18. Gershon Shafir, *Land, Labor and the Origins of the Israeli Palestinian Conflict, 1882–1914* (Cambridge, England: Cambridge University Press, 1989). Also see Uri Ram, "The Colonization Perspective in Israeli Sociology," *Journal of Historical Sociology* 6, no. 3 (September 1993): 327, n. 50.

19. At one point a public debate on post-Zionism was attended by over seven hundred people at Tel Aviv University in July 1994. An important locus for the development of new post-Zionist theoretical insights and methodologies scholars, especially younger ones, was the journal *Teoria vebikoret* (Theory and criticism).

20. Khalil Nakhleh, "Cultural Determinates of Palestinian Collective Identity: The Case of the Arabs in Israel," *New Outlook* 18, no. 7 (October 1975): 31–40. The Israeli Secret Service was unable to decide whether these nationalist poetry festivals were subversive acts or cultural events; it later harbored similar doubts about festivals organized by the Islamic movement in the 1980s.

21. It was published in English: Anton Shammas, *Arabesques*, translated by Vivian Eder (New York: Harper and Row, 1988).

22. Most notably, *The Secret Life of Saeed the Ill-Fated Pessoptimist*, translated by Salma Jayyusi and Trevor LeGassick (Columbia, La.: Reader's International, 1989).

23. Hannan Hever and Moshe Ron, eds., *Fighting and Killing without End: Political Poetry in the Lebanon War* (Tel Aviv: Hakibbutz Hameuhad, 1983) (in Hebrew).

24. This counternarrative is discussed in Yerah Gover, *Zionism: The Limits of Moral Discourse in Israeli Hebrew Fiction* (Minneapolis: University of Minnesota Press, 1994).

25. Dan Orian, *The Arab in Israeli Theatre* (Tel Aviv: Hakibbutz Hameuhad, 1998) (in Hebrew).

26. Typical plays that present the "Peace Now dilemma" are Benny Barabash, *Ehad Mishelanu* (One of us), 1988 and Yehoushu'a Sobol, *Hafalestinat* (The Palestinian woman), 1985.

27. I have discussed this adaptation and others in Ilan Pappé, "A Text in the Eyes of the Beholder: Four Theatrical Interpretations of Kanafani's *Men in the Sun*," *Contemporary Theatre Review* 3, no. 2 (1995): 157–174.

28. *Romeo and Juliet*, a coproduction of the Khan (an Israeli Jerusalemite theater) and al-Qasaba (a Palestinian Jerusalemite theater), directed by Fu'ad 'Awad and Eran Baniel, 1994.

29. Horowitz, this volume; Regev, "*Musica Mizrakhit*."

30. During the previous decade and in the wake of the 1982 Lebanon war, Shalom Hanoch had composed a popular song critical of Ariel Sharon, entitled "Does Not Stop on Red." The title was later borrowed by Uzi Benziman for his highly critical biography of Sharon; it appeared in English as *Sharon: An Israeli Caesar* (New York: Adamas, 1985).

31. Homi Bhabha, *The Location of Culture* (London: Routledge, 1994).

32. In English, the best source on *bourekas* films is Ella Shohat, *Israeli Cinema: East/West and the Politics of Representation* (Austin: University of Texas Press, 1989), 115–138. This same tension—between noble native and brutal primitive—also surfaced in the depictions of Mizrahis in plays and stand-up comedy during this period.

33. Shohat, *Israeli Cinema*.

34. This transformation is discussed in Nurith Gertz, *Motion Fiction: Israeli Fiction in Film* (Tel Aviv: Open University Press, 1993), 13–62 [in Hebrew]. There were some exceptions that prefigured the attempts in the 1980s and 1990s to counter these politics, such as Moshe Mizrahi's 1973 film *Habayit berehov Shelush* (The house on Chelouche Street). On *Habayit berehov Shelush* and its depiction of Mizrahi women, see Orli Lubin, "Women, Nationalism and Ethnicity," in *Fictive Looks: On Israeli Cinema*, edited by Nurith Gertz, Orli Lubin, and Jad Ne'eman (Tel Aviv: Open University Press, 1998), 120–127.

35. The film is discussed at length in Gertz, *Motion Fiction*, 365–380.

36. Judd Ne'eman, "The Empty Tomb in the Postmodern Pyramid: Israeli Cinema in the 1980s and 1990s," in *Documenting Israel: Proceedings of a Conference Held at Harvard University on May 10–12, 1993*, edited by Charles Berlin (Cambridge, Mass.: Harvard University Press, 1995).

37. For example, in the film *Avanti Popolo* (1986, directed by Rafi Bukai), an Egyptian soldier declares the message of human values common to both (Arab and Israeli) sides by quoting Shakespeare's Shylock—as if his own culture had no sources on which he could rely to buttress such a position.

38. One such film was Nissim Dayan, director, *Gesher Tzar Me'ad* (A very narrow

bridge), 1985. The prominent film critic and director Judd Ne'eman has argued that these films leveled a truly radical criticism of Zionism; see his "The Empty Tomb in the Postmodern Pyramid: Israeli Cinema in the 1980s and 1990s," in *Documenting Israel: Proceedings of a Conference Held at Harvard University on May 10–12, 1993*, edited by Charles Berlin (Cambridge, Mass.: Harvard University Press, 1995).

39. Moshe Zimerman, "The Holocaust and the 'Otherness,' or the Additional Value of the Film 'Al Tigu Li Bashoa," in *Fictive Looks: On Israeli Cinema*, edited by Gertz, Lubin, and Ne'eman, 135–159.

40. Habiby, *The Secret Life of Saeed.*

CINEMAS AND
CYBERSPACES

CAROL BARDENSTEIN

Cross/Cast: Passing

in Israeli and

Palestinian Cinema

O ver the past two decades a notable number of Israeli and Palestinian films have exhibited what may be termed deliberate forms of play with or interrogation of Palestinian and Israeli identities. These films challenge the concept of identities as fixed, unambiguously and securely distinct from each other, and clearly delineated in largely binary terms in a nationalist logic. This period is likely to be drawing to a close, however, on the ruins of the Oslo Accords and in the wake of the onset of the al-Aqsa Intifada in September 2000, as we lurch further into a period of the unbridled rise and domination of univocalizing discourses along national, ethnic, and religious lines in the Israeli-Palestinian context, as in so many others.

I examine this phenomenon of play as embodied in the gestures of cross-casting and role switching in a selection of Israeli and Palestinian feature films from the 1980s and 1990s.[1] By cross-casting, I am referring to the extradiegetic practice, outside of the narrative frame or plot of the film, of casting actors in particular roles and its effects: the casting of Palestinian actors, or Palestinians with Israeli citizenship, for example, in the roles of Israeli Jewish characters, or the casting of Israeli Jewish actors as Palestinians. By role switching, I am referring to the diegetic phenomenon in the narrative or plot of the film in which an Israeli Jewish character (played by an Israeli Jewish actor) takes on the role of, or passes as, a Palestinian character, or vice versa.[2] I also touch on nonbinary role switching, in which, for example, the role of one "kind" of Palestinian (according to hegemonic typologies of "who's who" that delineate such different "kinds") is played by a different "kind" of Palestinian actor.[3]

I find that instances of cross-casting and role switching along Palestinian and Israeli lines may be roughly divided into three groupings: (1) those that offer very controlled representations of the "other," in ways that merely serve to reaffirm stereotypes and reinscribe fixed identity categories in hegemonic narratives; (2) those that substantially or even radically challenge or subvert hegemonic configurations of social identity; and (3) those that occupy more of a middle ground, in that they engage in toying with or blurring fixed identity categories and hierarchies, but in modes that are largely ephemeral or quasi-utopian, leaving dominant social hierarchies and categories securely in place. I focus exclusively on the analysis of instances of crossing and switching in the second and third categories. In the case of Palestinian and Israeli cinema, it is possible to map the enactments of identity boundary crossing along a socioethnic spectrum of multiple points. This range of categories is a more differentiated spectrum than is usually identified in the theoretical literature about boundary crossing enacted in impersonation, mimicry, or passing, which tends to be implicitly engaged with binary-inflected configurations (male/female, black/white, white/not quite white), even if these binaries are problematized in the process of analyzing acts or figures of crossing. The majority of the enactments of identity boundary crossings in these films take place between the subjectivities of Mizrahi Israeli Jews and Palestinians with Israeli citizenship, and the rest shift between points on the spectrum that are similarly in close proximity to each other in the social hierarchy.[4] In spite of the fact that this very proximity between particular multiple points along the social spectrum is what enables many of the instances of cross-casting and role switching to work in the ways they need to, this fact is largely submerged in the films themselves. One effect of this is to enable liberal fantasies of the collapse of boundaries dividing the binarisms of Arab/Jew and Israeli/Palestinian.

The Constructed and Contingent Subject and Impersonation, Mimicry, and Passing

That social identities and subjectivities of all kinds are constructed, contingent, fluid, and nonessential; that the boundaries that appear to delineate and distinguish between them are slippery, indeterminate, and malleable is largely an accepted truism in much contemporary Western academic discourse. Some of the most elaborate and seminal explorations of identity as socially constructed have focused on the sites of impersonation, mimicry, and passing. The possibility of an ostensible x impersonating, mimicking, or passing for an ostensible y can be pointedly effective in exposing essentialized or reified social identities as constructed performative fantasies.[5] I present the phenomena of cross-casting and role switching as analogous to impersonation, mimicry, and passing in certain aspects of their modes of operation, functions, and effects. Role switching and cross-casting provide another rich site of identity boundary crossing, at which the contingency and slippery fluidity of social identities can get exposed and the social hierarchies and categories may be thrown into disarray, blurred, and challenged.[6]

Yet, while the relevant theoretical literature on impersonation, mimicry, and passing sheds some light on aspects of cross-casting and role switching, it also faces some limitations in the context of Palestinian and Israeli filmic representation. Work by Butler, Garber, and Bhabha on identity and boundary-crossing figures and enactments all assert in powerful ways that there is no secure, authentic identity (or binarisms of identity) beneath performative "masks."[7] Moreover, all assert that the very fact of boundary crossing through impersonation, mimicry, or passing is implicitly subversive and undermines hegemonic authority and its concomitant social categories. I argue, in contrast, that it cannot be assumed that all instances of mimicry, hybridity, or passing are transgressive or subversive, or even that they necessarily substantially interrogate social categories and hierarchies delineated by hegemonic discourses.[8] They may in some instances do so, and certainly the boundary crossing enacted in cross-casting and role switching creates a potentially hospitable arena for these processes. But if role switching and cross-casting do interrogate or transgress category boundaries, the degree to which they do so, what is at stake, and the nature of the boundary crossing can be established only on a case-by-case basis.

Impersonation and mimicry do not in themselves constitute challenges to hegemonic hierarchies; there are social boundary crossings that are not transgressions or acts of trespassing. However, when impersonation and mimicry are enacted along a spectrum of social identities in a charged and asymmetrical power configuration with concomitant exclusionary practices and unequal access to power, then representations of boundary crossings, such as those in some Israeli and Palestinian feature films, can be transgressive and may indeed be calling hegemonic social categories and discourses into question in subversive ways. Also, it is only in such contexts of unequal power that passing becomes a meaningful and distinct category.

Even in this context, however, boundary crossing is not always subversive (as, for example, Garber asserts transvestism is)[9] but may be enacted or represented in the service of reactionary, progressive, liberal, or subversive agendas.[10] And if social boundary crossings can be identified and interpreted as transgressive or subversive, how this transgression is articulated varies. In some instances, passing is only successful and subversive if it remains completely undetected, allowing for infiltration or blurring of hegemonic social boundaries. In other instances (such as certain types of transvestism), calling attention to and exposing the very fact of mimicry is a central component of the subversive nature of the act (exposing "the hairy knee under the silk skirt").[11]

I am also arguing that it is necessary to qualify and expand on the relevant theoretical literature to adequately describe and analyze the range of Israeli and Palestinian crossings found in these films. Bhabha's work only accounts for instances of "mimicking up" or partial or necessarily failed attempts to pass *up* the social hierarchy, whereas the film corpus includes instances of impersonating and sometimes passing up, down, and across the social spectrum. Similarly, Bhabha's particular examples (Indian/Anglicized-but-not-English/English; white/not quite white) are dependent on the mimic man's difference being detectable and readable on a visible surface. This assumption does not always pertain to the Palestinian-Israeli context. As a result, successful or "seamless" passing becomes possible, an option not accounted for in Bhabha's conception of colonial mimicry. The spectrum of hierarchized social identities along which boundary crossing occurs in the films examined is not binary, nor does it consistently offer enactments in which the slippage between identity and difference is readily detectable (and, of course, the degree of visibility is also dependent in part on the beholder).

Although a central aim of the theoretical literature addressed above is to expose hegemonic social (racial, gender, ethnic) categories as fabricated, constructed, and imposed on a fluid and varied spectrum, it identifies these hegemonic categories as binary and focuses on figures, sites, and enactments of crossing from one side of the binary to the other (man/woman, black/white, white/not white) or posits a "third" or "hybrid" figure.[12]

The spectrum of social (ethnic, national) identities along which boundary crossing occurs in the Israeli and Palestinian films includes six or seven different points arranged in order of the relative power each category wields in the Israeli-Palestinian social context. At one far end of the spectrum is the "idealized" pole or "empty" category of the white hegemonic subject (sometimes also identified as the colonizer-occupier). The next point on the spectrum is the Ashkenazi Israeli (Zionist) Jew, who, although also a hegemonic subject, is already "not quite white" or "off-white" in ways that have been described by Karen Brodkin and others.[13] The next point is the Mizrahi Israeli (Zionist) Jew, who is variably both hegemonic and subaltern subject, followed by the Palestinian with Israeli citizenship. Adjacent to this category is the Palestinian without Israeli citizenship, specifically in the West Bank or Gaza Strip (i.e., under occupation, thus in extensive and intimate contact of an interpenetrating nature: Israeli occupying presence in these places, as well as Palestinian presence in Israeli realms, as part of the mobile labor force as well as other points of contact). The Palestinian without Israeli citizenship, in exile outside of Israeli reach (guerrilla fighters in Lebanon, etc.), is the next point on the spectrum, followed by other Arabs who are not Palestinian, such as Egyptians. Nearly all instances of social boundary crossing in cross-casting and role switching take place between immediately adjacent points on this spectrum, usually between Mizrahi Israelis and Palestinians with Israeli citizenship.[14] This proximity along the spectrum is in part what enables the enactment of some of these crossings; it means that the slippage between identity and difference in impersonation, mimicry, and passing is not always readily detectable on a visible surface.[15] That said, these films rarely make explicit that it is those in proximate points along this spectrum who are impersonating or passing for each other. The boundary crossings in these films are generally transposed back into the more reductive binaries of Arab/Jew or Palestinian/Israeli.

From Likud's Rise to Power to the Unraveling of Oslo: Historical Contexts and Asymmetries

Several scholars have identified a combination of historical and political factors that account in part for new representations of Arabs and Palestinians and of Palestinian-Israeli relations and interactions in Israeli cinema starting in the 1980s. As Na'aman summarizes, until the early 1980s, "Arabs were only minor characters in Israeli cinema . . . they rarely delivered lines . . . were mainly seen in groups, in long shots, deprived of any individuation," and fell into three categories: the primitive but benign Arab, the evil Arab, and the exotic and forbidden other.[16] These stereotyped representations changed in the early 1980s, giving rise to increasingly three-dimensional characterizations, some focalization through Arab characters' points of view, and explicit treatment of the Israeli-Palestinian conflict, in what Shohat has dubbed "the Palestinian wave" in Israeli cinema. She also refers to the phenomenon as "the return of the repressed," in that this wave brought back into view on the screen an Arab Palestinian presence that had either been portrayed reductively in the pre-1948 fledgling cinema of the early Jewish *Yishuv* (Jewish settlers in Palestine prior to the establishment of Israel) and through the "heroic-nationalist" films of the 1950s and 1960s, or largely repressed in most subsequent Israeli film genres (*bourekas* films, "personal cinema") of the 1960s and 1970s. Scholars of Israeli cinema have generally concurred with Shohat's account and have elaborated it in their own distinct ways.[17]

A combination of factors contributed to the new trend in Israeli cinema sketched above, including portrayals of identity crossing and blurring starting in the early 1980s. In 1977 the right-wing Likud Party rose to power, defeating the more liberal Labor Party bloc for the first time since the founding of the state. In the election's aftermath, left-leaning artists and intellectuals found themselves relatively marginalized in the new political configuration, and much more sharply alienated from the new political mainstream, "cut off from their economic and moral base of support," in the words of Raz Yosef.[18] This dissociation increased further in the wake of Israel's invasion of Lebanon in 1982 and its actions in that war. The left's response took the form of political protest, the emergence of dovish movements such as Peace Now (in 1978), and, as Shohat noted, "oppositional artistic practices in the form of poems, plays, photographs and films thematizing the political situation."[19] In this context, Israeli filmmakers created a considerable number of films presenting sympathetic and humanizing portrayals of Arab Palestinian characters and contemplation of nonadversarial relations with them. A small subset of these films uses boundary-crossing enactments in cross-casting and role switching to achieve this aim. Shohat suggests that some of the films of the 1980s articulated the emerging notion in left-wing Israeli discourse that it was no longer suitable to portray a "David/Goliath ideological perspective [Israel as David, the Arabs as Goliath] when the Jewish side [wielded] disproportionate power in relation to the Palestinian."[20]

Israeli films of the 1980s and 1990s were certainly not always or even often direct reflections of the particular historical events and political developments in Israel pertaining to the evolving Palestinian-Israeli conflict (i.e., one does not necessarily find a particular film that explicitly reflects the initial post-Oslo euphoria, or another film that shows the subsequent disillusionment on the part of certain Israeli liberal sectors). Artistic and cultural expression cannot be presumed to operate in such explicit ways or to be wholly reducible to "national allegory." Nonetheless, it is important to outline some of the additional relevant political and historical developments in Israel of the 1980s and 1990s to adequately contextualize the readings of the films to follow, and specifically the instances of cross-casting and role switching in them.

The peace camp continued through the 1980s and into the 1990s to voice opposition to Israel's continued occupation of the territories of the West Bank, Gaza Strip, and Golan Heights (seized in 1967), even after the 1978 peace agreement with Egypt. Liberal protest in political, intellectual, and artistic forms was expressed with renewed vigor after the onset of the first Palestinian Intifada in 1987 and the brutal Israeli attempts to crush this grassroots uprising. The first Intifada also paved the way for Palestinians with Israeli citizenship—previously referred to exclusively as Israeli Arabs in Israeli public discourse—to express their solidarity and affiliation with Palestinians under Israeli occupation in the West Bank and Gaza. In the 1990s, intellectual and cultural elites continued to produce oppositional works from the political margins, including filmic portrayals that contemplated the Palestinian other in relatively humanized and sympathetic ways, with some hope, even if ephemeral or quasi-utopian, for transcending differences and finding common ground between Israeli and Palestinian adversaries.

The Gulf War gave way to negotiations for a political settlement to the Palestinian-Israeli conflict (Madrid and Oslo, resulting in the 1993 Oslo Peace Accords) and Yitzhak Rabin's election as prime minister in 1992. The pre-Oslo and immediately post-Oslo euphoria and optimism felt by some liberal Israelis found expression in film, in semi-utopian works (e.g., *Cup Final*, made in 1992 though set in 1982, which included intra-Palestinian across-casting). After Rabin's assassination by a right-wing Israeli Jew in 1995 and the election of ultraconservative Benjamin Netanyahu in 1996, liberal Israeli Oslo euphoria was substantially compromised, only to be revived again briefly under Ehud Barak's aegis. It has now been virtually extinguished with the decisive unraveling of the Oslo Accords, the onset of the al-Aqsa Intifada in September 2000, and the unchecked rise to power of Ariel Sharon in 2001.

As in so many other realms, the process of situating Palestinian films in historical and cultural terms is asymmetrical and radically distinct from the filmic and political-historical contextualization of the Israeli films outlined above, an asymmetry reproduced in my own selection of films for inclusion in this piece (two Palestinian, five Israeli). First, there is a gross structural disparity between what I have loosely referred to as Israeli cinema and Palestinian cinema. The absence of a Palestinian sovereign state in this period is paralleled by the absence of the most rudimentary kinds of concomitant institutions, both political and cultural. Just as there is no Palestinian national library, no Palestinian national art museum, no national site for commemorative purposes (much of the fifty-year commemoration of 1948, or the *Nakba*, took place in cyberspace), there is no entity or institution that can unambiguously be identified as Palestinian cinema, and certainly no Palestinian film industry. There are Palestinian filmmakers, but many of their films fall into the category articulated by Hamid Naficy as the "accented" cinema of exilic and diasporic filmmaking.[21] Both of the Palestinian filmmakers included in this essay, Michel Khleifi and Elia Suleiman, are living in exile (both are from the Galilee in present-day Israel), occasionally coming to visit and film in locations in Israel and Palestine, but with film production and most funding based abroad. Other Palestinian filmmakers not included in this study (because their films do not pertain to my focus on cross-casting and role switching) operate under similar circumstances or under the intensely compromised conditions of Palestinians based inside of Israel or in the West Bank or Gaza Strip.

For these and other reasons, there are far fewer Palestinian than Israeli feature films. Those that do exist originate from and circulate in different, sporadic and shifting locations. There is no place where Palestinian films accumulate into an aggregate body of work, about which genres and periodizations are asserted or debated by film critics and academics and in other, less elite venues. In contrast to the substantial body of criticism on Israeli cinema, criticism on Palestinian films has been largely confined to journal reviews or blurbs of screenings at international film festivals (i.e., largely outside of Palestine), or in fact, perhaps not surprisingly, to treatment by a number of Israeli film and cultural critics.[22] Precisely because of the scattered diasporic condition of Palestinian cinema, it is impossible to map particular Palestinian films along the same kind of political-historical timeline that seems straightforward and unified in contexts of collective national and geographic emplacement (as in the Israeli case).

Trying to map a film like Elia Suleiman's *Chronicle of a Disappearance* along these lines, for example, highlights these indeterminacies. Technically, the film falls within a post-Oslo chronological framework, set and filmed in 1996. But where does one place this film? Geographically, it is set in modern-day Israel, but one that is simultaneously portrayed as a Palestinian place that has become Israel, or more precisely, as the strange place in which a series of daily "disappearing acts" of the Palestinianness of Palestinians with Israeli citizenship takes place. Or is it the exilic-eye view, the positionality and sensibility of the filmmaker hailing from New York, that most centrally shapes or places this film? Similar questions are raised concerning Khleifi's 1987 *Wedding in Galilee*. It may be viewed as a markedly pre-Intifada film on a Palestinian historical timeline, portraying a relative lack of resistance on the part of the Palestinian population. But is the film's markedly nostalgic texture a product of Khleifi's many years in exile? Might this same exilic sensibility account for what otherwise might appear to be a sloppy anachronism: that he portrays the Galilee of the early 1980s as being under the kind of military regulations that pertained from 1948 to 1967? Although Palestinian and Israeli histories (onto which feature films may be mapped) may be very much affected by each other, they are radically asymmetrical, as are the overarching conditions of their national institutions and cultural production. The historical and contextual sketch presented here cannot transcend and thus undoubtedly reproduces these structural asymmetries.

I examine instances of role switching and cross-casting in seven films, which range from those that play with identity blurring in fairly safe ways to those that use such passings or nonpassings to radically challenge and subvert the boundaries between various hegemonic categories of identity.

Beyond the Walls: *Utopia in Prison*

The 1984 Israeli film *Beyond the Walls* presents a gritty and unsavory portrayal of prison life, yet it simultaneously offers a quasi-utopian and contrived space for the forging of an otherwise hard-to-imagine solidarity between Palestinians and Israelis. These Palestinians are "political prisoners," imprisoned for violent and nonviolent forms of resistance; the Israelis are mostly Mizrahim in prison for criminal offenses. The flatly malevolent and corrupt Ashkenazi Israeli prison director makes an artificially easy common enemy, against whom traditional adversaries can unite. In this idealized arena, where traditional divisions along ethnic lines are transcended or blurred, we find a practice I describe as a forerunner or variant of the more explicit cross-casting in later films. As Shohat points out, the director engages in a "chromatic inversion" of stereotyped identities in his casting choices in this film. The leader of the Palestinian prisoners, Isam, is played by the blue-eyed, fair-skinned, fair-haired Muhammad Bakri, and the (Mizrahi) leader of the Israeli Jewish prisoners, Uri, is played by the darker, swarthier Arnon Tzadok.[23] The chromatically inverted casting calls attention to and unsettles entrenched stereotypes and, in the context of this quasi-utopian film, simultaneously raises the hope (of the film's predominantly Israeli audience) that the unfixing of ethnic and social categories may enable the forging of peaceful solidarity between the two traditional adversaries, an effect reinforced by the sympathetic portrayal of both characters. Although the chromatic differences between Palestinians and Israelis have been accentuated rather than submerged, it is still noteworthy that the film's "partners for peace" are a Mizrahi Israeli and a Palestinian. Like many instances of middle-ground identity blurring, this one invites the Israeli Jewish spectator to contemplate such inversions in optimistic terms, to toy with the potentially liberating fluidity of identity, but from a safe position, in ways that seem to promise not to spill out into the fabric of everyday life. The ramifications of such inversions remain contained within the contrived world of the prison, as the film's original Hebrew title, *Behind Bars* (*Me'aḥorei hasoragim*), signals more clearly than its English title.

Wedding in Galilee: *Playing the Part (Not Quite) Right*

Michel Khleifi's 1987 film *Wedding in Galilee* contains instances of both cross-casting and role switching. Set in the early 1980s, the film portrays the inhabitants of a Palestinian village straining to engage in ordinary events, such as marriage, under Israeli domination. The mukhtar of the village, which is under curfew, seeks permission from the Israeli authorities to hold his son's wedding. Permission is granted, but only on the compromising condition that the military commander and an entourage of officers attend as guests of honor. The military commander is played by the well-known Palestinian Israeli actor (i.e., a Palestinian with Israeli citizenship) Makram Khoury. Khoury has played Israeli military personnel in other films (e.g., the Israeli films *On a Narrow Bridge*, dir. Nissim Dayan, 1985; *Smile of the Lamb*, dir. Shimon Dotan, 1986). In *Wedding in Galilee*, this appears to be a deliberate and marked casting choice, as the other Israeli soldiers in the film are all played by Israeli Jewish actors. This cross-casting leads to a shift between two adjacent points in the socioethnic spectrum: a Palestinian with Israeli citizenship impersonates a Mizrahi Israeli character, as Khoury's character is supposed to be of Syrian origin, born and partly raised in Aleppo. Khleifi might be tacitly signaling the possibility that there are cultural and historical connections or commonalities between "us" and at least some of "them." But the audience is reminded in the same breath of the commander's superseding category as Israeli hegemonic subject-occupier. When smacking his lips over the food at the wedding, he comments on how the food is even better in Lebanon, a reference to the recent Israeli invasion and presence there (marking his position as Israeli aggressor). However, he then adds that "there's nothing like the food in Aleppo," something the Ashkenazi Israeli members of his entourage cannot even begin to imagine, thereby marking his position as possibly benign Mizrahi Syrian Jew and distinguishing him from Ashkenazi Israeli hegemony.

In his role as a Syrian-born Israeli, Khoury passes seamlessly in Hebrew, which is fluent-sounding and unmarked. But there are some interesting imperfections and inconsistencies in this portrayal. Khoury's character speaks that special linguistic variety one might dub Israeli army Arabic, a broken, sloppy mix of formal Arabic and Palestinian colloquial, rife with mistakes and stereotypical Ashkenazi mispronunciations. So when the mukhtar insists that the military commander and his soldiers stay "until the end of the wedding" ("Hatta nihayat al-'urs"), Khoury repeats after him, conspicuously mispronouncing the utterance as "Khatta nihayat al-urs." Both the diegetic character of the Syrian Israeli military commander and the extradiegetic actor Khoury are native speakers of Arabic who would not make such pronunciation mistakes. Khoury impersonates the Mizrahi Israeli, but this category converges with that of commander as hegemonic Israeli subject, and associated features of Ashkenaziness bleed into the impersonation. Khleifi's casting a Palestinian Israeli in the role of the Israeli military commander and the inconsistencies in the enactment of the role call attention to the fluidity and unfixedness of social and ethnic categories. If there are inconsistencies or imperfections in the impersonation, it is not the actor's Palestinianness that gives him away, but a hypercorrection in the portrayal that displays stereotyped Ashkenazi features at the expense of internal consistency and for the sake of the strong association between Ashkenaziness and Zionist hegemony.

Social identities are also blurred at the diegetic level in this film. When Tali, the female Israeli soldier, is overwhelmed and faints in the face of the threat of Palestinian energies at the wedding, she is whisked away to the women's quarters, where they try to bring her back to consciousness. The Palestinian women remove her soldier's uniform and dress her up in traditional Palestinian women's clothing, a process to which she willingly and dreamily submits. In this eroticized and Orientalized scene, the film seems to signal that Tali, forced unnaturally into the masculine role of soldier in Israeli culture, can only experience her "natural" femininity and the comforting company of women through the liberating but ephemeral act of shedding the trappings of her Israeliness and passing into Palestinianness. In this instance, the passing is "down" the social and power hierarchy, from Ashkenazi Israeli woman to dress-up as Palestinian woman. Notably, Tali has to be unconscious, passive, and acted on to cross into Palestinianness.

Khleifi's portrayals of identity boundary crossing, when taken together with other overarching, recurrent themes in the film, seem in part to be fantasies about the possibility of Israeli disappearance, or of the blurring of the Israeli as occupier and aggressor. Some Israeli films partake of analogous fantasies, as in *Fictitious Marriage*, which presents the fantasy of an Israeli Arab who is unthreatening because he is uninterested in asserting any distinct Palestinian subjectivity, and an Israeli Jew who is keen to experience "how the other half lives."

Fictitious Marriage:
Palestinian Like Me and Israeli Uncle Tom

The 1989 Israeli film *Fictitious Marriage* has a series of instances of role switching. I address only two: the Israeli Jewish protagonist, Eldi, gets mistaken for and then passes as a Palestinian construction worker, and Bashir, a Palestinian Israeli hotel worker, aspires to Israeliness, in contrast to Eldi's apparent disaffiliation.[24] In the throes of a midlife crisis, Eldi leaves his Jerusalem home, gets mistaken for a Palestinian in Tel Aviv, and goes along with the mistake. His mode of passing down is distinctive: he is markedly passive and succeeds because his visible surface is bivalent, thus subject to two (or more) possible readings; he succumbs to whichever reading of him is made by others. His appearance is bivalent in the sense that the same surface that makes him passable as an Israeli Jew is the surface that renders him "readable" as a Palestinian: clad in casual sweatshirt, having brown-hued skin, brown hair, and a mustache, eating a sesame *ka'k* or ring of bread that is bivalent in the sense that it is consumed (though not prepared) by both Israelis and Palestinians. As Na'aman notes, Eldi also carries a plastic bag instead of the briefcase that would be more likely to signal his Israeli Jewishness in a Tel Aviv setting.[25] Eldi's Israeli ethnicity is not explicit in the film, but it is likely that he is of Mizrahi background, although an upwardly mobile, somewhat Ashkenized Mizrahi, to use Shohat's term. He thus passes along two points on the spectrum of relative power, from Mizrahi Israeli to Palestinian from the Occupied Territories. The relative proximity between these points on the spectrum contributes to his ability to pass without immediate detection of his "difference." Thus, when the construction workers gather around Eldi and read his surface as Palestinian, he is able to sustain this reading by simply not speaking. Playing mute is predominantly a passive role; to sustain both his muteness and his Palestinianness ultimately requires some action on Eldi's part (such as using sign language). But for the most part, his passing is achieved by not enacting his other (Israeli) valence and allowing himself to be read as Palestinian.[26]

Thus, while I concur with many aspects of Na'aman's reading of this film as an Israeli representation of Palestinianness, including her analysis of role switching in the film, I disagree with the assertion that Eldi's passing involves "an elaborate visual transformation."[27] What is actually striking about his passing is how little effort it takes: once Eldi is read as Palestinian, the workers only need to put a woolen cap on his head to make his transformation complete. While there are minor imperfections to his passing, for the most part it seems both effortless and seamless: he is only given away when he exerts active agency at the end of the film. The effortlessness of his passing seems commensurate with its being utterly subordinate to his larger personal crisis as an Israeli. As a byproduct, however, Eldi's passing in this bivalent mode blurs boundaries between social categories and has the potential to instill "the fear of the dissolution of the self, represented by fusion with the other."[28] In Eldi's passing, the fear of fusion does not stem from biological or racial miscegenation, but from the exposure of social identity (and, by extension, social hierarchies) as slippery, based on a combination of performance and shifting readings by others. Any secure or clear-cut hegemonic distinction of "us" and "them" is rendered precarious.

While passing as Palestinian, Eldi is exposed to "how the other half lives," experiencing the construction workers' often denigrating conditions. In a more benign vein, he tries, repeatedly and unsuccessfully, to comic effect, to mimic their way of eating in a squatting position: he falls over backward each time he attempts this. This "not quite Palestinian" imperfection in his impersonation does not give him away, however, and he learns to successfully mimic other habits, such as the use of bread as a utensil for swiping and eating food and dips, ostensibly unfamiliar to Israeli Jews.[29] The privilege of sexual access remains securely and exclusively in his grasp, in both of his valences, as Palestinian worker and as Israeli emigrant.[30]

Eldi is shaken to his senses when he mistakenly suspects his Palestinian coworkers of planting a bomb in a playground and shouts out in Hebrew to warn the children playing nearby, dropping his cover completely. He knows once again and unambiguously who he is, who his people are, and who "they" are: the lines are very clearly redrawn. The incident enables Eldi, the real "mattering subject," to return to his real life, his crossing-passing experience as a Palestinian having served its purpose in resolving his midlife crisis. No ideological agenda inspires or results from his "Palestinian like me" experience. The only thing at stake in Eldi's passing down was self-imposed deprivation of access to privilege, which he quickly regains on exposing his passing. He keeps one safe souvenir of his passing experience: the final shots of the film show his young son, who is able to squat in the Palestinian workers' manner without losing his balance, giving Eldi great pleasure. The son, however, is squatting on decorative tile in their home, visibly a formerly Arab-owned home in a formerly Arab-inhabited neighborhood in Jerusalem. This scene is portrayed as an unproblematic happy ending, further affirmation that this film is clearly not aimed at any kind of radical interrogation or subversion of social or political hierarchies. In spite of Eldi's crossing of ethnic boundaries, this film offers a classic example of quasi-liberal play with Palestinian and Israeli identity boundaries in ways that allow everyone to return safely to their places after the role-playing game is over.

While Eldi takes a detour into Palestinianness to find his way back to his true Israeli personhood, Bashir, the Palestinian hotel worker, is static and content throughout the film as an Uncle Tom wannabe Israeli. He partakes eagerly of quintessential Israeli Jewish collective rituals such as rooting avidly for the Maccabi Israeli basketball team on television. He speaks Hebrew all the time, even when talking to himself or when addressed in Arabic. He is an Israeli fantasy: an Arab completely filled and thereby contained by the desire to enact Jewish Israeliness. Not surprisingly, however, Bashir's mimicry of Israeliness is conspicuously imperfect and "not quite," in Bhabha's sense, portrayed here along stereotyped, caricatured lines that ridicule and mock the native's flawed attempts to mimic, without at all having the effect Bhabha attributes to mimicry: the "menace" of undermining the authority of hegemonic discourse and its categories.[31] Bashir's lines contrive to accentuate his "stereotypically Arab" mispronunciation of Hebrew. His character is buffoonlike, overeager to please, endearingly ignorant, and conspicuously emasculated, with a very high-pitched, effeminate voice. Bashir secretly tries on Eldi's clothes in his hotel room, and imitates his nonnative-sounding Arabic recitation of a proverb. In spite of the multiple role switching here—a Mizrahi Jewish actor impersonating a Palestinian Israeli who imperfectly mimics Jewish Israeliness, including imperfect Jewish Israeli mimicking of Arabness—none of this serves to disrupt or interrogate hegemonic Zionist categories, but in fact reinscribes them. The film, released in 1989, with the first Intifada in full swing and unprecedented identification on the part of Israel's Palestinian citizens with Palestinians in the Occupied Territories, enabled the Israeli Jewish spectator to indulge in a fantasy of Israel's non-Jewish population as a non-Palestinian minority content with their lot, aspiring only to be more "Israeli."

Avanti Popolo: *The Only Good Palestinian*
Is an Egyptian or a Jew

Rafi Bukai's *Avanti Popolo* (1986) shows a differently inflected kind of contemplation of the Palestinian other achieved through the enactment of identity boundary crossing at the extradiegetic level. In this case, Palestinian Israeli actors are cast as Egyptian soldiers wandering in the Sinai near the end of the 1967 war. This film is distinct in that it does not use cross-casting per se (i.e., casting subject to being remapped in a Palestinian/Israeli binary), but across-casting along different points of the socioethnic spectrum in indirect and layered ways. The "Egyptian" characters speak Palestinian colloquial dialect rather than Egyptian Arabic. There is no attempt whatsoever to Egyptianize these characters, which has the effect of evoking "a Palestinian framework of feelings."[32] The characters thus present a more substantial and three-dimensional Palestinian presence in their appearance as Egyptians than in Israeli films in which they appear as Palestinians. This across-casting serves, as Anton Shammas says, to "return the Palestinian to Israeli consciousness through the back door."[33] It appears that genuinely nonreductive and sustained consideration of Palestinianness is possible only if filtered through or projected onto a more distant, less threatening Egyptianness (which was ostensibly friendlier at the time, in the wake of the 1978 peace treaty with Egypt).

To what degree are Palestinianness and Egyptianness culturally intelligible or distinguishable on a visible and audible surface to Israeli audiences? It seems that "the Israeli ear," as Shammas says,[34] may not distinguish between the two, and so can easily accept Palestinianness (because of not hearing or seeing it) presented as Egyptianness. This inability exists despite decades of contact between Israelis and Egyptianness in film through the weekly "Friday Egyptian movie" aired on Israeli television,[35] and live contact with Egyptians in the years of Israeli tourism to Egypt in the wake of the peace treaty, not to mention live contact with Palestinians and Palestinianness in Israel and the Occupied Territories. Jewish Israelis whose native language is Arabic could certainly distinguish Egyptian from Palestinian and other dialects, both in the Friday Egyptian movie and in *Avanti Popolo*. But most others would be reading the film's subtitles, a Hebrew filter mediating their contact with Egyptianness. Live contacts are probably not much less filtered in practice. Most contacts between Israeli Jews and Palestinians with Israeli citizenship, for example, are conducted in Hebrew, not surprising given recognized dynamics of majority-minority languages in asymmetrical power configurations. Yet this contact serves to condition the Israeli eye and ear to a filtered and only partial version of Palestinianness.[36] Bhabha might focus on the effect or menace such a partial performance or mimicry of Jewish Israeliness by Palestinians (with Israeli citizenship) could have in undermining the hegemonic Zionist category of Jewish Israeliness. I would venture to turn Bhabha's analysis in the other's direction here and suggest that this only partial mimicry or performance by Palestinians of Palestinianness can create the menace of putting the category of Palestinianness under erasure, giving rise to the kinds of structures of "disappearance" so eloquently articulated in both film (Elia Suleiman's *Chronicle of a Disappearance*) and literature (Emile Habiby's *The Strange Events Surrounding the Disappearance of Happy Go-Unlucky the Opsimist*).[37] In this sense, one could say that *Avanti Popolo* offers a presentation of Palestinianness that is about as visible and sustained as it is going to get.

There is an additional role-playing twist in the film. At one point, after becoming both drunk and delirious from wandering in the desert heat, one of the two soldiers (Khalid, played by Salim Dau) gives an impassioned performance of Shylock's famous lines from *The Merchant of Venice*, in English, to the Israeli soldiers they have encountered: "I am a Jew. Has not a Jew eyes? Has not a Jew hands? . . . If you tickle us, do we not laugh? If you poison us, do we not die?" Khaled tells the soldiers that he played Shylock out of desperation as a frustrated actor in Egypt, and that afterward he was branded "the Jew" and found it difficult to get other roles. The Israeli soldiers' reaction to his performance of Shylock is aloof indifference: "What nonsense is he talking? He's gotten his roles mixed up!" One reading of this scene, with its complex configuration of mixed-up roles, is that once again, for Palestinianness to be allowed into view, a filtering device seems to be required: the refraction of Palestinianness through the performance of Jewishness (particularly the exilic Jewishness of Shylock) renders it un-menacing.[38] The setting of the film, the Sinai desert, plays no small part in these enactments. As the place where the Hebrews became Jews, it may be cast in this film as a liminal space where Palestinians can also become Jews, or even Egyptians—anything, it seems, except Palestinians.

Cup Final: *The Reassuring Face of the Guerrilla*

The 1992 Israeli film *Cup Final* (directed by Eran Riklis) is set in 1982, just after Israel's invasion of Lebanon, and focuses on an Israeli soldier who has been taken captive by Palestinian guerrilla fighters in Lebanon. Two of the guerrillas are played by Mohammed Bakri and Yusuf Abu Warda, both Palestinians with Israeli citizenship who are familiar faces in Israeli film, theater, and television culture. This instance of across-casting takes place between Palestinians with Israeli citizenship and Palestinian guer-rillas in Lebanon (i.e., Palestinians without Israeli citizenship and not under occupation in the West Bank and Gaza). In ways loosely analogous to *Beyond the Walls*, this film creates a very controlled and contrived set of circumstances in which (Israeli Jewish) spectators can contemplate the possibility of shared humanity and interests that can seem to transcend differences, albeit briefly, between Israelis and Palestinians. More specifi-cally, the Israeli character able to forge these relations with the Palestinians is a Mizrahi Israeli, and the Palestinian characters are those played by Pales-tinians with Israeli citizenship. The Ashkenazi Israeli soldier initially cap-tured by the guerrillas is portrayed as incapable of engaging in this human-izing type of interaction and is killed early in the film. It seems that relative proximity along the spectrum of socioethnic categories enables both the forging of mutually humanizing relationships as well as the smooth enact-ment of identity boundary crossing through impersonation.

The film's liberal sensibility allows this humanizing contemplation to happen in a guilt-free manner. The power configuration at the time—Israel's invasion of Lebanon—is inverted in the film. Israeli military power and aggression are rendered almost invisible; what is foregrounded until the last few minutes of the film is Israeli powerlessness, in the form of one vulnerable unarmed soldier held captive by a group of armed Palestinian guerrillas. The Israeli soldier (played by the ubiquitous Moshe Ivgi) is small, utterly nonaggressive, and clearly cast for cuteness. The film allows indul-gence in the fantasy of the Israeli—even in the midst of a massive incursion into Lebanon—as innocent, powerless, and naïve. Adversarial aspects of the relationship between captive and captors are submerged in a number of ways, most prominently by the fact that both Palestinian and Israeli characters are rooting for the same team in the World Cup soccer tournament. The main Palestinian characters are portrayed sympathetically, as rational, educated people engaged in a legitimate cause. The casting of Abu Warda and Bakri in the roles of (non-Israelized) Palestinian guerrillas may be viewed, on the one hand, as serving to refract this more threatening kind of Palestinian into reassuringly familiar terms. This transformation seems to be necessary to allow for Israeli Jewish contemplation of Palestinian guerrillas as having human, recognizable faces and human concerns, such as interest in soccer tournaments and legitimate aspirations to self-determination. The problematic assumption in Israeli hegemonic discourse that there is such a thing as an Israeli Arab, contained and safely distinct from the Palestinian Arab, is implicit in the reassuring effect of Abu Warda and Bakri. In the same gesture, though, a more unsettling possibility is raised for the Israeli Jewish spectator: Could "our" kind of Arab, a supposedly contained '48-er like Mohammed Bakri or Yusuf Abu Warda, possibly turn into "the other" kind of Palestinian? The successful impersonation of the latter by the former threatens to erase the line created by Zionist hegemony that distinguishes and separates '48-er from non-'48-er Palestinians, a line increasingly challenged during and after the first Intifada and still more sharply since the onset of the recent al-Aqsa Intifada.[39] For someone like Bakri, who in his recent film about Jenin (*Jenin, Jenin*) blurred to the point of erasure any such boundary between different kinds of Palestinians, the stakes and questions of allegiance raised by impersonating and passing for an armed guerrilla fighter may be troubling. While Bakri the actor condemns violent means of resistance, such as those used by his character, and although the film narrative submerges the prevailing power configuration at the extradiegetic level, through this film's casting, these questions seep beyond comfortably circumscribed borders.[40]

Chronicle of a Disappearance: Subversive Acts of Unpassing

I close with two examples in which such circumscribed borders of Palestinian and Israeli social identity appear to be deliberately transgressed and blurred in ways that more radically interrogate and subvert given categories. The first is a rather ambivalent instance of passing or unpassing in Elia Suleiman's 1996 *Chronicle of a Disappearance*.

On his return to the land of his birth, the filmmaker casts a sharp, wry eye on the experience of being a Palestinian with Israeli citizenship inside of Israel. In one scene, his friend 'Adan tries to rent an apartment in the Jewish sector of West Jerusalem. Her passing as non-Arab while making apartment inquiries by phone is partial, imperfect, and calls attention to itself fairly quickly through give-away utterances as basic as the pronunciation of an 'ayn when saying her name. Her "difference" is detected almost immediately: "Adan, what a pretty name. What kind of name is that?" and "Adan, that's not a Jewish name, is it?" and "Finally, a Russian who can speak Hebrew! What? You're not Russian? Then what exactly is your accent?" At times, she preemptively exposes her Arabness in response, identifying her name as Arab, pointedly asking if the landlord rents to Arabs. She is decidedly not trying to pass seamlessly; she is nothing at all like Bashir the wannabe Israeli. Although she can pass vocally, she will not submerge her Palestinianness from view, but instead exposes it to radically challenge the categories that exclude her from privilege. Her exercise in unpassing is a challenge to those who would deny her the right to live in any part of Jerusalem not as someone who can pass seamlessly as an Israeli but as an Arab, and an Arab who could but will not try to pass as an Israeli Jew. In these scenes, it is clear that the radical interrogation or subversion of ethnic and social hierarchy is achieved through explicit exposure of the Palestinian who wields Hebrew, the hairy knee underneath the silk skirt, rather than through any attempt to successfully pass as other. In this film, *not* passing is the desired aim; one cannot call this an attempt (or failure) to pass "up" because 'Adan's subversive enactments have thrown the up-down terms of the social hierarchy into disarray.

In a later scene, 'Adan again enacts partial passing as a Hebrew-speaking Israeli to engage in a ventriloquism that confounds the Israeli police and security apparatus and lends a Palestinian voice to the Israeli national anthem. Using a communication device left behind by Israeli police, she issues orders in coded Hebrew, dispatching police units to various "security incidents" (i.e., attacks by Palestinians). After scattering the units on a wild goose chase, she sings to them over the walkie-talkie a wistful rendering of "Hatikva," the Israeli national anthem, in Hebrew, interspersing her commands with comments such as "Jerusalem is no longer unified" and "Oslo is not going to arrive. Oslo is not even calling on the phone." 'Adan's actions are a more radical interrogation of social and ethnic hierarchies and categories than a mere binary flip, such as the singing of a Palestinian national anthem or plotting a real act of terror. Her unpassings challenge such binaries, asserting instead a call for their suspension. At the same time, her calls to be heard, not treated as an enemy, not kept out of Jerusalem, to be included in a national anthem seem to be utterable only in Hebrew.

Kadosh: A Sheep in Wolf's Clothing or a Wolf in Sheep's Clothing?

The final and arguably most subversive example of social boundary crossing through cross-casting is (perhaps unexpectedly) found in Amos Gitai's film *Kadosh* (1999) about an infertile couple in the Orthodox Jewish community of Jerusalem. The couple is forced to separate by the man's father, the rabbi of this tightly knit community, played by the Palestinian Israeli actor Yusuf Abu Warda. Again, the crossing and impersonation happen between two adjacent points on the socioethnic spectrum: a Palestinian with Israeli citizenship playing the role of a Mizrahi Israeli rabbi. Clearly, Gitai could easily have found a more obvious choice than Abu Warda for this role; his choice to cross-cast is a loaded one and gives rise to a potentially unsettling blurring of boundaries. There is a long tradition of Israeli Jewish characters, readers, and spectators who take comfort in portrayals of Arab characters who emulate or imitate Israeli Jewish practices. But what happens when the impersonation and mimicry are *too* good? Yusuf Abu Warda passes utterly seamlessly in his impersonation of the Orthodox Jewish rabbi. (In fact, having viewed this film in a theater in the United States, I realized that the fact and effect of this role being played by a Palestinian was invisible to U.S. audiences, though it would be immediately apparent in Israel.) To an Israeli spectator, his performance could be taken as some kind of "deferring compliment," if an uncanny one, producing admiration for his ability to imitate Jewish Israelis. Or it could be viewed as vaguely threatening, in that he passes too completely, particularly when some Palestinian suicide bombers have passed disguised as Orthodox Jews.

The film contains pointed instances in which a layered ventriloquism is enacted, creating an opening between the traditionally distinct realms of the diegetic film narrative and the extradiegetic realm of casting to raise the possibility of a blurring of social categories and identificatory boundaries. For example, when the rabbi tells his son to take action in the face of his childlessness, he emphasizes how important it is to bring Jewish children into the world: "Children are our strength. Only with children is it possible to defeat them." His son asks, "To defeat whom?" After a pregnant pause, the rabbi answers, "The others. The godless heathens who rule this state," and goes on to describe theirs as a holy struggle. He adds: "Our children are our future, the future of our religion, do you understand? The others? They don't have children! Thanks to our children, the future is ours!" Here, within the narrative diegetic frame, the rabbi articulates the sensibility of the Orthodox Jewish other pitted against secular Zionist hegemony, identifying fertility as a vital weapon. But of course, the notion of a "demographic struggle" has been widely articulated with regard to Israeli Jews and Palestinians, both '48-ers and others (giving rise to settlement campaigns with names like the Judaization of the Galilee—Israeli initiatives in response to the "threat" of higher reproductive rates in the Palestinian sector). For the viewer who is familiar with Yusuf Abu Warda, it is difficult to suppress the extradiagetic layer at play in this scene: it is easy to hear these words coming out of the mouth of the actor as an articulation of Palestinian agency in a struggle with Israeli Jewish hegemony. At the same time, considering the scathing portrayal of Orthodox Jewish life in Gitai's squarely secularist film and his known left-of-center political orientation, it is unclear whether Gitai was indeed drawing some kind of parallel in pairing two of secular Zionist hegemony's others, or if he was creating an ambiguously bivalent figure in Abu Warda qua rabbi: a sheep in wolf's clothing or a wolf in sheep's clothing?

Conclusion

Instances of social boundary crossing enacted through impersonation, mimicry, or passing in Palestinian and Israeli feature films must be mapped along a socioethnic spectrum that differentiates along the lines of ethnicity and national and positional subjectivities with greater specificity than do the reductive binaries of Palestinian/Israeli and Arab/Jew. A more differentiated spectrum, while still offering points in the form of identity categories that are constructed and schematized in hegemonic discourse, is of greater descriptive and explanatory value in accounting for these enactments of social boundary crossing. The majority of instances of boundary crossing in these films occur between relatively proximate points on this differentiated spectrum, usually between points that are immediately adjacent to each other. The most common of these adjacent crossings are between Mizrahi Israeli Jewish and Palestinian Israeli subjectivities; others include crossing between the subjectivities of Palestinian Israelis and either Palestinians without Israeli citizenship (under occupation in the West Bank or Gaza or guerrillas in Lebanon) or "Egyptians." This relative proximity is part of what allows crossing to take place, because it facilitates the minimizing of detectable difference, in some instances rendering such distinctions virtually invisible. There also seems to be a correlation between this relative proximity of socioethnic categories and largely liberal scenarios of possible rapprochement and solidarity between adversarial protagonists. Films that portray narratives of possible reconciliation or mutual humanization between the traditional Palestinian-Israeli adversaries frequently show this process taking place between Mizrahi Israelis and protagonists or actors who are Palestinians with Israeli citizenship.

It is also the case that, with the exception of across-casting (intra-Palestinian and Palestinian-to-Egyptian), this differentiation is relatively submerged in the films examined, and the questions or challenges these crossings raise are mostly rearticulated back in binary terms. These questions seem to cohere around two main sentiments: Maybe we are not so different after all, perhaps there is some common ground that might lead to less adversarial relations, and Maybe there is no clear-cut distinction between us and them, and aren't the implications of that seriously unsettling, or perhaps downright dangerous? Although all the instances of crossing examined in the preceding analysis raise questions about social identity categories and boundaries, the responses to these questions vary. Some serve to fairly easily reinscribe hegemonic categories and boundaries, others engage in safe play or contemplation of these categories as fluid, and still others seem to engage in more radically subversive and transgressive interrogation of these boundaries, creating the kind of "crisis of category" alluded to by Garber. Finally, these radical instances of boundary crossing often take forms more complex than simple "passing as subversion," such as the transgressive unpassings in *Chronicle of a Disappearance* and the multilayered connotations of Yusuf Abu Warda's ventriloquism in *Kadosh*.

I speculate that the period of both middle-ground play and more radical interrogation of social categories in Palestinian and Israeli films is drawing to an end, as ranks close around circumscribed, univocalizing, and reified categories of ethnic, social, and religious identity. There is no play whatsoever involved in today's most common enactments of passing in the Palestinian-Israeli context: Israelis passing in undercover units long enough to commit extrajudicial assassinations of Palestinians, and Palestinians passing long enough to detonate themselves and Israelis around them in suicide bombings. Filmic or literary representations like those of the preceding two decades, and their questions and challenges to identity, are unlikely to reappear for some time.

Notes

I would like to thank the editors, Rebecca Stein and Ted Swedenburg, for their extensive editorial feedback and input on this essay.

1. The films examined include *Me'ahore Hasoragim* [Beyond the walls], directed by Uri Barabash, 1984; *Avanti Popolo*, directed by Rafi Bukai, 1986; *'Urs al-Jalil* [Wedding in Galilee], directed by Michel Khleifi, 1987; *Nisuim Fictiviyim* [Fictitious marriage], directed by Haim Bouzaglo, 1989; *Gemar Gavia* [Cup final], directed by Eran Riklis, 1992; *Sijill Ikhtifa'* [Chronicle of a disappearance], directed by Elia Suleiman, 1996; and *Kadosh*, directed by Amos Gitai, 1999.

2. As I show presently, the spectrum along which impersonation and passing occurs is not as reductively binary as "Palestinian" and "Israeli"; both categories are internally differentiated, with, for example, Ashkenazi and Mizrahi Israelis, Palestinians with and those without Israeli citizenship, and so on.

3. An example would be a '48-er Palestinian Israeli actor (a Palestinian who remained or was born in what became Israel after its establishment in 1948 and who has Israeli citizenship) cast in the role of a non-'48-er Palestinian, such as a refugee or a guerrilla fighter in Lebanon. The terminology for referring to the Muslim and Christian Arab population living in Palestine that came under Israeli rule with Israel's formation in 1948 and who were granted Israeli citizenship (though not full rights or parity with their Jewish compatriots) is one that varies considerably depending on *when* they are being referred to, by whom, and in what context. In Israeli hegemonic discourse, they were referred to as Israeli Arabs to signal a minority within an unquestioned Israeli Jewish Zionist frame of sovereignty and to differentiate, or more precisely, to posit a distinction between them and their brethren, who were already situated or ended up outside of Israel's post-'48 borders in the West Bank or Transjordan, in the Gaza Strip, or as refugees elsewhere in the Arab world and abroad. Until sometime close to the Oslo Accords of 1993, it was taboo for those designated Israeli Arabs to be called or to call themselves Palestinians in public discourse inside of Israel or to affiliate openly as such. Since Oslo, it has become increasingly acceptable for a significant range of people to use the P-word in Israeli public discourse, so that "Palestinians with Israeli citizenship" and "Palestinian Israelis" have become increasingly widespread in use. From outside Israel's boundaries, reference to this same population as '48-ers is also common, reflecting the fact that this population fell within Israel's 1948 boundaries, but without specifying state structure or naming national affiliation. It is less cumbersome than some other formulations. In this essay, I alternate among these articulations. When I use the term "Israeli Arabs," I mean a minority as understood within the dominant Zionist ideological framework.

In other contexts, Zionist hegemonic discourse has made further distinctions based on religious affiliation: Muslim, Christian, Druze. Such distinctions are not made in the instances of boundary crossing exhibited in the films examined.

4. A more elaborate account and treatment of this spectrum is presented below.

5. As scholars have argued, part of the core problem with identity—the same problem that enables and thus links the practices of impersonation, mimicry, and passing (but does not equate them)—is an apparent paradox: that it "is predicated on the false

promise of the visible as an epistemological guarantee," that is, that things or people *are* what they appear to be, and that what they *are* can be detected by careful enough scrutiny of the visible surface. Amy Robinson, "It Takes One to Know One: Passing and Communities of Common Interest," *Critical Inquiry* 20 (1994): 716. On the other hand, of course, what enables these phenomena is the fact that the visible surface does *not* reveal an unambiguous epistemological truth. See Robinson, and the introduction to Eileen Ginsburg's *Passing and the Fictions of Identity* (Durham, N.C.: Duke University Press, 1996) for further elaboration of this paradox.

6. I emphasize that it "may," as opposed to automatically "does," challenge social categories and hierarchies, for reasons taken up shortly.

7. Judith Butler, *Bodies That Matter: On the Discursive Limits of "Sex"* (New York: Routledge, 1993) and *Gender Trouble: Feminism and the Subversion of Identity* (New York: Routledge, 1990); Marjorie Garber, *Vested Interests: Cross-Dressing and Cultural Anxiety* (New York: Routledge, 1992); Homi Bhabha, "Of Mimicry and Man: The Ambivalence of Colonial Discourse," *October* 28 (spring 1984); "Signs Taken for Wonders: Questions of Ambivalence and Authority Under a Tree Outside Delhi, May 1817" in *Europe and Its Others*, vol. 1. edited by Francis Barker et al. (Colchester: University of Essex Press, 1985); *The Location of Culture* (London: Routledge, 1984).

8. See Anne McClintock's critique of Bhabha in *Imperial Leather: Race, Gender and Sexuality in the Colonial Contest* (New York: Routledge, 1995), 61–66, which addresses the absence of an account of historical (colonized) agency in his work on mimicry and hybridity and, by extension, his failure to account for differences between colonial and *anti*colonial mimicry, resistance, and other strategies of the disempowered that go beyond "ambivalences of form" (66). She also questions the efficacy of overly broad application of a formulation of ambivalence, the effect of which is to cease to distinguish between very different kinds of ambivalence and ambiguity, including between those that are subversive and those that are not.

9. Garber, *Vested Interests*, 17.

10. As Anne McClintock notes, for example, "When marines in the U.S. army deck themselves in drag or put on blackface, white power is not necessarily subverted nor is masculinity thrown into disarray" (*Imperial Leather*, 67). Enactments such as these may, in fact, merely serve to reinscribe hegemonic social roles and categories.

11. Ibid., 65.

12. Garber, *Vested Interests*, 11–13; Homi Bhabha, "Of Mimicry and Man."

13. Karen Brodkin, *How Jews Became White Folks and What That Says about Race in America* (New Brunswick, N.J.: Rutgers University Press, 1998).

14. Others have treated the topic of Ashkenazi representation of the Mizrahi subject, both in Ashkenazi direction and production of films and in Mizrahi roles being played by Ashkenazi actors in ways that reinscribe controlled and stereotyped representations in Orientalist modes. Such representations do not appear explicitly in the films I examine. For these reasons, it is beyond the scope of this essay to include them in my analysis. See, for example, Ella Shohat's exhaustive treatment of this in chapter 3 of *Israeli Cinema: East/West and the Politics of Representation* (Austin: University of Texas Press: 1987), and Dorit Na'aman's "Orientalism as Alterity in Israeli Cinema," *Cinema Journal* 40, no. 4 (2001): 36–54.

15. This is not to say, of course, that the slippage between identity and difference between all points along the spectrum, or even between adjacent points, is always invisible. Only that difference, especially between certain adjacent points, *can* be rendered minimal or virtually absent and in visible terms in certain instances, both in controlled filmic representations and in real life.

16. Na'aman, "Orientalism as Alterity in Israeli Cinema," 29. She uses the term Arab to describe a range of Palestinian and Palestinian Israeli subjectivities. For a more thorough treatment of this with close readings of individual films, see Shohat, *Israeli Cinema*.

17. Shohat, *Israeli Cinema*. See Judd Ne'eman, "The Empty Tomb in the Postmodern Pyramid: Israeli Cinema in the 1980s and 1990s," in *Documenting Israel: Proceedings of a Conference Held at Harvard University on May 10–12, 1993*, edited by Charles Berlin (Cambridge, Mass.: Harvard University Press, 1995); Na'aman, "Orientalism as Alterity in Israeli Cinema"; Raz Yosef, "Homoland: Interracial Sex and the Israeli/Palestinian Conflict in Israeli Cinema," GLQ: *A Journal of Lesbian and Gay Studies* 8, no. 4 (2002): 553–579.

18. Yosef, "Homoland," 554.

19. Shohat, *Israeli Cinema*, 237.

20. Ibid., 244.

21. Hamid Naficy, *Accented Cinema: Exilic and Diasporic Filmmaking* (Princeton: Princeton University Press, 2001).

22. The recent Palestinian Film Festival hosted by Columbia University in New York City (2003) may be viewed as an attempt to provide a site for Palestinian cinema in exile.

23. Shohat, *Israeli Cinema*, 251, 269. The "chromatic" or color-coded stereotypes are so ingrained that even in the captions of the photos from *Beyond the Walls* that were used to illustrate the "chromatic inversion" Shohat was describing in her book, the editors misidentified the actors' names, realigning the stereotyped "lighter" actor as playing the Israeli character and the "darker" one as the Palestinian.

24. Eldi actually engages in double-passing, as a Palestinian and as a different kind of Israeli: a *yored*, or Israeli emigrant living in the United States. But treatment of this is beyond the scope of this essay. Na'aman has touched on this briefly in her "Orientalism as Alterity in Israeli Cinema."

25. Na'aman, "Orientalism as Alterity in Israeli Cinema," 34.

26. The bivalent or passive dynamics described earlier also pertain to his passing as an Israeli who has left Israel and lives in the United States. When he arrives at the hotel, he is bivalent in the sense that he could, with the same visible surface, be read as either an Israeli emigrant or as a "regular" Israeli, living in Israel but visiting Tel Aviv. Judy, the Israeli hotel worker, utterly smitten with the United States, reads Eldi as an Israeli emigrant, and he goes along with her. Detailed analysis of his inter-Israeli passing is beyond the scope of this essay.

27. Na'aman, "Orientalism as Alterity in Israeli Cinema," 34.

28. Raz Yosef writes this with regard to portrayals of what he identifies as interracial (Palestinian-Israeli) sexual relationships in Israeli cinema ("Homoland," 561).

29. In this scene, the category of Israeli Jews is implicitly generalized to mean

Ashkenazi. The habit of using bread to swipe and eat food is portrayed as non-Israeli, alien to both this Mizrahi Israeli Jewish character, who has to learn to do it, and to the Ashkenazi Jewish characters in whose presence he accidentally does it (which meets with disapproval), nearly exposing his underground Palestinianness.

30. In his incarnation as a Palestinian construction worker, Eldi is the one who gains sexual access to the artist living opposite the construction site (the workers have drawn lots to determine which of them will have the privilege of, as she puts it, "filling the crack" in her wall). In his incarnation as an Israeli emigrant (the identity he performs for both Bashir and Judy, the hotel receptionist), he becomes sexually involved with Judy. In both instances, the Palestinian characters remain excluded from such access, content to look on from their marginal positions of exclusion (e.g., the construction workers cheering him on from across the street; Bashir in the service of Eldi's sexual exploits with Judy, bringing refreshments to their bedside).

31. For Bhabha, the very fact of the "partial presence" that colonial mimicry enacts becomes a "menace" and threatens colonial authority and its categories by exposing the fact that, for instance, Englishness or whiteness can be partial and is not an unassailable whole. See Homi Bhabha, "Of Mimicry and Man," *The Location of Culture* (London: Routledge, 1994), and "Signs Taken for Wonders: Questions of Ambivalence and Authority under a Tree Outside Delhi, May 1817," in *Europe and Its Others*, vol. 1, edited by Francis Barker et al. (Colchester: University of Essex Press, 1985). Some might be eager to read Bhabha's "menace" of colonial mimicry as the threat of an achieved resemblance that can tres/pass as Other or the threat of the presence of a colonized agency. However, his explicit articulation of the concept of mimicry's menace remains largely confined to its internal discursive ambivalence.

32. Shohat, *Israeli Cinema*, 249.

33. Anton Shammas, "He Got the Roles Mixed Up" [Hu hitbalbel ba-tafkidim], preface to *Avanti Popolo* (Jerusalem: Kinneret Publishing House, 1990), 14.

34. Ibid.

35. Particularly in the years before cable television was introduced in Israel (i.e., when a large selection of channels became available) and before more state channels were added, one could be certain of extensive viewership of just about anything on the main Israeli state television station, including the Friday Egyptian movie, because there was very little else to choose from.

36. While the range of encounters in the contact zone between Israeli occupying soldiers in, for example, the West Bank and Gaza in the period under discussion is too broad and varied to address here, I venture to say that they, too, would be multiply filtered.

37. This is my preferred translation of the title of the work usually referred to in English as *Sa'eed the Pessoptimist*. Emile Habiby, *The Secret Life of Saeed the Ill-Fated Pessoptimist* [al-Waqa'i' al-ghariba fi ikhtifa' sa'id abi al-nahs al-mutasha'il], translated by Salma Jayyusi and Trevor LeGassick (Columbia, La.: Reader's International, 1989).

38. Though it is doubtful that the director, Rafi Bukai, had this in mind, to certain viewers this scene could easily resonate with the portrayal of Palestinians as being "the Jews of history," as articulated by poet Muzaffar al-Nawwab and others.

39. The recent years of the al-Aqsa Intifada have featured events and incidents

that have further blurred this dividing line: demonstrations against Israeli actions by Palestinians with Israeli citizenship, their getting the same treatment as Palestinians without Israeli citizenship (being shot at and killed at such demonstrations), and suicide bombs and other terror operations against Israeli Jews undertaken by Palestinians with Israeli citizenship.

40. Events surrounding the screening of Bakri's film *Jenin, Jenin* became complicated along these lines. Converging in the same time frame were the release of the film, its being banned in Israel, and a relative of Bakri's being accused of involvement in suicide bombing. In this highly charged context, Bakri reiterated his condemnation of suicide bombings and other acts of violence.

LALEH KHALILI

Virtual Nation:
Palestinian
Cyberculture in
Lebanese Camps

In the early evening hours, the Web café in the Burj al-Barajna camp in Beirut is filled with young Palestinians. The walls of the center are decorated with calendars and posters in Palestinian national colors downloaded from the Internet and reproduced on ordinary printer paper. A few older customers use the centrale telephones to contact relatives and friends; the youth, however, use the computers. Teenage girls sit at the terminals in small giggling groups; one engages in a chatroom conversation or instant message (IM) session. Women in their early twenties surf Arabic-language news sites and young men use the e-mail software. Numerous adolescent boys boisterously play computer games and fill the café with the disembodied noise of cybershooting and high-speed chases in digital landscapes.

Burj al-Barajna is one node in the worldwide network of computer users through which the quotidian cultural practices of Internet usage have insinuated themselves in the lives of millions.[1] In one sense, the ability to switch identities in cyberspace, the ease of border crossings, and the decentering of information flows all highlight the *possible* instabilities and fluidity of identities and cultural boundaries online. I argue, however, that *embodied* identities, *territorialized* spaces, and real-world institutions extend deeply into the realm of cyberspace, and that Palestinian virtual culture has nonvirtual social roots and histories.[2] In both the utopian and dystopian visions of cyberspace, technology brings with it a certain teleology, preordaining cultural forms and contents.[3] In my examination of Palestinian cyberculture in the refugee camps of Lebanon, based on fieldwork conducted in 2001–2003, I interrogate both these positions. My approach is a grounded exploration of the politics of cyberculture and its "communicative and cultural possibility,"[4] rather than a technologically determinist position that is either haunted by dystopian visions of infinite fragmentation and dehumanization or intoxicated by the ecstatic postcorporeal liberties of cyberspace fetishized in a late capitalist context.

In much of the research on the Internet, the focus is on technically prodigious users.[5] For example, in his study of Islamism on the Internet, Jon Anderson focuses extensively on professionals and technocrats.[6] I examine instead ordinary users who may not have sophisticated technological skills and who do not necessarily utilize cyberspace to showcase their technical virtuosity. Another characteristic of various technotheories of cyberspace is the outsized role they grant the Internet in restructuring cultures and societies.[7] By contrast, I discuss the concrete existence of those whose cyberculture does not disengage itself from spatialized identities and their cultural markers, nor does it necessarily encourage social alienation and dehumanization. Palestinian youth "excorporate" the resources provided by high-tech capitalism and use the ideological concepts developed in their diaspora to form a cyberculture in which transnational nationalisms play the dominant role.[8]

The Palestinian youth who are the primary Internet users in Lebanon's camps use the Internet as another mode of addressing their nonvirtual concerns, desires, and ideas. Although border crossings and imagined cybercommunities provide extensive and fluid cultural *possibilities*, ultimately, the realities of quotidian experiences and *lived* political and social relations of the young cyberusers constrain these possibilities. Instead of undergoing "identity travel," their national and political identities function as an integrative transnational force.[9] For these young people, the Internet further distributes modes of nationalist understanding, using images and leaflets, across borders. Far from destabilizing national identities, their virtual practices, whether quotidian or contentious, animate their "long-distance nationalism."[10] National-political identity influences most facets of their online interactions and even affects domains of romance and play that are ostensibly separate from nationalist politics. Nationalist tropes of martyrdom and of the anthropomorphized nation are prevalent in virtual artifacts, and references to concrete Palestinian spaces, landscapes, and geographies are common in the ephemeral and deterritorialized space of the Internet.

I develop this argument as follows. First, to provide context, I describe the everyday lives of the Palestinian youth who constitute the creative forces behind Palestinian cyberculture. Second, I examine the ways Palestinian nationalism is enunciated through the quotidian cyberculture of the youth in the camps via game playing, news gathering, virtual courtship, and on-line pseudonyms. Third, I analyze the nationalist instrumentalization of the Internet for cross-border political debates, circulation of contentious images, and cyberleafleting. Fourth, I discuss the Across Borders Project, which institutionalizes cyberrelations, both routine and contentious, between Palestinians in the Occupied Territories and those in the diaspora. I conclude by discussing the significance of Palestinian cyberculture for both technotheories and theories of popular culture.

Everyday Lives of the Palestinian
Youth in the Camps of Lebanon

Of the 380,000 Palestinian refugees in Lebanon who are registered with the United Nations Relief and Works Agency (UNRWA), more than 60 percent are under thirty years of age, the great majority of whom live in twelve UNRWA-managed refugee camps.[11] The camps are tightly packed, with narrow, winding alleys separating houses that have been enlarged to accommodate natural population growth in strictly circumscribed spaces. The camp households lack telephone lines, but social and political institutions and telephone centrales are connected to the Cypriot and Lebanese networks.[12] Electric supplies to the camps are erratic and daily power outages last for hours. Families whose breadwinners have secure employment can afford televisions, and almost all families with televisions have affordable satellite connections and access to a wide range of Arabic- and English-language channels. Because of hardware expenses, the irregularity of electricity supplies, and the absence of telephone lines, very few families have home computers and none have home access to the Internet. Most young Palestinian men and women who live in the camps are unable to secure employment, as the Lebanese government prohibits Palestinians access to over seventy different occupations.[13] Since 2002, the imposition of heavy fees on Palestinians attending public universities in Lebanon has led many to set aside plans for continuing education.[14] Prior to the al-Aqsa Intifada in 2000, many Palestinians in Lebanon felt abandoned by the Palestinian Authority (PA) and considered their predicament, opinions, and demands overlooked in the peace negotiations. The youth in particular regarded their condition as refugees pathological and humiliating, and often preferred to mask their Palestinian identities when in a Lebanese context. Mayssun Sukkariya, a local activist working with Palestinian youth, describes their mood: "Before the [al-Aqsa] Intifada, when I interviewed them, they would introduce themselves as Muslim rather than as Palestinian, because the Palestinian identity was denigrated. But now, they are more proud of being Palestinian and there is even a revival of *Al-'Awda* [the right of return]."[15]

Throughout the 1990s, Palestinian youth in Lebanon were forced into assimilation under the pressure of being "unwanted guests" in a hostile environment. To better disguise their otherness, they changed their accents, modified their clothes and behavior, and in some instances even denied their Palestinian background. They found it easier to declare themselves Muslims, and hence part of a respected community, rather than Palestinian *refugees*. The importance of an identity that garners the respect of a host community indicates the possibility of shifting between alternative extant identities (Muslim, Palestinian). Nonetheless, the range of potential identities is demarcated by access (or lack thereof) to the cultural resources that identity requires. Cyberspace has provided access to these nationalist symbolic resources.

Quotidian Cyberculture

The introduction of the Internet in the camps has been more or less concomitant with the al-Aqsa Intifada and the withdrawal of Israeli forces from southern Lebanon. Since the reopening of the Israel-Lebanon border zone, many Palestinian youths from the camps have traveled to the area to see with their own eyes the contours of Galilee, which their progenitors left behind in 1948. These visual pilgrimages to Palestine from behind barbed-wire borders have encouraged young Palestinians in Lebanon increasingly to relocate themselves in an imagined Palestinian territory and have intensified their interest in cross-border connections, in the landscapes of the homeland, and in the kin and compatriots who occupy these landscapes. The Internet has facilitated such cross-border connections, and quotidian virtual practices—visits to the Web cafés, online news gathering, virtual courtship, and game playing—have led to a revivification of *political* national identities already present in a nonvirtual social context.

In his celebratory account of the Internet, W. J. Mitchell writes that for community gatherings, "you need to *go* someplace . . . to the agora, the forum, the piazza, the café, the bar, the pub, Main street, the mall, the beach, the gym, the bathhouse, the college dining hall, the common room, the office, or the club . . . But the world-wide computer network—the electronic agora—subverts, displaces, and radically redefines our notions of gathering place, community, and urban life."[16] In the camps in Lebanon, however, the cyberusers still need to go somewhere to use computers. Thus, the Web cafés and Internet centers have joined the slender ranks of public gathering places for young Palestinians. Salah Salah, the founder of al-Ajial, an NGO that aims to provide cultural and social services to Palestinian youth, laments their condition: "They have no place to go, so they keep moving around in the camps and in the streets."[17] Outside the camp, young Palestinian men often face harassment by the Lebanese security forces. In most camps, the local municipality has appropriated for parking lots the peripheral fields formerly used as football grounds. The mosques are often used by older men; young people rarely frequent them unless they are enrolled in classes there. The small NGO libraries and art centers have limited hours and access. Young women use house visits to interact with one another; young men gather on doorsteps and rooftops or in alleyways.

The Internet centers and cafés not only provide cyberaccess, they also offer new gathering places that somewhat mitigate the absence of public spaces for camp youth. At the time of my fieldwork, almost all refugee camps possessed multiple NGO-run Internet centers and at least one Web café. The cafés are private enterprises that utilize the communal telephone lines to provide access to the Internet for a small fee (£1,000 or $0.67). Internet centers run by NGOs and the UNRWA also charge a small fee, but they provide computer classes and generally have superior access speed. Because public spaces are scarce in the camps, the Web cafés and Internet centers have quickly become part of the range of "acceptable" places for young men and especially young women to go.[18] The young people who manage these centers use the walls to display information and items they have received in e-mails or found online; thus, the centers act as bulletin boards for dissemination of political news as well as exhibition of nationalist artifacts. As gathering places, the cybercafés highlight the rootedness of practices of cyberusage, as even Palestinians who do not use the Internet check in to hear of the latest boycott effort or see the posted demonstration notices.

The political sentiment of Palestinian cyberculture is also apparent in young people's cyberhandles, which often incorporate Palestinian place-names or refer to nationalist symbols. The descendants of those who left their villages in Palestine in 1948 choose e-mail monikers named for these lost villages; for example, SAFFURIEH2001@aaa.com commemorates the village of Saffuria in Galilee; WALID_FARA@aaa.com refers to Fara, Walid's grandfather's village in the Safad province.[19] The numeral 48 appears repeatedly in the virtual pseudonyms, commemorating the year of the Nakba. The names also incorporate certain nationalist tropes. For example, a sixteen-year-old student from Burj al-Barajna uses MASHADI2000@aaa .com as her e-mail address. She chose the name after her neighbor "MArtyr SHADI" Anas was killed by the Israeli Defence Forces (IDF) in October 2000.[20] In these examples, even the most basic aspects of Internet use and online identity take on a national cast.

Palestinian identity and nationalist politics also influence the use of the Internet as a source of news. Though Palestinians regularly watch various Arab satellite television stations, the Internet provides them with the ability to track down particular stories and access news sources that supply analyses and coverage unavailable elsewhere. Some Palestinian cyberusers access U.S. or European news, but they trust and prefer Arabic-language sources. Interestingly, when convincing their families of the virtues of Internet access, women name news gathering as their primary motive for Internet usage. Because access to news of the homeland is considered to be unfrivolous, even strict parents allow their daughters to go to Web cafés (though they may regulate the hour and length of their attendance). Women may also engage in news gathering more than the men do because they are less imbricated in the networks of political factions and their gatherings, which have their own modes of news dissemination.

The primary intent of news gathering in the camps is to follow the conflicts in the Occupied Territories. Instantaneous access to the images and events of the Territories and the "reading together" of digital images and content have been crucial in the cultivation of the Palestinian "imagined community" across borders.[21] Images provide a basis for constituting the Palestinians in the Occupied Territories as "people who look like me and speak like me" and "who, like me, are suffering," as some of the young men and women assert, thereby creating a notion of community before personal communication has taken place. The consumers of cybercontent create narratives from news items and images that place the Palestinians in the Occupied Territories and those in the camps of Lebanon in the same community of suffering: referring to the al-Aqsa Intifada, a Palestinian youth in Lebanon writes, "Our pain is one and the suffering is one."[22] What distinguishes the consumption of news in this manner is the consumer's ability to *actively* seek out what he or she needs to construct a meaningful story of the world and the conflicts within it. Many of the youth self-consciously filter news items such that the mélange of information is almost always culled from sympathetic news sources. The news gatherers accept critical accounts only when they emanate from a trusted insider source. Thus, the nationalist sympathies of the news gatherers influence their narratives of cross-border community as shaped by political news.

Aside from cybernews gathering, the most prevalent reason for Internet use is personal communication and, increasingly, intimate cyberrelations; these interactions are also influenced by issues of Palestinian identity. Chatrooms that permit Arabic scripts have become a virtual meeting place for men and women who engage in flirtation and transgress the boundaries of ordinarily acceptable behavior without fear of being unmasked. Chatroom and IM romances frequently develop between Palestinians and other *Palestinians* rather than other Arabic speakers, highlighting the importance of national identity even in virtual flirtation. The language used for e-mails and chats is a hybrid of colloquial Arabic and English, where the primary vocabulary and diction is colloquial Arabic, but English words and idioms—OK, Bye, I love U, and I miss U—are used liberally. This novel form of bilingualism is distinctly different from the language used in everyday face-to-face interactions; it provides a space in which young Palestinian men and women can deploy nondominant modes of verbal expression and therefore, to some extent, are freed from the implicit significances and the weight of meaning of their primary language. Many unmarried Palestinian women who would never declare their love to a man in a face-to-face conversation in Arabic do so more freely online, protected by the less pregnant English-language I LUV U.

The use of colloquial Arabic words and diction online, and the intensity of interaction between Palestinians in Lebanon and their compatriots in the Occupied Territories, have revived Palestinian words that had fallen out of use in Lebanon. Over several generations, due to chosen or forced assimilation, many in Lebanon lost their Palestinian accents. Because the Palestinian accent is considered a significant marker of national identity, I was told that its loss is perceived as a sign of "humiliation and betrayal." Thus, the recuperation of an "authentically" Palestinian accent through virtual conversations with homeland Palestinians is a significant nationalist move; it can even form the basis of romance across borders. In more than one instance, I observed the fervent preference of Palestinian men and women in Lebanon for their counterparts in the Occupied Territories. They construed the connection as authentic because their interlocutors in the Territories used colloquial expressions and vocabularies that had been lost to them through Lebanonization. Hearing the accents of their friends on conference calls or in videoconferences similarly reinforced their notion of the authentic Palestinian at home to whose friendship and affection they aspired. One young Palestinian woman who had established virtual relations with a young West Bank man waxed rhapsodic about "his wonderful Palestinian accent," to which she had only been privy through electronic texts.[23] This search for Palestinian authenticity introduces nationalist sentiments into even the romantic domain and blurs the boundaries between what is overtly considered political and personal, even playful, aspects of life.

Palestinians' struggle for national self-definition even informs moments of play. Adolescent boys in the camps, who use the Web café computers primarily for game playing, describe these activities in nationalist terms. Boys ten to fifteen fervently use and discuss the wide array of computer games available in the cafés. Because families protectively prevent their sons from "playing with guns until they are older," violent computer games allow the boys to circumvent these prohibitions. Most parents consider these games a distraction for the boys, "to keep them out of trouble," and they justify the game playing by adding, "If they can't play with computers, what is left for them to play with?" While game playing aids manual-visual skills, in the camps, the games (which are overwhelmingly of the chase-and-shoot variety) also act as a staging ground for the development of what many young men consider defensive skills.[24] They consider these skills necessary because, on the one hand, masculinity is still largely bound up with notions of armed resistance, and on the other hand, internal Palestinian tensions and ongoing, though subsurface, conflict with Lebanese and Syrian security forces create a sense of vulnerability which the young men believe they can challenge only through a show of masculine (and armed) strength. As such, game playing is not simply child's play, but a rite of passage for young boys. While many of these games are bootlegged copies of software produced in the United States, in February 2003 they were joined by the Hizbullah-developed game *Special Force*, which allows the players to chase Israeli soldiers and practice target shooting against Ariel Sharon. The software box invites the players to join "the heroes of the Islamic Resistance in Lebanon" and to "fight, resist and destroy your enemy in the game of force and victory." The Hizbullah game is already widely available on various Web café computers and wildly popular with adolescent boys, attesting to the nationalist character of even game playing. Since its arrival in the camps, many of the boys have abandoned the competing U.S. games, speaking gleefully about *Special Force* as a game that is "about us" and "for us." Many are aware of similar U.S. chase-and-shoot games where the targets are sometimes Arabs portrayed as terrorists; the boys consider *Special Force* a worthy counterweight against such games and as a playful representation of national resistance.

As we have seen, other domains of Internet usage in the camps, such as news gathering, e-mail, and online romances, are similarly infused with political and nationalist symbols and meanings. The inseparability of politics from the everyday lives of the youth partially explains this saturation; but also, and perhaps more importantly, reflexive attempts at self-definition play a significant role in cyberactivities, whether quotidian or contentious.

Contentious Cyberculture

The virtual mobilization of populations under duress has become familiar since the Zapatistas of Chiapas launched their cybercampaign to garner solidarity for their cause in 1994.[25] The Internet has also been used to disseminate images of and testimonies about the al-Aqsa Intifada. The April 2002 reoccupation of West Bank cities and the destruction of refugee camps were reported by conventional media outlets, especially regional satellite stations such as Al-Jazeera and Abu Dhabi. In addition to these behemoths, however, independent news-delivery organizations used the Internet as their primary medium of reporting. Along with the Palestinian Information Centre, Electronic Intifada, and Indymedia, International Solidarity Movement activists launched digital diaries written in English and broadcast to European and U.S. audiences.[26] These news sources are not subject to IDF press office censorship or the Israeli requirements for acquisition of press permits.[27]

Contemporaneously, another set of computer-mediated flows traversed international boundaries. These electronic communications traveled in the periphery, between the camps and cities of the West Bank and the Palestinian camps in Lebanon. Despite the IDF's systematic attacks on cultural centers, shutting down of Internet Service Providers (ISPs), and looting of computer hard drives in the West Bank, these exemplars of "diasporic cultural nationalism" have circulated at increasing rates across borders.[28] The dissemination of nationalist virtual content at the grassroots level has been far more significant than any information issued through the offices of factional elites. The writers, recipients, and circulators of nationalist cybercontent are ordinary young men and women. These circulations eschew the denationalized and universally homogeneous language and cultural forms (read English and Eurocentric) promulgated through fluid global media connections. They do not discard nonvirtual political identities in favor of imagined virtual selfhoods. Instead, Palestinian cybernationalism has striven to unify the dispersed Palestinian communities across borders into a nation, and has demanded a convergence of needs, desires, concerns, and identities between the diasporic community and the Palestinians in the homeland.[29] To do so, Palestinians have propagated national(ist) symbols in images and texts and employed cyberleaflets and debate forums for national(ist) mobilization.

Palestinian organizations have used PalTalk discussion forums to encourage public exchanges with members of the Palestinian political elite about membership in the nation, political claims of the refugees, and the legitimacy of the PA in the eyes of Palestinian refugees.[30] Palestinians in Lebanon gleefully recount heated debates with Sari Nusseibeh, who is well-known for advocating the abandonment of the right of return by Palestinian refugees outside the Occupied Territories in return for Palestinian statehood.[31] A Palestinian youth from Burj al-Shamali who regularly attends PalTalk debates says, "Whenever Nusseibeh is online, lots of people are out there, ready to go after him." The number of Palestinians in the camps who actually know of such forums and who enter these debates is relatively small; nonetheless, the news of the debates has spread via word of mouth. The debates have gradually expanded, allowing for an independent public space in which discussions can occur openly and with minimum monitoring and surveillance by officials of various political factions or representatives of the PA in the camps. If the introduction of inclusive political debates encourages the emergence of a national public space, these forums can provide one method of extending such debates.

In addition to ongoing deliberation of what constitutes the nation, shared symbols and images also provide a basis of collective imagining about the national self. Palestinian youth across borders capture or create newspaper articles, cartoons, slideshows, and digital images in cyberspace and circulate them far and wide, thus disseminating the semiotics of nationalism. Virtual images of Palestinian places and landscapes have been crucial in *reterritorializing* Palestinians and reinforcing their ties to concrete locales and spaces. The individual youths who produce these images send them to long e-mail lists that include both their Palestinian friends and their foreign interlocutors. Sixteen-year-old Hiba from Burj al-Barajna camp explains: "I receive pictures and photographs all the time. I don't make them myself, but I send them to all my friends. The one that I most

FIGURE 4. Image circulated from Shatila camp: "All people have a homeland in which they live; we have a homeland which lives in us."

liked was this picture of Haifa before and after Israel. It was shocking to see the Israeli flag over mosques and over Palestinian buildings. They were so beautiful beforehand!"[32]

Utilization of digital images on the Internet to remind refugees of "what once was and no longer is" significantly expands the ability of Palestinians in the diaspora to imagine and commemorate the homeland. Images of pre-1948 Haifa are objects of nostalgia, but when combined with post-1948 images, they become potent nationalist symbols of a lost homeland whose mosques and "Palestinian buildings" are desecrated by the enemy flag. The naturalization of *ordinary* dwellings as *national* markers of a "lost homeland" is thus reinforced online.

Similarly, photographs of Jerusalem are particularly prevalent. Using pictures readily available online, young Palestinian men and women create nationalist collages featuring the Dome of the Rock and Jerusalem. The Dome of the Rock in figure 4 is set against a romantic landscape of Jerusalem at sunset and is framed by the familiar colors of the Palestinian flag (black, red, white, and green). The image also contains a contradiction which it does not address: on the one hand, the written text declares that the Palestinian homeland is contained *within* Palestinians; on the other hand, it subverts this notion by foregrounding a photograph of those most concrete physical symbols of Palestinianness: the Dome of the Rock and the map of Mandate Palestine. In effect, imagining the nation of Palestine as an unpartitioned whole recognizes neither Israel nor the PA's Palestine: it explicitly declares the defiant position of the diasporans who consider themselves excluded from the political concerns of the PA.

Other images focus on the connections between the refugees in the camps of Lebanon and the Palestinians in the Occupied Territories. These connections are reinforced through digital graphic and textual artifacts that weave images of the Intifada with refugee slogans and emphasize the joint destinies of Palestinians across borders. Though the photographs showcase the Intifada, the text refers to both the refugees and the Intifada. In fact, the juxtaposition of these texts and Intifada images makes a case for the claims of refugees being at the heart of Palestinian resistance: as long as there is no return, Palestinian women will defy bulldozers and Palestinian children will throw stones at tanks. There is no mention of armed resistance or martyrdom, otherwise constitutive elements of Palestinian nationalist semiotics, perhaps because the intended audience includes foreigners averse to the language of martyrdom. The audience for some of these images is intended to be a foreign one: the Palestinian map in one image, on which Israel and the proto-state of Palestine are geographically distinct, differs from the map in figure 4, where Palestine is imagined as unpartitioned. The different sources and audiences of the images influence the way Palestine is cartographically drawn. Figure 4 was produced in the diaspora by marginalized refugees who continue to hope for a return to their lost homes. As such, their map is the pre-Mandate one. The other, described above, was produced in the Occupied Territories; thus, it contains the details of the proto-state of Palestine but no visual references to pre-1948 Palestine, save the undifferentiated yellow expanse that is left unnamed but is nonetheless recognizable (and thus implicitly recognized) as the state of Israel.

Along with representations of Palestinian locales, images of bloodied bodies are widely circulated throughout the camps in Lebanon. These digital descendants of martyrs' commemorative posters chronicle grievances against Israeli occupation and anthropomorphize Palestine. In addition to harrowing photographs of wounded children, slideshows such as DiariesOfAChild.pps circulate through the camps. DiariesOfAChild.pps contains over thirty images of arrested, injured, or murdered children, arranged around a narrative told in the voice of a child. Among images of bloodied children, that of Muhammad al-Durra crouching under his father's arm has become emblematic and is even used as a background to other images of injured children.[33] Durra became a potent symbol of Palestinian nationalism and Palestinian solidarity and sympathy in diaspora. In Lebanon, songs are sung to him and *dabke* (the Palestinian national folk dance) troupes are named after him. The iconic figure of the young boy felled in his father's arms also exemplifies the death of innocents at the hand of IDF soldiers. Because the image shows a father desperately attempting to protect his son, it speaks to the Israeli propagandists' claim that "Palestinians don't love their children," of which the refugees in Lebanon are bitterly aware. Using Durra's image to frame the picture of wounded children extends the protective though helpless arm of the father over the body of the other injured child as well and normalizes the image of Durra as the perpetual fate of Palestinian children. The author of the collage uses the authority of the injured child to call the Israelis terrorists, inverting the usual direction of the accusation. By comparing Israelis to Nazis, the author further lays claim to a universal inheritance of suffering. The usage of George W. Bush's "axis of evil" slogan and a U.S. flag with a Star of David extends the blame for the children's injury to the super-power as well. The purpose is to move viewers, and perhaps move them to action, but by portraying suffering and victimization rather than active and defiant resistance. The content of the slogan and the use of English indicate that this appeal is intended to reach a foreign audience and to evoke their sympathy. Before the Internet, such immediate and urgent appeals required more centralized and resource-heavy forms of public relations.[34] Now, though, grassroots activists with Internet connections and basic software construct composite images to further their cause.

In another widely circulated image, IDF soldiers pose for a trophy photograph over a dead Palestinian body.[35] Taken by a Reuters photographer on February 21, 2002, at Baqa' al-Sharqiya, the photo shows the two soldiers smiling, one looking down at the barefoot body of the dead Palestinian. A third soldier, with his back to the photographer, is himself capturing the scene on film. As circulated by the Palestinians, the image (whose electronic file was variously named "Embodiment of Evil," "Evil Israelis," or something similar) is intended to personalize the institutional injustices perpetuated and defended by the IDF; the soldiers are taken as the embodiment of occupation. The virtual circulation of embodied cruelty, of injury and death, and the contrasting digital collages of slaughtered children all underline the persecution and victimization of the nation. The dialectical positioning of good against evil and the symbolic reproduction of the virtues of innocence, youthful martyrdom, and paternal protectiveness are familiar nationalist tropes. The images of wounded bodies represent the dissected body of an anthropomorphized nation and are viscerally evocative to the Palestinian diaspora in Lebanon, who have lived through a long and bloody civil war and who consider themselves cut off from the nation's body. Photographs and collages with images of Palestinian locales, flags, kufiyas, embroideries, and stone-throwing children, which previously appeared on material media such as postcards, paintings, and posters, are thus digitally reborn and fortify the semiotic language of a shared national identity.[36] In these images, the Palestinian is elided to the nation so that the

Palestinian person-nation is married to symbolic and figurative representations of the land, thus evoking the man-land bond so often at the center of nationalist paradigms.

Palestinian nationalist mobilization also extensively utilizes cyberleafleting. Leafleting has been recognized as one of the most prominent methods of protest in the Palestinian repertoire of contention during the first Intifada in the late 1980s.[37] But whereas the leaflets of the first Intifada were issued by an underground leadership committee, printed on paper, and disseminated on the streets of the Occupied Territories, a variety of writers produced the cyberleaflets of the al-Aqsa Intifada, the majority young, and none in a leadership position of any sort. Some resided in the Occupied Territories; others were scattered throughout the diaspora's camps. The lack of a centralized authorship reflected the absence of a centralized protest authority. In the first Intifada, a central oppositional leadership claimed the loyalty of most Palestinians; the al-Aqsa Intifada is a far more fragmented movement. New technologies available to Palestinians encouraged this form of decentralized mobilization. Internet users have produced the al-Aqsa leaflets throughout both the Occupied Territories and the diaspora and have circulated them regionally and internationally. The leaflets contained eyewitness accounts of Israeli reoccupation of the West Bank, laments for martyrs, polemics against perceived Arab impotence, calls for boycotts of corporate supporters of Israel, and invitations to protest.

Rabiha 'Alan 'Alan from Ramallah wrote her daily sketches of occupation and lyrical polemics for an exclusively Arabic-speaking readership. Twenty-three-year-old Rula of Nahr al-Barid camp, who circulated all of 'Alan's texts, said: "She tells us what is going on better than any news. With her, I feel how Palestinian she is, because of the way she writes. To me she is a female Mahmud Darwish."[38] Comparisons to Darwish, Palestine's most prominent national poet, indicate the respect 'Alan garners for the nationalism, and lyricism, of her prose. The intimacy of her writing conveys the details and urgency of life under occupation "better than any news." 'Alan's writings appeared in the e-mail boxes of many young men and women in different camps in Lebanon and were widely discussed. Many young women who read her prose sought to emulate her openly nationalist writing style.

Leaflet writing occurs throughout the diaspora, and a leaflet written by a young woman in Lebanon in the aftermath of a suicide operation took the U.S. secretary of state to task for his lopsided condemnation of Palestinians:

Colin Powell says that America condemns terrorist acts that target innocent civilians . . . But are *they* innocents? They live in settlements while
. . . the original owners of the land are thrown to the open air after their
houses had been destroyed and their lands are taken so that Israelis
build settlements . . . They attack and kill Palestinian men, women
and children, they burn Palestinian crops, they attack mosques and kill
Palestinians while praying . . . These innocent civilians are waiting for
their elected President [*sic*] Sharon to get rid of all the Palestinians. They
elected him knowing well his history in crimes and massacres.[39]

The text is written in the rhythmic oratory style prevalent in the leaflets of
the first Intifada and is presented in both Arabic and English for Palestinian
and foreign audiences. The occupation and settlement of land, attacks on
women and children, and destruction of Palestinian crops are all motifs
that appear regularly in oral accounts of the Nakba as told by the Palestinian refugees in Lebanon. The language used to assail Israeli occupiers is
geographically nonspecific in its description of particular grievances, thus
allowing for universalization of the claims to justice over time and space.
The leaflet establishes a connection between diaspora and homeland Palestinians through its generalized litany of inequities and by establishing a
common enemy. In condemnation of Israeli reoccupation of West Bank
towns, the writer reminds her readers of Sharon's responsibility for the
Sabra and Shatila massacres in Lebanon. The chronicle of atrocities is thus
a *national* history of suffering, inflicted by the same enemy of the nation.

Another leaflet written by a Palestinian in the Burj al-Shamali camp in
Lebanon as a letter of support for the Intifada invokes thyme, olives, stones,
jasmine, and fields of poppies, all part of the pastoral semiotics of Palestinian nationalism:[40]

Salutations from . . . our country's thyme, and from the olives of Galilee.
From the stones of Acre, and processions of jasmine, and the mourn-
ful songs of the flute, and the fields of poppies which grow upon our
wounds, and the flocks of Jerusalem doves who sing every day in the
name of peace. Salutations upon our righteous martyrs, Palestine's
martyrs who opened their chest to the fire of our enemy . . . It is your
faith that keeps us alive, and keeps the Cause alive. Peace be upon the
souls of the martyrs . . . Peace be upon you, Muhammad al-Durra.[41]

Alluding to both cultivated crops and wild flora, the writer claims the
land as a national birthright. In addition to the peasant heritage of Pales-

tinian nationalism, martyrdom is also praised as an essential element of the national cause. The format of the text mimics Intifada leaflets; however, this and other lyrical leaflets stop short of organizing a particular action. Instead, the very invocation of national symbols is its purpose. By reproducing and disseminating nationalist symbols and establishing a web of communication between the diaspora and the Occupied Territories, Palestinians use these leaflets to expand the national public sphere across borders.

Other, more prosaic cyberleaflets explicitly call for action: another letter of solidarity demands that the "Arab leaders intervene to stop the Palestinian bloodbath."[42] Cyberleaflets titled "The Anti-Arab Summit" and "Invitation to Palestinian and Lebanese Youth Groups" organize sit-ins, demonstrations, and boycott meetings. In one of the most successful instances of virtual mobilization, Palestinians in Lebanon launched a boycott of products produced by multinational companies with substantial investments in Israel. The boycott calls were initiated in the camps and spread from one personal e-mail list to another. Palestinians produced boycott posters in the centers and displayed them on the walls. These often included logos of targeted companies alongside images of bloodied corpses of children. Though some cyberusers voiced their discomfort over the use of photos of brutalized children, those images remained on the walls and dared the viewer to buy products from the likes of McDonalds, Coca-Cola, and Revlon. Whether organizing a specific action or disseminating symbolic or supportive content, cyberleafleting and graphic images have fostered nationalism through joint action, generation of solidarity, and articulation of national(ist) signs.

Institutionalized Cyberusage

The institutionalization of virtual border crossings resulted in the creation of the Across Borders Project (ABP). Birzeit University launched the project in May 1999 to rectify the "increasing division of the [Palestinian] community along regional lines and the consequent narrowing of political vision leading to the exclusion of refugee rights from the concerns of Palestinian negotiators."[43] It also aimed to provide a voice for the community "unmediated by other interests" and to join "families that have been divided for fifty years."[44] As of this writing, ABP has established six Internet centers in the Occupied Territories and one each in the Burj al-Shamali and Nahr al-Barid camps in Lebanon. In all these camps, ABP has created Web sites that present histories and images of the camp and stories of its individual residents for other Palestinians and "the rest of the world."[45]

During the al-Aqsa Intifada, Palestinians in Lebanon have used the intercamp connection to convey their support for their counterparts in the camps of the Occupied Territories. Muna Hamzeh, the ABP coordinator in Dheisheh (West Bank) recounts that "about a dozen letters of solidarity arrived from teenagers in Burj el-Shamali Refugee Camp. I'm printing them out and faxing them to the local Bethlehem TV station and to local journalists in Gaza and Ramallah. It is important for Palestinians here to know what Palestinians in the Diaspora are saying and doing . . . and vice versa of course."[46] Despite the fact that the camp Web pages route hundreds of e-mails from around the world, the young Palestinian men and women of the camps in Lebanon are overwhelmingly interested in developing relations mainly with the Palestinians in the Occupied Territories. There is a shared statelessness and political indeterminacy that ties the diasporan Palestinians to the refugees in the Territories. Additionally, however, the refugees in Lebanon realize that a Palestinian state will most likely—if at all—arise in the Occupied Territories, and as such they are intensely interested in cultivating relations with the future citizens of such a state. Through "virtual reunifications" of Palestinians across borders, ABP encourages this convergence of identities and aims.[47] "Visits" are enabled by videoconferencing equipment provided by the Project. Even the Project's name indicates its intent to reterritorialize the refugees, allowing them to solidify relationships with the homeland through communication.

Paradoxically, these virtual reunifications have also created tension. Since the beginning of the Oslo process, the status of refugees (whether inside or outside the proto-state of Palestine) has become far more precarious, as the negotiators have relegated the issue to the back burner and the PA has raised the possibility of vacating the right of return. However, the refugees inside the former borders of Mandate Palestine have a better chance of becoming citizens of a future Palestinian state than do the refugees outside. This perceived competition is a source of tension, as is the contested meaning of citizenship vis-à-vis the proto-state of Palestine. In the winter of 2003, when Mona Abu Rayyan, ABP coordinator for Lebanon, suggested an online poll of Palestinian refugees concurrent with the planned January 2003 elections in the Occupied Territories, she faced vehement opposition from some in the West Bank who considered even a nonbinding poll to be an "intrusion into the domestic politics" of the Occupied Territories.[48]

Although ABP emphasizes the homogeneity of the refugees as members of the Palestinian nation, it also paradoxically (and unintentionally) reinforces the borders between them: as the Palestinians across borders interact, differences in their respective aims and values become more apparent. The imagined equivalence of diasporic and home communities thus erodes in the cyberinteractions between Palestinians. Where Beirut was the heart of the Palestinian nation before 1982, the Occupied Territories now assume that role, and the cyberconnections facilitated and institutionalized by ABP reinforce this shift in territorial and community importance. In these cyberinteractions, sometimes the interests of '48 Palestinians are pitted against those of the '67 Palestinians and the '48-for-'67 bargain becomes a major source of contention. Disagreements over whether political compromises are more effective than continued armed resistance also play a role in these tensions, because although the diasporans and the Palestinians in the Occupied Territories do not adhere monolithically to one or the other tactic, the refugees in the diaspora are far more uniformly opposed to a political solution that would compromise their rights. These differences, which emerge out of interaction, in effect demystify the notion of belonging to the nation as something unitary and uniform. The emergence of contradictory processes by which the nation is at once unified and fragmented is familiar in all nationalist movements. For Palestinian refugees, ABP's institutionalization of cross-border connections has foregrounded debates about membership in the nation.

Conclusion

Whether in celebration or in mourning, the death knell of the nation-state as the site of politics is sounded again and again in descriptions of globalization, of which cyberspace is a significant component and metaphor.[49] Although many critics have conceptualized globalization as a series of disjunctures, they celebrate the possibilities of transnational or deterritorialized imaginings encouraged by cross-border (tele)communication.[50] Even ambivalent approaches to the potential of the Internet refer to this overcoming of national boundaries. Shohat cautiously argues that cyberspace can allow "geographically dispersed communities to interact beyond the literal and metaphorical boundaries of nation-states."[51] One of the concurrent characteristics of the alleged death of the nation-state is a conception of the liberties of disembodied cyberinteraction, where "our very rootedness to place is attenuated," and "the creation of an identity [is] so fluid and multiple that it strains the limits of the notion of" identity.[52] To be sure, cyberspace can *theoretically* accommodate deterritorialization and multiplicity of identities. However, nonvirtual identities and national imaginaries still wield considerable force, structure feelings,[53] mobilize collectivities, and shape and transform daily practices and social relations in both the real and cyber worlds.

Furthermore, the crossing of borders is still, perhaps increasingly, facilitated by access to the citizenship *privileges* of *privileged* sovereign states. Therefore, when Appadurai flattens all categories of border crossers into a community of "tourists, immigrants, refugees, exiles, guest workers, and other moving groups and individuals," he is effectively effacing certain disparities of power.[54] A jet-set tourist with a U.S. passport can enter any country in the world with few obstacles; a Palestinian refugee cannot even secure the passport of a sovereign state, much less travel to Europe or North America without enduring intense monitoring and restriction. The border crossings of cyberspace are negotiated not at Customs and Immigration checkpoints, but through access to cyberskills and technology. Nonetheless, the Internet's ability to undermine the sovereignty of nation-states and forge new political and national identities is underutilized.[55] In fact, the decentralized nature of cybertechnology allows diasporic communities to emphasize their ties to a homeland.

Finally, celebrations of deterritorialization in cyberspace have tended to ignore the problem that to become deterritorialized one has to have a territory and a homeland in the first place, and to forsake one's identity for the fluidities of diasporic or liminal identity play, one has to be able to claim an identity not only in political contestations but also in something as mundane as a passport. As Henry Louis Gates Jr. has argued, "Subaltern [groups] have to explore and reclaim [their] identity before critiquing it."[56] Palestinian cyberculture in the Lebanese camps thus facilitates exploration of the "nation" across borders and understanding of its extents, uniformities, and lines of fracture. Palestinian cyberculture highlights questions about who constitutes a compatriot and how distance and proximity between members of an imagined community are to be negotiated when national borders, passport requirements, and superpower politics are in the last instance a great barrier to face-to-face closeness.

Notes

1. In my description of cyberculture, I am indebted to Arturo Escobar, who credits it with "the rituals [cyberuse] originates, the social relations it helps to create, the practices developed around them by various users, the values it fosters." Arturo Escobar, "Welcome to Cyberia: Notes on the Anthropology of Cyberculture," *Current Anthropology* 35, no. 3 (1994): 211–233.

2. See William J. Mitchell, *City of Bits: Space, Place, and the Infobahn* (Cambridge, Mass.: MIT Press, 1995) on "despatialization of interaction" (10), "disembodied electronic identity" (11), and his celebration of how "spatially defined power erodes in cyberspace" (149). I use "real world" as shorthand for material and embodied institutions, relations, and interactions that take place in noncyberspace.

3. On utopian, see ibid.; Mark Poster "Cyberdemocracy: The Internet and the Public Sphere," in *Virtual Politics: Identity and Community in Cyberspace*, edited by David Holmes (London: Sage, 1997), 212–228; Sherry Turkle, *Life on the Screen: Identity in the Age of the Internet* (New York: Simon and Schuster, 1995). On dystopian, see Andrew Herman and John H. Sloop, " 'Red Alert!' Rhetorics of the World Wide Web and 'Friction-Free' Capitalism," in *The World Wide Web and Contemporary Cultural Theory*, edited by Andrew Herman and Thomas Swiss (London: Routledge, 2000), 77–98; David Holmes, "Virtual Identity: Communities of Broadcast, Communities of Interactivity," in *Virtual Politics: Identity and Community in Cyperspace*, edited by David Holmes (London: Sage, 1997), 26–45; Robert McChesney, "So Much for the Magic of Technology and the Free Market: The World Wide Web and the Corporate Media System," in *The World Wide Web and Contemporary Cultural Theory*, edited by Andrew Herman and Thomas Swiss (London: Routledge, 2000), 5–36; Michele Willson, "Community in the Abstract: A Political and Ethical Dilemma?" in *Virtual Politics: Identity and Community in Cyberspace*, edited by David Holmes (London: Sage, 1997), 145–162.

Castells, Jordan, Shohat, and Travers are all more ambivalent about the Internet. See Manuel Castells, *The Internet Galaxy: Reflections on the Internet, Business, and Society* (Oxford: Blackwell, 2001); Tim Jordan, *The Culture and Politics of Cyberspace and Internet* (London: Routledge, 1999); Ella Shohat, "By the Bitstream of Babylon: Cyberfrontiers and Diasporic Vistas," in *Home, Exile, Homeland: Film, Media, and the Politics of Place*, edited by Hamid Naficy (New York: Routledge, 1999), 213–232; Ann Travers, *Writing the Public in Cyberspace: Redefining Inclusion on the Net* (New York: Garland, 2000).

4. Paul Willis, *Common Culture: Symbolic Work at Play in the Everyday Cultures of the Young* (Milton Keynes, England: Open University Press, 1990), 136.

5. See, for example, Castells, *The Internet Galaxy*, where, in a wide-ranging study of the Internet, he attends more extensively to the technoelite, hackers, and entrepreneurs than he does to virtual communities on the Net (39–61), which he labels "networked individualism" (130).

6. Jon Anderson, "The Internet and Islam's New Interpreters," in *New Media and the Muslim World: The Emerging Public Sphere*, edited by Dale Eickelman and Jon Anderson (Bloomington: University of Indiana Press, 1999), 41–56.

7. See, for example, Manuel Castells, *The Rise of Network Society*, vol. 1: *The Information Age: Economy, Society and Culture* (Oxford: Blackwell, 1996).

8. "Excorporation is the process by which the subordinate make their own culture out of the resources and commodities provided by the dominant system." John Fiske, *Understanding Popular Culture* (New York: Routledge, 1989), 15.

9. Ella Shohat and Robert Stam, *Unthinking Eurocentrism: Multiculturalism and the Media* (New York: Routledge, 1994), 356.

10. Benedict Anderson, *The Spectre of Comparisons: Nationalism, Southeast Asia and the World* (London: Verso, 1998).

11. FAFO, UNRWA's *Financial Crisis and Socio-economic Conditions of Palestinian Refugees in Lebanon*. Study commissioned by the Royal Norwegian Ministry of Foreign Affairs, available at: http://www.fafo.no, 2000.

12. The Lebanese government has been reluctant to allow connections between most camps and the Lebanese telephone networks.

13. The Republic of Lebanon Ministry of Labour Decision No. 621/1 stipulates that most professional and managerial positions (including occupations in the service industry), small business ownership, engineering, and teaching professions are open only to the Lebanese. Additionally, even illegal day jobs in the construction sector are becoming increasingly scarce as the Palestinian workers face competition from lower-wage Syrian migrant laborers.

14. These fees are now 700,000 Lebanese liras (equivalent to nearly $500), which is beyond what most camp students or their families can afford. Since the imposition of these fees, many Palestinian students have dropped out of universities or have put their university plans on hold.

15. Interview with author, Beirut, January 17, 2002. Palestinian right of return is supported by the Universal Declaration of Human Rights (1948), which stipulates, "Everyone has the right to leave any country, and to return to his country" (Article 13, paragraph 2). The International Covenant on Civil and Political Rights (Article 12, paragraph 4); the International Convention on the Elimination of All Forms of Racial Discrimination (Article 5 (d) (11)); Protocol No. 4 of the European Convention for the Protection of Human Rights and Fundamental Freedoms (Article 3, paragraph 2); the American Convention on Human Rights (Article 2, paragraph 5); and the African Charter on Human Rights and People's Rights (Article 12, paragraph 2) similarly support *all* refugees' right of return to their home countries. Palestinian refugees specifically are supported by the United Nations General Assembly Resolution 194, which "resolves that the refugees wishing to return to their homes and live at peace with their neighbours should be permitted to do so at the earliest predictable date" (paragraph 11). See Jaber Suleiman, "The Palestinian Liberation Organization: From the Right of Return to Bantustan," in *Palestinian Refugees: The Right of Return*, edited by Naseer Aruri (London: Pluto Press, 2001), 88–89.

16. W. Mitchell, *City of Bits*, 7–8.

17. Interview with author, Beirut, December 19, 2001.

18. Where open courtship in the camp would be subject to surveillance and sanction, the courting couples can "meet" in the same Web café, sit at opposite ends of the

same room, and engage in flirtatious virtual romance, undeterred and unobserved by others. Interview with Mona Abu Rayyan, Beirut, April 8, 2003.

19. In the interest of my interlocutors' anonymity, I have obscured the e-mail program's domain name.

20. During early October 2000 in the vicinity of the Israeli-Lebanese border, Palestinians held several demonstrations in protest against the Sharon visit to the al-Aqsa mosque, which was followed by many Palestinian deaths in the Occupied Territories. The usual insults and curses and the occasional stone thrown across the border by Palestinians (and answered by tear gas from the other side) escalated into throwing Molotov cocktails. In response, the IDF troops shot and killed two young Palestinian men, Shadi 'Anas of Burj al-Barajna camp and Hasan Hasanayn of Shatila.

21. Benedict Anderson, *Imagined Communities: Reflections on the Origin and Spread of Nationalism* (London: Verso, 1991).

22. Burj al-Shamali, "Support for al-Aqsa Intifada," previously available at: http://www.bourjalshamali.org/english/inti/support1.htm. Sadly, as this book was going to press, ownership of this site had changed hands, or it had been hacked.

23. Interview with Abu Rayyan, Beirut, April 8, 2003.

24. In his study of popular culture among English working-class youth, Willis (*Common Culture*) also notes the enthusiasm of young boys for computer games and optimistically interprets it as the creative development of their manual skills.

25. Nationalist movements such as the Basque movement in Spain, the East Timorese in Indonesia, and the Tamil in Sri Lanka have also extensively employed the Internet to garner support from around the world. In the Middle East, the Algerians and the Western Saharans have organized Internet campaigns to highlight their plight in the late 1990s (I am grateful to Shira Robinson for this information). On cyberactivism, see Jerry Everard, *Virtual States: Globalization, Inequality and the Internet* (London: Routledge, 1999); Alan Scott and John Street, "From Media Politics to E Protest? The Use of Popular Culture and New Media in Parties and Social Movements," in *Culture and Politics in the Information Age: A New Politics*, edited by Frank Webster (London: Routledge, 2001), 32–51. On Zapatistas, see Henry Cleaver, "The Zapatista Effect: The Internet and the Rise of an Alternative Political Fabric," *Journal of International Affairs* 51, no. 2 (1998): 621–640; Aaron Pollack, "Epistemological Struggle and International Organizing: Applying the Experience of the Zapatista Army of National Liberation," Working Paper Series No. 295 (The Hague: Institute of Social Studies, 1999).

26. Palestinian Information Centre, http://www.palestine-info.net; Electronic Intifada, http//www.electronicintifada.net; IndyMedia–Palestine, http://www.jerusalem.indymedia.org.

27. To obtain and maintain an Israeli press permit, journalists have to obey IDF's strict rules, for example, abstaining from venturing into closed areas designated by the IDF. Furthermore, the Israeli government press office is known to have successfully demanded the removal of "troublesome" reporters of major media organizations from Israel-Palestine.

28. Joe Lockard, "Babel Machines and Electronic Universalism," in *Race in Cyber-*

space, edited by Beth E. Kolko, Lisa Nakamura, and Gilbert B. Rodman (London: Routledge, 2000), 181.

29. I do not discuss the interrelations between the Palestinians in Lebanon and the Palestinians in Israel, as cyberconnections exist overwhelmingly between the diasporan Palestinians and those in the Occupied Territories.

30. PalTalk is an online forum that provides not only chatrooms and forums for debate, but the ability to conference and communicate using digital voice technologies readily available on most modern computers. It is open to publics across the world. Despite the uncanny possibilities, the Pal in its name does not refer to Palestine. Hanafi also mentions that an Internet discussion list intended for scientific discussions by professionals abroad eventually focused on debates around "culture, politics, economy . . . in far greater depth than the intended topics of strict technical expertise." See Sari Hanafi, "Reshaping the Geography: Palestinian Communities Networks in Europe and the New Media," *News from Within* 18, no. 1 (2002): 16.

31. Sari Nusseibeh is the scion of a prominent Jerusalem family and head of the Palestinian University of Jerusalem and, until recently, was the pa's representative in Jerusalem. He is considered by many to be an accommodationist and has advocated that within the framework of a two-state solution, Palestinian refugees cannot return to their homes inside Israel. For more on the debates and controversies surrounding Nusseibeh, see Sari Hanafi, "Opening the Debate on the Right of Return," *Middle East Report* 222 (2002): 2–7.

32. Interview with author, Buj al-Barajna camp, Beirut, April 4, 2003.

33. Muhammad al-Durra was a twelve-year-old Gazan boy whose slaying by the IDF on September 30, 2002, was captured on film.

34. Such forms of public relations, effectively employed by Israel, for example, include public relations officers and their research assistants who monitor newspapers and television channels for adverse reports. They counter these reports by persistently pressuring the media outlets. In addition, funding is often available for academic and semiacademic as well as literary works that would benefit a particular cause. Constant production of op-ed columns, as well as educational lobbying that employs a veritable army of eloquent lobbyists is part and parcel of such information dissemination projects.

35. I received this photo from sixteen different friends and acquaintances living in various camps in Lebanon.

36. See especially Mahmud Abdallah Kallam, *Naji al-'Ali: Kamil Turab al-Filastini* [Naji al-'Ali: The entirety of the Palestinian soil] (Beirut: Bissan, 2001); Shafiq Ridwan, *Al-Mulsaq al-Filastini: Mashakil al-Nishat wa al-Tatawwar* [Palestinian posters: Problems of genesis and development] (Damascus: Da'irat al-Thaqafa, Munazzamat al-Tahrir al-Filastini, 1992); and Ted Swedenburg, "The Palestinian Peasant as National Signifier," *Anthropological Quarterly* 63 (1990): 18–30.

37. Zachary Lockman and Joel Beinin, eds., *Intifada: The Palestinian Uprising against Israeli Occupation* (Boston: South End Press, 1989).

38. Interview with author, Nahr al-Barid camp, May 10, 2002.

39. Leaflet, dated April 20, 2002 (in English and Arabic).

40. Swedenburg, "The Palestinian Peasant."

41. Burj al-Shamali, "Letters of Solidarity with the Intifada," available at: http://www.bourjalshamali.org/arabic/inti/poems/rashed.htm. The translation of the Arabic text is my own.

42. Burj al-Shamali, "Letters of Solidarity with the Intifada," previously available at: http://www.bourjalshamali.org/arabic/inti/poems/bourj.htm.

43. Birzeit University, "Across Borders Project," available at: http://www.birzeit.edu/web/apb.html.

44. Across Borders Project, "Statement of Aims," available at: http://www.acrossborders.org.

45. Burj al-Shamali, previously available at http://www.bourjalshamali.org; Nahr al-Barid, http://www.nahrelbared.org.

46. Muna Hamzeh, *Refugees in Our Own Land: Chronicles from a Palestinian Refugee Camp in Bethlehem* (London: Pluto Press, 2001), 3.

47. Birzeit University, "Across Borders Project."

48. Interview with author, Beirut, April 8, 2003.

49. Arjun Appadurai, *Modernity at Large: Cultural Dimensions of Globalization* (Minneapolis: University of Minnesota Press, 1996); Roland Robertson, *Globalization: Social Theory and Global Culture* (New York: Sage, 1992); Saskia Sassen, *Globalization and Its Discontents: Essays on the New Mobility of People and Money* (New York: New Press, 1998) and "Spatialities and Temporalities of the Global: Elements for a Theorization," *Public Culture* 12, no. 1 (2000): 215–232.

50. Appadurai, *Modernity at Large* and "Grassroots Globalization and the Research Imagination," *Public Culture* 12, no. 1 (2000): 1–19; Hanafi, "Reshaping Geography"; Jordan, *The Culture and Politics of Cyberspace.*

51. Shohat, "By the Bitstream of Babylon," 230.

52. Turkle, *Life on the Screen*, 178, 118.

53. Raymond Williams, *The Country and the City* (Oxford: Oxford University Press, 1973), 12.

54. Appadurai, *Modernity at Large*, 33. See Rebecca L. Stein, "'First Contact' and Other Israeli Fictions: Tourism, Globalization, and the Middle East Peace Process," *Public Culture* 14, no. 3 (2002): 515–543.

55. Several studies have shown how gender and racial identities are reconfigured in cyberspace, see Beth E. Kolko, Lisa Nakamura, and Gilbert B. Rodman, eds., *Race in Cyberspace* (London: Routledge, 2000); Turkle, *Life on the Screen*. I have not been able to locate accounts of people switching nationalities online.

56. Quoted in Shohat and Stam, *Unthinking Eurocentrism*, 361, n. 15.

LIVIA ALEXANDER

Is There a Palestinian

Cinema? The National

and Transnational

in Palestinian Film

Production

Issues of nationalism are at the heart of Palestinian cinema, and cultural expressions of nationalism remain central to many Palestinian films. Yet Palestinian dispersal and the absence of a nation-state to support film production raise an important question: Is it possible to speak of a "Palestinian" cinema at all? Palestinian intellectuals have long debated the fragmentation of Palestinian experience and the means of conveying a sense of Palestinian identity and community in the face of exile and dispersal. Commenting on exiles like himself almost twenty years ago, the late Palestinian intellectual and scholar Edward Said maintained, "We are at once too recently formed and too variously experienced to be a population of articulate exiles with a completely systematic vision, and too voluble and troublemaking to simply be a pathetic mass of refugees."[1] More recently, writers both in Palestine and in exile, including Salim Tamari, Rosemary Sayigh, and Fawaz Turki, have begun to examine Palestinian identity by addressing issues such as nostalgia, memory, and class differences, thus transcending the unifying demands of the national struggle.[2] The return of Palestinian intellectual activists to areas controlled by the Palestinian Authority (PA) following the Oslo Accords yielded a new outpouring of literature that addressed the tensions among the image of Palestine carried in the authors' imaginations, their differing historical experiences as refugees or exiles, and the realities they confronted upon returning.[3]

The scattering of the exile population, combined with the absence of a

Palestinian state, has limited the process of Palestinian cinematic production. Scholars working on issues of Palestinian film thus lack the starting point of spatial and temporal continuity and context from which to discuss and analyze Palestinian filmmaking. As a result, it is difficult to speak of a specific style or genre of Palestinian cinema in the same way that one can speak about Italian neorealism or Egyptian popular cinema, except for the thematic focus of the political desire and dream for a Palestinian state. Until the 1980s, studies of national cinemas concentrated primarily on films made within the borders of a given nation-state. These studies frequently regarded films as reflective of a certain national spirit and focused on them as texts, neglecting industrial aspects of production, distribution, and exhibition.[4] In this essay, I follow Andrew Higson's call to examine national cinemas in a larger industrial and cultural context.[5] While these industrial aspects are vital to shaping any film production, in the case of Palestinian filmmaking, the specific context of cultural and geographical dispersion, as experiences of Palestinians both inside historic Palestine and the Occupied Territories and in the diaspora, is particularly important.

I also address the transnational and global influences shaping Palestinian cinematic output by examining film against the centrality of the national narrative and the struggle for independence. Facing two distinct demands, namely, the growing dominance of global capitalism and a Palestinian anticolonial nationalist movement, Palestinian filmmakers have striven for a cosmopolitan film language, which has been the hallmark of other contemporary nation-state cinemas seeking to make their imprint in world markets. My work examines how national affiliations and international awareness affect film production in a society dominated by national conflict. The discussion focuses on two dominant trends in the production of Palestinian films: the first promulgates the motif of land in defining the Palestinian nation and its struggle for decolonization; the second employs the filmic medium to offer a more intellectually complex notion of Palestinianness that supersedes defined geographic boundaries and focuses on individuals and their liberation.

I focus on a time that saw substantial transformations, both historically and cinematically: the first Intifada and the following so-called peace process, an era inaugurated by the Madrid 1991 conference and the Oslo Accords (also known as the Declaration of Principles signed between Israel and the Palestinians in 1993). The uprising signified an important shift in the Palestinian national struggle against Israel, from limited military operations directed by resistance groups in the diaspora to a sweeping popular revolt inside historic Palestine along with the emergence of nation-building institutions. The outbreak of the first Intifada was also a cinematic turning point in that it increased Palestinian access to film and media production, marking a new phase in the visual expression of the conflict's history. Following the signing of the Oslo Accords, the creation of the PA in 1994 established limited self-rule in parts of the Occupied Territories that eventually expanded and essentially created Palestinian enclaves in otherwise Israeli-controlled areas. Palestinian film production was further enhanced by the wider availability of European and U.S. funding from agencies and television stations seeking to encourage cultural production in PA-controlled areas, as well as by the establishment of the Palestinian Broadcasting Corporation and the emergence of numerous local Palestinian television stations and cultural centers. Additional factors contributing to the nascent film production infrastructure in the Occupied Territories were the easing of Israeli restrictions and the seeming promise of an independent Palestinian state and its institutions. In the context of this important era in the history of Palestinian nationalism, I trace some of the main themes and developments in Palestinian-made films against the confluence of the competing forces of nation and exile, local and global, and seek to open the question: What is Palestinian cinema?

National Cinema, Transnational Production

Ongoing struggles by ethnic, national, and religious groups within, but also across, existing national borders with the goal of establishing distinct independent political entities have led some critics to suggest that nationalism remains an important force shaping contemporary politics. Others (including Salman Rushdie and Homi Bhabha) have questioned the relevance of the "national" as a category of analysis and a means of identification in an era of global communications, internationalized markets, and mass migration.[6] When it comes to the national, vital differences exist between literary and cinematic production, as Sumita Chakravarty points out in her study of Indian popular cinema. One essential question concerns form and context, that is, "how cinematic (as opposed to literary) elaborations are 'tied to' a coherent recognizable entity called the nation-state (a political and legal entity of spatial boundedness) within which all discourses of the nation are ultimately anchored."[7] The central role of the state in the study of national cinemas has similarly led Stephen Crofts to propose labeling such cinemas "nation-state cinemas" and not simply "national cinemas."[8] Despite the various local and global challenges, the state plays a prominent role in providing government subsidies for film production, issuing tariffs on the import of films, regulating export, protecting copyrights, even imposing censorship. The Israeli-Palestinian dynamic of occupier-occupied and the absence of Palestinian political sovereignty differentiate the structure of Palestinian cinematic production from those of other nation-state cinemas. These differences have had a decisive influence on Palestinian filmmakers and their representation of and preoccupation with the nation, evident in films made primarily for international markets.

The Palestinian national struggle, on the one hand, and experiences of exile and displacement, on the other, place any discussion of Palestinian cinema between two existing bodies of literature: that of national cinemas, which focuses on films produced within the defined geographic boundaries of the nation-state, and that of exilic, or transnational, cinema that operates beyond national boundaries. Recent studies on national cinemas focus primarily on the postmodern predicament in which the homogenizing demands of national metanarratives give way to the acknowledgment of the diversity and multiplicity of identities and cultures in one given nation-state. In the context of third world cinemas, Ella Shohat and Robert Stam speak of a shift from a national revolutionary third worldist aesthetic to a postindependence, postcolonial alternative, examining the repressions and limits of nationalist discourse. Whereas early third worldist films focused on the public sphere and producing alternative histories to colonialism, later, postcolonial films produced primarily during the 1980s and 1990s "use the camera less as revolutionary weapon than as a monitor of gendered and sexualized realms of the personal and the domestic, seen as integral but repressed aspects of collective history."[9] Yet, many Palestinian filmmakers feel that the continued demands of resistance to occupation leave them unable to engage such postcolonial preoccupations; instead, they remain weighed down by the primacy, even urgency, of the national.

The unique predicament of Palestinian colonial reality now existing in a mostly postcolonial world can be further linked to the emergence of the transnational film genre, defined by Hamid Naficy as "a genre that cuts across previously defined geographical, national, cultural, cinematic, and meta-cinematic boundaries."[10] It is a genre that is produced by filmmakers whom Naficy defines as "accented," differentiating between diasporic filmmaking (the work of filmmakers with hyphenated identities informed along multiple axes) and exilic filmmaking, which focuses more closely on the homeland.[11] In the case of Palestine, neither experience fits squarely into these definitions. Because of the anticolonial struggle for national independence, hyphenated Palestinians are perhaps more preoccupied with their homeland than other hyphenated people. Furthermore, many exilic Palestinian filmmakers, like their colleagues from neighboring Arab countries, are now based in European capitals and make their films as European coproductions that aesthetically fit squarely within the European art house sensibility and circulate their work primarily on the international film festival circuit. But thematically, issues of the national—of oppression and experiences of occupation—continue to take a dominant role in these filmmakers' work. At the same time, the focus, perspective, and emphasis of Palestinian filmmakers often vary considerably between those operating in the Occupied Territories, within the boundaries of historic Palestine, and those in exile and in the diaspora.

Palestinian Cinema

The history of cinema in Palestinian society is closely connected to the conflict with Zionism. Shortly after their formation in the mid-1960s, Palestinian political liberation organizations, including Fatah and the Democratic Front for the Liberation of Palestine, established small film units to project the image of the *fida'i*, the revolutionary Palestinian freedom fighter, in order to mobilize Palestinian audiences in refugee camps throughout the Arab world and to document and promote the national struggle. The documentaries funded by these organizations represented various Palestinian ideological standpoints and experiences, but all were intended to foster Palestinian national identity and present a counternarrative to those of Zionism and Israel.[12] Yet, the multiplicity of small film units, their affiliation with contending Palestinian political groups, and their limited resources and technical know-how resulted in rather low production quantity and quality.[13] In addition, the scattering of Palestinians as refugees and their living in the West Bank first under Jordanian and later under Israeli rule further limited the development of Palestinian cinema. This genre of documentaries disappeared by the 1980s, when the main film organization, the PLO-sponsored Palestinian Film Institute, gradually dissolved after the organization's transfer to Tunisia.

The focus of Palestinian cinema changed radically in the 1980s, most dynamically following the start of the first Intifada in December 1987. For the first time in the history of Palestinian cinema, films were shot in historic Palestine. The earliest two examples of this development are the works of Michel Khleifi, *Fertile Memory* (*al-Dhakira al-khasiba*, 1980) and *Wedding in Galilee* ('*Urs al-Jalil*, 1987). The outbreak of the Intifada allowed filmmakers and media entrepreneurs in the Occupied Territories to assert control over the production of Palestinian imagery as part of the nation-building process that characterized the uprising. The Intifada also spurred the development of a local film production infrastructure due to changes in foreign media news coverage in the Territories. Before the Intifada, Israeli reporters provided news coverage from the Territories for international media networks. As the Intifada intensified and the risk increased for Israeli reporters working in the Occupied Territories, international television networks began handing out videocameras to local Palestinians to cover the events in the area. Foreign news networks gradually employed more Palestinians in a variety of positions, and Palestinian media personnel eventually became the backbone for foreign news coverage in the area. Newly formed Palestinian media companies, often established in collaboration with European and U.S. agencies, helped train Palestinian audiovisual practitioners, provided an environment for Palestinians to produce films about local issues, created the infrastructure for the development of a national cinema inside Palestine, and ultimately reconnected the geographic imagery of the land with its people after what was for many a separation lasting decades.[14]

Despite these attempts to establish a national film industry in Palestine, the reality of the Palestinian diaspora and the demands of the international film market have meant that Palestinian cinema, like other world cinemas today, operates in a transnational context. The absence of a nation-state to support the development of an indigenous film industry has accentuated filmmakers' need for external funding for production, distribution, and exhibition. In addition, despite rigorous efforts to train film personnel in Palestine, the nascent local film infrastructure and political realities often require Palestinian filmmakers to rely on European or Israeli film crews. Most contemporary Palestinian filmmakers were trained in Europe or the United States (including Michel and George Khleifi, Elia Suleiman, Sobhi al-Zobaidi, Azza El-Hassan, and Najwa Najjar). Others, such as Rashid Masharawi and Nizar Hassan, gained their initial experience by working in Israeli film and television. Palestinian filmmakers often must also comply with the demands of international funding agencies to employ a certain quota of their own nationals.[15] This incorporation of Palestinian filmmakers into the Euro-American system of production, distribution, and exhibition steered Palestinian films in the direction of global transnational markets.

The transnational context of Palestinian film production is reinforced by the absence of local venues inside historic Palestine and the Occupied Territories for exhibiting filmmakers' works, which further complicates the question of what Palestinian cinema is. As Paul Willemen points out, the large capital investment involved in film production means that unless a large domestic market is available, films increasingly appeal to international audiences to achieve the largest possible number of viewers and the greatest potential profit margins. These market conditions have shaped the creation of films addressing the broadest common denominator with an eye for global viewers.[16] In the case of Palestinian film, the local market is virtually nonexistent. Until the early 1990s, the only exposure Palestinians in Israel and the Occupied Territories had to Arab cinema was through the films, almost entirely Egyptian, that were shown on Israeli television and Arab channels. Palestinians might read about Palestinian films, but they had few chances to view them. In fact, people in New York are still more likely to watch a Palestinian film than are residents of Nablus.[17] Over several decades, the Israeli occupiers closed down cinemas in major Palestinian cities one by one, and the clashes of the first Intifada struck the final blow to any remaining theaters. Cinemas in Palestinian communities inside Israel also closed their doors due to the growing conservative influence of the Islamic movement as well as competition from home video. Attempts to develop local venues during the post-Oslo era came to a screeching halt with the outbreak of the second Intifada in September 2000, and their number remains limited.

In the late 1980s and through the 1990s, funding from institutions such as European television networks created a different frame of reference from Palestinian film production of the 1960s and inspired a move toward films made for international consumption. This trend has resulted in a cinema addressing universal sensibilities, the metropolitan in-vogue issues of identity politics and human rights. In this international context, Palestinian filmmakers often projected a unified image of Palestine that superseded the internal conflicts that had emerged in Palestinian society, especially as the Intifada wore on and the peace process that followed faltered. The use of Israeli funds by Palestinian filmmakers who are also citizens of Israel further complicates the picture, because their reliance on such funds limits the extent to which they can criticize Zionism, while they simultaneously risk promoting Israel's self-image as liberal and democratic. Israeli government institutions often view the sponsorship of such films as an amiable framework in which to promote their vision of coexistence without ever having to deal with Palestinian indignation toward the decades-old occupation. For Palestinian filmmakers, these issues raise an additional difficulty with labeling their films as Palestinian.[18] Furthermore, residents of the Occupied Territories, as well as other Arab states, have grown wary of the "Israeli connection" of these Palestinian-Israeli filmmakers, fearing that the presentation of such films at Arab film festivals may signal a normalization of relations with Israel.[19]

Tension between national ideology in film production, the realities on the ground inside historic Palestine and the Occupied Territories, and global patterns of training, funding, and exhibition all animate contemporary Palestinian filmmaking. Some theorists, such as Ernest Gellner and, more recently, Laura Marks, have called for the breakdown of the assumed correlation between nationalism and a geopolitical landscape and between culture and land, but in Palestinian cinema the link remains relevant. National factors, namely, the absence of a political entity and the centrality of the national struggle, continue to dominate and shape Palestinian production. Yet, Palestinians' physical and emotional displacement from their original homeland—even if they continue to live there as exiles, refugees, or occupied people—engenders a transnational context of film production. All these factors combine to create a cinema that is neither national nor transnational, but a hybrid cinema that offers a complex relationship between the two. The tension between these two poles in contemporary Palestinian filmmaking is most actively pronounced in the emergence of two dominant trends of cinema, both influenced and shaped by the contradictions of the national and the transnational, homeland and exile. The first trend focuses on a nationalist message that advocates liberation through the primacy of Palestinian land; the second, on the liberation, first and foremost, of the Palestinian people.

Cinema of National Liberation:
From Freedom Fighter to Victim

The dominant language of national struggle against Israel left little room for addressing the tensions, inner rivalries, and debates that emerged in Palestinian society as the Intifada continued. As Palestine remains occupied, is transformed or destroyed, Palestinian films concentrate on the need to liberate the usurped homeland. This focus has created a particular style of filmmaking that emphasizes the collective and often claustrophobic space to which individual members of society are subjected. Such films frequently use tight frames and are set in closed spaces: inside homes or courtyards or within the boundaries of a specific village. Naficy identifies this style in independent transnational cinema as a means of signaling liminal spaces between filmmakers' societies of residence and origin. Yet, in a nationally contested situation such as the Palestinian case, these same claustrophobic spaces are employed to mark out a national space that is a site of both home and exile, resistance and confinement.[20] Other films employ familiar images from the Palestinian collective visual archive that mark out the national space, such as olive groves, close shots of the land, and keys to Palestinian homes left behind in 1948.

The dominance of the Palestinian collective national narrative is nowhere more evident than in the plot and character development of many Palestinian films, as if, in the absence of a physical space, the mere production of the film can create a figurative space where the various aspects of the nation can be brought together. In *Long Days in Gaza* (*Ayyam tawila fi Ghazza*, 1991), produced for the BBC, Rashid Masharawi conceals his interviewees' names and places of residence, and by doing so further pushes the film's argument for the collective, sweeping, shared character of Palestinian resistance. In addition to numerous scenes shot in the interviewees' homes, *Long Days in Gaza* includes footage of daily street life in the Gaza Strip under the watchful eye of the Israeli army. Thus, the film creates a contrast between the external, foreign occupation and the inner world of Palestinians, where resistance is carried out ad infinitum.

In a similar fashion, Masharawi frames his film *Curfew* (*Hatta ish'arin akhir*, 1994) within the national struggle, which supersedes the protagonists' individual lives and subjectivity (see figure 5). *Curfew* portrays the Raji family as an undifferentiated unit representing the collective facets of the nation. Like other Palestinian films from this period, such as *Wedding in Galilee* and *The Milky Way* (*Darab al-tabbanat*, Ali Nassar, 1998), the film is a collage of local dialects and locations, jarring to the Arabic-speaking viewer.[21] Bringing together different parts of Palestinian society, the film presents the nation as its main protagonist. There is no single, conventional hero to carry the weight of the plot, but the sum of its fragments represented by the film's numerous characters. Marcia Landy points out that the family fulfills a particular function in national narrative: "The national narrative relies on a melodramatic scenario in which the forces of light and darkness collide to produce the enlightened and just nation . . . The lan-

FIGURE 5. Publicity still for *Curfew*. Photo courtesy of New Yorker Films.

guage of the nation state is built upon discourses of the family, the prodigal son, the obedient daughter, the wise father law-giver. The face of the loyal subject is the mirror of this family bred from the 'family of nations.'"[22]

Just as Landy describes, Masharawi conjures national and familial history by having each of the film's characters represent a particular aspect of the Palestinian nation, ultimately forming a collective identity. Through this use of allegory, which Ismail Xavier argues is a means of commenting on historical moments of violence and repression, the film promotes national virtues such as loyalty, suffering, service, sacrifice, and loss.[23] The trigger of pain and suffering is Israeli occupation, but good and evil are internal: the struggle between disloyal and patriotic Palestinians teases out the values hailed for creating a virtuous nation. *Curfew*, as well as *The Tale of the Three Jewels* (*Hikayat al-jawahir al-thalatha*, Michel Khleifi, 1994), discussed below, depicts exilic Palestinians in a negative light, as people who by their departure and pursuit of personal gain have betrayed their people and their land.[24] However, exile has a dialectical role in *Curfew*: the family stubbornly continues to read aloud a letter from a son living in Europe, who represents the scattered nation, despite constant interruptions by the Israeli occupying forces, and the voices inside the house eventually overcome the off-screen sounds of the Israeli army announcing another curfew.

Although tensions remain between exilic and resident Palestinians, they are inextricably part of the same nation, as the repeated reading of the letter throughout the film stands as a metonym for the threads tying them together as one nation.

The emphasis on nationalist discourse often results in a focus on the land as a recurring theme that captures the soul and essence of the Palestinian nation. From this emerges a particular type of character who possesses the Palestinian virtues of perseverance and sacrifice for the sake of reclaiming the land.[25] The dominance of the land in Palestinian film production raises important questions regarding the relationship between individuals and the demands of the national culture. The context of national struggle has generally resulted in a hegemonic public-national landscape for Palestinian filmmakers, though one often fraught with contending experiences of exile and displacement that breach the strong connection advocated between culture and land.

In *The Tale of the Three Jewels* land is a focus of nostalgia for Nazareth-born and Belgian-based Michel Khleifi. Like much of his other work, *The Tale of the Three Jewels* is filtered through Khleifi's exilic perspective as he reinscribes the imagery of the Gaza Strip, usually associated with poverty and crowded camps, with elements of bounty and the orange grove as a symbol of pre-1948 Palestinian prosperity. In doing so, Khleifi seeks to create a visual discourse of liberation deeply rooted in the land. A ground-level camera shows young Palestinian fighters as they emerge from among the low bushes, emphasizing their oneness with the land.[26] Though realist in its portrayal of the Palestinian struggle, this bond is depicted through melodramatic elements of love, magic, and primordial knowledge of the land and its history. Some of the more fantastic elements are derived from *A Thousand and One Nights*, effectively repackaging the story of the land in a manner palatable to cosmopolitan audiences. The love story between two children, the Gypsy girl 'Aida (Hana' Na'ma) and the Palestinian boy Yusuf (Muhammad Nahhal), takes place away from the Intifada, in beautiful sites such as a lush oasis on the fringes of a refugee camp and Gaza's beach. The open skies continuously interlaced into the film's texture suggest a figurative space in nature where Palestinians exist away from Israeli occupation. In these sites, as well as in Yusuf's dreams of magical figures of ancient wisdom, there is no sign of, and perhaps no room for, the enemy. Thus, elements of natural beauty and magic coalesce to cancel out and rise above the harsh reality of occupation, liberating the film's protagonists.

Curiously, the film reveals the tension in Khleifi's work between land and people. Gaza, as home for some but exile for many others, bears the impossible task of being the symbol of both Palestinians' connection to the land and their nomadic existence.

The triumph of transnational capitalism and globalism, however, has left its mark on these films that emphasize the urgency of liberating Palestinian land: in a trend that has shaped postcolonial third world filmmaking in general, the revolutionary nationalist third worldist cinema popular in the 1960s and 1970s has withered, replaced by a depoliticized, universally humanist cinema.[27] In spite of increased militancy in Palestinian society, the films set in the first Intifada period display little violence and do not foreground the armed struggle. On one level, this is in keeping with the Palestinian political movement's departure from the image of the terrorist to that of the stone thrower during this period. On another level, Palestinian filmmakers, predominantly working on coproductions for international consumption, have shied away from images that would reinforce Western stereotypes of the violent Palestinian. Instead, filmmakers seeking to go beyond redundant renditions of Israeli-Palestinian confrontations have focused on the humanist aspect of their struggle, highlighting the Palestinian plight under the heavy boot of Israeli occupation. Thus, the press release for *Chronicle of a Disappearance* (*Sijill Ikhtifa'*, Elia Suleiman, 1996) includes the following statement: "*Chronicle of a Disappearance* does not take a position on the political impasse in the Middle East. Rather, the film is a personal meditation upon the spiritual effect of political instability on the Palestinian people, their psyche, their identity. As such, it is an invaluable contribution to the struggle for peace in the region."[28] As is the case with other reviews of Palestinian films in the U.S. press, a review of *The Tale of the Three Jewels* in *Variety* conveys the film's strong humanist appeal to cosmopolitan audiences in similar words: "The stark contrast between the grim realities of life in contemporary Gaza and a young boy's liberating imagination imbue the Palestinian *Tale of the Three Jewels* with a haunting quality . . . [It] has a universality that should earn it a berth on the fest circuit and selected arthouse dates in sophisticated markets."[29]

The Tale of the Three Jewels uses universal themes of nonviolent resilience that emphasize Palestinian victimhood and peace-seeking goals. While such a focus helps reverse the common dichotomy of a peace-seeking Israel and terrorist Palestinians, this approach both deprives Palestinians of their greatest asset—the vitality of their long and active struggle against Israeli occupation—and echoes Israel's own long-standing claim of victimhood. Because the national metanarrative has been so dominant in these productions, some Palestinian filmmakers have avoided tackling other issues that pervade daily life and form the basis of numerous debates on television and newspapers in the Occupied Territories, such as whether Palestinians would take up the right of return; the challenges encountered by women returning from Israeli jails; and debates between Fatahists and Islamists about negotiating with Israel.

Cinema of People's Liberation

The contradictory realities of the post-Oslo era—liberation on the one hand, and continued occupation on the other—has led some Palestinian filmmakers to display a tenuous relationship to their homeland. They have taken on what Shohat defines as a "post-Third-Worldist perspective," an approach that examines the factions that divide third world nations, while still accepting the legitimacy of the anticolonial movement.[30] In Israel-Palestine, these divisions were literal and geographical. The 1993 Oslo Accords presumably liberated parts of the land, but Israeli occupation continued in much of the West Bank and Gaza, with major restrictions on Palestinians' movement, limited job opportunities, and continued land confiscation. The construction of settlements and bypass roads reinforced the Bantustanization of the Occupied Territories.

The establishment of the Palestinian Authority in 1994 and the return of Palestinian leadership from exile carried the promise of a first step toward an independent Palestinian state. Yet, PA officials, enjoying access to resources and power, often abused their newly acquired means of control, and corruption, mismanagement, and excessive use of repressive measures became commonplace. The factionalism of the late first Intifada era intensified as the various groups vied for their share of the new regime.

The frenzied debates of this period inspired filmmakers to address a variety of internal issues, including women's rights, social taboos, domestic violence, and environmental damage.[31] During this period, the national liberation motif persisted in Palestinian film, but this shift in focus to the people of Palestine marks a second trend, characterized by the rise and demise of hopes for Palestinian independence, a trend that more critically explores the common icons of Palestinian nationalism and focuses on the need for people's liberation. In contrast to the prevailing representation of the Palestinian subject as fixed in history, characteristic of the national liberation trend, some films of this second trend, particularly in this post-Oslo era, have gone on to criticize the concept of a "pure" Palestinian.

Perhaps not surprisingly, the two filmmakers who lead this trend, Elia Suleiman and Nizar Hassan, are 1948 Palestinians, a minority in Israel who have steadfastly held on to cultural identity in the face of the territorial loss of Palestine to the Jewish state. Ironically, these two vociferous critics are among those who also most adamantly express Palestinian demands for national recognition. But the demand surpasses geographic borders and focuses instead on the individuals who compose the nation and their set of cultural references, as both filmmakers appear in their films in journeys of self-investigation and social exploration characteristic of the transnational genre and the critical inquiries prevailing among Western intellectual circles. In postmodernist fashion, both Hassan and Suleiman avoid telling a linear story, but instead provide small vignettes arranged to form a rhizome, a botanical term that Deleuze and Guattari employ to suggest something that has "no beginning or end; it is always in the middle, between things, interbeing, *intermezzo*."[32]

In one of the intertitles in *Chronicle of a Disappearance*, Suleiman sarcastically asks, "To be or not to be Palestinian?" This question animates most of his work, marked by his bifocal approach as both an insider and an outsider, a filmmaker returning to his homeland after twelve years of voluntary exile. While he ridicules vacuous national slogans of land and identity, be they Israeli, Palestinian, or Arab, he demonstrates a yearning to belong. Framing his film through doors and windows or gazing into spaces, Suleiman conveys his position as an eternal outsider, but also as an astute social commentator. He concludes the first part of the film, labeled as a personal diary and taking place in his hometown of Nazareth, by looking at slides taken from the film the way one would thumb through one's own journal. The act of looking at these images, his own among them, complicates his position as a filmmaker creating his composition, as object of a self-reflective gaze, and toward his other filmic subjects. Suleiman does not seek to represent all Palestinian experience. Refusing to anchor the film in any specific "realistic" set, he moves his films to the level of allegorical contemplations on identity. The Palestinian reality is colonial, but Suleiman prefers a symbolic exploration of its postcolonial terms dominant in the metropolitan centers of the West by focusing on the fragmentation of space and meaning. One may argue that the film is a disconnected meditation, yet it anchors the collective identity above all in the individuals that constitute it, a perspective informed by the fact that Suleiman himself owes his Palestinian identity not to his presence in the land of Palestine, but to his relationship with his parents. He dedicates the film to them, whom he calls "the last homeland."

In many ways, *Chronicle of a Disappearance* is a direct continuation, both thematically and cinematically, of Suleiman's earlier work. As in *Introduction to the End of an Argument* (*Muqaddima li-nihayat jidal*, 1990) and *Homage by Assassination* (1991), he relies on visual, nonverbal strategies to provoke questions about Palestinian identity, the Israeli-Palestinian conflict, media misrepresentations, and the touristic marketing of Palestine. It is a strategy that is characteristic of what Laura Marks defines as intercultural cinema preoccupied with excavating cultural memory. This cinema, she argues, demonstrates "a lack of faith in the visual archive's ability to represent cultural memory." Alternatively, silence, absence, and hesitation all expose an elusive sense of memory dominated by the gaps that exist in between available records of official history and memory.[33] Suleiman, playing the main character in both *Homage by Assassination* and *Chronicle of a Disappearance*, remains silent, and his attempts to communicate fail. His emphasis on the absurd transforms bleakly familiar images into comical parodies. He pokes fun at the consumption of Palestine as the Holy Land, promoted by a vigorous Israeli tourism industry, by including a shot of "the natives," a bored Suleiman and a friend merely sitting at a storefront smoking. Suleiman presents tourist consumption and Israeli Zionist discourses of heroism, an ancient connection to the land, and agricultural bounty associated with Zionist pioneer ideology through postcard images aimlessly swinging on a squeaky rack.

For Suleiman, Palestinians have little cultural memory left to retrieve because Zionism has appropriated the past of both the country and its people. His Palestinian characters are suspended in a detached present. As Marks points out, even after the deconstruction of colonial history is complete, "no simple truth is uncovered," which sparks the realization that "the histories that are lost are lost for good."[34] Instead of retrieving this lost cultural memory, *Chronicle of a Disappearance* shows the evaporation of Palestinian identity in the context of post-Oslo realities. The film is framed by lethargy, opening and closing with images of people sleeping, laced throughout with characters napping or staring sullenly into the distance. It depicts a reality dominated by nothingness; the film documents repeated scenes of empty acts. Men are constantly fighting and making up. Nazareth is a city where nothing happens; Jerusalem is empty of its inhabitants. Space is very focalized: a house, a theater, a café, a store. Similarly, characters appear individually on the screen or in small groups, telling short anecdotes. There is no real public space, either physically or psychologically, where broader groups socialize or interact. There is no "story." There is only an individualized space, both intimate and constricting, both home and exile, both self and nation.

In contrast to Suleiman's films, Nizar Hassan's work is more organically rooted in a place and its people, his film being targeted, as he testifies, first and foremost at Palestinian audiences.[35] His work is most often discussed in Israeli intellectual circles, however, so his success in reaching Palestinians during this time is debatable.[36] Though he strives to create a new radical voice in Palestinian cinema, he is also a recipient of funding and critical acclaim from the same Israeli establishment that he seeks to examine for its responsibility for his people's oppression. Hassan, however, avoids the theme of victimization found in other Palestinian films and sets out instead to explore the dynamics of personal, social, political, and cultural relations dominating primarily Israeli Palestinian society.[37] His films show the interlocking effects of inner Palestinian conflicts and contradictions on the one hand, and Israeli occupation on the other. Palestinian citizens of Israel are subjected to tensions on multiple levels. They live in their own homeland within a Jewish state, yet also outside of it. They are a part of Palestinian society, but live as second-class citizens in a Zionist Israeli state. These tensions create a collage of various gradations of identity that have placed 1948 Palestinians in the unique historical predicament that Hassan depicts.

Hassan constructs his films as journeys of inquiry into the intricacies of Palestinian society. There is no "answer" to his questions, nor does he seek a finite conclusion, a single understanding of the nationalist or, alternatively, Zionist paradigms. Hassan sees himself and his work as Palestinian above all, but the question of what a Palestinian is remains open. This debatable identity is evident in his documentary film *Ustura* (1998, literally meaning "fable," although not translated by the filmmaker). In the film, the Nijm family passes around the cover of a magazine; no one can agree on the identity of the family member depicted there. The knotty trajectory of the Nijm family crisscrosses ideological paths and geographic borders, its members dispersed from the pre-1948 Palestinian village of 'Asfuriya to Jordan, to Germany, and back to Palestine-Israel. Left in Palestine with his grandparents, Salim, arguably a collaborator, meets only partial success in his attempts to reunite his family in Palestine. Salim's aunt and mother, arguing about the details of their departure from Palestine, open a discussion of the slippery dynamics of memory with the passage of time and its interpretation. In the process, *Ustura* deconstructs the concept of return (*'awda*), central to Palestinian national ideology, into little splinters of a tragic reality that has torn apart the Nijm family.

An anthropologist by training, Hassan adopts the discipline's self-reflexive approach in his films, placing himself within his films' discursive formations. In *Ustura*, whereas his Palestinian protagonist Salim remains passively quiet, Hassan demands from outside the frame that Salim's Israeli employer answer questions that Salim would or could not ask himself. Hassan employs camera angles and character positioning in the frame to suggest or subvert existing power hierarchies between filmmaker and subject, men and women, Israelis and Palestinians. In *Yasmine* (1996), a documentary about a woman imprisoned for her involvement in the murder of her sister, Hassan includes a conversation with his sister that reveals his own complicity in the same problematic gender relations he seeks to criticize. The subjects' interaction with the filmmaker is an integral part of the story. The documentary's "truth" is constantly questioned as the filmic subjects, including Hassan, discuss, debate, and argue about it.

For Hassan, the act of filmmaking is an essential ingredient in the film's narrative. In a sense, the film crew is the main protagonist, as Hassan uses clips of the crew at work as continuity shots, connecting the interviewees and crew to the production of the film. By emphasizing the construction process of filmmaking, Hassan teases out his role as a storyteller drawing on different parts of society that might be brought together only by such a film as *Ustura*. The film is based on the family legend, yet, as the title suggests, it is also a fable or a myth in that it is arranged by Hassan's stream-of-consciousness, storyteller-style voice-over. He tells stories of individual people and refuses to offer any simple closure.

Conclusion

I have attempted to provide an analytical framework in which to discuss Palestinian films produced during the period corresponding with the first Intifada and the "peace process." In nation-building institutions in the Occupied Territories, Palestinian filmmakers found a new locus for the development of Palestinian film production. At the same time, this period also saw the integration of Palestinian filmmakers into transnational markets of production, distribution, and exhibition. The confluence of the national and transnational elements informs both trends of Palestinian filmmaking—national liberation and people's liberation—identified in this essay. These two trends, however, cannot be regarded as two distinct modes of filmmaking that correspond to discrete time periods marked first by the Intifada and later by the circumstances of the post-Oslo era. Many of the national liberation films were actually produced immediately following Oslo and participated in the fortification of the Palestinian national narrative. Other films, focused on deconstructing the Palestinian national narrative, were actually in production during the first Intifada. The points of convergence and contrast between these two trends, however, serve as an important indicator of the challenges and shifts experienced by Palestinians during this significant period in Palestinian history.

The Palestinian struggle for independence continues to inform political as well as cultural discourse. The initial promise that came with the Oslo Accords, the budding state, the short-lived easing of Israeli restrictions in certain areas of Palestinian life, and the challenges that came with the increasing corruption of the PA and the Accords' failures contributed to the shaping of a more reflective though still nationally committed mode of Palestinian film production. The ongoing dominance of the national in Palestinian film is especially evident in films produced following the outbreak of the second, or al-Aqsa, Intifada in September 2000 and the renewed intensification of the national struggle. At the same time, an examination of the two trends dominating Palestinian film production must also be situated within the multiplicity of realities for Palestinian filmmakers working worldwide, demonstrating how issues such as nostalgia, exile, the dominance of national icons, and the lines demarcating the different experiences of 1948, 1967, and diasporic Palestinians continue to shape and inform their productions.

The absence of a nation-state to support local production has in one sense freed Palestinian filmmakers from any ties to a government-directed national project. Because of the anticolonial context of Palestinian film production and its presentation to international audiences, little scrutiny is directed toward the national narrative itself, as internal discourses within Palestinian society remain largely on the margins. Palestinian cinemas competing in the international art film market are partly driven by the perceived commercial demands of a market with a decidedly Western orientation. However, nationalism is also dominant for domestic audiences inside historic Palestine and the Occupied Territories. Filmmakers often feel compelled to focus on issues that intrigue the international market and flatter its tastes and sensibilities. Even poverty is packaged to look appealing or poetic. In spite of these limitations, filmmakers' need to operate in the context of world cinema has helped bring Palestinian filmmaking and the Palestinian national struggle to international attention. For many Palestinian filmmakers, the establishment of a national cinema is a self-evident aspiration that would affirm the existence of the nation. While a filmmaker like Suleiman might satirize the national narrative by employing Jacques Tati–like language inspired by French existentialism, that same Palestinian narrative continues to inform his films. The hybrid form that Palestinian filmmaking has taken is the result of ongoing tensions promoting the Palestinian homeland, representing the exilic experience of many of its practitioners, and producing cinema under transnational conditions.

Notes

1. See Edward Said, *After the Last Sky* (Boston: Faber and Faber, 1986), 6.

2. Salim Tamari, "Bourgeois Nostalgia and Exile Narratives," in *Homelands: Poetic Power and the Politics of Space*, edited by Ron Robin and Bo Strath (Berlin: Peter Lang, 2003); Rosemary Sayigh, "Palestinian Camp Women as Tellers of History," *Journal of Palestine Studies* 27, no. 2 (winter 1998): 42–58; Fawaz Turki, *Exile's Return: The Making of a Palestinian American* (New York: Free Press, 1993).

3. See, for example, Murid Barghuthi, *I Saw Ramallah* (Cairo: American University in Cairo Press, 2000); Ghassan Zaqtan, "Nafy al-manfa" [The negation of exile], *al-Karmil* 51 (spring 1997): 141–145. A number of other returnees' testimonies were published in the same issue of the latter source: see Hasan Khadar, "Hal kuntu huna?" [Was I here?], 115–124; Zakariya Muhammad, "Al-'uzm wa-al-dhahab" [Grandeur and gold], 125–140.

4. Stephen Crofts, "Concepts of National Cinema," in *World Cinema: Critical Approaches*, edited by John Hill and Pamela Church Gibson (Oxford: Oxford University Press, 2000), 2.

5. Andrew Higson, "The Concept of National Cinema," *Screen* 30, no. 4 (1989): 36–46.

6. In a 1997 article published in *Harper's*, Salman Rushdie questions the role of nationalism against a backdrop of globalization, a stance particularly relevant to the questions posed by this essay: "Closed systems have always appealed to writers. This is why so much writing deals with prisons, police forces, hospitals, schools. Is the nation a closed system? In this internationalized moment, can any system remain closed? Nationalism is that 'revolt against history' that seeks to close what cannot any longer be closed. To fence in what should be frontierless. Good writing assumes a frontierless nation. Writers who serve frontiers have become border guards." Salman Rushdie, "Notes on Writing and the Nation," *Harper's*, September 1997, 24. See also Timothy Brennan, *Salman Rushdie and the Third World: Myths of the Nation* (New York:

St. Martin's Press, 1989); Homi Bhabha, *The Location of Culture* (London: Routledge, 1994); Frederick Buell, *National Culture and the New Global System* (Baltimore: Johns Hopkins University Press, 1994).

7. Sumita S. Chakravarty, *National Identity in Indian Popular Cinema, 1947–1987* (Austin: University of Texas Press, 1993), 12.

8. Crofts, "Concepts of National Cinema," 2.

9. Ella Shohat and Robert Stam, *Unthinking Eurocentrism: Multiculturalism and the Media* (New York: Routledge, 1994), 288.

10. Hamid Naficy, "Phobic Spaces and Liminal Panics: Independent Transnational Film Genre," *East-West Film Journal* 8, no. 2 (1994): 1–30.

11. Hamid Naficy, *Accented Cinema: Exilic and Diasporic Filmmaking* (Princeton: Princeton University Press, 2001), 14.

12. Husayn al-'Awdat, *al-Sinima wa-al-qadiya al-Filastiniya* [Cinema and the Palestinian question] (Damascus: al-Ahali, 1987), 61–100; Walid Shamit and Guy Hennebelle, eds., *Filastin fi al-sinima* [Palestine in cinema] (Beirut: Fajr, 1980), 13–21.

13. Husayn al-'Awdat maintains that an important reason for the weakness of early Palestinian film production was the lack of cinematic unity, a crucial demand if film production is to be an important tool in the Palestinian national project. See al-'Awdat, *Al-Sinima wa-al-qadiya al-Filastiniya*, 83–100. Calls in support of uniting all film institutions appeared, for instance, in the periodical *Al-Sura al-Filastiniya*, no. 1 (1978): 1, and no. 2 (1979): 2–3.

14. Al-Quds Television Production (ATP) and the Jerusalem Film Institute (JFI), founded in 1990 and 1991, respectively, were the two main production companies established to train Palestinians in the audiovisual field and raise the profile of cinema in Palestine. The European Union program Med Media, the Ford Foundation, the National Endowment for Democracy, and the Soros Foundation, as well as IKON Television and the BBC, are but a few such agencies. Palestinian millionaires donating to charities, primarily the Welfare Association, have also supported various NGO promotional films as well as other Palestinian films, though this kind of funding played a smaller and more sporadic role.

15. The cinematography, editing, sound, and art direction of Elia Suleiman's *Chronicle of a Disappearance*, for example, were primarily European, while the film's executive director was an Israeli who facilitated the collaboration of Israeli institutions that would not otherwise have cooperated with a Palestinian project. A similar situation has persisted in other Palestinian films, especially features such as *Curfew*, *The Tale of the Three Jewels*, and *The Milky Way*.

16. Paul Willemen, *Looks and Frictions: Essays in Cultural Studies and Film Theory* (Bloomington: Indiana University Press, 1994), 211–212.

17. During my 1995 research trip to Palestine, most video-store owners were surprised at my inquiry about the availability of Palestinian films. "Palestinian films?" they would respond. "There are no Palestinian films." In the early 1990s al-Quds Media Production, a Palestinian media group, organized a film festival in Gaza. More recently, the Columbia University–based project *Dreams of a Nation*, in collaboration with Yabous Productions, launched a new Palestinian film festival held in Jerusalem,

Ramallah, Nazareth, and Gaza in February 2004. See http://www.yabous.org/filmfes/index.html.

18. In the Israeli English-language magazine *Jerusalem Report*, Ilene R. Prusher gives an account of Nizar Hassan's difficulties with the Israeli New Fund for Film and Television when he tried to label his film *Yasmine* (1996) Palestinian. Ilene R. Prusher, "Oslo Is Not Even Calling," *Jerusalem Report* (May 1, 1997): 42–43. The only Palestinian thus far to receive support from this fund, Hassan is obliged to include the Fund's logo, "Hebrew cultural production," at the opening of his films.

19. For example, Muhammad Bakri's film *1948* is reported in an Israeli newspaper to have been only clandestinely screened at the Cairo film festival; see Yirmi Amir, review of the Cairo International Film Festival, *Yidi'ot Aharonot*, December 9, 1998. Ali Nassar was unable to distribute his film *The Milky Way* in Tunis because he is an Israeli citizen; the same was true for Elia Suleiman, who made his debut feature, *Chronicle of a Disappearance*, with support from the Israeli Fund for the Promotion of Quality Films.

20. Naficy, "Phobic Spaces and Liminal Panics," 14–23.

21. Although *Curfew* takes place in Gaza, the characters' dialect reveals that the film was actually shot in Nazareth. See al-Amir 'Abaza, "Halamtu bil-Qahira . . . wa-lam ufakkir fi ja'izatiha al-dhahabiya!" [I dreamed of Cairo . . . but I never imagined first prize!], interview with Rashid Masharawi, *al-Kawakib*, December 21, 1993, 13. Palestinian directors' reliance on nonprofessional actors, or their mere negligence, could also be seen as a contributing factor to the medley of dialects. In *Wedding in Galilee*, for example, a few actors spoke with a Moroccan dialect, many with a Gaza dialect, and the rest were divided between urban and rural dialects. I am grateful to Salim Tamari for bringing this patchwork of dialects to my attention.

22. Marcia Landy, "History, Folklore, and Common Sense: Sembène's Films and Discourses of Postcoloniality," in *Postcolonial Discourse and Changing Cultural Contexts: Theory and Criticism*, edited by Gita Rajan and Radhika Mohanram (Westport, Conn.: Greenwood Press, 1995), 175–176. A different perspective is provided by Ismail Xavier, who discusses the role of the family in 1960s and 1970s Brazilian cinema not as a marker of unity but as an allegory for the social problems plaguing the nation. See Ismail Xavier, *Allegories of Underdevelopment: Aesthetics and Politics in Modern Brazilian Cinema* (Minneapolis: University of Minnesota Press, 1997), 246–254.

23. Ismail Xavier, "Historical Allegory," in *A Companion to Film Theory*, edited by Toby Miller and Robert Stam (Oxford: Blackwell, 1999), 360.

24. Incidentally, this view calls to mind the similar Israeli attitude toward Israelis who have left the country.

25. It was only after 1993, with the proliferation of local television stations, that social concerns began to be addressed on TV. Political issues, however, continue to be a thornier issue, as the PA's censorship has to some extent replaced Israel's repressive policies that curbed free political expression. Israeli policies that sought the fragmentation of the area in order to break down Palestinian resistance resulted in the multiplicity of television stations throughout the West Bank, such as Nablus TV in Nablus, Watan and al-Quds TV in Ramallah, al-Amal and al-Mustaqbal Television in Hebron,

and Shepards' TV in Bethlehem. Each isolated community had its own station. Despite limitations, producers took television cameras into the streets, opened phone lines for audiences to call the studio, and created a new public space where issues such as drug abuse, youth concerns, suicide, gender relations, education, and culture could be discussed. This constitutes an important step toward greater participation in discussing Palestinian daily life.

26. Nationally oriented Israeli films use similar strategies. See Ella Shohat's discussion of *Oded the Wanderer* (*Oded ha-noded*, Haim Halachmi, 1933) in *Israeli Cinema: East/West and the Politics of Representation* (Austin: University of Texas Press, 1989), 29–31.

27. See Robert Stam, *Film Theory: An Introduction* (Oxford: Blackwell, 1999), 281–282; Crofts, "Concepts of National Cinema," 1–10.

28. *Chronicle of a Disappearance*, International Film Circuit, Inc., press release, n.d.

29. Leonard Klady, review of *The Tale of the Three Jewels*, *Variety*, June 5, 1995. See also Lawrence Van Gelder, "As Life Goes on or Not," review of *The Milky Way* (film by Ali Nassar), *New York Times*, January 20, 1999.

30. Ella Shohat, "Framing Post-Third-World Culture: Gender and Nation in Middle Eastern/North African Film and Video," *Jouvert: A Journal of Postcolonial Studies* 1, no. 1 (1997), http://social.chass.ncsu.edu/jouvert/viii/shohat.htm.

31. Sobhi al-Zobaidi's documentary *Women in the Sun* (*Nisa' fi al-Shams*, 1998), a title inspired by Ghassan Kanafani's well-known novel *Men in the Sun*, explores a phenomenon previously considered taboo: the growing number of Palestinian youth committing suicide. In her film *The Veiled Hope* (*L'espoir Voilé: Femmes de Palestine*, 1996), Norma Marcos, a native of Bethlehem operating out of Paris, is one of the few women filmmakers to challenge the subjugation of women in Palestinian national discourse. The explosion of activities by Western-funded women's NGOs during this time also led to a surge of documentary films dealing with women's issues, such as *The Invisible Half* (*ul-Nusf al-Gha'ib*, Muhammad Sawalme, 1995), *Early Marriage in Palestine* (*al-Zawaj al-Mubakkar fi Filastin*, International Association for Family Planning, n.d.), and *Sinbad Is a She* (*Hiya Sinbad*, Azza El-Hassan, 1999). The heightened attention to gender issues in these films has sparked a spirited debate in Palestinian society regarding the implications of foreign financial influence identified by critics with the agendas of foreign donor agencies and less with the real needs of the local population.

32. Gilles Deleuze and Félix Guattari, *A Thousand Plateaus: Capitalism and Schizophrenia*, translated by Robert Hurley, Mark Seem, and Helen R. Lane (Minneapolis: University of Minnesota Press, 1983), 25.

33. Laura U. Marks, *The Skin of the Film* (Durham, N.C.: Duke University Press, 2000), 21.

34. Ibid., 25.

35. See Nizar Hassan, quoted in Roni Parcheck, "Lo oseh bidur la-liberalim" [I do not produce entertainment for liberals], *Ha'aretz*, August 30, 1994; Yael Israel, "Seret al busha" [A film about shame], *'Al Hamishmar*, August 26, 1994.

36. In recent years, Hassan's films have enjoyed more success and wider circulation among Arab audiences.

37. Hassan acknowledges that his films more specifically address the perils and concerns of Palestinians living in Israel, rather than Palestinians in the Occupied Territories or in the diaspora. As he says in an interview about his film *Yasmine*, "My film is a Palestinian cultural phenomenon taking place within the state of Israel . . . At the same time, this is a Palestinian-Israeli phenomenon: the accent, the mixing of Hebrew and Arabic, the clothes, some of the images. They're not the images of refugee camps." Nizar Hassan, quoted in Prusher, "Oslo Is Not Even Calling," 42–43.

III THE POLITICS
OF MUSIC

JOSEPH MASSAD

Liberating

Songs: Palestine

Put to Music

Who's a terrorist?

Me, the terrorist?

How am I a terrorist

When I am living in my own homeland?

—DAM, "Min Irhabi?" (Who's a terrorist?)

S tudies of nationalism have largely ignored the role of song in political struggles. Whether reflections or expressions of the political or
generative mechanisms of it, the role of songs has not been integrated into the political analysis of colonial or anticolonial nationalisms.
Theodor Adorno analyzed the role of music in German Nazism, but popular songs received short shrift in much of the literature on nationalism despite the fact that they have been around for centuries.[1] From the "Marseil-
laise" and the "Internationale" to revolutionary Soviet songs and the *nueva
canción* in Latin America and from national anthems to nationalist songs
in nineteenth- and twentieth-century Europe to songs of the anticolonial
struggles for national liberation in Asia and Africa, songs have played an
important role in mobilizing the masses. If national anthems exemplify
a kind of emotive music that represents the nation and presents itself as
an icon of the nationalist principle, nationalist songs carry that logic further in their mobilizing capacities to stir the emotions of the masses for
the nationalist cause. This is as true in the United States, with its use of
melodramatic emotive music (such as "America the Beautiful" and "God
Bless America") to galvanize the public into a hypnotic state of support for

"the American way," as it is in European colonial nationalisms, Asian and African anticolonial nationalisms, and Latin American anti-imperialism.

How do songs come to be inserted into the political field of nationalism? In this essay I focus on the Arab national movement and address one of its most central issues: the colonization of Palestine by the Zionist movement and the resulting Arab resistance. What has the role of song been in the struggle for Palestine? What is the nature of the relationship between popular sentiment and song? Are these songs part of a culture industry (as Horkheimer and Adorno dubbed it) that defines popular sentiment and generates political commitments, or are the images and metaphors they deploy expressions of such sentiment? By exploring these and other questions, I aim to chart the history of song in the Palestine tragedy and its impact on Palestinian and Arab popular memory and political agency. The aim is not to present an exhaustive survey, but to examine the effects of the most popular songs and those with the greatest impact. This is especially important in view of the lack of substantial scholarship on this question. Whereas most works dealing with individual singers discuss these singers' patriotic songs, there has been no major academic engagement with the overall history and role of patriotic, nationalist, and revolutionary songs in the modern Arab world (whether in Arabic or English), nor with their role in the Palestine tragedy specifically. I intend to fill this gap in scholarship about the history of songs in the Palestine struggle.

That history parallels the history of the struggle itself. Songs supporting Palestinian liberation in the late 1950s and the early 1960s expressed the confidence of the Nasserist revolution; post-1967 songs expressed the despair of defeat and hope in the Palestinian guerrilla movement that was emerging at the time. The Lebanese civil war and the ensuing Israeli invasions of Lebanon produced another crop of songs about the struggle, including the recent loss of Jerusalem. Until the 1970s, non-Palestinian Arab singers took the lead, with Palestinian singers moving to the forefront thereafter. More recently, and especially since 1998, a new spate of enthusiasm has expressed itself in songs for Palestine by both Palestinians and other Arabs. The more recent songs are reminiscent of those of the 1950s, at least in performance style, though not necessarily in lyrics and music.

While Palestinians and other Arabs express their sense of loss in a number of literary and artistic genres (including poetry, novels, paintings, film, and plays),[2] song, by its very nature the most popular of forms, probably reaches the largest number of people. This widespread exposure is due to the easy accessibility of songs, which can be listened to at home, in a car, and in public spaces, as well as recited anywhere. The element of cost is also key in this regard, especially because radios and later cassette players were affordable to all classes. As this essay shows, songs for Palestine not only reflected popular sentiments but were also instrumental in generating such sentiments. The insertion of popular songs in the political domain as critique and intervention has rendered the popular internal to the political, and not a manifestation external to it. The popular nationalist song is therefore not epiphenomenal or subservient to the political, but is generative of political sentiment in many domains.

Songs responding to the 1948 Palestinian catastrophe (the *Nakba*) urged the Palestinians and other Arabs to liberate the stolen homeland. They were performed by the leading singers of the day, including the Lebanese Najah Salam,[3] the Syrian Farid al-Atrash, and the Egyptian composer and singer Muhammad 'Abd al-Wahhab. 'Abd al-Wahhab's song "Filastin" (released in 1949, lyrics written in 1948 by 'Ali Mahmud Taha) stood out most sharply. 'Abd al-Wahhab, however, was to achieve his greatest influence celebrating the 1952 Egyptian Revolution and the new regime's hopes of liberating Palestine and Algeria, notwithstanding his earlier songs written in support of the monarchy brought down by the Revolution and his subsequent songs for Anwar al-Sadat's regime, which supplanted the Revolution. Indeed, many singers and artists (including Umm Kulthum, who sang for the monarchy and for Nasser but *not* for Sadat) proved to be more politically mobile than the constituencies their songs mobilized.

Studying the role of song in political struggles is crucial to the understanding of how the popular and the political interact. One of the major concerns of theorizing the popular is the question of its production and consumption. The public may consume cultural products that are identified as popular, but what role, if any, have the consumers had in the production of such artifacts? In the course of this essay, I identify the moments of elite production and the moments of public participation in the production of song and correlate them with the political contexts within which they emerged. I also discuss the connections or lack thereof that the cadre of artists and poets who produced such songs have to the culture industry as well as the similarity between the themes of these songs and themes used in other artistic genres, including poetry, novels, painting, theater, and cinema.

The theme of laments for Palestine has formed part of the political projects of various state institutions and political opposition and dissident groups in the Arab world of the past half-century, as well as part of popular consciousness across the Arab world. The political importance of the issue was reflected in the sponsorship of songs that lamented or celebrated Palestine and praised the struggle to liberate it. The popularity of song itself is mainly derived from the democratic means distributing it to the largest possible public. Radio was the main instrument of this distribution in the 1950s, and television became widely available in the 1970s in the cities and the countryside. The accessibility of these media ensured the spread of songs beyond a capitalized culture industry predicated on sales of records to consumers of specific income brackets. Although the production, consumption, and sale of cassette tapes became a major industry from the 1970s onward, many of the tapes that circulated were bootlegged copies of copies well into the early 1990s. The emergence of a new culture industry in the form of satellite channels sponsoring cultural products along with the expanded cassette tape industry has changed this pattern of distribution in recent years.

Revolutionary Egypt

Since the turn of the twentieth century, Cairo has been the undisputed cultural center of the Arab East. By 1952, when the Free Officers ousted King Faruq and unleashed their youthful revolution, the Egyptian entertainment industry (theater, cinema, dance, and song) had no rival in the Arab world and its products even reached non-Arab Iran. The role of the state in revolutionary Egypt was instrumental in the funding and support of song, especially through the new medium of state-owned television.[4] 'Abd al-Wahhab was the preeminent composer of the time, writing songs celebrating Arab unity, Egyptian socialism, and the short-lived political union with Syria (1958–1961)[5] and calling for the liberation of Palestine. These songs, which became instant classics, were performed with full orchestras and sung by the most important artists of the day, including Fayza Ahmad (Syrian Egyptian), 'Abd al-Halim Hafiz (Egyptian), Warda al-Jaza'iriya (Algerian), Fayda Kamil (Egyptian), Sabah (Lebanese), Najat al-Saghira (Syrian Egyptian), and Shadia (Egyptian), as well as the composer himself. Beginning with "Watani Habibi" (My beloved homeland, lyrics by Ahmad Shafiq Kamil, 1958), they went on to include "al-Jil al-Sa'id" (The rising generation, lyrics by Husayn al-Sayyid, 1961) and "Sawt al-Jamahir" (The voice of the masses, lyrics by Husayn al-Sayyid, 1963), which were also televised with corresponding footage showing people from all walks of life.[6]

The formal properties of the music reveal the cultural hybridity of Arab nationalism more generally. While the music of the 1949 song "Filastin" (also known as "Akhi jawaza al-zalimun al-mada" [Brother, the unjust have gone too far]) used both Arab and Western instruments ('ud, nay, qanun, riqq, hand drum, violins) and featured quarter tones mixed up in segments with Western scales, the music of the grand nationalist songs of the post-1958 period used almost exclusively Western instrumentation, scales, and style and resembled Western martial music (though the syncopation and rhythmic arrangements, as well as parts of the orchestration, bore 'Abd al-Wahhab's modernist Arab stamp). "Watani Habibi" and "Sawt al-Jamahir" were performed by large casts and featured choruses that sounded at times more like a choir. And while "Filastin" used a slow-moving melody to assert that the youth would protect the land of Palestine or die trying, "Watani Habibi" and "Sawt al-Jamahir" roused the masses with Western martial music, which 'Abd al-Wahhab punctuated with several bars of emotive melodies in his distinctive style. The lyrics of "Watani Habibi" address the Arab homeland with the words "The voice is your voice, Arab and free, and not an echo of West or East," but the orchestra lacked a single Arab instrument.

This hybridity is an important aspect of the persistence of the colonial legacy in postrevolutionary times. Although Arab music in Egypt was Westernized during the years of British colonialism under pioneers like Sayyid Darwish and 'Abd al-Wahhab, the Revolution, which coupled its anticolonialism with a commitment to a Western modernization project, did not object to the colonial pedigree of this music, especially because the inspiration for martial music may also have been the Soviet revolutionary songs of the period. Indeed, an antiessentialism characterized this aspect of Arab nationalism and its ambivalence toward the West and its own musical tradition. While "Watani Habibi" asserts pride in a pure Arab identity uncontaminated by East or West, it does so unhampered by essentialist arguments about what constitutes nationalist music. Nationalist music, then, was defined predominantly through lyrics that expressed the sentiments of the nation, while the musical genre was appropriated as global culture that has been Arabized. 'Abd al-Wahhab himself had performed "Watani Habibi" in rehearsal accompanied only by his 'ud, but that recording was not released until the late 1990s, several years after his death and almost four decades after the release of the original song. However, the two recordings are presented as different styles of the same song rather than in terms of "authenticity" or "Westernization."

While both "Watani Habibi" and "Sawt al-Jamahir" celebrate the anticolonial and revolutionary achievement of Egypt, they also address parts of the more widely imagined Arab nation yet to be liberated, most prominently Palestine and Algeria (but also Bahrain, Oman, and Aden, likewise still under European colonial rule). The rhyming refrain of "Sawt al-Jamahir" speaks of the Arab nationalist struggle as a unified mass movement:

> The voice of the masses is that which awakens the generations,
> It is the uprising of the strength and will of heroes,
> It is the one that speaks,
> The one that rules,
> It is the hero behind every struggle.

"Sawt al-Jamahir" is also very explicit with regard to the Palestinian Nakba, describing Palestinian liberation as a central goal of this nationalist mobilization:

> In the name of our union,
> Rise O struggle,
> And tell the aggressor Zionists,
> That the banner of Arabism
> Found its stars
> Ever since the year 1948.

> . . . the masses say that the hour
> Of revolutionary action has struck
> In Palestine, in the name of the masses.

The song's optimistic tone reflects the triumphalism that engulfed the Arab world after Gamal Abdul Nasser's nationalization of the Suez Canal Company in 1956 and the withdrawal of the invading British, French, and Israeli forces following the Suez War. Indeed, there was a widespread belief that the liberation of Palestine was at hand. The popularity of Nasser (whose name means "victor") multiplied during those optimistic years, and 'Abd al-Wahhab was at the forefront of those who lionized the young Egyptian president in popular songs. 'Abd al-Wahhab's mid-1950s martial song "Nasser" (lyrics written by Husayn al-Sayyid in colloquial Egyptian Arabic) was performed publicly at Cairo rallies, with an audience of tens of thousands acting as chorus and repeating the refrain "Nasser, beloved of all."[7] Indeed, Nasser himself was seen as the leader of the march on Palestine. In this vein, the song's lyrics state:

Your people, your people, O Palestine,
Will never let go of their revenge
For the liberation army is at the gates
Waiting to return home,
Your sun O Palestine shall rise,
And the rights of the refugees shall be restored,
All the Arab people are your weapon, [O Palestine],
And their weapons are unity and nationalism.

Nasser, your banner is Arab,
And the next step,
O Nasser [Victor], is against Zionism,
Nasser, beloved of all, Nasser.

The public performance of "Nasser" and the popular participation in such events exemplified the general mobilizational capabilities of the revolutionary regime. At the affective level, if not at the political level, such mobilization produced a sense of unity among the masses, especially as they formed a chorus chanting *in unison* their love for Nasser and the Revolution. The songs of this period reflected a conscious state strategy of mobilization for a revolution whose aims included the liberation of Palestine. In addition to the occasional rally, radio and television were the main instruments used to popularize these songs. Their themes also appeared in cinematic and theatrical productions of the time, as well as in poetry, novels, and painting, but the latter three forms were not sponsored by the state, although their distribution was subject to state censorship. The pedagogical role that song played in this period was Freiresque in its approach and aimed to create a new type of engagé revolutionary culture, wherein art not only related emphatically to the political struggle in which the masses were engaged, but became unequivocally part of it.[8]

The 1967 War and the Rahbani Brothers

While these songs helped stir the masses to support the Revolution and the Palestinian struggle, the 1967 defeat brought this mobilization to a temporary halt. Post-1967 songs echoed a mélange of sadness and despair combined with the hope vested in the *fedayeen*, as the Palestinian guerrillas were known. At the same time, Egypt's near-monopoly in song production and distribution declined measurably after its military defeat. During the

1970s, erstwhile revolutionary composers, including Muhammad 'Abd al-Wahhab, were co-opted by the new order. 'Abd al-Wahhab's chameleonic politics as a court artist for hire manifested in his songs celebrating Anwar Sadat, especially on the occasion of Sadat's return from the infamous 1977 trip to West Jerusalem. Sadat requested that 'Abd al-Wahhab celebrate him by singing the nationalist song "Biladi Biladi," which was written by the early-twentieth-century Egyptian composer Sayyid Darwish when Egypt was still under British occupation and since then had become a nationalist anthem across the Arab world.[9] Given the changes in Egypt's political role, new foci of song production in other Arab countries were becoming more prominent after 1967. The most important collaboration was that of the Lebanese singer Fayruz and her composers, the Rahbani brothers ('Asi, to whom Fayruz was married, and Mansur). Together, they produced the most popular political songs in this period.

The Fayruz-Rahbani team had released a militant martial song "Sayfun fal-yushhar" (A sword must be brandished, lyrics by Sa'id 'Aql) in early 1967, before the outbreak of the June war.[10] However, it is their paean to Jerusalem, "Zahrat al-Mada'in" (The flower of cities), that stands out as the most popular song of the time. The music is quintessentially Rahbani, with Western scales and instruments and a melody that vacillates between martial music, Byzantine Arab church hymns, and somber sentimentality. The song opens with a genuflection: "It is for you that I pray, O city of prayers, for you I pray, O Jerusalem." In contrast to the exclusivist Israeli nationalist songs popular in Israel before and after the Jewish conquest of the city (such as "Yerushalayim shel Zehav" [Jerusalem of gold], sung by Naomi Shemer), the lyrics include reference to Jerusalem's synagogues as well as to its churches and mosques. Nonetheless, the emphasis is on Christianity and Islam and their history in the city, and the threat posed to them by Zionism. While Jerusalem's plight, according to the song, is so sad that even "the child in the manger"[11] and "his mother Mary are two crying faces, crying for those who have been dispersed," the tone is one of resistance. Thus, Fayruz declares:

> The gate of our city shall not be locked,
> For I shall go to pray.
> I shall knock at the gates,
> And I shall open up the gates
> O River Jordan, you shall wash
> My face with your holy water

And you shall erase, O River Jordan,
The remaining footprints of the barbarians.

Indeed, as far as the song is concerned, the city will be reclaimed only through active resistance on the part of its dispossessed residents:

For Jerusalem is ours, and the house is ours
With our own hands we shall restore the glory of Jerusalem
With our own hands, we shall bring peace to Jerusalem
Peace shall come to Jerusalem.

The lyrics—written, like the music, by the Rahbanis—have immortalized this song, which was released after an Australian terrorist (popularly believed to have been acting at the behest of the Israeli government) burned parts of al-Aqsa Mosque in 1969. The song's importance continues to this day, to the extent that the Palestinian Authority's Ministry of Culture and Information awarded its first Jerusalem Prize for Culture to Fayruz in 1998.

Other songs by the Rahbanis tell the story of individual Palestinian cities, including "Jaffa" (sung by Joseph 'Azar) and "Bisan" (sung by Fayruz). The sad theme of "Bisan" recounts the peaceful life of this wintry village ("where April slept") being overtaken by the violent hatred of Zionism. In Fayruz's most moving song, "Sanarji'u Yawman" (We shall return one day), the nostalgia is such that the returning masses (perhaps in an ironic parallel to Moses) are terrified of dying before reaching Palestine:

O Heart, slow down,
Do not throw yourself
In exhaustion on the road of return,
For it pains us to see that tomorrow,
The flocks of birds will return
While we still remain here.

The theme of the jealousy felt by exiled Palestinians for migrating birds, who return to Palestine though the Palestinians cannot, is ubiquitous in literary and artistic forms of the period. Another song about dispossession that insists on Palestinian return is "Raji'un" (We are returning).

The Rahbanis also produced a famous Broadway-style musical, *Jibal al-Suwwan* (Mountains of flint), in 1969 to analogize the Palestinian tragedy under Israeli occupation. In a mythical Palestine renamed Jibal al-Suwwan, the people struggle against the foreign usurpers, who arrest the resisters and use psychological warfare to weaken the population. Fayruz plays the heroine, Ghurba (which means "exile"), the exiled daughter of the leader of the first anti-occupation rebellion who was killed by the enemy. Returning to her homeland to lead the new rebellion, Ghurba reassures the fearful yet steadfast population:

> Fear not, for there are not enough prisons to detain everyone
> They will arrest many, but many will remain
> And with those who remain, we will continue [the struggle].[12]

Like the Egyptian revolutionary songs before them, the themes that these lyrics deployed were also similar to those deployed in other cultural productions of the period. In this sense, the popular was indeed being defined by a class of artists and literary producers, who were not necessarily state functionaries or (with the exception of film) subject to a capitalized culture industry. Still, these figures were central to the articulation of what came to be known as popular sentiment. The Rahbanis, who also produced films, were certainly part of the capitalized culture industry, as only the wealthy could afford to attend their musicals. However, their songs (and later the musicals) were popularized, like Egyptian political songs before them, through the widely accessible means of radio and television and not simply through record sales.

The importance of the Rahbanis is such that renowned Palestinian poet Mahmud Darwish declared on the occasion of the death of 'Asi al-Rahbani in 1986: "It may not be clear that the Palestinian people were not as creative in producing their national song as was the Rahbani phenomenon, which mastered it for the Palestinians and for all Arabs. The Palestinians showed off their aesthetic identity through the Arab songs of the Rahbanis . . . so much so that [these songs] became the reference point for our hearts; they became the restored homeland, and the motivation for us to march forward on the long caravan road."[13]

Until 1967, the songs dealt with exiled Palestinians living in refugee camps in the areas surrounding their former country. With the occupation of what was left of Palestine in 1967, however, the songs began to deal as well with the Palestinian population that now fell under Israeli rule; Palestinian Israelis were still largely ignored in these songs. Like *Jibal al-Suwwan*, Fayruz's song "Shawari' al-Quds al-'Atiqa" (The streets of old Jerusalem) addresses the people of the occupied land, sending them greetings ("Salami lakum, ya ahl al-ard al-muhtallah" [I salute you, o people of the occupied land]). Still, diasporic Palestinians remained the object of most songs, as the vision of the return continued to predominate. In "Ya Jisran

Khashabiyan" (O wooden bridge) and "Jisr al-'Awda" (Bridge of return), Fayruz immortalized the bridges over the River Jordan across which Palestinians were driven out by Israeli soldiers in 1967. It is in such songs that the role of the recently emergent Palestinian guerrillas is celebrated and more explicitly martial lyrics become common. In "Jisr al-'Awda," for example, Fayruz sings of a Palestinian boy, still in exile, who receives for his twentieth birthday a machine gun to liberate the land of his forefathers. Umm Kulthum's sole song to Palestine (although she sang numerous songs for the Egyptian Revolution) proclaims her desire to join the revolutionaries in 1969 with "Asbaha al-ana 'indi bunduqiya" (I have now got me a rifle), a poem by the Syrian poet Nizar Qabbani set to music by 'Abd al-Wahhab:

> I have now got me a rifle, to Palestine, take me with you
> To hills that are sad, like the face of the Magdalene
> To the green domes and the prophetic stones . . .

> I am with the revolutionaries,
> I am of the revolutionaries
> Ever since the day I carried my rifle,
> Palestine became only meters away
> O revolutionaries, in Jerusalem, in Hebron,
> In Bisan, in the Jordan Valley, in Bethlehem,
> Wherever you may be O free men
> Advance, advance, advance to Palestine,
> For there is only one path to Palestine,
> And it passes through the barrel of a gun.

The revolution was also portrayed as a masculinizing ritual, wherein Arab women could transform themselves into men through participating in the liberation of Palestine. Umm Kulthum herself, whose status was beyond sex, as Hazim Saghiya argues, declared in "Asbaha al-Ana 'indi Bunduqiyyah," "I want to live and die as men do."[14]

Echoing Mao's "barrel of a gun," other images called on the recently occupied Palestinians to remain steadfast on the land. While the analogy to returning flocks of birds saddened the Palestinians and reminded them of their loss, other analogies were deployed as models for them to emulate. For example, the image of trees as symbols of steadfastness became commonplace in these songs. In "Jisr al-'Awda," Palestinians are enjoined to "remain like rooted trees that do not depart . . . like olive trees you shall reside, like the branches of time you shall remain present forever." In Fayruz's "Ahtarifu al-Huzna wa al-Intizar" (Sadness and waiting have become my occupation), the themes of waiting and of return continue to haunt the exiled Palestinians:

> I grew up on the outside
> I built another family
> Like trees, I planted them so they stood tall before me
> They even acquired a shadow on the ground
> But then anew, we were hit by the wave of hatred
> Here I am, inhabiting the void again,
> For I was dispersed from my people twice
> And I inhabited absence twice
> My land remains on my mind
> While I take up sadness and waiting as my profession.

Zionist oppression is represented here in its acts of repetition as a limitless force of hatred and violence that pursues Palestinians time and time again, causing them unceasing suffering.

Registering this suffering, Christian motifs were common in many of these songs, as they have been in Palestinian poetry and painting. The Egyptian singer 'Abd al-Halim Hafiz's 1967 song "Al-Masih" (The Messiah, lyrics by 'Abd al-Rahman al-'Abnudi and music by Baligh Hamdi) used Christ's Via Dolorosa as the main allegorical theme of Palestinian suffering. While other songs used Christian parallels, to my knowledge, "Al-Masih" is one of only two songs in the entire archive of Arab nationalist songs that deployed Christian anti-Semitic motifs, with the lyrics asserting that the son of Jerusalem, like the Messiah, has now been "crucified, by the same Jews." (The other song is Fayruz's 1968 "Jisr al-'Awda," which declares that "those who had crucified every prophet have crucified my people tonight.") "Al-Masih" has an operatic-style chorus and music composition interspersed with hymn-like melodic sections sung by Hafiz himself accompanied by Western instruments.[15]

The Palestinian Guerrillas and Songs of the Underground

With the rise of the Palestinian guerrillas in the 1960s and the hopes vested in them following the 1967 defeat of the Arab armies and the guerrillas' performance at the Battle of Karamah in 1968, a new crop of songs emerged that celebrated the resistance and anticipated Palestine's liberation. Both established performers and underground dissident singers wrote songs that cheered the guerrillas and became an important weapon in the struggle for Palestine. One of the most significant of these songs is "Ya Falastiniya" (O Palestinians), sung by famed Egyptian dissident singer Shaykh Imam 'Isa in 1969. This underground song became popular in Palestinian refugee camps and among the Palestinian guerrillas, as well as in dissident circles in Egypt and elsewhere in the Arab world. The blind Shaykh Imam accompanied himself on the 'ud, and in line with his quintessentially Arab compositions in the different *maqams*, he wrote the music for "Ya Falastiniya" in the *Saba al-Shadi maqam*, the most popular maqam in Arab music, and to the Sufi Ayyubite *iqa'* (rhythm).[16] The lyrics, written by the Egyptian dissident colloquial poet Ahmad Fu'ad Nagm, evoked solidarity with and sympathy for the sufferings of the Palestinians and drew on the stock themes of exile, nostalgia, and revolution:

> O Palestinians, the fusilier has shot you
> With Zionism which kills the doves that live under your protection.

> O Palestinians, I want to come and be with you, weapons in hand
> And I want my hands to go down with yours to smash the snake's
>   head
> And then Hulagu's law[17] will die.

> O Palestinians, exile has lasted so long
> That the desert is moaning from the refugees and the victims
> And the land remains nostalgic for its peasants who watered it
> Revolution is the goal, and victory shall be your first step.[18]

The song became so popular that when Yasir Arafat visited Cairo in August 1968, he insisted on meeting the shaykh, who sang it for him.[19] Arafat's interest in Shaykh Imam is emblematic of the relationship between song and politics, wherein political songs became part and parcel of the very struggle they were representing and expressing.

Songs produced in the contexts of established states were broadcast on national radio and television stations and released on records in demonstration of the regime's commitment to the liberation of Palestine; Egypt and Lebanon stand out in this regard.[20] As a rule, however, only songs seen as unthreatening to Arab regimes were broadcast throughout the Arab world, including the songs of Fayruz and the Rahbanis. Many of 'Abd al-Wahhab's songs, however, were banned outside Egypt because they mixed the socialist goals and rhetoric of the Egyptian Revolution (to which not all Arab regimes subscribed) with the safer messages of Arab nationalism and the liberation of Palestine. Even in Egypt, the songs of Shaykh Imam were banned; both he and his lyricist, the poet Nagm, were jailed by Nasser and Sadat for songs that questioned the government's commitment to the Egyptian people's welfare and the Palestinian cause. Shaykh Imam's songs have circulated mainly in the form of poor cassette tape copies since the 1970s.

Meanwhile, a new genre of songs for Palestine produced by Palestinian diaspora singers linked to the newly autonomous PLO began to emerge. These, too, were underground music, thereby escaping the censorship of the Arab regimes. Al-Firqa al-Markaziya (the Central Band), associated with Fatah, produced numerous revolutionary songs after its establishment in 1969. These songs make use of folk Palestinian tunes, sometimes combined with Western martial rhythms and tempos, but their lyrics are invariably Palestinian Arabic, sung in rural accents. In contrast to previous political songs performed by famous soloists, al-Firqa al-Markaziya's music was sung by a chorus of unknown and nameless male and female singers. These songs, which addressed both diaspora Palestinians and those living under occupation with a militant and confident revolutionism, include "Ya Jamahir al-Ard al-Muhtallah" (O masses of the occupied land), "La Tihzanu" (Do not be sad), "Ana Samid" (I remain steadfast), "Kalashnikov," "Fida'iya," and "'Ahd Allah Ma Nirhal" (By God we shall not depart).

The songs, which echoed the struggles of the Palestinian people and of the guerrillas who were fighting for them, were popularized through guerrilla radio transmitters in vans that drove around Amman and other areas of Jordan, broadcasting guerrilla news and nationalist songs. The Cairo-based radio station Sawt al-'Asifa–Sawt Fath (Voice of al-'Asifa–Voice of Fatah) was also an important conduit for the transmission of these songs. After the expulsion of the fedayeen from Jordan in 1971, the PLO established the Radio of the Revolution (Sawt Filastin–Sawt al-Thawra al-Filastiniya) in Lebanon. The station, along with others in Iraq, Syria, and Egypt, allowed guerrilla groups to broadcast and gave prominence to these songs, which became so popular in the region's refugee camps that most people knew them by heart.[21] By the mid- to late 1970s, when cassette tapes became affordable and available on a mass scale, these songs could be heard in most camp households in the West Bank, Gaza, Jordan, Lebanon, and Syria.

Another rising star of this genre of songs in the 1970s was Abu 'Arab, a Beirut-based Palestinian singer associated with the guerrillas who produced dozens of songs about the struggle. His music also used folk Pales-

tinian tunes, including popular *mawwal*s and *mijana* sung to revolutionary lyrics accompanied by 'ud, qanun, violin, hand drum, and riqq. Abu
'Arab's music, like that of al-Firqa al-Markaziya, always had a specifically
Palestinian flavor. Unlike al-Firqa, however, Abu 'Arab sang in both urban
and rural Palestinian accents. Under PLO auspices, another group, Firqat
al-Funun al-Sha'biya, was established in the second half of the 1970s and
performed Palestinian music and revolutionary songs at music festivals
across the Arab world.[22]

The songs of this period concerned the exiled Palestinians and those
living under occupation in the West Bank and Gaza. Many songwriters of
the time had a mission to record a geography irrevocably changed with the
razing of Palestinian villages and the appropriation of Palestinian towns
by the conquering Israelis. Towns like 'Akka, Jaffa, Lydda, Majdal, Ramleh,
Safad, and Tiberias, not to mention numerous villages, were invoked in
songs dedicated to them individually or together, not as abstract names but
as concrete references to the homes to which people could not return. By
naming and mapping these lost places, such songs not only expressed nostalgia but also asserted the continuing presence of this geography in Arab
and Palestinian memory. After 1976, however, when Palestinian Israelis
rose up against Israel's policy of Judaizing the Galilee by confiscating yet
more Palestinian land, songs began to embrace them as well. It was following the 1976 events, for example, that the Palestinian Tawfiq Zayyad's poem
"Unadikum" (I call upon you) was put to music and sung by the Lebanese
Ahmad Qa'bur.[23] This song, which became very popular in the early 1980s,
implores the diaspora and West Bank and Gaza Palestinians not to forget
their compatriots who had suffered the longest under Israeli colonialism.

Works by many Palestinian poets, especially Darwish, were now being
used widely as lyrics. These poem-based songs ranged from the famed
"Bitaqat Hawiya" (Identification papers), better known as "Sajjil Ana 'Arabi"
(Record, I am an Arab), which chronicles Palestinian Israelis' experiences
of racist Israeli Jewish pass laws, to songs combining struggle and romantic
love, such as "Rita wa-al-Bunduqiya" (Rita and the rifle). Portions of "Sajjil
Ana 'Arabi," which depicts an Israeli Palestinian at an Israeli Jewish checkpoint, were performed by George Qirmiz, a West Bank Palestinian living
in the United States:

Record,
I am an Arab
My identification number is 50,000

I have eight children
And the ninth arrives after one summer . . .

Does this anger you? . . .

My distinguishing marks are:
On my head I wear a *'iqal* atop a *kufiya*[24]
And my palm is as hard as rock
It scratches whoever touches it . . .

Record . . . at the top of the first page;
I do not hate people
And I aggress against no one
However, were I ever to get hungry
I would eat the flesh of my occupier
Beware, then, beware . . . of my hunger
And of my anger![25]

The accompanying music, played by Western instruments, is part sentimental Western pop, part martial; the latter tone accompanies the impera-
tive opening line: "Record, I am an Arab." The poem was also sung to a
different tune by the Lebanese singer Ahmad Qa'bur in the early 1980s.

In the 1970s and 1980s, Lebanese singer and composer Marcel Khalife
achieved immense popularity around the Arab world for singing Darwish
poems and songs of resistance to Israel's occupation of southern Lebanon.
His innovative musical style differed markedly from both the Rahbanis and
'Abd al-Wahhab in its use of Arab instruments and its merging of Arab
and Western melodic structures and scales. But Khalife, too, is ambivalent
about the Arab and Western musical traditions, at times cultivating a musical form more in tune with recognizable forms of the Arab musical heritage, and at others using highly Westernized forms (albeit on occasion with
'ud and qanun instrumentation). Khalife is probably the first Arab singer of
political songs to have become popular through cassette tape sales, which,
along with guerrilla radio stations, were the main method of distributing his songs. He later began to stage concerts across the Arab world and
beyond.

Khalife's songs of early Darwish poems (mostly from the 1960s) popularized these poems even beyond the reach of Darwish's renown, which
parallels that of a Western rock star, as tens of thousands attend his public
poetry readings across the Arab world. Along with "Rita wa al-Bunduqiya,"
Darwish's poem "Ila Ummi" (To my mother) became one of Khalife's most

popular songs, its lyrics and sad imploring music exemplifying as few other poems had Palestinian nostalgia and loss as well as the folk Palestinian deification of motherhood. The song registers the personal as the political insofar as Darwish's yearning for his mother, who lives inside Israel while he lives in exile separated from her, parallels that of many Palestinians split from their families by Israeli colonization of their country. The poem's opening lines assert:

I yearn for my mother's bread
And my mother's coffee
And my mother's touch
As [my] childhood grows up within me
Day upon the bosom of day
And I love my life,
For if I died
I would feel shame for my mother's tears.

Take me, if I ever return,
As a veil for your lashes
And cover my bones with grass
Baptized in the purity of your heel
Tie me to you
With a lock of your hair
With a thread that trails
In the train of your dress
Perhaps, I would then become a god
A god, I would become
If I touched the depths of your heart.[26]

By the late 1980s and early to mid-1990s, in the shadow of the first Intifada, a number of new Palestinian groups emerged in the diaspora as well as in Israel proper. Those years also saw the appearance of some local groups and singers in the West Bank and Gaza, such as Firqat al-Funun al-Sha'biya (not to be confused with its 1980s diaspora-based namesake), though their fame never went beyond their local and regional surroundings. Sabreen, a band comprising a female lead singer, the Palestinian Israeli Kamilya Jubran (who also plays the qanun), and four Palestinian male musicians from Israel and the West Bank, combined Palestinian folk songs and tunes with innovative musical techniques, including jazz and other Western influences. Though virtually unknown outside Israel and the Occupied Territories, Sabreen is probably one of the more talented Palestinian musical groups to appear in recent years.[27] Their first album, 'An al-Sumud (About steadfastness), released in 1982, is largely unknown. It was their second album, Dukhan al-Barakin (The smoke of the volcanoes), released in 1984 and registering the massacres of the Israeli invasion of Lebanon, that received attention due to its sophisticated musical and lyrical styles. Subsequent albums include Mawt al-Nabi (The death of the Prophet), Jay al-Hamam (Here comes the doves), and, more recently, Ala Fayn (Where to?). Jay al-Hamam was released in 1994; its songs and title echoed the hopes for peace, thought to be unfolding with the arrival of the Palestinian Authority. 'Ala Fayn was released in 2000, and, as its title indicates, was registering the uncertainty of the future in light of the horrid conditions of the "peace process." The group's music is composed by Sa'id Murad and its instruments include 'ud, riqq, qanun, hand drum, and buzuq, as well as violin, cello, and saxophone. The lyrics, from poems written by Palestinian poets Darwish, Husayn al-Barghuthi, and Samih al-Qasim, seem to be chosen for their fragmentary nonnarrative structure that veers away from the ideological songs of 'Abd al-Wahhab, the sometimes lachrymose mood of the Rahbanis, or the militancy of al-Firqa al-Markaziya. They sing in both classical Arabic and colloquial Palestinian, and their complex compositions, which incorporate different forms of jazz, resist the hegemony of melody so pervasive in contemporary Arab song. Their song "Thalathin Nijma" (Thirty stars, lyrics by Barghuthi) is illustrative:

> Thirty stars twinkling over the cypress valley
> Thirty stars twinkling
> My heart is an open cavern
> If only the pretty one
> Would understand
> That the moon is wounded
> But hope is strength.[28]

Other popular diaspora groups include Baladna and al-'Ashiqin. Their songs deal mostly with the Palestinian struggle against the occupation of the West Bank and Gaza Strip and also address the common themes of the return of the refugees and the restoration of the land. These groups became very popular during the first Intifada (1987–1993). Another emerging singer is Rim al-Banna, a Palestinian Israeli popular among Palestinians in Israel and increasingly in the Occupied Territories, where she sings at rallies and other political events.[29]

Since the late 1980s, Palestinian singers have been joined by other Arab musicians singing solidarity songs for Palestine. One of the most popular songs of the first Intifada, "Wayn al-Malayin" (Where are the millions?), by Lebanese resistance singer Julia Butrus, was a desperate cry for the Arab masses to rise in support of the resisting Palestinians. Another popular singer, the Syrian Samih Shuqayr, has a large repertoire of songs for Palestine and also about the Golan Heights. He is popular in Palestinian refugee camps in Jordan, Syria, and elsewhere and was invited, in the context of the al-Aqsa Intifada, to perform at Jordan's Jerash festival of culture in the summer of 2002.

An interesting development since the late 1990s is the appearance of Palestinian Israeli rap groups whose songs about Israeli racism and colonialism powerfully indict the Jewish State's "democratic" record. Dam and MWR were the first to emerge; the latter is influenced by African American rappers like Dr. Dre and the late Tupac Shakur.[30] Their songs address not only the horrors of Israeli colonial racism, but also the disunity of the Palestinian population within, especially as regards the religious and class divisions fostered by Israeli policies. While the music largely borrows from American hip-hop, produced by synthesizers and percussion, it is punctuated by Arab musical phrases and rhythms (using hand drums). MWR sings and raps in colloquial Palestinian, with an 'Akka (Acre) twang. Their song "R" (named for the band's lead rapper, Richie) emphasizes the issue of religious divisions. It insists:

> That is why things here are loose,
> because there is a distinction between us in religion . . .
> We are brothers, Muslims and Christians . . .
> there are people who live in our lands,
> who look at us with glee,
> seeing that we are at odds among ourselves.
> It does not matter who among us is Christian or Muslim,
> we are Arabs . . . and must be one hand.

MWR's social consciousness is also manifest in songs like "Masari" (Money), which reproaches rich Palestinians:

> Only money preoccupies you
> while you leave your people in the middle of a fight,
> this is why we have come,
> so that we can raise the consciousness of the downtrodden.

Their songs are pedagogical, aimed at "waking up our people" and raising their consciousness. "Ya Sha'bi" (My people) calls on the Arab people to be unified in confronting the enemy. MWR state clearly that their main weapon for "defend[ing] our people" is the microphone.

The second such group, Dam ("lasting" or "persisting," in Arabic; "blood," in Hebrew), founded in 1998 in the mixed city of Lydda, bill themselves as "the first Palestinian rap crew."[31] Their music is produced by synthesizers and Western drums and highly influenced by American rap, but most of their tunes have an Arab motif. Dam's songs are powerful in tenor and performative vigor. The members appear on the CD cover dressed in hip-hop fashion; above them appear their names, some in Arabic, others in English. Hanzala, the famous Palestinian cartoon character created by the late Palestinian cartoonist Naji al-'Ali, watches them from the bottom corner. Their choice of the hip-hop genre signifies the continuing openness of Palestinian and Arab culture to foreign musical influences, from classical Western music to jazz. Their political choice of rap also testifies to the parallels they see between the racially oppressive society from which African American rappers emerge and their own conditions under Israeli racial oppression. Dam was recently invited to perform for the first time in Ramallah to a packed audience.[32]

Their most popular song, "Min Irhabi?" (Who's a terrorist?), features some of the most powerful lyrics of resistance to the Israeli racist narrative and squarely addresses the Israelis as a collective. The refrain asks in colloquial Palestinian rhymed verse:

Who's a terrorist?
Me, a terrorist?
How am I a terrorist
When I am living in my own homeland?
Who's a terrorist?
You are the terrorist.
You have eaten me up
While I am living in my own homeland
You are killing me now,
Like you have killed my forefathers.

Dam ridicules Israeli claims that the Jewish state is based on law: "But you play the witness, the lawyer, and the judge, judging me." Not mincing words, "Min Irhabi?" proclaims:

You beat me up and then you cry,

And then you rush to complain about me [to the world]

When I remind you that you started the whole thing, you jump to say:

"You let small children throw stones

Do they have no parents to throw them inside their homes?"

What! Have you actually forgotten the time when you

Threw the parents under the rubble? . . .

Yet you call me the terrorist!

The Arab Dream

The 1990s witnessed a major retreat, if not outright defeat, of the dream of Arab unity that had continued to inspire the Arab masses throughout much of the century. Not only were all of Palestine, the Golan Heights, and southern Lebanon still in the hands of the Israeli occupiers, but the resistance of the Palestinians, Syrians, and Lebanese, continuing against all odds, found little actual support in the Arab corridors of power. Iraq's 1990 invasion of Kuwait and the U.S.-led invasion of the region in 1991 dealt a final blow to any notion of Arab unity, as Arabs became divided and allied against one another with foreign powers, long seen throughout the Arab world as imperial sponsors. Finally, Arafat's signing of the Oslo Accords divided the Palestinian people and almost destroyed their national movement.[33] Followed by the Jordanian-Israeli peace treaty, Oslo turned the Arab dream of unity into a nightmare of disunity and division.

In this dismal context, a new televised song, which included upwards of twenty singers and scores of musicians, debuted on Arab television stations in 1998 and became, quite unexpectedly, an instant hit continuously aired on Arab satellite channels. The song, "Al-Hulm al-'Arabi" (The Arab dream), was an attempt to replicate the form of 'Abd al-Wahhab's nationalist songs of the late 1950s and early 1960s. "Al-Hulm al-'Arabi" featured Arab singers from almost every Arab country (except Iraq, whose inclusion was reportedly vetoed by the Kuwaiti participants) and was funded by the Arab nationalist Saudi prince Walid bin Talal. The director of the production, Muhammad al-'Aryan, is a Palestinian. The tear-jerker documentary footage accompanying the music, which showed the succession of Arab defeats since 1948 (and the few "victories," such as the 1956 nationalization of the Suez Canal Company and the crossing of the Suez Canal and the Golan Heights' demilitarized zone during the 1973 war), evoked feelings of despair and loss at the end of a dream in the face of yet more defeats, death, and division. One novelty of the production was the presence of eight singers from the Gulf, a presence nowhere to be found in the songs of the preceding four decades. The emergence and growing popularity of Gulf singers since the 1980s and increasingly in the 1990s, coupled with increased Gulf funding for numerous art and music productions in other parts of the Arab world, account for this increased visibility.

The lyrics of "Al-Hulm al-'Arabi" were mild compared to its 1950s predecessors, expressing the lowest common denominator among the Arab regimes to avoid the song's possible banning. The music video (or video-clip) was more a Westernized Arab *taqtuqa* (ditty) played by Western instruments than the "operetta" the producers and the press alike had promoted. The refrain and the segments sung by each singer are repetitions of the same few sentimental bars, rendered evocative (and approaching melodrama) by the synchronic images of real suffering. When the singers performed the piece live in downtown Beirut in the summer of 1998, as many as 1 million people reportedly showed up to sing along. Each singer sang in her or his own national Arabic dialect, or an approximation of it, with subtitles on the screen so that all Arabs could follow and sing along. The song begins with the following lines:

> Generation after generation will live in the hope of realizing our
> dream
> As what we say today we will be called to account for throughout our
> lifetime.

The song then proceeds to the refrain, sung in Egyptian Arabic (known to most Arabs through movies and television):

> It is possible that the darkness of night
> May render us far from one another, but
> The beam of light can
> Reach the farthest of skies
> This has been our dream
> All of our lives:
> An embrace that will contain us all together.

Footage of Palestinians being expelled from their lands, killed by Israeli soldiers, bombed alongside the Lebanese by Israeli planes, resisting Israeli occupation, and other similar images dominated the song.

Since the beginning of the al-Aqsa Intifada, more such songs have emerged from around the Arab world. One of the more notable is the equally melodramatic "Al-Quds Hatirga' lina" (Jerusalem will return to us), sung by yet another group of Egyptian pop singers and featuring a couplet referring to the Palestinian child Muhammad al-Durra, whose televised murder by Israeli soldiers in the first days of the new uprising seemed to exemplify Israel's continuing brutality against all Palestinians. What is especially interesting during this period is the re-airing of 1950s and 1960s songs on Arab satellite stations, which, along with the daily televised images of resisting Palestinians, moved millions across the Arab world to demonstrate in solidarity. Indeed, Fayruz herself, whose political songs since the 1970s have focused on Lebanon's own tragic wars, recently has begun to include her late-1960s songs for Palestine and the Palestinians in the repertoire of her concerts, most recently in Paris in June 2002.[34] The emergence of privately and government-owned satellite channels combined with the expanded record industry have been instrumental in the recent production and distribution of these new songs. This transmission is made all the easier by the increasing affordability of satellite dishes, which dot the skyline of rich and poor neighborhoods across the cities and towns of the Arab world.

These songs have obviously not brought about the liberation of Palestine and the Palestinians. Nonetheless, the songs both express and register the changing dynamics of the Palestinian struggle, reflecting which segment of the Palestinian people is most prominent at the moment and which form of struggle is imagined as most effective. They have shifted in tone and content, ranging from songs of a united Arab front fighting for liberation and the return of refugees in the context of Arab unity, to songs celebrating the Palestinian guerrillas' fight for their people's independence, songs that describe the oppression of all Palestinians, and songs expressing a rejuvenated Arab solidarity with the second Intifada. These songs serve to record as well as to generate the feelings and aspirations of a dispossessed people without access to official state channels and forms for writing official histories. While the public has been the main receiving party of these cultural productions offered by a cadre of literary and artistic figures and state-sponsored radio stations, ordinary Palestinians have participated actively in producing songs through the guerrilla movement and groups like al-Firqah al-Markaziya and its successors. While elite and state-sponsored songs became parts of a politics of mobilization (as in Nasserist Egypt), nonelite and dissident songs formed part of revolutionary and dissident politics (as in the case of the Palestinian guerrillas and dissident and resistance singers Shaykh Imam, Ahmad Qa'bur, Marcel Khalife, and others). The reception of these songs and singers, including their adoption as unofficial national anthems, the popularity of their recordings, and the ticket sales for the concerts of singers such as Khalife gesture toward their adoption as, and transformation into, popular culture.

Notes

I would like to thank Nadia Abu El-Haj and Neville Hoad for their comments on earlier drafts, Muhammad Ayyub and Hasan Abu Haniyyah for sharing their encyclopedic knowledge of Palestinian musical groups, and the late Magda al-Nowaihi for her insights into the songs of the Nasserist period. I would also like to thank Ted Swedenburg and Rebecca Stein for inviting me to contribute to this volume and for their valuable comments on the text.

Unless otherwise noted, all song translations are mine.

1. Theodor W. Adorno, *Introduction to the Sociology of Music* (New York: Continuum, 1976).

2. On the role of Palestinian literature, see the important collection edited and introduced by Salma Khadra Jayyusi, *Anthology of Modern Palestinian Literature* (New York: Columbia University Press, 1992). On Palestinian painting, see Kamal Boullata, *Istihdar al-makan: dirasa fi al-fann al-tashkili al-Filastini al-mu'asir* [Conjuring up space: A study of contemporary Palestinian plastic arts] (Tunis: al-Munazzama al-'Arabiya lil-Tarbiya wa-al-Thaqafa wa-al-'Ulum, 2000). See also his "'Asim Abu Shaqra: The Artist's Eye and the Cactus Tree," *Journal of Palestine Studies* 30, no. 4 (summer 2001): 68–82. On Palestinian theater inside Israel, see Radi Shihada, *al-Masrah al-Filastini fi Filastin 48: bayna sira' al-baqa' wa-infisam al-huwiya* [Palestinian theater in 1948 Palestine: Between the struggle for survival and the splitting of identity] (Ramallah: Wizarat al-Thaqafa al-Filastiniya, 1998). On Palestinian film, see my "The Weapon of Culture: Palestinian Cinema and the National Struggle," in *Dreams of a Nation*, edited by Hamid Dabashi, forthcoming from Verso.

3. Salam sang "Ya za'ir mahda 'Isa" (O visitor of the cradle of Jesus) in 1948. The lyrics were by Bulus Salama. Hers is said to be the first such song for Palestine. See Ibrahim al-Tunub, "Najah Salam: al-Dimuqratiya fi al-Ghina' Haddama" [Najah Salam: Democracy in singing is destructive], *al-Hayah*, May 29, 2000, 15.

4. For an overview of the importance of Egyptian nationalism and the revolution in song and music production and the role of the revolutionary state in it, see Samhah al-Khuli, *Al-Qawmiya fi Musiqa al-Qarn al-'Ishrin* [Nationalism in the music of the twentieth century] (Kuwait: 'Alam al-Ma'rifa, 1992), 296–297.

5. For example, songs like Muhammad 'Abd al-Wahhab's 1959 "Ya Ilahi" (lyrics by Husayn al-Sayyid).

6. For a list of all of Abd al-Wahhab's nationalist songs, see Idward Halim Mikha'il,

Muhammad 'Abd al-Wahhab, Sab'un 'Aman min al-Ibda' fi al-Ta'lif al-Musiqi wa al-Talhin wa al-Ghina' [Muhammad 'Abd al-Wahhab: Seventy years of creativity in musical composition and singing] (Cairo: Maktabat Madbuli, 2002).

7. Lutfi Radwan, *Muhammad 'Abd al-Wahhab, Sira Dhatiya* [Muhammad 'Abd al-Wahhab, autobiography] (Cairo: Dar al-Hilal, 1991), 231.

8. See Paolo Freire, *Pedagogy of the Oppressed*, translated by Myra Bergman Ramos (New York: Herder and Herder, 1970).

9. Mikha'il, *Muhammad 'Abd al-Wahhab*, 118.

10. 'Aql is the Lebanese poet and political figure who in the 1970s, as godfather to the right-wing Maronite group Guardians of the Cedars, called for the expulsion of Palestinians from Lebanon. It is said that he later denied ever writing the poem, although all released CDs mention him as the author.

11. The actual word is *maghara* or "cave," which was the stable that in Arab Christian tradition designates the place where Jesus was born in Bethlehem.

12. For an interesting discussion of *Jibal al-Suwwan*, see Fawwaz Tarabulsi, "Jibal al-Suwwan: Filastin fi Fann Fayruz wa al-Rahabina" [*Jibal al-Suwwan*: Palestine in the art of Fayruz and the Rahbanis], *Al-Karmil* (Ramallah) 57 (autumn 1998): 203–213.

13. Mahmud Darwish, "Tilka al-Ughniya Hadhihi al-Ughniya" [This song, that song], *Al-Yawm al-Sabi'*, no. 126 (October 6, 1986): 13.

14. For an intelligent overview of Umm Kulthum's career, albeit one punctuated throughout with right-wing quasi-Orientalist polemics, see Hazim Saghiya, *al-Hawa Duna Ahlihi, Umm Kulthum, Siratan wa Nassan* [Passion bereft of its people: Umm Kulthum as biography and as text] (Beirut: Dar al-Jadid, 1991), 43–61. For an exploration of the masculine as model for nationalist women in the context of Palestinian nationalism, see Joseph Massad, "Conceiving the Masculine: Gender and Palestinian Nationalism," *Middle East Journal* 49, no. 3 (summer 1995): 467–483.

15. Hafiz performed the song only once, in London at the Royal Albert Hall. He never recorded it in a studio and indeed never sang it again, although the live performance was replayed on Arab radio and television stations for years. The song was finally released on compact disc in 1999 on the twenty-second anniversary of Hafiz's death. It was rumored that the Mossad threatened to assassinate Hafiz if he sang it again, although close friends of Hafiz deny the rumor. See 'Ali 'Abd al-Amir, "Ughniyat 'al-Masih' li-Awwal Marra 'ala Ustuwana li-'Abd al-Halim Hafiz" [The song "al-Masih" on an 'Abd al-Halim Hafiz record for the first time], *al-Ra'y* (Jordan), March 30, 1999. In contrast to Christian motifs, Islamic themes were rarely used in the songs of the period, although mention of prayer, God, and the Prophet Muhammad's night journey to Jerusalem punctuated some of the songs.

16. A *maqam* is a melodic mode based on a theoretical scale, notes of emphasis, and a typical pattern of movement. The octave is divided into smaller microtones to the interval resolution of one-ninth of a step, called a comma. See Ali Jihad Racy, "Arab Music," available: www.turath.org/ProfilesMenu.htm.

17. In reference to the Mongol leader and grandson of Çengiz Khan, who destroyed Baghdad in A.D. 1258 and who is seen in standard Arab accounts as a barbarian.

18. The lyrics of this song can be found in Ahmad Fu'ad Nagm, *Al-A'mal al-Kamila* [Complete works] (Cairo: Dar al-Ahmadi lil-nashr, 2002), 109–111.

19. See Shakir al-Nabulsi, *al-Aghani fi al-Maghani, al-Shaykh Imam 'Isa, Sira Faniya wa Musiqiya* [Songs in the art of singing: Al-Shaykh Imam 'Isa, an artistic and musical biography], *vol. 1, 1918–1969* (Beirut: al-Mu'assasa al-'Arabiya lil-Dirasat wa al-Nashr, 1998), 361.

20. The Lebanese context is quite different from the Egyptian, as the Lebanese state did not possess a monopoly on entertainment venues as the state did in Egypt.

21. On the popularity of these songs and an examination of their lyrics, see Nimr Sirhan, "al-Muqawama fi al-Fulklur al-Filastini" [Resistance in Palestinian folk culture], *Shu'un Filastiniya* 43 (March 1975): 114–136. See also Sirhan's "al-Ughniya al-Sha'biya al-Filastiniya: min al-Huzn ila al-Shawq ila al-Qital" [Palestinian popular songs: From sadness to yearning to fighting], *Shu'un Filastiniya* 19 (March 1973): 159–169.

22. See Isma'il Shammut's report "Al-Nashat al-Fanni al-Filastini" [Palestinian artistic activities], *Shu'un Filastiniya* 98 (January 1980): 138–139. Shammut is less than flattering in his assessment of the performance of the Mu'assassat al-Funun al-Sha'biya (Foundation of Popular Arts), of which the Firqa was part.

23. Tawfiq Zayyad, "Ashuddu 'ala Aydikum," part of the collection of poems by the same title, *Ashuddu 'ala Aydikum*, written in 1966, reprinted in Tawfiq Zayyad, *Diwan Tawfiq Zayyad* (Beirut: Dar al-'Awdah, n.d.), 122–124. *Unadikum* is the first word of the poem and not its title. At the time he sang "Unadikum," Qa'bur was a member of the Lebanese Communist Action Organization. He worked recently for the Mustaqbal (Future) television station owned by Lebanese Prime Minister Rafiq Hariri. Hariri ran clips of Qa'bur as part of his recent election advertising campaign. I would like to thank Elias Khoury for this piece of information.

24. The *'iqal* is the two-ringed black rope that is placed on top of the kufiya to hold it in place.

25. The poem was part of Darwish's first collection, titled *Awraq al-Zaytun* (The olive tree leaves) and published in 1964. See Mahmud Darwish, *Diwan Mahmud Darwish*, vol. 1 (Beirut: Dar al-'Awda, 1994), 71–74.

26. In Darwish, *'Ashiq min Filastin* [A lover from Palestine] (first published in 1966), reprinted in Darwish, *Diwan Mahmud Darwish*, 93–94.

27. For a review of their music in English, see Kamal Boullata and Joost Hilterman, "Improvisation and Continuity: The Music of Sabreen," *Middle East Report* 182 (May–June 1993): 32–35.

28. "Thalathin Nijma," written by Husayn Barghuthi in 1987 and included in Sabreen's album *Jay al-Hamam*, released in 1994.

29. A new group that has recently appeared in the Occupied Territories is Nawa, who sing the lyrics of modern Palestinian poets as well as of the medieval Sufi poet al-Hallaj, and who performed at concerts in besieged Ramallah in the summer of 2002 to rave reviews. See Yusuf al-Shayib, "Firqat Nawa al-Filastiniya Turahin 'ala al-Mustaqbal" [The Palestinian group Nawa bets on the future], *al-Haya*, June 24, 2002, 20.

30. On MWR, see Jason Keyser, "Israel's Arabs Find Revolution in Rap," Associated Press, June 25, 2002.

31. Dam did two tours of England in 2003 sponsored by Palestinian student

groups, and appeared in Paris. They were recently featured in a film by Israeli director Udi Aloni (son of politician Shulamit Aloni). Dam's members are known as Su (Suheil Nafar), Tn (Tamer Nafar), and Jocker (Mahmud Jrery).

32. Yusuf al-Shayib, "Firqat Dam al-liddawiya: al-rab li-mukafahat al-'unsuriya al-Isra'iliya" [The Lyddan Dam band: Rap fighting Israeli racism], *al-Haya*, January 7, 2004, 21. Dam and MWR are becoming known in Israel and in the U.S. and European diaspora, but remain virtually unknown in the Occupied Territories or among the Palestinian diaspora in the Arab World.

33. On the nature of the Oslo agreement and its effects on Palestinian politics, see Edward Said, *Peace and Its Discontents: Essays on Palestine in the Middle East Peace Process* (New York: Vintage Books, 1996), and *The End of the Peace Process* (New York: Pantheon, 1998); Joseph Massad, "Repentant Terrorists, or Settler-Colonialism Revisited: The PLO-Israeli Agreement in Perspective," *Found Object* 3 (spring 1994): 81–90. On Oslo's effect on the Palestinian national movement and Palestinian intellectuals, see Joseph Massad, "Political Realists or Comprador Intelligentsia: Palestinian Intellectuals and the National Struggle," *Critique* (fall 1997): 21–35, and "Return or Permanent Exile," in *Palestinian Refugees and the Right of Return*, edited by Naseer Aruri (London: Pluto Press, 2001). For an assessment of Oslo in relation to Zionism's overall strategy, see Joseph Massad, "The Ends of Zionism: Racism and the Palestinian Struggle," *Interventions* 5, no. 3 (2003): 440–451.

34. Arlit Khuri, "Fayruz Ghannat Filastin wa Lubnan fi Baris" [Fayruz sang Palestine and Lebanon in Paris], *al-Haya*, June 29, 2002, 20.

AMY HOROWITZ

Dueling Nativities:

Zehava Ben Sings

Umm Kulthum

It has been a long time since we rode donkeys in Yemen, went to synagogue three times a day, ate *jachnun*, and chewed on *gat*, we write and sing about being Yemenite Israelis in the here and now. —AVIHU MEDINA, interview with author, Tel Aviv, June 1, 1992

Following the mass migration of Jews from European, Middle Eastern, and North African homelands after World War II, Israel became a site for new genres of music combining the styles, instruments, and traditions of varied cultures. Jews from Islamic lands found in Israel a European-dominated national music that excluded their music for being too Arabic, too Turkish, or otherwise insufficiently Western.[1] Against a backdrop of cultural and political exclusion, Jews from Islamic lands developed their own musical genres and styles.

The pan-ethnic music genre they created, now called Mediterranean Israeli music, gives voice to the dynamic relationship between ethnic affinity and national identity that followed the immigration. Mediterranean Israeli music emerged in the late 1960s, as children of North African and Middle Eastern immigrants such as Avihu Medina, quoted above, wrestled with diverse musical forces in transit camps, development towns, and poor neighborhoods. It developed in the disjuncture between the European Zionist vision of a Jewish national homeland and the actuality of a Middle Eastern Israeli state. The music issued a visceral aesthetic challenge to the European Israeli sense of what the soundscape of a home/land should sound like and of who should control the reconstruction of home itself. Mediterranean Israeli music—its texts, melodies, vocal elaboration, and aesthetic intention—resists and reforms the physical and spiritual boundaries of disputed territory by producing Jewish music composed of conflicting national and aesthetic elements.[2]

The journey of Zehava Ben, a young Moroccan Israeli singer of Turkish tunes from a poor neighborhood in the peripheral southern town of Beersheba, to center stage at official Israeli, Jordanian, Palestinian, and French occasions provides an opportunity to observe the encounters between art and politics in this emergent genre. Zehava Ben's mellismatic vocals burst into Israeli public space in 1990 as the fragile Middle Eastern peace process began to draw attention. The Turkish melody "Tipat Mazal" (A drop of luck) had been circulating freely in the public domain when Moroccan composer Dani Shoshan found it, reupholstered it with Hebrew lyrics, and offered it to Zehava.[3] Before radio editors knew her name, Zehava's amplified voice blared in all directions from dozens of cassette booths that occupied retail space among vegetable, appliance, and clothing booths in Tel Aviv's Central Bus Station marketplace. Within three months there were unsubstantiated estimates that she had sold an astounding 80,000 copies of the "Tipat Mazal" cassette. When listeners flooded the radio with requests for the song, radio editors and record store buyers took notice. In January 1991, Leah Inbal wrote in the newspaper Yedi'ot Aharanot, "The producers on Israel's army radio station, Galei Tzahal were surprised by the requests for 'the Turkish song' by Zehava (meaning gold), but they didn't know who or what she was. A singer named Zehava? Maybe this is all a practical joke."[4] Yet, in working-class neighborhoods of Middle Eastern and North African Israeli Jews, Zehava Ben was indeed considered a golden girl; her Arab-style voice spoke to the residents of these neighborhoods, awakening memory and inspiring hope.

As Zehava's voice continued to invade mainstream Euro-aesthetic public spaces in the early 1990s, European Israelis began to comment on the eastward shift in the soundscape of Israeli popular music. The European Israeli writer Yonatan Gefen lamented a Turkified Tel Aviv when he indirectly referred to Zehava in a May 1992 Ma'ariv column: "As much as I tried I couldn't avoid hearing the 'Turkish' singer whose name I intentionally deleted and who blessed the State of Israel with a medley of Turkish melodies as the audience screamed. After 44 years of solitude we have returned to the roots of Istanbul. The Turks have conquered the city."[5]

Gefen's hostile response to Zehava Ben's music, and his use of the metaphor of political conquest, indicate the potentially turbulent power of such boundary-crossing music in a context of ethnic polarization and disputed territory.[6] The music under study, although an Israeli cultural process and product, emerges in the broader context of the multiple and often over-lapping asymmetries that exist between Israel and Palestine. While fully acknowledging and foregrounding the political reality of Israeli occupa-tion of Palestinian lands, cultures, and communities, it is important to avoid essentializing either group. In this essay I focus almost exclusively on parallel and intersecting internal asymmetrical relationships, the ongoing (despite claims to the contrary) ethnic struggles between European and Middle Eastern and North African Israeli Jews. I am not suggesting that these asymmetries are parallel to those that undergird the Israel-Palestine conflict, in which Israel is a state and Palestine a patchwork of occupied territories. I am, however, arguing that a close reading of those intra-Jewish Israeli power dynamics can ultimately contribute to a critique of the larger Israel-Palestine struggle and, I hope, contribute to a just resolution. My use of the term "disputed territory" to describe asymmetries among Jew-ish Israeli ethnic groups does not eclipse the national struggle over geo-graphic territory between Israel and Palestine. My discussion of disputed territory as a rubric to explore ethnomusical inequities among Israeli Jews exists in the context of a larger struggle over disputed territories—that is, the struggle to remedy the Israeli occupation of Palestinian lands.

I propose a model of dueling nativities to trouble the prevailing concepts of indigeneity, appropriation, and inheritance, and to suggest that Israeli Jewish musicians with roots in Islamic countries are both insiders and out-siders to the regional soundscape.[7] I suggest that some forms of musical borrowing, insofar as they entail the coexistence of multiple and shifting differences, can undermine political boundaries in disputed territory. In particular, I argue that a rhizomatic rather than hierarchical analysis of Zehava Ben's performances of the repertoire of the most famous twentieth-century Arab singer, Umm Kulthum, provides a basis for understanding how music can deterritorialize political boundaries.

In Deleuze and Guattari's terms, the rhizome is an antigenealogy: in-stead of charting linear influences or flows of information or chronologies, rhizomatic mappings are weblike, similar to soundwaves, both permeable and immediate. The rhizome "operates by variation, expansion, conquest, capture, offshoots."[8] Zehava Ben's performances create a tension between rhizomatic multiple coexisting inheritances, polarized identity-based terri-torial claims to ownership, and genealogical subversion when homage and ascription flow across enemy lines.

As boundaries shift and musics are deterritorialized, reterritorialized, or relocalized, context and inclusion also shift and groups are reconfigured to match the new genres just as genres are reconfigured by new coalitions. Both the European-dominated national music that became the mainstream soundscape of Israel, *Shirei Eretz Yisrael* (Songs of the Land of Israel), and the marginalized and excluded music genres created by Mizrahim involved appropriation and reappropriation.[9] Both genres can be described as pan-ethnic formations that borrowed melodies and visual aesthetics from local contexts in Russia, Poland, Czechoslovakia, Greece, Turkey, and Palestine and reconfigured them in new communal contexts in Palestine-Israel.

However, as I argue, the European appropriations and reconfigurations of East European melodies with Hebrew texts and appropriated local Palestinian or Yemenite motifs that were used to create a new national Israeli soundtrack are significantly different from Mizrahi appropriations of Arab, Turkish, Greek, and Persian tunes with Hebrew or Judeo-Arab texts. The difference depends on claims of inheritance and the power dynamics involved. In creating the dominant new Israeli national soundtrack out of reconstituted Russian folk songs, European Israelis drew on their East European musical inheritance to celebrate Jewish workers tilling ancient Hebrew soil. They appropriated local Palestinian and Middle Eastern and North African Jewish musical traditions, rather than engaging in a reciprocal musical encounter. Such an encounter could have resulted in a musical remixing of previously distinct Jewish communities and a musical dialogue with local Palestinian artists.

The genre of Mediterranean Israeli music rose out of the attempts of Middle Eastern and North African Jews in Israel to create a more inclusive national soundtrack. While European Israeli formations of national music were based on asymmetric appropriation of Mediterranean sounds, Mizrahi musicians engaged in reciprocal pan-ethnic appropriations that created this genre against the backdrop of their political struggle for equality. Mizrahi Jews claimed an inheritance of Middle Eastern and North African music as an extension of their centuries-old local traditions. Recent manifestations of the genre, such as Zehava Ben's performances, rely on rhizomatic appropriations that cross or defy political and ethnic borders and may open spaces for political challenges to these boundaries. Ben's rhizomatic appropriations are significant precisely because of the way their routedness reflects the situation of the Mizrahim, who were uprooted from Middle Eastern and North African communities and rerouted to a new local context that was at war with their former homelands.

Forebears: Scholarship on Mediterranean Israeli Music

The scholarship on Mediterranean Israeli music parallels the legitimizing process of this contested music genre itself. Mediterranean Israeli music's cassette debut in the marketplace in 1974 was accompanied by a handful of newspaper articles in the daily Hebrew-language newspapers that covered the music as either local gossip or as a sidebar to the story of the emerging Mizrahi ethnic revolution. In the early 1980s, the Syrian Israeli ethnomusicologist Amnon Shiloah and the European Israeli sociologist Erik Cohen copublished two landmark articles on the musical, social, and political dimensions of Israeli popular music. Shiloah and Cohen identify musical trends that describe immigrant musicians' expressions of their sudden encounter with a new culture as a result of geographical and social relocation. These trends are outlined as temporally chronological stages developing from the 1950s through the 1980s: Israelization, Orientalization, ethnicization, popularization, and academization.[10] Anthropologist Jeff Halper and ethnomusicologists Edwin Seroussi and Pamela Squires-Kidron similarly examined Mizrahi music to develop ethnographically grounded observations that unveil the "coded" musical meanings for creators and listeners.[11] They also distinguish the musical community, or "taste public," according to ethnicity and class identity, arguing that *Musiqa Mizraḥit* remains marginal not only because of its unaccepted sound, but because it is associated with "low culture." Similarly, Motti Regev's work on Israeli rock-and-roll explores questions of nativities and "foreign" musical influences.[12]

By focusing on Israelization and Israeliness, attempting to understand Mediterranean Israeli music as a context-sensitive Israeli local expression, Shiloah, Serrousi, and Regev provide a model for studying music as culturally situated but not wedded to particular "authentic" or "original" contexts. They provide the groundwork for my exploration of sounds separated from one context and recontextualized in another. I argue that Mediterranean Israeli music is best described as a web of soundscapes involving contiguous claims of shared roots by enemies in local conflict zones.

Counterhomelands and Rerouted Encounters

The emergence of Mediterranean Israeli music is a direct consequence of the mid-twentieth-century North African and Middle Eastern Jewish relocation to the newly established Israeli state. Although a small number of Middle Eastern Jews were already present in Palestine, this music genre must be understood in the context of the complex and mass encounter between some 300,000 immigrants from North Africa and the Middle East and some 300,000 European Holocaust survivors between 1948 and the mid-1950s. The magnitude and pace of this sudden mass meeting between diverse Jewish groups doubled the Jewish population in Palestine in less than a decade marked by war, national independence, international censure, and economic crisis. The migration also unsettled and reconfigured ethnic demographics, creating a puzzling rubric those Eastern European socialist architects of the new state were ill-prepared to manage. Israel's ethnic problems and the emergence of the Mizrahi pan-ethnic marker are rooted in cultural affinities as well as in the shortcomings of an absorption program characterized by unequal treatment and cultural insensitivities toward North African and Middle Eastern Jews.[13]

In Mizrahi Israeli neighborhoods and development towns in the 1950s, Jewish musicians interacted with each other and created new musical innovations emerging from and reshaping North African and Middle Eastern musics. These new encounters between Middle Eastern and North African Jewish musicians occurred in transit tent camps or "abandoned" Palestinian neighborhoods as Palestinian musicians were being uprooted from these very homes and rerouted into what also were imagined to be transitional camps, infusing the process with tragic irony.[14] Amid the final echoes of a vanished local Palestinian music scene resonant with an aesthetic that would have reminded them of home, North African and Middle Eastern Jewish musicians shared their diverse rural and urban, classical and folk, liturgical and secular musics, traditions that had evolved in concert with Muslim and Christian neighbors throughout the region. Walking through a neighborhood street on a Friday evening, one could hear the convergence of previously distant regional liturgical traditions as Yemenite and Bukharan, Syrian and Afghani *nigunim* (tunes) poured out of open windows. Weddings, births, bar mitzvahs, and religious holidays were occasions for musical transformation as well as celebration. Renowned Iraqi *qanun* and *'ud* players performed at Iranian, Libyan, Egyptian, and other Mizrahi community events. Yemenite singers became fluent in Iraqi and Kurdish folk songs. While the intermingling of styles had inspired the creation of new pan-ethnic formulations in earlier periods, such as the liturgical Jerusalemite-Sephardi cantorial style documented by renowned musicologist Abraham Zvi Idelsohn and later by Amnon Shiloah and others, this new North African and Middle Eastern musical encounter was unique in its demographic diversity.

Encountering the Eastern European
Israeli National Soundtrack

New immigrants from the Middle East and North Africa also encountered the dominant national soundtrack, Shirei Eretz Yisrael (Songs of the Land of Israel; henceforth, SLI), a popular music genre combining Russian folk tunes and Hebrew lyrics that emerged during the large waves of Eastern European immigration from the 1880s until the late 1940s. There were various subgenres and stylistic developments, but the music had one goal: to create a sense of Israeliness, rerooting diasporic Jews in the land of Israel.[15] Song and dance teachers traveled between Jewish settlements in Palestine teaching the newly composed national folk songs and dances to aid the nation-building project. This genre featured a Western or Eastern European structure and ethos, combined with selected Middle Eastern and Mediterranean textures and tunes. The songs were characterized by romantic nationalistic Hebrew lyrics idealizing worker, land, and communal mission and were usually set to Eastern European marching tunes, although some Yemenite, Bedouin, and even local Palestinian melodies were employed.[16] The SLI represents an asymmetrical appropriation primarily in its token use of stereotypical Orientalized musical styles. With the advent of national radio and recording companies, the market expanded locally and nationally (see figure 6).

Israel, like many African, Asian, and European countries that gained independence after World War II, established a state-controlled media for ideological and economic reasons. The Israeli government believed that by controlling access to the airwaves, ethnic variation could be minimized while new national songs helped shape a shared identity. But as Israeli national radio, television, and local recording industries developed in the 1960s, the gap between emerging Mizrahi neighborhood traditions and national folk, popular, and art musics intensified. Arabic and Mediterranean sounds were relegated to specific radio time slots or state folkloric occasions.[17] Only Middle Eastern and North African Israelis with European training, such as Yemenite singer Bracha Zefira, entered the mainstream musical establishment.[18] The arrival of renowned Jewish musicians from Islamic countries in the early 1950s might have provided an opportunity to broaden the local soundscape by fostering a mutually respectful dialogue between Eastern and Western music masters. But these rich and ancient Eastern Jewish traditions became reduced to motifs and local texture in a national music industry governed by European tastes.

FIGURE 6. This Shirei Eretz Yisrael album cover is emblematic of Ashkenazi attempts to incorporate Middle Eastern visual elements. Barefoot dancers wear embroidered costumes and musicians combine *darbuka* and *halil* with accordion in an attempt to localize the European frame. Album cover of the Oranim Zabar Israeli Troupe's *Shalom!*, 1959.

Emerging Mizrahi Styles:
Undermining the National Soundscape

As pan-Mizrahi musical styles began to coalesce in the 1960s, SLI became a nostalgic device through which European Israelis preserved memories of the Yishuv and the state's early days. However, for the children of recent Mizrahi immigrants growing up during this period, the music became a symbol of Shiloah and Cohen's category of Israelization, an attempt to realize the ideal of integration of the diasporas by assimilating their traditional musical styles to the predominant style of Israeli folk music.[19]

North African and Middle Eastern immigrants to Israel and their Israeli-born Mizrahi children were eager to participate in the national soundscape. Yet their attempts to offer Eastern cover versions of the SLI style were rejected. The pan-ethnic styles that emerged in Mizrahi neighborhoods—their texts, melodies, vocal elaboration, and aesthetic intention—challenged the European soundscape of the Israeli state by encompassing Hebrew, Arab, Persian, Turkish, and even East Indian sonic and linguistic elements. Simultaneously, the music's creators and performers troubled tendencies to reduce Israel's unfolding ethnic problem to a simple opposition of Ashkenazi versus Mizrahi. They complicated such equations through lyrical and melodic compositions that intentionally re-covered, re-formed, and remixed Western, Eastern European, and Arabic genres. Moreover, they considered the very process of selecting and remixing the diverse musical and lyrical traditions of European and Mizrahi Jews with Greek popular music or even rock as a continuation of their own multivocal cultural heritage.

Mizrahi musicians were frustrated by European attempts to preserve and freeze their creativity rather than embrace their emerging styles. Avihu Medina, a leading Mizrahi composer of Yemenite ethnic origin, lamented mainstream tendencies to privilege notions of Yemenite purity. Commenting on the exclusionary tendencies of the 1970s, he said, "It has been many years since Israelis left our Eastern and Western homelands. We have mixed together into one single, enormous muddle."[20] Medina's resistance to the preservationist treatment of Yemenite music coincided with the increasing influence of Mediterranean music in Israel. By the late 1960s and 1970s, media development helped undermine European Israeli attempts to create a coherent Israeli music. Responding to market interests, radio and television began to introduce Greek, French, Spanish, and other Mediterranean popular musics, as well as rock-and-roll.[21]

In Mizrahi neighborhoods, Mediterranean and Arab songs were copied from LPS and radio onto tape and distributed widely. By challenging dominant channels of communication and empowering grassroots distribution, these innovations further destabilized the nationally sanctioned music genre and made way for the emergence of new Mizrahi genres and viable alternative neighborhood networks. The Mediterranean trend of the 1960s and 1970s influenced Ashkenazi as well as Mizrahi musicians. Greek influences evoked ancient myth and reinvented national tradition, themes resonating with the unfolding modern Israeli project.[22] Greek music signified the meeting place of Eastern and Western influences, a safety zone between the "extremes" of the Arab East and the U.S. West. Greek and Mediterranean appropriations did not resonate with political overtones, whereas Arab and Turkish borrowings were seen as degrading invasions and touched a visceral chord in a national psyche committed to upholding a Eurovision of the Jewish state. At the same time that radio editors and record companies were accepting Ashkenazi appropriations of Greekness, they rejected offerings by Mizrahi composers such as Medina's Greek vocal overlay on "Lilkom Ba'adekh, Medina" (To fight for you, country), a 1970s Mizrahi composition influenced by the remake of the SLI song "Malu Asameinu Bar" (Our silos were filled with wheat).[23]

Each appropriation, each rejection, and each newly emerged style was read in a changing system of cultural values. In Israel's new musical laboratory, in which claims to origins could carry as much weight (and baggage) as claims to originality, musical appropriations mapped the confluence of several disputed territories. The dispute played out between West and East, Europeanizing and Orientalizing appropriations, modernity, premodernity, and the ancient world, but the contest itself was about participation in the national soundtrack of Israel. Claiming a stake in the soundtrack meant claiming a stake in the nation. In this context, the 1970s relocalization of Mediterranean Israeli music can be seen not only as a consolidation of the music genre, but of the political coalition of Israelis from North Africa and the Middle East. Mizrahi music covers of Mediterranean tunes proliferated in the 1970s; they abandoned emulation of the weighty messages and Russian marching tunes of sli songs in favor of lighter party music. Holiday parties and neighborhood clubs resounded with the electrified sounds and Arab dance movements that accompanied the Mizrahi *hafla* (Arabic slang for "party") songs. Where a Greek vocal style had supplemented a Russian marching tune in "Lilkom Ba'adekh," now Klezmer melodies such as "Hanale Hitbalbela" (Little Hanale got confused) were retuned in a Greek style. As the performers negotiated Greek, Arabic, rock-and-roll, Yiddish, and Hebrew elements, their mellismatic vocals centered the sound weave.[24] The lyrics of "Hanale Hitbalbela," written in 1933 by Natan Alterman (1910–1970), are social commentary and parody recounting a topsy-turvy love story and marriage between an Askenazi boy and a Mizrahi girl.[25] In this counterappropriation, Mizrahi musicians laid claim to a European text that poked fun at Ashkenazi and Mizrahi cultures as well as the notion of a mixed marriage. This double-voicedness inevitably confuses if not shifts the grounds of power.[26]

Mizrahi musicians chose Alterman's poem about a wedding as the basis for a song for good reason. Mizrahi singers had begun to consolidate their style in the synagogue and at neighborhood celebrations, especially weddings. In the 1960s and 1970s, Mizrahi neighborhood singers were primarily employed as wedding entertainers. Although most were Yemenites, they provided multiethnic vocals appropriate for each wedding party. They rearranged Turkish, Yemenite, and Kurdish songs with rock-and-roll and Mediterranean popular styles, and they reworked European songs using Middle Eastern elements. Wedding bands such as Tszliley Hakerem (Tunes of the vineyard) were adept at such ironic juxtapositions; in fact, their livelihood depended on this multivocality. Thus, North African and Middle Eastern Israeli weddings were locations where neighborhood singers con-

FIGURE 7. The cover of this Mediterranean Israeli Music songbook, produced by the Reuveni Brothers, features a gold cassette necklace, emblem of the Mizrahi music revolution. *Zemer Yam Tikhoni* [Mediterranean singer], ed. Aryeh Tsuberi (Tel-Aviv: Modan, 1987).

FIGURE 8. This CD cover features a headshot of Zehava Ben inscribed in the profile of Umm Kulthum. *Zehava Ben Sings Arabic*, 1995.

solidated a repertoire that provided both ethnically specific selections and pan-ethnic blends as it reconfigured sacred and secular proximities. Moreover, weddings were rituals in which Mizrahiyut was both consolidated and transgressed as Middle Easterners and North Africans, and Ashkenazim and Mizrahim entered mixed marriages.[27]

Asher Reuveni's tale of a 1970s wedding provides a genesis story of how the music of Mizrahim became consolidated as a genre called Mediterranean Israeli music. Significantly, the story combines post–Yom Kippur War sociopolitics with the use of a cassette recorder at a Yemenite wedding party:

> It all started with my wedding. I didn't have a real wedding with a band and dancing and drinking till the morning. My wife's only brother was killed in the [1973 Yom Kippur] war. Our happiness was shattered and we married in a quiet way in the offices of the Rabbinate. My friends promised that when the day comes, three months later, they will make it up to me with a real hafla. They brought the original Oud Band from Kerem Hateymanim [Yemenite Quarter]. With Daklon [Yossi Levy] and Ben Mosh [Moshe Ben Mosh]. Close to sixty people squeezed into my mother's living room, three by four meters, and Daklon and Ben Mosh played and sang songs from our father's home.

Asher and his brothers, Iranian owners of a record and electronics shop in a Yemenite neighborhood in Tel Aviv, Shkhunat Hatikva, recorded the wedding party. Using a new four-way duplicating machine, they made souvenir cassettes for their guests. The sound quality was poor, but the capacity to mass-produce the cassette was revolutionary. When someone offered them 100 lirot, they took notice.

> This was '74 when a lira was a lira, and don't forget, it was a "partisani" [grassroots] recording, it was very unsophisticated. So I said, "What's happening here?" My friends don't know how to read notes but they play and sing "alakefak" [cool] because it comes straight from the heart. It's good to know that music in this country finally runs according to our tap![28]

Reuveni's story is emblematic of the consolidation of the genre of Mediterranean Israeli music in individual communities and neighborhoods, and its ability to spread beyond those specific contexts by means of inexpensive mass duplication.

Mediterranean Israeli music became audible beyond the neighborhoods in the early 1970s as Mizrahi youth challenged the hegemonic state policies that had been termed "the mistakes of the '50s."[29] The Mizrahi cultural renaissance and social revolution of the 1970s attempted to redefine the artistic as well as political boundaries of Israeli society during a period of deep national and international transformation. The 1967 and 1973 wars altered the balance of power in profound ways. Ilan Halevi points out that "the acquisition of Arab territories was the end of the geocultural isolation of Israel in the Arab world."[30] The 1967 war presented a fundamental contradiction for a society that had fashioned its political philosophy on a supposedly egalitarian ideal. Michael Keren points to the ambivalence of artists and scholars who were aroused by the victory but repulsed by their new role as occupier: "For Israeli writers of the seventies and eighties, utopia is the reality of the past; the present nothing but a great and ugly dystopia. The new figure who appeared in the late 1960's gradually took over a central position in the literature of the 1970's and 1980's: the figure of the uprooted Israeli. In essence, the model of alienation and affliction, the pre-heroic model, reemerged from the deep unconscious of the nation's soul."[31] Ammiel Alcalay suggests that for Mizrahi Jews, the new proximity to Arab territories that resulted from Israeli occupation triggered buried memories of ancestral homelands, memories that had been sealed from consciousness in the process of acculturating to the Jewish state.[32] On a practical level, the acquisition of new territories brought about changes in Mizrahi status: there were increased job opportunities for Arabic speakers, who were needed to govern and administer the occupied territories.

After the Yom Kippur War (1973), the Ashkenazi power grip was shaken by an anti–Labor Party outcry from Israel's Mizrahi underclass. Mizrahi anger was fed by an experience of continued oppression even after service in the recent wars. Mizrahi activism was also intensified by the impact of the leftist cultural and political revolution in the United States represented by Black Power, antiwar, and student rights movements. One Mizrahi social activist group fighting for better housing, jobs, and education took the name Black Panthers. However, the Mizrahi music of the revolution, sometimes referred to as Panther music, cried out for inclusion in rather than eradication of the mainstream.[33] Libyan Israeli Eli Luzon's "Eyzo Medina" (What a country), a gentle critique of Israeli society, and "Avraham Avinu"

(Abraham our patriarch), Avihu Medina's subsequent commentary on the Israeli-Arab conflict, underscore the distance between U.S. protest music of the 1960s and 1970s and what Sephardi radio editor Shimon Parnas describes as Israel's little music revolution.[34]

As Asher Reuveni's wedding story demonstrates, the portable cassette recorder allowed Mizrahi entrepreneurs to mass-produce and distribute music excluded by the mainstream industry. The affordability and plasticity of the cassette facilitated commercial and musical growth, empowering community-based music and altering local soundscapes forever.[35] Using homemade cassettes, Mizrahi musicians and distributors were able to sidestep the state-controlled media that had rejected their raw combination of Middle Eastern and Mediterranean influences with Western pop music.[36]

When the Reuveni Brothers released a tape by an unknown Yemenite singer, Zohar Argov, they were already positioned as a prominent Mizrahi cassette company. The new tape, "Elinor," sold by the hundreds of thousands, taxing their production operation.[37] They quickly developed a distribution network by negotiating with several Iranian and Georgian merchants in Tel Aviv's open-air marketplace, and then entered other outdoor marketplaces throughout the country.

The formula for Argov's increasing popularity lay in his collaboration with another Yemenite musician: singer, composer, and arranger Avihu Medina. Medina crafted songs that selectively incorporated Spanish, Greek, and Western instrumentation and arrangements to embellish the Yemenite vocal line, which remained the most resilient element of the music. Medina's compositions for Argov, such as "Peraḥ Begani" (The flower in my garden), often began with the traditional Arabic *mawwal* (introduction to a song), highlighting Argov's mellismatic vocalization. In Bakhtinian terms, the prolonged *mawwal* itself can be considered a multivocal "uncrowning" of the authorial voice of Israeli culture.[38]

With Argov's commercial success in the early 1980s, Mediterranean Israeli music gained increased airtime. By 1981, the army's official station, Galei Tzahal, and Israel Radio's popular music channel, Reshet Gimel, had each added a two-hour weekly Mizrahi segment. While these were significant advances, Argov claimed ghettoization: "Over 55% of Israel is my audience, but to hear me on the radio they have to wait until 2 pm on Wednesday in the *Mizrahi* corner. We live in 1981 and those programs were old 10 years ago. We are fed up!!! Why are we being locked in a—I didn't say ghetto, that's your word. I only said it hurts. Scatter us on all the hours or don't play us at all."[39] The Mizrahi accusation was especially harsh for European Holocaust survivors, for whom the term ghetto touched a deep nerve. Also, Mizrahi appropriation of the word in the sense used by the U.S. Black Power movement, to signify poor sections of urban centers, was a wake-up call to a national identity built on egalitarian notions. A disenfranchised neighborhood music that had flourished at a grassroots level, despite being assigned to broadcast corners and heritage display, was now blasting out of the ghetto as the soundtrack to an emerging pan-ethnic political coalition. At the heart of the conflict were questions of appropriation and the rights to a musical inheritance.

The ghetto blasting moved in unexpected ways as a song by a Yemenite Israeli singer named Haim Moshe seeped across the border to Syria, Lebanon, and Jordan. Moshe's renditions of the popular Arabic song "Linda, Linda" resulted in fan mail from Arab listeners, testifying to his ability to blast through geopolitical ghettos and touch the hearts of Israel's enemies. Though the Arabic text and aesthetic features of Moshe's "Linda Linda" could touch a Syrian listener, they seemed remote from mainstream European Israeli taste. Nonetheless, in 1986, a refashioned "Linda Linda" became popular on the kibbutz scene and was choreographed for Israeli folk dance. With "Linda Linda," Moshe had simultaneously infiltrated both enemy airwaves and Israel's ideological heartland as symbolized by the kibbutz and official "Israeli" folk dance.[40]

By the late 1980s, Moshe's mainstream successes included appearances on prime-time television and at official state celebrations. He entertained Israelis and Palestinians at Donald Trump's Taj Mahal casino in Atlantic City. Morocco's royal palace was also on his tour schedule. He had succeeded in straddling mainstream, Mizrahi neighborhood, and Arab tastes. However, when Haim Moshe added "Ashkenazi" music to his repertoire, he was accused of trying to pass for Ashkenazi. In response, he claimed that he was "not Ashkenazifying" but composing music for the true nation: "I call it Israeli music, neither east nor west but made up of both, but if you want a name, well then call it country music, because it reflects what's really going on in the country—Stevie Wonder singing country music. Stevie is Yemenite, well a little to the left of Yemen. In another twenty years this music will be known as the real Israeli music, not eastern or western but the authentic sound."[41]

In the early 1990s, Mizrahi cassette company owners and performers, who had previously competed fiercely in a small market, joined together to bring issues of unpaid performance royalties, broadcasting discrimination, ghettoization, and illegal monopolization before a special Knesset committee. To maximize their credibility, they established two official organizations, Hapil, the Israeli Federation for Mediterranean Music, and AZIT, the Association for Mediterranean Song. In the process of creating an official framework, musicians and producers claimed and renamed their emergent genre, replacing largely pejorative designations based on class and ethnic slurs that called attention to the "inferior" cassette production and the working-class locations in which the music was played and sold. The press had bestowed on the genre names such as *musiqat qasetot* (cassette music), *musiqa shel hataḥana hamerkazit* (central bus station music), *musiqa mizrahit* (Eastern music), *musiqa etnit* (ethnic music), and *musiqa shora* (black music). The new name chosen by the genre's practitioners, *musiqa yisraelit yam tikhonit* (Mediterranean Israeli music), modified the designation of Israeliness by placing it in a regional context.

With the rising popularity of Mediterranean Israeli music, some singers headed east. They exchanged Western rock beats and Greek tunes for royalty-free Turkish melodies circulating in the public domain. Although Greek melodies contained Western elements that appealed to European Israeli ears, obtaining licensing agreements was often expensive and time-consuming. Turkish tunes, according to Meir Paz of ACUM, were free because Israel and Turkey had not yet established any copyright agreements. The music, like the Mediterranean basin, is a crossroads at which cultural forces meet and are reforged. Defiance of European categories and designations was also a political challenge to hegemonic media and national institutions that classify Mizrahi musical contributions as lacking in aesthetic legitimacy, commercial viability, and national coherency. Mizrahi creators viewed the hybrid nature of their music as appropriate to their multicultural identities. And some viewed the attempts of folklorists, musicologists, and composers to reduce their music into neat categories, as in the drive to preserve "authentic" Yemenite songs, as Ashkenazi appropriation.

In the mid- to late 1990s, Mediterranean Israeli music shifted from an illegitimate, contestive alternative network consisting of what Motti Regev had called a "poor imitation of Israeli rock," to an elevated position within mainstream Israeli popular music. The posthumous consecration of Yemenite singer Zohar Argov was expressed in an uptown avant-garde theater piece, a feature-length film, and a prime-time television documentary. Occasions of truly reciprocal interactions between Mizrahi and Ashkenazi singers were no longer surprising, and the nature of media attention had changed (covering the music itself rather than music as ethnic issue).

Now claims of continuing ethnic gaps in the field of music were deemed irrelevant. The proliferation of cable channels and decentralized local radio stations reconfigured access to broadcast channels, and local papers regularly reviewed new releases and concert appearances. Mediterranean Israeli music was, as Argov had wished, "scattered throughout the hours" rather than ghettoized in Oriental corners of radio and television.

At the same time, Mediterranean Israeli musicians returned to the ethnically specific rural and urban, classical and folk, Middle Eastern and North African music genres their parents and grandparents had been asked to abandon in the late 1940s, when ethnicity itself was illegitimate and the national musical task was a blending of exilic soundscapes. In the context of a burgeoning world music industry and increased acceptability of Middle Eastern and North African musics, Moroccan, Kurdish, Iranian, and other particular traditions found favor in the mainstream Israeli marketplace. The popularity of specific ethnic musics may have come out of a nostalgia that grew from the consolidation of Mizrahiyut. With increasing, though by no means fully realized, integration came an expression of longing for ancestral diaspora homelands. For Ashkenazi world music lovers, vicarious reclamation of North African and Middle Eastern music roots (what Yael Zerubavel would call recovered roots) may have signaled indigenousness as well as a more appealing and "aesthetically coherent" (i.e., "authentic") sound than previous Mediterranean Israeli music formulations.[42]

From Schizophonia to Rhizomatics

Steven Feld's discussion of schizophonia and schismogenesis in world music is helpful for understanding Mizrahi claims for indigeneity, heritage, and hybridity in popular music. According to Feld, schizophonia is Murray Schafer's term for the separation of sounds from their sources, and schismogenesis is how Gregory Bateson describes the way regroupings and reterritorializations create asymmetrical power relationships between groups competing for indigeneity.[43] In the case of Mizrahi regroupings (the creation of a pan-ethnic community) and reterritorialization (border crossings), the separation of sounds from their sources creates the possibility for enemy appropriation of musical styles in disputed territory. Emergence creates schisms, and schisms create unlikely emergences across enemy lines. In concert with the emergent music forms I have described, I propose three categories of power relationships.

In the first category, which I call *asymmetrical appropriation*, hegemonic groups, such as the European Israelis who were architects of the national soundscape, borrowed from subordinate Mizrahi groups. As is typical in asymmetrical relationships, European Israelis tokenized, trivialized, caricaturized, and exoticized the borrowed materials. Also, they freely transformed the material, while the Mizrahi musicians were regarded as vestiges of a disappearing Ur form and were thus discouraged from exploring musical transformation or innovation. Feld describes the asymmetry of this form of appropriation as a "succoring-dependence" or custodial relationship in which the custodians ensure the continued dependency of cultural practitioners from whom they mine creative resources.[44] This custodial dependence is an apt description of the Israeli power structure, in which European Israelis dominated not only economic, educational, and political spheres, but also the emerging music industry. In particular, I note two dimensions of asymmetrical appropriation: first, the tokenized use of Middle Eastern and North African musical motifs and instrumentation by mainstream European Israeli composers, and second, the appropriation of Middle Eastern and North African music for live or broadcast official heritage display. Both dimensions demonstrate schizophonia, or the separation of sounds from their sources. The first type of appropriation uses synechdoche to borrow parts of the music, and the second keeps the performance intact but removes it from its community context.

In the second category, which I call *pan-ethnic appropriation*, relationships are based on reciprocal rather than asymmetrical affiliations. In contrast to the hegemonic-subordinate relationships of the first category, these appropriations are characterized by shared experience, indigeneity that translates into claims of uninterrupted inheritance, or other kinds of belonging. The force driving pan-ethnic appropriations is not dominance and subordination, though there are indeed struggles within the emergent pan-ethnic group for territory, but a shared sense of rootedness and rootlessness. These appropriations demonstrate cultural affiliations that can map onto political identities and cultural styles that can trespass across geopolitical conflict lines. Both the European-dominated national music that became the mainstream soundscape of Israel and the marginalized and excluded music genres created by Mizrahim involved appropriation and reappropriation; both can be described as pan-ethnic formations that borrowed melodies and visual aesthetics from local contexts in Russia, Poland, Czechoslovakia, Greece, Turkey, or Palestine and reconfigured them in new communal contexts in Palestine-Israel. However, European appropriations and reconfigurations of East European melodies with Hebrew texts appropriated from Middle Eastern and North African Jewish musical traditions without engaging in a reciprocal musical encounter that could truly have represented a musical "remixing of the exiles." Mizrahi Jews, on the other hand, claimed an inheritance of Middle Eastern and North African music as an extension of their own Middle Eastern context. They envisioned a continuing development of the music of the region as part of the development of a new national style. Toward that end, they added Hebrew texts and drew on some aspects of the aesthetics being developed by European composers.

The third category of power relationship, *rhizomatic appropriation*, describes the loss of control by official culture or by the manufacturers of meaning (to use Bourdieu's term) and involves the proliferation of emergent styles that contest pure categories.[45] Music becomes inevitably "contaminated" as it travels through the airwaves across national boundaries, transgressing customs, checkpoints, and security zones. Rhizomatic appropriations describe relationships across geopolitical conflict lines and the performance of cultural identities that confirm, ignore, realign, transcend, or defy those borders. Uncontested appropriations belie their invented nature and can be deployed to create powerful political affiliations across enemy lines. The uncontested status is always temporary and always open to suspicion. It is unclear how porous to such infiltration a particular political landscape may be, because cultural boundaries and political boundaries are not necessarily parallel.

Music provides a particularly fertile ground for exploring porous boundaries, insofar as it recognizes that the map is not the territory and that soundscapes do not conform to either historical legacies or political landscapes. Ethnomusicologists and folklorists define cultural heritage claims expressed through aesthetic re-coverings and reformulations as borrowing, quotation, appropriation, parody, intertextuality, stylistic allusion, usage, pastiche, patchwork—terms that command literatures and scholarly discourses.[46] However, such lumping together and splitting of music's categories runs counter to the intentions of the Mizrahi musicians who created the Mediterranean Israeli music style.[47] Mizrahi performers like Avihu Medina and Zehava Ben can map their repertoire in terms they recognize, but they also subvert or blur these boundaries. Medina delineates his songs as *asli* (authentic), *asli im gvan yam tikhoni* (the real thing with mediterranean color), and *shirey meurav* (combination songs). His aim is integrational rather than oppositional.[48] Musicians' own cartographies of their repertoires encompass multiple and conflicting essentialisms. This proliferation of styles can be seen not only as an inheritance or a struggle over indigeneities but also as a model for coexistence, albeit a contested, conflictual, and unresolved one. As John Szwed has demonstrated, the goal of mapping style is not to insist on a direction of influence but to be able to observe multidirectionality, simultaneously fast-forwarding and rewinding.[49] When this multidirectionality trespasses across enemy lines, the potential for reciprocal exchange may take on a political meaning.

With the developments in the Palestinian-Israeli peace process and the continued ascendancy of world music in the early 1990s, the homespun genre of Mediterranean Israeli music was elevated to a new position in the mainstream Israeli imagination. Zehava Ben, who had previously offended journalists with her Turkish songs, now pushed against the borders of musical and political maps by singing the repertoire of Umm Kulthum.

In 1994–1995 Zehava Ben released a CD on her own label entitled *Zehava Ben Sings Arabic*. The silver and gold cover inscribes Zehava Ben within the profile of Umm Kulthum (see figure 8). The inner sleeve is adorned with images of Ben's pilgrimage to the graves of Umm Kulthum and Farid al-Atrash in Egypt. Umm Kulthum, whose career spanned over half a century, was able to attract Jewish, Muslim, and Christian audiences in Islamic countries.[50] Zehava Ben's performances of her repertoire demonstrate the dialogic relationship of appropriation. As an Israeli Jewish performer singing the repertoire of an Egyptian Muslim woman, Zehava Ben could be seen as reproducing the asymmetrical power relationships of the Middle East (what I have described as assymetrical appropriation). But Zehava Ben publicly positions herself as an heir to Umm Kulthum because of her North African ethnicity and Arabic-speaking background. Her performances of Umm Kulthum's repertoire also may be considered, therefore, a legitimate claim to a legacy, thereby endeavoring to remedy the asymmetry of the appropriation.

The political implications of an enemy claim to inheritance complicate the second category of pan-ethnic appropriation. An inheritance is significantly different from other kinds of appropriation, and this difference has enormous importance for cultures in disputed territory. The success of Zehava Ben's claim to the legacy of Umm Kulthum depends on the willingness of her audience to accept the supposedly fundamental contradiction of an Israeli Jew claiming to be the musical heir of an Egyptian Muslim. Audiences that accept Zehava Ben's performances either embrace a larger pan-ethnic formulation that can conceive of and include a Jewish Arab, or they simply ignore her Jewishness. Zehava Ben calls attention to aspects of her shared experience with Umm Kulthum: they are both women from poor, religious, rural, Arabic-speaking families. These connections compete with but never completely overshadow the political, national, and religious schisms between their contexts, as well as the temporal distance between them.

Zehava Ben's venture was risky; by reclaiming Arab music as her heritage, she opened herself up to criticism at home and in the Arab world. Her performances of Umm Kulthum took on very different meanings on different occasions: at an official ceremony commemorating the peace process, at an Egyptian Israeli wedding (nostalgia in older people for pre-state days in Alexandria), at a concert for Palestinians in Jericho (commercial entertainment and suspension of politics), at a chic Tel Aviv club frequented by European Israeli world music fans (Israeli claims to an indigenous "ethnic" soundscape), or at an outdoor antidrug concert in downtown Jerusalem.

It is possible to describe Zehava Ben as a nomadic figure, traversing imaginary cartographies that cannot be mapped by unidirectional appropriations and are better understood as rhizomatic invasions. If Zehava Ben's covers of Umm Kulthum opened her to Arab challenges of appropriating from their culture, they also helped her to consolidate her position as a representative of a Jewish-Arab-Israeli hybridity that was used as the soundtrack of border openings and crossing within Israel and between Israel and its enemies.

In the fall of 1995, in the aftermath of Prime Minister Rabin's assassination, Zehava Ben released her second Arabic CD, this time on the mainstream Helicon label. In the interim she had studied classical Arab music, language, and performance and developed competency in the repertoire of Umm Kulthum; now she employed the Arab Orchestra of Haifa to accompany her. As many Israelis and Palestinians shared in grieving over Rabin's death and the unsettling prospects for peace, Zehava Ben's CDs and appearances in Nablus and Jericho and at ceremonies marking the (cold) peace with Egypt resonated with musical, political, and commercial overtones. The children of North African and Middle Eastern Jewish immigrants who had kept Arabic music in the closet now turned up the volume in taxis and cafés. Palestinians seeking material signs of a fragile peace process also took notice of Ben's musical overture.

The question of the political consequences of these dueling nativities —especially the juxtaposition of Ben's national nativity (Israeli) with her musical choices (Arab, Turkish, Western rock, among others)—requires a model of cultural politics that relies less on unidirectional forces of influence and more on a weblike model of airwaves or soundscapes that are not bound by geographic or national borders, if nonetheless overdetermined. Perhaps the performers and listeners who manage dueling nativities as fields of integrations and contradictions, as the business of everyday life, produce the best critique of identity politics. Essentialism is not only academically unviable but also experientially impossible, at least in disputed territories. In these liminal spaces, identity is often strategic, and claims to lineage may have dramatic contemporary consequences that go beyond the preservation and transmission of an idealized past.[51]

Zehava Ben's performances allow her audience to invest in otherwise contradictory elements, to momentarily realign nonaligned political positions (most notably, Muslim and Jew, Israeli and Egyptian, European and Middle Eastern Israeli, disenfranchised and mainstream).[52] She allows her audiences to temporarily cross seemingly impenetrable borders. The subjectivity Ben represents is, like all subjectivities and identities, temporary and mobile. Her seemingly improvisational identity riffs call and respond to contextual particularities, shifting between centers of gravity as she performs Umm Kulthum, duets with Yemenite transvestite singer Dana International in a Meretz party election ad, and sings Arabic-language praise poems for Bibi Netanyahu at a Likud-sponsored barbecue.[53] Zehava Ben embodies and performs the dual and the dueling nativities that her audience recognizes in them. Despite our academic discomfort with such contiguous discontinuities, they nonetheless represent a part of life in disputed territories, for example, the way Moroccan Israeli soldiers affix Ben's "drop of luck" image to their weapons: on the one hand, they are Israeli soldiers looking for a drop of luck, on the other hand, they are Andalusian Arabs, frequently the butt of ethnic discrimination in Israel. It is discomforting that these contradictions come together in the form of a military decoration.

The contradictions extend to Ben's appropriations of the repertoire of an Egyptian singer who was a spokesperson for Gamal Abdul Nasser's Pan-Arab nationalism and anti-Israeli policies. It is precisely Ben's dueling nativities and inherited cultural styles that produce both investment and disdain in the context of the dispute. Her appropriation of Umm Kulthum is also a self-Orientalizing and relocalizing move that grants Ben status not just as a popular music star, but as an embodiment of those contradictory identities. Musical performances such as Ben's create a proliferation of routes in tension with a hierarchy of influence and appropriation, thereby challenging origin points and border crossings. I have described four ways that Zehava Ben's performances deterritorialize and reterritorialize: (1) by claiming a fluid lineage, (2) by providing contradictory and momentary realignments, (3) by occupying a temporary and mobile subjectivity, and (4) by temporarily crossing seemingly impenetrable borders.

The new paths taken by Mediterranean Israeli music in the 1990s go beyond the genre's initial struggle against categories of asymmetric appropriation (represented by sli) and pan-ethnic reciprocal appropriation, and open a space for a musical exchange that challenges and crosses borders that earlier manifestations of the genre could only imagine. In the 1970s, Mizrahi musicians lacked resources for learning the "correct" forms of either Eastern or Western music (as demonstrated by Avihu Medina's story about being told that learning to read music would alter his Yemenite authenticity). Mizrahi musicians like Medina and Argov were caught between the expectation that they retain the traditions of their forbears and the lack of resources to creatively continue their work.

The resources available to Mediterranean Israeli musicians such as Zehava Ben in the 1990s, from studying Arabic music with the Haifa Arab Orchestra and playing with the group Etnix to her covers of Umm Kulthum, need to be understood in the context of the development of Mediterranean Israeli music. Her contribution to the development of Mediterannean Israeli music is the deployment of borrowing as a legitimate and respectful enterprise creating flexibilities rather than rigidities. Her multidirectional move of covering Umm Kulthum allows her passage across Israel's borders into Arab lands and into the mainstream European Israeli domain that is longing for its own version of world music legitimacy. Her Umm Kulthum covers both adhere to the tradition and provide flexible, nomadic, multidirectional affiliations.

Zehava Ben's contribution to the development of Mediterranean Israeli music does not merely represent an interesting example of the difference between rhizomatic appropriations and the fiction of shared cultural styles. Her persona and performance also raise the question of whether cultural border crossings such as these can (even temporarily) override the hostilities in the Middle East, and whether that suspension of conflict can create any far-ranging possibilities for change. At the very least we can say that enemy appropriation made in a spirit of reverence and reclaimed lineage — to the extent that Ben inscribes her head within Umm Kulthum's profile — puts the complex dueling nativities of all of the players on the front lines.

I have argued that music and perhaps other cultural forms can retain or regain their distinctiveness and yet cross borders, thus creating new audiences who themselves reconfigure their imaginary identities. The proliferation of emergent hybrid genres, covers, and borrowings flies in the face of homogeneities and hegemonies of any kind, so that the stabilities at the root of cultural and political conflict are replaced by the instabilities of nomadic, rhizomatic connections. These cultural border crossings, creating the possibility for emergent, culturally distinctive forms in war zones, may not create peace. Yet, the instability they engender offers a dress rehearsal for more substantive dialogue after the concert's curtain call. If war assumes imaginary stabilities, these musical instabilities offer a temporary alternative imaginary that might have consequences for the rehearsal of peace. If these border crossings do not create peace, they do, at least temporarily, destabilize war.

Notes

I am grateful to the Center for Advanced Judaic Studies, University of Pennsylvania, and to the Mershon Center for Public Policy, The Ohio State University, for two fellowship years in which I was able to test these ideas with colleagues from several disciplines. Amy Shuman, Rebecca Stein, and Ted Swedenburg provided invaluable editorial and substantive support.

1. The rejection of Mediterranean Israeli music's raw, Eastern, pan-ethnic sound has parallels with other subversive genres that emerge and proliferate (despite their rejected status) in the process of relocation. For example, the popularity of rai music in France extends beyond the Algerian community and encompasses a pan–North African diasporic community. Similarly, Greek, Armenian, Turkish, and Arab musicians in the United States together created a pan-Eastern music that developed in neighborhood nightclubs and cafés. Joan Gross, David McMurray, and Ted Swedenburg, "Arab Noise and Ramadan Nights: *Rai*, Rap and Franco-Maghrebi Identities," in *Displacement, Diaspora and Geographies of Identity*, edited by Smadar Lavie and Ted Swedenburg (Durham, N.C.: Duke University Press 1996), 131.

2. This essay draws from ethnography that I conducted in Israel between 1986 and 1995, roughly the period from the beginning of the first Intifada through an idealistic phase of the Israeli Palestinian peace process. Methodologically, the ethnographic enterprise was collaborative and dialogic, suggesting the acknowledgment of informants as insider experts rather than patronized teachers from whom scholars mine the raw materials that create perspectives. I acknowledge my research assistant, Reuven Namdar, whose critical observations and artistic sensibilities helped me to put the dialogic into practice. I also analyzed newspaper articles, documentary films and television shows, and dozens of cassette recordings and artwork spanning the post–Yom Kippur War period (1974) until the initial reverberations of Chairman Arafat and Prime Minister Rabin's cnn White House handshake (1995).

3. Zehava Ben, "Tipat Mazal" [A drop of luck], audiocassette (Tel Aviv: Eli Banai Productions, 1992).

4. Leah Inbal, "Zehava," *Yedi'ot Aharonot*, January 4, 1991, Seven-day supplement, 32–33. The "joke" is that "Zehava" (gold) is both a name and a reference to a gold record.

5. Yonatan Gefen, "Ha'etzev Hu Ashkenazi" [Sadness is Ashkenazi], *Ma'ariv*, May 15 1992, Weekend supplement, 3.

6. Disputed territory refers to a geographically situated regional struggle in which Israel occupies Palestinian land and is also a metaphorical way of describing dissonant spaces such as exist between Jewish Israeli ethnic groups.

7. Amy Horowitz, "Musika Yam Tikhonit Yisraelit [Israeli Mediterranean music]: Cultural Boundaries and Disputed Territories" (PhD diss., University of Pennsylvania, 1994). See, Amy Horowitz, "Rerouting Roots: Zehava Ben between Shuk and Suk," in *The Art of Being Jewish in Modern Times*, edited by Barbara Kirshenblatt-Gimblett and Jonathan Karp (Philadelphia: University of Pennsylvania Press, forthcoming).

8. Territories assume a coterminous relationship among people, identities, places, ownership of culture, and self-determination. Deterritorialization is accomplished by taking apart any of these naturalized associations. Thus, Deleuze's concept of the rhizome substitutes endless nodes of connection for overdetermined associations. Giles Deleuze and Felix A. Guattari, *A Thousand Plateaus: Capitalism and Schizophrenia*, vol. 2, translated by Brian Massumi (Minneapolis: University of Minnesota Press, 1987), 10.

9. Natan Shahar, "Hashir haeretz Yisraeli vekeren kayemet leyisrael" [Eretz-Yisraeli song and the Jewish National Fund] (Jerusalem: Research Institute for the History of the Jewish National Fund, Land and Settlement, 1994).

10. Erik Cohen and Amnon Shiloah, "Major Trends of Change in Jewish Oriental Ethnic Music in Israel," *Popular Music* 5 (1985): 199–223.

11. Jeffrey Halper, Edwin Seroussi, and Pamela Squires-Kidron, "*Musika Mizrakhit*: Ethnicity and Class Culture in Israel," *Popular Music* 8 (1989): 131–141.

12. Motti Regev, "*Musiqa Miarakhit*, Israeli Rock and National Culture in Israel," *Popular Music* 15, no. 3 (1996): 275–284; "The Musical Soundscape as a Contest Area: 'Oriental Music' and Israeli Popular Music," *Media, Culture and Society* 8, no. 3 (1986): 343–355; and Motti Regev and Edwin Seroussi, *Popular Music and National Culture in Israel* (Berkeley: University of California Press, 2004).

13. There are over four decades of literature on Israeli ethnicity. See Myron J. Aronoff, "Myths, Symbols and Rituals of the Emerging State," in *New Perspectives on Israeli History: The Early Years of the State*, edited by Laurence J. Silberstein (New York: New York University Press, 1991), 175–192; David Ben Gurion, "The Call of Spirit in Israel," in *Rebirth and Destiny of Israel*, edited by David Ben Gurion (New York: Philosophical Library, 1954), 403; Philip V. Bohlman, "Central European Jews in Israel: The Re-urbanization of Musical Life in an Immigrant Culture," *Yearbook for Traditional Music* (1984): 67–82; Erik Cohen, "The Black Panthers and the Israeli Society," *Jewish Journal of Sociology* 14 (1972): 93–109; Henry Elkin Dietz, "The Military, Ethnicity, and Integration in Israel Revisited," in *Ethnicity, Integration, and the Military*, edited by

Maurice Jerrold Roumani (Boulder, Colo.: Westview, 1991), 51–81; S. N. Eisenstadt, *The Absorption of Immigrants: A Comparative Study Based Mainly on the Jewish Community in Palestine and the State of Israel* (London: Routledge Kegan and Paul, 1954); Itamar Even-Zohar, "The Emergence of a Native Hebrew Culture in Palestine: 1882–1948," *Poetics Today* 11, no. 1 (1990): 175–191; Harvey Goldberg, "The Mimouna and the Minority Status of the Moroccan Jews," *Ethnology* 17 (1978): 75–87; Calvin Goldscheider, "The Demography of Asian and African Jews in Israel," in *Ethnicity, Identity and History*, edited by Joseph B. Maier and Chaim I. Waxman (New Brunswick, N.J.: Transaction Books, 1983), 274; Guy Haskell, "The Development of Israeli Anthropological Approaches to Immigration and Ethnicity: 1948–1980," *Jewish Folklore and Ethnology Review* 11, nos. 1–2 (1989): 19–26; Jehoash Hirshberg, "Brakha Tsfira vetahalikh Hashinui bamusiqa beyisrael" [Brakha Tsfira and the process of change in Israeli music], *Pe'amim* 19 (1984): 29–46; Ella Shohat, *Israeli Cinema: East/West and the Politics of Representation* (Austin: University of Texas Press, 1989).

14. The notion of "abandoned" Palestinian houses obscures the fact that Palestinian residents justifiably feared for their lives as the Jewish army advanced on their neighborhoods. At the same time, they were assured by Arab leaders that if they fled they would soon return to their homes.

15. See discussion of the relationship between genre, technologies of production, and standardization in Amy Shuman, *Storytelling Rights: The Uses of Oral and Written Texts by Urban Adolescents* (Cambridge, England: Cambridge University Press, 1986). Constraints on the technologies of production (in this case, the recording industry) are used to enforce the boundaries of a genre.

16. Natan Shahar, "The Eretz-Yisraeli Song, 1920–1950: Sociomusical and Musical Aspects" (PhD diss., Hebrew University of Jerusalem, 1989), 5–6.

17. Pertaining to rai airing on local radio in France. "*Rai* played a significant part in the story of Franco-Arab mobilization and identity formation. It was aired widely on the local radio stations, such as the celebrated Radio Beur in Paris that sprang up to serve and instill pride into French North African communities." Gross, McMurray, and Swedenburg "Arab Noise and Ramadan Nights," 131. See Amnon Shiloah, *Jewish Musical Traditions* (Detroit: Wayne State University Press, 1992), 206.

18. Gila Flam, "Beracha Zefira: A Case Study of Acculturation in Israeli Song," *Asian Music* 17 (1986): 108–125; Hirshberg, "Bracha Tsfira Ve'Tahalikh Ha'Shinui Ba'Musika Be'Yisrael."

19. Cohen and Shiloah, "Major Trends of Change in Jewish Oriental Ethnic Music in Israel," 202.

20. Avihu Medina, interviewed by Amy Horowitz, Tel Aviv, June 1, 1992.

21. Cohen and Shiloah, "Major Trends of Change in Jewish Oriented Ethnic Music in Israel," 217.

22. Bohlman, "Central European Jews in Israel"; Yaron Sahish, "Hamoshava Hayevonit" [The Greek colony], *Iton Yerushalayim*, August 14, 1992, 26–27; Shiloah, *Jewish Musical Traditions*, 206. Also see Edwin Seroussi's discussion of Mediterranean categories in "Yam Tikhoniyut: Transformations of the Mediterranean in Israeli Music," in *Mediterranean Mosaic: Popular Music and Global Sounds*, edited by Goffredo Plastino (New York: Routledge, 2003), 179–197.

23. Tsliley HaKerem (Tunes of the vineyard), "Lilchom Biadech" [To fight for you, country], on *Songs That We Love* (Tel Aviv: Reuveni Brothers, 1986); "Malu Asamaynu Bar" [Our silos were filled with wheat], lyrics by David Zahavi, music by Pinchas Lander, in *Shiron* [A book of Hebrew songs], Jewish National Fund, n.d. This song can also be found in the three-volume collection, *1000 Zemer V'od Zemer* [The Israeli sing-along] (Tel Aviv: Kinneret, 1981), 57.

24. See Edwin Seroussi, "Hanale hitbalbela" [Hanale was rattled], in "Fifty to Forty Eight: Critical Moments in the History of the State of Israel," edited by Adi Ophir, special issue, *Teoria vebikoret*, 12–13 (1999): 269–278. "Hanale Hitbalbela" [Hanala got confused], lyrics by Natan Alterman (1944), tune by Tsliley Ha Kerem, on *Songs That We Love* (Tel Aviv: Reuveni Brothers, 1986). Seroussi notes that since this article was published they have identified the tune, previously considered Hassidic, as a klezmer tune. Examples can be heard at www.jewishmusic.com/index.asp (last accessed February 7, 2004).

25. See Yaacov Mazor and Edwin Seroussi, "Towards a Hassidic Lexicon of Music," *Assaph* 10 (1990): 91, 118–143.

26. See Gary Saul Morson's discussion of "the ways in which a parody subverts its target," in *The Boundaries of Genre: Dostoevsky's Diary of a Writer and the Traditions of Literary Utopia* (Austin: University of Texas Press, 1981), 107.

27. For an overview of the increase in intermarriage between ethnic groups in the 1970s, see Barbara S. Okun, "Ethnicity and Educational Attainment in Marriage Patterns: Changes among the Jewish Population of Israel, 1957–1995," *Population Studies* 55 (2001): 49–64. Okun attributes the rise to both increased interaction and the motivation to marry others with the same educational level. See also Haya Stier and Yossi Shavit, "Two Decades of Educational Intermarriage in Israel," in *Who Marries Whom? Educational Systems as Marriage Markets in Modern Societies*, edited by Hans-Peter Blossfeld and Andreas Timm (Oxford: Oxford University Press, 2004).

28. Interview with Asher Reuveni and interview with Chaim Moshe and Asher Reuveni, Tel Aviv, August 5, 1984, on *Side by Side: Creators on Restless Soil*, radio series, produced by Amy Horowitz, edited by Ziv Yonatan (Washington, D.C.: Private collection, 1986), 5 audiocassettes.

29. Interview with Jeff Halper, Tel Aviv, September 8, 1985, on A. Horowitz, producer, *Side by Side: Creators on Restless Soil*.

30. Quoted in Ammiel Alcalay, "Israel and the Levant: 'Wounded Kinship's Last Resort,'" *Middle East Report* 159 (July–August 1989): 18.

31. Quoted in Gershon Shaked, *The Shadows Within: Essays on Modern Jewish Writers* (Philadelphia: Jewish Publication Society, 1987), 193.

32. Alcalay, "Israel and the Levant," 18.

33. Cornell West, "A Bloodstained Banner," in *Twilight, L.A. 1992*, edited by Anne Deveare Smith (New York: Anchor, 1994), 41–48. West has long contended that the Black Panthers were attempting to change the system rather than destroy it, as is often claimed.

34. Eli Luzon and Yonni Roeh, "Eyzo Medina" [What a country], audiocassette (Tel Aviv: Ben Mosh Productions, 1986); Avihu Medina, "Avraham Avinu" [Abraham our

father], audiocassette (Petah Tikvah: A. M. Hafakot, 1992); Shimon Parnas, interviewed by Amy Horowitz, Jerusalem, August 12, 1984.

35. Roger Wallis and Krister Malm, *Big Sounds from Small Peoples: The Music Industry in Small Countries* (New York: Pendragon Press, 1984).

36. There are many cassette studies that focus on the impact of this technology on emergent and excluded music genres. See Lila Abu-Lughod, "Bedouins, Cassettes and Technologies of Public Culture," *Middle East Report* 159 (July–August 1989): 7–11; John Baily, "Cross-cultural Perspectives in Popular Music: The Case of Afghanistan," *Popular Music* 1 (1981): 105–122; Houston A. Baker Jr., *Black Studies, Rap, and the Academy* (Chicago: University of Chicago Press, 1993); Salwa El-Shawan Castelo-Branco, "Some Aspects of the Cassette Industry in Egypt," *The World of Music* (Berlin) 29 (1987): 32–44; Haifaa Khalafallah, "Unofficial Cassette Culture in the Middle East," *Index of Censorship* (1982): 10–12; Peter Manuel, *Cassette Culture: Popular Music and Technology in North India* (Chicago: University of Chicago Press, 1993); Jon Pareles, "Cassette Culture: Home Recording of Original Music on Cassettes," *Whole Earth Review* 5 (winter 1987): 110–111; Susan Rodgers, "Batak Tape Cassette Kinship: Constructing Kinship through the Indonesian National Mass Media," *American Ethnologist* 13 (1986): 23–42.

37. Zohar Argov, "Elinor" (Tel Aviv: Reuveni Brothers, 1980), audiocassette.

38. Katerina Clark and Michael Holquist, *Mikhail Bakhtin* (Cambridge, Mass.: Belknap Press/Harvard University Press, 1984), 276, 319.

39. Quoted in Michael Ohad, "Libi bamizraḥ" [My heart is in the East], *Ha'aretz*, September 25, 1981, 16–17.

40. Merav Moran, "Linda Goes to the Kibbutz," *Hadashot* (Tel Aviv), June 13, 1986, 19.

41. Chaim Moshe and Asher Reuveni, interviewed by Amy Horowitz, Tel Aviv, August 5, 1984.

42. Yael Zerubavel, *Recovered Roots: Collective Memory and the Making of Israeli National Tradition* (Chicago: University of Chicago Press, 1995).

43. Steven Feld, "From Schizophonia to Schismogenesis: On the Discourses and Commodification Practices of 'World Music' and 'World Beat,'" in Charles Keil and Steven Feld, *Music Grooves* (Chicago: University of Chicago Press, 1994), 258–262, 265.

44. Ibid, 265.

45. Deleuze and Guattari, *A Thousand Plateaus*, 2: 109. Style, rather than genre, is a significant dimension of category 4. Homi Bhabha, commenting on his own Parsee heritage and his wife's history as a German Jew whose family settled first in Bombay and then in Milan, notes, "And there is something about belonging to a community with a style or a flavour, rather than a tradition of tablets, which has a rather contemporary feel to it." Paul Thompson, "Between Identities: Homi Bhabha Interviewed by Paul Thompson," in *Migration and Identity: International Yearbook of Oral History and Life Stories*, edited by Rina Benmayor and Andor Skotnes (Oxford: Oxford University Press, 1994), 183. In discussing "what it means to be a Parsee," Bhabha cautions against "the promise of consensual culture . . . a belief that we can educate people out

of racism by exposure to or the knowledge of cultural diversity—Indian food, African dresses, and so on" (195).

46. A series of annual workshops on issues of copying and covers has been held at the University of Pennsylvania's Center for Folklore in honor of Professor Roger Abrahams. See http://www.sas.upenn.edu/folklore/center/conferenceArchive/voiceover .html and http://www.sas.upenn.edu/folklore/center/conferenceArchive/takecover .html.

47. Zerubavel, *The Fine Line.*

48. Avihu Medina interview.

49. James F. Szwed, "Vibrational Affinities," in *Keeping your Head to the Sky: Interpreting African American Home Ground,* edited by Grey Gundaker and Tynes Cowan (Charlottesville: University Press of Virginia, 1998).

50. Virginia Danielson, *The Voice of Egypt: Umm Kulthum, Arabic Song, and Egyptian Society in the Twentieth Century* (Chicago: University of Chicago Press, 1997). For information about the struggle to realize the museum (which eventually opened on the anniversary of the singer's ninety-ninth birthday February 22, 2003), see http:// www.cairolive.com/newcairo/live/classic/26-12.html and http://weekly.ahram.org .eg/2000/467/umm5/htm. In honor of the anniversary of Umm Kulthum's one hundredth birthday, the Tel Aviv Museum featured a special concert of her music entitled "Hightlights of Arab Classical Music" as part of its classical music series in 2004. See: http://www.tamuseum.com/museum/musicseason.htm.

51. See the discussion of strategic essentialism in Gayatri Spivak, "Can the Subaltern Speak?," in *The Post-Colonial Studies Reader,* edited by Gareth Griffiths and Helen Tiffin (New York: Routledge, 1995), 18–23.

52. See the discussion of alignment in Erving Goffman, "Footing," in *Forms of Talk* (Philadelphia: University of Pennsylvania Press, 1981), 124–157.

53. Adelide Reyes-Schramm, "Ethnic Music, the Urban Area and Ethnomusicology," *Sociologus* 29, no. 1 (1979): 1–21; Ted Swedenburg, "Saida Sultan/Danna International: Transgender Pop and the Polysemiotics of Sex, Nation, and Ethnicity on the Israeli-Egyptian Border," *Musical Quarterly* 81, no. 1 (1997): 81–108. Erez Laufer, producer, *Solitary Star: Zehava Ben,* vhs (Tel Aviv: Idan Productions, 1997).

TED SWEDENBURG

Against Hybridity:
The Case of Enrico
Macias/Gaston
Ghrenassia

Arab Jews played a major role in the development of modern Arab culture during the first half of the twentieth century, particularly in the
realm of music. After the creation of the state of Israel and the subsequent emigrations, forced or otherwise, of Jews from Arab countries,
the vital Jewish role in the Arab musical tradition gradually diminished. In
Arab countries this story has largely been forgotten, expunged from official history, or rewritten according to the imperatives of a simplistic anti-
Zionist ideology. Meanwhile, Arab Jewish, or Mizrahi, artists have continued to perform and record in Israel, where their brand of music has
not only survived but has undergone a revival and today enjoys crossover
popularity. A number of scholars have investigated this phenomenon and
argued effectively that Mizrahi music represents a kind of challenge to
hegemonic Ashkenazi-dominated and Eurocentric conceptions of Israel's
national identity.[1] By contrast, little attention has been paid to the ongoing
but mostly underground reception in the Arab world of music produced
by Arab Jews.[2]

The failure of scholars to consider this quite remarkable phenomenon
is understandable, given that the dynamics of Arab reception of Jewish
Arab music are quite different from those that characterize the position of
Mizrahi music in Israel. There, Mizrahi music has been produced in the
context of ethnic identity construction and the emergence of local political movements. Mizrahi music can be meaningfully studied by attention to
performers, spaces of consumption, mass media dissemination, and audience reception. It also makes sense, methodologically and theoretically, to

examine the effects and meanings of Mizrahi music in the framework of the Israeli nation-state.[3] In sum, music produced in Israel by Arab Jews, even though theirs has been regarded by hegemonic forces as an "inferior" culture, is readily available for ethnographic, historical, and ethnomusicological study.

By contrast, the investigation of the reception of Arab Jewish music in the Arab world since Israel's creation defies conventional research methods. Not only has it been illegal in most Arab countries for over fifty years to import *any* goods from Israel, it also is widely considered an act of treason to enjoy or consume commodities produced by "the enemy." Nonetheless, despite the hostilities, Arab audiences for Arab Jewish music do exist. However, they are understandably invisible and unconnected to any social movements, and there exist virtually no social spaces where such audiences might regularly congregate to consume such music.[4] Arab Jewish performers do not, with few exceptions, produce their music with audiences in Arab countries in mind.[5] Quite often, as in the case of contraband Dana International cassettes sold in Egypt, Arab Jewish music circulates in the Arab world through informal or black market channels. All of these factors render it difficult to study such phenomena and to gauge the music's social and political effects. In most cases, the only available evidence consists of negative reactions penned by commentators and reporters in Arab newspapers and magazines. From this negative evidence, one can deduce that some Arabs in fact *are* listening to Arab Jewish music, otherwise, why would writers bother raising the alarm about the dangers of Zionist cultural influence? In most instances, however, it is difficult to deduce precisely what the existence of such Arab audiences *means*. Does the act of listening to Mizrahi music signify resistance to official or oppositional rhetorics of Arab anti-Zionism? Political apathy when it comes to the question of Palestine? Sympathy for the state of Israel? A critique of monolithic notions of Arab identity? A nostalgia for the time when Jews were an important presence in the Arab countries? Or simply the appreciation of good music?

My task here is not to provide definitive answers to these questions. But the case I have chosen to investigate, that of French variety star Enrico Macias, has the advantage of offering much more evidence to the researcher than do most other examples of Arab Jews with Arab audiences.[6] Macias's musical master, Cheikh Raymond Leyris, was a giant of the Algerian *malouf* tradition, and as we shall see, his own career was entangled in important ways with Zionism and the question of Israel. Macias is an artist with a global reputation, whose ties to Israel are well documented and whose career has been punctuated by controversies regarding his positions in support of Zionist projects. He has received massive press coverage over the past four decades, has been the subject of several biographies, and has authored two autobiographies.[7]

Interzone

To suggest something of the context that produces a figure like Enrico Macias, I want to evoke the concept of the "interzone," about which I have written elsewhere, and stress three of its key aspects.[8] The notion of the interzone refers, first of all, to the long history of Jewish presence in the Middle East and to the Jews' active participation in Arab Islamic civilization. Until the creation of the state of Israel in 1948, Arabic-speaking Jews were native inhabitants of the Arab regions of the Middle East and cocreators of (if not always fully equal participants in) Arab culture.[9] Second, the notion suggests that classical Arab Islamic civilization at its height was a kind of mercantile crossroads, an intermediary between civilizations in Africa, Europe, and South and East Asia. As such, Arab Islamic civilization was rooted in long-distance trade and travel, cultural exchange and interconnections, cosmopolitan and polyglot cities, and far-flung connections, a reality that Ghosh evokes vividly in his book *In an Antique Land*. Third, during the colonial period in the Arab world, the racial and social lines separating European and native were more fluid than in other zones of European colonialism that are usually cited as typical colonial cases (e.g., southern Africa and India). A distinct hierarchy of European colonials existed in which those hailing from the Mediterranean (Italians, Greeks, Corsicans, Maltese, Spaniards, etc.) were regarded as inferior to those from northern Europe. Although Mediterranean Europeans certainly made every effort to distinguish themselves, the boundaries separating them from the "natives" were nonetheless often rather fluid, even in settler colonies such as Algeria.[10]

I do not mean to suggest, however, that the interzone was a premodern golden age of tolerance, cosmopolitanism, and flexible boundaries. European colonialism in the Middle East was as cruel and deadly as anywhere else in the globe. It is estimated, for instance, that 1 million Algerians lost their lives in the course of the Algerian independence struggle.[11] In addition, Jews and Christians were not the full political or juridical equals of Muslims under Islamic law, and the character of their treatment frequently depended on the whim of the particular ruler and the socioeconomic context. The second-class position occupied by Arab Christians and Jews under Islamic rule and their vulnerability to various forms of persecution and discrimination help explain the receptivity of many of them to colonial intervention. Moreover, in many instances, European rule in fact improved the position of Arabic-speaking Jews and Christians.[12]

The relatively weak position of Jews who participated in Arab civilization also helps make sense of their complicated relationship to Zionism. For contemporary Arab Jews, memories of times of persecution and humiliation frequently coexist with nostalgia for the music of Umm Kulthum and traditional Arab foods like *foul* and couscous. The fact that Mizrahi musicians in Israel are problematizing the Eurocentricity of hegemonic Ashkenazi culture is in no way inherently contradictory to a trend of Mizrahi political support for right-wing Zionist parties. Indeed, since the 1970s, the main base for the Likud in Israel, the party of Begin, Shamir, Netanyahu, and Sharon, has been the Mizrahi community. In some senses, therefore, Enrico Macias represents an entirely typical Arab Jewish cultural figure: the fact that he is a supporter of Zionism who at the same time is one of the foremost practitioners of the canonical Arab musical tradition is not a paradox, but entirely normal in the post-1948 context.

It is for such reasons that I employ the notion of the interzone rather than concepts such as cultural hybridity, so often invoked today in the postcolonial and cultural studies literature. Hybridity is not an appropriate term for this case, especially as it is so frequently employed to suggest new forms of identity or cultural resistance. Arab Jewish culture is not novel, but has deep roots going back over a thousand years. Nor is it inherently a form of resistance against colonialism or Jewish nationalism. It is also not useful here to regard the Mizrahim as a natural bridge between Arab and Jew, as is sometimes done in the critical literature on Israel and Palestine. On the other hand, the argument offered by some Arab critics that Arab Jews like Enrico Macias are guilty of "appropriating" Arab culture is equally unhelpful, given that we are speaking of a shared, Arab Muslim-Jewish heritage.

I am drawn to the case of Enrico Macias precisely because of the difficult questions it poses. His is clearly not an instance of exemplary cultural or political practice. Macias's story resists romanticization, and it provides no clear model for action. Instead, his case raises a number of thorny, and recalcitrant, questions about identity and politics. How is it possible to be a Zionist and a master practitioner of traditional Arab music? To be proud of one's background as a *pied-noir* (one of the European Algerian settlers who left Algeria after it gained independence) and a leftist? To be a supporter of Israel's conquest of East Jerusalem and a backer of a Palestinian state? The story of Macias offers no easy solutions, but instead forces us to confront tough questions.

Layla Murad, Dana International, and Others

Enrico Macias is certainly not the only prominent Arab Jewish singer to have won over audiences in the Arab world after 1948. It is impossible here to give any kind of complete accounting of this phenomenon. It is not a consistent story, for Arab Jewish musicians have at times aroused great opposition and controversy in the Arab countries and at other moments been warmly welcomed by Arab audiences. The great Egyptian vocalist and cinema star Layla Murad, a Jew who converted to Islam in 1946 when she married Egyptian actor Anwar Wagdi, represents an early example. In 1952, while on vacation in France, rumors circulated in Egypt that she had visited Israel and contributed money to the Israel Defense Forces. Murad returned to Egypt to give a few more concerts, but then, at the height of her brilliant career, she went into retirement rather than continue to face the ugly rumors. The Damascus-based Arab Boycott Committee banned Murad's music on the basis of the allegations of her support for Israel. Egyptian President Gamal Abdul Nasser, however, was able to convince Syria to lift its embargo of Murad in the course of negotiations over unification with Syria in the United Arab Republic in 1958.

Murad is, of course, a transitional case, from the 1948–1967 period during which Jews gradually disappeared from the Arab countries. Since 1967, the story of Arab Jewish music has mostly concerned Mizrahim located in Israel. In some instances, their music has been welcomed in the Arab world. For instance, in the 1980s, Yemeni Israeli singer Haim Moshe's hit "Linda, Linda" was broadcast over Israeli radio and enthusiastically greeted by listeners in neighboring Arab countries.[13] The late Israeli Yemeni singer Ofra Haza's recordings of traditional Yemeni music circulated on smuggled cassettes throughout Cairo in the late 1980s without setting off any contentious response from the media. During the second half of the 1990s, the Mediterranean fusion group Alabina, which features Israeli vocalist Ishtar (born Eti Zach) singing in Arabic, Spanish, and English, achieved great popularity in the Arab world and even performed in Tunisia and Morocco. Mizrahi music has been well liked among Palestinians in the West Bank and Gaza Strip since at least the 1970s, and Mizrahi cassettes and CDs circulate widely there. The Israeli Moroccan singer Zehava Ben played a number of well-publicized concerts in Palestinian cities in the Palestinian Authority between 1995 and 2000, entrancing audiences with her interpretations of the repertoire of Egyptian diva Umm Kulthum. I am told that the Mizrahi singer Sarit Haddad is now more favored in the Palestinian territories than Zehava Ben, and others, like Avi Cohen, said to be "the voice of Muhammad 'Abd al-Wahhab," enjoy popularity among Palestinians as well.[14]

Other Israeli Mizrahi singers whose music has circulated in the Arab countries have been far more controversial. Dance diva Dana International, of Yemeni origin, achieved massive popularity and notoriety in Egypt in 1995 and 1996, when it was estimated that Egyptians purchased roughly 1 million of her cassettes on the black market. For months, the Egyptian media was full of denunciations of Dana as a key weapon in Israel's plot to undermine and corrupt Egyptian youth. (The sexual innuendo of some of Dana's Arabic songs, as well as her transsexuality, also played a role in the Egyptian campaign against her.) Egypt's government banned her music again in 2001 as part of an antinormalization campaign.[15] The outbreak of the al-Aqsa Intifada has heightened Arab sentiment for a total embargo of Israeli culture. In July 2002, for example, Algerian rai star Khaled was threatened with boycotts when he toured Lebanon and Jordan because he had sung a duet in concert at a Meeting of Peace concert in Rome with Yemeni Israeli singer Noa (known in Israel as Achinoam Nini).[16]

Meanwhile, France has served as an important site for the revival of the careers of prominent Algerian Jewish musicians, including the late Reinette l'Oranaise (d. 1998), Lili Boniche, Maurice El Medioni, Line Monty, and Luc Cherki. After arriving in France from Algeria such artists mostly either went into retirement or performed solely on the ethnic Algerian Jewish wedding circuit. But over the past decade such artists have been drawing large audiences to public concerts and enjoying crossover success in France. The Beurs, the North African Arab residents and citizens of France, constitute an important part of the audience for these Arab Jewish artists, whom they regard as part of their own cultural formation.

It is in this larger context that it makes sense to turn now to the great French variety star Enrico Macias, and to the controversy, as well as acclaim, that attended his recent return to the classical Andalusian tradition of his Jewish Algerian youth. The controversy has been entangled with the issue of his ties to Israel as well as to the related question of the role of Algerian Jews in the history of French colonial adventure in Algeria.

The Constantine Pogrom of 1934

In 1934, four years before the birth of Gaston Ghrenassia (later known as Enrico Macias) in Constantine, that city witnessed the massacre of twenty-five members of its Jewish community by Muslim residents. Among the dead were some close relatives of Macias's mother.[17] The proximate cause was a rumor that a drunken Jew had profaned a mosque, but the deeper reasons were an accumulation of resentments between Jews and Muslims of Constantine. These were rooted in the fact that, although both communities spoke the same language (the Algerian Arabic vernacular), the Jews enjoyed the privileges of French citizenship, while the Muslims did not. According to several observers, the French far-right anti-Semitic organization Croix-de-Feu probably manipulated the pogrom from behind the scenes.[18]

Despite their long history of residence and integration into Algerian life, albeit in a second-class position prior to the French occupation, Algerian Jews retained a sense of vulnerability and unease during the colonial period.[19] The Jews' memories of events like the Constantine massacre help make sense of their attitudes toward the Zionist movement and the state of Israel. According to Macias, during the Palestine war of 1948, he and his Constantine family listened attentively to Kol Israel (Israel Radio) and were very concerned about the condition of the Jewish community.[20] But despite their sympathy for the Zionists, in general Algerian Jews were not inclined to make *aliyah* to Palestine (pre-1948) and later Israel, chiefly because they held French citizenship and were heavily invested in French culture and it was easy to settle in France. Between 1931 and 1961, it is estimated that only 7,600 Algerian Jews migrated to Palestine-Israel.[21]

It was not just memories of the humiliations of the precolonial era or the ongoing fear of violence at the hands of Muslims that fostered the unease of Algerian Jews, but also the anti-Semitism of European Algerians. It would be a mistake, therefore, to regard the Algerian Jews simply as the indigenous beneficiaries of colonialism, as pieds noirs traitors to the Algerian nation. They may have been French citizens, but many French Algerians did not regard Jews as fully legitimate French nationals. Anti-Semitism was rampant among the colonialists in Algeria, and according to Raphaël Draï, fights and disputes between Jews and anti-Semitic Christian Europeans were everyday occurrences in the city of Constantine.²² Algerian Jews suffered a heavy blow in 1940 with the German occupation of France and the establishment of the Vichy regime of Marshall Pétain. Jews lost their citizenship during the Vichy period, and Algerian Jews numbered among the victims of the Shoah.²³

Cheikh Raymond, Colonialism, and Zionism

In 1961, during the last year of the Algerian independence struggle, Gaston Ghrenassia/Enrico Macias's musical master and future father-in-law Cheikh Raymond Leyris began receiving anonymous threats. Raymond responded to the warnings, and to the deteriorating position of the Jewish community in Constantine, by traveling to France that May to investigate a possible relocation there. While he was away, rumors circulated in Constantine that Raymond had been jailed for belonging to the OAS (Secret Army Organization, the ultra-right *colon* terrorist organization) or that he had taken refuge in Israel. Raymond returned to Algeria, having decided against moving to France, and on June 21, a few days after he came back, he was assassinated in the streets of Constantine. Within a few weeks of Raymond's death, the Jewish community of Constantine had by and large abandoned the city.

Why was this great master of Algerian malouf, the classical musical tradition of Andalusia, assassinated, and why did his murder lead to the rapid evacuation of Constantine's Jewish community? Raymond Leyris was born out of wedlock in Aurés in 1912 to a Jewish father named Jacob Lévy and a Catholic mother named Céline Leyris. Because at the time mixed marriages were inconceivable, Céline had been forced to abandon Raymond after naming him, and he was adopted and raised as a Jew by the Halimis, a poor and pious Jewish family from Constantine (93). Raymond was a francophone, but his language of everyday speech was Arabic, he knew Hebrew from his religious studies, and he sang in classical Arabic. He apprenticed with Constantine malouf master and 'ud player Cheikh Abdelkrim Bestandji, a Muslim and a member of a family with a long musical history. Raymond later started his own musical group, in which he sang and played the 'ud, the Arab lute, and rapidly gained acknowledgment as one of Constantine's leading malouf practitioners. This musical tradition (malouf means "faithful to the tradition") was the classical music of Andalusia, of Arab Spain, composed by Jewish and Muslim Arab masters during what has come to be known as the Golden Age, between the ninth and fifteenth centuries (24). It was transmitted orally, from father to son, across the generations, and had been preserved in Constantine, more or less intact, for at least five hundred years, although some instruments (such as the European-style violin) had been added. Eventually, the title Cheikh ("master") was conferred on Raymond after he demonstrated to a panel of Muslim sages that he had memorized over five hundred verses of poetry. (Macias claims Raymond knew thousands of classical Arabic *qasa'id* [poetry verses].)

The musicians, Muslim and Jewish, who played with Cheikh Raymond constituted a kind of supergroup, all masters of their instruments in their own right. Raymond's violinist was Sylvain Ghrenassia, Gaston's father. Sylvain came from a musical family whose repertoire, like Cheikh Raymond's, was malouf. Born in 1938, Gaston (the future Enrico) grew up listening to Raymond's orchestra. His Algerian Jewish family had resided in Constantine since its expulsion from Arab Spain during the *reconquista* in the fifteenth century. Constantine was home to one of the most important Jewish communities in Algeria, and about one-third of its population was Jewish. The Cremieux Decree of 1870 had made the Jews of Algeria French citizens, and the Ghrenassias, like Cheikh Raymond, were francophones who believed in Algérie Française. Gaston's parents and grandparents spoke Arabic at home among themselves and French with their children. Although there were Muslim quarters and Jewish quarters in Constantine, the Ghrenassias lived in a mixed quarter of Jews, Muslims, and Europeans.

Young Gaston was apprenticed to Cheikh Raymond at age fifteen and played guitar in Raymond's group between 1954 and 1961. It was Raymond's, and Gaston's, innovation to incorporate guitar for the first time into malouf. Although the years of Gaston's work with his master are the same as those of the Algerian War, Cheikh Raymond's group retained its favored position during this period, playing concerts and at life cycle celebrations (weddings, circumcisions) in both Muslim and Jewish communities throughout the conflict. In his 2001 autobiography, Macias asserts that the Jews of Algeria did not, for the most part, support the Algerian revolutionaries of the Front de Libération National (FLN), because they were ignorant of their own history and had been *francisé* (148). Neither, he says, did they generally belong to the extreme rightist, paramilitary OAS. However, he adds, the Jews ignored the OAS's true nature and did nothing to stop its abuses (156).

Macias's representation of the Jewish position during the war is somewhat selective. The Jews of Algeria were for the most part neutral during the war, but, led by local Zionists, they did organize to defend themselves. The Zionists in Algeria, in fact, were more significant as organizers of self-defense than as orchestrators of aliyah. In May 1956, Algerian Muslims attacked a Jewish café in Constantine with a grenade, injuring thirteen Jews. The next day, when a group of Muslims entered another Jewish café, its patrons, fearing another attack, pulled out revolvers and killed the Muslims.[24] Local Zionists not only organized Jewish self-defense but also served as army interrogators whose knowledge of Arabic facilitated the questioning of suspected Algerian FLN sympathizers (321). In 1961 a number of young Jews joined the OAS, despite the fact that one of its most important elements was the ardently anti-Semitic Jeune Nation group (331). When the OAS attacked Muslims, however, it was Algerian Jews who bore the brunt of the revenge attacks, because their districts frequently straddled Muslim and European districts and many Jewish enclaves were located in Muslim quarters. In Constantine, the war between the OAS and Muslims was especially fierce and the Jewish quarter subject to repeated Muslim attacks (332).

It is still unknown who gave the order to assassinate Cheikh Raymond, but it is fairly clear that the action was carried out by FLN elements. According to Macias, Raymond was apolitical, although he was in favor of Algeria remaining French. Macias and others argue that Raymond was killed because he represented a kind of cultural bridge between the two communities, Muslim and Jewish, a symbol of the *convivencia*.[25] But it might also make sense to see Raymond as representing the epitome of the contradictory position of Algerian Jews, who were, at one and the same time, French citizens, supporters of keeping Algeria French, speakers of Arabic, pieds noirs, Israel sympathizers, francophones, and upholders of traditional Arab culture. It is hard to imagine, in fact, how a national liberation movement, mobilized on the basis of quite homogeneous notions of Arab and Muslim identity, could, after a very bloody anticolonial struggle, have accommodated Algeria's 140,000 Jews, despite the best intentions of some FLN leaders.

Macias, the June 1967 War, and the Arab Boycott

Gaston Ghrenassia was part of the Jewish and colon exodus from Algeria, and he landed in Marseille in July 1961. By 1964, he had adopted the name Enrico Macias and become one of France's leading singers of variety. That same year, he played his first dates in Israel, and thenceforth, he continued to visit Israel nearly every year to give concerts or take vacations. Macias happened to be in Israel in late May 1967, during the crisis with Syria and Egypt, and he performed at kibbutzim near the "hot borders." His wife's pregnancy forced him to return to Paris, where he participated in pro-Israel demonstrations.[26] On the night of June 4–5, Macias reports, Cheikh Raymond appeared to him in a dream and told him to pack his bags and return to his country, which he took to mean Israel. Macias and several of his musicians quickly boarded a plane bound for Tel Aviv; they entertained Israel's victorious troops in the Sinai and at the Suez Canal. Accompanied by Generals Moshe Dayan (minister of defense) and Uzi Narkis (the conqueror of Jerusalem), Macias was one of the first Jews to pray at the Wailing Wall in June 1967; he asserts that this was one of the two most important moments of his life.[27] In addition, Macias met with Prime Minister Levi Eshkol, who personally thanked him for the role he had played in Israel's victory.[28]

Macias's activities in support of Israel's victorious troops were widely publicized, and so it is unsurprising that his music was soon banned in the Arab world on the grounds that it represented pro-Israeli propaganda. In 1969, Radio Cairo asserted that Macias was being boycotted because he was a paid agent of Israel and a supporter of Israeli expansionism.[29] This did not dissuade him from continuing in his high-profile support for the Jewish state. On a 1970 visit he performed in several frontier kibbutzim; during the October 1973 war he was again in Israel with his musicians, playing for troops at the Sinai front and for wounded soldiers at Hadassah Hospital in Jerusalem.[30]

Macias, however, was anything but a stereotypical Zionist. Shortly after arriving in Marseille, still known as Gaston Ghrenassia, he married Cheikh Raymond's daughter Suzi and began to relaunch a musical career. At first, he and his father, Sylvain, performed the Andalusian repertoire of Cheikh Raymond, but French audiences greeted this classical Arab music with hostility and racism. So he opted for a more mainstream, acceptable route. In Constantine, he had mastered not only malouf, but also French variety music, particularly the Mediterranean-inflected brand performed by artists like Luis Mariano (the son of refugees from the Spanish Civil War), Charles Aznavour (born Varenagh Aznavourian to Armenian refugees from the Turkish massacres of 1915), and Dalida (born and raised in Egypt). In addition to playing with Cheikh Raymond, the teenage Gaston had joined a gypsy musical ensemble in Constantine. The band's leader was named Enrico, and Gaston was known in the group as "little Enrico." On the boat from Algiers to Marseille, Gaston composed a song about his sorrow over leaving Algeria called "Adieu Mon Pays," which he recorded for Pathé-Marconi in 1962, adopting the recording name Enrico. He planned to use the last two syllables of his family name, Nassia, as his second name, but the Pathé-Marconi secretary with whom he spoke on the phone mistranscribed it, so "Adieu Mon Pays" was released under the name Enrico Macias.

In October 1962, the song was broadcast on a national radio program focusing on the pieds noirs. It became an immediate sensation, selling 50,000 copies in just a few days, and Enrico Macias became the singer in France of the pieds noirs. In 1963, he cut another record, and in July of the same year, he was booked into the most famous cabaret in Beirut, where he was received as a star. Macias remained a favorite throughout the Mediterranean for the next thirty years, despite boycotts and bannings in the Arab world. In 1963, he received a letter from Algeria's minister of culture informing him that he was banned in Algeria—for his support for French colonialism, not because of his Zionism.

His variety music, he asserts, was from the start tinged with Andalusian sounds. In concert over the years he has played 'ud for one number, or featured belly dancers, or spotlighted his father Sylvain on Andalusian violin for one song.[31] He was not able to experiment in this vein a great deal, and the Andalusian element remained at the level of frills and embellishments rather than forming the musical basis for his work. An emphatic Arabic sound invariably incited negative reactions from French audiences. However, the pieds noirs (who have a reputation for being fiercely anti-Arab) typically greeted Macias's use of Andalusian features (and even his singing in Arabic) with enthusiastic applause and shouts of approval.[32]

Macias and Sadat

In September 1979, Egypt's president Anwar Sadat organized a festival of peace on the first anniversary of the Camp David Peace Accords. The Egyptian government invited Enrico Macias to participate, and contacted him—significantly—via the Israeli government.[33] Clearly, President Sadat did not see Macias as simply a knee-jerk supporter of Israel. During the 1970s, Macias continued to insert small doses of Arabic music into his live performances and recordings. In 1977, he composed and recorded "La Folle Esperance," a song based on a folkloric Arab melody that Cheikh Raymond had played. The song's lyrics praised Sadat's November 1977 visit to Jerusalem, and asserted, "We [Muslims and Jews] are brothers." Macias reports that, when he first performed the song, on French television, it was a big success and that the studio audience included many Maghrebis, who clapped and sang along enthusiastically.[34] Another song Macias composed in the early 1970s, "Le Grand Pardon," expressed his hopes that the "sons of Abraham" would achieve peace. In a 1974 interview, he went so far as to assert his sympathy for the Palestinians because they had been uprooted. He did not agree, however, that the Jews were responsible for the Palestinians' dispossession.[35]

Macias writes that when Sadat met him in Egypt, he "said first he invited me because his people like me. But he also said to me, 'I made peace with Israel, but I want also to make peace with all Jews in all the world, and for the moment you are the representative of these Jews.'"[36] The fact that Sadat chose an Algerian Jew who spoke Arabic to represent world Jewry at the peace festival, rather than an Ashkenazi, is certainly significant; this was not a choice based on European notions of Jewish "representativeness." Macias was warmly greeted in Egypt where, despite the boycott, his music was well-known due to the underground market. In Egypt, he did not simply perform his variety hits, but felt comfortable enough to indulge in his Arabic repertoire. At a private concert, for instance, he performed a song by one of Egypt's most beloved stars, Farid al-Atrash, in Arabic.[37] He played his third show in Egypt at Gazira Stadium for the general public, with his father joining the band on violin. The crowd of 20,000 was enthusiastic, knew the lyrics to his songs, and went wild when Macias took up the 'ud. He and his father were invited to an audience with Sadat at his winter palace in Ismailiya, and Macias performed a few songs for the small gathering, including "La Folle Esperance," which he sang in Arabic. Macias has called his encounter with Sadat "the crowning achievement" of his life.[38]

The Beurs and Liberal Humanism

Macias has always represented himself as a kind of liberal humanist who, due to his own exile experience, is deeply concerned about the plight of migrants, refugees, and exiles everywhere. Many of his most beloved songs deal with the issues of diaspora and displacement, such as "Spanish Jew" and "L'Etranger." Moreover, he has been a prominent advocate of the civil rights of Arabs in France, the traditional targets of ultrarightist violence and antipathy. During the mid-1980s, the Beurs mounted major mobilizations against endemic French racism and police brutality. In 1983, young Beurs organized a two-month-long walk across the country, from Marseille to Paris. Their march culminated with a huge demonstration in Paris, and Macias was among the "celebrity" participants.[39]

Even though Macias has been regarded as the singer of the pieds noirs, over the years he has had frequent run-ins with extreme rightists, particularly due to their anti-Semitism and anti-Arabism (222). In 1983 he confronted the wrath of the far right when Algerian president Chadhli Benjedid visited France and some pied noir organizations demonstrated against his visit. In a newspaper interview, Macias asserted his hopes that Benjedid's visit would help settle the problems of the *harkis* (Algerians who fought on the side of the French during the war of national liberation and who were exiled to France) and the pieds noirs. But it was time, he added, to turn the page and move ahead. The extreme right reacted by accusing him of treason (223). On another occasion, in July 1988, Macias was scheduled to sing at Marignane in the Midi. The extreme-right party, the Front National (FN), led by some of its pied noir members, called for a boycott of the concert. The FN castigated Macias for fighting racism and defending the rights of immigrants, and it distributed leaflets that went so far as to label him a "henchman [*suppôt*] of the Arabs" and a "Youpin" (Yid), a classic anti-Semitic epithet (69). In 1992, in his one venture into French electoral politics, he ran unsuccessfully for Parliament as part of Bernard Tapie's Energie Sud list in the south, in the Var department. (At the time, Tapie was the highly controversial president of the Olympique Marseille soccer team and the chief executive of Adidas). Macias participated in the elections as part of a larger and ultimately failed effort on the part of the left to block the political rise of the extreme right in the south.

During this period, Macias continued to be active in the Israel-Palestine issue and in characteristically complicated ways. In 1994, Israeli president Ezer Weizmann asked him to represent Israel at a meeting in Gaza, where Yasser Arafat addressed a gathering of about 150 journalists, intellectuals, and artists from the Arab world. Macias was the only Jew and the only emissary from Israel (232–233). According to Macias, in his address to the gathering Arafat called on the Arabs to retake Jerusalem and make it the capital of Palestine; Macias subsequently met with Arafat and told him that he rejected the idea that Jerusalem could be the capital of any country other than Israel. Macias was also active as a global humanitarian. In July 1997, UN Secretary General Kofi Annan named him as his first UN goodwill ambassador, a mostly celebrity appointment whose numbers have included such luminaries Magic Johnson, Luciano Pavarotti, Natacha Atlas, and Danny Glover.

In 1999, Macias made an unanticipated return to the Constantine malouf tradition of his master and father-in-law, Cheikh Raymond. The move resulted in the revival of his musical career but also plunged him into renewed controversy, revolving, once again, around the troubling and complex questions of his strong backing of Israel and the apparent contradiction of his being an Arab Jewish Zionist who is also a master practitioner of the Arab musical tradition.

By 1998, Enrico Macias had sold an estimated 60 million records worldwide. In Europe and the Mediterranean, he had achieved a stature comparable to that enjoyed by Frank Sinatra in the United States. In addition, he was a celebrity humanitarian, a prominent defender of the rights of immigrants and North Africans in France, a man of the left, and a champion of Israel who also believed that Palestinians had the right to their own state. But at the age of sixty, his musical output was regarded as somewhat old-fashioned and passé, especially by the younger generation in France. Moreover, the fact that Enrico Macias was viewed as a representative of pieds noirs culture also contributed to his has-been image.

As noted earlier, on his arrival in France Macias had tried to carry on the malouf tradition in the company of his father, but the French audience response was overwhelmingly hostile. Although the music he produced between 1962 and 1999 was frequently spiced with the Andalusian spirit and occasionally marked by the use of "Oriental" instruments, according to Macias, for the most part malouf, the essential part of his cultural formation, remained dormant and sleeping, and he had "forbidden" himself from returning to what he considered a "sacred repertoire." One factor that slowly drew him back to his heritage was the Beur mobilization, particularly its cultural dimensions. North African music, especially Algerian rai, gradually achieved mainstream status in France during the 1990s, in the face of tremendous anti-Arab sentiment. The Beur struggle had helped foster an increasing openness among French audiences, particularly among progressive youth, toward North African and Middle Eastern culture. Such tolerance and acceptance had simply not existed in the 1960s and 1970s.[40] Macias himself was an early supporter of rai music and rai artists in France, and the French public regarded him as an integral part of the North African cultural wave. Meanwhile, other Algerian Jewish singers were gaining prominence and wider publics in France, chief among them the great *hawzi* vocalist and 'udist Reinette L'Oranaise (d. 1998). Another significant factor that encouraged Macias's re-embrace of malouf was the new official receptivity in Algeria of him and his music. The Algerian government's overtures were motivated in part by its keen interest in currying favor with the French government and public at a time when it was engaged in a very bloody and repressive war with Algerian Islamists, which had broken out in 1992. Whatever the Algerian government's motives, its initiatives did offer important opportunities and incentives for Macias.

The first signal from Algeria came in 1993. In September, the Algerian ambassador to France organized an evening of solidarity with the people of Algeria. Enrico Macias was officially invited as a representative of Algerian culture and was warmly received. As was typical on such occasions, journalists asked for his opinion regarding the Palestine question. He asserted that as he himself was in exile, he understood "perfectly" the Palestinian refugee problem. As for Jerusalem, he asserted once again that it was the capital of Israel, but he added that the Palestinians had a right to their own state with their own capital (22–23).

The next official overture on the part of Algerian officialdom occurred in March 1999, when the Algerian cultural center in Paris organized a concert in honor of Cheikh Raymond. This was truly a remarkable event, given the fact that Raymond's memory had essentially been obliterated from Algeria's cultural history after his assassination. Among those present was Leila Shahid, the PLO's representative in France. Macias attended the concert together with his brother-in-law, Cheikh Raymond's son Jacques Leyris. The Constantinois violinist Taoufik Bestandji led the group. Macias recounts that, after Raymond's death, he had been certain that no one possessed the necessary talent to revive his master's music, but the playing of Bestandji's group proved him wrong (24). At the close of the concert, Bestandji invited Macias onstage, and he sang two of the Cheikh's songs to great acclaim.

Jacques Leyris subsequently encouraged Macias to continue his collaboration with Bestandji. Leyris had known Bestandji since 1990, when the latter had moved to France, and together they had brought out four CDs of Cheikh Raymond's music.[41] Taoufik is the grandson of Cheikh Abdelkrim Bestandji, who was Cheikh Raymond's master. Bestandji and Macias were determined to reestablish the centuries-old cultural link between Jews and Arab Muslims in Algeria that had been broken since the early 1960s, and they began to rehearse for a concert in Brouges in April.[42] Macias reports that he had no trouble returning to the music as a guitarist, but that because he had not sung with Raymond's group, he had to work extremely

hard to master the difficult task of performing vocals in classical Arabic. He seems to have succeeded, because his concerts with Bestandji were great triumphs, performed in front of mixed audiences (Arabs, Jews, and French non-Semites). Macias and Bestandji's group released a live double CD, entitled *Hommage à Cheikh Raymond* (recorded at Brouges in April) as well as a concert DVD.[43] The CD's sales of 100,000 were double the normal sales of Macias's recordings over the past few years. The tribute to Cheikh Raymond also brought Macias renewed credibility with younger audiences, including North Africans. One song from the album, "Koum Tara," is a duet with rai singer Cheb Mami, who became a global star that same year on the strength of his "Desert Rose" duet with Sting.

Macias was quite explicit about what he considered to be the political implications of his collaboration with Bestandji. At the opening of the concert recorded on DVD, he tells the audience, "From this night the two communities, Jews and Muslims, are reconciled and *retrouvés*." Although his statement rang true insofar as the concert audience, in other domains his "return" underscored, despite his optimistic hopes, the existence of continued divisions and an absence of reconciliation. At first, Macias's concert statement seemed prescient. Soon after Bouteflika's election in April 1999 (the same month as the Macias-Bestandji concert at Brouges), the Algerian president made a point of paying public tribute to Cheikh Raymond, to the Jews of Algeria, and to Enrico Macias. That summer, on the occasion of Constantine's 2,500th anniversary, Bouteflika again paid homage to Cheikh Raymond and called on Macias to return to his country of birth (33–34). In October, Macias, his family, and the family of Cheikh Raymond attended a very amiable dinner at the Algerian ambassador's residence. Finally, in February 2000, President Bouteflika met Macias at an official reception in Paris and formally extended him an invitation to visit Algeria, which he had not seen since 1961. Bouteflika told Macias that the assassination of Raymond had been a grave mistake, representing the death of a part of Algerian culture. He added that when Macias visited Cheikh Raymond's tomb in Constantine, he would be by his side (39–40).

Macias began to make plans to tour Algeria in mid-March 2000, where he would give several performances featuring both his variety and his malouf repertoires, accompanied by the Bestandji group as well as his regular group. He was to be joined on the trip by a group of one hundred Algerian Jews, including members of his own family. The trip was to include a visit to Constantine, where he would stay overnight in his birth house at the invitation of the family who lived there (40). But news of Macias's impending visit quickly touched off loud opposition in Algeria. Several groups there, mostly Islamists and conservative members of the FLN opposed to normalization with Israel, objected that Macias's presence was the first step toward the establishment of diplomatic relations between Algeria and the Jewish state. Algerian MP Mohieddin Ameimour asserted that Macias's visit "had to be stopped" because it "was nothing more than an [Israeli] attempt to gain access to Algerian society and create an atmosphere conducive to normalizing relations with Israel." Macias's concerts, claimed Ameimour, "were designed to act as a launching pad for the [Israeli] penetration of the whole Maghreb."[44] Those opposed to the visit spread rumors that Macias's family had committed crimes during the Algerian war of liberation. Some accused Macias himself of having belonged to the ultra-right OAS or to the Territoriale, the pied noir organization that fought on the side of the French army. Abdallah Djaballah, former head of the moderate Islamist party An-Nahda, declared at a meeting in Constantine that the singer's visit was forbidden by Islam, and one of Djaballah's aides accused the Jewish nation of being at the root of all the ills of the Muslim nation.[45] The former leader of Ahmed Ben Bella's dissolved Movement for Democracy in Algeria (MDA), Khaled Bensmaïn, recalled that Macias had sung for Israeli soldiers during the 1967 war.[46] Bensmaïn also claimed that Macias's aim of visiting the tomb of Raymond Leyris would "touch the values of the [Algerian] revolution," as Leyris had been executed for belonging to the OAS.[47]

Other opponents raised suspicions about President Bouteflika's intentions regarding Israel. They asserted that he had been undertaking "secret contacts" with Israel since the previous year, when he met Israeli officials at the funeral of Moroccan monarch Hassan II in July 1999 and shook the hand of Israeli prime minister Ehud Barak.[48] More nonpartisan observers saw Bouteflika's initiatives regarding Macias and Israel as part of a strategy to open up Algeria to the West and to attract foreign investment, particularly from the United States.[49] In any case, the outcry over Macias eventually forced Bouteflika to cancel the visit. In the aftermath, journalist Addi Lahouari wondered "why, each time the question of Enrico Macias and Algeria comes up, [Algerian] journalists, consciously or unconsciously, speak of Israel? What does Israel have to do with this case?"[50] Lahouari is of course correct to suggest that the case was about more than simply Israel, although this should not blind us to Algerian sentiments regarding the plight of the Palestinians. Israel served as an important ideological weapon the opposition forces were able to use in political struggles with Bouteflika. In addition, the uproar over Macias is symptomatic of the anxiety that exists in Algeria over the possibility that Algerian Jews might make legal claims regarding properties lost in the wake of independence.

Intifada and Roubaix

During the same period, the issue of Enrico Macias and his relation to Israel erupted into controversy in France as well. Shortly after the outbreak of the al-Aqsa Intifada in Palestine, on October 10, 2000, pro-Israel groups in Paris organized a demonstration of 8,000–10,000 in support of the Jewish state and to protest an upsurge of anti-Semitic incidents in France. Henri Hadjenberg, president of the Representative Council of Jewish Organizations in France, was prevented from speaking at the demonstration because he had shaken the hand of Yasser Arafat. Macias did address the crowd and sang "Yerushalaim."[51] In statements to the Jewish media, he asserted that because the French media were failing to do their job and were doctoring news information with regard to Israel and the Palestinians, he tunes into CNN.[52]

The following month, Macias and the Bestandji group were scheduled to give a concert of Cheikh Raymond's music in Roubaix, a town located near the Belgian border with a population composed of roughly 40 percent immigrants. A number of Arab groups called for a demonstration and a boycott of the concert to protest Macias's pro-Israel stance. They accused Macias of participating in a demonstration alongside rightist Zionist parties, especially the Likud, and of refusing to denounce the massacre of Palestinians. Local socialists condemned the "blackmail directed at the singer's visit" and the Greens asserted that Macias had "nothing to do with the Israeli right wing and bears no responsibility for the present situation in the Middle East."[53] Two hundred pro-Palestinian protestors picketed the concert, chanting, "Stop the massacres, free Palestine, Barak assassin." The demonstration was as much a sign of the tremendous alienation of unemployed young Beurs, the victims of severe racism in France, as a sign of solidarity with Palestine.[54] Inside the Roubaix concert hall, meanwhile, an audience of about one thousand, including Arabs and Jews, enjoyed the music of Cheikh Raymond.

Since the furor over these controversies has died down, Macias has continued with his usual activities. After his Cheikh Raymond tribute, he has gone back to variety-style recording, but now with a more obvious integration of Andalusian elements. He continues to be active on both the Beur/Algerian and pro-Israel arenas, playing benefits in both camps. Recently, for instance, he performed at a benefit organized in November 2002 for the victims of the November 10 floods in Algiers that took over one thousand lives. Among those performing on the same stage were such well-known Arab artists in France as Khaled, Cheb Mami, and Djamel Allam.[55]

Conclusion

We have not learned much in this essay about the Arab audiences for the music of Enrico Macias and other Arab Jewish artists. The fact that such audiences exist, despite the ongoing violence in Palestine-Israel, offers at least one slim thread of hope for reconciliation. But music alone cannot bridge the gap, although it may be a beginning. Given the widespread dissemination of crude anti-Semitic discourse (mostly drawn from European sources) in the Arab world, the fading of memories of people's everyday experiences with Arab Jews prior to their emigration, the lack of decent books or research on Arab Jews or translations of studies written in other languages, ignorance about Arab Jews is on the increase in the Arab world. The escalating levels of Israeli violence against the Palestinians, the occupation of the West Bank and Gaza—now nearing its fourth decade—and the Zionist ideology which asserts the total identification of the category

"Jew" with Israel, only heighten prevailing tendencies in the Arab world toward binary thinking and black-and-white categorization when it comes to Israel and Palestine, Arab and Jew.

To realize the promise that the Arab audiences for Macias might portend, established modes of thinking will have to be radically shifted. It is in this spirit that I advance the notion of the interzone. It suggests that we conceptualize Arab Islamic civilization and tradition as cosmopolitan and open rather than closed and homogenizing. The interzone proposes regarding Arab Islamic civilization as one in which Jews and Christians actively participated in developing. But the interzone also reminds us of the abuses and persecutions to which Jews and Christians living under Islam frequently fell victim. Only by taking this history seriously, acknowledging the realities of Jewish life in the Arab world rather than romanticizing the Golden Age of Andalusia, can one begin to comprehend the apparent complexities of someone like Enrico Macias. Jews in Algeria may have benefited from colonialism, but they also suffered greatly from the pogrom of Constantine, their loss of French citizenship during the Vichy era, and the death camps of the Shoah (which, despite hegemonic definitions, did not just eliminate European Jews).

The interzone also proposes a shift in our binary thinking about colonialism.[56] Otherwise, how are we to make sense of the colons, the pieds noirs, in France, who since the 1960s have greeted Enrico Macias's forays into Andalusian music, including his use of Arabic language, with wild enthusiasm?[57] To stereotype France's estimated 1 million pieds noirs as simply anti-Arab racist Le Pen supporters is to crudely oversimplify.[58] The case of Enrico Macias, as well as that of his remarkable master and father-in-law, Cheikh Raymond Leyris, calls for a radical rethinking of the nature of French colonial experience in Algeria, a reexamination that would stress the heterogeneity, contradictions, and internal divisions within colon society, as well as the nature of everyday pieds noirs, and especially Jewish, interactions with Muslim Algerians.[59]

All this is not, however, to suggest in any way that the politics of Enrico Macias are exemplary. I find his blind spots when it comes to Palestine-Israel to be quite disturbing, particularly the fact that he can claim to identify with Palestinian exiles while denying the fact that Zionist violence produced those refugees. The circumstances that engendered the historical plight of the Palestinian refugees deserve to come to light and be acknowledged just as much as do the circumstances of Cheikh Raymond's murder. I fully appreciate, however, Macias's courage in defending the rights of France's estimated 4 million Arabs and the role he has played in making Arab culture more acceptable in France. Moreover, in his recent autobiography, *Mon Algérie*, he acknowledges that French colonialism manipulated the Algerian Jews and expresses empathy for the Algerian national movement. Although there is not space to discuss this subject here, France at present represents the most hopeful site for the development of a dialogue between Arab Muslims and Arab Jews on such issues.

Despite Macias's recent moves, and despite his leftist and humanitarian instincts, he remains someone deeply concerned about anti-Semitism in France and willing to stand next to members of the Likud Party in support of Israel. Given the history and context discussed here, I would argue that it makes sense that Enrico Macias is both a strong (if Labor-leaning) Zionist and a preeminent master of Arab Andalusian music. This is not a paradox but a normal condition for tens of thousands of Arab Jews. If the normality of this situation is to be changed, it will take a tremendous amount of hard political and intellectual work.

Notes

An earlier version of this paper was presented at the International Summer Academy on "Cultures of Conflict: Reflections on Middle East Dilemmas," sponsored by the Institute for the History of the Jews in Austria and the Austrian Institute for International Affairs, July 2, 2003, Vienna. Thanks to Rebecca Stein and Sari Hanafi for their very tough and useful comments. Thanks as well to David McMurray for general inspiration and assistance with the finer points of French; to Ammiel Alcalay, for prompting my initial interest in the music of Arab Jews; and to Bruce Masters, for warning me against romanticizing the picture of Arab-Jewish relations in the Middle East.

Unless otherwise noted, all translations are mine.

1. See, for instance, Ammiel Alacalay, *After Jews and Arabs: Remaking Levantine Culture* (Minneapolis: University of Minnesota Press, 1993) and "Israel and the Levant: 'Wounded Kinship's Last Resort,'" *Middle East Report* 159 (July–August 1989): 18–25; Amy Horowitz, "Performance in Disputed Territory: Israeli Mediterranean Music," *Musical Performance* 1, no. 3 (1997): 43–53, and in this volume; Motti Regev and Edwin Seroussi, *Popular Music and National Culture in Israel* (Berkeley: University of California Press, 2004); Motti Regev, "*Musica mizrakhit*, Israeli Rock and National Culture in Israel," *Popular Music* 15, no. 3 (1996): 275–284, "Present Absentee: Arab Music in Israeli Culture," *Public Culture* 7, no. 2 (1995): 433–445, and "The Musical Soundscape as a Contest Area: 'Oriental Music' and Israeli Popular Music," *Media, Culture and Society* 8, no. 3 (1986): 343–355.

2. The only exception I am aware of is my own study of Dana International's (earlier known as Danna International) reception in Egypt; see Ted Swedenburg,

"Saida Sultan/Danna International: Transgender Pop and the Polysemiotics of Sex, Nation, and Ethnicity on the Israeli-Egyptian Border," in *Mass Mediations: New Approaches to Popular Culture in the Middle East and Beyond*, edited by Walter Armbrust (Berkeley: University of California Press, 2000), 88–119.

3. There are, however, important Mizrahi communities outside of Israel. Kay Kaufman Shelemay's ethnomusicological study of the liturgical music of Syrian Jews in Brooklyn is one of the few examinations of such diasporic musical communities of which I am aware; see *Let Jasmine Rain Down: Song and Remembrance among Syrian Jews* (Chicago: University of Chicago Press, 1998).

4. Exceptions are Mizrahis who perform in the Palestinian territories, Arab Jews who play for Arab audiences in Europe, and the odd Mizrahi or Israeli who give concerts in the Arab world, like Enrico Macias in Tunisia at the Carthage Festival (Tunis) and the Hammamet Festival and Noa at the Sacred Music Festival in Fez, Morocco, both in summer 1999 (before, significantly, the outbreak of the second Palestinian Intifada).

5. Exceptions include the Arab songs recorded by Dana International, aimed at least in part at Arab audiences outside Israel, and analyzed by Swedenburg, "Saida Sultan/Danna International." Ishtar of the group Alabina also seems to have had Arab world audiences in mind when she recorded songs in Arabic; during its existence, the group was quite popular in the Arab world.

6. The exceptions I am aware of are Mizrahi singers who perform for and are appreciated by Palestinians in the West Bank and Gaza, some of whom are discussed briefly below.

7. Because biographies of popular music stars are not considered serious and therefore are not regularly collected by academic libraries, I have been able to consult only one Macias biography: Martin Monestier, *Enrico Macias: L'enfant de tous pays* (Paris: Encre Editions, 1980). Autobiographies are Enrico Macias with Jacques Demarny, *Non, je n'ai pas oublié* (Paris: Éditions Robert Laffout, 1982); Enrico Macias with Florence Assouline, *Mon Algérie* (Paris: Plon, 2001). Subsequent references to the latter are cited in parentheses in the text.

8. Ted Swedenburg, "Musical Interzones: The Middle East and Beyond," paper presented at the Center for the Humanities, Wesleyan University, September 23, 2000. I borrow the term interzone from William Burroughs's fictional writings on Tangier, most notably *Naked Lunch* and *Interzone*. My use of the concept is inspired by his vision of Tangier but has a much wider historical, geographic, and sociological reach.

9. Of the voluminous sources on this subject, among the most accessible are Alcalay, *After Jews and Arabs*; Amitav Ghosh, *In an Antique Land* (New York: Vintage Books 1994); and S. D. Goitein, *Jews and Arabs, Their Contacts through the Ages* (New York: Schocken Books, 1964). For a very fine comprehensive review of the literature, see Sarah Abrevaya Stein, "Sephardi and Middle Eastern Jewries since 1492," in *The Oxford Handbook of Jewish Studies*, edited by Martin Goodman (Oxford: Oxford University Press, 2002), 327–362.

10. Although there is no space here for a definitive comparison between the racialist character of European colonialism in the Arab world as opposed to more canonical

cases of colonialism, it is clear that the kind of obsessive racial boundary maintenance that was developed in the Dutch colonies and is described by Ann Laura Stoler did not, for the most part, characterize European colonies in the Middle East. *Race and the Education of Desire: Foucault's History of Sexuality and the Colonial Order of Things* (Durham, N.C.: Duke University Press, 1995).

11. According to Ali Ahmida, .5 million Libyans died in battle or lost their lives due to starvation, disease, or thirst during the Libyan independence struggle. *The Making of Modern Libya: State Formation, Colonization, and Resistance, 1830–1932* (Albany: State University of New York Press, 1994), 1.

12. For an account dealing with Christians and Jews in the Arab provinces of the Ottoman Empire, see Bruce Masters, *Christians and Jews in the Ottoman Arab World: The Roots of Sectarianism* (Cambridge, England: Cambridge University Press, 2001).

13. Horowitz, this volume.

14. Personal communication, Pnina Motzafi-Haller, May 2003. Muhammad 'Abd al-Wahhab (d. 1991) was one of Egypt's most renowned singers and composers of the twentieth century.

15. Reported by United Press International, August 6, 2001.

16. The song they performed was John Lennon's "Imagine." A recorded version of the duet was released on Khaled's 1999 album *Kenza*. (The song is conspicuously absent, however, from the U.S. version of the album.) In the Israeli context, Noa is well-known as a partisan of peace, of the Peace Now variety.

17. Two Muslims died as well. Dozens of Jews were wounded, and hundreds of stores in Jewish neighborhoods sacked. See Jean-Luc Allouche, "Constantine, La Necessaire," in *Les Juifs d'Algérie: Images et Textes*, edited by Jean Laloum and Jean-Luc Allouche (Paris: Éditions du Scribe, 1987), 122.

18. Raphaël Draï, *Lettre au président Bouteflika* (Paris: Éditions Michalon, 2000), 52.

19. The Constantinois Jew Raphaël Draï writes that his grandmother recounted to him (in Arabic) that the Jewish community of Constantine welcomed the coming of French troops because Turkish rule was oppressive to the Jews. Draï writes as well that the image that Constantine Jews retain in their memory of the French assault on Constantine is of the dey (the local Turkish ruler) tying local Jews to the stock of his cannons in the hopes of keeping French troops from firing on them (Draï, *Lettre au président Bouteflika*, 49).

20. Macias, *Non, je n'ai pas oublié*, 83.

21. Joelle Bahloul, "Les Pionniers de Regavim," in *Les Juifs d'Algérie*, 304.

22. Draï, *Lettre au président Bouteflika*, 50.

23. Among them, the great doyen of classical Andalusian singing from Oran, Saoud El Medioni, popularly known as Saoud El Oranais. El Medioni, who was the master of the next generation of Algerian Jewish artists from Oran, including Reinette l'Oranaise and Lili Boniche, and was the uncle of Maurice El Medioni, met his end at Sobibor concentration camp (Poland) in March 1943. See Annie Teboul, "Les Musiciens," in *Les Juifs d' Algérie*, 278.

24. Michael Laskier, *North African Jewry in the Twentieth Century: The Jews of Morocco, Tunisia, and Algeria* (New York: New York University Press, 1994), 320–321.

25. Other observers have noted that Raymond also represented a bridge with Christianity, given that his mother was French Catholic.

26. Monestier, *Enrico Macias*, 87.

27. The other moment was meeting Anwar Sadat in 1979, discussed below.

28. Macias, *Non, je n'ai pas oublié*, 288–291.

29. Monestier, *Enrico Macias*, 11.

30. Macias, *Non, je n'ai pas oublié*, 311, 316.

31. To my ears, the Arab influence on his variety recordings is quite subtle and requires some effort to hear.

32. Monestier, *Enrico Macias*, 55.

33. Ibid, 178.

34. Macias, *Non, je n'ai pas oublié*, 327.

35. Monestier, *Enrico Macias*, 145.

36. Richard Cromelin, "Macias: Singer for the Dispossessed," *Los Angeles Times*, November 22, 1985, part 6, p. 1.

37. Farid al-Atrash (d. 1974) was a Syrian Druze whose entire career as singer, 'udist, and movie actor was based in Egypt. He is one of the most renowned Egyptian singers of the twentieth century.

38. Monestier, *Enrico Macias*, 183.

39. Frank J. Prial, "Parisians March Against Racism," *New York Times*, December 5, 1983, section 1, p. 20.

40. Josette Alia, "La france et la culture arabe," *Nouvel Observateur* 1726, December 4, 1997; David McMurray, "La France Arabe," in *Post-Colonial Cultures in France*, edited by Alec G. Hargreaves and Mark McKinney (London: Routledge, 1997), 26–39.

41. Cheikh Raymond, *Concert Public De Malouf*, Vols. 1–3, CD (Paris: Al Sur, 1995); *La Desirée* (Paris: Al Sur, 1999). On these recordings you can also hear the teenage prodigy Gaston Ghrenassia (Macias) playing guitar.

42. Interestingly, Macias claims that PLO representative Leila Shahid informed him ahead of time that she would attend his Bourges concert in tribute to Cheikh Raymond. Veronique Mortaigne, "Enrico Macias, ambassadeur de la reconciliation des juifs et des musulmans," *Le Monde*, April 19, 1999.

43. Enrico Macias accompanied by Taoufik Bestandji and the Foundok Ensemble, *Hommage à Cheikh Raymond*, CD (Paris: Trema/Sony Music, 1999); Enrico Macias accompanied by Taoufik Bestandji and his ensemble, *Enrico Macias en concert en hommage à Cheikh Raymond*, DVD (Paris: TFI Video, 2000).

44. Mohieddin Ameimour, "Bouteflika Hit 'Several Birds with One Stone' by Rapping Algerian Journalists over Israeli Trip," *Mideast Mirror* 14, no. 125 (July 3, 2000), translated from *Al-sharq al-awsat*.

45. Hassane Zerrouky, "Enrico Macias déchaîne les passions," *L'Humanité*, March 7, 2000.

46. Agence France Presse, "Un parti islamiste dénonce la visite d'Enrico Macias en Algérie," February 15, 2000.

47. Hassane Zerrouky, "Constantine attend l'enfant du pays," *L'Humanité*, March 4, 2000.

48. Françoise Germain-Robbin, "Enrico Macias reporte sa tournée en Algérie," *L'Humanité*, March 6, 2000.

49. Nitzan Horowitz, "Algerian President Warms to Israel," *Ha'aretz*, October 31, 1999.

50. Addi Lahouari, "Abdelaziz Bouteflika a du renoncer à inviter Enrico Macias," *Liberation*, March 9, 2000, 9.

51. "Yerushalaim Shel Zahav" (Jerusalem the golden), one of Israel's most beloved folk anthems. Curiously, Macias was not prevented from speaking, although he too had met Arafat, in 1994.

52. Henri Tincq, "Les fils de la diaspora defilent à Paris devant l'ambassade d'Israel," *Le Monde*, October 12, 2000.

53. Bertrand Bollenbach, "Concert by Singer for Peace Sparks Mideast Boycott Rumpus," Agence France Presse, November 25, 2000.

54. Sara Daniel, "Enrico Macias et la 'haggra,'" *Nouvel Observateur* 1882, November 30, 2000.

55. Amel Bouakba, "Beur FM vient au chevet des sinistrés de Bab El Oued," *La Tribune* (Algiers), February 11, 2002, available at: http://allafrica.com/stories/200202110457.html.

56. Of course, many postcolonial theorists have advocated such a move. My interest here is in using the interzone concept to think through some of their proposals. For a useful account of antibinary thinking with regard to colonialism, see Michael Hardt and Antonio Negri's chapter on "The Dialectics of Colonial Sovereignty," in their *Empire* (Cambridge, Mass.: Harvard University Press, 2000), 114–136.

57. Monestier, *Enrico Macias*, 55.

58. This is to suggest that not only are the pieds noirs not all racists, but that even the "racists" among them might have quite an ambivalent relation to both French and Arab culture. A useful analogy here might be the contradictory position of the Mizrahim in Israel.

59. I am a great admirer of the work of Ann Laura Stoler, but I do not think that her *Race and the Education of Desire* serves as a useful model of colonialism in this instance.

IV REGIONAL AND GLOBAL CIRCUITS

REBECCA L. STEIN

"First Contact" and
Other Israeli Fictions:
Tourism, Globalization,
and the Middle East
Peace Process

In the summer of 1994, several days before the signing of the Washington
Declaration that would end the official state of war between Israel and
Jordan, one of Israel's most popular daily newspapers documented the
"first" Israeli visit to Petra, the Nabatean city in southern Jordan. A two-
page spread, featured in the front section of *Yedi'ot Aharonot* and illustrated
with photographs, recounted the clandestine voyage of two Israeli travelers
who had crossed the border into Jordan illegally with their European passports. "I Got to the Red Rock!" the headline proclaimed. Dramatic, first-
person prose recounted the travelers' mounting anticipation as they neared
Petra in a Jordanian taxi, their constant fear of discovery, and, at last, the
thrill of arrival. "And then it happened. Suddenly, between the crevices of
the giant stones, 100 meters from us, [we caught our] first glimpse of the
red structures hewn in rock. Tears came to our eyes . . . 'Photograph me,'
we said to each other in the same breath."[1]

Israeli voyages into the Arab Middle East received extensive coverage in
the mainstream Israeli media of the mid-1990s. The figure of the Israeli
tourist and the grammar of a tourist imagination constituted crucial discursive tools by which popular newspapers represented the so-called Middle East peace process and its effects to mass reading publics. Stories about
tourism were important vehicles of translation. While the intricacies of diplomacy and political economy could be difficult to convey in the popularized vocabularies of the press, stories about leisure travel were not. The

figure of the tourist was highly intelligible, even banal in its intelligibility. Tales of the Jewish Israeli leisure traveler, traversing borders into neighboring states heretofore off-limits, were deployed to narrate the effects of regional reconfiguration. Through the image of the traveling tourist body, crossing borders made porous by "peace," the press illustrated Israel's new diplomatic and economic place in the Middle East. Through the highly recognizable figure of the tourist, newspaper readers contended with new maps and new meanings of the Israeli nation-state in an increasingly regionalized and globalized age.

Using the tourist as a lens, this essay examines the ways in which the Oslo process and the shifting relations between Israel and the Arab Middle East were represented and managed in popular Israeli media of the mid-1990s.[2] My investigation is framed by the tenure of the Rabin-Peres Labor-led administration (1992–1996), the formative years of the so-called peace process, which began in earnest with the Oslo Accords of 1993, as the Israeli state negotiated a political settlement with the Palestinians and neighboring Arab countries. Through the Oslo process, the Labor administration hoped to build a regional economy and common market with Tel Aviv at its center, a political blueprint celebrated euphemistically as the "New Middle East." For the Israeli business community, "peace" held economic promise on a far grander scale; analysts argued that diplomatic and economic agreements with the Palestinians and neighboring Arab countries, in accordance with liberalization in the nation-state, would enable Israel's fuller integration into the global economy. For the Labor administration, the Oslo Accords were also designed as a security arrangement in which the Palestinian Authority would collaborate in the work of the Israeli occupation to ensure the safety and integrity of the Jewish state.

Although the Oslo process failed to alter the regional balance of power, it had a profound effect on the "national order of things" within Israel.[3] As the state and private sectors developed stronger diplomatic and economic ties with neighboring Arab states and as territorial borders became flexible in new ways, cultural and ideological borders began to shift and come to crisis. At issue were a new set of questions and anxieties about Israeli identity in the era of "peace" and the place of a Jewish state in the Middle East. Tourism was at the center of these multiply shifting terrains. As a market, it was both product and progenitor of Israel's integration into new regional and global economies; as a field of both representational and spatial practices, it was a crucial tool by which differently situated Israeli communities explored and contended with the meaning of Israeliness in the peacetime era.

This essay investigates the popular grammar of the Oslo era by focusing on representations of tourism in Israel's most widely consumed Hebrew-language daily newspapers, *Yedi'ot Aharonot* and *Ma'ariv*.[4] I look at two narratives that were repeatedly deployed during this period. The first is a story of "first contact," in which the Jewish Israeli tourist was cast as discoverer in and of the so-called Arab world. Through a grammar of discovery, which reiterated the stock conventions and gestures of imperial travelogues, such tales of discovery functioned to shore up the boundaries of the Israeli nation-state, to preserve the fiction of Israel as a discrete territorial and cultural unit at precisely the moment that borders were being traversed by new kinds of regional and global flows. The second is a less laudatory tale about incoming tourism *from* Arab countries. Whereas the Jewish Israeli tourist was portrayed as a heroic traveler, freely traversing borders into Arab lands hitherto untouched by an Israeli presence (or so the press suggested), the Arab tourist seeking entry into Israel was the object of considerable anxiety. Through the menacing and often illegible figure of the Arab tourist, the press evoked and managed the threats posed by the permeable borders of the New Middle East and the incoming flows of Arab persons, cultures, and things that the Oslo process was beginning to deliver.

Citizenship was supremely at stake in these tourism narratives. Indeed, the question Who is a tourist?, as enunciated through both legal and popular cultural registers, could often be read as Who is a citizen? The relationship between these key terms (tourist, citizen) was highly variable. Stories about Israeli tourists traveling into Arab countries turned on an isomorphic relationship, whereby good tourist looked like good citizen. In stories about Arab tourists in Israel, however, the very authenticity of the tourist depended on his or her difference from the (Israeli) citizen. In the case of the former narrative, good tourists-citizens had very particular profiles; despite the diverse populations of Israelis traveling through the region during this period, this figure was perpetually cast as Ashkenazi, a Jew of European descent,[5] a move consistent with the Ashkenazi bias of the popular Hebrew press and, more pointedly, with the hegemonic terms of Israeliness on which the state had been founded.[6] In turn, stories about incoming Arab tourists (or the threat thereof) worked to shore up the borders of the nation-state, preserving its Jewishness in the face of shifting demographics and regional geopolitics that threatened Israel with Arabization. Yet the popular press was an ambivalent text; in the slippages and anxieties that attended stories about tourism, newspapers exposed precisely the instabilities of dominant Israeli ideology in the Oslo era and the possibilities for its remaking.

In the broadest terms, I am suggesting that "the tourist" be read as a surrogate: a figure that stood in for something else. This is not to discount the material importance of tourism in the Oslo process and its emerging markets but to suggest that the significance of tourism in the popular press exceeded the register of political economy, even as it was articulated through it. In Israeli newspapers, stories about tourism were simultaneously stories about the nation-state, about the meaning and boundaries of Israeli identity, citizenship, and culture during the peacetime era. Their function was twofold: they worked to regulate the flows of bodies, culture, and things (both real and imagined) across the border, in and out of the Israeli nation-state, and to performatively reproduce a set of knowledges about the nation-state and its subjects during this period of both regional and national flux. These stories demarcated the difference between home and away, consolidating the ideological boundaries of the nation-state, at precisely the moment that physical borders were becoming porous in new ways. The highly legible and recognizable figure of the leisure traveler illustrated the reorganization of political alliances, economies, and circuits of labor in the New Middle East of the Oslo era.

In part, this essay emerges out of, and seeks to complicate, the discussion and deployment of tropes of travel by cultural theorists of the past two decades. In the early 1990s, images of travel and the traveler were used to illustrate postmodern hybridity and to shatter the presumed isomorphism of community, culture, and place by theorizing and historicizing subjects at points of transience and flux.[7] More recently, traveling subjects have been marshaled as illustrations of globalization or transnationalism, offered in the form of a laundry list ("tourists, immigrants, refugees, exiles, guest workers").[8] As Caren Kaplan has suggested, the traveling subject as trope of global flow tends to obscure the historical conditions of travel for differently situated communities and the discrepant relations of power that attend them.[9] In other words, laundry lists risk an equivalence effect, whereby differences among disparate histories and experiences of travel are smoothed over or ignored. Rather than merely dismiss such tropes for their leveling effects, this paper explores the meanings and effects of their deployment in a particular historical context in an effort to take these tropes seriously as both effects and catalysts of larger political, economic, and social processes. By conjoining discourse analysis with political economy, I seek to complicate the prevailing scholarship on the Oslo process with its relatively singular attention to the macroeconomic effects and diplomatic histories of peacemaking, by considering some of the quotidian discursive economies in and by which Oslo was represented and managed. My reading also seeks to illustrate the uneven regional geographies of mobility, prosperity, and power that Oslo generated, even as it suggests the relative fragility of Israeli hegemony in the global era.

This study of Israeli tourism discourses must be read in the context of multiple histories of travel and movement that far exceed the scope of this essay. They include the Zionist migration to Palestine beginning in the late nineteenth century; the flight and expulsion of some 700,000 Palestinians in the course of the 1948 war; the Mizrahi emigration of the 1950s and subsequent decades of state-sponsored peripheralization; the itineraries of Israeli soldiers and settlers in Arab places, in the context of occupation or military incursion (in Lebanon, Sinai, the West Bank, and Gaza Strip); and the ways that tourism practices and discourses have been enlisted in the material and symbolic service of the Israeli occupation. My study of leisure travel articulates with and because of these histories.[10]

The Oslo Process and Its Economies

While negotiations between Israel and neighboring Arab states have been openly pursued since the 1967 war, the Oslo Accords of 1993 were celebrated in the Israeli and international media as the first significant breakthrough in Israeli-Palestinian negotiations.[11] Yet, as many Palestinian critics have argued, the Accords did little to alter the geopolitical balance of power in the region: signed by Yasser Arafat in an attempt to secure his regime in a time of political and economic crisis, the Oslo Accords reconfigured the terms of Israeli power in the West Bank and Gaza Strip through a new partnership with the Palestinian Authority but did not achieve a significant redistribution of that power.[12] The Accords stipulated mutual recognition between Israel and the Palestine Liberation Organization (PLO) and the beginning of Israeli withdrawal from Palestinian territories occupied in 1967. They offered the Israeli government the economic and political gains of an internationally recognized rapprochement with the Palestinian people but necessitated little territorial compromise, leaving Israel in control of land, security, the economy, and all matters pertaining to the Jewish settlements in the West Bank and Gaza Strip. Despite the symbolic trappings of statehood (e.g., Palestinian postage stamps, passports, and uniformed immigration officers), the Palestinian governing entity and its territorial borders remained "legally subordinate to the authority of the [Israeli] military government."[13]

The Oslo Accords had profound effects on the Israeli economy.[14] "Peace" with the Palestinians paved the way for Jordan and Israel to sign the Washington Declaration in July 1994, thereby ending the official state of war between the two countries; in turn, Arab nations ended their forty-year boycott of Israeli goods and commercial partnerships and their ban on third-party dealings with Israel.[15] By many accounts, the "Arab boycott" had long been a public fiction, belied by a history of covert trade between Israel and the Arab states in everything from arms to agriculture.[16] Yet the official dismantling of the boycott regime had serious effects.[17] Without the boycott as obstacle, Israeli companies began to look toward neighboring nations as potential markets, suppliers of cheap labor, subcontractors, business partners, and targets of investment. Israel increased its trade with North African countries (particularly Morocco and Tunisia) and opened trade representation offices in Qatar and Oman. The Israeli private sector pursued regional ventures with Jordan, Egypt, and the Palestinians in the areas of tourism, transportation, water, and the environment. Israeli textile firms began to transfer plants over Israel's eastern and southern borders in search of inexpensive labor.[18] At issue was less an emerging regional economy, as proclaimed by the Israeli state and private sector, than a regionalized Israeli economy that was beginning to mine Arab countries for new markets, sites of production, and labor pools, thereby fortifying the pre-Oslo balance of power.[19]

The dismantling of the secondary and tertiary tiers of the Arab boycott banning third-party dealings with the Jewish state produced major economic gains for Israel. Prior to the 1990s, Israel had been largely ignored by European and Asian multinationals. In the first two years after the Oslo Accords, Israel's national economy grew significantly due to a surge in foreign investment and consumer confidence. Total foreign investment in Israel increased by $4.7 billion to $19.6 billion, and several U.S. high-tech corporations (including Intel, IBM, and Microsoft) announced major new investments in the country, investments made possible by a large, skilled workforce of Russian immigrants trained in science and technology.[20] In turn, Israeli companies began to globalize, working through regional channels. The Israeli textile industry was a self-proclaimed pioneer in this regard;

in the 1990s, raw cotton was being purchased in Egypt, sent to Turkey for spinning and weaving, to Israel for designing, to Jordan for sewing and packaging, and finally shipped for sale in the United States. In tandem, Israeli capital was flowing to Asia as never before; following the end of the boycott, Israeli companies began exploring markets in Malaysia, India, Vietnam, and Indonesia. Government ministers spoke of Israel as the future "Singapore of the region," a hub between Asia and Europe.[21] Through the channel of the regional, Oslo was globalizing the Israeli economy. Indeed, the process was dialectical: the regional processes generated by Oslo enabled global ones, even as the globalization of the Israeli economy had regional effects.

In accordance with the dual axes of commerce and security on which the Oslo process turned, globalization depended on Israel's violent containment of the occupied Palestinian territories. In March 1993, the Labor administration began to pursue a policy of military closure by which the West Bank and Gaza Strip were effectively sealed off from each other, the Jerusalem area, and Israel proper in an effort to protect Jewish citizens from "Arab terror." The number of Palestinians granted permits for work inside Israel fell dramatically, from approximately 120,000 daily in 1992 to 36,000 in 1996. To replace the Palestinian blue-collar workforce, the government began importing workers from nations where non-Arab labor could be contracted at minimal costs (Romania, Thailand, Nigeria, Ghana, the Philippines). Due to a history of Palestinian dependence on the Israeli economy, the policy of closure produced high rates of unemployment (escalating from 11 percent in 1993 to 28 percent in 1996), vastly reduced levels of Palestinian trade and production, and heightened poverty.[22] In keeping with the terms of the Oslo Accords, Israel maintained control over the perimeters of Palestinian areas and prevented Palestinian access to Israeli markets while ensuring Israeli access to Palestinian ones.

The mid-1990s was also a period of tremendous social and political change in Israel, change enabled by shifts on regional and global scales. Israeli Jews of North African, Asian, and Middle Eastern descent (Mizrahim) were demanding and gaining new kinds of political visibility and electoral power in Israel. Although they had long constituted the Jewish majority in the state, at least until the large-scale Russian immigration of the 1990s, they had historically occupied the lowest rungs of Israeli Jewish society—victims of state-sponsored peripheralization, underdevelopment, and racism. During the 1990s, as Israel pursued "peace" with its Arab neighbors, Mizrahi voters began to mobilize in unprecedented ways.

As a result, Israel's only Mizrahi-identified party, SHAS (Shomrei Torah Sephardim; Sephardic Torah Guardians), greatly increased its parliamentary numbers and power during the national elections of 1996 and 1999, with a strident critique of Ashkenazi hegemony.[23] At the same time, Palestinian citizens of Israel were increasingly demanding their civil rights as citizens of the state and reaching new audiences in the Parliament and popular media alike. Toward the end of the Labor tenure, the first Palestinian Israeli politician announced plans to run for prime minister in the 2000 race.

These shifts in Israeli political culture were attended by demographic changes in the nation-state that increasingly threatened the Jewish character of the state (in the words of right-wing analysts). Israel's Christian communities grew markedly during this decade, as a result of the mass immigration to Israel of non-Jews from the former Soviet Union (the spouses of Jewish immigrants).[24] At the same time, Israel's population of blue-collar foreign workers was growing and beginning to settle in Israeli towns and cities; by 1998, they made up one-sixth of the population of metropolitan Tel Aviv. Perhaps of greatest consequence, population analysts warned, was the precipitous rise in Arab birthrates, both among the Palestinian population living within the borders of Israel and the Arab population within the region as a whole, and the coextensive decline in Jewish fertility (indeed, this warning had been anxiously voiced since the early years of state formation). In the mid-1990s, some demographers anticipated an Arab majority in the area of Israel-Palestine by the early decades of the twenty-first century.[25] Such statistics seemed to foretell the demise of the Jewish state. As Israel moved toward greater economic and political integration in the Arab Middle East, the ability of the dominant culture to remain both Jewish and European was the subject of considerable anxiety.

Tourism and "Peace"

The Oslo process also had a profound effect on the tourism sector in both Israel and the Middle East as a whole.[26] Indeed, it was in the field of tourism that "peace" generated some of the most substantial regional cooperation and seemed to hold its greatest financial promise, at least in the first few years after the Oslo Accords. In fall 1995, Israel joined Turkey and Egypt in establishing the Eastern Mediterranean Tourist Association to coordinate joint marketing of regional itineraries. Simultaneously, the Israeli government announced plans for a series of tourism projects in cooperation with

Jordan, including a Dead Sea park spanning the border, joint airport facilities in Aqaba and Eilat, and a "Peace Road" connecting Haifa and Irbid.[27] In 1995, as the Israeli Ministry of Tourism hailed "the year of peace tourism," the number of incoming visitors peaked at a record 2.2 million, generating $3.1 billion.[28] With tourism revenues representing over 30 percent of Israel's income from service exports in 1993 ($2.5 billion), the development of regional tourism promised growth to an already crucial Israeli market.[29] Optimists anticipated a 250 percent rise in revenue as a result of regional marketing, air links between Israel and Asia, newly opened and eased border crossings, and the rise in consumer confidence generated by political stability.[30]

The Oslo Accords also substantially affected the itineraries of Israeli travelers, as diplomatic and economic agreements between Israel and its neighbors made the Middle East newly available and attractive to tourists. Jordan was the most popular, and the most possible, new Middle Eastern destination. In the first six months following the Washington Declaration (1994), some 60,000 Israelis crossed the eastern border for weekend visits to sites that had been off-limits since 1948.[31] Between 1995 and 1997, over 100,000 Israelis paid a visit to the Hashemite Kingdom.[32] Israeli tourism to Morocco also increased during this period following the establishment of low-level diplomatic relations with Rabat in 1994; some 40,000 Israelis, many of Moroccan descent, visited in 1995, a dramatic increase from the 2,000 Israelis who had come annually (and illegally) since the 1980s.[33] Growing numbers of Israelis traveled to Egypt and the Sinai Peninsula during the post-Oslo period, despite over a decade of "peace" with Egypt. Some 200,000 visited in 1994, a 70 percent increase from the previous year.[34]

No less monumental was the shifting imagination of Israeli armchair travelers as sites in Arab countries that remained restricted to Israeli passport holders in the mid-1990s were becoming available as objects of tourist fantasy. As talks between Israel and Syria progressed in spring 1995, the Hebrew press began to prepare its readers for their impending trips to Damascus, Beirut, and Tunis. In tandem, Israeli tourist agencies began to prepare their clients for travel across a Middle East uninterrupted by borders or political conflict (see figure 10). Prior to peace, dominant Israeli discourse had conceptualized the distance between Israel and its Arab neighbors largely in terms of military threat. In the mid-1990s, this geography began to change. The New Middle East was now being offered to Israeli consumer-citizens as a singular geography—not of conflict but of leisure.

FIGURE 10. Figurative image of the "New Middle East," in *Eastern Mediterranean Tourism/ Travel Magazine*, 1994.

The Oslo process also stimulated geographies of leisure within the nation-state, sanctioning new forms of Ashkenazi curiosity in Palestinian Israeli culture. Israeli Jews had long conceptualized the distances between Jewish towns and Palestinian villages as indices of enmity, real and imagined (similar to the ways they had regarded distances between Israel and its Arab neighbors). In the mid-1990s, they began to reconceptualize these proximities, traveling into Palestinian villages and towns for weekend leisure, returning to places they had visited in the uniform of the Israeli army or deliberately skirted for fear of politically motivated violence. Palestinian and Jewish entrepreneurs took advantage of the new curiosity and developed a market in ethnic tourism (trafficking in foods, folklore, cultural practices, and historical narratives), and it soon gained the symbolic and fiscal support of the Ministry of Tourism.[35] Only certain forms of Palestinian culture were sanctioned by the state and deemed attractive to the Ashkenazi tourist-consumers who frequented this market: those that bore the recognizable marks of "authenticity" (the rural untouched by modernity) and the cultural diacritics of a desituated "Arabness," stripped of the threatening traces of Palestinian ethnonationalism.[36]

Yet, not all proximities were cause for celebration. The possibility of Amman, Damascus, and Beirut as potential tourist sites in the pages of the Hebrew press was predicated on the simultaneous absence of the cities and towns that "peace" could less easily abide. Even as Jewish tourists began crossing the border into Jordan or traveling north to the Palestinian Galilee for weekend leisure, they continued to avoid the cities and towns of the West Bank and Gaza Strip, as they had since the first Intifada (1987–1991). More than touristic appeal or "safety" was at issue here. The new geography of Jewish Israeli leisure obeyed the political and cultural logic of the New Middle East with its provisional links between Israel and neighboring states and its highly regulated divides between Israel and its occupied Palestinian territories.

Tales of Discovery

How did the mainstream Israeli press contend with the Oslo process? How did it make sense of Israel's changing relationship to the Arab Middle East and its new participation in regional and global economies? The figure of the Israeli tourist traversing Arab lands was a popular means of representing these cultural and political-economic processes to mass Israeli readerships. The narrative of first contact, in which the Jewish tourist was celebrated as discoverer in and of Arab landscapes previously unavailable to Israeli passport holders, was particularly prominent in the Hebrew press during this period. Through stories of discovery, which relied on an imagined history of noncontact between Israel and its Arab neighbors, the Oslo process could be lauded as heroic for its rupturing effects. Jordan was the foremost object of Israeli discovery, both because it was the first Arab state to open its borders to Israeli travelers during this decade and because of its alluring proximity.[37]

So let us return to the press account of the "first" Israeli tourists in Petra with which this essay began. The Israeli arrival in Petra could only be imagined in heroic terms; Petra was a place long immortalized in Israeli myth, the subject of collective longing, popular song, and children's stories. Beginning in the 1950s, clandestine travel to this Nabatean city had been a virtual rite of passage for young Israeli men who risked their lives in enemy Jordanian territory for a glimpse of the city's celebrated red sandstone cliffs.[38] By the mid-1990s, the desire for Petra was firmly embedded in the national Israeli imagination. In the press, the Israeli tourist was installed to consummate that desire:

> Now we are here, descending on foot on the donkey path, and my heart is beating wildly. When no one is around, we speak in Hebrew—certainly the first conversation that has been heard here, in this language,

for many years. Suddenly, standing out from two sides of the narrow path, the giant red rocks rise proudly, casting a menacing glance on the small figures that move between them . . . And then it happened. Suddenly, between the crevices of the giant stones, 100 meters from us, [we caught our] first glimpse of the red structures hewn in rock. Tears came to our eyes . . . "Photograph me," we said to each other in the same breath.[39]

The thrill of arrival depended on a companion narrative of secrecy and disguise. Our visitors speak a careful Hebrew, only out of earshot, in a place where Israeli Jews had long feared to tread. The text is rife with the standard tropes of discovery drawn from the archive of colonial travel: the ardor of a clandestine voyage, the mounting anticipation as the site is neared, the victorious testimonial upon arrival, the virtual invisibility of indigenous bodies or subjects that might sully the landscape and mitigate the rhetoric of first contact.[40] The act of discovery is explicitly thematized and its excitement preserved through recourse to a perpetual present tense: "Today, at this moment, [Petra] is being discovered by two Israeli journalists with the excitement of children. I pinch myself to confirm it."[41]

The narrative of discovery was substantiated by a photograph (see figure 11). Like the televised images of this scene of first contact, shot by the same journalists with a handheld camera and aired that evening on the Hebrew news, the quality of the photograph is poor. The image is grainy and overexposed, with the Israeli journalist squarely at its center, posing before Petra's mythic red rocks with a compact camera worn like a medal of honor. In its composition and amateurism, the photograph is recognizable as "the tourist snapshot." The thrill and drama of the clandestine arrival depends on this quotidian portrait, on the story of common travelers crossing state lines. Through the very familiarity of its tropes, through its evocation of the conventional signifiers of leisure travel, the photograph constitutes the proof of presence. It assures us not simply that "they were there" but that "being there" happened in familiar ways. As the companion narrative suggests ("*photograph* me") the discovery must be documented and witnessed to be true.[42] Indeed, the story of first contact depends on a double act of verification: on site, with handheld camera, and by readers of the press, through consumption and recognition of the image.

Discovery was also an act of subject formation. In the consummate moment of arrival, and the rituals of documentation that attend it ("*photograph me*"), the discoverer-subject is made visible; that is, the "I" is re-

FIGURE 11. "I Got to the Red Rock," *Yediot Aḥaronot*, 1994.

constituted at the moment of first contact ("*I* Got to the Red Rock"). For newspaper readers, the very recognizability of the discoverer qua tourist functions as a moment of interpellation, albeit one that can be refused. Through consumption and recognition of the photograph and the standard tropes of tourism that attend the narrative, the reader is hailed as tourist-discoverer. Given that a collective Israeli longing for Petra began just after state formation, discovery was considerably belated. Yet, however belated, the narrative's present tense rendered discovery both immediate and always already new ("Today, at this moment, Petra is being discovered"). Through consumption of texts like this one, readers of the Hebrew press discovered Jordan and were hailed as Israeli discoverers over and over again.

Similar stories of first contact proliferated in the pages of the Israeli press during the period. Indeed, the scene of discovery in Jordan would be restaged less than one month later. On August 12, 1994, three days after the border legally opened to third-party passport holders, images of "the first Israeli tourists to return from Jordan" appeared again on the front page of a popular Hebrew daily. And this scene would recur in November, when the border was officially opened to all Israeli travelers regardless of passport (prior to this date, representatives from the tourism ministry explained, Israeli tourists had crossed the border in violation of international agreements). In the months that followed, the press announced the first private Israeli vehicles to cross into Jordan, the first flights between Tel

Aviv and Amman, and the first direct bus service to the Jordanian capital.[43] Some firsts were more quotidian, such as tales of Hebrew spoken by tourists in select Jordanian towns "for the very first time." Some were cautionary, as in "the first time since [peace] that a Jordanian newspaper printed a racist article against Israeli tourists."[44] As the Oslo process grew in scope, stories of first contact were told of other places, announcing the arrival of Israelis to Yemen and Tunisia. And this narrative was mobilized to anticipate future routes to places that remained inaccessible to Israeli civilians: Syria, Lebanon, and the Gulf States. The power and credence of this narrative relied on its sheer proliferation. And yet, in proliferation, the narrative of "newness" was perpetually undone. Each successive first required the forgetting of its antecedent.

The idiom of the tourist guide was critical in producing the story of first times and introducing the geography of the Middle East to Jewish Israeli readers. These narratives worked to secure the ideology of discovery and to realign the threatening political geography of the Arab Middle East as a cartography of leisure. As Israel pursued negotiations with Syria in the winter of 1994, newspapers acquainted their reading publics with the streets and sites of Damascus.[45] One offered tips on shopping, museum going, and proper ways of bargaining.[46] Another offered its readers "Thirty Things You Didn't Know about Syria," with lists of useful facts and attractive vistas.[47] Regional itineraries were shifting dramatically for the Israeli tourist. With Arab countries becoming available in new ways, the merits of particular Arab cities could now be measured relationally: "[The Damascus market] is all very authentic. There's no system of double prices—one for tourists, one for locals—like in Jordan. And they don't ask for *baksheesh* like in Egypt."[48] North Africa, Yemen, and the Gulf States were also being inscribed onto an Israeli tourist cartography in new ways, following diplomatic and economic advances in the Oslo peace process. On the occasion of Shimon Peres's first visit to Qatar, the press introduced its readership to "The Qatari: Our New Friend in the East" through an imagined encounter with Israelis "in the world of tourism."[49] In spring 1996, newspapers announced "Yemen: Starting to Open to the World" and featured Tunisia as an "Oasis in the Sahara."[50] When snapshots of first contact were unavailable, they had to be anticipated; the streets of Tunis were depicted with a photograph of an empty marketplace, above the caption: "Soon to be a center of Israeli tourism."[51]

The "discovery" of the Arab Middle East required a narrative on geography. To dramatize the heroism of first contact, the proximity between

Israel and its Arab neighbors was cast in the idiom of astonishment. The press deployed a narrative of the "surprisingly near," that is, of a geography of contiguity that "peace" had only now made visible and available. Newspapers assured readers that Arab places were much nearer than expected and articulated the allure of neighboring states through the wonder of their proximity. Headlines announced "Closer Than You Think!" and articles reminded readers that "it's closer than Turkey . . . or even Egypt."[52] The same idiom was employed to entice readers with future itineraries in Syria, stressing Damascus's negligible distance from Israeli urban centers ("An Hour and a Half from Tiberias").[53] Whether articulated in temporal or spatial terms, proximity was represented as an effect of regional realignment and its anticipated future. "Peace" was creating "new conditions of neighborliness," changing the way Israeli national geography could be told and understood, making the distance and difference between Israel and its Arab neighbors thinkable in new ways.[54] Distances and differences that were once legible only through the coordinates of enmity were now possible to remap through the idiom of leisure travel. Yet distance had no absolute value; Israel's ability to contain Palestinian proximity during this period is what made the celebration of regional proximity possible.

Diasporic Itineraries

On what did first contact depend? What was at stake in its perpetual reiteration? The story of Israeli newness in Arab countries depended on a set of constitutive exclusions and historical revisions that worked to stabilize the New Middle East, to make the regional geography of contiguity and proximity safe for dominant Jewish culture. Tales of discovery consolidated Israel's difference from the region at precisely the moment that flows of labor, commerce, and capital between Israel and its neighbors seemed to make borders porous in ways that threatened the integrity of the Israeli nation-state. The myth of first contact stabilized the border as both a geographic and cultural divide.

Of course, first contact was a fiction, one that relied on an imagined history of noncontact that "peace" effectively ruptured, one that operated through the elision of prior histories of contact between Israel and its Arab neighbors. Although these tales of discovery borrowed from the archive of colonial travel, the nature of their elisions differed in important ways. Critical to the colonial travelogue and its narrative of discovery was the process of distorting and forgetting local knowledges and practices of a place—a discursive practice which in turn enabled the place to be "found" by the Western traveler.[55] The Israeli case was different. At issue in the Israeli press was less a revision of "local" knowledges or histories than a willful forgetting of Israeli ones, that is, of prior Jewish Israeli histories in Arab places. Of particular consequence were those pertaining to the Israeli army and to the violent Israeli itineraries born of war, occupation, and incursion. The forgetting of these histories enabled the discovery of Beirut as Israeli tourist destination, despite the 1982 invasion of the capital city, when many Israeli soldiers passed through its historic districts. A similar process of forgetting enabled the emergence of Tunis as first-time leisure destination, despite a history of Israeli efforts to monitor (and assassinate) PLO leadership in this city. The story of the first time did the work of historical revision at a moment when national economic interests were supremely at stake. To forget these histories of aggression in Arab places was to enable new modalities of both collaboration and exploitation in the emerging markets of the New Middle East.

The fiction of first contact also depended on a set of elisions and revisions pertaining to the Israeli tourist population itself. To sustain the myth of discovery, contact between tourist and host was represented as an interface across the lines of difference, and the tourist carried the onus of that difference. In the pages of the mainstream Hebrew press, Israelis visiting Arab countries were represented not merely as Jews but as Jews of European descent (Ashkenazim). The tourist's European identity was illustrated through accounts of his or her confusion in Arab places. Numerous articles described the tourist's failure to comprehend Arabic in the middle of the Arab metropolis and celebrated (in the case of Jordan) the ability of hotel and restaurant workers to converse in Hebrew.[56] Newspaper accounts frequently described an Israeli tourist populace unable to comprehend the quotidian Arab landscape; the press did the work of decoding this foreign landscape for the Jewish reader qua traveler, translating unfamiliar Arab places and cultural practices into a legible "Israeli" lexicon and geography.

In truth, there were many kinds of Israelis traveling through the Middle East at this moment, with many different itineraries. Despite the press's portrait of the Ashkenazi peacetime traveler, there were many Mizrahi Israelis touring the region during this period, and many lacked the linguistic and cultural incompetence that the press presumed. In the 1980s and increasingly after the Oslo Accords, Jews of Moroccan descent began touring Morocco in unprecedented numbers, a voyage made possible by low-level diplomatic agreements with Israel in 1994 and a Moroccan government eager for revenue from an incoming Jewish market.[57] Moreover, during this period Mizrahi travelers numbered heavily among the Israeli tourists visiting Turkey (attractively situated in the interstices of Europe and the Middle East). Yet the press's story of first contact, and its presumption of the culturolinguistic newness of the Middle East, made no conceptual space for these travelers and their itineraries. The same was true of articles that anticipated and invited future travel to Arab places not yet available to Israeli tourists; "Thirty Things You Didn't Know about Syria," a 1995 exposé of Damascus cast as proto–tourist guide, was not addressed to Arab Jewish travelers with prior knowledge of Syria's cultural and political landscapes; the allure of travel in the region relied on a narrative of sights heretofore unseen. Mizrahi travel could not be mobilized to tell a heroic story of discovery or a tale of "peace" as rupturing event and thus was not featured in the popular media.

Nor were all Israeli travelers Jewish. Indeed, notwithstanding the presumptions of the press, the vast majority of Israelis traveling to Jordan in the mid-1990s were Palestinian citizens of the state.[58] As with Mizrahi travelers, their presence among the Israeli tourist masses was invisible in a discovery narrative dependent on an Orientalist binary (Europe meets the Arab world). These traveling subjects could not represent the nation-state in the pages of its newspapers; although citizens of the state, they continued to be actively excluded from the national collective ("the people of Israel") as they had been since Israel's founding. The invisibility of these Palestinian travelers was heightened by the relative visibility granted Palestinian tourists from the occupied territories, whose voyages to Jordan, though never celebrated as "discoveries," were sometimes chronicled in the back pages of the Hebrew press. Consider the following excerpt, from an article entitled "They Were There," which offered tips on Jordan to the prospective Jewish Israeli tourist amassed from West Bank informants: "Naseer Adin Nashashibi . . . recommends a visit to the Jerash festival . . . He discourages hitchhiking . . . Sako, an employee in a camera store who requested anonymity, often travels to visit his family. He recommends the Jabri chain of restaurants, especially the one with American-style [food] . . . Daoud Maoli, a cook at the Munateen restaurant, recommends a visit to the King's castle."[59] The reporter finds his informants in East Jerusalem's service sector, in the commercial contact zones (camera store, restaurant) where Israeli Jews and Palestinians most frequently meet. These informants are marked as Palestinians only in name; indeed, many offer advice under the protection of anonymity. Here, the idiom of the tourist guide obscures a history of Palestinian diaspora and its migratory routes between Israel, the Occupied Territories, and neighboring Arab countries. In turn, in standard tourist register, the story of a family visit is overshadowed by recommendations for restaurants and entertainment venues. Local knowledge of the place and appropriate behavioral norms ("he discourages hitchhiking") is implicitly ascribed to a history of leisure rather than to the legacy of dispossession that necessitated the journey between Jordan and the West Bank—the itinerary that retraces a path of exile. In this telling, to have "been there" (recall the headline) was to have been a tourist.

What were the effects of the press's very selective portraits of the Israeli traveler? They policed the borders around national identity and culture. They regulated and performatively reinstated the portrait of normative Israeliness on which the state had been founded, sustaining the terms of the dominant Israeli discourse in which "Israeli" connoted both and only the European and Jewish subject. This production of normativity relied on a central dyad: because the scene of first contact was meant to be understood as an interface between nation-states and not merely leisure travelers after a history of enmity, discovery depended on the isomorphism of tourist and citizen, that is, tourist as representative of his or her nation-state. In the slippage between these terms (tourist and citizen), the Ashkenazi Jew was installed not only as normative Israeli tourist but also as normative Israeli citizen-subject. As I have suggested, normativity was constituted through a logic of difference, not only in the difference between the Israeli tourist and Jordanian host but between Jew and Arab. The aforementioned photograph of first contact provides a graphic illustration of this logic in the dyadic relationship between the foregrounded Israeli tourist and (presumably) backgrounded Bedouin laborer, visible only in profile (figure 11). The banality of this image, clearly legible as the tourist snapshot, helps to naturalize the narrative. Handheld camera is to tourist as Ashkenazi Jew is to Israeli. The link between signifier and signified is offered as incontestable: equally recognizable, equally banal. The press's tales of tourism worked to preserve the disappearance of this foundational fiction about Israel and its citizenry, to reproduce and secure it, in the face of its vanishing.[60]

The Tourist as Mimic

Regional travel during the Oslo era was not unidirectional. In the mid-1990s, Arab tourists from neighboring states were beginning to appear

in the Israeli metropolis. Jordanians composed the largest tourist population. In 1994, following the Washington Declaration, some 25,000 Jordanians toured the Jewish state, and by 1995, this number had risen to over
80,000.[61] As travel agents in Amman attested, the demand was far greater
than the number of visas granted due to rigid Israeli screening of potential
applicants in an effort to sort bona fide travelers from migrant laborers, terrorists, and those seeking permanent residence—or so the state argued.[62]
In 1994, as the mainstream Israeli press celebrated the first-time journeys
of Ashkenazi tourists in Jordan, it uneasily anticipated the beginning of
this tourist influx ("They Are Coming to See Eilat").[63] Two years later, headlines predicted "A Million Arab Tourists Will Visit Jerusalem and Bethlehem."[64] Small numbers of Muslim Arabs from neighboring countries had
visited Israel in the years before the Oslo Accords, often illegally or through
third-party passports. Yet, with the emergence of a regional "peace," the
Israeli state and private sector predicted unprecedented numbers of Arab
visitors—a prediction that generated considerable concern.

Not all Arab tourists were regarded equally.[65] The Israeli press and private sector eagerly anticipated "the wealthy of Amman" and the Gulf States,
"tempted by Eilat's nightclubs and the availability of alcohol," destined for
Tel Aviv's malls and tourist complexes.[66] Yet, more often than not, this
incoming population was depicted as an underclass mob. In the wake of
the Washington Declaration, as rumors circulated about a "major influx
of Muslim pilgrims," newspapers assured their readers that "black clad
women from Iran are not [yet] thronging the streets of Tel Aviv."[67] In an
image drawn from the Orientalist archive, the "throng" threatened in both
its magnitude and its illegibility.

In winter 1995, the Israeli press began to describe illegitimate Arab tourists with unrecognizable itineraries. Of particular concern was the growing
population of Jordanians seeking tourist visas for travel in Israel. Popular
newspapers began to investigate cases of Jordanians who "came to visit and
stayed" in violation of their visas. Articles documented scores of Jordanian
men working in construction and Jordanian women selling sex in northern
Israeli towns.[68] One headline warned, "Arab Towns [in Israel] Being Used
as Hiding Places for Illegal Tourists."[69] Newspapers exposed such crimes
and encouraged readers to participate in the regulatory work of the state.

Indeed, many "tourists" were working in Israel during this period in violation of the terms of their visas. They infiltrated with relative ease, thanks
to the growing number of foreign workers imported by the Labor Ministry
to replace the blue-collar Palestinian workforce from the West Bank and

Gaza, *now* deemed a political risk.[70] By 1995, some 89,000 foreign laborers (from Ghana, Romania, Thailand, and the Philippines) worked legally in Israel and some 100,000 more worked illegally on tourist visas.[71] For the state, foreign labor promised a certain kind of clarity. Unlike the Palestinian workforce they had replaced, these laborers were obligated to leave after the expiration of their work visas. But perhaps more critically, they bore a marked difference from both Jews (qua good citizens) and Arabs (qua proto-terrorists), an ethnoracial difference inscribed on their bodies, thereby easing the labor of policing their movements. Amid growing Israeli concern for their rising numbers, the accounts of foreign workers began to appear in the Hebrew press in spring 1996. True to the terms of their visas, many spoke in tourist idioms: "I'm meeting a lot of girls. It's interesting for me here, because it's another country."[72]

Jordanians also populated the illegal workforce during this period.[73] Yet, unlike the foreign worker on tourist visa, who blended easily in the laboring crowd, the fraudulent Jordanian worker-tourist could be easily recognized, or so the press assured its readers. At issue was a failure of resemblance: they simply didn't look like tourists in any normative sense. One prominent daily newspaper described a typical scene at the Israeli-Jordanian border. Many alleged tour groups crossed the border together, the article reported, only to disband on the other side: "Immediately after the border crossing, they separate and each one travels to a different place. There are some who come with mattresses and equipment, and it's clear that they aren't exactly tourists that are coming to tour and then return to Jordan."[74]

A crime is being documented here, that of Jordanians who try to pass as tourists. Their fraudulence is transparent ("it's clear that they aren't exactly tourists"). Criminality is deduced from the truth of the visible, from material artifacts that do not bear the standard markers of leisure travel. In the place of a handheld camera, we see mattresses and kitchen implements, objects connoting homecoming, not tourism.

This tale of tourism and criminality forestalled a much more threatening narrative about the New Middle East. Like accounts of Palestinian travel to Jordan in which familial visits were recast as leisure itineraries, this story of tourism/criminality displaced the legacy of exile and diaspora. Contrary to the discourse of the press, these visitors had little need to hide, and this was precisely their threat. Most Jordanians on tourist visa were of Palestinian origin; thus, their ability to pass as laborers, or as citizens of Israel, rested in a history of familial or ethnonational ties to the Palestinian communities and populations in which they sought refuge. They had little need for concealment: their bodies could look "at home" in Israel in ways that the state could not easily control.

On what, then, did criminality depend? The fraudulence of the Jordanian visitor rested not merely on the failure of resemblance, but also on the threat of likeness. Unlike the case of Israeli tourism in the Arab Middle East where tourist and citizen were offered as isomorphic terms, the authenticity of the Arab tourist rested precisely in her or his visible *difference* from the Israeli citizen. Indeed, suspicion arose at precisely the moment when visitors began to look at home. Their menace cohered at this place of liminality where lines could not be drawn clearly. Anxiety came to the fore at the moment of mimicry, when the alleged tourist began to resemble the citizen. The press intervened to regulate the difference.

Whom did the Arab travelers resemble? First and foremost, they bore an ethnonational resemblance to Palestinian laborers from the Occupied Territories and Palestinian citizens of the state, thus enabling their successful concealment in Israeli towns and work sites. But their likeness, and its menace, was broader still. In the mid-1990s, these visitors raised the specter of an unpleasant past, one the state had long ignored. Images of laden travelers recalled the mass flight of Palestinians after the founding of Israel, travelers similarly burdened with mattresses and kitchen implements, fleeing with their home on their back. But the figure of the Arab traveler also signaled a future that Jewish Israel imagined with considerable trepidation. These figures seemed to foretell the mass return of Palestinian refugees to their homes inside Israel.[75] As documented in the Israeli press, many Jewish Israelis feared that the peace process would make this return possible: "We are going to gain in this 'peace,' but maybe, at the same time, lose everything: our country, our Jewish identity, and, in the end, the opportunity to live in what we once called the land of Israel . . . They expect millions of tourists [here] from the whole world. The foreigners will fill the streets of our cities in masses, until it is no longer clear who lives here and who is a tourist."[76] What exactly was tourism's menace in the age of the Oslo process and the globalization of the Israeli economy and culture? As this passage from the Israeli press suggests, in words spoken by a prominent Jewish environmentalist, its menace lay in mimicry. In the midst of an urban crowd, at the heart of the Jewish Israeli metropolis, the line between tourist and citizen had the potential to blur. Israelis feared that persons from outside the nation-state might suddenly make themselves at home, protected by the cloak of resemblance. In the urban crowd, as foreigners mingled with citizens, as visitors walked the streets of Israel, making themselves at home in the nation-state, these tourists-mimics had the capacity to unsettle dominant Israeli geographies, notions of national identity, accounts of its history. These spectral figures threatened to render home itself unrecognizable.

Alternative Maps

Much scholarship of the past decade has encouraged us to think "beyond the nation"—to consider the unbundling of nation-states in the age of global capitalism.[77] Discussion of borders has tended to focus on new degrees of permeability. Traveling subjects, traversing state lines, have been privileged illustrations of global processes. As Katherine Verdery has noted, the prefix trans- in transnationalism seems to connote both border crossing and transcendence: the transcendence of "the national" form.[78] Yet the case of mid-1990s Israel requires a different account. The diplomatic and economic reconfiguration of the region in the peace process era, with its cross-border flows and circuits, necessitated the fortification of the nation-state and the remaking and remapping of Israel's territorial and symbolic contours. Rather than tell a story of (Israeli) denationalization or deterritorialization in the global era, my analysis illustrates processes of both renationalization and reterritorialization in the midst of globalizing processes.[79] Flows across state lines produced the need to defend and remake Israel's spatial and ideological divides, to shore up the borders around normative Jewish Israeli identity, culture, and territory.

The mid-1990s was a period of tremendous social and political change in Israel and on its borders. While politicians and businesspeople could predict the future economic landscape of Israel and the Middle East (or so many of them thought), the sociopolitical effects of regional realignment remained uncharted, and threateningly so. For even as "peace" promised to globalize Israel, it also threatened to Arabize it, hence the fear of a tourist mob. The press's stories of first contact respond to this anxiety by shoring up the borders of the nation-state, demarcating clear parameters around Israeli identity and the subjects that could claim it, preserving Israeliness as a Jewish and European domain in the face of shifting geopolitics and newly flexible borders. Of course, Israel was always already Arabized, and this was precisely the issue, the locus of fear and anxiety. The possibility of resemblance—of Arab tourist to citizen—threatened the fiction of Ashkenazi normativity by making visible the history of Palestinian dispossession and Mizrahi disfranchisement on which this fiction depended.

Yet, the anxiety that attends the tourist mob also suggests that the present and future geography of Israel and the Middle East was not and is not under control in any strict sense. Although the Israeli state could prevent the emergence of a sovereign Palestinian state (as it continues to do), it cannot control the changing demographics in the region and nation-state and the promise of a Palestinian majority in the area of Israel-Palestine in the next half-century. Although the Israeli state could and can regulate the movement of bodies on its borders through militarized checkpoints and visa restrictions, it could not and cannot determine the multiple effects produced by the continued globalization of Israeli economies, cultures, and knowledges. The haunting images in the Israeli press of Palestinian Arabs in tourist guise, returning to claim their homeland, might yet foretell an alternative Israeli future.

Notes

An earlier version of this essay appeared in *Public Culture* 14, no. 3 (2002): 515–543. Many thanks to Ann Anagnost, Joel Beinin, Yael Ben-Zvi, Robert Blecher, Elliot Colla, Andrew Janiak, Kaylin Goldstein, Jake Kosek, Donald Moore, Andy Parker, Matthew Sparke, and *Public Culture*'s anonymous reviewers for a wealth of insightful readings and suggestions.

1. Gad Lior, "Higa'ti lasel'a haadom" [I got to the red rock], *Yedi'ot Aharonot*, July 18, 1994, sec. 1, p. 10.

2. I use the terms "Middle East peace process," "Oslo process," and "peace process" interchangeably to refer to the bilateral, trilateral, and multilateral negotiations conducted during the 1990s between Israel, the Palestinian Authority, and Arab states. My use of the word "peace" and the phrase "New Middle East" is not intended to endorse the political ideologies and processes that they denote, but aims to draw attention to the ways this rhetoric circulated in dominant Hebrew discourse.

3. Liisa Malkki, "Refugees and Exile: From 'Refugee Studies' to the National Order of Things," *Annual Review of Anthropology* 24 (1995): 70.

4. These newspapers, both published in Tel Aviv, had daily circulations of 250,000 and 160,000, respectively, during this period. My analysis also includes reference to the Hebrew dailies *Ha'aretz* and *Davar Rishon*; the regional and/or urban Hebrew weeklies *Kol Ha'ir* (Jerusalem) and *Kol Hatzafon*; and the *Jerusalem Post* and the *Jerusalem Report*, Israel's primary English-language publications of this period.

5. Ashkenazi Jews of Russian, Polish, German, and Central European descent have historically made up Israel's elite class and have dominated Israel's cultural, economic, and political institutions since the early years of state formation. Although largely excluded from elite institutions, the Mizrahi Jewish population (including Jews from North Africa, the Middle East, and the Levant) constituted the majority of Israel's Jews in the decades following their mass migration to Israel in the 1950s.

With the arrival of some 700,000 Jews from the former Soviet Union in the first half of the 1990s, this majority status was lost. Despite their ethnonational origins, these immigrants have not been able to claim Ashkenazi privilege due to their class background, lack of schooling in Zionist culture, and numerous rabbinical challenges to their Jewishness. Jews who migrated to Israel from England, South Africa, and the United States have historically exercised Ashkenazi privilege and yet have been largely excluded from dominant positions in Israel's elite institutions. See Sami Shalom Chetrit, "Mizrahi Politics in Israel: Between Integration and Alternative," *Journal of Palestine Studies* 29, no. 4 (2000): 51–65, and Youseff Courbage, "Reshuffling the Demographic Cards in Israel/Palestine," *Journal of Palestine Studies* 28 (1999): 21–39, for analyses of changing ethnoracial demographics and power relations in Israel during the 1990s.

6. The readership of *Yedi'ot Aharonot* and *Ma'ariv* has long been relatively diverse, including Jews of European descent (Ashkenazim), Jews who immigrated to Israel from Arabic-speaking countries (Mizrahim), and Palestinian Arabs with Israeli citizenship. Despite this broad consumer base, both papers have historically observed the terms of dominant Israeli ideology by focusing on Ashkenazi cultures, political circuits, and institutions. Eli Avraham, *Hatiqshoret beyisrael: Siquran shel 'ayarot hapituah* [The media in Israel: Coverage of the development towns] (Tel Aviv: Breirot, 1993).

7. See James Clifford, "Notes on Theory and Travel," *Inscriptions* 5 (1989): 177–187, "Traveling Cultures," in *Cultural Studies*, edited by Lawrence Grossberg, Cary Nelson, and Paula A. Treichler (New York: Routledge, 1992); bell hooks, "Representing Whiteness in the Black Imagination," in *Cultural Studies*, edited by Lawrence Grossberg, Cary Nelson, and Paula Treicher (New York: Routledge, 1992).

8. Arjun Appadurai, *Modernity at Large: Cultural Dimensions of Globalization* (Minneapolis: University of Minnesota Press, 1996), 33.

9. Caren Kaplan, *Questions of Travel: Postmodern Discourses of Displacement* (Durham, N.C.: Duke University Press, 1996).

10. Following the 1967 war and Israel's occupation of Arab and Palestinian lands, Jews flocked to the East Jerusalem Old City for "authentic" Arab food, to the Sinai coast for natural beauty and Bedouin culture, and to the markets and restaurants of Bethlehem and Ramallah for inexpensive shopping on Friday afternoons. See Smadar Lavie, "Sinai for the Coffee Table: Birds, Bedouins, and Desert Wanderlust," *Middle East Report* 18, no. 1 (1988): 40–44, and *The Poetics of Military Occupation: Mzeina Allegories of Bedouin Identity under Israeli and Egyptian Rule* (Berkeley: University of California Press, 1990).

After the Camp David Accords of 1978, hundreds of thousands of Israeli Jews visited Cairo and Alexandria. The first Palestinian uprising put a temporary end to West Bank leisure itineraries. After the Oslo Accords, Jewish settlements in the West Bank and Gaza began to develop tourist facilities, but few Israeli Jews returned as tourists to Palestinian towns and cities. See Rebecca Stein, "Itineraries of Peace: Remapping Israeli and Palestinian Tourism," *Middle East Report* 25, no. 5 (1995): 16–19.

11. Yaacov Bar-Siman-Tov, *Israel and the Peace Process, 1977–1982: In Search of Legitimacy for Peace* (Albany: State University of New York Press, 1994); William B. Quandt,

Peace Process: American Diplomacy and the Arab-Israeli Process since 1967 (Berkeley: University of California Press, 1993).

12. Emma Murphy, "Stacking the Deck: The Economics of the Israeli-PLO Accords," *Middle East Report* 25, no. 3/4 (1995): 35–38; Mouin Rabbani, "Palestinian Authority, Israeli Rule: From Transition to Permanent Arrangement," *Middle East Report* 26, no. 4 (1996): 2–6. By the early 1990s, political and economic conditions in the West Bank and Gaza Strip were deteriorating: the PLO was crippled by the loss of revenue and military support from the former USSR and Gulf patrons following the Gulf War; the Intifada had fallen out of favor with the Western media, partially due to Arafat's alliance with Saddam Hussein; and as poverty grew in the West Bank and Gaza Strip alongside dissatisfaction with Arafat's regime, the Islamic movement Hamas was becoming an increasingly popular alternative to the PLO. Naseer H. Aruri, *The Obstruction of Peace: The United States, Israel, and the Palestinians* (Monroe, Maine: Common Courage, 1995).

13. Aruri, *The Obstruction of Peace*, 223, 213.

14. Gershon Shafir and Yoav Peled, "Peace and Profits: The Globalization of Israeli Business and the Peace Process," in *The New Israel: Peacemaking and Liberalization*, edited by Gershon Shafir and Yoav Peled (Boulder, Colo.: Westview, 2000).

15. The primary Arab boycott against Israeli products was instituted in the late 1940s. The secondary boycott, established in 1952, blacklisted firms that traded with Israel, followed by a tertiary boycott imposed on firms that traded with Israel. On October 1, 1994, the Gulf Cooperation Council—including Saudi Arabia, Bahrain, Kuwait, Oman, Qatar, and the United Arab Emirates—ended its blacklist of Israeli goods and companies with Israeli ties. See Ofira Seliktar, "The Peace Dividend: The Economy of Israel and the Peace Process," in *The Middle East Peace Process: Interdisciplinary Perspectives*, edited by Ilan Peleg (Albany: State University of New York Press, 1998).

16. Israel Shahak, "Drugs and Vegetable: The Israeli Trade with Arab Countries," in *Open Secrets: Israeli Nuclear and Foreign Policies* (London: Pluto Press, 1997), 107–122.

17. Seliktar, "The Peace Dividend."

18. Ibid.; Shafir and Peled, "Peace and Profits."

19. As of 1998, Israel's per capita GNP was six to ten times higher than that of neighboring states. Guy Mundlak, "Labor in a Peaceful Middle East: Regional Prosperity or Social Dumping?", in *The Middle East Peace Process: Interdisciplinary Perspectives*, edited by Ilan Peleg (Albany: State University of New York Press, 1998), 202.

20. Joel Beinin, "Palestine and Israel: Perils of a Neoliberal, Repressive Pax Americana," *Social Justice* 25, no. 4 (1998): 20–39.

21. Many Israeli economists and market analysts were more cautious in predicting Israel's place in an emerging regional economy, citing "xenophobic restrictions on foreign trade and investment" and popular fears of neocolonial domination in the Arab Middle East, in addition to the gross disparities between national economies. See Seliktar, "The Peace Dividend"; Ben-Zion Zilberfarb, "The Effects of the Peace Process on the Israeli Economy," *Israel Affairs* 1 (autumn 1994): 84–95.

22. Yacov Ben Efrat, "Close Minded: Changing the Nature of Control," *Challenge* (May–June 1993): 6–7; Leila Farsakh, "Under Siege: Closure, Separation, and the Palestinian Economy," *Middle East Report* 30, no. 4 (2000): 22–24.

23. See Courbage, "Reshuffling the Demographic Cards in Israel/Palestine"; Chetrit, "Mizrahi Politics in Israel."

24. Demographer Youssef Courbage explains: "With the massive arrival of Jews from the former Soviet Union beginning in 1991, the Law of Return was de facto extended to include the non-Jewish spouses of Jewish immigrants. As a result, the proportion of Jews among the immigrants fell from about 97 percent in 1990 to 75 percent in 1997." He notes that Israel's Christian community grew from 107,000 persons in 1990 to 183,000 in 1996, a tenfold increase. Courbage, "Reshuffling the Demographic Cards in Israel/Palestine," 28.

25. Ibid., 30.

26. The Jordanian private sector was equally optimistic about the effects of peace and began massive state-sponsored development of the national tourist infrastructure to accommodate the anticipated boom. Yet tourist numbers and revenues decreased rapidly in the late 1990s despite initial growth, fueling popular opposition to peace and to normalized relations with Israel. For analysis of Jordan's 1990s tourism economy, see Patrick Clawson, *Tourism Cooperation in the Levant*, Policy Focus Series, no. 26 (Washington, D.C.: Washington Institute for Near East Policy, 1994); Waleed Hazbun, "Mapping the Landscape of the 'New Middle East': The Politics of Tourism Development and the Peace Process in Jordan," in *Jordan in Transition*, edited by George Joffé (New York: Palgrave, 2002).

27. See Government of Israel, *Development Options for Cooperation: The Middle East/East Mediterranean Region* (Jerusalem: Government Publishing House, 1996).

28. Margo Lipschitz Sugarman, "Tourists with Reservations," *Jerusalem Report*, October 31, 1996, 47–48.

29. Ministry of Finance, Government of Israel, *Focus on the Economy: Possible Economic Implications of the Peace Treaty* (Jerusalem: Government Publishing House, 1994).

30. See Mordecai Ben Ari, *Peace Tourism Update* (Jerusalem: Israeli Ministry of Tourism, 1996) and Margo Lipschitz Sugarman, "Make Tours, Not War," *Jerusalem Report*, August 25, 1994, 34–36.

31. Nicky Blackburn, "Reaching the Threshold," *Link: Israel's International Business Magazine* (fall 1995): 21.

32. Most Israeli tourists visiting Jordan went to Petra only, and many just for the day. See Hazbun, "Mapping the Landscape of the 'New Middle East.' "

33. See André Levy, "To Morocco and Back: Tourism and Pilgrimage among Moroccan-born Israelis," in *Grasping Land: Space and Place in Contemporary Israeli Discourse and Experience*, edited by Eyal Ben-Ari and Yoram Bilu (Albany: State University of New York, 1997); Gil Sedan, "Moroccan Jews Mourn Death of King," *Jewish News of Greater Phoenix*, July 30, 1999, available at: http:// www.jewishaz.com/index.html.

34. Betsy Hiel, "Tourism Revival in the Land of the Pharaohs," *Arab DataNet*, June 2, 1995, available at: http://www.arabdatanet.com.

35. See Rebecca Stein, "National Itineraries, Itinerant Nations: Israeli Tourism and Palestinian Cultural Production," *Social Text* 56 (1998): 91–124.

36. Ibid.

37. The story of first contact was also deployed by the Hebrew press to describe Israeli tourism to Egypt in the wake of the Camp David Accords of 1978, ending the formal state of war between Israel and Egypt. Yet this narrative was mitigated by the breadth of popular and academic (notably archaeological) Israeli knowledge about ancient Egypt. Thus, unlike the story of Israeli tourism to Jordan in the wake of the Washington Declaration, the popular narrative of Israeli first visits to Egypt did not presume discovery of the previously unknown, but rather its rediscovery in the "modern" age.

38. Petra was first introduced to Western travelers in the nineteenth century through John Lewis Burckhardt's *Travels in Arabia: Comprehending an Account of Those Territories in Hedjaz Which the Mohammedans Regard as Sacred* (London: Henry Colburn, 1829). A century of travelers followed Burckhardt's lead, including Orientalist scholars who traveled in disguise as Muslim pilgrims, and Christian pilgrims who traversed the Holy Land in search of biblical geography.

39. Lior, "Higa'ti lasel'a haadom."

40. See Stephen Greenblatt, *Marvelous Possessions: The Wonder of the New World* (Chicago: University of Chicago Press, 1991); Mary Louise Pratt, *Imperial Eyes: Travel Writing and Transculturation* (London: Routledge, 1992).

41. Lior, "Higa'ti lasel'a haadom."

42. Mary Pratt describes a similar phenomenon in Victorian discovery rhetoric and the role of material evidence in making it "real": "The 'discovery' itself, even within the ideology of discovery, has no existence of its own. It only gets 'made' for real after the traveler (or other survivor) returns home, and brings it into being through texts: a name on a map, a report to the Royal Geographical Society, the Foreign Office." Pratt, *Imperial Eyes*, 240.

43. Revital Levinshtein, "Masof 'aravah niftah lema'avar klei rekhev pratiim" [Arava border crossing opens to private vehicles], *Ha'aretz*, April 8, 1996, sec. 1.

44. Khalid Abu-Tuma, "Iton beyarden: Hatayarim hayisraelim qamtzamim veokhlim raq falafel" [Newspaper in Jordan: The Israeli tourists are stingy and only eat falafel], *Yerushalayim*, September 8, 1995.

45. Aviv Lavi, "Natbag 2000" [Airport 2000], *Kol Ha'ir*, December 29, 1995.

46. David Shalit, "Haya'ad haba: Dameseq" [The next destination: Damascus], *Ha'aretz Supplement*, November 25, 1994, 33–35.

47. Moshiq Lavi, "Shloshim devarim shelo yad'atem 'al suriah" [Thirty things you didn't know about Syria], *Yedi'ot Aharonot*, December 1, 1995.

48. Ibid.

49. Ben Kaspit, "Haqatari: Yedidenu hehadash mimizrah" [The Qatari: Our new friend from the east], *Ma'ariv*, April 5, 1996, 27.

50. "Teiman: Mathilah lehitpateah la'olam" [Yemen: Starting to open to the world], *Ma'ariv*, April 5, 1996, Tayarut section, 26; "Tunisia: Neot midbar basaharah" [Tunisia: Oasis in the Sahara], *Ma'ariv*, April 5, 1996, Tayarut section, 27.

51. Alon Shehori, "Kamah medinot 'araviyot yifteḥu bashevu'ot haqerovim netzigut tayarutit betel-aviv" [Several Arab countries will open tourist offices in Tel Aviv in upcoming weeks], *Israel Tourist Guide*, February 1, 1996, 1.

52. Yossi Cohen, "20 dinar lezug, kolel mizug avir" [Twenty dinars per couple, including air conditioning], *Kol Ha'ir*, July 22, 1994, sec. 1, 65; Carl Schrag and Steve Rodan, "Closer Than You Think," *Jerusalem Post Magazine*, July 29, 1994, 11.

53. Edna Iss, "Sha'ah vaḥetzi miteveriah" [An hour and a half from Tiberias], *Yedi'ot Aḥaronot*, December 8, 1995.

54. Appadurai, *Modernity at Large*, 29.

55. Pratt, *Imperial Eyes*.

56. Y. Cohen, "20 dinar lezug, kolel mizug avir."

57. A. Levy, "To Morocco and Back."

58. Haim Shapiro, "Israelis Flock to Jersash Festival," *Jerusalem Post*, July 12, 1995, 3; Ehud Ya'ari, "The Jordanian Option," *Jerusalem Report*, February 9, 1995, 2830.

59. Y. Cohen, "20 dinar lezug, kolel mizug avir."

60. As noted above, this fiction was being challenged in unprecedented ways during the 1990s: by the growing parliamentary power and public visibility of SHAS, Israel's Mizrahi party; by the mobilization of Palestinians with Israeli citizenship; by rising numbers of non-Jews in the nation-state (foreign workers and Russian immigrants); and by the looming question of how to retain the Jewishness of the state in the midst of a New Middle East.

61. Israeli Ministry of Tourism, *Tourism to Israel, 1995: Statistical Report* (Jerusalem: Government Publishing House, 1996), 14, and *Tourism to Israel, 1997: Statistical Report* (Jerusalem: Government Publishing House, 1998), 19. By law, Palestinian residents of Jordan were permitted entry into Israel and the Occupied Territories after the 1967 occupation in the framework of family reunification; in practice, the number of visas granted by Israel was limited.

62. R. Stein, "Itineraries of Peace."

63. Betsalel Rubin, "Hem baim lirot et Eilat" [They are coming to see Eilat], *'Erev 'Erev*, December 26, 1994.

64. Avshalom Kaveh, "Milyon tayarim 'araviim yevaqru biyerushalayim uveveitlehem 'im heskem Oslo bet" [A million Arab tourists will visit Jerusalem and Bethlehem with the realization of Oslo 11], *Davar Rishon*, January 23, 1996.

65. The Israeli state's policy on incoming Arab or Muslim tourism was contradictory and perpetually shifting. See Israeli Ministry of Tourism, *Regional Tourism Cooperation Development Options*. (Jerusalem: Government Publishing House, 1995), i. The Israeli Ministry of Tourism declared Israel open to "all Muslim and Arab travelers"; two months later, Ministry spokespersons "clarified" that Muslim tourism to Jerusalem would not be "encouraged" at a time when the political status of the city was so fiercely contested. Eyal Hareuveni, "Hasar Bar'am neged tayarut muslemit" [Minister Baram is against Muslim tourists], *Kol Ha'ir*, September 1, 1995.

66. Savar Plotzker, "Haḥalom evar kan" [The dream is already here], *Yedi'ot Aḥaronot*, July 25, 1994; Sugarman, "Make Tours, Not War."

67. Haim Shapiro, "Across the Great Divide," *Jerusalem Post Magazine*, October 13, 1995, 20.

68. Hillel Cohen, "Shalom 2: Palestinim ezraḥei yarden baim ketayarim veni-sharim beyisrael" [Peace 2: Palestinian citizens of Jordan come as tourists and stay in Israel], *Kol Ha'ir*, October 27, 1995; Dani Sadeh, "6,000 yardenim bau leviqur venisharu bashetaḥim" [6,000 Jordanians came to visit and stayed in the territories], *Yedi'ot Aḥaronot*, September 3, 1995.

69. Yuli Dar, "Yishuvei ha'aravim meshamshim mekom mistor letayarim bilti ḥuqiim" [Arab towns used as a hiding place for illegal tourists], *Kol Hatzafon*, January 26, 1996.

70. Because of their ability to "pass," some Jordanian travelers were victims of police violence intended for Palestinians from the occupied territories. See Hillel Cohen, "Shalom 1: Tayar Yardeni mitlonen 'al alimut shotrim yisraelim" [Peace 1: Jordanian tourist complains about violence from Israeli police], *Kol Ha'ir*, October 27, 1995; Kamal Ja'afari, "Foreign Arab Workers in Israel," *Challenge* (January–February 1996): 14–15.

71. "Foreign Workers in Israel," *Migration News* 4, no. 8 (August 1997). Available at http://migration.ucdavis.edu/mn/.

72. Shuli Sapir, " 'Arbev et hatiaḥ, Jonny" [Mix the plaster, Jonny], *Davar Rishon*, March 26, 1996.

73. Unlike other foreign workers, Jordanian laborers were not provided with housing, which radically cut corporate costs for Israeli companies. Salaries in Israel were often three times that available for comparable labor in Jordan and Egypt. Ja'afari, "Foreign Arab Workers in Israel."

74. Sadeh, "6,000 yardenim bau leviqur venisharu bashetaḥim."

75. In the 1990s, this nightmare was beginning to materialize, as Palestinians with deeds to property inside Israel (particularly West Jerusalem) began to explore legal restitution. Hillel Cohen, "Heḥanu et hacheck" [We prepared the check], *Kol Ha'ir*, February 16, 1996.

76. Rubin, "Hem baim lirot et Eilat."

77. See Appadurai, *Modernity at Large*; Linda Basch, Nina Glick Schiller, and Cristina Szanton Blanc, *Nations Unbound: Transnational Projects, Postcolonial Predicaments, and Deterritorialized Nation-States* (Langhorne, Penna.: Gordon and Breach, 1994); Pheng Cheah and Bruce Robbins, eds., *Cosmopolitics: Thinking and Feeling beyond the Nation* (Minneapolis: University of Minnesota Press, 1998).

78. Katherine Verdery, "Beyond the Nation in Eastern Europe," *Social Text* 38 (1994): 1–19.

79. See Appadurai, *Modernity at Large*; Saskia Sassen, *Globalization and Its Discontents: Essays on the New Mobility of People and Money* (New York: New Press, 1998), and "Spatialities and Temporalities of the Global: Elements for a Theorization," *Public Culture* 12, no. 1 (2000): 215–232. I am drawing on James Ferguson and Akhil Gupta's account of reterritorialization: "Beyond 'Culture': Space, Identity, and the Politics of Difference," *Cultural Anthropology* 7 (1992): 6–24.

MELANI McALISTER

Prophecy, Politics,

and the Popular:

The *Left Behind*

Series and Christian

Evangelicalism's

New World Order

In the fall of 2001, about six weeks after the events of September 11, a novel called *Desecration* was released. The book was part of the path-breaking *Left Behind* series written by conservative evangelist Tim LaHaye and writer Jerry Jenkins, which describes the "end of times," the rise of the Antichrist and the final battle of Armageddon, all of which figure prominently in Christian apocalyptic theory. *Descecration* went on to become the best-selling hard-cover book of the year, moving John Grisham out of the number 1 spot he had held every year since 1994, and it did so after only three months on the shelves. *Desecration* built on the remarkable success of its predecessors. To date, eleven books of the planned fourteen-book series have been released, and the last five have all debuted at number 1 on the best-seller lists. In total, they have sold more than 32 million copies (excluding graphic novels and children's versions) since the first book appeared in 1995.[1]

The *Left Behind* novels are unabashedly fundamentalist fiction, based on literalist interpretations of the "end of time" as understood through the prophetic books of the Bible. Although the popular success of the series was already well established before September 11, the events of that day spurred a new interest in the books and the larger field of biblical prophecy. For many evangelicals in the United States, the terrorist attacks were more than simply horrific political crisis or personal loss, they were further proof that the end of times predicted in biblical prophecy was imminent. Those who mine the apocalyptic books of the Bible for signs of the Second Coming of Christ often argue that "wars and rumors of wars" as well as great sorrow and tribulation are key indicators of the quickening of God's plan.[2] When that plan unfolds, the Middle East will be the stage and Israel will be at the heart of the story, as Jesus Christ himself returns to fight on the side of his Chosen People against the Antichrist.

The *Left Behind* novels describe the experiences of a group of newly committed Christians who live through the terrible events leading up to Armageddon and Christ's return. In accordance with biblical prophecies, these believers must face the rise of the Antichrist, who will persecute Christians and Jews, take over as dictator of a one-world government, lead a global crusade against Israel, and eventually bring the world to Armageddon.[3] LaHaye and Jenkins have constructed fast-paced and plot-driven stories that are also generic hybrids, combining traditional evangelical homily with science fiction–like threats and action adventure thrills, complete with plenty of male bonding and high-flying action.

Until recently, the series was all but invisible in liberal and intellectual circles, though that is changing; in 2002, authors LaHaye and Jenkins were the center of friendly interviews on CNN, ABC, NPR, CBS, CNBC, and *Time* magazine, among others.[4] Despite extraordinary newspaper and television coverage, however, each account of the *Left Behind* phenomenon finds it necessary to introduce the books to an audience who presumably find their very existence to be news. Fundamentalism itself appears as a novelty to the major media, yet as many as 40 percent of Americans define themselves as evangelical or "born again," depending on how you ask the question.[5] (Fundamentalists are best defined as a subset of evangelical Christians who are generally more literal in their biblical interpretations and often more interested in prophecy than are other evangelicals, mainline Protestant denominations, and Catholics.)[6] The popularity of *Left Behind* is no doubt connected to the much broader growth in the sales of religious-themed cultural products in the United States, ranging from books on New Age spirituality and Jewish dating to Christian T-shirts and Hindi lunch boxes. Sales of religious items have grown by over a third in the past six or seven years. Kmart executives, for example, have said that religious and inspirational writing is the chain's fastest growing category.[7]

The *Left Behind* books are remarkably popular not only with the evangelicals who form their core readership, but also with casual readers who pick up the books when they see the displays at Walmart and Kmart, or visit the special sales section at Amazon, or see the ads reading "Read the Future" and "leftbehind.com" blazoned on the side of a car at NASCAR races in recent years. As one scholar describes it, "In office settings, these things are being passed around like Stephen King novels or the *Sports Illustrated* swimsuit issue."[8] Indeed, as each new installment races to the top of the hardcover charts, paperback versions of earlier books in the series continue to dominate the paperback charts.[9] In addition, the series has spawned two movies, five soundtracks, calendars, mugs, and an impressive line of screensavers and e-greetings.[10] What we are seeing, then, is a remarkable mainstreaming of evangelical pop culture, in which nonevangelicals seem to be willing to read overtly proselytizing messages as long as they are delivered in a reader-friendly genre.

But the novels are also indicative of the reenergized political and cultural power of the Christian Right that in the late 1990s seemed in retreat. In hindsight, that retreat may have been genuine at the political level, as exemplified by the decline of the Christian Coalition and the failure of several evangelical campaigns for president, but it is far less genuine when one considers the politics of culture: by 1996, the *Left Behind* books were already under-the-radar best-sellers. These extraordinary novels marry their evangelical religious commitments to a political agenda that combines traditional social conservatism, an emergent evangelical racial liberalism, and a strongly developed interest in contemporary Middle East politics, in which Israel is central to the unfolding of God's plan for the end of time.

These days, that interest is certainly not expressed or experienced only in novelistic form. As the conflict in Israel-Palestine escalated in the past two years, evangelical preachers and their communities have rushed to "Stand for Israel," organizing support rallies, letter-writing campaigns, and tours of the Holy Land that are linked directly to the Israeli right.[11] These Christian Zionists seem to be having a very real influence on the Bush administration's policies, as they fire off e-mails, hold lobbying days, and organize rallies to insist that the United States take the strongest stance in favor of right-wing Israeli policies to fully subjugate Palestine. The link between political ideology and cultural consumption is never simple or direct, but in the past five years, and especially since September 11, the power of *Left Behind* as a major cultural phenomenon has had an undeniable link with the resurgence of millennialist pro-Israel activism on the Christian right and the extraordinarily dangerous directions taken by the U.S. "war on terrorism" in the Middle East.

In this essay I explore the *Left Behind* series as an exemplary cultural text, one that is simultaneously a symptom of and a strategy for the revitalization of Christian Zionism. I analyze the novels as part of a larger project of evangelical mapping, placing evangelicals on the U.S. political map as a modernized and mainstreamed political force who have moved far beyond the subcultural status that marginalized them even in the heyday of the Moral Majority. This project simultaneously maps the Middle East in highly specific ways. As it looks to biblical passages as support for the "restoration" of Jews to Palestine, and as it marks Israel as the site of God's action in history, the fundamentalist vision of *Left Behind* makes Palestine and Palestinians literally invisible. And as Palestine is wiped off the evangelical map, it is also removed from a sizable audience of potential U.S. readers.

The Future Is Coming

The first novel of the *Left Behind* begins when, without warning, a large group of people from all over the world suddenly and mysteriously disappear, leaving clothes and jewelry behind. The disappeared are committed Christians who have been taken up bodily into heaven, an event that fundamentalists call the Rapture. Nonbelievers are left on earth to face the tribulations—natural disasters, plagues, war, and persecution—that accompany the rise of the Antichrist and the countdown to the final battle of Armageddon. Having been "left behind," one small group of Americans realize what has happened and are converted into committed believers.

The group quickly forms itself into an anti-Antichrist underground which they dub the Tribulation Force. Over the course of several novels, the membership of the force evolves, but the key players are four: Rayford Steele, an expert pilot in his forties who becomes the official leader of the group; his daughter, Chloe, recently a college student; Chloe's husband, Buck, a crack journalist; and, eventually, Tsion Ben-Judah, an Israeli Jew who, after carefully studying the prophecies in the Bible, converts to believing that Jesus of Nazareth was the predicted Jewish Messiah. By stating his newfound conviction to the world, Ben-Judah becomes one of the first of the 144,000 Witnesses, Jewish converts who testify to the world that they accept Christ as their Messiah. He becomes the spiritual mentor of the Tribulation Force and eventually of the new believers who begin to spring up around the world.

As the seven-year period of the Tribulation moves forward, the novels describe the Tribulation Force's struggle against the rising power of the Antichrist. Nicholae Carpathia, a Romanian national and former head of the United Nations, now rules the world as the head of the newly formed Global Community (GC). Carpathia builds himself a gleaming capital city from which to rule, a shining symbol of the totalitarian one-world order, in New Babylon, Iraq. As Carpathia takes over the world, the Tribulation—God's judgments, designed to bring those who are left to a recognition of His power—is unleashed. The Tribulation begins with a terrifying and devastating series of plagues in which millions of people are killed; they include earthquakes, water turning to blood, drought, and invasion by death-dealing horsemen of the air, who kill with fire, sulfur, and smoke. Writing over the Internet (from an untraceable connection at the Tribulation Force headquarters in suburban Chicago), Ben-Judah speaks to the millions of newly converted believers around the globe about the biblical meaning of unfolding events.

The Christian core at the center of the stories are modern, strong, and resourceful. Many of them are tough, competent men of action, several of whom are professional pilots and can thus zip around the world in Gulf-streams or old Egyptian fighter planes. They face dramatic plagues and terrible dangers as well-equipped international travelers with access to private jets, untraceable cell phones, untouchable bugging devices, and advanced laptop computers that are described in loving detail. The novels thus gesture toward Tom Clancy in their style, Stephen King in their sensibility, and Ian Fleming in their plot structures. Humorous yet also featuring detailed statements of evangelical doctrine, they are worlds away from the older, didactic terrain of prophecy exegesis. Instead, they exhibit what can best be described as evangelical worldliness, a melding of traditional subcultural views with a mass culture style and a broad, mainstream appeal.

Since September 11, the reviews and responses to the *Left Behind* books have often related them to Christian conservatives' support for Israel. LaHaye tells interviewers repeatedly that Israel's existence is one of the "super signs" that signal the coming of the end times; he refers inevitably to the biblical injunction, so frequently cited by evangelicals, that "God promised he will bless those who bless Israel and curse those who curse Israel."[12] Although it is appropriate to link *Left Behind* to Christian activism in support of Israel, media discussions of the issue often make one of two mistakes: either they present the novels as examples of a Christian fascination that is entirely new and that somehow emerged full blown in recent years; or they suggest that the revitalized Christian right is simply a return of the repressed, a new Moral Majority. Neither view is correct, and both approaches can lead to mistaken analyses of the current situation. If, for example, we fail to understand the long and deep history of the prophecy tradition in U.S. evangelical culture (and to a lesser but still significant degree, its power in mainstream popular culture), we will fail to see the emotional and intellectual force of current trends. Yet we must also not fail to appreciate what is new, to see how the worldview embraced and exemplified by the *Left Behind* novels links biblical literalism and a traditional Christian Zionist interest in prophecy to what is in many ways a broader, even liberalizing sensibility—more sophisticated, more multicultural, and certainly more consciously "modern" than anything that has come before. These transformations have helped to bring what was once a culturally marginal branch of "old-time religion" into the mainstream of postmodern American life.[13]

The *Left Behind* series is deeply embedded in a long-established tradition in fundamentalist thought that looks to the books of Ezekiel, Daniel, and Revelation for information about the end times and the Second Coming of Christ. Fundamentalists generally regard the Bible as literal truth, but, in the face of the allusive and elusive texts of the prophecies, they must become hermeneutic experts, unpacking highly metaphorical passages for their predictive value. Drawing on the interpretations developed by John Darby in the nineteenth century and popularized in the 1909 Scofield Reference Bible, generations of fundamentalists have held that the Bible's accuracy can be tested and confirmed by political developments, especially those concerning Israel.[14] The doctrinal specifics vary among different groups, but all agree that in the Bible, one important signal of the approach of the Second Coming of Christ is the return of Jews to the Holy Land. Then, according to prophecy, as the end time approaches, an Antichrist will arise, claiming to bring peace. During the Tribulation under the Antichrist, both Jews and Christians will be persecuted. (Various groups disagree about whether the Rapture of believers will happen before or after the Tribulation. The *Left Behind* novels are exemplars of the theory of pre-Tribulation Rapture. Pat Robertson is a well-known proponent of the belief that the Rapture will happen after the Tribulation.) All agree that as God shows his hand and the truth of the Christian Bible's prophecies are revealed, there will be mass conversion of Jews to the recognition that Jesus was their Messiah. At the end of seven years, Israel, threatened by a confederacy of most of the nations of the world, will face down her enemies at a final, terrible battle of Armageddon, during which Christ himself will return to do battle for Israel. After Christ's return, the millennial reign of peace begins.[15]

Evangelical enthusiasm for prophecy study quickened after the founding of Israel in 1948, but it was mobilized to a near frenzy when, after the 1967 Arab-Israeli war, the Israelis occupied all of Jerusalem, just in time for the revival of fundamentalism in the United States. For many, Israeli control of the Holy City was a crucial indication, perhaps *the* indication, that this generation will see the coming of Christ. In 1970, Hal Lindsey published *The Late, Great Planet Earth*, a popularization of fundamentalist doctrines of the end times that used accessible language and a pseudo-hip writing style to target worried baby boomers on the edge of the counterculture. It went on to became the best-selling nonfiction book of the 1970s.[16]

Lindsey, like others before and after him, highlighted the *political significance* of his interpretations of biblical prophecy: the Middle East wars that had happened and those that were coming were predicted and explained in the Bible. Lindsey also aimed to bring the study of prophecy a new kind of panache: he wanted to reach audiences, particularly young audiences, who might be interested in politics first and convinced of Christian revelation as a result. At the same time, he also pushed hard against traditional fundamentalist opposition to worldliness: Christians *must* begin to pay attention to politics, he argued, especially to foreign policy, because the Middle East, particularly the nation of Israel (and its allies and enemies), would be central to the greatest *religious* test of all time. In this context, political events become important because of how they fit into a biblical scheme, and interpreting that scheme is a complex and politically saturated process.[17] Many mainline Protestant leaders have spoken out against end times theology in general, and even evangelicals have strong theological disagreements with an approach that focuses heavily on the possibility of an imminent Second Coming.[18] Yet the appeal remains quite powerful. *Left Behind* uses images, character types, and even whole scenes from the subcultural industry of novels and movies that, since the early 1970s, have been making prophecy, the Rapture, and Armageddon staples of evangelical popular culture.[19] As one scholar of evangelicalism has pointed out, evangelical fascination with end times theology can in part be explained by the fact that prophecy interpretation can be *fun*: fundamentalists debate what the founding of the European Union signifies, or how the oil crisis or Desert Storm fit into the prophetic scheme. Thus, both politics and religion are energized by their relationship to each other.[20]

These general views about prophecy and politics were explicitly part of the fundamentalist Christian activism of the late 1970s, when evangelicals began making themselves felt as a political force. In 1978, Jerry Falwell told reporters, and later repeated in his preaching, that Christians must involve themselves politically in such a way as to guarantee that the United States would support Israel: "I believe that if we fail to protect Israel, we will cease to be important to God . . . We can and must be involved in guiding America towards a biblical position regarding her stand on Israel."[21] When the Moral Majority was founded in 1979, one of its founding principles was: "We support the state of Israel and the Jewish people everywhere."[22]

The writers of the *Left Behind* novels hail from that earlier era, in the 1970s and 1980s, when fundamentalism's political power was on the rise. LaHaye, who provides the biblical commentary and prophecy interpretation that structures each novel, was active in the Moral Majority; in 1987 he was deposed as cochairman of Jack Kemp's presidential campaign for having called Catholicism a "false religion" and for blaming Jewish suffering on the Jewish rejection of Jesus.[23] Jenkins, who does all of the actual writing, was a staff writer for the fundamentalist powerhouse the Moody Bible Institute, as well as the collaborator on Billy Graham's autobiography and ghost writer for several sports autobiographies before he turned to the series. Although LaHaye has until recently enjoyed less visibility than television preachers like Falwell and Robertson, his intellectual and cultural influence has been tremendous. He is married to Beverly LaHaye, founder of the conservative Concerned Women for America, the antigay, antifeminist, anti-abortion, and pro-creationist enterprise that currently claims to be "the largest public policy women's organization" in the country.[24] Even before the *Left Behind* series, he published more than forty books on marriage and family, "sexual adjustment," and biblical prophecy. Recently, Jerry Falwell established the Tim LaHaye School of Prophecy at Liberty University in Lynchburg, Virginia.[25]

Given these credentials, it is not surprising that the other major response of secular commentators has been to see the novels as the vanguard for a revival of 1980s-style political fundamentalism. And at one level, this view is entirely justified. As Michelle Goldberg argued in *Salon.com* recently, it is surely significant that "the most popular fiction in the country creates a gripping narrative that pits American Christians against a conspiracy of Satan-worshipping, abortion-promoting, gun-controlling globalists—all of it revolving around the sovereignty of Israel."[26] With Representatives Dick Armey (R-TX), Tom DeLay (R-TX), and Jim Inhofe (R-OK) vying to become the most visible and most hard-line of Israel's congressional supporters, the political power of Christian Zionism is undeniable. In an MSNBC interview in 2002, Armey called for the transfer of the Palestinian population out of the West Bank, before offering a half-hearted retraction the next day; Inhofe said on the House floor that Israel should keep the West Bank "because God said so."[27] Grassroots churches are increasingly joining the mix, raising money to fund Jewish immigrants to populate Israeli settlements, for example, and joining the estimated 16,000 congregations who participated in Pray for Israel day in October 2002. When President Bush called for Israel to withdraw its tanks from Palestinian territory in the spring of 2002, Falwell and others organized the religious right to send nearly 100,000 e-mails to the White House to protest the request. When the Christian Coalition held its Rally for Israel in October 2002, President Bush sent a videotaped message and Tom DeLay and the mayor of Jerusalem both gave speeches.[28] In fact, the enthusiastic embrace of Israeli security and Israeli settlements includes not only a strong push in Congress, but a close alliance with Israeli leadership. This alliance goes back to the Labor Party's embrace of fundamentalism in the 1970s, when the Israeli government began courting evangelical leaders, hosting Holy Land tours for well-known preachers (including Falwell, and Bailey Smith of the Southern Baptist Convention), and which only intensified under the right-wing Likud government elected in 1978.[29] In January 2002, the Israeli embassy in Washington held the first of a series of meetings with conservative Christian leaders and launched a drive to encourage Christian tourism to Israel; later in the year, Ariel Sharon spoke to an enthusiastic crowd of thousands of evangelicals in Jerusalem.[30] Observers argue that these activities are making a real difference, for quite pragmatic political reasons. While it cannot be ignored that President Bush has every reason to want to secure the position of Jeb Bush in Florida, where his strong support for Israel is also winning him increasing support from Jewish voters, this is only a small part of the story.[31] Many Congressional Republicans have few Jewish constituents but a large number of conservative Christian ones, and their support has been seen as instrumental in pushing Congress to more hawkish positions.[32] As one commentator in the *Jerusalem Post* put it, "The U.S. is Israel's best friend largely because the American Christian community wills it to be so."[33]

To the degree that critics of the Christian right see these actions as *only* a revitalizing version of Reagan-era Christian activism, however, they are likely to miss the important ways the political culture of fundamentalism is changing, maintaining deeply conservative views on Israel and U.S. foreign policy generally, but revamping its cultural politics. In the *Left Behind* novels, we see not only what one reviewer has called the "conspiratorial balderdash" of fundamentalist political ideology, but also a significant outward reach, in terms of both style and content.[34] The *Left Behind* novels claim to be about the future: "Prophecy is history written in advance," LaHaye once said. But they are also very much about the present and a new kind of conservative evangelical self-fashioning that self-consciously reaches out to the larger world, in part to evangelize that world, certainly, but also to construct a complex set of connections to it. As evangelical performance, these novels struggle to enact modernity and to establish both for their protagonists and implicitly for their readers the kind of broad cultural reach that might authorize fundamentalist mappings of U.S. global politics.

Not Your Father's Fundamentalism

Chang Wong is seventeen years old, cocky and tough, a new convert to Jesus. He is also the technical czar for Nicholae Carpathia's Global Community government, working out of the headquarters in New Babylon. Carpathia and his team fully trust Chang, for he appears to have the Antichrist's "mark of loyalty" on his forehead. The young Chang is a computer wiz, and from his position in the belly of the beast, he controls the computers and surveillance system with which the Antichrist keeps track of the population and tries to hunt down those who oppose his rule: Christian converts and Orthodox Jews. But Chang is actually a spy for the Tribulation Force, able to thwart Carpathia's system at every turn. At a key moment, as the Antichrist prepares to interdict the Jews who have retreated to Petra (where they will be protected by God), Chang is able to force the simultaneous broadcast of spiritual leader Tsian Ben-Judah's sermon over every television channel, radio station, and Web site on the Internet. While he is doing that, he is also listening to the plotting of Carpathia and his henchmen via the absolutely secure bugging device that the Tribulation Force has installed on the Antichrist's personal plane. As he listens, automatic filters provide interpretation of conversations held in languages other than English. When Chang hears that the security team is about to track down some key members of the Tribulation Force, he immediately enters the computer system and erases all trace of them in the database. He isn't worried that he'll be caught, because his system is so thoroughly encrypted—it has a "revolving encoder"—that it is impenetrable even by the forces of the one-world government.

In this scene, and hundreds of others like it over the course of the series, LaHaye and Jenkins establish their characters as more modern than modern. Making the most of the fact that the events they describe must necessarily be the future (though a rather near-term future, in their view), the novels present a world in which our Tribulation Force members are unfailingly knowledgeable about and outfitted with an impressive array of the best possible equipment, from guns to high-end suvs, from Gulfstream jets to the "computer without limitations" ordered by the Tribulation Force from an underground dealer. Leaving aside how the novels' various fantasies of the power of perfect gear actually expose a certain technological naïveté, the embrace of *matériel* (equipment) is not simply decorative; it performs important cultural work. If fundamentalists at the turn of the century still carry a residual reputation as old-fashioned and unsophisticated, these characters leave no doubt about their up-to-dateness. They are unflappable globetrotters, as comfortable whipping out their cell phones during a rescue mission as they are witnessing to an unconverted colleague while piloting the most advanced aircraft in the world.

This tech savvy is present not only in the novels, but in the marketing of the series as well. Though *Left Behind* sales have a strong base in Christian bookstores and superstore chains centered in the heartland, the series is also supported by a highly sophisticated Web page that its managers claim receives 60,000 visitors a day. Leftbehind.com has a younger, hipper presence that is far less apparent in the other marketing efforts for the series (such as the NASCAR promotions); it includes visual images that can be downloaded as screensavers and e-cards, message boards and discussion groups, online polls, advertising for products, an e-mail newsletter, and more.[35] The message boards on leftbehind.com have many active threads at once, with several posting hundreds of entries at any given time. The sections designed to promote the graphic novel versions of the books and the separate series for children, *Left Behind: The Kids*, are visually arresting, with the pulsating text and moving images that characterize video games. On the official site, and on several nonofficial fan pages, there is a great deal of the fan accouterment that the Internet has made routine: quizzes, games based on the characters, chatrooms for fans who want to meet each other on the Internet, and, perhaps most important, postings of fan fiction. The fiction entries are generally short stories, usually penned by people in their teens and twenties; they often add new, younger characters to the series. Yet despite the impressive Web presence, the use of the Web sites is a more complicated question; as with many fan-based sites, the vast majority of posters are a rather small group of participants (no more than three hundred), almost all of whom are under thirty. Tyndale Publishers has said that the average buyer of the books is a Southern, white, married female age twenty-five to fifty-four.[36] It is easy to imagine that many of those buyers pick up the books at Walmart, read them and perhaps even share them with friends, without ever visiting a Web site. This worldliness and ease with modernity is doubly striking in that it frames and perhaps in some sense even cushions the uncompromising religious views propounded in the novels. At the level of fundamentalist doctrine, the *Left Behind* series is unreconstructed and proud of it: there is only Jesus Christ, and Christianity is the only truth, and winning converts is the primary moral duty of the characters (and, one presumes, of the novels themselves). This purity is contrasted with the evil one-world faith propounded by the Antichrist and led by a pompous, ritual-obsessed fraud who, before the Rapture, was a Catholic archbishop. The one-world faith defines itself as eclectic, open to all beliefs, including atheism, as long as those faiths are "tolerant," but in fact, it does little more than provide a platform for the eventual worship of the Antichrist while encouraging decadence and immorality. Thus, when, in one of the early novels, the leader of this syncretic abomination calls the Tribulation Force members a "right-wing, fanatic, fundamentalist faction," readers are invited to consider the source and take it as a compliment (*Soul Harvest*, 359). It is not despite but *because of* this doctrinal conservatism that the novels also insist throughout on a certain kind of secular situatedness for their characters. With their high-powered jobs and their impressive access to the best computers and the fastest planes, these end times Christians speak the high-tech language of the unbelieving world around them.

Speaking that language also means operating in its preferred generic registers, and nothing is more striking about the *Left Behind* series than formal intersections with, even slavish devotion to, the conventions of popular science fiction and horror. The fundamentalist world, at least during the years of the Tribulation, is littered with lower-level supernatural creatures: demons and angels in the flesh, ghostly horsemen in the sky who can be seen only by believers, and of course, Satan incarnate in the person of the Antichrist. Here, for example, is the description of the first demonic invaders of the Tribulation, called Apollyon: "Buck stared out the window, and his heart thundered against his ribs. From out of the smoke came flying creatures—hideous, ugly, brown and black and yellow flying monsters. Swarming like locusts, they looked like miniature horses five or six inches long with tails like those of scorpions. Most horrifying, the creatures were attacking, trying to get in" (*Apollyon*, 305). We also learn that these creatures have a man's face, long flowing hair, and a golden crown (315–317). They attack nonbelievers in a swarm, attaching themselves to the body, stinging and biting their victims. Christian believers are immune. In one scene, a loyal but unconverted household employee is caught outside, attacked, and felled by the creatures. He lies screaming and writhing until Buck, fearful but protected, rushes outside to combat the invaders and rescue him (307). The debt to science fiction tales of alien attack and horror narratives of monstrous invasion is obvious here, right down to the hero who must leave the safe house to rescue his buddy from the creatures. In the Tribulations faced by those left behind, the invaders who torment nonbelievers are satanic forces that are nonetheless in the service of God. The Christian heroes of the novels face them with the mix of awe, fear, and hope that so often has attended accounts of alien abduction: the superior beings, their nightmarish bodily invasions and probings, who leave the vivid impression that this encounter indicates malevolent intent and perhaps future destruction.

The science fiction address of the series is even more apparent in the Web page images designed to accompany each book, which draw on the look and feel of popular action and sci-fi movies: weapons, anxious people fleeing a scene, and images of nightmarish nuclear war–style devastation that are familiar to anyone who has seen *Terminator* or *Mad Max*. The e-card/screensaver for *Apollyon* is a perfect apocalyptic cliché: in the background, a destroyed building, with only the half-standing outline of the structure left, strange orange clouds dominating the sky, fires burning on the street; in the foreground, a large, almost distended image of a man, middle-aged, probably white, his eyes bulging, fearful (see figure 12). The image for *The Mark*, the eighth book in the series, shows a futuristic urban skyline: tall, streamlined buildings against a darkening sky. In the middle of the scene is a harshly lit building guarded by men in suits with machine guns, with lines of people streaming into it. This is the "loyalty mark enforcement center," where people are forced to receive the mark of loyalty to the Antichrist or face execution. The building is easy to recognize: it is any of those station stops in the world after *1984*, where unwilling victims

© 2000, Tyndale House Publishers, Inc.

FIGURE 12. Science fiction–style images highlight the books' links to mainstream popular fiction. Screensaver offered at www.leftbehind.com for *Apollyon*, book 5 in the *Left Behind* series. Copyright 2000, Tyndale House Publishers, Inc. Used with permission.

go to face lobotomy, alien takeover of their mind, or mandatory execution at age thirty.

The science fiction connection makes sense, plot-wise. The dramatic nature of the events is plausible only in the sense that the entire end times scenario is *supposed* to be otherworldly—it is, after all, the story of the Judgment of God and the rise to power of supernatural evil. So when the Antichrist takes over the United Nations and then takes control of the world's military, police forces, and finances, the level of his power and the extent of his malice are credible precisely to the degree that the reader either believes in the general outlines of the fundamentalist interpretation of the prophetic books of the Bible, or to the degree one is willing to suspend disbelief to enjoy the pleasures of a story of conflict between great evil and great good. The science fiction tie also works at the level of form, functioning much like the technology fetish in the stories. The invading demons, narrow escapes, flawed but brave heroes, and the race to get the fancy technology to do your bidding, always just in time—fundamentalism has made popular modernity its calling card; here, *Buffy* meets *Bond* on the way to the church social.

The voice of the *Left Behind* series is distinctly modern in another way: it suggests that although the chosen believers at the end of times may be doctrinally narrow, they are culturally and racially expansive. The rather striking racial liberalism in the books has both a domestic politics and a global reach, and it is linked to the maps that structure the cultural politics of the novels: that is, race politics works both to map fundamentalism onto mainstream U.S. domestic politics and to make mainstream in U.S. foreign policy the evangelical mapping of a Holy Land without Palestine or Palestinians.

Domestically, the history of fundamentalism in the United States has often been one of racial exclusivity and prejudice. In the 1960s, the largely southern base for white fundamentalists and evangelicals helped to establish their firm opposition to racial integration.[37] In the 1980s, the Moral Majority and then the Christian Coalition did little more than pay lip service to issues of race, despite the fact that the doctrines of many black Christians were clearly evangelical, but in the 1990s, with the rise of the Promise Keepers and other new parachurch organizations, evangelicals began to talk more extensively about crossing racial barriers, and did so in ways that brought discussions of racism into the heart of white evangelism. It perhaps shouldn't be surprising, then, that LaHaye and Jenkins put the white characters who form the core of the Tribulation Force through their multicultural paces: at various times, they work closely with at least two African American male characters, one set of Chinese Christians, a Native American woman, two Muslim Arab converts, and uncountable numbers of Israeli Jews. The plot consistently presents racial liberalism as the norm for the characters, and implicitly for the readers as well.

In the fourth book, for example, the first of two important African American characters is introduced into the plot. Dr. Floyd Charles is a young physician who helps save Buck's wife when she is pregnant, injured, and on the run from the forces of the Antichrist. Charles is soon making regular visits to the Tribulation Force's safe house; he eventually ends up living there and falling in love with a woman in the group, Hattie. When he reveals his feelings for Hattie to Rayford Steele, who functions as the Force's leader, Rayford expresses deep concern. This concern, however, is not framed as an issue of race; the fact that Charles is black and Hattie is white goes unmentioned in their discussion. Instead, Rayford is worried that Hattie is simply not a good enough person for Charles, as she is both unconverted and remarkably selfish. Though Charles conveniently dies before he can even declare his love to Hattie, much less act on it, it is nonetheless remarkable that the *Left Behind* series would present an interracial relationship as so utterly noncontroversial (what *is* controversial is falling in love with a nonbeliever). It says volumes about the ways white fundamentalism has changed its self-presentation, both within the community itself and in terms of its public voice on issues of race.

Although LaHaye and Jenkins have obviously made a conscious decision to bring African Americans into close proximity to the core characters, the novels nonetheless register a particular self-consciousness about this fact that at times borders on self-parody. On several occasions, for example, Buck or Rayford make what the authors seem to think are rather cute jokes that play off the parallels between the concept of brothers in Christ and the trope of African American men as brothers. At another point, an older and uglier stereotype appears: when Rayford and Dr. Charles are in trouble, Rayford asks the other African American male character, T. M. Delanty ("T"), to help him by trading cars with Charles. T has never met Charles, but Rayford explains that T can recognize him because of the vehicle he is driving and the fact that he "looks a lot like you." A few pages later, LaHaye and Jenkins have T refer back to this stereotype as useful in carrying out an escape plan. This character is forced, in other words, to testify in favor of the subtle racism of the books.

The global racial and religious politics of the novels are even more complex, and equally problematic. As the Tribulation Force expands its global reach, the white American members encounter believers all over the world. In one novel, an Israeli Jew who has converted to Christianity gets a friendly lesson on avoiding stereotypes from a Native American woman named Hannah Palemoon (*The Mark*, 215); later in the series, the young Chinese man, Chang, moves to the forefront of the action as he battles with his father over his Christian beliefs. Soon, Chang's sister Ming becomes a leading character; her emerging romance with a Korean believer is being followed enthusiastically.

These international characters are among the most popular on the fan sites, and it is here that one gets the strongest sense of a worldview in which multiculturalism, albeit of a rather limited type, is the presumptive norm. One female fan, for example, has written a series of stories on a fan Web site about a young man named Jonathan Palemoon, whom she describes as Hannah Palemoon's younger brother. On the story site, she listed among her character's strengths his "family and his heritage" and his martial arts skills (www.tribforcehq.com/fiction; series: "SpiritWalker's Song"). Early in the series, the African American man T was frequently listed by contributors to the message boards as their favorite; since the most recent books were released, Chang, the young computer hack with parent problems, has been widely embraced.[38]

The internationalism of this vision is precisely of a piece with the stark doctrinal narrowness of the stories: *anyone* can convert, but conversion to (born-again) Christianity is necessary to be recognized by God. This has been the source of concern for a good many Jewish and Israeli commentators, who have pointed out that the fundamentalist love of Israel comes at the price of a belief in the massive conversion of Jews at the end of time: 144,000 Jewish witnesses recognize Jesus as the Messiah and join with the non-Jewish believers to fight the Antichrist. As Gershom Gorenberg has argued, this seeming embrace of Jews and Israel is merely instrumental at best. At worst, it is vicious: Israeli Jews exist to testify, in the end, to the truth of Christianity.[39] On the other hand, the views about conversion are entirely consonant with the larger fundamentalist view of the "narrow road" to heaven. When conservative Christians insist that Jews and Muslims and all others must be converted in order to see God, this is perhaps best understood less as racism or anti-Semitism per se than as simple doctrinal conservatism.

Arabs and Muslims, however, fare much worse, though they are also subject to a version of the deadly love offered to Jews. Since September 11, the news media have reported a rather extraordinary series of anti-Muslim slurs by conservative evangelical leaders, including Franklin Graham's comment that Islam is an "evil and wicked religion" and Jerry Falwell's infamous declaration on *60 Minutes* that "Mohammad was a terrorist."[40] Yet in the *Left Behind* series, Arabs and Muslims are woven into the much more complicated cultural tapestry. Besides Suhail Akbar, the demonic Pakistani who is the Antichrist's head of security (and who joins a virtual Rainbow Coalition of evil, including the Antichrist himself, Romanian Nicholae Carpathia; his "right hand man," the Italian American Leon Fortunato; the leader of the abominable one-world faith, the former U.S. Catholic bishop Peter Matthews; and later, the Chinese security expert Walter Moon), there have been several moments over the course of the series in which Islam or Arabs figured importantly. In the most recent novel, there is a fairly long scene in which a group of Chinese Muslims prove themselves to be holdouts against the Antichrist and are thus about to be executed. The views of

Islam are summarized briefly but respectfully; just before they are about to die, a group of the Muslims convert to Christianity and thus assure their assent to heaven (*Remnant*, 282–297). In the earlier novels, two key Arab characters emerged, both of whom are Muslims who convert after the Rapture. Both are presented as highly positive individuals. One, "Al-B" or Albie, is described as a native of Al Basrah, Iraq, which in later novels is glossed as simply "north of Kuwait." He plays a key role in many of the novels' most daring rescues and escapes. The second is Abdullah Smith; "The name looks weird," his friend Mac explains. "But he has his reasons" (*Apollyon*, 333). He is a Jordanian pilot and is almost always named as a favorite character on the fan sites: one young person has even taken his name as her nom de Web, and he is often featured in fan fiction as well. In fact, Smith is one of the central characters in the entire last half of the series. As one of the pilots who can ferry the Tribulation Force members back and forth between the United States and the Middle East, he is key to the plot. But he is also figured as a good friend to several of the key male characters at the heart of the story, particularly the Tribulation Force leader, the pilot Rayford Steele. Smith is one of the tough men of action who provide the story's emotional center; he is laconic but has a rough and earthy sense of humor that allows him to trade friendly insults with another pilot, a white American named Mac. When Smith first appears, his broken English is presented as the source of amusement for the readers and other characters (*Apollyon*, 353; *Assassins*, 136). Later, as he becomes more central to the Tribulation Force, he and Mac trade the kind of ethnic jokes that are supposed to be the staples of locker room and battlefield bonding: he makes fun of Mac's "Texan" talk and calls him a "cowboy"; Mac responds by calling him a "camel jockey" (*Remnant*, 350–353). Here, as with the African American characters in the earlier novels, LaHaye and Jenkins exhibit a genuine but awkward embrace of diversity and yet a none too subtle racism: Abdullah Smith is warmly welcomed into the fraternity of Christian believers, but he must consistently perform as a (racially) marked man.

The more subtle but perhaps more important signifier in the world of *Left Behind* is the fact that Smith is Jordanian, not Palestinian. In fact, there are *no* Palestinian Arabs in a series where much of the action takes place in Jerusalem and the surrounding areas. There are Arabs, presumably, in the masses who gather to hear the Antichrist when he speaks in Jerusalem, but in those moments, it is Jews and Israel that *matter*: Israeli Jews are key doctrinally, and they are key characters in the novels as they convert, provide leadership to other believers, and, in one of the recent novels, find themselves gathered and protected in the city of Petra as the Antichrist gathers his forces. (On the other hand, and surely this is not incidental, there are no American Jews in *Left Behind*.)

So it is that the mapping of characters' identities is also a mapping of the space of Palestine-Israel precisely because the very notion of "Palestinian" is made invisible, impossible. There are Muslims and there are Arabs in *Left Behind*, but there are no Arab Christians and there are no Palestinians. In the logic of the series, Palestinians cannot convert like Abdullah Smith or Albie, and they cannot resist like the righteous Chinese Muslims, because they are simply outside the representational possibilities of the *Left Behind* world. Dick Armey's suggestion that Palestinians should be removed from the West Bank and Gaza and Pat Robertson's insistence that Israel should never compromise one bit of land are enacted in the novels as wish fulfillment: there is no Palestinian problem on the evangelical map.

Conclusion

In the summer of 2002, *Time* magazine featured the *Left Behind* series on its cover, just in time to usher in the release of *The Remnant*. With several closely related stories, including a flattering portrait of LaHaye, *Time* explained the popularity of the novels as a sign of the times: in a post–September 11 world, the stories provide hope, a certainty about the future, and a promise that the good guys win in the end. There might be *some* problems with the series: *Time* pointed out that there is a sense of unease among some religious scholars about the books' enthusiasm for the violence and devastation afflicted during the end times. As the theologian Harvey Cox suggested, it is impossible to read the series without getting the impression that a certain "lip-licking anticipation of all the blood" is involved.[41]

What mattered most about the *Time* story was not its ideological slant—it carried the requisite combination of reporting balance, slightly snide tone, and empty summations that are *Time*'s standards for most stories—but the fact that it was there at all. *Left Behind* had reached the very heart of mainstream media and had been received both as a doctrinal juggernaut—fundamentalist views on the apocalypse were reported in impressive detail—and as a popular culture sensation. The sense was that fundamentalist culture was not only tapping into the mainstream of American life, but indeed might *be* the mainstream of American life. After all, *Time* reported, its own poll with CNN showed that 59 percent of Americans believe that the events in Revelation are going to come true.[42]

In the summer of 2002, fighting between Palestinians and Israelis escalated; the Oslo process all but over, there were increasing numbers of suicide bombings by Palestinians against Israeli civilians, followed by Israeli ground incursions and then missile attacks on Palestinian refugee camps. The death toll rose, anger and despair were heightened all around, and the U.S. media feverishly recounted each new atrocity. With the U.S. "war on terrorism" stalled, having provided remarkably little in the way of satisfying vengeance or morally righteous certainties, the Israeli-Palestinian conflict took on the tenor of a proxy battle, where anger about Osama bin Laden and fear of terrorism might find expression in support for Israel in its struggle with the Palestinians.

In this context, righteous Israeli Jews, fighting an Antichrist located in New Babylon, might well begin to look like history written in advance. In fact, one *Left Behind* fan suggested as much to a *Time* reporter, when he explained that he was sure the Antichrist is already among us: "He's probably a good-looking man," he said. "I'm sure he's in politics right now and probably in the public eye a little bit." *Left Behind*, he explained, "helped me to look at the news that's going on about Israel and Palestine" and to understand that it "is just ushering in the End Times, and it's exciting for me."[43] In the context of prophecy interpretation, that excitement makes sense: Israel is fulfilling its biblical destiny in its conflict with the Palestinians, who may or may not have connections with the Antichrist, who may or may not be Saddam Hussein or Osama bin Laden. But for those of us hoping to find the hard path to secular justice and worldly peace, that excitement is nothing less than deadly.

Notes

I would like to thank the following colleagues for their help in formulating this essay and for reading and commenting on it: Mohammed Bamyeh, Carl Conetta, Jane Gerhard, Ruth Feldstein, Michael Kazin, Shelly MacKenzie, Kirsten Swinth, and Priscilla Wald.

1. Tim LaHaye and Jerry Jenkins, *Desecration* (Wheaton, Ill.: Tyndale House, 2001); Daisy Maryles, "Few Surprises in the Winners' Circle," *Publishers Weekly*, March 18, 2002, 53. Nancy Gibbs, "The Bible and the Apocalypse: The Biggest Book of the Summer Is about the End of the World," *Time.com*, June 23, 2002. The first book in the series is Tim LaHaye and Jerry Jenkins, *Left Behind: A Novel of the Earth's Last Days* (Wheaton, Ill: Tyndale House, 1995). The following books and their release dates

are, in order: #2: *Tribulation Force*, 1996; #3: *Nicolae*, 1997; 4: *Soul Harvest*, 1998; #5: *Apollyon*, 1998; *Assassins*, 1999; *The Indwelling*, 2000; *The Mark*, 2000; *Desecration*, 2001; *The Remnant*, 2002; *Armaggedon*, 2003. References to specific books are cited in the text in parenthesis. The final book will be followed by a prequel and a sequel; the series is scheduled to end in 2006. See John Cloud, "Meet the Prophet: How an Evangelical and Conservative Activist Turned Prophecy into a Fiction Juggernaut," *Time.com*, July 23, 2002.

2. Kevin Sack, "Apocalyptic Theology Revitalized by Attacks," *New York Times*, November 23, 2001.

3. The *Left Behind* series does not refer to the end times converts as Christians, but as the Tribulation Force or Believers, or, later, as followers of Tsion Ben-Judah (Judahites). This is because, according to the biblical interpretations put forward by LaHaye, the post-Rapture converts are not referred to in the scriptures as Christians (those are already Raptured), but as Tribulation Saints. See Tim LaHaye and Jerry Jenkins, *Are We Living in the End Times?* (Wheaton, Ill: Tyndale House, 1999), especially 95–120.

4. *American Morning*, CNN, November 8, 2002; *Fresh Air*, NPR, October 28, 2002; *Up Close*, ABC, July 30, 2002; CBS *Saturday Early Show*, July 13, 2002. *Time*'s cover story, "The Bible and the Apocalypse" by Nancy Gibbs ran on June 23, 2002, with several accompanying stories and an interview with LaHaye.

5. The Pew Forum on Religion and Public Life published a September 2004 report that put the number of evangelical at 26 percent of Americans. John Green, "The American Religious Landscape and Politics, 2004" Available at: http://pewforum.org/publications/surveys/green.pdf. Historian of religion Grant Wacker estimates that about 50 million are interested in biblical prophecy; Caryle Murphy, "At Millennium, Finding Salvation: Popular Series by Evangelical Christian Authors Retells Book of Revelation," *Washington Post*, November 28, 1999, C1.

6. Evangelism has many definitions, but perhaps the best is the simplest: those Christians who believe that evangelizing others is a central requirement of their faith and who argue for more direct or literal interpretations of the Bible. The term "fundamentalist," though less frequently used today than in the 1980s, is useful in demarking evangelism's most conservative wing. See Randall Balmer and Laura Winner, *Protestantism in America* (New York: Columbia University Press, 2002); see also R. Marie Griffith's discussion of the definitions in *God's Daughters: Evangelical Women and the Power of Submission* (Berkeley: University of California Press, 1997).

7. Martha MacNeil Hamilton, "Retailing's New Testament Faith; Sales of Items Tied to Spirituality Are Booming, and Not Just through Traditional Religious Venues," *Washington Post*, October 15, 2001, H01.

8. Larry Eskridge of the Institute for the Study of American Evangelicals, quoted in Ann Rodgers-Melnick, "Evangelical Fiction Cracks the Bestseller List," *Pittsburgh Post-Gazette*, May 6, 2001, A1.

9. Dermott McEnvoy and Daisy Maryles, "The Right Name Makes the Game: Trade Paper Sales Continue to Climb, Fiction Rules in Mass Market," *Publishers Weekly*, March 19, 2001, 37.

10. The movies are *Left Behind* (2000, directed by V. Sarin) and *Left Behind II: Tribu-*

lation Force (2002, directed by B. Corcoran), both produced by Cloud Ten pictures, a small evangelical production company. LaHaye and Jenkins are said to be very unhappy with the low-budget, straight-to-video approach of the films, and are currently in litigation to regain rights to the films.

11. "Stand for Israel" (www.standforisrael.com) is a project of the International Fellowship of Christians and Jews, which is led jointly by Rabbi Yechial Eckstein and Ralph Reed, formerly of the Christian Coalition. Eckstein also heads the Jerusalem Friendship Fund, which recently funneled more than $15 million in evangelical contributions to support Jewish immigration to Israel. Yair Sheleg, "Christian Generosity Becomes Rabbinical Nightmare," *Ha'aretz*, October 16, 2002, translated and reposted at: http://www.bintjbeil.com/articles/en/021016_sheleg.html.

12. This is LaHaye's paraphrase in one of many similar interviews. Sandi Dolbbe, "Second-Coming Attraction: Best-selling, Apocalypse Author Is Drawn to the End Times," *San Diego Union-Tribune*, November 15, 2002, E-1. The biblical verse is Genesis 12:1–3. See also CNN *American Morning* with Paula Zahn, November 8, 2002, transcript no. 110814CN.V74.

13. For an informative discussion of apocalyptic religious views of all kinds as organized on the Internet, see Brenda Basher, *Give Me That Online Religion* (San Franciso: Jossey-Bass, 2001).

14. For a good discussion of the basics of this theology, see Paul Boyer, *When Time Shall Be No More: Prophecy Belief in Modern American Culture* (Cambridge, Mass.: Harvard University Press, 1992).

15. James Hunter, "The Evangelical Worldview since 1890," *Piety and Politics: Evangelicals and Fundamentalists Confront the World*, edited by Richard Neuhaus and Michael Cromartie (Washington, D.C.: Ethics and Public Policy Center, 1987), 19–53; Nancy Ammerman, "North American Protestant Fundamentalism," in *Media, Culture, and the Religious Right*, edited by Linda Kintz and Julie Lesage (Minneapolis: University of Minnesota Press, 1998), 55–114.

16. Hal Lindsey with C. C. Carlson, *The Late, Great Planet Earth* (Grand Rapids, Mich: Zondervan, 1970). I discuss Lindsey in some detail in *Epic Encounters: Culture, Media, and U.S. Interests in the Middle East, 1945–2000* (Berkeley: University of California Press, 2001), 165–178.

17. Presbyterian Gary DeMar has written a debunking treatise, *End Time Fiction: A Biblical Consideration of the Left Behind Theology* (Nashville, Tenn.: Thomas Nelson, 2001). There are also many Web sites devoted to various arguments with the theology, though these are often from the perspective of those who disagree over the timing of the Rapture.

18. Karen Long, "*Left Behind* and the Rupture over the Rapture," *Washington Post*, May 5, 2001, B09. In December 2000, the Office of the President of the Lutheran Church, Missouri Synod, released a statement, "The Left Behind View Is Out of Left Field," at www.cms.org/predient/statements/leftbehind.asp.

19. See, for example, *A Thief in the Night* (1972, directed by D. Thompson), which was a sensation in churches throughout the 1970s, and the *Apocalypse* series (*Caught in the Eye of the Storm* [video, Cloud Ten Pictures, 1998], *Apocalypse II—Revelation*

[video, Cloud Ten Pictures, 1999], *Apocalypse III—Tribulation* [video, Cloud Ten Pictures, 2000], *Apocalypse IV—Judgment* [video, United American, 2001], all directed by André van Heerden).

20. Randal Balmer and Lauren Winner, *Protestantism in America* (New York: Columbia University Press, 2002), quoted in David Van Biema, "The End: How It Got That Way," *Time.com*, June 23, 2002, available at: www.time.com/time/covers/1101020701/theology.html.

21. Jerry Strober and Ruth Tomczak, *Jerry Falwell: Aflame for God* (Nashville, Tenn.: Thomas Nelson, 1979), 167.

22. David Snowball, *Continuity and Change in the Rhetoric of the Moral Majority* (New York: Praeger, 1991), 16. See also my discussion in *Epic Encounters*, 193–197.

23. Rodgers-Melnick, "Evangelical Fiction Cracks the Best-Seller List."

24. For more information on this organization, see the "Right Wing Watch" section of the People for the American Way Web site, www.pfaw.org.

25. David Mehegan, "Appeal Spreads for Series that Spreads the Word," *Boston Globe*, February 27, 2002, G1.

26. Michelle Goldberg, "Fundamentally Unsound," *Salon.com*, July 29, 2002.

27. For a discussion of Armey's statements from a moderate conservative who nonetheless fears the influence of the Christian right on pro-Israel policy, see Peter Beinart, "Bad Move," *New Republic*, May 20, 2002, 6. Inhofe's statement is quoted by Gershom Gorenberg, "Unorthodox Alliance: Israeli and Jewish Interests Are Better Served by Keeping a Polite Distance from the Christian Right," *Washington Post*, October 11, 2002, A37. In May 2002, the House passed 352–21, a resolution supporting Israel "as she wages war against terrorists who would mercilessly kill her citizens." Bruce Alpert, "Support for Israel Bridges Old Divides," *Times-Picayune* (New Orleans), May 3, 2002, 4.

28. Jason Keyser, "Hundreds of Americans Move to Israel: Mass Immigration Is Paid For in Part by Evangelical Christian Groups," *Seattle Post-Intelligencer*, July 20, 2002, A1; Ken Ellingwood, "A Christian Day of Prayer for Israel," *Los Angeles Times*, October 21, 2002. Other groups that support Jewish immigration to Israel (e.g., the "ingathering" of Jews they believe to be predicted in the Bible) are Christians for Israel, which operates a project called "Exobus," and John Hagee Ministries of Texas. See also Tatsha Robertson, "Evangelicals Flock to Israel's Banner: Christian Zionists See Jewish State Bringing Messiah," *Boston Globe*, October 21, 2002, A3; Avram Goldstein, "Christian Coalition Rallies for Israel in Comeback Bid," *Washington Post*, October 12, 2002, B1.

29. I discuss these connections from the 1970s and 1980s in detail in chapter 4 of *Epic Encounters*. See also Don Wagner, "For Zion's Sake," *Middle East Report* (summer 2002): 52–58. Currently, there are dozens of groups linking conservative Christians and conservative Jews, both American and Israeli, including the International Fellowship of Christians and Jews headed by former Christian Coalition leader Ralph Reed and Rabbi Yechiel Ekstein. The IFCJ claims to have raised more than $60 million for Israel (Wagner, "For Zion's Sake"). In April 2002, the *New York Times* touted the alliance between former Republican presidential candidate Gary Bauer and William Kristol, editor of the *Weekly Standard*. Alison Mitchell, "Mideast Turmoil: The Conser-

vatives, Israel Winning Broad Support from the U.S. Right," *New York Times*, April 21, 2002, 1. Bauer is also cochair, with Rabbi Daniel Lapin, of the American Alliance of Jews and Christians. Other Christian Zionist organizations include Friends of Israel, based in New Jersey; Bridges for Peace, which has contributed more than $20 million to programs in Israel in the past five years; and the International Christian Chamber of Commerce, which actively promotes Israeli businesses.

30. On the meetings at the Israeli embassy, see T. Roberston, "Evangelicals Flock to Israel's Banner." Mark O'Keefe, "Israel's Evangelical Approach: U.S. Christian Zionists Nurtured as Political, Tourism Force," *Washington Post*, January 26, 2002, B11, discusses both the meetings and the push for tourism. Sharon's talk is mentioned by T. Roberston and also on ABC, "God and Country," *Nightline*, November 26, 2002.

31. Katty Kay and Roland Watson, "Influential U.S. Jews Like What They Hear," *Times* (London), June 26, 2002, n.p.

32. Marshall Whitmann of the Hudson Institute, and former lobbyist for the Christian Coalition, quoted by Abraham McLaughlin and Gail Russell Chaddock, "Christian Right Steps in on Mideast," *Christian Science Monitor*, April 16, 2001, 1. In April 2002, Bush called Ariel Sharon a "man of peace"; several observers have seen Bush's pro-Israeli policies, which differ significantly from his father's, as motivated by a combination of political pressure and true belief. Gay Alcorn, "Bush Follows His Conservative Heart Back to Israel," *The Age* (Melbourne), April 20, 2002, 5. Gary Bauer also makes claims for the right's success in pressuring Bush, and Pat Buchanan, who is very critical of the conservative tilt toward Israel, concurs (Alpert, "Support for Israel Bridges Old Divides").

33. David Klinghoffer, "Just Be Gracious," *Jerusalem Post*, August 16, 2002, 7B.

34. Andrew Gumbel, "The Profits of Doom," *The Independent*, November 12, 2000, 7, 9–10.

35. On how the series has affected Tyndale, the series' publisher, see Corrie Cutrer, "Left Behind Has Been Very, Very Good to Tyndale," *Christianity Today.com*, October 17, 2000, www.christianitytoday.com/ct/2000/013/20.26.html.

36. Mehegan, "Appeal Spreads for Series That Spreads the Word," G1. In terms of the self-representation of Internet posters, I am aware of the arguments about the performativity of age and gender on the Internet, but other research suggests that the vast majority of people present themselves realistically, at least on these basics, and there is reason to suspect that most people who join a fundamentalist community are inclined to self-represent accurately. In fact, there is some evidence to support this, as there are clearly demarcated ways participants *do* perform across gender, ethnicity, and age via the handles they take when they sign onto the message boards. For example, the handle Abdullah (in the series, a converted Jordanian pilot in his early thirties) belongs to a person who, in her profile, describes herself as a teenage girl. In these situations, performance is allowed and even encouraged via character identification, which thus clears the "profiles" as a space for authenticity. See David Gauntlett, "Web Studies: A User's Guide," in *Web Studies: Rewiring Media Studies for the Digital Age*, edited by D. Gauntlett (New York: Oxford University Press, 2000); Kevin Robbins, "Cyberspace and the World We Live In," in *The Cybercultures Reader*, edited by David Bell and Barbara Kennedy (New York: Routledge, 2000).

37. Among the many histories of fundamentalism that trace this legacy, see William Martin, *With God on Our Side: The Rise of the Religious Right in America* (New York: Broadway Books, 1996). David Chappell's *A Stone of Hope* (Chapel Hill: University of North Carolina Press, 2004) argues that evangelical churches in the South were not in fact particularly active in opposing integration, and that their quiescence was important to the defeat of segregationists.

38. One of the most recent threads of fan fiction on the leftbehind.com Web site features Chang as the protagonist, and in an earlier, 2001 thread (now unavailable; message boards are not archived at leftbehind.com), Chang was often mentioned as a favorite character. When I posted a query about Chang on the message boards on August 12, 2002, I received several replies, most of which said Chang was one of their favorite characters (often running behind Buck, or, interestingly, David Hassid, the converted East European Jew who succeeded Chang as the new mole inside New Babylon). Remembering that there are literally dozens of characters in the series and that each book introduces at least three or four new characters, it is no small thing for a character to be a greater favorite than the central four characters of the Tribulation Force.

39. Gershom Gorenberg, *The End of Days: Fundamentalism and the Struggle for the Temple Mount* (New York: Free Press, 2000).

40. Franklin Graham made his comments in an interview with NBC Nightly News, as reported by Gustav Niebuhr, "Muslim Groups Seeks to Meet Billy Graham's Son," *New York Times*, November 20, 2001, 5. Falwell made his infamous comment in an interview on *60 Minutes*: Bob Simon reporting, "Zion's Christian Soldiers," *60 Minutes*, October 6, 2002.

41. Cloud, "Meet the Prophet." *Time* also mentioned controversy over the fact that LaHaye and Jenkins are reported to have both made about $50 million, with more to come. Both authors have been asked repeatedly in interviews about their newfound wealth, and both insist that the money brings with it an enormous responsibility of "stewardship" and to giving a good deal of it away. There have been few suggestions that either of them has embarked on an extravagant lifestyle.

42. Gibbs, "The Bible and the Apocalypse," 2.

43. Kelly Sellers, interviewed and quoted in ibid.

MARY N. LAYOUN

Telling Stories in
Palestine: Comix
Understanding
and Narratives of
Palestine-Israel

Although every image embodies a way of seeing, our perception or appreciation of an image depends also upon our own way of seeing. —JOHN BERGER, *Ways of Seeing*

The visual is *essentially* pornographic. —FREDRIC JAMESON, *Signatures of the Visible*

Make no mistake, everywhere you go, not just in Marvel comics, there's parallel universes. —JOE SACCO, *Palestine*

What are comics, or, in a clever contemporary turn on the category, comix?[1] Why should we pay attention to them? And, especially given the current dire political context of Palestine-Israel, what does a comic book have to tell us about stories of Palestine-Israel that is not superfluous or even frivolous? In the dreadful context of daily life for Palestinians and, increasingly, though less starkly and pervasively, for Israelis, the political and human situation is so urgent, the need for wise local and international intervention so pressing, that the form of comics may seem a slim reed on which to rest any part of the burden of understanding Palestine. Nor, in the United States, is popular capacity (or desire) to critically understand the situation in Palestine-Israel particularly capacious. And comics, particularly in the United States, are scarcely a widely acknowledged genre, especially for renditions of historical, political, or social complexity.[2]

Joe Sacco's *Palestine* is a succinct and stunning account of daily Palestinian (and, by extension, at least some aspects of Israeli) life in the Occupied Territories during the early 1990s.[3] *Palestine* is also about a "transnational circuit" of media images and headlines that travels well beyond Israel or Palestine. But *Palestine*—in its specific content as well as in its specific form and generic structure—performs within the text and implicitly solicits outside of it an alternative recognition of the ways we learn to make differential sense of (parts of) a bigger picture. Sacco's *Palestine* alludes to the bigger picture of Palestine-Israel and its transnational circuits by illuminating a series of small and individualized stories, facts, and reports, numerous accounts of daily Palestinian life witnessed by the narrator and by Palestinians and, occasionally, by Israelis with whom the narrator speaks. This is not to suggest that *Palestine* proposes or enacts some simple accretion of multiple individual stories or facts and statistics, a kind of marketplace proliferation of detail. Instead, *Palestine* proposes and enacts an always partial and differential effort to read the relations between those details. Sacco's comic questions the relationship between the audience and the story, in part through the changing roles and perceptions of its narrator. Finally, *Palestine* implicitly indicts the "visual as pornographic," a way of seeing that would allow audience and narrator to willfully ignore their relationship to the Palestine (and Israel) that the comic depicts. This effort is its most powerful contribution to popular understandings of Palestine-Israel.

Comics-as-a-Genre and Joe Sacco's Palestine

Only recently have comics been more widely accepted in the United States. Still a popular cultural form, comics remain linked to, but not narrowly defined by, the superhero and action comics or *Classics Illustrated* that were the inception of the genre in the United States. Internationally, the status of comics as both an art form and a popular cultural genre is far less equivocal. The pervasive popularity of comics in Japan dates back several centuries to the Edo period's illustrated "chapbooks." In Europe and in Latin America, comics are more readily considered a popular genre of noteworthy attention. Though such acknowledgment came rather more belatedly in the United States, in recent years comics have been increasingly recognized as a genre capable of subtlety and complexity and of addressing diverse topics. In 1992, the Pulitzer Prize was awarded to Art Spiegelman's *Maus*. The American Book Award was given to Joe Sacco's *Palestine* in 1996, and the Will Eisner Award for the Best Original Graphic Novel to Sacco's *Safe Area Gorazde* in 2001. Sacco also won a Guggenheim Fellowship in 2001 and the vpro Grand Prix of Haarlem in 2002.⁴ Additionally, the notable success of (nonanimated) films based on comic books of the past two decades, including *X-Men, From Hell, Ghost World,* and *Spiderman,* suggests a further shift in the popular appreciation of comics in the United States.⁵ Comics, then, are no longer (and, in fact, haven't been for decades, in their alternative form) simply "kid stuff."

The expanding possibilities of the genre of comics is apparent in the earliest work of Joe Sacco, collected in *War Junkie*: the (occasionally self-indulgent) story of an American punk band's tour of Europe ("In the Company of Long Hair"), a chronicle of a stay in his native Malta ("A Disgusting Experience"), and three stories of modern war and its casualties ("When Good Bombs Happen to Bad People," "More Women, More Children, More Quickly," and "How I Loved the War").⁶ In *War Junkie*, the characteristic style of Sacco's work is already present in the comic's ironic narrative perspective and the painfully astute questions embedded in that ironic posture, in its attention to visual and historical contradiction, in a trenchant awareness of the perspectives and situations of those behind or left altogether out of the news headlines,⁷ and in the intensely detailed cross-hatched style of Sacco's artwork.

But it is in Sacco's nine-book series *Palestine* that the potential of comics-as-a-genre is most stunningly realized. The sequential narrative of deliberately juxtaposed words, images, and panels that characterizes comics-as-a-genre allows *Palestine*, in its own particular configuration of narrative, image, and word, to productively exploit that form in a rendering of the complex historical, political, social, and personal realities of Palestine-Israel. Moreover, Sacco's unique engagement with the comics genre offers a particularly efficacious way to understand the meaning-making process that occurs in coming to understand historical or political or personal complexity and relationship. *Palestine* draws that complexity and a witness's relationship to it in the comic's structural foregrounding of partial, particularized visual frames to suggest a larger (unvisualized and unvisualizable) narrative. In this aberrantly synecdochic process of reading and understanding, partial and particularized images are structurally suggested (by the comic) and perceived (by a reader) as standing for a larger but absent picture.⁸ If we understand synecdoche as substituting, or more precisely, *assuming*, the part for the whole, the structural organization of comics presents the sequential but always partial and particular panels of comics for synecdochic understanding. This apparently simple proposition, true of the simplest comics, is far less simple in the context of a process of historical and political understanding. In what might be seen as a latter-day turn on the venerable literary and philosophical question of *mimesis* (the figural relation of visual or narrative representations to reality or truth or the real), comics in general, and *Palestine* in particular, tell the story of precisely that relation of (partial) comics representation to a reality that can be suggested or implied but never completely represented or observed.

In this compelling and even confrontational assemblage of detail and stories in comics format, which also continually calls attention in its very structural organization to the ways details and stories are framed, Sacco's "comics journalism" demonstrates an ability to "transcend comic book culture" that comics scholar Matthew Pustz asserts as a necessity for comics.[9] In a unique tribute to Sacco's ability to approach Pustz's goal, the reprinted single-volume edition of *Palestine* bears a poignant introduction by Edward Said, the renowned Palestinian American scholar and public intellectual; political columnist Christopher Hitchens contributed the introduction to Sacco's subsequent comic, *Safe Area Gorazde*.[10] In the challenge to media images and words as we know them, with an insistence—most often ironic or clever, sometimes grimly humorous, but always insightfully serious— on attending to the visual and verbal details of local stories, Sacco's comics trace the outlines of those local stories' implication in and framing by both their viewing audiences and the larger (transnational) landscape on which local stories and transnational audiences dwell.

One would therefore ignore a crucial point if one were to focus only on the historical and factual content of Palestine "the comic" or on Palestine "the place and peoples and histories," the former contextualized in Joe Sacco's scrupulous authorial explanations and the latter contextualized in the references of Palestine's narrator to reports, testimonials, and quantifiable data.[11] The narrator begins his journey in search of

> The real-life adaptation of all those affidavits I've been reading. (1:10)

> Gunshot injuries! Broken bones! Amputees! The intifada I know from appendices in small press books! With names, places, and dates of incident! The intifada you can count! (2:4)

> The Occupation is crawling with do-gooders, human rights monitors, nuns and Quakers, international jurists with clipboards, all of 'em willing to pile us high with documents and studies. (3:7)

But there is never a moment in which all the stories or all the facts or all the details are possessed and controlled by a narrator (or, implicitly, by a reader). In the course of the comics series, the quantifiable data that *Palestine*'s narrator initially claims control over and in which he relishes — "The intifada you can count!"—is supplanted (though *not* renounced) by multiple stories of individual people, of generations of Palestinians living under occupation. It is these small stories of individual experiences told to or observed by the narrator and, as significant, his effort to account for the relations between those stories and the bigger picture of Palestine-Israel that is a crucial aim of *Palestine*. It is this exemplary effort to figure *structural relations* rather than just the (painful, moving) individual stories of the comic that makes *Palestine* such an accomplished narrative of Palestine.

Structures of Seeing

One of the most powerful of the structural relations traced in *Palestine* is its turn on the comics' convention of parallel universes. That convention is, as the phrase literally suggests, the graphic side-by-side representation of apparently discrete but simultaneous universes. Those universes may or may not be recognized as such by characters in the comic. But, in their manifest juxtaposition on the comics page, they must necessarily be recognized by the implied comics audience. Comics make graphically visible the proposition that "other universes are parallel to ours and may be quite close to ours, but of which we'd never be aware. They may be completely different with completely different laws of nature operating."[12] If comics are the deliberate sequential juxtaposition of panels of words and images that tell a story, the convention of parallel universes in comics is a visual culmination of the genre's possibilities. Superhero comics offer familiar examples of parallel universes, such as those in *Superman*, occupied by Clark Kent/Superman, or in which something is happening on Earth in one panel while something else is happening simultaneously on another planet in the next panel. While virtually no one *in* the *Superman* comic other than Superman/Clark Kent (and his archenemy) knows about the existence of those parallel universes, they are explicitly arrayed in the visual layout of the comic for the necessary recognition of the implied reader.

It is in the transformation of this near-cliché of the genre that Sacco's *Palestine* is most visually provocative. In the visual juxtaposition of parallel universes, *Palestine* ironically explores what Fredric Jameson has perhaps scandalously suggested in the opening lines of his *Signatures of the Visible* as characteristic of the visual itself: that it is *"essentially* pornographic." "Which is to say," Jameson continues, "that it has its end in rapt, mindless fascination; thinking about its attributes becomes an adjunct to that, if it is unwilling to betray its object."[13] The visual juxtaposition of parallel universes in *Palestine* makes most clear that the object of its narrative gaze is not merely the often ignored parallel universes that exist for Palestinians in Palestine. But the object of *Palestine*'s narrative gaze is equally, perhaps more scathingly, the narrator himself and, implicitly, the audience looking over the shoulder of that narrator.

In fact, one way of understanding Joe Sacco's comic book series is to see it as primarily about the visual as pornographic. *Palestine*'s indictment of the pornographic visual—of the world (of Palestine-Israel, of the Arab world) rendered as a series of collectable images, like a naked body for visual possession and mastery by the viewer—is figured precisely in its juxtaposed frames. This juxtaposition is writ both small and large in the series. It is, for example, *visible* in the distant comparison of the tumultuous opening splash page of the first comic and the almost banal and anticlimactic closing page of the ninth. Metaphorically, the narrator's entry into the Arab world (and by extension, into Palestine) is marked precisely by the words and images that dominate a familiar transnational circuit: a stereotypically overwhelming and chaotic crush of Cairene cars, dirt, noise, passion, and angry politics. But *Palestine*'s critical indictment occurs in the construction of a trajectory between that point of entry and the subdued and anticlimactic confusion that marks the narrator's point of departure from Palestine. That point of departure is the conclusion of *Palestine* as an Israeli bus driver loses his way in Gaza on the way to the Egyptian border. Between the turbulent assault of Cairo and the subdued and bewildered displacement in Gaza, between entry to and departure from Palestine, the narrative frame of *Palestine* traces a change in its narrator's way of seeing that is never quite articulated in words. The object of Sacco's work is not simply transparent reportage of the facts on the ground in Palestine but, equally, the way that situation is perceived and understood. And that way of seeing operates simultaneously on the level of the narrator's gaze and on that of the comic series as a whole.

If, as the narrator comes to realize, there's no single image or story of Palestine and its people that captures the complex whole,[14] the comics series itself reiterates this insight in its very structure. In the radically synecdochic proposition of comics' structure, the broader picture may be "perceived" in *Palestine*, but it is never "observed." The part must necessarily stand for an unrepresented (and unrepresentable) whole. And, if there's no single photo or story that gets the picture, the mimetic value of any narrative—visual or verbal, artistic or literary or historical—depends not simply on the facts it marshals but on the narrative frame in which it situates, organizes, and re-presents those facts.[15]

Frames in and for Palestine

It is this visual and verbal narrative frame in which stories of Palestine are embedded that gives the stories themselves, as the entirety of Sacco's *Palestine* series, its most compelling power. The history of Palestine, the poignant testimonials of Palestinians living under grievous conditions of occupation or exile or imprisonment, the betrayals by international and national leaders, the miscalculations and mistakes are stories that have been told before. The most powerful contribution of the comic is not exactly the novelty of *Palestine*'s stories, but the manner in which those stories are organized and recounted in the comic's narrative frame. It also lies in the personalization of that frame and of those stories in the trajectory by which the initially presumptuous and self-serving narrator becomes the somber, chastened, and thoughtful commentator in conclusion. That trajectory implicitly offers a model of understanding for an implied reader who might seek to understand the relations among complex parts. The series of comic books that make up *Palestine* are a suggestive and even daring illustration of a mode of seeing, of reading and understanding Palestine. In its enactment of the acquisition and exercise of a "relational literacy" operating precisely in relation to popular notions of Palestine, Sacco's comics series is at least implicitly an address, perhaps even an injunction, to transnational circuits of seeing, reading, and (mis)understanding. And the comic itself shrewdly comments on the workings of the transnational production and consumption of Palestine-Israel in popular cultural understanding.

Palestine's trenchant illustration of and commentary on the transnational production and consumption of visual meaning are immediately if implicitly apparent in the nine front covers of the original comic book series. Taken collectively, those front covers in relation to the inside cover of each comic constitute the first in a series of crucial parallel universes to which *Palestine*/Palestine calls attention. The only color images in *Palestine*, those front covers mime international news photo images of violence, anguished or brutal faces, demonstrations, bloody and tortured bodies, children throwing stones, funerals, and grave sites (see figure 13). Given the particular and intense graphic style that marks all of Sacco's artwork, the difference of the visual frame and content of *Palestine*'s front covers parallel familiar enough public images of Palestine and of the Palestinian-Israeli conflict. But these exterior, public images are in striking contrast to, and are radically recontextualized by, the sequence of inside covers, in which a parallel universe of individualized perception is juxtaposed to that of public media images.

Each of the nine inside covers are full-page black-and-white images of the narrator inked in black against the gray of his changing surroundings. Their sequence chronicles the increasing implication of the narrator in and with those changing surroundings, progressing from the first comic in the series, with an opening back shot of a solitary observer high on the rampart walls of the Old City of Jerusalem, overlooking the scene below, to the inside cover of the ninth and final comic book, with its virtually parallel perspective high on Jerusalem's rampart walls (see figure 14). In an example of the pointed visual subtlety that marks *Palestine* throughout, that initial image of the narrator recurs later in the first comic book (1:18) as a segment of a larger picture, revealing the narrator on the rampart walls not alone, as in the cover image, but flanked by two Israeli soldiers and an American Jewish family visiting Israel. They're looking down at a demonstration in the Arab village of Silwan (in the occupied West Bank) against the illegal seizure of Palestinian homes by Jewish settlers. Not simply a casual observer on his own, as he might at first have seemed, the narrator's perspective is literally one shared by American tourists and Israeli soldiers. The implications of the transnational circuit that funds and supports the Israeli occupation are visually striking, if not explicitly commented on verbally. In the final inside cover the apparently solitary narrator of the first comic is joined by two Israeli women. All three look down from the same gate on the rampart walls of Jerusalem at the same Palestinian village, eight weeks (and eight comic books) earlier. The Israeli flags planted by the Jewish settlers who forcibly evicted the Palestinian residents and occupied their homes are still flying. "And nothing's changed," notes the narrator when that full-page image, too, is reproduced and recontextualized later in the same comic book (9:2).

What *has* changed, though, between the inside covers of the first and the ninth comic, is the narrative perspective that frames *Palestine*'s stories and, implicitly but no less importantly, that models a way of seeing for its audiences. What has changed is the narrator's (and the narrative's) frame for seeing and understanding Palestine. If "every image embodies a way of seeing," our perception "depends *also* on our own way of seeing."[16] *Palestine* is an evocative illustration of other ways to see and narrate the stories

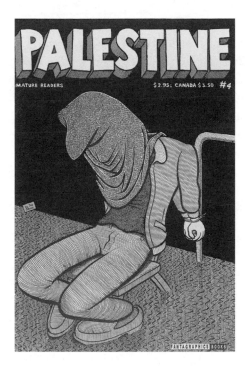

FIGURE 13. Joe Sacco,
Palestine #4. © 1996 Joe Sacco.
Used with permission.

FIGURE 14. Joe Sacco,
Palestine #1. © 1996 Joe Sacco.
Used with permission.

of lives that are not our own but that are, as the comic insists, nonetheless complexly intertwined with our stories and lives. It is precisely this way of seeing and hearing and of subsequent retelling the story, this kind of relational reading ability, that has been so sorely missing in the transnational circuit from Palestine-Israel to the United States and back again. It is this ability that is missing from the media shots of violence, grief, and death on the outside covers. Juxtaposed to one another, however, the inside and outside covers call for a crucial relational reading of life in Palestine-Israel and of an English-speaking audience's relation to that life, especially in the United States.

From the Visual as Titillation to the Visual as Testimonial

The lure of the pornographic visual is depicted with grim humor in the initially prurient gaze of *Palestine*'s narrator, from the media shots of the front covers to the narrator's coy dissembling in individual stories in the first comic in the series. "Blind Dates," the story of the narrator's arrival in Palestine and his putative fluency in the local idiom, immediately follows on the opening episode in Cairo. "I'm good at this, watch his reaction," the narrator boasts, in reference to a Palestinian shopkeeper he encounters on the street of the Old City of Nablus. "We both know I don't belong, now watch this . . . I've got him . . . I'm gracious . . . a perfect guest of Palestine . . . a real charmer . . . a real innocent."[17] The narrator's presumptuous fluency is reiterated in the second comic, in his brash insistence on depicting a badly wounded young Palestinian man in the hospital who asks not to be photographed, while claiming to abide by the man's wish (2:6). In "A Thousand Words,"[18] the opening section of the third comic, the narrator presses the Japanese photojournalist Saburo for photographs of a baby with congenital birth defects, reportedly due to prenatal tear gas exposure. Saburo photographs the child only at the repeated insistence of the Palestinians who have taken him to see the baby. But he doesn't offer those photographs to the narrator. And the narrator's comment on Saburo's anguished reluctance? "I'm a sceptic. Journalistically speaking, you gotta be a Doubting Thomas; you gotta make sure. It's good to get your finger in the wound. Your whole head would be better . . . Man, I wish I'd seen the soldiers firing tear gas . . . I wish I'd seen that baby" (3:25). *Palestine*'s narrator is at least initially always looking for that image (or story) that will titillate the eye of a media audience, that will elicit the "rapt, mindless fascination" that popular media photographs occasion. He accepts with scarcely a moment's hesitation the photos of young Palestinian men killed by Jewish settlers (3:19). Saburo doesn't want the photos; they're "too heavy." But for the narrator, what's too heavy today might not be tomorrow, "Cause faces are what it's all about, man" (3:19). "My comics blockbuster depends on conflict; peace won't pay the rent" (3:24); "A comic needs some bangbang" (5:2). But the narrator's preoccupation with pictures (and stories) of violence and injury and conflict, his titillation by those stories and images, begins to turn on itself by the middle of the series.

That shift is figured in outline in the visual sequence of the comics' nine inside covers. If the narrator's salacious search for visual titillation dominates the early books in the series and is continually referenced in the comics' front covers, the nine inside covers tell a frame narrative not of titillating violence but of a witness's implication in far more complex and nuanced stories than the cover images or the narrator's initial bravado can ever indicate. The sequence of those inside covers visually traces the narrator's literal *transfiguration* from the first inside cover image of apparent uninvolvement as the narrator surveys the scene from high above the action (1);[19] to the slightly bewildered narrator on the ground in Jerusalem, holding a travel guide to Israel (2); to a relatively expressionless narrator walking through an Arab marketplace (3); to the narrator's furrowed brow and down-turned mouth as, walking down a residential street, Palestinian residents call out to him in greeting (4); to a close-up of the narrator's tense, sweating face and even more furrowed brow (5); to the gendered, social context of the narrator, with his back partially turned to the viewer/reader, sitting in conversation over coffee and tea with Palestinian men (6); to the virtual invisibility of the narrator behind the foregrounded image of a glowing television set outlined in black, around which a group of men are gathered (7);[20] to the narrator's reappearance, again outlined in black ink against the details of a gray background scene, beside (and in fact, almost identical in posture, dress, and facial expression to) Sameh, his Palestinian translator and guide (8); to the narrator's return to his point of entry to Palestine, on the rampart walls of Jerusalem overlooking the Palestinian village of Silwan in the company of two Israeli women (9).[21]

This trajectory of images, figured in the person of the narrator, is emblematic of the narrative direction and transfiguration of *Palestine* itself. It challenges and counters the charge of the visual as pornographic in its tracing of a verbally unarticulated change in its narrator's way of seeing. Instead, the transformation is suggested only visually, as in the trajectory of the narrator's depiction and positioning in each of the inside front covers. If the uncritically circulated and consumed visual is *essentially* pornographic, then the comic series' critically ironic way of seeing, attentive to the fascinating allure of such images, engages in a betrayal of its object. This way of seeing operates simultaneously on the level of the narrator's gaze and on that of the comic series as a whole. It is a way of seeing made explicit in the reoccurrence of parallel universes in the comic series.

Seeing Parallel Universes

The visual and narrative "bang-bang" that sells comics (and attracts popular press editors and audiences) begins to shift, initially perhaps through sheer force of accumulation. Amid countless stories of arrests, detentions, imprisonment, and torture, the narrator asks a Palestinian man: "Has *he* ever been interrogated? . . . Beaten? How were you beaten? Can you describe it?" (4:13).[22] One of the men obliges the narrator by playing Israeli interrogator. "Sit down," he tells the narrator. "This way, without the backrest . . . SIT! SIT! HANDS BEHIND! LEAN BACK!" (4:14). A white arrow directs our attention to the next panel, in which the Palestinian-as-Israeli-interrogator begins to bring his fist down on the crotch of the narrator-as-Palestinian-prisoner, the latter with a grotesque grimace on his startled face. "Don't worry," the narrator reassures his audience. "He stops short . . . He doesn't do it . . . He spares me" (4:14). In a verbal gesture to the parallel universes that inhabit comics as a genre,[23] that the narrator himself will introduce a few pages later (4:22), and that will increasingly come to dominate *Palestine*, the Palestinian man continues, "The door he closes, and the world cannot see." But of course, the audience for the comic *does* see what the Palestinian prisoner does not, both and simultaneously the universe within the prison cell and that beyond the prison. Those parallel universes are also gendered. From a "Doubting Thomas" at the conclusion of the third comic in the series to the titillating fascination with the "itsy-bitsy details, descriptions of the crunching sounds" of torture of young Palestinian men, the narrator meets his match of sorts, and begins to surrender his arrogant incredulity, with the introduction in "The Tough and the Dead" (4:17) of "one tough [female] cookie . . . a Palestinian woman about my age . . . who did 18 days in Jerusalem's notorious Russian Compound courtesy of the Shin Bet." She tells him, in reference to one of the men who, under torture, had given her name to the police, that "even if they beat him on the genitals, its hurts once, it hurts twice . . . And after that, she says, you don't feel it so much." In a textually explicit indication of the narrator's willingness to perceive what he can't observe or experience directly, he comments to his audience, "I beg to differ of course, but who am I to take issue with a person of her mettle . . . she's done months in prison, she's been arrested four times" (4:17). The power of gendered telling of and listening to Palestinian stories in *Palestine* is even more compellingly illustrated in the last two sections, "Women" and "Hijab," of the fifth comic. There the narrator is confronted with the complexity of gender (and class) difference, which he cannot control but with which he nonetheless wants to engage.[24]

Despite the narrator's wry insights into parallel universes of gender in Palestine, perhaps the most extended and visually graphic illustration of parallel universes is in the concluding section of the fourth comic, " 'Moderate Pressure': Part 2," on the extralegal detention and torture of Palestinians in Israeli prisons. The narrator introduces that section with an admonition: "Make no mistake, everywhere you go, not just in Marvel comics, there's parallel universes" (4:22). This section affords a painful illustration of exactly how parallel universes work *in* Palestine (and in *Palestine*). One universe is Ghassan's living room, where his daughter sleeps on his lap; another is that of the Israeli military on the street outside. Ghassan recounts an evening when the tenuous barrier between the two—literally, the door of his home—"gets bashed down" by Israeli security and policemen.

In increasingly tightly bound panels of diminishing size, with black gutters and black-bordered pages, *Palestine* visually and verbally figures Ghassan's story of subsequent imprisonment, torture, and multiple appearances in an Israeli court until his release nearly three weeks later. The parallel worlds of which Ghassan is painfully aware as he is forced from one (his home) to another (the prison cell) is characterized by the narrator in the beginning of the segment: "On the surface streets: traffic, couples in love, falafel-to-go, tourists in jogging suits licking stamps for postcards . . . And over the wall behind closed doors: other things—people strapped to chairs, sleep deprivation, the smell of piss" (4:22).

But Ghassan is not the only one aware of parallel universes. So are the Israeli police and security men who seize, detain, and torture him. So is *Palestine*'s narrator, though at a temporal and spatial remove. But in the comic's visual rendition of parallel universes, the point of view from which the panels are framed is scarcely ever that of Ghassan.[25] Blindfolded and then with a hood over his head for virtually the entirety of his imprisonment, he sees only darkness. The parallel universe of imprisonment and torture behind closed doors is presented for an onlooker on the prison's outside. Occasionally, it is also, more contentiously, perhaps, presented as for the Israeli police (4:27, most distinctly). For the implied audience of these grim pages, *Palestine*'s parallel universes, and the perception of one from the *outside* of another,[26] are characterized by increasingly smaller and darker panels. The visual movement of the panels mirrors not Ghassan's visual perspective, but his experience itself—as observed from the outside. Ever more cramped, dark, crowded, pressured, the already intense cross-hatch artwork that characterizes Sacco's visual style grows more so with each frame. The figments of Ghassan's hallucinations as he wears down after days of abuse are arrayed on the ground at his feet: the "dead" bodies of his daughter, his father, his brother, his uncle, the image of his mother sick and in the hospital and then arrested by the Israelis. For the comic's implied audience, the parallel universe of Ghassan's hallucinations is rendered visually. So there are multiple parallel universes in these pages displayed for the comic's audience. Yet no single character in the comic has access to the whole. Only the narrator and the implied audience see all the parallel universes—at a spatial and temporal remove. Ghassan, his captors, the comic's narrator, and *Palestine*'s implied audience are each aware of a different configuration of parallel universes. Some of them are shared; for Ghassan and his captors, for example, the parallel universes in and outside of the prison. Some are not. Ghassan's captors may be aware that he is hallucinating, but they don't see the bodies of his family at his feet.

The toll of such knowledge of parallel universes is sharply differential. Looking at a comics panel of torture, or even engaging in the torture of another, is not the inscription of that torture on the viewer's or the torturer's own body. But a central object of *Palestine*'s critical scrutiny is the choice to ignore the existence of parallel universes at all—in *Palestine*, in Palestine, or elsewhere. For, *Palestine*'s narrator wryly observes at the outset of his venture from the West Bank to Gaza in the last four books of the comics series, "some of the world's blackest holes are out in the open for anyone to see" (6:1)—or for anyone to ignore. Of course, "anyone" doesn't typically see those "blackest holes," even though the narrator provides a UNRWA (UN Relief and Works Agency for Palestinian refugees) phone number for "anyone" interested in participating in a tour.[27] And the next double-page spread provides a painstakingly detailed long shot for the observer of "Refugeeland" (see figure 15).

There are two further instructive examples in *Palestine* of the powerful exploitation of the comics convention of parallel universes. One accompanies the narrator's story of an unsuccessful effort to convince a Palestinian

FIGURE 15. Joe Sacco, *Palestine* #6, pp. 2–3. © 1996 Joe Sacco. Used with permission.

woman that her statement "Jews are dogs" is both offensive and wrong (see figure 16). "This time I can't let it go . . . I tell her talk like that makes me wince . . . anyway lots of Jews don't agree with the occupation, I say, including *Israeli* Jews." He proceeds to tell her a story of an Israeli soldier who approached him in Nablus, who seemed to have some appreciation for the old section of the Palestinian city he was occupying. The narrator's Palestinian audience is impassive, and his own summation of the effect of his story is dispirited: "I suppose one loose anecdote doesn't bridge any gulfs." But the interesting visual disjuncture here on the page is that the anecdote *has* bridged a gulf as the narrator tells his story. On the page, people apparently and actually occupying diametrically opposed positions—a Palestinian woman holding her baby on her lap in a Madonna-like pose and an Israeli soldier holding a gun in militaristic pose—are visually brought together, side by side, even though the narrator protests, "It's not like I'm here to mediate." But the very page layout itself, if not the narrator's story or its reception by his audience in the comic, suggests otherwise. The dis-

FIGURE 16. Joe Sacco, *Palestine #3*, p. 33. © 1996 Joe Sacco. Used with permission.

juncture in content between one panel and the next speaks otherwise in the visual proximity and juxtaposition of those same panels. The gap is closed, if only for a moment, on a single comics page, and only for those who are not direct participants in the struggle that *Palestine* narrates, but who seek to perceive and understand it. The comic visually constructs a tenuous bridge between parallel universes.

The final comic in the *Palestine* series opens by considering the relations between Palestine and Israel "through other [gendered] eyes,"[28] and ends with the reiteration of elements that have characterized the narrator's two months in Palestine-Israel: an American tourist (9:29), (the memory of a meeting with) Palestinians, Israeli peace activists and U.S. NGO workers (9:29–30), Jewish settlers (9:32), the Israeli military (9:33), and young Palestinian boys waiting to throw stones (9:33). The anticlimactic final panel of the comic shows nothing more than the bus driver again losing his way and asking for further directions at an Israeli army post. And in a final example of parallel universes, that lost way is metaphorized here (9:29–31) through parallel universes of memory.

On the bus as he leaves Palestine-Israel, the narrator's conversation about "peace" with an American Jewish tourist returning to New York spurs the memory of another conversation about a peace that "isn't described identically by all who wish to imagine it" (9:29). In a conversation among a Palestinian, an Israeli peace activist, and two U.S. NGO workers in the back room of an Arab jewelry shop in Jerusalem, "The Israeli listened to our little debate for awhile, then said—Ultimately I don't think peace is about whether there should be one state or two. Of course that issue is important. But what is the point of *two* racist states or *one* racist state . . . Or one racist state dominating another? The point is whether the two peoples can live side by side as equals" (9:31).

This is the final statement in *Palestine* about peace. It is perhaps not a coincidence in this comic that it is an Israeli man who speaks of that vision of cohabitation.

The comic's graphic suggestion to imagine a Palestine-Israel otherwise is tempered by the narrator's memory of another incident, another lost way. His recollection follows immediately after the question of "whether the two peoples can live side by side as equals." Lost on the road out of Palestine, from within two parallel universes of memory, the narrator recalls another incident, in which "a group of Israeli soldiers stopped a Palestinian youth of 12 or 13 . . . The soldiers took cover under an awning and they made the boy remove his keffiyeh and pointed to where he should stand—in the rain.

Perhaps for the boy it was one of dozens of humiliations, bad enough in his personal scheme of things, but no worse than others he'd experienced . . . I'd come for the occupation and I found what I'd come to find and here it was again, and something else, too" (9:30). The visual framing and content of the three horizontal panels on the page powerfully and suggestively implicate ways of seeing and of reading relations (see figure 17). As the narrator recounts how "the boy stood there and answered their questions, and what choice did he have?" the angle of the panel is from behind the boy's shoulders, the faces of the Israeli soldiers only half visible. It is the angle from which an onlooker might see the scene. In the next panel, to the boy's upturned face in the rain, the narrator asks the question: "But what was he thinking . . . here is something else—a boy standing in the rain, and what is he thinking?" The panel frames the boy's face from above. He squints up through the falling rain, presumably at his military interlocutors. But it is the narrator who asks the question. It is, implicitly at least, the narrator, occupying the position of the Israeli soldiers, at whom the young boy looks. He also peers up at the comic's implied audience. The third and last panel on the page offers a side view of the (dry) face of one of the soldiers as the young boy looks up at him: "And if I'd guessed before I got here, and found with little astonishment once I'd arrived, what can happen to someone who thinks he has all the power, what of this—what becomes of someone when he believes himself to have none?"

Sacco's response to this question is not only the retrospective look back at the comic series and the experiences, stories, and images of life under occupation and the first Intifada (1987–1993) that it narrates. An extratextual response to this question, inadvertently prophetic in its implications, is also the second Intifada and the nearly decade-long exacerbation of the miserable living conditions for Palestinians in the West Bank and Gaza, both at the hands of the Palestine Authority and ever so much more atrociously at the hands of the Israeli government and military.

If the object of image and word in *Palestine* is the experience of Palestinians in the winter of 1990–1991, and if, as John Berger suggests, "every image embodies a way of seeing" but "our perception or appreciation of an image depends also upon our own way of seeing," *Palestine*'s narrator and the combination of word and image in *Palestine* itself have brilliantly and scathingly figured that process. From "getting the story" or the image to understanding the relations between the stories themselves and between the stories and "our own way of seeing," *Palestine* makes a powerful case for understanding (spoken and silent, visible and not) relations. And, implicitly at least, it makes a powerful indictment against willful ignorance of those connections. If, as Jameson cautions, "the visual is *essentially* pornographic," then *Palestine* and its narrator point to ways the visual is "betrayed." It does not rely on a purist refusal of the visual to do so. Nor does it revel in its "pornography." In addition to its brilliant exposition in word and image of the excruciating experiences of Palestinians living under occupation, in addition to its astute use of comics conventions in the service of a stunningly insightful comics-journalism, *Palestine* also takes as the object of its narrative, and "betrays" in the process, the visual itself as pornographic gaze or stare. It indicts a seeing or hearing without fluency in understanding relations either on or beyond the surface of what is seen or heard. Sacco therefore also indicts the represented and the *un*represented objects of that seeing and hearing: the narrator in the former instance, the implied audience, looking over the shoulder of the narrator, in the latter. The explicit and implicit viewer is equally, if in the latter case metaphorically, an object of the comic's gaze.

The Sites behind the Image: "The Words under the Words"

"Answer, if you hear the words under the words," urges Naomi Shihab Nye, "otherwise it is just a world with a lot of rough edges, difficult to get through, and our pockets full of stones."[29] From presumptuous conceit and bravado in the first comics in the series to the tone of sober recognition in the later, *Palestine* is a narrative of learning to "listen to the words under the words." It traces a way of seeing that perceives the relations between the objects of its gaze and itself as seer. It is a verbally implicit but often visually explicit (and even confrontational) performance of the acquisition and exercise of reading relations—relations between what is presented visually and verbally, between cultures, between communities, and between the apparently disparate stories and scenes witnessed by its narrator. Based on that reading of relations, the story is retold in a narrative of the history of a people, of past and present events, of desires and memories. For *Palestine* is, crucially and simultaneously, a comics narrative of the history and contemporary experiences of Palestinians (and Israelis) in the Occupied Territories. But it is also, and no less importantly, the story of the way those experiences and that history are related to one another and to the observer, who, listening and watching attentively, may just be able to productively tell the story again.

Finally, neither the comics form of Sacco's *Palestine* nor its content are

FIGURE 17. Joe Sacco, *Palestine* #9, pp. 30–31. © 1996 Joe Sacco. Used with permission.

scandalous or frivolous. *Palestine* accomplishes something more than providing a unique comics format of words and images about Palestine-Israel.
What is scandalous *for* Palestine-Israel and *in* the comic series *Palestine* is
the proffering of pornographically titillating images that "ask us to stare
at the world *as though* it were a naked body" for collection and possession,
and the hollow fascination evoked by such images. Such a gaze willfully
ignores any relationship with or implication in the images and the events,
places, and people they represent beyond that of titillating fascination. This
"mindless" and uncritical gaze (or stare) is the object of *Palestine*'s visual
(and verbal) perspective. It is this way of seeing that *Palestine* indicts, and
this "*essentially* pornographic" visual that *Palestine* "betrays"—pointedly,
sometimes poignantly, relentlessly.

Notes

1. That is the "co-mix" of words and images.
2. Nonetheless, noteworthy comics in the United States include accomplished and
critically acknowledged works of social and historical complexity, such as Art Spiegelman's well-known *Maus*, Joe Kubert's *Fax from Sarajevo*, Phoebe Gloeckner's *A Child's
Life*, Larry Gonick's *Cartoon History of the Universe*, and Ho Che Anderson's *King*.
3. *Palestine*, volumes 1–9, was originally published by Fantagraphics Books between 1993 and 1995 as a series of nine comic books. It was subsequently issued in a
two-volume book edition, *Palestine Book 1: A Nation Occupied* (Seattle: Fantagraphics
Books, 1994) and *Palestine Book 2: In the Gaza Strip* (Seattle: Fantagraphics Books,
1996) and, most recently, in a single-volume edition with an introduction by Edward
Said, *Palestine* (Seattle: Fantagraphics Books, 2002). References in the text are to the
original comic book series and are cited parenthetically by volume and page number.
   For an excellent and succinct political history of Palestine-Israel and the Arab-
Israeli conflict, see "Palestine, Israel and the Arab-Israeli Conflict: A Primer," available
at the MERIP (Middle East Research and Information Project) Web site: http://www
.merip.org/palestine-israel_primer/toc-pal-isr-primer.html. The site has an equally
excellent account of the second Intifada, "MERIP Primer on the Uprising in Palestine,"
by Phyllis Bennis, Deborah J. Gerner, Steve Nivan, and Rebecca Stein.
4. In 1996, in its presentation of the seventeenth annual American Book Award
to *Palestine*, the Before Columbus Foundation recognized Sacco for his "outstanding
contribution to American literature" and also noted that *Palestine*'s publisher, Fantagraphics, should "be honored for their commitment to quality and their willingness
to take risks that accompany publishing outstanding books and authors that may not
prove 'cost-effective' in the short run." Quoted on the Fantagraphics Web site page:
http::/www.fantagraphics.com/artist/sacco/sacco.html.
5. The contemporary popularity of these films based largely on comic book superheroes or on dark challenges to superheroes, and the equally popular and lucrative

spinoff marketing from them, is a striking cultural and sociopolitical phenomenon, worthy of consideration in its own right.

6. The material compiled in *War Junkie* was originally published in *Yahoo* and *Drawn & Quarterly* between 1989 and 1995. It has been recently republished with additional materials as *Notes from a Defeatist*. In his wonderful and poignant introduction to the most recent single-volume edition of *Palestine*, Edward Said amusingly characterizes *War Junkie* as "exceptionally weird." "Homage to Joe Sacco," introduction to *Palestine* by Joe Sacco (Seattle: Fantagraphics Books, 2002), iv.

7. Born in Malta, Sacco grew up hearing his parents' stories of the bombing of their homeland by Axis forces. His family moved to Portland, Oregon, when he was fourteen. He graduated from the University of Oregon with a degree in journalism and currently lives in Queens, New York.

8. This is what comics critic Scott McCloud attempts to account for in his characterization of perception and of reading comics as a process of "observing the parts but perceiving the whole," in *Understanding Comics: The Invisible Art* (New York: Harper Perennial, 1994), 62–63.

9. Matthew Pustz, *Comic Book Culture: Fanboys and True Believers* (Jackson: University Press of Mississippi, 1999), 24.

10. *Safe Area Gorzade*, which has been prominently featured in media such as the *New York Times*, the *New York Times Book Review*, *Time*, *Utne Reader*, *The Times of London*, the *Washington Post*, *The Boston Globe*, *The Economist*, and *The Atlantic Monthly* has sold approximately 16,000 copies in the United States, with close to 20,000 copies in print. But total sales for *Palestine*, already or soon to be released in Brazil, France, Germany, Great Britain, Italy, Korea, Portugal, Spain, and Sweden, are 26,000, with 30,000 copies in print (figures from Fantagraphics). Sacco's *The Fixer* (Montreal: Drawn and Quarterly Publications, 2003), on life in the battered city of Sarajevo following the Balkan war, was first released in December 2003 and is already in a second printing. It has been widely and favorably reviewed; see Drawn and Quarterly's "news" page for Joe Sacco at http://www.drawnandquarterly.com/artBio.php?artist= a3dff7dd55575b.

11. See the "Cartoonist's Note" on the inside back cover of the first comic (1:25). For online biographies of Sacco and his work, see http://www.fantagraphics.com/artist/sacco/sacco_bio.html and http://www.drawnandquarterly.com/artBio.php?artist=a3 dff7dd55575b.

12. Michael Duff (Professor of Theoretical Physics, University of Michigan, Ann Arbor), BBC Two, "Horizon" and "Parallel Universes" (February 14, 2002), available at: www.bbc.co.uk/science/horizon/2001/paralleluni.shtml.

13. Fredric Jameson, *Signatures of the Visible* (New York: Routledge, 1992), 1.

14. "The intifada is over, especially when *I* don't get the picture," a Palestinian photographer contends to the narrator about a demonstration in Jerusalem. "Yeah, but *I* did," the narrator boasts in an aside to his audience (3:5). In fact, his putatively "Pulitzer Prize-winning photograph" of " 'the violence' " of that Jerusalem demonstration turns out to be "nothing." Nothing, that is, that a wire service editor wants to circulate.

15. This *relational* construction suggests the workings of another kind of kind

of trope, metaphor, that constructs a not-readily-apparent relationship between one thing and another.

16. John Berger, *Ways of Seeing* (London: Penguin, 1973), 10 (emphasis added).

17. ". . . and, by the way," he adds, "*not* with Israeli intelligence" (1:5).

18. As in, of course, "A picture is worth a thousand words." Though there is not time or space here to detail the amazing visual work the comic does, it's worth noting the careful structural attention paid in this section to the relation of word balloons to images and text. In *Palestine*, the square word balloons consistently indicate the running ironic commentary of the narrator; the round word balloons perform their conventional role in comics of indicating characters' speech. On pages 2 and 6, as the narrator refers to the "inverted pyramid lead paragraph," the visual composition of the pages mimics that journalistic convention. In this third comic, the narrator is obsessively concerned with "getting the picture." He doesn't. Or at least, he doesn't get the picture he thinks he wants.

19. But see the discussion above of the narrator flanked in a later image in the first comic of the series by American tourists and Israeli soldiers.

20. In fact, his face, no longer delineated and emphasized in darker ink, is hidden behind the text that provides publication information. The TV is drawn in precisely that darker ink used in previous comics in the series to outline the narrator as an "authoritative" narrative voice. In this instance, his position is taken over, not by the television itself, as it might at first appear, but by an illegal video playing on the television of the torture of Palestinians in Israeli prisons.

21. The inside front cover of the final comic in the series finds the narrator acting as guide and "translator"—"I know my Jerusalem!" (9:1)—for Paula and Naomi, two Israeli women from Tel Aviv in Jerusalem for the day. The inside cover of the last comic is a perhaps pointed *visual* suggestion about future narrators of the stories of *Palestine*. For in this last inside cover in the series, against the gray line drawing of Silwan, all *three* figures are drawn in the darker ink that has been a visual convention in *Palestine* for the narrator's position. It is also noteworthy that the narrator doesn't mention in his conversation with the two Israeli women the Peace Now activists whose considerable participation in solidarity with the Palestinians demonstrating in Silwan he has already narrated early in the series (1:19). The implied audience of the comic, again, knows more than the characters in the comic.

22. "I'm numbed by so many accounts of incarceration that the sort of thing that raises my brow is a male in his mid-20s who *hasn't* been arrested. I want to ask him *why the hell not?*" (4:1).

23. In addition to synchronic parallel universes in the comic—while A is happening here, B is happening there—there are also parallel universes of memory and of desire. A familiar convention not only in comics but in literature and popular culture, another world of a remembered past or a longed-for or fantasized future intersects or interrupts the narrative present.

24. Nonetheless, the comic's tentative closure on its discussion of gender is an ironic display of (a transnational) patriarchal male community, "Still One of the Boys," that marks the increasing constraint of the narrator's coy presumptuousness.

25. Of 148 panels, only a few are framed from below looking up, as the impris-

oned Ghassan would have been positioned. The rest are all angled and framed for the observer's gaze, looking in at Ghassan and at his captors, lawyers, or judges.

26. That is, the apprehension of the universe inside the prison that is parallel to that outside of it and, as well, the perception of both that are parallel universes of memory for the narrative present of the comic. It is perhaps the privilege of such a point of view, distant from the bodily or mental experience to which that perspective is witness, that is an example of Jameson's "*essentially* pornographic" visual, the "mindless rapt fascination" of seeing something without the bodily and mental toll of experiencing it directly, indulging in a titillating voyeurism of willful nonengagement.

27. "They'll set you up, drive you there themselves, admission is free . . . but you'll want your refugee camp experience to be an intimate thing" (6:1).

28. In which the narrator is joined by two Israeli women to whom he tries to explain his sojourn in Palestine and with whom he returns to his point of entry to Palestine/*Palestine* on the walls above Jerusalem. His gendered, national audience here is a suggestive signpost for extratextual audiences for *Palestine* and its stories. See the discussion above.

29. Naomi Shihab Nye, "The Words under the Words," in *Words under the Words: Selected Poems* (Portland, Ore.: Eighth Mountain Press, 1995), 37.

ELLIOTT COLLA

Sentimentality
and Redemption:
The Rhetoric of
Egyptian Pop
Culture Intifada
Solidarity

Although it was produced long before the outbreak of the al-Aqsa Intifada, the LiveAid-style pop ballad "al-Hulm al-'arabi" (The Arab dream) was transformed into an anthem to the Palestinian struggle in the months following the beginning of the uprising.[1] Like other pop tributes to pan-Arab unity and Palestine, "al-Hulm al-'arabi" was frequently broadcast in Egypt, both on radio and as a slickly produced video.[2] The original video, replete with images of real Arab suffering drawn from the first Intifada and the Gulf War, was revised after October 2000, adding footage of Muhammad al-Durra and others killed during the uprising. Featuring singers from Egypt and all over the Arab world, the song presents an uplifting but ultimately vague pan-Arab message:

> Generation after generation, we will live on our dream
> And what these generations say today will last our lifetime . . .
> That's our dream, for all our life
> An embrace that gathers all of us together.

In terms of its musical style, Intifada imagery, and lyrical message, "al-Hulm al-'arabi" is not extraordinary. Its sculpted vocals, earnest tenor and seamless production resemble those of many other popular music videos from the Arab world about the al-Aqsa Intifada. The song's seemingly sincere gesture of Arab unity and solidarity with Palestine also seems straightforward, even unremarkably so. Moreover, because such gestures have been so ubiquitous in contemporary Egyptian popular culture in the past several years, it may be difficult to think of them as complicated or requiring anything but a cursory glance.

However, despite the apparent earnestness of these pop gestures of solidarity, there is an undeniably ambiguous quality to them. The cloyingly sentimental tone of "al-Hulm al-ʿarabi" was not lost on Egyptian audiences long familiar with sentimental genres in music and film.[3] Although popular, the message of "The Arab Dream" was more than once turned on its head in parody. One version, renamed "al-Hashish al-ʿarabi" (The Arab hashish), equates pan-Arab dreams with drug use:

> Toke after toke ruins our lungs
> And what we smoke today cuts our lives in half
> Perhaps a joint will get us stoned
> Or we'll get sky high with just a bit of hash.

Another parody, titled "al-Fil al-ʿarabi" (The Arab elephant), turned the original, "ajyal baʿd ajyal" (generation after generation) into the ludicrous "afyal baʿd afyal" (elephants upon elephants). Other versions punctured the original pop anthem's inflated sentiments with different needles.

These parodies were not broadcast in venues of mass culture, but circulated around their margins, on Web sites and in cafés. Admittedly, such parodic texts exist in a secondary and parasitical relation to pop culture. Nonetheless, their humor derives from mimicking a recognizable original textual referent. What the parodies of "al-Hulm al-ʿarabi" all share is the way they caricature the original's overly emphatic, earnest tone. In so doing, these versions point to ambiguities in the original text: the disconnection between the song's pan-Arab rhetoric and the reality of inter-Arab politics, or between the singers' high-minded moral posture and their openly commercial presentation.

We might read the parodies of "al-Hulm al-ʿarabi" as a special form of cultural criticism, as each presents a skeptical *close reading* of the original's rhetoric. Each parody diverges from the original, but its humor invariably depends on its ability to exploit an ambiguity already present in the original text. Although such parodies surface and disappear far from the mass media, they show how audiences can rewrite pop culture texts to suit their own tastes and ideologies. Moreover, they can play a crucial function for the analysis of popular culture, because they draw attention to rhetorical structures that are all too often thought to be unworthy of second thought.

In this sense, parody serves to expose what Roland Barthes called myth. For Barthes, myth was associated with a certain kind of text that presents itself as transparent and commonsensical, whose meanings are received as self-evident, taken for granted. The mythical text is that which disavows its own rhetorical status, presenting itself as if it were something natural and unadorned.[4] The parodies of "al-Hulm al-'arabi" thus perform a critical function by deconstructing the rhetorical structures of their mythmaking. It may seem counterintuitive to place the sort of irony we find in these parodies at the forefront of a consideration of Egyptian pop solidarity with Palestine, especially given the heavy political valence of these texts and their earnest style of presentation. But parody is useful, because it high-lights ambiguities in the rhetorical constructs of those texts.

I argue that most gestures of solidarity with Palestine that have be-come a staple of Egyptian pop culture are mythological in this Barthe-sian sense: they present Egyptian-Palestinian political solidarity as natural (rather than constructed) and images of Palestinian resistance as if they were nonrhetorical, transparent representations, akin to "reality" itself.[5] The rhetoric of Egyptian pop solidarity is dominated by two familiar kinds of narrative: sentimentality and redemption. However, rhetorical analysis, like that prompted by the existence of parodic texts, reveals that the seem-ingly straightforward narratives of sentimentality and redemption contain complex and often self-contradictory messages. Their emphatic and some-times catachrestic rhetoric suggests that even the most earnest gestures of pop solidarity with Palestine cannot be taken at face value.

Because the analysis of popular culture in the Middle East has some-times assumed relatively stable, reflective models of representation, the place of irony—and rhetorical analysis—has often been too marginal. In this essay, I discuss the current state of criticism on Middle East popular culture and argue that Egyptian pop Intifadiana shows the usefulness of the rhetorical analysis suggested by Barthes in *Mythologies* and elsewhere. I next consider some prominent rhetorical issues in texts from Egyptian pop Intifadiana, which make an interesting test case for rhetorical study because they are usually seen as transparent indicators of popular senti-ment. Finally, I consider some of the ways these rhetorical concerns impact the expression of political solidarity more generally. The lessons offered by rhetorical analysis are not just crucial for reading pop Intifadiana, they also serve to illuminate divergent understandings of what it means to be in political solidarity. In this regard, I consider the rhetoric of solidarity with Palestine from two different perspectives: from contemporary critical discussions of solidarity and from Jean-Luc Godard's *Ici et ailleurs*, which puts ambiguity, irony, and the self-reflexive consideration of filmic rhetoric at the heart of a politics of solidarity. By way of conclusion, I argue that other rhetorics of solidarity are a useful gauge, not just for measuring the shortcomings of the mythological forms of solidarity that dominate Egyptian pop Intifadiana, but also for imagining others forms of political alliance.

Rhetoric and Cultural Studies

Recent cultural criticism on the Middle Eastern pop culture can be divided into three groups. One body of literature tends toward macroanalysis of pop culture networks and "public spheres." In these accounts, mass culture appears as an arena of "information" in which texts clearly reflect larger social phenomena.[6] Another body of criticism provides ethnographic accounts of cultural reception.[7] Both kinds of analysis often forgo the close reading of individual texts in favor of broader sociological descriptions. In these literatures little attention is paid to rhetorical issues—especially those raised by parody, irony, and ambiguity—that might complicate reflective theory. This aversion to rhetorical analysis is surprising given the array of Middle Eastern popular cultural genres and traditions that thrive on ambiguity and irony.

However, the ambiguities of rhetoric, form, and performance have been an important part of a third segment of the critical literature on Middle Eastern pop culture. Critics have noted unstable rhetoric around certain topics, from the traditional *mawwal* to drag performance, in Middle Eastern music, just as they have commented on traditions of ironic literature, from the *maqama* to the comic strip, and the ambiguities contained in erotic oral poetry.[8] However, with regard to *visual* mass media (photography, film, and video) in Egypt, cultural critics have tended to read texts as if they were reflective of social and political phenomena and to imply that this reflection is transparent and stable.[9] This tendency is due in part to the centrality of didactic generic traditions in Egyptian culture, such as social realism, which asserts claims about identity and "authenticity" (*asala*).[10] In Egyptian cinema, the question of identity has been dominant and thematically connected with the twin legacies of modernization and colonial rule. As Viola Shafik observes, it is no accident that realism's referential style predominates in Egyptian cinema's late colonial and early postindependence period: "Because of its sociopolitical commitment and anti-colonialist attitude, realism was considered, more than other genres, as an expression of national culture . . . Realism performs a conserving and reflective function that is immensely important for the formerly colonized, who were deprived even of their own image."[11]

Although Shafik's comments about the centrality and motivation of social realism ring true, she, like other critics, tends to accept the rhetoric of cinemagraphic realism in Egypt as if the image of authentic Egyptian identity it offered existed in a stable relationship with a sociological type. In such cases, the rhetoric of the film text is treated as if it were natural and transparent; indeed, though much has been said about the *narrative* structures of Egyptian realist cinema, much less has been said about its *visual* structures. Some realist films may indeed suggest transparent and referential readings, but the rhetoric of other important genres in Egyptian cinema, especially melodrama, problematize such readings.[12] Similarly, the hyperbolic and often *camp* quality of melodrama draws attention to its own rhetorical excesses and disrupts the genre's apparently earnest and sincere assertions.[13] To read texts as complicated, even conflicted, is not to privilege irony and ambiguity, but to insist on their place in pop culture production and cultural studies analysis. Nonetheless, some critics have been reluctant to read for such irony in realist cinema and other ostensibly "straight" genres. There may be good reasons for this hesitancy. As Walter Armbrust has pointed out, there are dangers that arise when critics from different cultures attempt the rhetorical reading of texts: "Americans may view classically 'bad' films with a kind of ironic detachment. I rarely noticed this with my Egyptian friends, but it is very hard to judge irony even in a tradition one knows thoroughly and even among people one has grown up with. To be sure of attitudes is hard."[14] Likewise, Armbrust argues, this ironic detachment is also a register for articulating class-based notions of taste, one that allows critics to denounce (as vulgar) or celebrate (as kitsch) texts encountered in popular culture. Because Armbrust is acutely attuned to the ironic possibilities in Egyptian popular culture, his wariness cannot be easily disregarded. Nevertheless, his warning is directed against confusing the rhetorical possibilities of a text with the responses, the "attitudes," of actual audiences, in this case, American and Egyptian viewers. And though he is attentive to the internal rhetoric of popular texts, his focus is, in the end, on how they are received in the "real lives" of audiences. His focus, in other words, is on an understanding of rhetoric to be about performance and response, elocution and response, in an empirical sense.

Yet, as Roland Barthes noted, the empirical understanding of rhetoric does not exhaust the possibilities of the term, because for much of its history that tradition was more concerned with the exhaustive description of figures.[15] Although it may seem strange to argue for the contemporary relevance of rhetoric as the study of figure, such a method is uniquely suited for sifting through the complicated and often self-contradictory texture of Egyptian pop culture. What, other than apparently archaic rhetorical terms, such as *auxesis* (the augmentative form of *hyperbole*) and *bathos* (an abrupt shift from an elevated to a commonplace theme), can more precisely describe the rhetorical basis on which rest the parodies of "al-Hulm al-'arabi"?

Myths of Solidarity: Pop Intifadiana

Alongside the popular protests that erupted in Egypt during fall 2000 (at the outset of the al-Aqsa Intifada), and then again in spring and summer 2002, a new pop culture of solidarity with Palestine emerged. Nowhere was this more evident than in the state media. Unlike earlier moments in the Arab-Israeli conflict, when the Egyptian media, including the opposition press, paid little, if any attention to events in the Occupied Territories, news of Palestinian suffering and militancy became a regular and prominent feature in newspapers and on state TV.[16] The host of the press review program *Editor-in-Chief* urged the audience to honor the boycott against Israel and contestants on the Egyptian version of *Who Wants to Be a Millionaire?* were asked trivia questions about martyr operations (suicide bombings) in the Occupied Territories. The once oppositional stance of antinormalization became the official editorial policy of the state news agencies. In Egypt's state and private media, songs, videos, films, and advertising offering frankly mercantile stereotypes of Palestinian struggle began to appear in late 2000. Images of raised guns, the Dome of the Rock, Palestinian flags, and kufiyas began to adorn cassette tapes of pop stars—even those who did little more than croon sentimental ballads. Following the siege of Yasser Arafat's compound in Ramallah in April 2002, a new snack food appeared in the slums of Cairo: Abu 'Ammar Corn Snacks featured a cartoon of a confused-looking Arafat wearing fatigues.

Perhaps no image was so ubiquitous as that of Muhammad al-Durra, the young boy killed in October 2000 by Israeli gunfire. Within months, the boy's picture had appeared in countless music videos and films and on products from T-shirts to boxes of Kleenex. Arguably, the primary significance of al-Durra's image lay in the fact that it seemed to record, without embellishment, a horrific death suffered by Palestinian civilians at the hands of the Israeli military.

The video image of Muhammad al-Durra first appeared in Egyptian pop culture (and elsewhere) as a picture of the truth of Israeli crimes and Palestinian life in the Occupied Territories.[17] Even if the image was deployed metaphorically, as a particular example of a wider pattern of atrocities (as opposed to the record of a single event), this did not mean the image itself was anything like a metaphor. The fact that al-Durra's death was recorded in real time and in unembellished video footage suggested that this was a literal (rather than figurative) image of a boy being killed, that it was an actual (rather than metaphorical) image of Israeli atrocity.

Admittedly, much of what lends pathos to the image is indeed its literal quality, an unadorned depiction of something that really happened. But the image, which appears to need no explanation, was always accompanied from the earliest broadcasts by commentary and narrative that helped to shape its meaning. For instance, when the video was first shown, viewers were informed that this was footage of a boy "about to be killed."[18] Thus, the framing commentary played a crucial role for transforming the footage from an image of death into a familiar narrative genre: *tragedy*. By drawing attention to the narrative rhetoric of the image, I am not suggesting that its indexical gesture is indeterminate or denying that it is the record of an event that happened. Rather, I want to draw attention to how the presentation of al-Durra's image includes not just the horrific events as recorded by the video footage, but also a voice-over narrative that tells, in advance, the horrible outcome of the event before it appears visually. It is undeniably horrifying that al-Durra dies before our eyes and that we know it to be an actual event. But what is *tragic* is that we know the outcome before we see the event and yet are powerless to stop it from transpiring.

The foretold death of Muhammad al-Durra is not the only tragic aspect of the image. Importantly, it also shows Muhammad's father holding him, trying to squeeze their bodies into an impossible space between a barrier and a wall. The father attempts to shield his son's body from the bullets raining down on them. This depiction of the father's failure to save the life of his own son is no less significant to the rhetoric of the image. The image is able to depict the *pathos* of both loss and death at the same time. This pathos of Muhammad's death is interwoven with another, as the image depicts the brutally public exposure, of a powerless and intimate fatherly sentiment that is normally the provenance of the private sphere. This aspect of the image was not lost in the culture of Egyptian pop solidarity; indeed, the pop performer Sha'ban 'Abd al-Rahim recorded a hit, "Qataluni ya-Ba!" (They've killed me, Father!) that spells out the pathos of this father-son tragedy.[19]

The public desecration of what is normally domestic is central to the way al-Durra's image communicates innocence and violation. This particular narrative of victimization — the public violation of familial intimacy — is a common feature of sentimental narrative. In this way, al-Durra's image does more than record an unembellished fact of death and atrocity. It also narrates, through recognizable structures, a story of foretold outcomes, powerlessness, and the violation of domestic innocence. In this sense, we might say that the way al-Durra's image circulates in Egyptian pop culture exemplifies mythology in the Barthesian sense: its putative meaning (the literal image of death and suffering) obtains only by obscuring the rhetorical constructs (the framing commentary, the tragic and sentimental narrative structures) at work in the text. If al-Durra's image has circulated in Egyptian pop culture as the unembellished truth of Israeli war crimes in the Occupied Territories, it is largely because it has been presented as if it were a nonrhetorical representation.

Yet, some in Egypt recognized the rhetorical quality of al-Durra's image, even if only to protect its mythological status. Troubled about the deployment of the image on so many different cultural goods, state censor Madkour Thabet intervened: "Al-Durra's photo has appeared on most cassette tape covers, no matter what's inside. To protect this sacred symbol from vulgar commercial exploitation, I have now banned its use, except in cases where it is related to the theme of the album."[20] This intervention into the excessive use of al-Durra's image suggests that, at least from Thabet's point of view, there need to be norms guiding its deployment and rules for distinguishing appropriate uses from inappropriate ones. But why would inappropriate uses threaten the "sacred" character of al-Durra's image? In the language of rhetoric, what Thabet feared — the inappropriate use of al-Durra's image — might be best called *catachresis*, the strained use (or misuse) of a figure. The central significance of al-Durra's image in the culture of pop solidarity is mythological, an effect of the way it presents itself as a literal (as opposed to figurative) image, as unadorned truth rather than rhetorical affect. The image of al-Durra circulates as if it were a pure signified. Its misuse draws attention to the fact that it is not a signified, but a signifier, a piece of rhetoric. But al-Durra's image remained a "sacred symbol" only insofar as it appeared as something natural whose meaning was self-evident, nonconstructed, generalizable. Herein lies the threat posed by catachresis to mythmaking: by drawing attention to the rhetorical structures underlying the image, excessive or strained use exposes the mechanics of mythmaking. In this way, the attention that the text's rhetoric draws to its constructed status (its figurative quality) undermines its status as sacred.

The mythology presented in the video image of al-Durra's death was a sentimental narrative about Palestinian sacrifice and tragedy. This narrative was intentionally attached to others that developed the theme by exploring images of redemption and victory. Take, for instance, the videoclip for "Ya Quds" (O Jerusalem) by the Syrian popular performer Majd Qasim, which appeared in Egypt via regional satellite stations such as Arab TV and Dream TV. In Qasim's videoclip, the singer croons as his visage, framed against an empty black background, dissolves into a dizzying montage of images: funeral mourners fade into the Jordan Arab Legion and then into a seascape; Lebanese cedars fade into pairs of cute, nesting birds, which fade into views of Jerusalem and then into an image of Arafat in tears; images drawn from Yousef Chahine's 1963 epic *Salah al-Din al-Ayyubi* (Saladin) are transposed with clips from Mustafa Akkad's 1981 tale of anticolonial resistance in Libya, *Lion of the Desert*; footage of the 1973 October war cuts into archival footage from the 1936–39 revolt in Palestine; images of fedayeen appear next to pictures of Ben Gurion, Dayan, and Meir; a Quranic verse with special reference to martyrdom is juxtaposed with pictures of the Crucifixion, pilgrims at Mecca, a Jewish West Bank settlement, and the Dome of the Rock. Some of these images, such as *Saladin* and the Dome of the Rock, make sense individually and seem to build organically on themes in the lyrics. The relevance of others is less direct but connected to the theme of anticolonial resistance. Still others, such as nesting artic birds, suggesting innocence and domesticity, seem quite tangential. Taken together, these images seem to form a rhetorical hodgepodge, yet the exaggerated polysemy of the visual montage is apparently meant to amplify the message of the lyrics. What is revealing about the text's catachrestic rhetoric is that its very excess lays bare the various symbolic orders invoked by the images: the images of domesticity, violation, mourning, and personal sacrifice invoke a discourse of sentimentality, innocence, and redemption for Palestinians; the iconography of Muslim and Christian piety, and the special sanctity of Jerusalem for Christians and Muslims, suggests both the transsectarian unity of Arabs and their essential difference from the Jewish state's barbarism; and the symbolism of armed struggle creates a transhistorical movement that links all Arabs fighting forms of colonial rule, from Crusaders to Italian fascists to Israelis. In this sense, it is the *strained use* of images that helps to reveal their rhetorical contours and to suggest how they might compose a single coherent narrative where the sentimental narrative, the Israeli violation of Palestinian Jerusalem, would find redemption in decisive military action on the part of a unified pan-Arab community.

The rhetorical strain of another popular Intifadiana video, "Ubrit thawrat abtal" (Operetta of the heroes' revolution), is even more problematic. "Operetta" opens with flames, behind which a group of performers chants and sways and fades into a scene of Middle Eastern urban ghetto, with graffiti and crowds of kufiya-clad youths waving Palestinian flags. Confronting soldiers whose helmets are emblazoned with the Star of David, the main hero of the operetta, Palestinian vocalist Yusuf al-Katri, faces the Israeli troops and sings defiantly: "Our revolution is a revolution of heroes / We stand, with stones, to die for you [Palestine]!" (see figure 18).

One by one, Egyptian pop performers (Ahmed Gohar, Hasan 'Abdel Mageed, Ahmad al-Shawki, Walid al-Husayni) pick up the song's thread. Each performer steps forward and delivers his lyrics in the face of Israeli soldiers. Behind them, against an ornate set more reminiscent of Cairo's dilapidated streets than of Gaza, "Palestinian" youths ceaselessly wave flags and hurl stones toward the camera. At times, the lyrics present a call and response. Al-Katri sings, "My roots are Palestinian, stubborn / Dying, stone in hand," and Hasan 'Abd al-Mageed sings back in empathy, "Ahhhhhh! / And we're coming / to Jerusalem, the Pure, the Luminous!" followed by the refrain, "We're not afraid, nor have we retreated a single step." By this moment, it has become clear that the "we" of the refrain refers not just to those Palestinians taking part in the Intifada but also to those Egyptians who stand with them in their struggle. This is the myth offered by the video: that Egyptians and Palestinians are naturally unified and essentially defiant. Like other pop solidarity texts, "Ubrit" makes use of video footage in the attempt to argue that its assertions reflect a literal reality. Yet, the exaggerated quality of video's earnest tone is more problematic than may first appear.

As al-Katri begins to sing, he is posed squarely *against* the camera, stone in hand, and his face is framed by his armed opponents. The lens never wavers from this position, squared against the performers, the point of view of the Israeli outpost. This contrary visual perspective serves to heighten the defiant tone of the performers' stance and, along with the gesture of solidarity, is arguably the main theme of the song itself. While the lyrics of the song are at times addressed to Palestine, the static and contrary camera angle compels the viewer to observe the operetta from the soldiers' viewpoint. Put differently, while the video's audio text is aimed at Egyptian and Arab audiences, its visual rhetoric addresses its audience as if they were Israelis.

Though meant to underscore the stance of opposition, the angle of the video lens is only one way in which the text's visual rhetoric conflicts with the apparent message of the song's lyrics. The images of nonstop street action are juxtaposed with familiar footage of real-life scenes: funeral processions, the faces of grieving relatives, bloody confrontations, wounded casualties. The effect of the video footage initially seems indexical, intended to root the operetta in actual events taking place in Palestine. But the repetitive media images of suffering and oppression begin to jar with the scripted tenor of the music video. Moreover, as much as the video footage appears to signal real-life events, the repetition of stock-footage imagery in this video (as in others), gives it a clichéd, already-seen quality. Thus, while the rhetorical use of video footage gestures again toward the real, the hyperbole of these real-life images draws attention to their generic status. Likewise, the sets and costumes, apparently designed to create a real sense of urban occupation grit, also appear exaggeratedly composed.

The point is not to criticize "Operetta" for being unrealistic, but to show that its inflated rhetoric, intended to emphasize the real-life quality of its depiction of Palestinian defiance, is more complicated and confused than might first appear. Moreover, the video's stance of solidarity is muddled, not simply because its hyperbolic gesture of defiance undermines itself, but also because it combines symbols and genres whose meanings do not cohere. The serious moral message of the text—drawing a sharp division between occupier and occupied, oppressor and resister—is perhaps badly suited to the music video genre, with its performers' slick choreographed movements, crisp costumes, and the elaborate set.

Amid the text's rhetorical confusion, other symbolic systems also fail to cohere. Throughout the video, flames are superimposed over the checkpoint scene. Like other Egyptian pop culture texts that draw analogies between present-day Palestinian suffering and the past suffering of European Jews, the video's superimposition of flames marks an attempt to invoke the Holocaust for the Palestinian cause. But this rhetorical gesture is juxtaposed to a frankly racist graffito—"la li-l-yuhud" (No Jews)—prominently

FIGURE 18. Palestinian singer Yusuf al-Katri, "Operetta of the Heroes' Revolution" video.

FIGURE 19. "No Jews": Egyptian singer Ahmed Gohar, "Operetta of the Heroes' Revolution" video.

emblazoned on one wall of the set (see figure 19). In the context of the video's other messages, this slogan seems to reverse the usual lessons of the Holocaust and suggests that European Jews deserved to suffer genocide. It also appears to interpret Palestinian suffering as the result not of Zionist colonialism, but of Jewish existence itself.

Here it is obvious that the rhetoric of the video operetta is not just confused but *preposterous*. The term remains useful, as Jonathan Goldberg has argued, for exploring discursive confusions. The preposterous is the Anglicization of the term from classical Greek rhetoric, *histeron proteron*, "a form of disordered speech in which the cart is put before the horse."[21] In the context of this video, we might correctly call preposterous the reversals in which Israeli racism toward Arabs is answered with anti-Jewish slogans and the Holocaust is suggested to belong more properly to Palestinian than Jewish history. To call a rhetorical figure, such as the use of a symbol or slogan, preposterous is to criticize its impropriety. But what other word better describes the video's attempt to reverse sedimented symbols of anti-Semitism and the Holocaust by invoking them alongside the defiant, political slogans of the lyrics, alongside the pop style of the emphatic choreography and the sentimental singing, alongside video footage that gestures toward tragedies from the actual Intifada? What causes problems for "Operetta of the Heroes' Revolution" is, for the most part, not images, camera angles, and slogans that are "improper." Rather, it is the exaggerated attempt to combine them in a rhetorical equation that proves impossible to sustain. Again, the strained deployment of figures reveals the mythical contours of the text: the attempt to expose Israeli crimes against Palestinians by linking it to the history of European anti-Semitism; the assertion that pan-Arab unity and militancy is natural; the attempt to illustrate the urgency of the Palestinian situation by couching it in a sentimental register of suffering, loss, and mourning.

At first glance, no statement of pop solidarity could seem more straightforward and earnest than the message of the most spectacular example of pop Intifadiana, Sha'ban 'Abd al-Rahim's infamous hit, "Akrah Isra'il" (I hate Israel), released in fall 2000. Against an indomitable dance beat, Sha'ban belts out lines like:

> I hate Israel, and will say so if asked
> God willing, I'll be killed for it or thrown in prison . . .
> I hate Israel, and I hate Ehud Barak
> Because he's got no sense of humor and everyone hates him.

When the song first came out, the Israeli ambassador officially complained to the Egyptian government, creating a minor diplomatic crisis. Most critics have interpreted the song's text as an unambiguous declaration that resonates with popular Egyptian opposition to Israel's policies toward the Palestinians. Likewise, Egyptian critics, especially leftists, sought to claim Sha'ban as a voice of popular opposition, expressing in direct and simple phrases the natural solidarity between Egyptians and Palestinians. Yet, further consideration of the song in light of Sha'ban's notorious career suggests that its rhetoric may not be so simple.

The words that most offended Israel's ambassador, and bluntly indicated Sha'ban's oppositional views, were those of the title and its repeated refrain: "I hate Israel." However, the emphatic words originated not with the performer or his lyricist, who had titled the song "I Don't Like Israel," but with the state censor, Madkour Thabet, who changed the title to "I Hate Israel" to better reflect "the state of people's feelings."[22] Likewise, Sha'ban was reportedly encouraged to balance his attacks on Israeli leaders with praise for the Mubarak regime. Thus, "I Hate Israel" includes lines such as:

I love Hosni Mubarak because his heart is so big
He weighs every step he takes with his conscience . . .
I love 'Amr Moussa, his thinking is judicious . . .
I love Yasser Arafat, he's the dearest one to me.

Sha'ban's energetic praise for Mubarak and Egypt's foreign minister 'Amr Moussa begs the first question of panegyric verse: Is the singer sincere? Here, the character of the poet is an important context for evaluating his sincerity, and Sha'ban's reputation is one that undermines any such claim, for he has always bragged about his drug use, lack of education, and rough and thuggish lifestyle.[23]

Only months before "I Hate Israel," Sha'ban released another hit, "Habattal al-sigayyir" (I'm going to quit smoking), which appears to embrace a message of middle-class morality and to decry the ills of carousing:

I'm going to quit smoking, and become a new person
On January 1, it's over! I'm going to start working out . . .
I'm going to chew king-size seeds, and drink my tea light
I'm going to go down to the market and buy a clean new shirt.

Barely able to stop from laughing as he sings, Sha'ban goes on to list the various ways he is going to straighten out. Although he does mention the health dangers associated with smoking, his noble intentions are put into doubt by his playful delivery. And, as he sings about relaxing on the grass ("al-hashish"), it is clear that the "grass" to which he refers may not be so innocent. The message of this text is certainly at odds with the surface of the word. It is hard to imagine that listeners, hearing the hyperbolic lyrics and his comic delivery, thought that Sha'ban actually meant to change his life to suit in accordance with mainstream norms. Quite the opposite: the song itself, by mimicking those values to such exaggeration, holds them up to ridicule.

What about Sha'ban's praise for Mubarak's regime in "I Hate Israel"? Despite (or because of) his hyperbolic rhetoric, no one would argue that his music voices an official position. Sha'ban remains barred from state radio and television on the grounds of his "vulgarity." The parliamentary media committee chair declared: "Sha'ban does not represent any artistic or cultural value. In addition, his weird attire, which is far from good taste, affects our youth who are influenced by what they see on television."[24] But do Sha'ban's exclusion from state media and the mass popularity of his tapes make him an oppositional figure? Again, the answer seems ambigu-

ous.[25] But even then, no one could credibly argue that Sha'ban himself ad-
heres to any line of solidarity with the Palestinian uprising, for, as he made
clear in interviews, the motivation for his song had to do with business, not
politics: "I'm really happy that our politicians feel it's so important to talk
about a simple man like me. These people say that I'm a rough man. But
who cares? Every time they talk about me, I sell more records."[26] Meanwhile, in 2001, as thousands of Egyptians began to boycott U.S. corporations that do business with Israel, Sha'ban was hired by McDonald's to sing
a jingle about their new McFalafel sandwiches: "If you eat one bite, you
can't stop before finishing the whole roll."[27] Sha'ban was fired shortly thereafter, when the American Jewish Committee pressured the company to
drop him. This nexus of state censorial management, commercial appeal,
and oppositional posturing that helped to produce and broadcast Sha'ban's
supposedly straightforward anti-Israeli pop hit illustrates the ambiguity
that stands at the heart of Egypt's pop culture of solidarity with Palestine.[28]

Myth and Solidarity

Solidarity is not discovered by reflection, but created. — RICHARD RORTY, *Contingency,
Irony, Solidarity*

Solidarity does not include unqualified support . . . rather it excludes unqualified support. — AGNES HELLER AND FERENC FEHÉR, "Citizen Ethics and Civic Virtues"

Given the ambiguity of Egyptian pop Intifadiana, it is difficult to say what
sort of solidarity politics it enables. Moreover, the implicit politics of pop
solidarity diverge strongly from the oppositional politics of Egypt's anti-
normalization movement. Antinormalization, at least at its high point in
the 1980s, foregrounded images of collective action and historical narratives of opposition.[29] Far from being part of the mainstream of commercial culture institutions and the state media, antinormalization discourse critiqued them from outside. The rhetoric of today's pop Intifadiana,
by contrast, tends to highlight—mythologize—the actions of individuals
motivated by spontaneous, eruptive feelings rather than historical understandings.

The narrative structures of sentimentality and redemption constitute
the bulk of the messages offered by the pop culture of solidarity, and the
myth of the Palestinian uprising they construct is a problematic one. In

the pop myth of the *sentimental* Intifada, Palestinians appear as innocent victims, passive recipients of Israeli barbarism. Palestinians occupy one of the positions offered by the al-Durra image: the dying child or the grieving parent. In pointing out that such images form the basis for a familiar, generic narrative of innocence, I am not suggesting that they do not reflect actual and sadly common occurrences. Rather, I am drawing attention to how they construct a particular narrative, one in which Palestinians appear as objects of Israeli history rather than subjects of their own history. Alongside sentimentalism operates the other central myth, the Intifada as *redemption*. This narrative focuses on the heroic images of armed militants and the iconography of martyrs, both unintentional (like al-Durra) and intentional (suicide bombers). Whereas the sentimental narrative tells a story of passivity, the redemptive one articulates a particular sense of Palestinian agency. The first narrative highlights the dispossession and violation of Palestine, the second, its recovery through exceptional acts of violence and sacrifice. Again, such acts are indisputably a part of contemporary Palestinian experience. Nonetheless, Palestinian intellectuals have criticized the mythologization of martyrdom actions.[30] For instance, filmmaker Sobhi al-Zobaidi has pointed out that the glorification of the Palestinian martyr leaves little space for collective action.[31] Moreover, this narrative privileges violence over other important means (boycotts, peaceful demonstrations, steadfast refusal to leave) by which Palestinians resist the occupation. Such narratives elevate the singular over the collective, the heroic over the mundane, and privilege spectacular forms of resistance over others.

As I have been arguing, these pop Intifadiana texts share the tendency to present images as natural and transparent, as inherent truths rather than as figures deliberately created and juxtaposed. Such images circulate not so much to exemplify or symbolize, but to *be* the victimization of the Palestinians living under military occupation. As myth, where "things appear to mean something by themselves," the images presented by Egyptian pop solidarity appear as facts.[32] Rhetorical analysis shows that not only do these texts actively work to construct narratives, but they do so in a way that consistently disavows this agency. I have been arguing that it is the disavowed presentation of sentimental (or pathetic, or redemptive) images as natural, transparent truth that constitutes the mythical quality of Egyptian pop solidarity discourse. But this argument begs a series of questions: What might other, less mythological solidarity politics look like? What kind of solidarity politics might be enabled by a practice of representation that did not seek to disavow the agency of mediation but to own it? Finally, might not rhetorical construction be seen as a form of agency, one that was not at odds with, but rather a constitutive part of political solidarity?

These questions appear all the more urgent given their strong resonance with the critical literature on solidarity, whose recurring argument is whether this state is natural or willed, and whether it is based on an assertion of shared identity or one of difference. In contemporary philosophical and sociological literature, there is a rough consensus that political solidarity is not a relationship of natural unity, nor does it reflect a shared identity. Anthony Giddens, for whom political solidarity implies reciprocal obligation, ties the concept of solidarity to Durkheim's observation about modern shifts from "community" (received social bodies) to "association" (actively constructed social organizations).[33] For his part, Jürgen Habermas associates solidarity with a Sartrean notion of "commitment," that is, a willed, active engagement.[34] The question of solidarity has had an especially central place in the work of Richard Rorty, who has developed it along antiessentialist, anti-identitarian lines. Solidarity, he writes, "is not thought of as recognition of a core self, the human essence, in all human beings. Rather, it is thought of as the ability to see more and more traditional differences as unimportant when compared to similarities with respect to pain and humiliation—the ability to think of people wildly different from ourselves as included in the range of us."[35] In Rorty's "liberal ironist" conception, solidarity is made, not given; moreover, it is a dialectical process, where any sense of "we" moves to consideration of "them." Michael A. Principe has further developed this active sense of political solidarity, stressing that rather than being associated with shared identities, solidarity is precisely a mode for thinking through coalition based on difference. His argument begins with the observation that some concepts (such as Rorty's) privilege the notion of "being in solidarity" over "acting in solidarity." Drawing on a Sartrean concept of responsibility, Principe overturns the notion that solidarity is primarily concerned with commonality, a notion he associates with the term "being." For him "acting in solidarity" stresses that solidarity is not about the assertion of shared identity, but is the ability of different groups to act in alliance: "[An] advantage of this theorization of the relationship of solidarity to responsibility is that it makes much more sense of how we can stand in solidarity with those that are unlike us. It seems important that we be able to act in solidarity with those that are at least in some important senses not 'one of us.' "[36]

It may seem abrupt to bring this literature to bear on the texts of Egyptian pop Intifadiana, but this juxtaposition does reveal one of its mythical assumptions: that Egyptian solidarity with Palestine is natural and based on an implied identity shared by Egyptians and Palestinians. The fact that terms (such as obligation, responsibility, dialectical relationship) associated with this critical tradition of theorizing solidarity are notably absent from the texts of pop solidarity further underscores the problematic nature of Egyptian solidarity myths.[37]

There is a small body of aesthetic works that take solidarity with the Palestinian liberation movement as their theme and root their articulation of solidarity in a critical reflection on the media through which such representations occur.[38] Perhaps no filmic text better embodies these insights than *Ici et ailleurs* (Here and elsewhere). In spring 1970, Jean-Luc Godard's collaborators, Anne-Marie Mieville and Jean-Pierre Gorin, traveled to Jordan to shoot a film not just about the Palestinian resistance movement but in solidarity with it. Commissioned by the PLO and the Arab League, Mieville and Gorin shot some of the most interesting footage extant about this phase of the Palestinian struggle. In accordance with the original producers, the footage was initially organized under five slogans of the Palestinian resistance: "The Will of the People," "The Armed Struggle," "Political Work," "The Prolonged Struggle," and "Until Victory." Had the September 1970 events not intervened, this might have turned out to be a straightforward propaganda film, a myth of solidarity par excellence. However, after the September slaughter of thousands of Palestinians by the Jordanian army, this unedited footage took on new significance. Many of the fedayeen who had been filmed were now dead, and so was the guerrilla movement in Jordan. *Ici et ailleurs* did not appear for another four years, by which time the fedayi image of Palestinian liberation had been eclipsed by images of Palestinian terrorists whose name, Black September, commemorated the death of armed resistance from Jordan and inaugurated another, increasingly media-focused strategy of struggle.

When the revised film appeared in 1974, the images of the murdered revolution had been reassembled so as to reflect critically on the formal problems of political and aesthetic representation. Using the very elements of mythmaking—from the five slogans to cliché images of Palestinians in armed struggle—Godard's film presents a solidaristic text that simultaneously asserts and deconstructs its gesture of solidarity. The form of solidarity that *Ici et ailleurs* articulates is one that constantly problematizes itself by embedding its message in a critical analysis of the conditions of its own rhetorical construction. At no time does Godard's assertion of solidarity appear taken for granted, natural. Indeed, much of what the film has to say—about the vanguardism of Palestinian leadership, the European and Palestinian fetishization of revolution, or even the gesture of making political film—is critical to the point where it is easier to see how it diverges from, rather than allies itself with, those people and projects it depicts. But this very difference is a marker of the unique kind of solidarity it has to offer.

Ici et ailleurs presents a systematic lesson in the rhetoric of cinematic texts. It begins by considering molecular units of the cinematic medium, still photographs, commenting on the new meanings created when two images are juxtaposed next to one another. Thus, the presentation of an image of Hitler next to Lenin begins to imply a troubling association, if not equation between Nazism and Sovietism. Later, when images of Kissinger and Moshe Dayan are added, these associations widen to include U.S. power and Zionism. The film then reflects on the metaphoric play of montage, the quick replacement of one image by another that creates the illusion of the moving picture. Next, the film didactically shows how sound creates and intensifies the meanings at play on the visual register. Finally, *Ici et ailleurs* adds voice-over commentary that at times overscores and at times undermines the audiovisual text of the film. At each level, *Ici et ailleurs* is concerned with how meaning is created by the juxtaposition and substitution (through editing) of different texts: whether it is one image placed next to another in a single frame, images that replace one another sequentially through montage, or a sound placed next to an image, and so on.

To a large extent, it is the flexibility and precision of the film's framing pair of metaphors, *here* and *there*, that allows it to explore so thoroughly a range of issues around the filmic medium. The film reflects on the play of signification in these terms: *here* stands in for the images (or sounds) presented, and *there* becomes the meaning created by their juxtaposition and montage. At times, one sense of *here* in the film is associated with the material signifiers (images, sounds) of the text, while *there* is associated with the signifieds (such as those created by the startling associations of images). But, even as the film creates associations (such as those between Nazism, Sovietism, Americanism, and Zionism), it does so in a way that deliberately avoids positing identities between signifiers and signifieds. At no point does the film explicitly draw an equation between Hitler, Kissinger, and Dayan, though the suggestion is quite strong. The very instability and contingency of these significations is signaled by the terms *here* and *there*, terms that, we should remember, point only to a shifting relationship and never an actual place.

Ici et ailleurs also interrogates the relationship of the photographic image and the material thing it purports to represent. In this way, *here* again signals to the filmic text's signifiers, and *there* indicates the referents they depict. Again, the metaphors suggest that this relationship between signifier and referent is one of radical difference. Indeed, any notion of an identity between Godard's images of Palestinian revolution and actual Palestinian revolution is made tenuous by the fact that the 1970 image depicted something that no longer existed in 1974. In this sense, Godard's images of revolution eclipsed the movement. The film thus radically reconsiders what is sometimes assumed to be the most natural meaning of the photographic image: its capacity to record. Godard's critical engagement with the filmic medium underscores the fact that it is not an index of an existing referent, but the index of an absent referent. Indeed, rather than suggesting a sense of *here*, the filmic signifiers of the text suggest something else, an *elsewhere*.[39] In this way, *Ici et ailleurs* insists on a relationship with its putative object of study—Palestinian revolution—that stresses critical difference rather than mimetic identity.

It is at this moment that Godard's critique of representational *politics* begins to show itself. Rather than assume identities, whether between signifiers and signifieds or between signifiers and referents, Godard reflects on the formal means by which the filmic medium poses such identities in the first place. The film suggests that such assertions are the effect of substitutions: the signified that replaces the signifier, the signifier that replaces the referent. For Godard, this act of substitution is at the heart of mythical forms of solidarity; indeed, what *Ici et ailleurs* suggests is that the solidaristic text that presents images of others' struggles as if they were natural and transparent (as if they were noninterpretative, as if they were facts) is to replace actual struggle with its image, to replace a movement with representations. This act of substitution is, for Godard, an act of violence.

But this act of violence is more than an issue of the filmic medium, for the substitutive logic of the mythical form of aesthetic representation is also that of vanguardist forms of political representation. One of the many senses of *here* and *there* developed in *Ici et ailleurs* is the distance between the vanguardist leader/film director and the movement/image of his creation. Like realist cinema, the ideology of vanguardism disavows any distance between here/there, image/revolution, party/people. This disavowal is crucial if the second term, the created figure, the text is to take on a life that appears to be independent of the author. Godard's critique shows that this blurring serves to hide the first terms (here, image, party, author), while also privileging them over the second terms (there, revolution, people, text). In this vein, *Ici et ailleurs* returns often to the staged quality of the relationship between leaders who speak on behalf of the Palestinian movement and the people in the movement who are spoken for. At one point in the film, a young Palestinian woman speaks to the camera in an apparently unscripted moment about her aspirations for the revolution. Later, the film replays this footage, though this time there is a woman's voice-over revealing that the moment has been scripted by the director: not only is the spokeswoman not who she first seemed to be, but we are told that her words were fed to her by a director who stands off-camera. This standing off-camera constitutes the mythical disavowal of political vanguardism and its central problematic: the image and the party become (and *stand in for*) the revolution and the people; it effectively speaks for the movement while admitting only to an act of speaking about.[40] As such, the discourse of vanguardism proposes a language of presence and transparency, while its grammar functions in terms of proxy and replacement. *Here* becomes *there* by means of a series of equations and proxy substitutions, a technique the film associates explicitly with fascism. Godard's aesthetic strategy is to put these rhetorical structures back into the frame of the film so as to denaturalize the kind of ventriloquism that drives actors, whether they act in film or in political movements. In Barthesian terms, *Ici et ailleurs* presents both the myth of the solidarity (vanguardist) text and its deconstruction.

But, as the film asserts, the move to deconstruct is not opposed to the gesture of solidarity. That is because the other sense of *here* and *there* developed in *Ici et ailleurs* quite explicitly critiques what it takes to be empty forms of solidarity. Throughout the film, images of Palestinians in struggle are contrasted with images of a bourgeois family (including the filmmakers) involved in the mundane rituals of commodity culture, from eating dinner to watching television. The juxtaposition is startling and suggests that if there is solidarity between the French middle class and Palestinians in revolt, it is neither dialectical nor one of mutual obligation. It is the utter failure to *act* in solidarity with Palestinians that shows the emptiness of the claim to *be* in solidarity. Coming in the wake of 1968, some of the text's sharpest barbs are directed at the failures of revolution in France, or, in the terms of the film, revolution *here*. When a voice-over repeats the enigmatic statement "Pauvre revolutionaire: millionaire des images," it addresses the status of the image that third world revolution came to have in small circles of French intellectual life following 1968.[41] In so doing, it poses uncomfortable questions about solidarity politics that turn first world intellectuals toward third world struggles and that make the term "Palestine" synonymous with "revolution" and "elsewhere," where revolution *over there* might serve as a consolation for the failure, or postponement, of revolution *here*.

It is this last point that contains some of the most profound critiques for rethinking the sort of solidarity politics offered by Egyptian pop Intifadiana. In the text of *Ici et ailleurs*, the failures of the PLO in the 1970s are ascribed not just to mythical forms of propagandistic culture and to problems in the representational politics of vanguardism, but also to the place of solidarity in the field of revolutionary political practice. Importantly, Godard's critique of these failures is offered sympathetically—not to denounce the political struggle of Palestinians, but to learn from it. No less important, especially for the concept of solidarity, Godard associates these issues formally and materially with radical French politics in the late 1960s: the critique of the rhetorical structures of Palestinian struggle is brought to bear on the politics of the French left as well. In this vein, Godard argues that solidarity with others elsewhere may be a slogan raised by militants unable (or unwilling) to engage in meaningful revolutionary action in their own local contexts. As *Ici et ailleurs* suggests, the rhetorical drawing together of divergent struggles may be the condition of solidarity politics, but such a politics always rubs up against the mythical sort of image critiqued in the film. Such an image may serve to replace the revolution that it purports to depict *there*, and also the revolution that needs to take place *here*, whether that place refers to Amman, Paris, Cairo or even to the place from which I am writing, Providence.

Notes

1. Produced and aired on satellite channels in 1998, the song features singers from around the Arab world (except Iraq) with a special emphasis on Gulf stars. Performers sing in their own national dialect of Arabic, enacting a tableau of unity-through-variation that stands in stark contrast to the actuality of inter-Arab politics during this period. For a critique of the song, its lyrics, and history, see Joseph Massad, "Liberating Songs: Palestine Put to Music," *Journal of Palestine Studies* 32, no. 3 (spring 2003): 21–38, and in this volume.

2. Others include 'Amr Diab's "Jerusalem" and Walid Tawfiq's "Cry of the Stone."

3. See Lila Abu-Lughod, "The Objects of Soap Opera: Egyptian Television and

the Cultural Politics of Modernity," *Worlds Apart: Modernity through the Prism of the Local*, edited by Daniel Miller (London: Routledge, 1995), 190–210. On melodrama in Egyptian cinema, see Yves Thoraval, *Regards sur le cinéma égyptien 1895–1975* (Paris: L'Harmattan, 1996), 21–78; Viola Shafik, *Arab Cinema: History and Cultural Identity* (Cairo: American University in Cairo Press, 1998), 128–143.

4. Barthes invokes the word "myth" to describe the semiological process involved in the transformation of values into fact, or of figurative language (which is rhetorical and value-laden) into language that is said to be transparent, literal, and value-free. The point is not to deny the possibility of truth claims generally, but to explore a specific kind of truth claim that poses itself as nonrhetorical. See *Mythologies*, translated by Annette Lavers (New York: Hill and Wang, 1972), 130. For Barthes, one of the most seamless forms of myth was "the fact," a statement that, in modern society, has come to have the highest form of authority precisely because it is a sort of description that is ostensibly free of interpretation, value, and rhetoric. For a more recent consideration of the rhetorical figure of the fact, see Mary Poovey, *A History of the Modern Fact: Problems of Knowledge in the Sciences of Wealth and Society* (Chicago: University of Chicago Press, 1998). Barthes's link between myth and nature is provocative: "What the world supplies to myth is an historical reality . . . what myth gives in return is a natural image of this reality . . . A conjuring trick has taken place; it has turned reality inside out, it has emptied it of history and has filled it with nature" (*Mythologies*, 142).

5. For the sake of clarity, I draw a distinction between the commercial, Egyptian pop culture of solidarity with Palestine (which is the subject of this essay) and other, more activist-based forms of Egyptian political solidarity with Palestinians. Indeed, the depth of oppositional solidarity practices among Egyptian leftists and Islamists has been profound at times; importantly, its tones both jibe and conflict with the account of pop culture solidarity I am presenting here.

6. See Jon Anderson, "The Internet and Islam's New Interpreters," in *New Media in the Muslim World: The Emerging Public Sphere*, edited by Dale Eickelman and Jon Anderson (Bloomington: Indiana University Press, 1999), 41–56; Dale F. Eickelman, "Communication and Control in the Middle East: Publication and Its Discontents," in *New Media in the Muslim World*, edited by Eickelman and Anderson, 29–40.

7. See Katherine E. Zirbel, "Playing It Both Ways: Local Egyptian Performers between Regional Identity and International Markets," in *Mass Mediations: New Approaches to Popular Culture in the Middle East and Beyond*, edited by Walter Armbrust (Berkeley: University of California Press, 2000), 120–145; Walter Armbrust, *Mass Culture and Modernism in Egypt* (Cambridge, England: Cambridge University Press, 1996), especially the chapter entitled "Popular Commentary, Real Lives," 116–164.

8. See, for example, Virginia Danielson's careful attention to the rhetoric of musical performance—stress, repetition, and embellishment—in *The Voice of Egypt: Umm Kulthum, Arabic Song, and Egyptian Society in the Twentieth Century* (Chicago: University of Chicago Press, 1997); Ted Swedenburg on the multiple, divergent meanings created by transgender performance, "Saida Sultan/Danna International: Transgender Pop and the Polysemiotics of Sex, Nation, and Ethnicity on the Israeli-Egyptian Border," in *Mass Mediations: New Approaches to Popular Culture in the Middle East and Beyond*, edited by Walter Armbrust (Berkeley: University of California Press,

2000), 88–119; Marilyn Booth, on the unstable rhetoric of irony in the early twentieth-century literature, *Bayram al-Tunisi's Egypt: Social Criticism and Narrative Strategies* (Oxford: Ithaca Press, 1990); Walter Armbrust's close reading of *Ghazal al-binat* in "The Golden Age before the Golden Age," in *Mass Mediations*, edited by Armbrust, 292–327; Allen Douglas and Fedwa Malti-Douglas on the formal qualities of cartoon genres, *Arab Comic Strips: Politics of an Emerging Mass Culture* (Bloomington: Indiana University Press, 1994); and Lila Abu-Lughod's delicate reading of the ambiguities at play in colloquial poetry, *Veiled Sentiments: Honor and Poetry in a Bedouin Society* (Berkeley: University of California Press, 1986).

9. A welcome exception to this is Ibrahim Fawal, *Youssef Chahine* (London: British Film Institute, 2001).

10. On *asala* and the recurring figure of *ibn al-balad*, see Armbrust, *Mass Culture and Modernism in Egypt*, 25–7 and Jessica Winegar, "Claiming Egypt: The Cultural Politics of Artistic Practice in a Postcolonial Society," PhD diss., New York University, 2003, 148–161. On social realism in Egyptian cinema, see Thoraval, *Regards sur le cinéma égyptien 1895–1975*, 21–78; Shafik, *Arab Cinema*, 128–143.

11. Shafik, *Arab Cinema*, 211, 212.

12. Additionally, as Hosam Aboul-Ela has argued, Isma'il Yasin's classic comedies, especially his parodies of popular films (such as *Isma'il yuqabil Raya wa-Sakina* [Isma'il meets Raya and Sakina]), thrive on exposing the rhetorical quality of categories like identity and authenticity on the levels of both narrative and image, and throw them into confusion ("Subverting the Dominant Paradigm: Ismail Yaseen and the Picaresque Hero in Egyptian Cinema," paper delivered at the Middle East Studies Association annual meeting, San Francisco, November 2001).

13. See Ien Ang, *Watching Dallas: Soap Opera and the Melodramatic Imagination* (New York: Routledge, 1989), and Lila Abu-Lughod, "Finding a Place for Islam: Egyptian Television Serials and the National Interest," *Public Culture* 5 (1993): 493–513, and "The Objects of Soap Opera," 190–210.

14. Armbrust, *Mass Culture and Modernism in Egypt*, 196–197.

15. Roland Barthes, "The Old Rhetoric: An Aide-mémoire," in *The Semiotic Challenge*, translated by Richard Howard (New York: Hill and Wang, 1988), 11–93. "Figure" derives from the Latin *figura*, meaning "the made" or "the composed." In the long history of the study of rhetoric, it has most often been paired with (and opposed to) the term "trope," from the Greek *tropein*, meaning "to turn," or "to swerve." Since Quintilian, rhetoricians have defined these terms in different ways, though most often the definitions have sought to distinguish "figurative language" from "normal language." Metaphor, metonymy, and synedoche are just three examples of figures whose meanings are said to diverge from "normal," "proper," or "literal" uses of language. Since Aristotle, the philosophical study of rhetoric has been motivated by a desire to divide reason and logic (which is associated with language assumed to be plain, transparent, unadorned, and nonfigurative) from poetry and eloquence (associated with "turn of phrase," or trope, and "composition," or figure). One of the chief accomplishments of poststructuralist thought has been to show that these divisions between reason and rhetoric (and between normal and figurative language) are arbitrary and untenable. For a lucid summary, see "Figure, Scheme, Trope," in T. V. F. Brogan, ed., *The New*

Princeton Handbook of Poetic Terms (Princeton: Princeton University Press, 1994), 90–93.

16. See Mustapha K. El-Sayed, "Egyptian Popular Attitudes toward the Palestinians Since 1977," *Journal of Palestine Studies* 18, no. 4 (summer 1989): 37–51; Karem Yehia, "The Image of the Palestinians in Egypt, 1982–85," *Journal of Palestine Studies* 16, no. 2 (winter 1987): 45–63, and "All Our Destinies," *Al-Ahram Weekly*, July 4–10, 2002. On the discourse of antinormalization and the new forms of solidarity politics in Egypt, see my "Solidarity in the Time of Anti-Normalization: Egypt Responds to the Intifada," *Middle East Report* 224 (fall 2002): 10–15.

17. In the Arab world and elsewhere, there was little debate about the truth of the image. However, in the United States, many aspects of the image's truth were disputed in the mainstream press: quoting Israeli army spokesmen, the *New York Times* first implied that Muhammad al-Durra had been killed by Palestinian rather than Israeli bullets, then later acknowledged that while he may have been struck by Israeli fire, it happened during a cross-fire with Palestinian gunmen. Other commentators in Israel and the United States asserted that al-Durra's father bore primary responsibility for bringing the boy to such a dangerous place. Still others argued that Palestinian militants, when they realized the political capital to be gained from such an image, moved so as to draw Israeli fire toward the father and son. Two and a half years after the event, James Fallows has summarized the history of the ideological struggle for control over the image, giving special privilege to the scientific exactitude of Israeli accounts while describing Palestinian accounts as rhetorical and mythological. Despite the logical incoherences of its "radical indeterminacy" assertions, Fallows's essay asserts that (1) it was probably not an Israeli bullet that killed him; (2) al-Durra was perhaps not even killed; (3) his death was staged by Palestinians to make myth; and (4) we will never know definitively because "the case will remain in the uncomfortable realm of events that cannot be fully explained or understood." James Fallows, "Who Shot Mohammed al-Durra?", *Atlantic Monthly*, June 2003.

18. In this sense, al-Durra's image resonates with Barthes's analysis of the image of the convict Lewis Payne on the eve of his execution. In his discussion, Barthes describes the disconcerting fact that the photograph records not just the image of someone who is dead, but also someone who is going to die. Roland Barthes, *Camera Lucida: Reflections on Photography*, translated by Richard Howard (New York: Hill and Wang, 1981), 94–97. Barthes's curiosity, even skepticism, about the recording capacity of the photographic image shows that even what appears to be the most transparent aspect of the most "non-figurative" of expressive mediums exceeds itself.

19. From Sha'ban 'Abd al-Rahim's cassette "al-Karh shay' qalil, ya Isra'il!" [Hate is a small thing, Israel], Cairo, al-Wadi li-l-intaj, 2002.

20. Quoted in "Intifada Becomes Theme of Egyptian Films, Songs, Art," *Middle East Times*, September 26, 2001.

21. Jonathan Goldberg, *Sodometries* (Stanford: Stanford University Press, 1992), 4.

22. Andrew Hammond, "When Israel Talks, Cairo Listens," *Washington Report on Middle East Affairs*, September 1, 2001.

23. Tarek Atia, "Shaaban," *Al-Ahram Weekly*, January 18–24, 2001.

24. Quoted in *Christian Science Monitor*, January 18, 2002.

25. The influential literary journal *Akhbar al-Adab* debated whether to compare Sha'ban to Shaykh Imam, whose populist songs inspired an earlier generation of leftist activists: "There is another culture that we don't know anything about, and that is the culture of the lower classes . . . It is a culture marginalized by resentment and arrogance from the cultural elite." Quoted in Hammond, "When Israel Talks, Cairo Listens." On Shaykh Imam, see Kamal Abdel-Malek, *A Study of the Vernacular Poetry of Ahmad Fu'ad Nigm* (Leiden: E.J. Brill, 1990).

26. Quoted in *Christian Science Monitor*, January 18, 2002.

27. Associated Press, June 16, 2001.

28. See Joel Gordon, "Singing the Pulse of the Egyptian-Arab Street: Shaaban Abd al-Rahim and the Geo-Pop-Politics of Fast Food," *Popular Music* 22, no. 1 (2003): 75–90.

29. See, for example, *Samidun* (Standing fast), a magazine published by university staff members in the National Committee for Solidarity with the Palestinian and Lebanese People in 1983–1984; *al-Muwajiha* (Confrontation), published by the Committee for Defense of National Culture during the 1980s. On antinormalization cultural politics, see Barbara Harlow, "*Mismar Goha*: The Arab Challenge to Cultural Dependency," *South Atlantic Quarterly* 87, no. 1 (winter 1988): 109–129.

30. On the debates about the discourse of martyrdom in Palestine, see Lori Allen, "There Are Many Reasons Why: Suicide Bombers and Martyrs in Israel," *Middle East Report* 223 (summer 2002): 34–37.

31. See Sobhi al-Zobaidi's remarkable video diary of life under occupation, *Crossing Kalandia* (Tel Aviv: FPAD, 2002). See also Rema Hammami, "Interregnum: Palestine after Operation Defensive Shield," *Middle East Report* 223 (summer 2002): 18–27.

32. Barthes, *Mythologies*, 143.

33. Anthony Giddens, *Beyond Left and Right: The Future of Radical Politics* (Stanford: Stanford University Press, 1994), 124.

34. Jürgen Habermas, *Autonomy and Solidarity: Interviews with Jürgen Habermas*, edited by Peter Dews (New York: Verso Press, 1992), 60–61.

35. Richard Rorty, *Contingency, Irony, Solidarity* (Cambridge, England: Cambridge University Press, 1989), 192.

36. Michael A. Principe, "Solidarity and Responsibility: Conceptual Connections," *Journal of Social Philosophy* 31, no. 2 (summer 2000): 143–144.

37. Importantly, a few pop Intifadiana texts do attempt to express solidarity with the Palestinian struggle by reflecting on their own rhetorical figures and their media of expression, and do assert a difference (rather than natural identity) between Egyptians and Palestinians. For instance, the popular Egyptian film *Ashab walla biznis* (Friends or business) uses the Palestinian Intifada to present a moral lesson about the Egyptian mass media. *Ashab Walla Biznis* (video, Al-Duqqi: al-Sibka Vidiyufilm, 2002, directed by 'Ali Idris) presents solidarity between Egyptians and Palestinians as a relationship learned and made (rather than naturally assumed); it underscores the different and divergent roles played by Egyptians and Palestinians working in solidarity with one another; and it includes a formal consideration of its medium within the frame of its representation and suggests that representation is a constitutive act (rather than window onto) acts of political solidarity.

38. A short list of works in this vein would have to include Elias Khoury, *Bab al-Shams* (Beirut: Dar al-Adab, 1999) and Jean Genet, *Un captif amoreux* (Paris: Gallimard, 1986).

39. Here, Godard's exploration of the medium resonates with Barthes's discussion of death and the photograph in *Camera Lucida* and André Bazin's discussion of the photographic image as a process of mummification in "The Ontology of the Photographic Image," *What Is Cinema?* (Berkeley: University of California Press, 1967), 9–16.

40. The phrasing is from Gayatri Spivak, *A Critique of Postcolonial Reason: Toward a History of the Vanishing Present* (Cambridge, Mass.: Harvard University Press, 1999), 258–259.

41. It is significant to note how exceptional the solidaristic gestures of Godard and Genet were in the context of progressive French intellectual circles that have been traditionally unsympathetic to Palestine. See Joseph Massad, "The Legacy of Jean-Paul Sartre," *al-Ahram Weekly* 623, January 30–February 5, 2003; and Adam Shatz, *Prophets Outcast: A Century of Dissident Jewish Writing about Zionism and Israel* (New York: Nation Books, 2004).

BIBLIOGRAPHY

Publications

'Abaza, al-Amir. "Halamtu bi-al-Qahira . . . wa-lam ufakkir fi ja'izatiha al-dhahabiya!" [I dreamed of Cairo . . . but I never imagined first prize!]. Interview with Rashid Masharawi. *Al-Kawakib*, December 21, 1993, 13.

'Abd al-Amir, 'Ali. "Ughniyat 'al Masih' li-Awwal Marra 'ala Istiwana li-'Abd al-Halim Hafiz" (The song "al Masih" appeared for the first time on a record of 'Abd al-Halim Hafiz). *Al-Ra'y* (Jordan), March 30, 1999.

Abdel-Malek, Kamal. *A Study of the Vernacular Poetry of Ahmad Fu'ad Nigm*. Leiden: E.J. Brill, 1990.

Abou-Ela, Hosam. "Subverting the Dominant Paradigm: Ismail Yaseen and the Picaresque Hero in Egyptian Cinema." Paper delivered at the Middle East Studies Association annual meeting, San Francisco, November 2001.

Abu El-Haj, Nadia. *Facts on the Ground: Archaeological Practice and Territorial Self-Fashioning in Israeli Society*. Chicago: University of Chicago Press, 2001.

Abu-Lughod, Lila. "Bedouins, Cassettes and Technologies of Public Culture." *Middle East Report* 159 (July–August 1989): 7–11.

———. "Finding a Place for Islam: Egyptian Television Serials and the National Interest." *Public Culture* 5 (1993): 493–513.

———. "The Objects of Soap Opera: Egyptian Television and the Cultural Politics of Modernity." In *Worlds Apart: Modernity through the Prism of the Local*, edited by Daniel Miller. London: Routledge, 1995.

———. *Veiled Sentiments: Honor and Poetry in a Bedouin Society*. Berkeley: University of California Press, 1986.

———, ed. *Remaking Women: Feminism and Modernity in the Middle East*. Princeton: Princeton University Press, 1998.

Abu-Tuma, Khalid. "Iton beyarden: Hatayarim hayisraelim qamtzamim veokhlim raq falafel" [Newspaper in Jordan: The Israeli tourists are stingy and only eat falafel]. *Yerushalayim*, September 8, 1995.

Adorno, Theodor W. *Introduction to the Sociology of Music*. New York: Continuum, 1976.

Ahmida, Ali. *The Making of Modern Libya: State Formation, Colonization, and Resistance, 1830–1932*. Albany: State University of New York Press, 1994.

Air, Eyal Ben, and Yoram Bilu. *Grasping Land: Space and Place in Contemporary Israeli Discourse and Experience*. Albany: State University of New York Press, 1997.

Alacalay, Ammiel. *After Jews and Arabs: Remaking Levantine Culture*. Minneapolis: University of Minnesota Press, 1993.

———. "Israel and the Levant: 'Wounded Kinship's Last Resort.'" *Middle East Report* 159 (July–August 1989): 18–25.

Alcorn, Gay. "Bush Follows His Conservative Heart Back to Israel." *The Age* (Melbourne), April 20, 2002, 5.

Alexander, Livia. "Conflicting Images: Palestinian and Israeli Cinemas, 1988–1998." PhD diss., New York University, 2001.

Alia, Josette. "La France et la culture arabe." *Nouvel Observateur* 1726, December 4, 1997.

Allen, Lori. "There Are Many Reasons Why: Suicide Bombers and Martyrs in Palestine." *Middle East Report* 32, no. 2 (summer 2002): 34–37.

Allouche, Jean-Luc. "Constantine, La Necessaire." In *Les Juifs d'Algérie: Images et Textes*, edited by Jean Laloum and Jean-Luc Allouche. Paris: Éditions du Scribe, 1987.

Almog, Oz. *The Sabra: The Creation of the New Jew*. Berkeley: University of California Press, 2000.

Alpert, Bruce. "Support for Israel Bridges Old Divides." *Times-Picayune* (New Orleans), May 3, 2002, 4.

Ameimour, Mohieddin. "Bouteflika Hit 'Several Birds with One Stone' by Rapping Algerian Journalists over Israeli Trip." *Mideast Mirror* 14, no. 125 (July 3, 2000). [Translated from *Al-sharq al-awsat*.]

Amir, Yirmi. Review of the Cairo International Film Festival. *Yedi'ot Aharonot*, December 9, 1998.

Ammerman, Nancy. "North American Protestant Fundamentalism." In *Media, Culture, and the Religious Right*, edited by Linda Kintz and Julie Lesage. Minneapolis: University of Minnesota Press, 1998.

Anderson, Benedict. "Exodus." *Critical Inquiry* 20, no. 2 (1994): 314–327.

———. *Imagined Communities: Reflections on the Origin and Spread of Nationalism*. London: Verso, 1991.

———. *The Spectre of Comparisons: Nationalism, Southeast Asia and the World*. London: Verso, 1998.

Anderson, Jon. "The Internet and Islam's New Interpreters." In *New Media in the Muslim World: The Emerging Public Sphere*, edited by Dale Eickelman and Jon Anderson. Bloomington: Indiana University Press, 1999.

Ang, Ien. *Watching Dallas: Soap Opera and the Melodramatic Imagination*. New York: Routledge, 1989.

Appadurai, Arjun. "Grassroots Globalization and the Research Imagination." *Public Culture* 12, no. 1 (2000): 1–19.

———. *Modernity at Large: Cultural Dimensions of Globalization*. Minneapolis: University of Minnesota Press, 1996.

Armbrust, Walter. "The Golden Age before the Golden Age." In *Mass Mediations: New Approaches to Popular Culture in the Middle East and Beyond*, edited by Walter Armbrust. Berkeley: University of California Press, 2000.

————. *Mass Culture and Modernism in Egypt*. Cambridge, England: Cambridge University Press, 1996.

————, ed. *Mass Mediations: New Approaches to Popular Culture in the Middle East and Beyond*. Berkeley: University of California Press, 2000.

Aronoff, Myron J. "Myths, Symbols and Rituals of the Emerging State." In *New Perspectives on Israeli History: The Early Years of the State*, edited by Laurence J. Silberstein. New York: New York University Press, 1991.

Aruri, Naseer H. *The Obstruction of Peace: The United States, Israel, and the Palestinians*. Monroe, Maine: Common Courage, 1995.

Ashrawi, Hanan. "The Contemporary Palestinian Poetry of Occupation." *Journal of Palestine Studies* 7, no. 3 (1978): 77–101.

Atia, Tarek. "Shaaban." *Al-Ahram Weekly*, January 18–24, 2001.

Augustin, Ebba, ed. *Palestinian Women: Identity and Experience*. London: Zed Books, 1993.

Avraham, Eli. *Hatiqshoret beyisrael: Siquran shel 'ayarot hapituah* [The media in Israel: Coverage of the development towns]. Tel Aviv: Breirot, 1993.

'Awdat, Husayn al-. *Al-Sinima wa-al-qadiya al-Filastiniya* [Cinema and the Palestinian question]. Damascus: al-Ahali, 1987.

Azoulay, Ariela. "With Open Doors: Museums and History and the Israeli Public Space." *Teoria vebikoret* 4 (1993): 79–96 [in Hebrew].

Badarna, Muhammad. *Yafa: 'Arus al-Bahr* [Jaffa: Bride of the sea]. Jaffa: Rabita Publications, 1997.

Badran, Margot. *Feminists, Islam, and Nation: Gender and the Making of Modern Egypt*. Princeton: Princeton University Press, 1995.

Bahloul, Joelle. "Les Pionniers de Regavim." In *Les Juifs d'Algérie: Images et Textes*, edited by Jean Laloum and Jean-Luc Allouche. Paris: Éditions du Scribe, 1987.

Baily, John. "Cross-cultural Perspectives in Popular Music: The Case of Afghanistan." *Popular Music* 1 (1981): 105–122.

Baker, Houston A., Jr. *Black Studies, Rap, and the Academy*. Chicago: University of Chicago Press, 1993.

Balmer, Randal, and Lauren Winner. *Protestantism in America*. New York: Columbia University Press, 2002.

Bar-Siman-Tov, Yaacov. *Israel and the Peace Process, 1977–1982: In Search of Legitimacy for Peace*. Albany: State University of New York Press, 1994.

Barbour, Nevill. *Nisi Dominus: A Survey of the Palestine Controversy*. Beirut: Institute for Palestine Studies, 1969.

Barghuthi, Murid. *I Saw Ramallah*. Cairo: American University in Cairo Press, 2000.

Barthes, Roland. *Camera Lucida: Reflections on Photography*. Translated by Richard Howard. New York: Hill and Wang, 1981.

————. *Mythologies*. Translated by Annette Lavers. New York: Hill and Wang, 1972.

————. *The Semiotic Challenge*. Translated by Richard Howard. New York: Hill and Wang, 1988.

Basch, Linda, Nina Glick Schiller, and Cristina Szanton Blanc. *Nations Unbound:*

Transnational Projects, Postcolonial Predicaments, and Deterritorialized Nation-States. Langhorne, Penna.: Gordon and Breach, 1994.

Basher, Brenda. *Give Me That Online Religion.* San Francisco: Jossey-Bass, 2001.

Bayly, C. A. *Empire and Information: Intelligence Gathering and Social Communication in India, 1780–1870.* Cambridge, England: Cambridge University Press, 1996.

Bazin, André. "The Ontology of the Photographic Image." In *What Is Cinema?* Berkeley: University of California Press, 1967.

Beinart, Peter. "Bad Move." *The New Republic,* May 20, 2002, 6.

Beinin, Joel. "Intellectual and Political Limits of New Israeli History." Unpublished manuscript. n.d.

———. "Palestine and Israel: Perils of a Neoliberal, Repressive Pax Americana." *Social Justice* 25, no. 4 (1998): 20–39.

———. "2002 Presidential Address: Middle East Studies after September 11, 2001." *Middle East Studies Association Bulletin* 37, no. 1 (2003): 2–18.

———. *Was the Red Flag Flying There? Marxist Politics and the Arab-Israeli Conflict in Egypt and Israel, 1948–1965.* Berkeley: University of California Press, 1990.

Ben Ari, Mordecai. *Peace Tourism Update.* Jerusalem: Israeli Ministry of Tourism, 1996.

Ben-Arieh, Yehoshua. *Jerusalem in the 19th Century.* Vol. 1, *The Old City in Context.* New York: St. Martin's Press, 1984.

Ben Efrat, Yacov. "Close Minded: Changing the Nature of Control." *Challenge* (May–June 1993): 6–7.

Ben Gurion, David. "The Call of Spirit in Israel." In *Rebirth and Destiny of Israel,* edited by David Ben Gurion. New York: Philosophical Library, 1954.

Bennett, Tony. "Introduction: Popular Culture and the 'Turn to Gramsci.'" In *Popular Culture and Social Relations,* edited by Tony Bennett, Colin Mercer, and Janet Woollacott. Milton Keynes, England: Open University Press, 1986.

———. "The Politics of the 'Popular' and Popular Culture." In *Popular Culture and Social Relations,* edited by Tony Bennett, Colin Mercer, and Janet Woollacott. Milton Keynes, England: Open University Press, 1986.

Bennett, Tony, Colin Mercer, and Janet Woollacott, eds. *Popular Culture and Social Relations.* Milton Keynes, England: Open University Press, 1986.

Bennis, Phyllis. *From Stones to Statehood: The Palestinian Uprising.* New York: Olive Branch Press, 1990.

Bennis, Phyllis, Deborah J. Gerner, Steve Niva, and Rebecca Stein. "MERIP Primer on the Uprising in Palestine." MERIP (Middle East Research and Information Project). Available at: http://www.merip.org/new_uprising_primer/primer_intro.html.

Benziman, Uzi. *Sharon: An Israeli Caesar.* New York: Adamas, 1985.

Berger, John. *Ways of Seeing.* London: Penguin, 1973.

Beshara, Azmi. "On the Question of the Palestinian Minority in Israel." *Teoria vebikoret* 3 (1993): 7–21 [in Hebrew].

Bhabha, Homi. *The Location of Culture.* London: Routledge, 1994.

———. "Of Mimicry and Man: The Ambivalence of Colonial Discourse." *October* 28 (spring 1984): 125–133.

————. "Signs Taken for Wonders: Questions of Ambivalence and Authority under a Tree outside Delhi, May 1817." In *Europe and Its Others*, vol. 1, edited by Francis Barker et al. Colchester: University of Essex Press, 1985.

Bisharat, George. *Palestinian Lawyers and Israeli Rule: Law and Disorder in the West Bank*. Austin: University of Texas Press, 1989.

Blackburn, Nicky. "Reaching the Threshold." *Link: Israel's International Business Magazine* (fall 1995): 21.

Blecher, Rob. "Citizens without Sovereignty: Ethnic Cleansing and Transfer in Israel." Forthcoming, *Comparative Studies in Society and History*.

Bohlman, Philip V. "Central European Jews in Israel: The Reurbanization of Musical Life in an Immigrant Culture." *Yearbook for Traditional Music* (1984): 67–82.

Bollenbach, Bertrand. "Concert by Singer for Peace Sparks Mideast Boycott Rumpus." Agence France Presse, November 25, 2000.

Booth, Marilyn. *Bayram al-Tunisi's Egypt: Social Criticism and Narrative Strategies*. Oxford: Ithaca Press, 1990.

Bouakba, Amel. "Beur FM vient au chevet des sinistrés de Bab El Oued." *La Tribune* (Algiers), February 11, 2002. Available at: http://allafrica.com/stories/200202110457.html.

Boullata, Kamal. " 'Asim Abu Shaqra: The Artist's Eye and the Cactus Tree." *Journal of Palestine Studies* 30, no. 4 (summer 2001): 68–82.

————. *Istihdar al-makan: dirasa fi al-fann al-tashkili al-Filastini al-mu'asir* [Conjuring up space: A study of contemporary Palestinian plastic arts]. Tunis: al-Munazzama al-'Arabiya lil-Tarbiya wa-al-Thaqafa wa-al-'Ulum, 2000.

Boullata, Kamal, and Joost Hilterman. "Improvisation and Continuity: The Music of Sabreen." *Middle East Report* 182 (May–June 1993): 32–35.

Boyarin, Jonathan. *Palestine and Jewish History: Criticism at the Borders of Ethnography*. Minneapolis: University of Minnesota Press, 1996.

Boyer, Paul. *When Time Shall Be No More: Prophecy Belief in Modern American Culture*. Cambridge, Mass.: Harvard University Press, 1992.

Brennan, Timothy. *Salman Rushdie and the Third World: Myths of the Nation*. New York: St. Martin's Press, 1989.

Brodkin, Karen. *How Jews Became White Folks and What That Says about Race in America*. New Brunswick, N.J.: Rutgers University Press, 1988.

Brogan, T. V. F., ed. *The New Princeton Handbook of Poetic Terms*. Princeton: Princeton University Press, 1994.

Buell, Frederick. *National Culture and the New Global System*. Baltimore: Johns Hopkins University Press, 1994.

Burckhardt, John Lewis. *Travels in Arabia: Comprehending an Account of Those Territories in Hedjaz Which the Mohammedans Regard as Sacred*. London: Henry Colburn, 1829.

Burke, Timothy. *Lifebuoy Men, Lux Women: Commodification, Consumption and Cleanliness in Modern Zimbabwe*. Durham, N.C.: Duke University Press, 1996.

Butler, Judith. *Bodies That Matter: On the Discursive Limits of "Sex."* New York: Routledge, 1993.

————. *Gender Trouble: Feminism and the Subversion of Identity*. New York: Routledge, 1990.

Cassanelli, Lee V. "Qat: Changes in the Production and Consumption of a Quasi-legal Commodity in Northeast Africa." In *The Social Life of Things: Commodities in Cultural Perspective*, edited by Arjun Appadurai. Cambridge, England: Cambridge University Press, 1986.

Castells, Manuel. *The Internet Galaxy: Reflections on the Internet, Business, and Society*. Oxford: Blackwell, 2001.

————. *The Rise of Network Society*. Vol. 1, *The Information Age: Economy, Society and Culture*. Oxford: Blackwell, 1996.

Castelo-Branco, Salwa El-Shawan. "Some Aspects of the Cassette Industry in Egypt." *The World of Music* (Berlin) 29 (1987): 32–44.

Cattan, Henry. *The Dimensions of the Palestine Problem, 1967*. Beirut: Institute for Palestine Studies, 1968.

Chakravarty, Sumita S. *National Identity in Indian Popular Cinema, 1947–1987*. Austin: University of Texas Press, 1993.

Chappell, David. *A Stone of Hope: Prophetic Religion and the Death of Jim Crow*. Chapel Hill: University of North Carolina Press, 2004.

Cheah, Pheng, and Bruce Robbins, eds. *Cosmopolitics: Thinking and Feeling beyond the Nation*. Minneapolis: University of Minnesota Press, 1998.

Chetrit, Sami Shalom. "Mizrahi Politics in Israel: Between Integration and Alternative." *Journal of Palestine Studies* 29, no. 4 (2000): 51–65.

Clark, Katerina, and Michael Holquist. *Mikhail Bakhtin*. Cambridge, Mass.: Belknap Press/Harvard University Press, 1984.

Clawson, Patrick. *Tourism Cooperation in the Levant*. Policy Focus Series, no. 26. Washington, D.C.: Washington Institute for Near East Policy, 1994.

Cleaver, Henry. "The Zapatista Effect: The Internet and the Rise of an Alternative Political Fabric." *Journal of International Affairs* 51, no. 2 (1998): 621–640.

Clifford, James. "Notes on Theory and Travel." *Inscriptions* 5 (1989): 177–187.

————. "Traveling Cultures." In *Cultural Studies*, edited by Lawrence Grossberg, Cary Nelson, and Paula A. Treichler. New York: Routledge, 1992.

Cloud, John. "Meet the Prophet: How an Evangelical and Conservative Activist Turned Prophecy into a Fiction Juggernaut." *Time.com*, July 23, 2002.

Cobban, Helena. *The Palestinian Liberation Organisation: People, Power and Politics*. Cambridge, England: Cambridge University Press, 1984.

Cohen, Erik. "The Black Panthers and the Israeli Society." *Jewish Journal of Sociology* 14 (1972): 93–109.

Cohen, Erik, and Amnon Shiloah. "Major Trends of Change in Jewish Oriental Ethnic Music in Israel." *Popular Music* 5 (1985): 199–223.

Cohen, Hillel. "Heḥanu et hacheck" [We prepared the check]. *Kol Ha'ir*, February 16, 1996.

————. "Shalom 1: Tayar Yardeni mitlonen 'al alimut shotrim yisraelim" [Peace 1: Jordanian tourist complains about violence from Israeli police]. *Kol Ha'ir*, October 27, 1995.

————. "Shalom 2: Palestinim ezraḥei yarden baim ketayarim venisharim beyisrael" [Peace 2: Palestinian citizens of Jordan come as tourists and stay in Israel]. *Kol Ha'ir*, October 27, 1995.

Cohen, Yossi. "20 dinar lezug, kolel mizug avir" [Twenty dinars per couple, including air conditioning]. *Kol Ha'ir*, July 22, 1994, sec. 1, p. 65.

Colla, Eliott. "Solidarity in the Time of Anti-Normalization: Egypt Responds to the Intifada." *Middle East Report* 224 (fall 2002): 10–15.

Coughlin, Ellen K. "As Perceptions of the Palestinian People Change, Study of Their History and Society Grows." *Chronicle of Higher Education*, February 19, 1992, A8.

Courbage, Youseff. "Reshuffling the Demographic Cards in Israel/Palestine." *Journal of Palestine Studies* 28 (1999): 21–39.

Crofts, Stephen. "Concepts of National Cinema." In *World Cinema: Critical Approaches*, edited by John Hill and Pamela Church Gibson. Oxford: Oxford University Press, 2000.

Cromelin, Richard. "Macias: Singer for the Dispossessed." *Los Angeles Times*, November 22, 1985, part 6, p. 1.

Cutrer, Corrie. "Left Behind Has Been Very, Very Good to Tyndale." *Christianity Today.com*. October 17, 2000. Available at: http://www.christianitytoday.com/ct/2000/013/20.26.html.

Daniel, Sara. "Enrico Macias et la 'haggra.'" *Nouvel Observateur* 1882, November 30, 2000.

Danielson, Virginia. *The Voice of Egypt: Umm Kulthum, Arabic Song, and Egyptian Society in the Twentieth Century*. Chicago: University of Chicago Press, 1997.

Dar, Yuli. "Yishuvei ha'aravim meshamshim mekom mistor letayarim bilti ḥuqiim" [Arab towns used as a hiding place for illegal tourists]. *Kol Hatzafon*, January 26, 1996.

Darwish, Mahmud. *Diwan Mahmud Darwish*. Vol. 1. Beirut: Dar al-'Awda, 1994.

———. "Tilka al-Ughniya Hadhihi al-Ughniya" [This song, that song]. *Al-Yawm al-Sabi'*, no. 126 (October 6, 1986): 13.

Darwish, Mahmud, Samih al-Qasim, and Adonis. *Victims of a Map*. Edited and translated by Abdullah al-Udhari. London: Al Saqi Books, 1984.

Davis, Rochelle. "Ottoman Jerusalem." In *Jerusalem 1948: The Arab Neighbourhoods and Their Fate in the War*, edited by Salim Tamari. Jerusalem: Institute of Jerusalem Studies, 1999.

Deleuze, Gilles, and Félix Guattari. *A Thousand Plateaus: Capitalism and Schizophrenia*. Translated by Robert Hurley, Mark Seem, and Helen R. Lane. Minneapolis: University of Minnesota Press, 1983.

———. *A Thousand Plateaus: Capitalism and Schizophrenia*. Vol. 2. Translated by Brian Massumi. Minneapolis: University of Minnesota Press, 1987.

DeMar, Gary. *End Time Fiction: A Biblical Consideration of the Left Behind Theology*. Nashville, Tenn.: Thomas Nelson, 2001.

Dietz, Henry Elkin. "The Military, Ethnicity, and Integration in Israel Revisited." In *Ethnicity, Integration, and the Military*, edited by Maurice Jerrold Roumani. Boulder, Colo.: Westview, 1991.

Diyab, Imtiyaz. *Yafa: 'Utr Madina* [Jaffa: Perfume of a city]. Beirut: Dar al Fati al-Arabi, 1991.

Dodd, Peter, and Halim Barakat. *River without Bridges: A Study of the Exodus of the 1967 Palestinian Arab Refugees.* Beirut: Institute for Palestine Studies, 1969.

Dolbbe, Sandi. "Second-Coming Attraction: Best-selling, Apocalypse Author Is Drawn to the End Times." *San Diego Union-Tribune,* November 15, 2002, E-1.

Domínguez, Virginia R. *People as Subject, People as Object: Selfhood and Peoplehood in Contemporary Israel.* Madison: University of Wisconsin Press, 1989.

Douglas, Allen, and Fedwa Malti-Douglas. *Arab Comic Strips: Politics of an Emerging Mass Culture.* Bloomington: Indiana University Press, 1994.

Doumani, Beshara. *Rediscovering Palestine: Merchants and Peasants in Jabal Nablus, 1700–1900.* New York: Columbia University Press, 1991.

Draï, Raphaël. *Lettre au président Bouteflika.* Paris: Éditions Michalon, 2000.

Dumaniki, A. S. Marmarji. "Nazra fi Ta'rikh yafa" [A view of the history of Jaffa]. *Al-Mashriq,* no. 10 (1928): 729–735; no. 11 (1928): 826–833.

Dupee, F. W. Afterword to *Sentimental Education.* By Gustave Flaubert. New York: New American Edition, 1972.

Eickelman, Dale F. "Communication and Control in the Middle East: Publication and Its Discontents." In *New Media in the Muslim World: The Emerging Public Sphere,* edited by Dale F. Eickelman and Jon W. Anderson. Bloomington: Indiana University Press, 1999.

Eickelman, Dale F., and Jon W. Anderson, eds. *New Media in the Muslim World: The Emerging Public Sphere.* Bloomington: Indiana University Press, 1999.

Eisenstadt, S. N. *The Absorption of Immigrants: A Comparative Study Based Mainly on the Jewish Community in Palestine and the State of Israel.* London: Routledge and Kegan Paul, 1954.

El-Sayed, Mustapha K. "Egyptian Popular Attitudes toward the Palestinians Since 1977." *Journal of Palestine Studies* 18, no. 4 (summer 1989): 37–51.

Ellingwood, Ken. "A Christian Day of Prayer for Israel." *Los Angeles Times,* October 21, 2002.

Emmett, Ayala H. *Our Sisters' Promised Land: Women, Politics, and Israeli-Palestinian Coexistence.* Ann Arbor: University of Michigan Press, 1996.

Escobar, Arturo. "Welcome to Cyberia: Notes on the Anthropology of Cyberculture." *Current Anthropology* 35, no. 3 (1994): 211–233.

Even-Zohar, Itamar. "The Emergence of a Native Hebrew Culture in Palestine: 1882–1948." *Poetics Today* 11, no. 1 (1990): 175–191.

Everard, Jerry. *Virtual States: Globalization, Inequality and the Internet.* London: Routledge, 1999.

Eyal, Gil. "Between East and West: The Discourse on the Arab Village in Israel." *Teoria vebikoret* 3 (1993): 39–56 [in Hebrew].

FAFO (Institute for Applied Social Science, Norway). *UNRWA's Financial Crisis and Socio-economic Conditions of Palestinian Refugees in Lebanon.* Study commissioned by the Royal Norwegian Ministry of Foreign Affairs. Available at: http://www.fafo.no, 2000.

Fallows, James. "Who Shot Mohammed al-Durra?" *Atlantic Monthly,* June 2003.

Farsakh, Leila. "Under Siege: Closure, Separation, and the Palestinian Economy." *Middle East Report* 30, no. 4 (2000): 22–24.

Fawal, Ibrahim. *Youssef Chahine*. London: British Film Institute, 2001.

Feld, Steven. "From Schizophonia to Schismogenesis: On the Discourses and Commodification Practices of 'World Music' and 'World Beat.'" In Charles Keil and Steven Feld, *Music Grooves*. Chicago: University of Chicago Press, 1994.

Ferguson, James, and Akhil Gupta. "Beyond 'Culture': Space, Identity, and the Politics of Difference." *Cultural Anthropology* 7 (1992): 6–24.

Finkelstein, Norman. *Image and Reality of the Israel-Palestine Conflict*. New York: Verso, 1995.

Fiske, John. *Understanding Popular Culture*. New York: Routledge, 1989.

Flam, Gila. "Beracha Zefira: A Case Study of Acculturation in Israeli Song." *Asian Music* 17 (1986): 108–125.

Flapan, Simha. *The Birth of Israel: Myths and Realities*. New York: Pantheon, 1987.

"Foreign Workers in Israel." *Migration News* 4, no. 8 (1997). Available at: http://migration.ucdavis.edu/mn/more/php?id=1299_0_5_0.

Freire, Paolo. *Pedagogy of the Oppressed*. Translated by Myra Bergman Ramos. New York: Herder and Herder, 1970.

Freitag, Sandria B. *Collective Action and Community: Public Arenas and the Emergence of Communalism in North India*. Berkeley: University of California Press, 1989.

———. "Popular Culture in the Rewriting of History: An Essay in Comparative History and Historiography." *Peasant Studies* 16, no. 3 (1989): 169–199.

Garber, Marjorie. *Vested Interests: Cross-Dressing and Cultural Anxiety*. New York: Routledge, 1992.

Gauntlett, David. "Web Studies: A User's Guide." In *Web Studies: Rewiring Media Studies for the Digital Age*, edited by David Gauntlett. New York: Oxford University Press, 2000.

Gavish, Dov. "The Old City of Jaffa, 1936: A Colonial Urban Renewal Project" [Mivtz'a Yafo: Shipur Coloniali shel Pnei 'Ir]. *Eretz Israel* 17 (1984): 6–73.

Gefen, Yonatan. "Ha'etzev Hu Ashkenazi" [Sadness is Ashkenazi]. *Ma'ariv* (Tel Aviv), May 15, 1992, Weekend supplement, 3.

Gelvin, James. *Divided Loyalties: Nationalism and Mass Politics in Syria at the Close of Empire*. Berkeley: University of California Press, 1998.

Genet, Jean. *Un captif amoureux*. Paris: Gallimard, 1986.

Germain-Robbin, Françoise. "Enrico Macias reporte sa tournée en Algérie." *L'Humanité*, March 6, 2000.

Gertz, Nurith. *Myths in Israeli Culture: Captives of a Dream*. London: Valentine Mitchell, 2000.

———. *Motion Fiction: Israeli Fiction in Film*. Tel Aviv: Open University Press, 1993 [in Hebrew].

Ghanem, As'ad. *The Palestinian-Arab Minority in Israel, 1948–2000: A Political Study*. Albany: State University of New York Press, 2001.

Ghosh, Amitav. *In an Antique Land*. New York: Vintage Books, 1994.

Ghoussoub, Mai, and Emma Sinclair-West. *Imagined Masculinities: Male Identity and Culture in the Modern Middle East*. London: Saqi Books, 2000.

Gibbs, Nancy. "The Bible and the Apocalypse: The Biggest Book of the Summer Is about the End of the World." *Time*, June 23, 2002.

Giddens, Anthony. *Beyond Left and Right: The Future of Radical Politics*. Stanford: Stanford University Press, 1994.

Gilroy, Paul. *The Black Atlantic: Modernity and Double Consciousness*. Cambridge, Mass.: Harvard University Press, 1993.

Ginsberg, Elaine, ed. *Passing and the Fictions of Identity*. Durham, N.C.: Duke University Press, 1996.

Gluck, Sherna Berger. *An American Feminist in Palestine: The Intifada Years*. Philadelphia: Temple University Press, 1994.

Goffman, Erving. *Forms of Talk*. Philadelphia: University of Pennsylvania Press, 1981.

Goitein, S. D. *Jews and Arabs: Their Contacts through the Ages*. New York: Schocken Books, 1964.

Goldberg, Harvey. "The Mimouna and the Minority Status of the Moroccan Jews." *Ethnology* 17 (1978): 75–87.

Goldberg, Jonathan. *Sodometries*. Stanford: Stanford University Press, 1992.

Goldberg, Michelle. "Fundamentally Unsound." *Salon.com*, July 29, 2002.

Goldscheider, Calvin. "The Demography of Asian and African Jews in Israel." In *Ethnicity, Identity and History*, edited by Joseph B. Maier and Chaim I. Waxman. New Brunswick, N.J.: Transaction Books, 1983.

Goldstein, Avram. "Christian Coalition Rallies for Israel in Comeback Bid." *Washington Post*, October 12, 2002, B1.

Gordon, Joel. *Revolutionary Melodrama: Popular Film and Civic Identity in Nasser's Egypt*. Chicago: University of Chicago Press, 2002.

———. "Singing the Pulse of the Egyptian-Arab Street: Shaaban Abd al-Rahim and the Geo-Pop-Politics of Fast Food." *Popular Music* 22, no. 1 (2003): 75–90.

Gorenberg, Gershom. *The End of Days: Fundamentalism and the Struggle for the Temple Mount*. New York: Free Press, 2000.

———. "Unorthodox Alliance: Israeli and Jewish Interests Are Better Served by Keeping a Polite Distance from the Christian Right." *Washington Post*, October 11, 2002, A37.

Gover, Yerah. *Zionism: The Limits of Moral Discourse in Israeli Hebrew Fiction*. Minneapolis: University of Minnesota Press, 1994.

Government of Israel. *Development Options for Cooperation: The Middle East/East Mediterranean Region*. Jerusalem: Government Publishing House, 1996.

Graham-Brown, Sarah. "The Political Economy of the Jabal Nablus, 1920–48." In *Studies in the Economic and Social History of Palestine in the Nineteenth and Twentieth Centuries*, edited by Roger Owen. Carbondale: Southern Illinois University Press, 1982.

Gramsci, Antonio. *Selections from Cultural Writings*, edited by David Forgacs and Geoffrey Nowell-Smith. Translated by William Boelhower. Cambridge, Mass.: Harvard University Press, 1991.

———. *Selections from the Prison Notebooks*. Edited and translated by Quintin Hoare and Geoffrey Nowell-Smith. London: Lawrence and Wishart, 1970.

Green, John. "The American Religious Landscape and Politics, 2004." Washington, D.C.: Pew Forum on Religion and Public Life, 2004. Available at: http://pewforum.org/publications/surveys/green.pdf.

Greenblatt, Stephen. *Marvelous Possessions: The Wonder of the New World*. Chicago: University of Chicago Press, 1991.

Griffith, R. Marie. *God's Daughters: Evangelical Women and the Power of Submission*. Berkeley: University of California Press, 1997.

Gross, Joan, David McMurray, and Ted Swedenburg. "Arab Noise and Ramadan Nights: *Rai*, Rap and Franco-Maghrebi Identities." In *Displacement, Diaspora and Geographies of Identity*, edited by Smadar Lavie and Ted Swedenburg. Durham, N.C.: Duke University Press, 1996.

Grossberg, Lawrence. "History, Politics, and Postmodernism: Stuart Hall and Cultural Studies." In *Stuart Hall: Critical Dialogues in Cultural Studies*, edited by David Morley and Kuan-Hsing Chen. London: Routledge, 1996.

———. "Pedagogy in the Present." In *Popular Culture, Schooling, and Everyday Life*, edited by Henry Giroux and Roger Simon. New York: Bergin and Garvey, 1989.

Gumbel, Andrew. "The Profits of Doom." *The Independent*, November 12, 2000, 7.

Habermas, Jürgen. *Autonomy and Solidarity: Interviews with Jürgen Habermas*, edited by Peter Dews. New York: Verso Press, 1992.

———. *The Structural Transformation of the Public Sphere: An Inquiry into a Category of Bourgeois Society*. Translated by Thomas Burger. Cambridge, Mass.: MIT Press, 1991.

Habiby, Emile. *The Secret Life of Saeed the Ill-Fated Pessoptimist*. Translated by Salma Jayyusi and Trevor LeGassick. Columbia, La.: Reader's International, 1989.

Hall, Stuart. "Popular Culture and the State." In *Popular Culture and Social Relations*, edited by Tony Bennett, Colin Mercer, and Janet Woollacott. Milton Keynes, England: Open University Press, 1986.

Halper, Jeffrey, Edwin Seroussi, and Pamela Squires-Kidron. "*Musika Mizrakhit*: Ethnicity and Class Culture in Israel." *Popular Music* 8 (1989): 131–141.

Hamilton, Martha MacNeil. "Retailing's New Testament Faith: Sales of Items Tied to Spirituality Are Booming, and Not Just through Traditional Religious Venues." *Washington Post*, October 15, 2001, H01.

Hammami, Rema. "Interregnum: Palestine after Operation Defensive Shield." *Middle East Report* 223 (summer 2002): 18–27.

———. "Women's Political Participation in the Intifada: A Critical Overview." In *The Intifada and Some Women's Social Issues*. Ramallah: Bisan Center for Research and Development, 1991.

Hammond, Andrew. "When Israel Talks, Cairo Listens." *Washington Report on Middle East Affairs*, September 1, 2001.

Hamzeh, Muna. *Refugees in Our Own Land: Chronicles from a Palestinian Refugee Camp in Bethlehem*. London: Pluto Press, 2001.

Hanafi, Sari. "Opening the Debate on the Right of Return." *Middle East Report* 222 (2002): 2–7.

———. "Reshaping the Geography: Palestinian Communities Networks in Europe and the New Media." *News from Within* 18, no. 1 (2002): 16.

Hardt, Michael, and Antonio Negri. *Empire*. Cambridge, Mass.: Harvard University Press, 2000.

Hareuveni, Eyal. "Hasar Bar'am neged tayarut muslemit" [Minister Baram is against Muslim tourists]. *Kol Ha'ir*, September 1, 1995.

Harlow, Barbara. "*Mismar Goha*: The Arab Challenge to Cultural Dependency." *South Atlantic Quarterly* 87, no. 1 (winter 1988): 109–129.

———. *Resistance Literature*. London: Routledge, 1987.

Haskell, Guy. "The Development of Israeli Anthropological Approaches to Immigration and Ethnicity: 1948–1980." *Jewish Folklore and Ethnology Review* 11, nos. 1–2 (1989): 19–26.

Hazbun, Waleed. "Mapping the Landscape of the 'New Middle East': The Politics of Tourism Development and the Peace Process in Jordan." In *Jordan in Transition*, edited by George Joffé. New York: Palgrave, 2002.

Heller, Agnes, and Ferenc Fehér. *The Postmodern Political Condition*. New York: Columbia University Press, 1989.

Herman, Andrew, and John H. Sloop. "'Red Alert!' Rhetorics of the World Wide Web and 'Friction-Free' Capitalism." In *The World Wide Web and Contemporary Cultural Theory*, edited by Andrew Herman and Thomas Swiss. London: Routledge, 2000.

Herman, Andrew, and Thomas Swiss, eds. *The World Wide Web and Contemporary Cultural Theory*. London: Routledge, 2000.

Hever, Hannan, and Moshe Ron, eds. *Fighting and Killing without End: Political Poetry in the Lebanon War*. Tel Aviv: Ha-Kibbutz Ha-Meuhad, 1983 [in Hebrew].

Hiel, Betsy. "Tourism Revival in the Land of the Pharaohs." *Arab DataNet*, June 2, 1995. Available at: http://www.arabdatanet.com.

Higson, Andrew. "The Concept of National Cinema." *Screen* 30, no. 4 (1989): 36–46.

Hiltermann, Joost. *Behind the Intifada: Labor and Women's Movements in the Occupied Territories*. Princeton: Princeton University Press, 1991.

Hirshberg, Jehoash. "Brakha Tsfira Vetahalikh Hashinui bamusiqa beyisrael" [Brakha Tsfira and the process of change in Israeli music]. *Pe'amim* 19 (1984): 29–46.

Holmes, David. "Virtual Identity: Communities of Broadcast, Communities of Interactivity." In *Virtual Politics: Identity and Community in Cyberspace*, edited by David Holmes. London: Sage, 1997.

———, ed. *Virtual Politics: Identity and Community in Cyberspace*. London: Sage, 1997.

hooks, bell. "Representing Whiteness in the Black Imagination." In *Cultural Studies*, edited by Lawrence Grossberg, Cary Nelson, and Paula Treichler. New York: Routledge, 1992.

Horowitz, Amy. "Musika Yam Tikhonit Yisraelit [Israeli Mediterranean music]: Cultural Boundaries and Disputed Territories." PhD diss., University of Pennsylvania, 1994.

———. "Performance in Disputed Territory: Israeli Mediterranean Music." *Musical Performance* 1, no. 3 (1997): 43–53.

————. "Rerouting Roots: Zehava Ben between Shuk and Suk." In *The Art of Being Jewish in Modern Times*, edited by Barbara Kirshenblatt-Gimblett and Jonathan Karp. Philadelphia: University of Pennsylvania Press, forthcoming.

Horowitz, Nitzan. "Algerian President Warms to Israel." *Ha'aretz*, October 31, 1999.

Hunter, James. "The Evangelical Worldview since 1890." In *Piety and Politics: Evangelicals and Fundamentalists Confront the World*, edited by Richard Neuhaus and Michael Cromartie. Washington, D.C.: Ethics and Public Policy Center, 1987.

Inbal, Leah. "Zehava." *Yedi'ot Aharonot*, January 4, 1991, Seven-day Supplement, 32–33.

International Film Circuit, Inc., "Chronicle of a Disappearance." Press release, n.d.

"Intifada Becomes Theme of Egyptian Films, Songs, Art." *Middle East Times*, September 26, 2001.

Israel, Miton. *Communications and Power: Propaganda and the Press in the Indian Nationalist Struggle, 1920–1947*. Cambridge, England: Cambridge University Press, 1994.

Israel, Yael. "Seret al busha" [A film about shame]. *'Al Hamishmar*, August 26, 1994.

Israeli Ministry of Tourism. *Regional Tourism Cooperation Development Options*. Jerusalem: Government Publishing House, 1995.

————. *Tourism to Israel, 1995: Statistical Report*. Jerusalem: Government Publishing House, 1996.

————. *Tourism to Israel, 1997: Statistical Report*. Jerusalem: Government Publishing House, 1998.

Iss, Edna. "Sha'ah vahetzi miteveriah" [An hour and a half from Tiberias]. *Yedi'ot Aharonot*, December 8, 1995.

Ja'afari, Kamal. "Foreign Arab Workers in Israel." *Challenge* (January–February 1996): 14–15.

Jameson, Fredric. *Signatures of the Visible*. New York: Routledge, 1992.

Jansen, Michael E. *United States and the Palestinian People*. Beirut: Institute for Palestine Studies, 1970.

Jawhariyyeh, Wasif. *Ahwal al-Quds al-'Uthmaniya fil Mudhakkarat al-Jawhariya* [Ottoman Jerusalem in the Jawhariya memoirs]. Vol. 1. Edited by Issam Nassar and Salim Tamari. Jerusalem: Institute of Jerusalem Studies, 2003.

Jayyusi, Lena. "The Voice of Palestine and the Peace Process: Paradoxes in Media Discourse after Oslo." In *After Oslo: New Realities, Old Problems*, edited by George Giacaman and Dag Jrund Lonning. London: Pluto Press, 1998.

Jayyusi, Salma Khadra. *Anthology of Modern Palestinian Literature*. New York: Columbia University Press, 1992.

Jiryis, Sabri. *The Arabs in Israel*. Translated by Inea Bushnaq. New York: Monthly Review Press, 1976.

————. *The Arabs in Israel, 1948–1966*. Translated by Meric Dobson. Beirut: Institute for Palestine Studies, 1969.

Johnson, Penny. "Ramallah Dada: The Reality of the Absurd." *Jerusalem Quarterly File* 16 (fall 2002). Available at: http://www.jqf-jerusalem.org/2002/jqf16dada.html.

Jordan, Tim. *The Culture and Politics of Cyberspace and Internet.* London: Routledge, 1999.

Kahn, Susan Martha. *Reproducing Jews: A Cultural Account of Assisted Conception in Israel.* Durham, N.C.: Duke University Press, 2000.

Kallam, Mahmud 'Abdallah. *Naji al-'Ali: Kamil Turab al-Filastini* [Naji al-'Ali: The entirety of the Palestinian soil]. Beirut: Bissan, 2001.

Kanaaneh, Rhoda Ann. *Birthing the Nation: Strategies of Palestinian Women in Israel.* Berkeley: University of California Press, 2002.

Kanafani, Ghassan. *'A'id ila Haifa* [Return to Haifa]. 3rd ed. Beirut: Mu'assasat al-Abhath al-'Arabiya, 1985.

Kaplan, Caren. *Questions of Travel: Postmodern Discourses of Displacement.* Durham, N.C.: Duke University Press, 1996.

Kaspit, Ben. "Haqatari: Yedidenu hehadash mimizrah" [The Qatari: Our new friend from the east]. *Ma'ariv*, April 5, 1996, 27.

Katriel, Tamar. "Remaking Place: Cultural Production in an Israeli Pioneer Settlement Museum." *History and Memory* 5, no. 2 (fall–winter 1993): 104–135.

Kaveh, Avshalom. "Milyon tayarim 'araviim yevaqru biyerushalayim uveveit-lehem 'im heskem Oslo bet" [A million Arab tourists will visit Jerusalem and Bethlehem with the realization of Oslo II]. *Davar Rishon*, January 23, 1996.

Kay, Katty, and Roland Watson. "Influential U.S. Jews Like What They Hear." *Times* (London), June 26, 2002, n.p.

Kayali, Hasan. *Arabs and Young Turks: Ottomanism, Arabism, and Islamism in the Ottoman Empire, 1908–1918.* Berkeley: University of California Press, 1997.

Kayyali, 'Abd al-Wahhab. *Palestine: A Modern History.* London: Croom Helm, 1978.

Kazir, Sara, and Shlomo Swirski. "Ashkenazim and Sephardim: The Making of Dependence." *Mahbarot lemehkar vebikoret* 1 (1978): 21–59 [in Hebrew].

Keller, Adam. *Terrible Days: Social Divisions and Political Paradoxes in Israel.* Amstelveen, Netherlands: Cypres, 1987.

Keyser, Jason. "Hundreds of Americans Move to Israel: Mass Immigration Is Paid For in Part by Evangelical Christian Groups." *Seattle Post-Intelligencer*, July 20, 2002, A1.

———. "Israel's Arabs Find Revolution in Rap." Associated Press, June 25, 2002.

Khadar, Hasan. "Hal kuntu huna?" [Was I here?]. *Al-Karmil* 51 (spring 1997): 115–124.

Khalaf, Issa. *Politics in Palestine: Arab Factionalism and Social Disintegration 1939–1948.* Albany: State University of New York Press, 1991.

Khalafallah, Haifaa. "Unofficial Cassette Culture in the Middle East." *Index of Censorship* (1982): 10–12.

Khalidi, Rashid. *Palestinian Identity: The Construction of Modern National Consciousness.* New York: Columbia University Press, 1997.

Khalidi, Walid. *All That Remains: The Palestinian Villages Occupied and Depopulated by Israel in 1948.* Washington, D.C.: Institute for Palestine Studies, 1992.

———, ed. *From Haven to Conquest: Readings in Zionism and the Palestine Problem until 1948.* Beirut: Institute for Palestine Studies, 1971.

Khoury, Elias. *Bab al-Shams.* Beirut: Dar al-Adab, 1999.

Khuli, Samhah al-. *Al-Qawmiya fi Musiqa al-Qarn al-'Ishrin* [Nationalism in twentieth-century music]. Kuwait: 'Alam al-Ma'rifa, 1992.

Khuri, Arlit. "Fayruz Ghannat Filastin wa Lubnan fi Baris" [Fayruz sang Palestine and Lebanon in Paris]. *Al-Hayah*, June 29, 2002, 20.

Kimmerling, Baruch. *Zionism and Territory: The Socio-Territorial Dimensions of Zionist Politics*. Berkeley: University of California Press, 1983.

Kimmerling, Baruch, and Joel S. Migdal. *The Palestinian People: A History*. Cambridge, Mass.: Harvard University Press, 2003.

Klady, Leonard. Review of *The Tale of the Three Jewels*. *Variety*, June 5, 1995.

Klein, Chaim H., ed. *The Second Million: Israel Tourist Industry, Past, Present, and Future*. Jerusalem: Amir, 1973.

Klinghoffer, David. "Just Be Gracious." *Jerusalem Post*, August 16, 2002, 7B.

Kolko, Beth E., Lisa Nakamura, and Gilbert B. Rodman, eds. *Race in Cyberspace*. London: Routledge, 2000.

Kunzle, David. *The History of the Comic Strip*. 2 vols. Berkeley: University of California Press, 1973.

LaHaye, Tim, and Jerry Jenkins. *Are We Living in the End Times?* Wheaton, Ill.: Tyndale House, 1999.

———. *Desecration*. Wheaton, Ill.: Tyndale House, 2001.

———. *Left Behind: A Novel of the Earth's Last Days*. Wheaton, Ill.: Tyndale House, 1995.

Lahouari, Addi. "Abdelaziz Bouteflika a du renoncer à inviter Enrico Macias." *Libération*, March 9, 2000, 9.

Laloum, Jean, and Jean-Luc Allouche, eds. *Les Juifs d'Algérie: Images et Textes*. Paris: Éditions du Scribe, 1987.

Landy, Marcia. "History, Folklore, and Common Sense: Sembène's Films and Discourses of Postcoloniality." In *Postcolonial Discourse and Changing Cultural Contexts: Theory and Criticism*, edited by Gita Rajan and Radhika Mohanram. Westport, Conn.: Greenwood Press, 1995.

Laskier, Michael. *North African Jewry in the Twentieth Century: The Jews of Morocco, Tunisia, and Algeria*. New York: New York University Press, 1994.

Lavi, Aviv. "Natbag 2000" [Airport 2000]. *Kol Ha'ir*, December 29, 1995.

Lavi, Moshiq. "Shloshim devarim shelo yad'atem 'al suriah" [Thirty things you didn't know about Syria]. *Yedi'ot Aharonot*, December 1, 1995.

Lavie, Smadar. *The Poetics of Military Occupation: Mzeina Allegories of Bedouin Identity under Israeli and Egyptian Rule*. Berkeley: University of California Press, 1990.

———. "Sinai for the Coffee Table: Birds, Bedouins, and Desert Wanderlust." *Middle East Report* 18, no. 1 (1988): 40–44.

Levi-Barzilai, Vered. "Muhammad Bakri: Had Tzdadi" [Muhammad Bakri: One-sided]. Interview with Muhammad Bakri. *Ha'aretz*, June 9, 2002, weekend supplement.

LeVine, Mark. *Overthrowing Geography: Jaffa, Tel Aviv and the Struggle for Palestine*. Berkeley: University of California Press, 2004.

Levinshtein, Revital. "Masof 'aravah niftaḥ lema'avar klei rekhev pratiim" [Arava border crossing opens to private vehicles]. *Ha'aretz*, April 8, 1996, sec. 1.

Levy, André. "To Morocco and Back: Tourism and Pilgrimage among Moroccan-born Israelis." In *Grasping Land: Space and Place in Contemporary Israeli Discourse and Experience*, edited by Eyal Ben-Ari and Yoram Bilu. Albany: State University of New York Press, 1997.

Levy, Yail. "A Militaristic Policy, Interethnic Relationship and Domestic Expansion of the State: Israel 1948–1956." *Teoria vebikoret* 8 (1996): 203–224 [in Hebrew].

Lindsey, Hal, with C. C. Carlson. *The Late, Great Planet Earth*. Grand Rapids, Mich.: Zondervan, 1970.

Lior, Gad. "Higa'ti lasel'a haadom" [I got to the red rock]. *Yedi'ot Aḥaronot*, July 18, 1994, sec. 1, p. 10.

Lockard, Joe. "Babel Machines and Electronic Universalism." In *Race in Cyberspace*, edited by Beth E. Kolko, Lisa Nakamura, and Gilbert B. Rodman. London: Routledge, 2000.

Lockman, Zachary. *Comrades and Enemies: Arab and Jewish Workers in Palestine, 1906–1948*. Berkeley: University of California Press, 1996.

———. "Original Sin." In *Intifada: The Palestinian Uprising against Israeli Occupation*, edited by Zachary Lockman and Joel Beinin. Boston: South End Press, 1989.

Lockman, Zachary, and Joel Beinin, eds. *Intifada: The Palestinian Uprising against Israeli Occupation*. Boston: South End Press, 1989.

Long, Karen. "*Left Behind* and the Rupture over the Rapture." *Washington Post*, May 5, 2001, B09.

Loshitzky, Yosefa. *Identity Politics on the Israeli Screen*. Austin: University of Texas Press, 2002.

Lubin, Orli. "Women, Nationalism and Ethnicity." In *Fictive Looks: On Israeli Cinema*, edited by Nurith Gertz, Orli Lubin, and Judd Ne'eman. Tel Aviv: Open University Press, 1998 [in Hebrew].

Lustick, Ian. *Arabs in the Jewish State: Israel's Control of a National Minority*. Austin: University of Texas Press, 1980.

Macias, Enrico, with Florence Assouline. *Mon Algérie*. Paris: Plon, 2001.

Macias, Enrico, with Jacques Demarny. *Non, je n'ai pas oublié*. Paris: Éditions Robert Laffout, 1982.

Malkki, Liisa. "Refugees and Exile: From 'Refugee Studies' to the National Order of Things." *Annual Review of Anthropology* 24 (1995): 495–523.

Manuel, Peter. *Cassette Culture: Popular Music and Technology in North India*. Chicago: University of Chicago Press, 1993.

Marks, Laura U. *The Skin of the Film*. Durham, N.C.: Duke University Press, 2000.

Martin, William. *With God on Our Side: The Rise of the Religious Right in America*. New York: Broadway Books, 1996.

Maryles, Daisy. "Few Surprises in the Winners' Circle." *Publishers Weekly*, March 18, 2002, 53.

Massad, Joseph. "Conceiving the Masculine: Gender and Palestinian Nationalism." *Middle East Journal* 49, no. 3 (summer 1995): 467–483.

————. "The Ends of Zionism: Racism and the Palestinian Struggle." *Interventions* 5, no. 3 (2003): 440–451.

————. "The Legacy of Jean-Paul Sartre." *Al-Ahram Weekly* 623 (January 30–February 5, 2003). Available at: http://weekly.ahram.org.eg/2003/623/op33.htm.

————. "Liberating Songs: Palestine Put to Music." *Journal of Palestine Studies* 32, no. 3 (spring 2003): 21–38.

————. "Political Realists or Comprador Intelligentsia: Palestinian Intellectuals and the National Struggle." *Critique* (fall 1997): 21–35.

————. "Repentant Terrorists, or Settler-Colonialism Revisited: The PLO-Israeli Agreement in Perspective." *Found Object* 3 (spring 1994): 81–90.

————. "Return or Permanent Exile." In *Palestinian Refugees and the Right of Return*, edited by Naseer Aruri. London: Pluto Press, 2001.

————. "The Weapon of Culture: Palestinian Cinema and the National Struggle." In *Dreams of a Nation*, edited by Hamid Dabashi. London: Verso, forthcoming.

Masters, Bruce. *Christians and Jews in the Ottoman Arab World: The Roots of Sectarianism.* Cambridge, England: Cambridge University Press, 2001.

Mayer, Tamar, ed. *Women and the Israeli Occupation: The Politics of Change.* New York: Routledge, 1994.

Mazor, Yaacov, and Edwin Seroussi. "Towards a Hassidic Lexicon of Music." *Assaph* 10 (1990): 91, 118–143.

McAlister, Melani. *Epic Encounters: Culture, Media, and U.S. Interests in the Middle East, 1945–2000.* Berkeley: University of California Press, 2001.

McChesney, Robert. "So Much for the Magic of Technology and the Free Market: The World Wide Web and the Corporate Media System." In *The World Wide Web and Contemporary Cultural Theory*, edited by Andrew Herman and Thomas Swiss. London: Routledge, 2000.

McClintock, Anne. *Imperial Leather: Race, Gender and Sexuality in the Colonial Contest.* New York: Routledge, 1995.

McCloud, Scott. *Reinventing Comics.* New York: Harper Collins, 2000.

————. *Understanding Comics: The Invisible Art.* New York: Harper Perennial, 1994.

McEnvoy, Dermott, and Daisy Maryles. "The Right Name Makes the Game: Trade Paper Sales Continue to Climb, Fiction Rules in Mass Market." *Publishers Weekly*, March 19, 2001, 37.

McLaughlin, Abraham, and Gail Russell Chaddock. "Christian Right Steps in on Mideast." *Christian Science Monitor*, April 16, 2001, 1.

McMurray, David. "La France Arabe." In *Post-Colonial Cultures in France*, edited by Alec G. Hargreaves and Mark McKinney. London: Routledge, 1997.

Mehegan, David. "Appeal Spreads for Series That Spreads the Word." *Boston Globe*, February 27, 2002, G1.

Mikha'il, Idward Halim. *Muhammad 'Abd al-Wahhab, Sab'un 'Aman min al-Ibda' fi al-Ta'lif al-Musiqi wa-al-Talhin wa-al-Ghina'* [Muhammad 'Abd al-Wahhab: Seventy years of creativity in musical composition and singing]. Cairo: Maktabat Madbuli, 2002.

Ministry of Finance, Government of Israel. *Focus on the Economy: Possible Eco-*

nomic Implications of the Peace Treaty. Jerusalem: Government Publishing House, 1994.

Mitchell, Alison. "Mideast Turmoil: The Conservatives, Israel Winning Broad Support from the U.S. Right." New York Times, April 21, 2002, 1.

Mitchell, Timothy. "The Limits of the State: Beyond Statist Approaches and Their Critics." American Political Science Review 85, no. 1 (1991): 77–96.

Mitchell, William J. City of Bits: Space, Place, and the Infobahn. Cambridge, Mass.: MIT Press, 1995.

Monestier, Martin. Enrico Macias: L'enfant de tous pays. Paris: Encre, 1980.

Monk, Daniel Bertrand. An Aesthetic Occupation: The Immediacy of Architecture and the Palestine Conflict. Durham, N.C.: Duke University Press, 2002.

Moran, Merav. "Linda Goes to the Kibbutz." Hadashot (Tel Aviv), June 13, 1986, 19.

Morson, Gary Saul. The Boundaries of Genre: Dostoevsky's Diary of a Writer and the Traditions of Literary Utopia. Austin: University of Texas Press, 1981.

Mortaigne, Veronique. "Enrico Macias, ambassadeur de la reconciliation des juifs et des musulmans." Le Monde, April 19, 1999.

Muhammad, Zakariya. "Al-'uzhm wa-al-dhahab" [Grandeur and gold]. Al-Karmil 51 (spring 1997): 125–140.

Mundlak, Guy. "Labor in a Peaceful Middle East: Regional Prosperity or Social Dumping?" In The Middle East Peace Process: Interdisciplinary Perspectives, edited by Ilan Peleg. Albany: State University of New York Press, 1998.

Murphy, Caryle. "At Millennium, Finding Salvation: Popular Series by Evangelical Christian Authors Retells Book of Revelation." Washington Post, November 28, 1999, C1.

Murphy, Emma. "Stacking the Deck: The Economics of the Israeli-PLO Accords." Middle East Report 25, no. 3/4 (1995): 35–38.

Muslih, Muhammad Y. The Origins of Palestinian Nationalism. New York: Columbia University Press, 1988.

Na'aman, Dorit. "Orientalism as Alterity in Israeli Cinema." Cinema Journal 40, no. 4 (2001): 36–54.

Nabulsi, Shakir al-. Al-Aghani fi al-Maghani, al-Shaykh Imam 'Isa, Sira Faniya wa Musiqiya [Songs in the art of singing: Al Shaykh Imam 'Isa, an artistic and musical biography]. Vol. 1, 1918–1969. Beirut: al-Mu'assassat al-'Arabiyyah lil-Dirasat wa-al-Nashr, 1998.

Naficy, Hamid. An Accented Cinema: Exilic and Diasporic Filmmaking. Princeton: Princeton University Press, 2001.

———. The Making of Exile Cultures: Iranian Television in Los Angeles. Minneapolis: University of Minnesota Press, 1993.

———. "Phobic Spaces and Liminal Panics: Independent Transnational Film Genre." East-West Film Journal 8, no. 2 (1994): 1–30.

Najjar, Aida Ali. "The Arabic Press and Nationalism in Palestine, 1920–1948." PhD diss., Syracuse University, 1975.

Najm, Ahmad Fu'ad. Al-A'mal al-Kamila [Complete works]. Cairo: Dar al-Ahmadi lil-nashr, 2002.

Nakhleh, Khalil. "Cultural Determinates of Palestinian Collective Identity: The Case of the Arabs in Israel." *New Outlook* 18, no. 7 (October 1975): 31–40.

Nassar, Jamal R., and Roger Heacock, eds. *Intifada: Palestine at the Crossroads.* New York: Praeger, 1990.

Ne'eman, Judd. "The Empty Tomb in the Postmodern Pyramid: Israeli Cinema in the 1980s and 1990s." In *Documenting Israel: Proceedings of a Conference Held at Harvard University on May 10–12, 1993,* edited by Charles Berlin. Cambridge, Mass.: Harvard University Press, 1995.

Nevo, Yoseph. "The Palestinians and the Jewish State, 1947–48." In *We Were Like Dreamers,* edited by Y. Wallach. Tel Aviv: Massada, 1985 [in Hebrew].

Niebuhr, Gustav. "Muslim Group Seeks to Meet Billy Graham's Son." *New York Times,* November 20, 2001, 5.

Nimr, Abbas. "Jaffa . . . The Eternal Longing." *Al-Quds,* May 17, 1997.

Nye, Naomi Shihab. *Words under the Words: Selected Poems.* Portland, Ore.: Eighth Mountain Press, 1995.

Office of the President of the Lutheran Church, Missouri Synod. "The Left Behind View Is Out of Left Field." December 2000. Available at: http://www.cms.org/predient/statements/leftbehind.asp.

Ohad, Michael. "Libi bamizraḥ" [My heart is in the East]. *Ha'aretz,* September 25, 1981, 16–17.

O'Keefe, Mark. "Israel's Evangelical Approach: U.S. Christian Zionists Nurtured as Political, Tourism Force." *Washington Post,* January 26, 2002, B11.

Okun, Barbara S. "Ethnicity and Educational Attainment in Marriage Patterns: Changes among the Jewish Population of Israel, 1957–1995." *Population Studies* 55 (2001): 49–64.

Oncu, Ayse, and Petra Weyland. *Space, Culture and Power: New Identities in Globalizing Cities.* London: Zed Press, 1997.

1000 Zemer V'od Zemer [The Israeli sing-along]. Tel Aviv: Kinneret, 1981.

Orian, Dan. *The Arab in Israeli Theatre.* Tel Aviv: Ha-Kibbutz Ha-Meuhad, 1998 [in Hebrew].

"Palestine, Israel and the Arab-Israeli Conflict: A Primer." MERIP (Middle East Research and Information Project). Available at: http://www.merip.org/palestine-israel_primer/toc-pal-isr-primer.html.

Pappé, Ilan. *The Making of the Arab-Israeli Conflict, 1947–1951.* New York: I.B. Tauris, 1992.

———. "The New History of the 1948 War." *Teoria vebikoret* 3 (1993): 95–114 [in Hebrew].

———. "Post-Zionist Critique on Israel and the Palestinians: Popular Culture." *Journal of Palestine Studies* 26, no. 4 (1997): 60–69.

———. "Post-Zionist Critique: Part 1. The Academic Debate." *Journal of Palestine Studies* 26, no. 2 (winter 1997): 29–41.

———. "The Post-Zionist Discourse in Israel, 1991–2000." *Holy Land Studies* 1, no. 1 (September 2002): 9–35.

———. "A Text in the Eyes of the Beholder: Four Theatrical Interpretations of Kanfani's *Men in the Sun.*" *Contemporary Theatre Review* 3, no. 2 (1995): 157–174.

Parcheck, Roni. "Lo oseh bidur la-liberalim" [I do not produce entertainment for liberals]. *Ha'aretz*, August 30, 1994.

Pareles, Jon. "Cassette Culture: Home Recording of Original Music on Cassettes." *Whole Earth Review* 5 (winter 1987): 110–111.

Peled, Yoav, ed. *Shas: The Challenge of Israelism*. Tel Aviv: Yediot Aḥronot, 2001 [in Hebrew].

Peretz, Don. *Intifada: The Palestinian Uprising*. Boulder, Colo.: Westview Press, 1990.

Peteet, Julie M. *Gender in Crisis: Women and the Palestinian Resistance Movement*. New York: Columbia University Press, 1991.

Plotzker, Savar. "Haḥalom evar kan" [The dream is already here]. *Yedi'ot Aḥaronot*, July 25, 1994.

Pollack, Aaron. "Epistemological Struggle and International Organizing: Applying the Experience of the Zapatista Army of National Liberation." Working Paper Series No. 295. The Hague: Institute of Social Studies, 1999.

Poovey, Mary. *A History of the Modern Fact: Problems of Knowledge in the Sciences of Wealth and Society*. Chicago: University of Chicago Press, 1998.

Porath, Yehoshua. *The Emergence of the Palestinian-Arab National Movement, 1918–1929*. London: Frank Cass, 1974.

———. *The Palestinian Arab National Movement, 1929–1939*. London: Frank Cass, 1977.

Poster, Mark. "Cyberdemocracy: The Internet and the Public Sphere." In *Virtual Politics: Identity and Community in Cyberspace*, edited by David Holmes. London: Sage, 1997.

Potter, Russell A. *Spectacular Vernaculars: Hip-Hop and the Politics of Postmodernism*. Syracuse: State University of New York Press, 1995.

Pratt, Mary Louise. *Imperial Eyes: Travel Writing and Transculturation*. London: Routledge, 1992.

Prial, Frank J. "Parisians March Against Racism." *New York Times*, December 4, 1983, sec. 1, p. 20.

Principe, Michael A. "Solidarity and Responsibility: Conceptual Connections." *Journal of Social Philosophy* 31, no. 2 (summer 2000): 143–144.

Prusher, Ilene R. "Oslo Is Not Even Calling." *The Jerusalem Report* (May 1, 1997): 42–43.

Pustz, Matthew J. *Comic Book Culture: Fanboys and True Believers*. Jackson: University Press of Mississippi, 1999.

Quandt, William B. *Peace Process: American Diplomacy and the Arab-Israeli Process since 1967*. Berkeley: University of California Press, 1993.

Quandt, William, Fuad Jabber, and Ann Mosely Lesch, eds. *The Politics of Palestinian Nationalism*. Berkeley: University of California Press, 1973.

Rabbani, Mouin. "Palestinian Authority, Israeli Rule: From Transition to Permanent Arrangement." *Middle East Report* 26, no. 4 (1996): 2–6.

Rabinovich, Itamar. *The Road Not Taken: Early Arab Negotiations*. New York: Oxford University Press, 1991.

Rabinowitz, Dan. "Oriental Nostalgia: The Transformation of the Palestinians into 'Israeli Arabs.'" *Teoria vebikoret* 4 (1993): 141–152 [in Hebrew].

———. *Overlooking Nazareth: The Ethnography of Exclusion in Galilee*. Cambridge, England: Cambridge University Press, 1997.

Radwan, Lutfi. *Muhammad 'Abd al-Wahhab, Sira Dhatiya* [Muhammad 'Abd al-Wahhab, Autobiography]. Cairo: Dar al-Hilal, 1991.

Ram, Uri. "The Colonization Perspective in Israeli Sociology." *Journal of Historical Sociology* 6, no. 3 (September 1993): 327–350.

———. "Glocommodification: How the Global Consumes the Local. McDonald's in Israel." *Current Sociology* 52, no. 1 (2004): 11–31.

Regev, Motti. "*Musica mizrakhit*, Israeli Rock and National Culture in Israel." *Popular Music* 15, no. 3 (1996): 275–284.

———. "The Musical Soundscape as a Contest Area: 'Oriental Music' and Israeli Popular Music." *Media, Culture and Society* 8, no. 3 (1986): 343–355.

———. "Present Absentee: Arab Music in Israeli Culture." *Public Culture* 7, no. 2 (1995): 433–445.

Regev, Motti, and Edwin Seroussi. *Popular Music and National Culture in Israel*. Berkeley: University of California Press, 2004.

Reyes-Schramm, Adelide. "Ethnic Music, the Urban Area and Ethnomusicology." *Sociologus* 29, no. 1 (1979): 1–21.

Ridwan, Shafiq. *Al-Mulsaq al-Filastini: Mashakil al-Nishat wa al-Tatawwur* [Palestinian posters: Problems of genesis and development]. Damascus: Da'irat al-Thaqafa, Munazzamat al-Tahrir al-Filastini, 1992.

Robbins, Kevin. "Cyberspace and the World We Live In." In *The Cybercultures Reader*, edited by David Bell and Barbara Kennedy. New York: Routledge, 2000.

Robertson, Roland. *Globalization: Social Theory and Global Culture*. New York: Sage, 1992.

Roberston, Tatsha. "Evangelicals Flock to Israel's Banner: Christian Zionists See Jewish State Bringing Messiah." *Boston Globe*, October 21, 2002, A3.

Robinson, Amy. "It Takes One to Know One: Passing and Communities of Common Interest." *Critical Inquiry* 20 (1994): 715–736.

Rodgers, Susan. "Batak Tape Cassette Kinship. Constructing Kinship through the Indonesian National Mass Media." *American Ethnologist* 13 (1986): 23–42.

Rodgers-Melnick, Ann. "Evangelical Fiction Cracks the Bestseller List." *Pittsburgh Post-Gazette*, May 6, 2001, A1.

Rorty, Richard. *Contingency, Irony, Solidarity*. Cambridge, England: Cambridge University Press, 1989.

Rouhana, Nadim N. *Palestinian Citizens in an Ethnic Jewish State*. New Haven: Yale University Press, 1997.

Royal Institute of International Affairs. *Great Britain and Palestine, 1915–1945*. London: Oxford University Press, 1946.

Rozen, Rami. "Hashalom hashaḥor hazeh" [This black peace]. *Ha'aretz Supplement*, September 9, 1994, 50.

Rubin, Betsalel. "Hem baim lirot et Eilat" [They are coming to see Eilat]. *'Erev 'Erev*, December 26, 1994.

Rushdie, Salman. "Notes on Writing and the Nation." *Harper's*, September 1997, 22, 24.

Sabin, Roger. *Adult Comics: An Introduction*. New York: Routledge, 1993.

———. *Comics, Comix and Graphic Novels: A History of Comic Art*. New York: Phaidon, 1996.

Sacco, Joe. *Palestine*. 9 vols. Seattle: Fantagraphics Books, 1993–1996.

———. *Palestine*. Introduction by Edward Said. Seattle: Fantagraphics Books, 2002.

———. *Palestine Book 1: A Nation Occupied*. Seattle: Fantagraphics Books, 1994.

———. *Palestine Book 2: In the Gaza Strip*. Seattle: Fantagraphics Books, 1996.

———. *Safe Area Gorazde: The War in Eastern Bosnia, 1992–95*. Seattle: Fantagraphics Books, 2000.

———. *Soba: Stories from Bosnia*. Montreal: Drawn and Quarterly, 1998.

———. *War Junkie: Illustrated Tales of Combat, Depression, and Rock 'n' Roll*. Seattle: Fantagraphics Books, 1995.

Sack, Kevin. "Apocalyptic Theology Revitalized by Attacks." *New York Times*, November 23, 2001.

Sadeh, Dani. "6,000 yardenim bau leviqur venisharu bashetahim" [6,000 Jordanians came to visit and stayed in the territories]. *Yedi'ot Aharonot*, September 3, 1995.

Saghiya, Hazim. *Al-Hawa Duna Ahlihi, Umm Kulthum, Siratan wa Nassan* [Passion bereft of its people: Umm Kulthum as biography and as text]. Beirut: Dar al-Jadid, 1991.

Sahish, Yaron. "Ha moshava Hayevanit" [The Greek colony]. *Iton Yerushalayim*, August 14, 1992, 26–27.

Said, Edward. *After the Last Sky*. Boston: Faber and Faber, 1986.

———. *The End of the Peace Process*. New York: Pantheon, 1998.

———. "Homage to Joe Sacco." Introduction to *Palestine*. By Joe Sacco. Seattle: Fantagraphics Books, 2002.

———. *Orientalism*. New York: Vintage, 1979.

———. *Out of Place: A Memoir*. New York: Vintage, 1999.

———. *Peace and Its Discontents: Essays on Palestine in the Middle East Peace Process*. New York: Vintage Books, 1996.

———. *The Question of Palestine*. New York: Vintage Books, 1979.

Sakakini, Khalil al-. *Kadha Ana Ya Dunia* [Such is my life]. Beirut: al-Ittihad al-'Amm lil-Kuttab wa-al-Suhufiyin al-Filastiniyin, al-Amana al-'Amma, 1982.

Sakr, Naomi. "Satellite Television and Development in the Middle East." *Middle East Report* 29, no. 1 (1999): 6–10.

Samara, Adel. *Industrialisation in the West Bank: A Marxist Socio-economic Analysis, 1967–1991*. Jerusalem: Al-Mashriq Publications for Economic and Development Studies, 1992.

Sapir, Shuli. "'Arbev et hatiah, Jonny" [Mix the plaster, Jonny]. *Davar Rishon*, March 26, 1996.

Sassen, Saskia. *Globalization and Its Discontents: Essays on the New Mobility of People and Money*. New York: New Press, 1998.

————. "Spatialities and Temporalities of the Global: Elements for a Theorization." *Public Culture* 12, no. 1 (2000): 215–232.

Sassoon, Anne Showstack. "Hegemony, War of Position and Political Intervention." In *Approaches to Gramsci*, edited by Anne Showstack Sassoon. London: Writers and Readers, 1982.

Savage, William W., Jr. *Comic Books and America, 1945–1954.* Norman: University of Oklahoma Press, 1990.

Sawwaf, Husni. "Foreign Trade." In *Economic Organization of Palestine*, edited by Sa'id Himadeh. Beirut: AUB Press, 1938.

Sayigh, Rosemary. "Palestinian Camp Women as Tellers of History." *Journal of Palestine Studies* 27, no. 2 (winter 1998): 42–58.

Sayigh, Yezid. *Armed Struggle and the Search for State: The Palestinian National Movement 1949–1993.* Oxford: Oxford University Press, 1997.

Schrag, Carl, and Steve Rodan. "Closer Than You Think." *Jerusalem Post Magazine*, July, 29, 1994, 11.

Scott, Alan, and John Street. "From Media Politics to E-Protest? The Use of Popular Culture and New Media in Parties and Social Movements." In *Culture and Politics in the Information Age: A New Politics*, edited by Frank Webster. London: Routledge, 2001.

Sedan, Gil. "Moroccan Jews Mourn Death of King." *Jewish News of Greater Phoenix*, July 30, 1999. Available at: http:// www.jewishaz.com/index.html.

Segev, Tom. *The Seventh Million: The Israelis and the Holocaust.* New York: Henry Holt, 2000.

Seliktar, Ofira. "The Peace Dividend: The Economy of Israel and the Peace Process." In *The Middle East Peace Process: Interdisciplinary Perspectives*, edited by Ilan Peleg. Albany: State University of New York Press, 1998.

Seroussi, Edwin. "Hanale hitbalbela" [Hanale was rattled]. In "Fifty to Forty Eight: Critical Moments in the History of the State of Israel," edited by Adi Ophir. Special issue, *Teoria vebikoret* 12–13 (1999): 269–278.

————. "Yam Tikhoniyut: Transformations of the Mediterranean in Israeli Music." In *Mediterranean Mosaic: Popular Music and Global Sounds*, edited by Goffredo Plastino. New York: Routledge, 2003.

Shafik, Viola. *Arab Cinema: History and Cultural Identity.* Cairo: American University in Cairo Press, 1998.

Shafir, Gershon. *Land, Labor and the Origins of the Israeli-Palestinian Conflict, 1882–1914.* Cambridge, England: Cambridge University Press, 1989.

Shafir, Gershon, and Yoav Peled. *Being Israeli: The Dynamics of Multiple Citizenship.* Cambridge, England: Cambridge University Press, 2002.

————. "Peace and Profits: The Globalization of Israeli Business and the Peace Process." In *The New Israel: Peacemaking and Liberalization*, edited by Gershon Shafir and Yoav Peled. Boulder, Colo.: Westview, 2000.

Shahak, Israel. "Israeli Trade with Arab Countries: Vegetables and Drugs." In *Open Secrets: The Israeli Trade with Arab Countries.* London: Pluto Press, 1997.

Shahar, Natan. "The Eretz-Yisraeli Song, 1920–1950: Sociomusical and Musical Aspects." PhD diss., Hebrew University of Jerusalem, 1989.

————. "Hashir haeretz yisraeli vekeren kayemet leyisrael" [Eretz-Israel song and the Jewish National Fund]. Jerusalem: Research Institute for the History of the Jewish National Fund, Land and Settlement, 1994.

Shaked, Gershon. *The Shadows Within: Essays on Modern Jewish Writers*. Philadelphia: Jewish Publication Society, 1987.

Shalev, Michael. *Labour and the Political Economy in Israel*. Oxford: Oxford University Press, 1992.

Shalit, David. "Haya'ad haba: Dameseq" [The next destination: Damascus]. *Ha'aretz Supplement*, November 25, 1994, 33–35.

Shamit, Walid, and Guy Hennebelle, eds. *Filastin fi al-sinima* [Palestine in cinema]. Beirut: Fajr, 1980.

Shammas, Anton. *Arabesques*. Translated by Vivian Eden. New York: Harper and Row, 1988.

————. "He Got the Roles Mixed Up" [Hu hitbalbel ba-tafkidim]. Preface to *Avanti Popolo*. Jerusalem: Kinneret, 1990.

Shammut, Isma'il. "Al-Nashat al-Fanni al-Filastini" [Palestinian artistic activities]. *Shu'un Filastiniya* 98 (January 1980): 138–139.

Shapira, Anita. *Visions in Conflict*. Tel Aviv: 'Am 'oved, 1987 [in Hebrew].

Shapira, Yonathan. "The Historical Origins of Israeli Democracy." In *Israeli Democracy under Stress*, edited by Ehud Sprinzak and Larry Diamond. Boulder, Colo.: Lynne Rienner, 1993.

Shapiro, Haim. "Across the Great Divide." *Jerusalem Post Magazine*, October 13, 1995, 20.

————. "Israelis Flock to Jerash Festival." *Jerusalem Post*, July 12, 1995, 3.

Sharabi, Hisham. *Palestine Guerrillas: Their Credibility and Effectiveness*. Beirut: Institute for Palestine Studies, 1970.

Sharoni, Simona. *Gender and the Israeli Palestinian Conflict: The Politics of Women's Resistance*. Syracuse: Syracuse University Press, 1995.

Shatz, Adam. *Prophets Outcast: A Century of Dissident Jewish Writing about Zionism and Israel*. New York: Nation Books, 2004.

Shayib, Yusuf al-. "Firqat Dam al-liddawiya: al-rab li-mukafahat al-'unsuriya al-Isra'iliya" [The Lyddan Dam band: Rap fighting Israeli racism]. *Al-Haya*, January 7, 2004, 21.

————. "Firqat Nawa al-Filastiniya turahin 'ala al-mustaqbal" [The Palestinian group Nawa bets on the future]. *Al-Haya*, June 24, 2002, 20.

Shehadeh, Raja. *When the Birds Stopped Singing: Life in Ramallah under Siege*. South Royalton, Vt.: Steerforth Press, 2003.

Shehori, Alon. "Kamah medinot 'araviyot yiftehu bashevu'ot haqerovim netzigut tayarutit betel-aviv" [Several Arab countries will open tourist offices in Tel Aviv in upcoming weeks]. *Israel Tourist Guide*, February 1, 1996, 1.

Sheleg, Yair. "Christian Generosity Becomes Rabbinical Nightmare." *Ha'aretz*, October 16, 2002. Translated and reposted at: http://www.bintjbeil.com/articles/en/021016_sheleg.html.

Shelemay, Kay Kaufman. *Let Jasmine Rain Down: Song and Remembrance among Syrian Jews*. Chicago: University of Chicago Press, 1998.

Shemesh, Moshe. *The Palestinian Entity, 1959–1974: Arab Politics and the* PLO. London: Frank Cass, 1988.

Shihada, Radi. *Al-Masrah al-Filastini fi Filastin 48: bayna sira' al-baqa' wa-infisam al-huwiya* [Palestinian theater in 1948 Palestine: Between the struggle for survival and the splitting of identity]. Ramallah: Wizarat al-Thaqafa al-Filastiniya, 1998.

Shiloah, Amnon. *Jewish Musical Traditions.* Detroit: Wayne State University Press, 1992.

Shiron [A book of Hebrew songs]. Jewish National Fund, n.d.

Shohat, Ella. "By the Bitstream of Babylon: Cyberfrontiers and Diasporic Vistas." In *Home, Exile, Homeland: Film, Media, and the Politics of Place,* edited by Hamid Naficy. New York: Routledge, 1999.

———. "Framing Post-Third-World Culture: Gender and Nation in Middle Eastern/North African Film and Video." *Jouvert: A Journal of Postcolonial Studies* 1, no. 1 (1997), http://social.chass.ncsu.edu/jouvert/v1i1/shohat.htm.

———. *Israeli Cinema: East/West and the Politics of Representation.* Austin: University of Texas Press, 1989.

———. "Reflections of an Arab Jew." *Emergences* 3, no. 4 (1992): 39–45.

———. "Sephardim in Israel: Zionism from the Standpoint of Its Jewish Victims." In *Dangerous Liaisons: Gender, Nation, and Postcolonial Perspectives,* edited by Anne McClintock, Aamir Mufti, and Ella Shohat. Minneapolis: University of Minnesota Press, 1997.

Shohat, Ella, and Robert Stam. *Unthinking Eurocentrism: Multiculturalism and the Media.* New York: Routledge, 1994.

Shuman, Amy. *Storytelling Rights: The Uses of Oral and Written Texts by Urban Adolescents.* Cambridge, England: Cambridge University Press, 1986.

Silberstein, Lawrence J. *The Postzionism Debates: Knowledge and Power in Israeli Culture.* New York: Routledge, 1999.

Sinnema, Peter. *Dynamics of the Picture Page: Representing the Nation in the "Illustrated London News."* Aldershot, England: Ashgate, 1998.

Sirhan, Nimr. "Al-Muqawama fi al-Fulklur al-Filastini" [Resistance in Palestinian folk culture]. *Shu'un Filastiniya* 43 (March 1975): 114–136.

——— "Al-Ughniya al-Sha'biya al-Filastiniya. min al-Huzn ila al-Shawq ila al-Qital" [Palestinian popular songs: From sadness to yearning to fighting]. *Shu'un Filastiniya* 19 (March 1973): 159–169.

Slyomovics, Susan. *The Object of Memory: Arab and Jew Narrate the Palestinian Village.* Philadelphia: University of Pennsylvania Press, 1998.

Smith, Michael. *Transnational Urbanism.* London: Blackwell, 2001.

Smooha, Sammy. *Israel: Pluralism and Conflict.* London: Routledge and Kegan Paul, 1978.

———. *The Orientation and Politicization of the Arab Minority in Israel.* Haifa: Haifa University Press, 1980.

Snowball, David. *Continuity and Change in the Rhetoric of the Moral Majority.* New York: Praeger, 1991.

Spivak, Gayatri. "Can the Subaltern Speak?" In *The Post-Colonial Studies Reader,* edited by Gareth Griffiths and Helen Tiffin. New York: Routledge, 1995.

————. *A Critique of Postcolonial Reason: Toward a History of the Vanishing Present.* Cambridge, Mass.: Harvard University Press, 1999.

Stam, Robert. *Film Theory: An Introduction.* Oxford: Blackwell, 1999.

Stein, Rebecca L. " 'First Contact' and Other Israeli Fictions: Tourism, Globalization, and the Middle East Peace Process." *Public Culture* 14, no. 3 (2002): 515–543.

————. "Israeli Leisure, 'Palestinian Terror,' and the Question of Palestine (Again)." *Theory and Event* 6, no. 3 (2002).

————. "Itineraries of Peace: Remapping Israeli and Palestinian Tourism." *Middle East Report* 25, no. 5 (1995): 16–19.

————. "National Itineraries, Itinerant Nations: Israeli Tourism and Palestinian Cultural Production." *Social Text* 56 (1998): 91–124.

Stein, Sarah Abrevaya. "Sephardi and Middle Eastern Jewries since 1492." In *The Oxford Handbook of Jewish Studies,* edited by Martin Goodman. Oxford: Oxford University Press, 2002.

Stevens, Richard P. *Zionism and Palestine before the Mandate: A Phase of Western Imperialism.* Beirut: Institute for Palestine Studies, 1972.

Stier, Haya, and Yossi Shavit. "Two Decades of Educational Intermarriage in Israel." In *Who Marries Whom? Educational Systems as Marriage Markets in Modern Societies,* edited by Hans-Peter Blossfeld and Andreas Timm. Oxford: Oxford University Press, 2004.

Stokes, Martin. *The Arabesk Debate: Music and Musicians in Modern Turkey.* New York: Oxford University Press, 1992.

Stoler, Ann Laura. *Race and the Education of Desire: Foucault's History of Sexuality and the Colonial Order of Things.* Durham, N.C.: Duke University Press, 1995.

Strober, Jerry, and Ruth Tomczak. *Jerry Falwell: Aflame for God.* Nashville, Tenn.: Thomas Nelson, 1979.

Sufian, Sandy. "Anatomy of the 1936–1939 Revolt: Images of the Body in Political Cartoons of Mandatory Palestine." *Journal of Palestine Studies,* forthcoming.

Sugarman, Margo Lipschitz. "Make Tours, Not War." *Jerusalem Report,* August 25, 1994, 34–36.

————. "Tourists with Reservations." *Jerusalem Report,* October 31, 1996, 47–48.

Suleiman, Jaber. "The Palestinian Liberation Organization: From the Right of Return to Bantustan." In *Palestinian Refugees: The Right of Return,* edited by Naseer Aruri. London: Pluto Press, 2001.

Swedenburg, Ted. *Memories of Revolt: The 1936–1939 Rebellion and the Palestinian National Past.* Fayetteville: University of Arkansas Press, 2003. First published 1995 by University of Minnesota Press.

————. "Musical Interzones: The Middle East and Beyond." Paper presented at the Center for the Humanities, Wesleyan University, September 23, 2002.

————. "The Palestinian Peasant as National Signifier." *Anthropological Quarterly* 63 (1990): 18–30.

————. "Saida Sultan/Danna International: Transgender Pop and the Polysemiotics of Sex, Nation, and Ethnicity on the Israeli-Egyptian Border." *Musical Quarterly* 81, no. 1 (1997): 81–108. Reprinted in *Mass Mediations: New Approaches to Popu-*

lar Culture in the Middle East and Beyond, edited by Walter Armbrust. Berkeley: University of California Press, 2000.

Swirski, Barbara, and Marilyn P. Safir, eds. Calling the Equality Bluff: Women in Israel. New York: Teachers College Press, 1991.

Swirski, Shlomo. Israel: The Mizrahi Majority. London: Zed Books, 1989.

Szwed, John F. "Vibrational Affinities." In Keeping Your Head to the Sky: Interpreting African American Home Ground, edited by Grey Gundaker and Tynes Cowan. Charlottesville: University Press of Virginia, 1998.

Tamari, Salim. "Bourgeois Nostalgia and Exile Narratives." In Homelands: Poetic Power and the Politics of Space, edited by Ron Robin and Bo Strath. Bern: Peter Lang, 2003.

———. "Factionalism and Class Formation in Recent Palestinian History." In Studies in the Economic and Social History of Palestine in the Nineteenth and Twentieth Centuries, edited by Roger Owen. Carbondale: Southern Illinois University Press, 1982.

Tammuz, Benjamin. Hapardes [The orchard]. Tel Aviv: Hakibbutz Hameuhad, 1971.

Tarabulsi, Fawwaz. "Jibal al-Suwwan: Filastin fi Fann Fayruz wa al-Rahabina" [Jibal al-Suwwan: Palestine in the art of Fayruz and the Rahbanis]. Al-Karmil (Ramallah), no. 57 (autumn 1998): 203–213.

Taylor, Alan. Prelude to Israel: An Analysis of Zionist Diplomacy, 1897–1947. Beirut: Institute for Palestine Studies, 1970.

Teboul, Annie. "Les Musiciens." In Les Juifs d'Algérie: Images et Textes, edited by Jean Laloum and Jean-Luc Allouche. Paris: Éditions du Scribe, 1987.

"Teiman: Mathilah lehitpateah la'olam" [Yemen: Starting to open to the world]. Ma'ariv, April 5, 1996, Tayarut section, 26.

Thompson, Paul. "Between Identities: Homi Bhabha Interviewed by Paul Thompson." In Migration and Identity: International Yearbook of Oral History and Life Stories, edited by Rina Benmayor and Andor Skotnes. Oxford: Oxford University Press, 1994.

Thoraval, Yves. Regards sur le cinéma égyptien 1895–1975. Paris: L'Harmattan, 1996.

Tincq, Henri. "Les fils de la diaspora défilent à Paris devant l'ambassade d'Israel." Le Monde, October 12, 2000.

Travers, Ann. Writing the Public in Cyberspace: Redefining Inclusion on the Net. New York: Garland, 2000.

Tucker, Judith. In the House of the Law: Gender and Islamic Law in Ottoman Syria and Palestine. Berkeley: University of California Press, 1998.

"Tunisia: Neot midbar basaharah" [Tunisia: Oasis in the Sahara]. Ma'ariv, April 5, 1996, Tayarut section, 27.

Tunub, Ibrahim al-. "Najah Salam: al-Dimuqratiya fi al-Ghina' Haddama" [Najah Salam: Democracy in singing is destructive]. Al-Haya, May 29, 2000, 15.

Turki, Fawaz. Exile's Return: The Making of a Palestinian American. New York: Free Press, 1993.

Turkle, Sherry. Life on the Screen: Identity in the Age of the Internet. New York: Simon and Schuster, 1995.

"Un parti islamiste dénonce la visite d'Enrico Macias en Algérie." Agence France Presse, February 15, 2000.

Van Biema, David. "The End: How It Got That Way." *Time.com*, June 23, 2002. Available at: http://www.time.com/time/covers/1101020701/theology.html.

Van Gelder, Lawrence. "As Life Goes on or Not." Review of *The Milky Way*, directed by Ali Nassar. *New York Times*, January 20, 1999, sec. E, p. 5.

Veicmanas, B. "Internal Trade." In *Economic Organization of Palestine*, edited by Sa'id Himadeh. Beirut: AUB Press, 1938.

Verdery, Katherine. "Beyond the Nation in Eastern Europe." *Social Text* 38 (1994): 1–19.

Wagner, Don. "For Zion's Sake." *Middle East Report* 32 (summer 2002): 52–58.

Wallis, Roger, and Krister Malm. *Big Sounds from Small Peoples: The Music Industry in Small Countries*. New York: Pendragon Press, 1984.

Warnock, Kitty. *Land before Honour: Palestinian Women in the Occupied Territories*. New York: Monthly Review Press, 1990.

Weingrod, Alex, ed. *Studies in Israeli Ethnicity: After the Ingathering*. New York: Routledge, 1985.

West, Cornell. "A Bloodstained Banner." In *Twilight, L.A. 1992*, edited by Anne Deveare Smith. New York: Anchor, 1994.

Willemen, Paul. *Looks and Frictions: Essays in Cultural Studies and Film Theory*. Bloomington: Indiana University Press, 1994.

Williams, Raymond. *The Country and the City*. Oxford: Oxford University Press, 1973.

———. *Keywords: A Vocabulary of Society and Culture*. Revised ed. Oxford: Oxford University Press, 1985.

Willis, Paul. *Common Culture: Symbolic Work at Play in the Everyday Cultures of the Young*. Milton Keynes, England: Open University Press, 1990.

Willson, Michele. "Community in the Abstract: A Political and Ethical Dilemma?" In *Virtual Politics: Identity and Community in Cyberspace*, edited by David Holmes. London: Sage, 1997.

Winegar, Jessica. "Claiming Egypt: The Cultural Politics of Artistic Practice in a Postcolonial Society." PhD diss., New York University, 2003.

Witek, Joseph. *Comic Books as History: The Narrative Art of Jack Jackson, Art Spiegelman, and Harvey Pekar*. Jackson: University Press of Mississippi, 1989.

Xavier, Ismail. *Allegories of Underdevelopment: Aesthetics and Politics in Modern Brazilian Cinema*. Minneapolis: University of Minnesota Press, 1997.

———. "Historical Allegory." In *A Companion to Film Theory*, edited by Toby Miller and Robert Stam. Oxford: Blackwell, 1999.

Ya'ari, Ehud. "The Jordanian Option." *Jerusalem Report*, February 9, 1995, 28–30.

Yehia, Karem. "All Our Destinies." *Al-Ahram Weekly*, July 4–10, 2002.

———. "The Image of the Palestinians in Egypt, 1982–85." *Journal of Palestine Studies* 16, no. 2 (winter 1987): 45–63.

Yiftachel, Oren. "State Policies, Land Control and an Ethnic Minority: The Arabs in the Galilee, Israel." *Society and Space* 9 (1991): 329–362.

Yiftachel, Oren, and Avinoam Meir, eds. *Ethnic Frontiers and Peripheries: Landscapes of Development and Inequality in Israel*. Boulder, Colo.: Westview, 1998.

Yosef, Raz. *Beyond Flesh: Queer Masculinities and Nationalisms in Israeli Cinema*. New Brunswick, N.J.: Rutgers University Press, 2004.

———. "Homoland: Interracial Sex and the Israeli/Palestinian Conflict in Israeli Cinema." *GLQ: A Journal of Lesbian and Gay Studies* 8, no. 4 (2002): 553–579.

Young, Elise G. *Keepers of the History*. New York: Teachers College Press, 1992.

Zaqtan, Ghassan. "Nafy al-manfa'" [The negation of exile]. *Al-Karmil* 51 (spring 1997): 141–145.

Zayyad, Tawfiq. *Diwan Tawfiq Zayyad*. Beirut: Dar al-'Awda, n.d.

Zerrouky, Hassane. "Constantine attend l'enfant du pays." *L'Humanité*, March 4, 2000.

———. "Enrico Macias déchaîne les passions." *L'Humanité*, March 7, 2000.

Zertal, Idit. *Zhavam shel hayehudim: Hahagirah hayehudit hamahtardit Le-Eretz Yisrael, 1945–1948* [From catastrophe to power: Jewish intellectual immigration to Palestine, 1945–1948]. Tel Aviv: Am Oved, 1996.

Zerubavel, Yael. *Recovered Roots: Collective Memory and the Making of Israeli National Tradition*. Chicago: University of Chicago Press, 1995.

Zilberfarb, Ben-Zion. "The Effects of the Peace Process on the Israeli Economy." *Israel Affairs* 1 (autumn 1994): 84–95.

Zimerman, Moshe. "The Holocaust and the 'Otherness,' or the Additional Value of the Film Al Tigu Li Bashoa." In *Fictive Looks: On Israeli Cinema*, edited by Nurith Gertz, Orli Lubin, and Judd Ne'eman. Tel Aviv: Open University Press, 1998 [in Hebrew].

Zirbel, Katherine E. "Playing It Both Ways: Local Egyptian Performers between Regional Identity and International Markets." In *Mass Mediations: New Approaches to Popular Culture in the Middle East and Beyond*, edited by Walter Armbrust Berkeley: University of California Press, 2000.

Zureik, Elia. *Israel: A Study in Internal Colonialism*. London: Routledge and Kegan Paul, 1979.

Films

Abu Sa'ud, Ibrahim, producer. *Ya Quds*. With Majd Qasim. Videoclip. Cairo: Studio 10. n.d.

'Awad, 'Adil, producer. *Ubrit Thawrat Abtal* [Operetta of the Heroes' Revolution]. With Yusuf al-Katri. Video. Distributed by Ibrahim Sami, n.d.

Bakri, Muhammad, director. *1948*. Video. Tel Aviv: Ozen hashelishit, 2000.

———. *Jenin, Jenin*. Video. Seattle: Arab Film Distribution, 2002.

Barabash, Uri, director. *Me'ahore Hasoragim* [Beyond the walls]. Video. Tel Aviv: GMC Home Video, 1993 [1984].

Benshitrit, David, director. *Miba'ad Lire'alat Hagalut* [Behind the wall of exile]. Video. Jerusalem: Shidure keshet, 1998 [1992].

———. *Ruah Qadim* [Kaddim wind-Moroccan chronicle]. Video. Hod Hasharon, Israel: Akedia Productions, 2002.

Bouzaglo, Haim, director. *Nisuim Fictiviyim* [Fictitious marriage]. Video. Teaneck, NJ: Ergo Media, 1992 [1989].

Bruner, Benny, director. *The Seventh Million.* Video. Amsterdam: Viewpoint Productions: 1995.

Bukai, Rafi, director. *Avanti Popolo.* Video. Tel Aviv: Golan Globus Video, 1988 [1986].

Chitrit, Sami Shalom and Eli Hamo, director. *The Black Panthers (In Israel) Speak.* Video. Münster, Germany: mec film, 2002.

Corcoran, B., director. *Left Behind II: Tribulation Force.* Video. Cloud Ten Productions, 2002.

Dayan, Nissim, director. *Gesher Tzar Me'od* [On a narrow bridge]. Video. Not distributed. 1985.

Dotan, Shimon, director. *Hiuh Hagedi* [Smile of the lamb]. Video. Tel Aviv: Orev Films, 1986.

El-Hassan, Azza, director. *Sinbad Is a She* [Hiya Sinbad]. Video. Distributed by director, 1999.

Ganani, Gideon, director. *Esh Tzolevet* [Crossfire]. Video. Teaneck, NJ: Ergo Media, 1989.

Gerretson, Peter, director. *Apocalypse—Caught in the Eye of the Storm.* Video. Cloud Ten Pictures, 1998.

Gitai, Amos, director. *Bait* [House]. Video. Tel Aviv: Amos Gitai, 2000.

———. *Kadosh.* Video. Paris: UGC International. 1999.

Godard, Jean-Luc, Jean-Pierre Gorin, and Anne-Marie Mieville, directors. *Ici et ailleurs.* Video. Paris: JR Films, 1975.

Hasan, Nizzar, director. *Istiqlal* [Independence]. Video. Distributed by director, 1994.

———. *Ustura* [Fable]. Video. Distributed by director, 1998.

———. *Yasmine.* Video. Distributed by director, 1996.

Idris, 'Ali, director. *Ashab walla biznis* [Friends or business]. Video. Al-Duqqi, Egypt: Al-Sibka Films, 2002.

International Association for Family Planning, director. *Early Marriage in Palestine* [Al-Zawaj al-mubakkar fi Filastin]. Video. n.d.

Katz, Nisan, director. *Thank God for India.* Video. Tel Hai, Israel: Hamerka tikshoret Tel Hai, 1995.

Khleifi, Michel, director. *Al-Dhakira al-Khasiba* [Fertile memory]. DVD. Seattle: Arab Film Distribution, 1980.

———. *Hikayat al-Jawahir al-Thalatha* [The tale of the three jewels]. Video. Oley, Pennsylvania: Bullfrog Films, 1994.

———. *'Urs al-Jalil* [Wedding in Galilee]. Video. New York: Kino Video, 1987.

Kishon, Efraim, director. *Salah Shabati.* Video. New York: International Video Center, 1983 [1964].

Laufer, Erez, producer. *Solitary Star: Zehava Ben.* Video. Tel Aviv: Idan Productions, 1997.

Loevy [Levi], Ram, director. *Ani Ahmed* [I am Ahmed]. Video. Tel Aviv: Haozen hashelishit, 1991 [1986].

———. *Close, Closed, Closure* [Seger]. Video. New York: First Run/Icarus Films, 2002.

———. *Sipur Hirbet Hizah.* Video. Not distributed. 1976.

———. *Leḥm* [Bread]. Video. Not distributed. 1985.

Marcos, Norma, director. *The Veiled Hope* [L'espoir Voilé: Femmes de Palestine]. Video. New York: Women Make Movies, 1996.

Masharawi, Rashid, director. *Ayyam Tawila fi Ghazza* [Long days in Gaza]. Video. Ramallah: Cinema Production Center, 1991.

———. *Hatta Ish'arin Akhir* [Curfew]. Video. New York: New Yorker Films, 1994.

Mizrahi, Moshe, director. *Habayit berehov Shelush* [The house on Chelouche Street]. Video. Sandy Hook, N.J.: Video Yesteryear, 1983 [1973].

Moshensons, Ilan, director. *Roveh Huliot* [The wooden gun]. Video. Teaneck, N.J.: Ergo Media, 1987 [1979].

Nassar, Ali. *Darab al-tabbanat* [The milky way]. Video. Seattle: Arab Film Distribution, 1998.

Riklis, Eran, director. *Gemar Gavi'a* [Cup final]. New York: First Run Films, 2002 [1992].

Sarin, V., director. *Left Behind.* Video. Cloud Ten Productions, 2000.

Sawalme, Muhammad, director. *The Invisible Half* [Al-Nusf al-gha'ib]. Video. Distributed by director, 1995.

Suleiman, Elia, director. *Homage by Assassination.* Video. Distributed by director, 1991.

———. *Muqaddima li-Nihayat Jidal* [Introduction to the end of an argument]. Video. Seattle: Arab Film Distribution, 1990.

———. *Sijill Ikhtifaa'* [Chronicle of a disappearance]. Video. Seattle: Arab Film Distribution, 1996.

Telalim, Asher, director. *Al Tigu Li Bushoah* [Don't touch my Holocaust]. Video. Tel Aviv: Set Haṭakot, 1996.

Van Heerden, André, director. *Apocalypse II—Revelation.* Video. Cloud Ten Pictures, 1999.

———. *Apocalypse III—Tribulation.* Video. Cloud Ten Pictures, 2000.

——— *Apocalypse IV—Judgement.* Video. United American Video, 2001.

Wolman, Dan, director. *Mikha'el Sheli* [My Michael]. Video. Teaneck, N.J.: Ergo Media, 1987 [1975].

Zobaidi, Sobhi al-, director. *Crossing Kalandia.* Video. Tel Aviv: FPAD, 2002.

———. *Nisa' fi al-shams.* [Women in the sun]. Video. Distributed by director. 1998.

Music and Sound Recordings

'Abd al-Rahim, Sha'ban. *Insa ya 'Amr!* [Forget it, Amr!] Cairo: Super li-l-Intaj, 2000.

———. *Mati'darsh* [You can't]. Cairo: al-Wadi li-l-Intaj, 2001.

———. *Al-Karh shay' qalil, ya Isra'il* [Hate is a small thing, Israel!]. Cairo: al-Wadi li-l-Intaj, 2002.

Alterman, Natan. "Hanale Hitbalbela" [Hanala got confused]. Lyrics by Natan

Alterman (1944). Music by Tsliley Ha Kerem. On *Songs That We Love*. Tel Aviv: Reuveni Brothers, 1986.

Argov, Zohar. "Elinor." Audiocassette. Tel Aviv: Reuveni Brothers, 1980.

Ben, Zehava. "Tipat Mazal" [A drop of luck]. Audiocassette. Tel Aviv: Eli Banai Productions, 1992.

Cheikh Raymond. *Concert Public De Malouf*. Vols. 1–3. CD. Paris: Al Sur, 1995.

———. *La Desirée*. CD. Paris: Al Sur, 1999.

Hekerem, Tszliley. "Likom Ba'adekh, Medina" [To fight for you, country]. On *Songs That We Love*. Tel Aviv: Reuveni Brothers, 1986.

Horowitz, Amy. *Side by Side: Creators on Restless Soil*. Radio series. Produced by Amy Horowitz. Edited by Ziv Yonatan. 5 audiocassettes. Washington, D.C.: Private collection, 1986.

Luzon, Eli, and Yonni Roeh, "Eyzo Medina" [What a country]. Audiocassette. Tel Aviv: Ben Mosh Productions, 1986.

Macias, Enrico. *Hommage à Cheikh Raymond*. CD. Paris: Trema/Sony Music, 1999.

———. *Enrico Macias en concert en hommage à Cheikh Raymond*. DVD. Paris: TF1 Video, 2000.

Medina, Avihu. "Avraham Avinu" [Abraham our father]. Audiocassette. Petah Tikvah: A. M. Hafakor, 1992.

CONTRIBUTORS

Livia Alexander is executive director of ArteEast, a nonprofit organization promoting the visibility of the arts and cultures of the Middle East in the United States. She has curated and consulted on numerous Middle East film festivals. She has a PhD in Middle Eastern cinemas from New York University, where she completed her dissertation on Israeli and Palestinian cinemas between the two Intifadas.

Carol Bardenstein is Associate Professor of Arabic and Comparative Literature at the University of Michigan. Her book, *Translation and Transformation in Modern Arabic Literature: The Indigenous Assertions of Muhammad 'Uthman Jalal*, is forthcoming from Harrassowitz Press, 2004. She is completing a monograph entitled *Cultivating Attachments: Palestinian and Israeli Discourses of Rootedness and Dispersion*.

Elliott Colla is Assistant Professor of Comparative Literature at Brown University, where he teaches modern Arabic literature. He is writing *Conflicted Antiquities*, a study of the figures of Egyptian antiquities in European travel writing, museum discourses, and modern Egyptian literature. He is on the editorial committee of *Middle East Report*.

Amy Horowitz is a fellow at the Mershon Center for Public Policy and a lecturer in the Department of International Studies at the Ohio State University. Her dissertation is entitled *Musika Yam Tikhonit Yisraelit (Israeli Mediterranean Music): Cultural Boundaries and Disputed Territories*. She is the founder and executive director of Roadwork: Center for Responsible Citizenship.

Laleh Khalili is a lecturer in politics at the School of Oriental and African Studies, University of London. Her doctoral research focused on the mnemonic practices of the Palestinian refugees in Lebanon and the ways commemorative performances frame their political claim making.

Mary Layoun is Professor and Chair of the Department of Comparative Literature, University of Wisconsin, Madison. Recent work includes *Wedded to the Land? Gender, Boundaries and Nationalism in Crisis* (Duke University, 2001); "Visions of Security: Impermeable Borders, Impassable Walls, Impossible Home/Lands?"; "The Sixth Day of Compassion: The Fiction of Andrée Chedid and the Gendering of Life towards Death"; and "The Stories That GATT/WTO Tell: Narrative Authority, National Boundaries, and 'Intellectual Property.'"

Mark LeVine is Associate Professor of Modern Middle Eastern History, Culture, and Islamic Studies at the University of California, Irvine. His publications include *Overthrowing Geography: Jaffa, Tel Aviv and the Struggle for Palestine* (University of California Press, 2005); *Why They Don't Hate Us: From Culture Wars to Culture Jamming in the Global Era* (Oneworld Publications, forthcoming); *Religion, Social Practice, and Contested Hegemonies: Reconstructing Muslim Public Spheres*, coedited with Armando Salvatore (Palgrave, forthcoming), and *Twilight of Empire: Responses to Occupation*, with Viggo Mortensen and Pilar Perez (Perceval Press, 2003).

Joseph Massad is Assistant Professor of Modern Arab Politics and Intellectual History at Columbia University. His books include *Colonial Effects: The Making of National Identity in Jordan* (Columbia University Press, 2001), and *Desiring Arabs* (Harvard University Press, forthcoming).

Melanie McAlister writes and teaches about foreign policy, popular culture, religion, and globalization. She is the author of *Epic Encounters: Culture, Media, and U.S. Interests in the Middle East, 1945–2000* (University of California Press, 2001) and has published analysis about U.S. perceptions of the Middle East in the *New York Times*, the *Washington Post*, *The Chronicle of Higher Education*, and *The Nation*. She is currently working on a study of Christian evangelicals, popular culture, and foreign policy.

Ilan Pappé is Professor in the Political Science Department at the University of Haifa. He is the author of *A History of Modern Palestine: One Land, Two Peoples* (Cambridge University Press, 2004); *The Making of the Arab-Israeli Conflict 1947–1951* (I.B. Tauris, 1992); and *Britain and the Arab-Israeli Conflict, 1948–1951* (St. Martin's Press, 1988) and editor of *The Israel/Palestine Question* (Routledge, 1999).

Rebecca L. Stein is Assistant Professor of Cultural Anthropology at Duke University. She is on the editorial board of *Middle East Report*, and her writing on Israeli political culture has appeared in *Social Text, Public Culture*, and *Theory and Event*. She is the coeditor, with Joel Beinin, of *The Struggle for Sovereignty in Palestine and Israel, 1993–2004* (Verso, forthcoming) and is completing a monograph on articulations of tourism and settler-nationalism in contemporary Israel.

Ted Swedenburg is Professor of Anthropology at the University of Arkansas. He is the author of *Memories of Revolt: The 1936–39 Rebellion and the Palestinian National Past* (University of Arkansas Press, 2003) and coeditor of *Displacement, Diaspora and the Geographies of Identity* (Duke University Press, 1996). He is currently working on a book about Middle Eastern-related "border" music, called *Radio Interzone*.

Salim Tamari is Professor of Sociology at Birzit University, the director of the Institute of Jerusalem Studies, and editor of *Jerusalem Quarterly File: Hawliyat al-Quds*. His recent books include *Ahwal al-Quds al-'Uthmaniya fi al-Mudhakkarat al-Jawhariya* [Ottoman Jerusalem in the Jawharia memoirs] (Institute of Jerusalem Studies, 2003) and *The King of Palestine and Other Essays on the Social History of Palestine* (forthcoming), coedited with Issam Nassar.

Armey, Dick, 295–96, 306

Ashkenazim, 103, 107, 261, 274, 276, 280, 281 n.5; hegemony of, 82, 88, 266; and music, 216–17; racism of, 90. *See also* identity; Israelis; Jews

audiences, film: Arab, 232; cosmopolitan, 160; French, 241; international, 161, 167; Israeli, 118; Palestinian, 165. *See also* cinema

authenticity, 268; in Egypt, 341; of music, 220

automobiles: consumption in Mandatory Palestine, 60, 67. *See also* advertising; commodity

a'yan: in Jerusalem, 31, 43; mistresses of, 45

Barak, Ehud, 105, 249

Barthes, Roland, 340, 345, 358, 360 n.4

Beersheba, 203. *See also* Israel

Beirut, 143, 242, 274. *See also* Lebanon

Bensmaïn, Khaled, 248

Beurs, 236, 242–43, 245, 250, 252. *See also* Arabs; France

Bhabha, Homi, 86, 101, 112, 114, 122 n.8, 124 n.31, 229 n.45. *See also* mimicry

bilingualism, 132

binary, 120; Arab/Jew, 9, 103, 119, 251; Orientalist, 275; Palestinian/Israeli, 5, 103, 119, 161. *See also* hybrid

Birmingham School (cultural studies), 7–9, 14

Black Panthers (Israeli), 79, 214. *See also* Mizrahim

borders: as confining, 14; crossing of, 10, 14, 126, 127, 144, 218, 223–25, 260, 262, 271; permeable, 261, 280; virtual, 141–42. *See also* Across Borders Project; boundaries

boundaries: artistic, 214; blurring, 111, 116, 118, 125 n.40; colonial, 233; crossing of, 101–3, 119–20, 203; crossing national, 69; ethnoconfessional, 28–39; fluid, 233; political, 214; porous,

220. *See also* Across Borders Project; borders; transnational

bourekas, 86, 104. *See also* cinema

bourgeoisie, Palestinian. *See* class

Bouteflika, President, 247–49

boycott: Arab, 235, 242, 264, 283 n.15; consumer, 141; Egyptian, 343, 352. *See also* normalization

Burke, Timothy, 60

Bush, George W., 138, 311 n.32; and Christian Zionists, 290, 296

businessmen: Jaffa, 58, 61; popular culture of Jaffa Palestinians, 65. *See also* advertising; commodity

bypass roads, 162

cafés, 222; in Egypt, 339; Internet, 126, 129–30; Israeli, and discourse on leisure, 22 n.48; in Jerusalem, 36, 43–44, 46–47

Cairo, 178. *See also* Egypt

Camp David, 113, 242

capitalism, global, 151. *See also* commodity; globalization

cartography: of Middle East, 11; musical, 220–21. *See also* geography; mapping; space

cartoons, in Palestinian press, 56, 59, 73 n.20

cassette: companies, 216; necklace, 212; players, 177; recorders, 215; tapes, 85, 178, 188, 190, 203, 206, 217, 343, 345. *See also* music

CDs: *Hommage à Cheikh Raymond*, 247; *Zehava Ben Sings Arabic*, 212, 221

censorship: Egyptian state censor, 345, 350; by Palestinian Authority, 170 n.25

Chadhli Benjedid, President, 244

children, Palestinian, 137–38. *See also* youth

Christian: Coalition, 296, 307; Right, 290; Zionists, 14, 290, 292, 294, 296, 310 n.29. *See also* Antichrist;

Way], 158, 170 n.19; *al-Dhakira al-Khasiba* [Fertile Memory], 155; *Esh Tzolevet* [Crossfire], 8; *Gemar Gevi'a* [Cup Final], 115–16; *Hatta Ish'arin Akhir* [Curfew], 158–60, 170 n.21; *Hikayat al-Jawahir al-Thalatha* [The Tale of the Three Jewels], 159–62; *Homage by Assassination*, 164; *Ici et ailleurs*, 355–59; *Jenin, Jenin*, 116, 124 n.39; *Jibal al-Suwwan* [Mountains of flint] (musical), 183–84; *Kadosh*, 118–19; *Me'ahore Hasoragim* [Beyond the Walls], 107–8; *Miba'ad Lire'alat Hagalut* [Behind the Wall of Exile], 89; *1948*, 89, 170 n.19; *Nisa' fi al-Shams* [Women in the Sun], 171; *Nisuim Fictiviyim* [Fictitious Marriage], 110–12; *Ustura* [Fable], 165–66; *Yasmine*, 166, 172 n.37. *See also* cinema

first contact, 261, 269, 272–73, 275, 285 n.37; FLN (Front de Libération National), 239–40. *See also* colonial; postcolonial

flows, 273; global, 261; regional, 261. *See also* borders, boundaries

foreign workers. *See* workers

Foucault, Michel, 33 n.21

France: leftists in, 359; 1968, 358–59; racism in, 241. *See also* Beurs

Freitag, Sandria, 68

fundamentalism, 289, 293, 301, 308 n.6; fundamentalist fiction, 288; and love of Israel, 304; and racial exclusivism, 202; and racial liberalism, 302–4. *See also* Antichrist; Armageddon; Christian; end times; evangelicalism; *Left Behind* series; Rapture; Second Coming; Tribulation

Galron, Nurit, 85–86
Gates, Henry Louis, Jr., 144
Gaza, 244, 318; Gaza Strip, 158, 160
gaze, 331, 334; self-reflexive, 163. *See also* visual

Gefen, Yonatan, 203
gender: femininity, 110; masculinity, 133, 185; and masculinization, 185; modern women, 62; and motherhood, 191; Palestinian women, 166; roles, 62, 324–25; women in Palestinian film, 171 n.31; women singers, 222; women's rights, 162

genre: comics as, 314–16; film, 151, 153
geography: of consumption, 13; of contiguity, 273; of leisure, 267–68; of Middle East, 272; of mobility, 263; national, 273; of power, 263; regional, 273. *See also* maps; space

Ghrenassia, Gaston. *See* Enrico Macias
globalization, 143, 161, 262; of capital, 161; of economy, 260; of Israeli economy, 264–65, 279, 281; of labor, 13; of media, 13. *See also* commodity; geography; New Middle East

grammar, popular, 260
Gramsci, Antonio, 7–9, 21 n.29
Gulf States: singers, 196; tourists to Israel, 277

Habiby, Emile, 83, 90, 114
Haifa, 136
Hall, Stuart, 7–9
Hebrew, 118, 269–70, 272, 274; lessons, 63; pronunciation of, 117
hegemony, 8–9, 21 n.29, 21 n.31; hegemonic discourse, Israeli, 116
hip-hop, Palestinian-Israeli, 13, 193–95. *See also* music; musicians; songs
history: collective, 153; deconstruction of colonial, 164; forgetting of, 274; historiography, 9; Israeli, 77; Israeli new historians, 81, 92 n.10; Jewish Israeli, 274; national, 140; Palestinian historiography, 9, 80; postmodernist historiography, 81; revisionist, 4; rewriting, 70; Zionist historiography, 80, 82. *See also* academia; Middle East Studies

Hizbullah, 133
Holocaust, 82, 238, 251, 348–49; in
Israeli film, 88; survivors, 80, 207,
216. *See also* anti-Semitism
homeland, 164, 202; Palestinian, 162;
return to, 163. *See also* diaspora
horror literature, 299–300
al-Husayni, Hashim, 27
al-Husayni, Husayn, 34–35, 45
Husayni, Musa Qadhim, 35
Husaynis, 31, 33, 49 n.13
hybrid: generic, 289; hybridity, 29, 66,
102, 122 n.8, 168, 222, 225, 234, 262.
See also binary
hygiene, 66. *See also* cleaning products

identity, 99, 102, 121 n.5; blurred, 100,
108–9, 116; chromatic inversion of,
107, 123 n.23; class, 206; constructed,
100; contradictory, 223; Egyptian,
341–42; embodied, 126; ethnic, 207,
231; European, 274; and European
Jewish subject, 276; fellaheen, 55, 59,
68, 70, 140; fluid, 100; hegemonic,
100; improvisational, 223; Israeli,
260, 262; national, 202, 231; online,
131, Palestinian, 132–33, 164; Russian
immigrants, 265; strategic, 223; and
subject formation, 270; subverted,
100–101. *See also* Ashkenazim; Beurs;
gender; Mizrahim; Palestinians
images: of bodies, 138; digital, 131, 135–
37; montage of, 356; mythical, 359;
national, 135, 138–39; as transparent
truth, 353; unified, of Palestine, 156;
and rhetoric, 344–45; strained use of,
347, 350
India, 75 n.49
Inhofe, Jim, 294–95
Institute for Palestine Studies, 2, 17 n.7.
See also academia, Israeli; Palestinians
intellectuals: Israeli, 104; Palestinian,
53. *See also* academia, Israeli; Israel
studies; history; Middle East Studies;
Palestinians

Internet, 13, 126, 129, 131, 144, 292,
297–98, 311 n.36, 339; centers, 141;
chat, 132; romance on, 134–35. *See also*
cyberspace
interzone, 233–34, 251, 253 n.8
Intifada: al-Aqsa, 12, 90, 124 n.39, 128,
131, 134, 139, 167, 197, 199, 249, 343,
352–53; culture of, 12; first (1987–
1993), 3, 80–81, 83, 85–86, 105,
137, 139, 151, 154, 161, 192, 330; Intifadiana, in Egypt, 340, 343–53, 359,
363 n.37
Islamists: Algerian, 246, 248
Israel: militarism in, 82; racial oppression in, 194; ties with Arab states,
260, 264. *See also* academia; Ashkenazim; Barak, Ehud; Beersheba;
cinema: Israeli; Eilat; Eshkol, Levi;
Haifa; identity; Intifada; Jerusalem;
Jews; Labor Party; Likud; Meretz;
Mizrahim; Netanyahu, Benjamin;
1948 war; 1973 war; 1967 war; Oslo
Accords; Palestinians in Israel; Peace
Now; post-Zionism; Rabin, Yitzhak;
settlers; Sharon, Ariel; Shas; Tel Aviv;
Zionism
Israeli-Egyptian peace treaty (1978), 113,
242. *See also* Egypt
Israelis: Israeliness, 280; normative
Israeliness, 274; as Nazis, 138; as
peace-seeking, 161. *See also* Ashke-
nazim; Mizrahim; Palestinians in
Israel
Israelization, 209
Israel studies, 22 n.39. *See also* Middle
East Studies

Jaffa, 50: as backward, 54; as civilized,
61; contemporary, 70; as cosmopolitan, 62–64; as cultural center, 54–55;
films in, 61; Jewish neighborhoods in,
64; port, 56; urban development in,
57; Zionist encroachment on, 57. *See
also* Palestinians
Jameson, Fredric, 317–18

Jawhariyyeh, Jiryis, 31, 39, 42
al-Jazeera, 12, 134
Jenkins, Jerry, 288, 295, 298, 302–3, 312 n.41
Jerusalem, 46, 118, 164, 182–83, 244, 246, 346; daily life in, 36–37; early Mandate, 29; growth outside walls, 37–38; Israeli occupation of, 294; Jews of, 38; Late Ottoman, 28–29, 43; modernity, 27, 43; Old City, 28, 320; in photographs, 136; quarters, 28, 37
Jerusalem Film Institute, 169
Jewish: diaspora, 80; European ethnic subject, 276; Israeli history, 274; Israeli youth; 85; musicians in Algeria, 236; neighborhoods in Jaffa, 64; orange exporters, 63; return, 293
Jews: mass conversion of, 291, 293, 304; as musicians, 42–43; Orthodox, 91, 118–19; in Ottoman Palestine, 41. *See also* anti-Semitism; Arab Jews; Holocaust; Mizrahim
Jordan, 277
Jordan River, 185
journalists, Palestinian, 53, 55, 72 n.15
juxtaposition, 315–18, 322, 356

Klezmer, 211
kufiya, 56, 138, 329, 343

Labor Party (Israel), 79, 252, 260, 296
LaHaye, Tim, 288, 295, 298, 302–3, 312 n.41
land: Palestinian, 160–61, 185; and Zionism, 164. *See also* homeland
language. *See* accents; bilingualism; dialect, Arabic; grammar; popular; Hebrew
The Late, Great Planet Earth, 294
Lebanon: 1982 war, 3, 80, 83, 86, 104, 115, 274
Left Behind series, 288–95, 297–306; Arabs and Muslims in, 304–5; and high tech language, 299; internationalism in, 304; invisibility of

Palestinians in, 305–6; and Israeli Jews, 305; marketing tech savvy, 298; multiculturalism in, 303–4. *See also* Antichrist; Armageddon; Christian; end times; evangelicalism; fundamentalism; Rapture; Second Coming; Tribulation
Leyris, Jacques, 246
Likud, 79, 90, 223, 234, 250, 252, 296
Lindsey, Hal, 294
Literature. *See* cartoons; comics; horror literature; poetry; science fiction
Lockman, Zachary, 9

Mahalla (Jerusalem), 28, 37
Mahallat al-Sa'diya, 32, 36
malouf, 232, 238, 245. *See also* Andalusia: music of
mapping: evangelical, of Palestine-Israel, 306; of Israel, 260; of Middle East, 10–11; of Palestine, 137. *See also* cartography; geography; space
maqam, 187, 199 n.16
martyrdom, 127, 137, 141, 353. *See also* victimization
martyr operations. *See* suicide bombings
Masabni, Badi'a (musician), 44
masculinity. *See* gender
McDonald's, 352
media: Israeli, 260; mass, 341; state, 215, 351. *See also* cyberspace; Internet; newspapers; radio; television
Mediterranean Israeli music, 85, 203, 205–7, 213–14, 218, 220, 224, 225 n.1. *See also* Mizrahim: music of
melodrama, and Egyptian cinema, 342
memory, 166, 237; cultural, 164
Meretz, 223
Michael, Sami, 83–84
Middle East Research and Information Project (MERIP), 17 n.8
Middle East studies, 1, 11; Middle East Studies Association, 3, 16 n.4. *See also* academia; Israel studies
military rule, of Palestinian Israelis, 83

mimicry, 100, 102, 112, 114, 118, 122 n.8; menace of, 112, 114, 124 n.31. *See also* Bhabha, Homi

Mitchell, W. J., 129

mixing, social, 64

Mizrahim, 12, 77–79, 82, 86, 90–91, 100, 103, 107–10, 115, 119, 205–7, 214–15, 218–20, 224, 234, 265–66, 280, 281 n.5; fiction of, 83–84; film directors, 88; music of, 85–86, 206, 231, 236, 253 n.3. *See also* Black Panthers; identity

modernity: colonial, 69; evangelical, 293, 297; of fundamentalism, 301; in Jaffa, 57, 63–63; of Tribulation Force, 301; modernization, 341; modernization of Arab music, 42, 179

Moody Bible Institute, 295

Moral Majority, 295, 302

Moshe, Haim, 216, 235

Mubarak, Hosni, 350–51

music: borrowing, musical, 204; copyright and, 217; country, 216; European soundscape, 209; French variety, 240–41; Greek, 210, 217; Israeli rock, 210, 217; jazz, 191–92; martial music, 188; re-Arabizing of Israeli music, 211; soundscape, 202, 204, 206, 215, 222–23; Turkish, 203, 217; at wedding parties, 211, 213, 222, 236, 239; Western, 188; world music, 218, 221–22. *See also* Andalusia: music of; hip-hop; *malouf*; Mediterranean Israeli music; Mizrahim; musicians; *muwashshahat*; songs; *taqtuqa*

musicologists, 217; ethno-, 220

al-Mutran School, 34

muwashshahat, 33–34, 49 n.10, 49 n.12

MWR (musicians), 193–94

myth, 166, 340–41, 345, 347, 352–53, 359, 360 n.4; Israeli, 90, 269

Na'aman, Dorit, 110–11

Nakba, 80, 83, 140, 177

narrative, 318–20, 331, 342, 344, 353; of discovery, 270; national, 158, 162, 167; Palestinian, 87; Palestinian national metanarrative, 162; Zionist, 77

Nashashibi, Fakhri, 44

Nashashibi, Raghib, 36, 49 n.13

Nasser, Gamal Abdul, 180, 188, 223, 235

nation: absence of nation-state, 151, 155, 167; Arab nationalism, 29, 41; diasporic nationalism, 134; death of nation-state, 143; ethnic nationalism, 47; the national, 152–53; national allegory, 105; national form, 280; national ideology, 157; national imaginaries, 144; nationalism, 175–76; nationalist song, 175–76; nationalist symbols, 130, 135–36, 141; national paradigm, 5, 9, 14, 165; national slogans, 163; national soundtrack, 208, 211; national struggle, 153, 157, 160, 162, 167, 180; nation-building, 152, 166; nation-state, 143, 152, 232, 262; Palestinian nationalism, 38, 40, 51–52, 67, 69, 137, 150–51, 153, 160, 162; Palestinian nationalist song, 176–77; pan-Arab nationalism, 223; as protagonist, 158; renationalization, 280; virtuous, 159

Nazareth, 163–64. *See also* Palestinians: in Israel

neighborhood: music, 207, 213, 216; parties, 211

Netanyahu, Benjamin, 105, 223

New Middle East, 267–69, 278. *See also* Oslo Accords

news gathering, on Internet, 131–32. *See also* cyberspace; Internet

newspapers, 71; communal reading of, 68; Egyptian, 343; Israeli, 261–62, 269, 271–72, 274–77, 282 n.6; in Jaffa, 50–51, 55, 57, 67; lack of, 70; local, 218; Palestinian, 72 n.15; Zionist, 54. *See also* media

1948 war, 80–81, 237

1973 war, 79, 214

1967 war, 113, 181, 214, 241, 294

normalization, 248; anti-,14, 236, 343, 352. *See also* boycott; Oslo Accords

normativity, 276; Ashkenazi, 280

nostalgia, 107, 136, 160, 234. *See also* memory

Nusseibeh, Sari, 135, 148 n.31

OAS (Secret Army Organization), 238–39, 248–49

occupation, Israeli. *See* Occupied Territories

Occupied Territories, 85, 155, 184, 250, 265, 283 n.12, 314, 327, 330–31, 344; Israel's reoccupation of, 140

online identity. *See* cyberspace

oranges, 61, 66; grove as symbol, 160; Jaffa, 58; Jewish exporters of, 63

Orientalism, 277; in cinema, 109. *See also* Said, Edward

Orientalizing, 208; self-, 223

Oslo Accords (1993), 4, 91, 105, 150–51, 162, 195, 201, 260, 263–64, 266–67; Oslo process, 261, 265, 279. *See also* globalization; New Middle East; normalization; peace

Palestine. *See* Arafat, Yasir; Gaza; al-Husayni, Musa Qadhim; Intifada; Jaffa; Jerusalem; Nashashibi, Raghib; Nazareth; Nusseibeh, Sari; Occupied Territories; Oslo Accords

Palestine Liberation Organization (PLO), 188, 263, 355, 359

Palestine Research Center, 2

Palestinian Authority (PA), 150, 152, 162, 167, 183, 263

Palestinian Broadcasting Corporation, 152

Palestinian Film Institute, 154

Palestinians, 86, 115, 116, 119, 140, 142; exilic, 103, 159–60; in Israel, 77–79, 82, 90–91, 100, 103, 105, 108–9, 115–16, 119, 121 n.3, 125 n.39, 163,

165, 184, 189, 266; in Israeli scholarship, 79–82; in Lebanon, 128–29, 134–36; in Occupied Territories, 103, 119, 125 n.39, 131, 134–36, 140, 142, 157; resident, 160. *See also* fedayeen; fellaheen

PalTalk, 135, 148 n.30

pan-ethnicity, 225 n.1; Mizrahi, 205, 207, 218, 221. *See also* ethnicity; identity

parallel universes, 317–18, 324–26, 329, 337 n.26

passing, 100–102, 110–11, 117, 120, 287 n.70; down, 110, 112; not, 117; up, 102

peace: camp, in Israel, 105; in Palestine-Israel, 329; process, 4, 11–12, 151, 221–22, 260, 263, 265–66, 279–80; struggle for, 161. *See also* New Middle East; Oslo Accords; Washington Declaration of Israel-Jordan Peace

Peace Now, 84, 87, 90, 104, 336 n.21. *See also* Israel

peasants, Palestinian. *See* fellaheen

personal liberation: in Palestinian cinema, 151, 162–67

Petra, 259, 269–72, 285 n.38

phonograph, 28, 31, 27, 43–15, 59; record companies, 208; records, 44, 184, 187

photograph, 270–71, 276, 356; montages, 58; news, 74 n.26; in popular media, 322–23, 335 n.14; as trophy, 138

pieds noirs, 235, 242, 244, 256. *See also* Algeria; colonialism; France

poetry: classical Arabic, 239; of Jewish Israelis, 83; of Palestinian Israelis, 82–83

poets: 'Aql, Sa'id, 182, 199 n.10; al-Barghuthi, Husayn, 192; Darwish, Mahmud, 139, 184, 189–92; Nagm, Ahmad Fu'ad, 187–88; Qabbani, Nizar, 185; al-Qasim, Samih, 83, 192; Zayyad, Tawfiq, 83, 189

popular culture, 11, 14–15, 53–54, 71; confrontational, 69; cultural criti-

taqtuqa (pl., taqatiq), 34, 49 n.12, 196
Tati, Jacques, 168
Tel Aviv: Arabs in, 64; Central Bus Station, 203; film in, 61; Museum, 230; open-air marketplace, 215
telephone, 128
television, 178, 181, 184, 187; cable, 218; Egyptian, 343, 351; French, 242; international networks, 155; Israeli, 89–90, 114, 155, 208, 216; Palestinian stations, 152, 170 n.25; satellite, 128, 178, 197
terrorists: Israelis as, 194–95; Palestinians as, 79, 161
theater, Israeli, 84
torture, 324–26
tourism: Arab, to Israel, 261, 276–80, 286 n.65, 287 n.70; Christian, to Israel, 296; ethnic, in Israel, 268–69; illegal, 277; Israeli, 11, 164, 259–63, 266–76; Israeli, to Jordan, 267, 269–72; Israeli, to Morocco, 267, 274; Israeli, to Palestinian villages in Israel, 22 n.41; Israeli, to Turkey, 275; Israeli Palestinian, to Jordan, 275; to Jaffa, 70; Mizrahi, 274–75; Palestinians of Occupied Territories, to Jordan, 275
tourist: citizen, 276; mimics, 280; mob, 277, 281. *See also* traveler
transnational, 10; circuit, 314, 319, 322; markets, 166; relationality, 10; transnationalism, 151, 168, 262, 280, 319. *See also* flows; global
transvestism, 102
travel: colonial, 270, 273; imperial travelogue, 261; leisure, 273; by Palestinian bourgeoisie, 59. *See also* tourism
Tribulation, 291–93; Tribulation Force, 291, 297, 303, 305. *See also* Armageddon; Christian; end times; evangelicalism; fundamentalism; *Left Behind* series; Rapture; Second Coming
tropes, 262; metaphor as, 336; nation-

alist, 127; of tourist, 271. *See also* narrative
Tunisia, 272, 274

'ud, 31, 34, 43, 238
uda, 32, 45–47
undercover units, Israeli, 120
unemployment, Palestinian, 265. *See also* Occupied Territories; Palestinians
United States, 81, 175; flag, 138
UNRWA (United Nations Relief and Works Agency), 128, 326
USSR, 81

vanguardism, 356–57
Vichy, 238, 251
victimization, 138; Israeli, 162; as narrative, 345; Palestinian, 88, 161, 165, 353
villagers, Palestinian. *See* fellaheen
virtual culture. *See* cyberspace
visual: as betrayed, 331, 334; as pornographic, 314, 317–18, 322–24, 331, 334, 337 n.26. *See also* ways of seeing

Wadi Salib, riots of, 78. *See also* Black Panthers; Mizrahim
Wailing Wall, 241
war on terrorism, 14, 307. *See also* September 11, 2001
Washington Declaration of Israel-Jordan peace, 264. *See also* New Middle East; Oslo Accords
ways of seeing, 320, 323–24, 350. *See also* visual
Wedding in Galilee (film), 107–10, 155, 158, 170 n.21
women. *See* gender
Wonder, Stevie, 216
workers: Jordanians, in Israel, 278–79; Palestinians, in construction, 110–11, 124 n.30; Palestinians, in hotels, 110; third world or foreign workers, in Israel, 12, 265, 277–78
worldliness, evangelical, 292; of *Left Behind* readers, 299

Xavier, Ismail, 159, 170 n.22

Yemen, 202, 272
Yemenites, in Israel, 211; music of, 210, 217
youth: escapist Israeli youth culture, 13; Israeli Jewish, 85; Palestinian, 55, 127, 130; suicide, 171 n.31

Zapatistas, 135
Zionism, 29, 113, 156, 165, 182; as corruption, 56; history of, 4; ideology of, 11, 86, 121 n.4, 164, 250; mainstream, 91; secular, 119, 233. *See also* anti-Zionism; post-Zionism
Zionists, in Algeria, 239–40

Rebecca L. Stein is Assistant Professor of
Cultural Anthropology at Duke University.

Ted Swedenburg is Professor of Anthropology
at the University of Arkansas.

Library of Congress Cataloging-in-Publication Data
Palestine, Israel, and the politics of popular culture /
edited by Rebecca L. Stein and Ted Swedenburg.
p. cm.   Includes bibliographical references and index.
ISBN 0-8223-3504-2 (cloth : alk. paper)
ISBN 0-8223-3516-6 (pbk. : alk. paper)
1. Popular culture—Political aspects—Palestine.
2. Arab-Israeli conflict. 3. Palestinian Arabs—Social conditions.
4. Israel—Social life and customs. 5. Palestine—Ethnic
relations. I. Stein, Rebecca L. II. Swedenburg, Ted.
DS113.P35 2005   306′.095694—dc22   2004027164